A Field Guide
to Trees and Shrubs

THE PETERSON FIELD GUIDE SERIES
EDITED BY ROGER TORY PETERSON

1. A Field Guide to the Birds–R. T. Peterson

2. A Field Guide to Western Birds–R. T. Peterson

3. A Field Guide to Shells of the Atlantic and Gulf Coasts and the West Indies–Morris

4. A Field Guide to the Butterflies–Klots

5. A Field Guide to the Mammals–Burt and Grossenheider

6. A Field Guide to Pacific Coast Shells (including shells of Hawaii and the Gulf of California)–Morris

7. A Field Guide to Rocks and Minerals–Pough

8. A Field Guide to the Birds of Britain and Europe–R. T. Peterson, Mountfort, and Hollom

9. A Field Guide to Animal Tracks–Murie

10. A Field Guide to the Ferns and Their Related Families of Northeastern and Central North America–Cobb

11. A Field Guide to Trees and Shrubs (Northeastern and Central North America)–Petrides

12. A Field Guide to Reptiles and Amphibians of Eastern and Central North America–Conant

13. A Field Guide to the Birds of Texas and Adjacent States–R. T. Peterson

14. A Field Guide to Rocky Mountain Wildflowers–J. J. Craighead, F. C. Craighead, Jr., and Davis

15. A Field Guide to the Stars and Planets–Menzel

16. A Field Guide to Western Reptiles and Amphibians–Stebbins

17. A Field Guide to Wildflowers of Northeastern and North-central North America–R. T. Peterson and McKenny

18. A Field Guide to the Mammals of Britain and Europe–van den Brink

19. A Field Guide to the Insects of America North of Mexico–Borror and White

20. A Field Guide to Mexican Birds–R. T. Peterson and Chalif

21. A Field Guide to Birds' Nests (found east of Mississippi River)–Harrison

22. A Field Guide to Pacific States Wildflowers–Niehaus

23. A Field Guide to Edible Wild Plants of Eastern and Central North America–L. Peterson

24. A Field Guide to the Atlantic Seashore–Gosner

25. A Field Guide to Western Birds' Nests–Harrison

26. A Field Guide to the Atmosphere–Schaefer and Day

THE PETERSON FIELD GUIDE SERIES

A Field Guide to Trees and Shrubs

Field marks of all trees, shrubs, and woody vines that grow wild in the northeastern and north-central United States and in south-eastern and south-central Canada

BY GEORGE A. PETRIDES

Second Edition

Illustrations by
GEORGE A. PETRIDES (*leaf and twig plates*)
ROGER TORY PETERSON (*flowers, fruits, silhouettes*)

HOUGHTON MIFFLIN COMPANY BOSTON

ISBN: 0–395–13651–2 hardbound
ISBN: 0–395–17579–8 paperbound

Library of Congress Catalog Card Number: 76-157132
Printed in the United States of America

A   15   14   13   12   11

To

MY MOTHER

and

MY WIFE

Editor's Note

A *Field Guide to the Birds*, the first book in the Peterson Field Guide Series, was published in 1934 and the principle on which it was founded — a schematic approach pointing out the visual or field differences between species — proved a sound one. Checklist or phylogenetic order was often subordinated to an artificial but more practical arrangement of the figures on the plates. For example, the chimney swift was placed with the swallows and the Philadelphia vireo and ruby-crowned kinglet were compared with the confusing fall warblers.

It was inevitable that a field guide to trees, shrubs, and woody vines should follow. In fact, as far back as 1941 I had planned to do such a book and had actually started on it when I learned that George Petrides was deep in the identical project. Upon examining his work I concluded that his version adhered to the basic principles of the *Field Guide* system even more than mine, so I turned to other projects, offering him bits of supplementary material — tree silhouettes, drawings of fruits and flowers, etc. — that would have gone into my own book. He had based his approach mostly on leaf, twig, and bud characters.

Dr. Petrides, a veteran field naturalist with a record of teaching and research, first in the National Park Service and U.S. Wildlife Service and now at Michigan State University, had long felt the need of an approach to plant recognition that his students in ecology and game management would understand. It is well enough to be tutored in basic plant taxonomy, but more often than not the student even after considerable training is still confused when confronted by many problems of identification.

This *Field Guide* in a sense is a pictorial key using obvious similarities and differences of form and structure by which the beginner can quickly run down his tree, shrub, or vine. True, some botanists may raise their eyebrows because the plants are not in the traditional order of their relationships, but there are many formal botanies so arranged; it would have been pointless to produce another. This guide is a shortcut. Actually the student will learn the relationships too (even if indirectly), for a key in the appendixes makes these quite clear.

The leaf and twig plates are the ingenious and painstaking labor of Dr. Petrides, while the other figures (silhouettes, drawings on legend pages, etc.) are mine. To Devereux Butcher I express thanks for his offer of the use of his photographs of trees, several of which were used as reference material in the silhouette section. I only wish that shortage of space had not prohibited a similar section of drawings of the bark of trees. Had this been included, some of the keys would have had to go. These, particularly the winter keys, were deemed indispensable to the usefulness of the book.

This, the first extensive revision in fourteen years, brings numerous refinements to a *Field Guide* that has already been used by more than 250,000 students, botanists, and amateur naturalists. The plates have been reorganized so as to bear a more convenient relation to the updated text, facilitating quick reference.

In the ecology-oriented years ahead, use this handy book to inform yourself about the green mantle of plants that clothe our "small blue planet," the only home we've got.

ROGER TORY PETERSON

Preface

THERE IS growing concern that man is destroying the environment on which he depends for his prosperity and even for his survival. This is not the place to review the many ways in which not only industrialized but also developing societies are degrading or destroying their necessities of life. However, many of modern man's ills are related to his destruction of plants. The human animal, like all others, is totally dependent on green plants, since these convert inorganic chemicals into organic foods and also help to maintain essential atmospheric gases in a healthful balance.

In any area the presence or absence of certain plant species or their tendencies to increase or decrease may provide indications of the erosion, over-exploitation, or pollution in that particular spot. In addition to their serving as indicators of environmental quality, trees and shrubs also have immensely important aesthetic and monetary roles because of their beauty. If there is any doubt that ecology and economics are interlinked, one can consult a forester, a soils scientist, watershed biologist, wildlife ecologist, fisheries limnologist, or hydrologist. Simpler yet, though, he can ask any real estate broker — or any urban dweller whose separation from the soil has induced a lowered morale.

Learning to know plants, in at least some respects, is like collecting stamps. I can well remember that as a youngster I had no particular interest in acquiring, say, the 1915–18 issues from Afghanistan until somehow I had managed to accumulate about half of them. Then I could not wait to fill in the gaps of the series. In a similar way, one who knows four or five hickories is stimulated to find and identify the others in his locality or even farther afield. Unlike the first few stamps, which can be purchased from a dealer, the first few hickories (or other trees) must be acquired through some real effort on the part of the collector. But with each plant learned the next becomes easier, and soon the enjoyment of wanderings and travels is vastly enhanced by an interest in looking out for new collector's items and the companion plants and habitats with which they are associated.

This second edition offers a reorganized format, making the *Field Guide* easier to use. Many minor improvements that gradually accumulated during the eleven printings of the first edition have all been incorporated here, along with numerous alterations and clarifications. A new key to the hickories has been inserted and one species of ash has been added.

The visual plan that illustrates the features of the five plant groups is now placed more prominently in the front of the book. The reader at a glance can see how the book is laid out.

The plate illustrations have been relocated so that each of the five text Sections is followed by its associated plates, on which there are color triangles in the upper right-hand corners to divide even the closed volume into its five easily found portions. Running heads throughout the book now incorporate the Section number to further facilitate use of the book.

Persons wishing to identify unknown plants often are baffled by botanical manuals and sometimes even by books designed as popular guides. Several obstacles to identification commonly are encountered. First, the technical language used is so involved that it dampens enthusiasm. We shall return to this point later. Second, a "popular" book may not include all species and one is left in doubt as to whether or not his specimen really is the one the book seems to indicate it to be. Third, if one has a book on trees alone or only on shrubs, what is done with a ten-foot woody plant of unknown identity? If it is a young tree then a shrub guide is of no assistance, and if it is a shrub species a tree guide cannot be used. Yet often before one can decide definitely whether it is a tree or a shrub the plant's identity must be known, and so neither book is needed. Fourth, in some books final identification depends on floral characteristics, and the specimen at hand may lack flowers. Or if leaf characteristics are given, then the identification of winter specimens may not be provided for.

It is hoped that this *Field Guide* avoids these obstacles (1) by limiting the use of technical terms, as discussed later, (2) by including all wild woody species in the area covered, (3) by treating trees and shrubs as well as woody vines in the same volume, and (4) by stressing characteristics of twigs and leaves which are present the year round.

The book essentially is a diagrammatically illustrated field key with accompanying text descriptions. It does not provide technical botanical descriptions of either vegetation or flowers. Such treatments are available elsewhere. This volume for the most part describes characteristics essential to the identification of unknown plants in both summer and winter conditions, plus some secondary characteristics considered desirable to confirm identification.

The area treated is the northeastern and north-central United States and southeastern and south-central Canada. It extends in the north from Newfoundland and islands of the Gulf of St. Lawrence along the 49th parallel to northwestern Minnesota. On the west it follows the western boundaries of Minnesota and Iowa and thence along the 96th meridian to include eastern Nebraska and Kansas. To the south the border is the southern boundaries of Virginia, West Virginia, Kentucky, Missouri, and eastern Kansas. Eastward it is limited by the Atlantic Coast.

Within this area all native trees, shrubs, and vines whose stems are woody, as well as those of foreign origin which regularly survive and reproduce successfully there, are considered.° The only exceptions are the brambles (*Rubus, Rosa*), and the hawthorns (*Crataegus*), whose many species and hybrids are not always identifiable even by specialists. Examples from these groups, however, are discussed. Botanical varieties and forms beneath the rank of species are not considered unless they differ from the typical species to such an extent that they may create confusion in identification. There are 646 species in 186 genera discussed, including 17 in the above three genera. In addition, important varieties are identified; seven are sufficiently distinct to be given separate accounts.

Beyond the described area, this manual still should be useful in identifying species that are distributed more widely. The extent to which each species ranges throughout North America (north of Mexico) is given.

The area, the scientific names used, and the woody species considered are the same as in *Gray's Manual of Botany*, 8th ed., by Merritt Lyndon Fernald (New York: American Book Company, 1950). Although Fernald is a standard technical reference for the area, not all botanists agree with his treatment of some plant groups. There might have been some advantages in adopting the analyses of special groups by other authorities, but it was felt that the disadvantages in possibly confusing the average reader with a battery of synonymous scientific and common names outweighed any benefits. Where technical data beyond those necessary for ordinary field identification are desired, it is thus possible to make direct use of Fernald's manual by merely looking up the scientific names used here.

With further regard to terminology, the following description is a concocted one but is not unbelievably extreme: "Stoloniferous shrub; leaves subcoriaceous, cuneate-ovate to lanceolate, denticulate, glabrescent; twigs terete, glaucous; buds glabrous or glutinous, divaricate, acuminate; inflorescence a thyrse-like panicle, pubescent during anthesis; flowers polygamodioecious, 9-merous," etc. It is sometimes claimed that anyone seriously

---

° Some partly woody plants of general interest are included, but such largely herbaceous plants as canes (*Arundinaria*), Buckwheat-vine (*Brunnichia*), Salt-wort (*Salicornia*), False-spirea (*Sorbaria*), Kudzu-vine (*Pueraria*), Rue (*Ruta*), Pachysandra (*Pachysandra*), prickly-pears (*Opuntia*), Diapensia (*Diapensia*), Pyxie-moss (*Pyxidanthera*), periwinkles (*Vinca*), Climbing-dogbane (*Trachelospermum*), Gutierrezia (*Gutierrezia*), and worm-woods (*Artemesia*) are omitted. The yuccas (*Yucca*) technically have woody stems, but there is no erect or visible trunk or branches; the nonflowering parts of the plants are completely covered by long bayonet-shaped leaves.

interested in the subject will be willing to learn such terminology. And it is true that certain terms are necessary to prevent unduly long descriptions, but this is not so for others. There seems little point to describing a leaf shape as "cordate," for instance, when a botanical glossary defines the word as merely meaning heart-shaped. One might as well say heart-shaped from the beginning. Similarly, "stoloniferous" means with runners, "coriaceous" is leathery, "cuneate" means wedge-shaped, "ovate" is egg-shaped, "lanceolate" means lance-shaped, "denticulate" is with fine teeth, and so on. Many botanical terms can be translated easily into plain English with no loss in accuracy. This book uses a simplified terminology, trusting that new interests in plant identification will be encouraged thereby. Where one attempts to avoid technical language, however, the danger of oversimplification and loss of accuracy arises. It is hoped that a satisfactory compromise has been made on this point.

It was while I was serving as a naturalist with the National Park Service that the need for a recognition volume on trees and shrubs first became apparent to me, a volume planned in the schematic tradition of the Peterson Field Guide Series. Even before that, the late Professor W. C. Muenscher had stimulated my interest through his fine course in woody plants at Cornell University. His *Keys to Woody Plants* (Ithaca, New York, 1950) still is exceptionally good.

I wish to express my most sincere appreciation to Dr. George W. Parmelee, Curator of Woody Plants, Michigan State University, for his painstaking review of this work and for his many excellent suggestions. Very considerable help was given by Dr. Roger Tory Peterson, who contributed much to the book as editor of text and artwork and supplied the tree silhouettes as well as the drawings of flowers and fruits that appear on the legend pages. Miss Helen Phillips of Houghton Mifflin Company has devoted many hours to careful crosschecking and editing; she has worked on both editions and I am most appreciative of her generous help. I am grateful also to Drs. John Cantlon, Carleton Ball, Leslie Gysel, and Anton de Vos, who each contributed several helpful ideas. My thanks are due to the authorities in charge of the herbaria at the Smithsonian Institution, University of Georgia, University of California, Ohio State University, Texas A & M College, and Michigan State University who made their facilities available. Mrs. E. Musser assisted with lettering originally planned for the book. My mother encouraged my efforts, and my wife Miriam also devoted many hours of assistance in the preparation of the manuscript.

GEORGE A. PETRIDES

Contents

Editor's Note   vii

Preface   ix

Illustrated Plan of the Five Main Sections   xvi

How to Use This Book   xix

Tree Silhouettes   1

Section I.   Plants with Needlelike or Scalelike Leaves;
    Mostly Evergreens   15
      Conifers with Needles in Clusters: Pines   16
        Larches   20
      Conifers with Flat Needles   20
      Conifers with 4-sided Needles; Spruces   23
      Conifers with Scalelike or 3-sided Leaves   24
      Needle-bearing, Non-Cone-bearing Evergreens   27
      Plates   32

Section II.   Broad-leaved Plants with Opposite Compound
    Leaves   46
      Vines with Opposite Compound Leaves   47
      Plants with Opposite Compound Leaves   48
      Trees with Opposite Feather-compound Leaves: Ashes,
        Ashleaf Maple, and Corktree   49
      Trees with Opposite Fan-compound Leaves: Buckeyes   52
      Plates   55

Section III.   Broad-leaved Plants with Opposite Simple
    Leaves   66
      Low Creeping and Trailing Shrubs (and American
        Mistletoe)   67
      Vines with Opposite Simple Leaves (includes climbing
        honeysuckles)   69
      Honeysuckles: Erect Shrubs   72
      Dogwoods   75
      Miscellaneous Plants with Opposite Leaves Not Toothed   78

Plants with Opposite or Whorled Heart-shaped Leaves
  That Are Not Toothed   84
Miscellaneous Shrubs with Opposite Toothed Leaves   86
Viburnums   90
Maples   95
Plates   99

Section IV.   Broad-leaved Plants with Alternate Com-
pound Leaves   122
  Prickly Brambles   123
  Erect Thorny Trees and Shrubs   126
  Thornless Trifoliates   130
  Sumacs   133
  Walnuts and Similar Trees   135
  Hickories   138
  Miscellaneous Species with Alternate Once-compound
    Leaves   142
  Thornless Plants with Leaves Twice-compound   146
  Plates   149

Section V.   Broad-leaved Plants with Alternate Simple
Leaves   168
  Low Creeping or Trailing Shrubs   174
  Greenbriers   181
  Grapes (and Ampelopsis and Boston Ivy)   184
  Moonseeds   188
  Miscellaneous Vines Climbing without Tendrils   189
  Miscellaneous Upright Thorny Plants   191
  Hawthorns   197
  Thorny Currant and Gooseberries   198
  Thornless Currants   201
  Miscellaneous Plants with Fan-lobed Leaves   203
  Plants with Leaves Fan-lobed or Fan-veined   206
  Poplars   210
  Oaks   213
  Magnolias   223
  Elms and Water-elm   224
  Ironwood, Hornbeam, Hazelnuts, and Alders   227
  Birches   231
  Cherries and Thornless Plums   235
  Juneberries   240
  Willows   246
  Miscellaneous Plants with 3 Bundle Scars   261
  Miscellaneous Plants with 3 (or more) Bundle Scars   269
  Spireas   272
  Hollies   274
  Blueberries   277
  Huckleberries, Bilberries, and Relatives   279

Azaleas   283
Evergreen Heaths   286
Nonevergreen Heaths with Toothed Leaves   289
Miscellaneous Plants with 1 Bundle Scar   290
Plates   297

Appendixes
  A. Winter Key to Plants with Opposite Leaf Scars   375
  B. Winter Key to Plants with Alternate Leaf Scars   378
  C. Key to Trees in Leafy Condition   390
  D. Key to Trees in Leafless Condition   395
  E. Plant Relationships   401
  F. The Meaning of Botanical Terms   405
  G. Table for Converting Inches to Millimeters   410

Index   411

Illustrated Plan of the
Five Main Sections

The plants are divided according to the types and arrangements of leaves diagrammed on these two pages. Details
of leaf shapes, etc., are considered in each Section.

The green color was provided to aid identification by
emphasizing leaf shape; it does not represent the precise
shade of green of the plants.

> NOTE: For convenience in quick reference the
> following symbols are used opposite the plates.
>   ↟ Tree
>   ↟ᵥ Small tree or shrub (may be either)
>   ⋁ Shrub
>   ʃ Vine

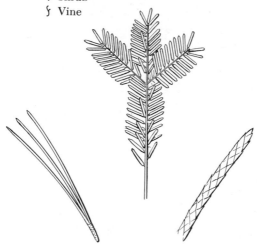

SECTION I

PLANTS WITH
NEEDLELIKE OR SCALELIKE LEAVES
Plates 1–6, pp. 32–45. Text p. 15

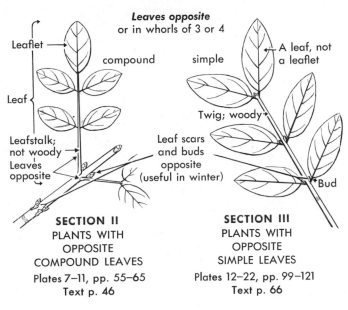

Leaves opposite
or in whorls of 3 or 4

Leaflet

compound

simple

A leaf, not
a leaflet

Leaf

Twig; woody

Leafstalk;
not woody
Leaves
opposite

Leaf scars
and buds
opposite
(useful in winter)

Bud

SECTION II
PLANTS WITH
OPPOSITE
COMPOUND LEAVES
Plates 7–11, pp. 55–65
Text p. 46

SECTION III
PLANTS WITH
OPPOSITE
SIMPLE LEAVES
Plates 12–22, pp. 99–121
Text p. 66

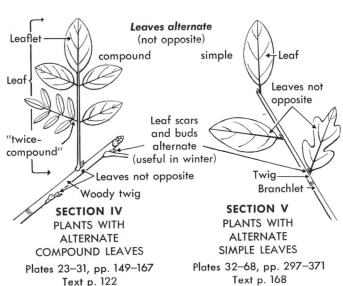

Leaves alternate
(not opposite)

Leaflet

compound

simple

Leaf

Leaf

Leaves not
opposite

"twice-
compound"

Leaf scars
and buds
alternate
(useful in winter)

Leaves not opposite

Woody twig

Twig

Branchlet

SECTION IV
PLANTS WITH
ALTERNATE
COMPOUND LEAVES
Plates 23–31, pp. 149–167
Text p. 122

SECTION V
PLANTS WITH
ALTERNATE
SIMPLE LEAVES
Plates 32–68, pp. 297–371
Text p. 168

xvii

How to Use This Book

GENERAL LAYOUT

THE BOOK is divided into five principal sections:

   I. Plants with needlelike or scalelike leaves.
   II. Plants with opposite compound leaves.
   III. Plants with opposite simple leaves.
   IV. Plants with alternate compound leaves.
   V. Plants with alternate simple leaves.

Sections II–V contain the broad-leaved plants.

The five basic leaf types and arrangements are illustrated on pages xvi–xvii. They can be learned in a few minutes. In summer, plants can be easily assigned to one of these sections. In winter, plants without leaves can be placed in the combined opposite-leaved (Sections II and III) or alternate-leaved (Sections IV and V) categories according to leaf-scar arrangements (see drawings of leaf types and arrangements preceding the plates in each Section, pp. 55, 99, 149, 297).

Keys, which are explained below under "Identifying Unknown Plants," further assist in identifying species in summer. Winter keys to all nonevergreen species are to be found in the Appendixes and deal respectively with plants with opposite leaf scars (Appendix A) and alternate leaf scars (Appendix B). Additional keys are provided as Appendixes C and D. These should be useful in identifying plants that obviously are trees, being 25 feet or over. A summary of family and other relationships of woody plants is provided as Appendix E. The meanings of some terms are summarized in Appendix F. Appendix G permits conversion of inches to millimeters.

LEAF TYPES

In leafy condition, all woody plants fall into one of the five major categories described above under "General Layout" and illustrated in the drawings on pages xvi–xvii.

Plants whose leaves obviously are not needlelike or scalelike are *broad-leaved plants*.

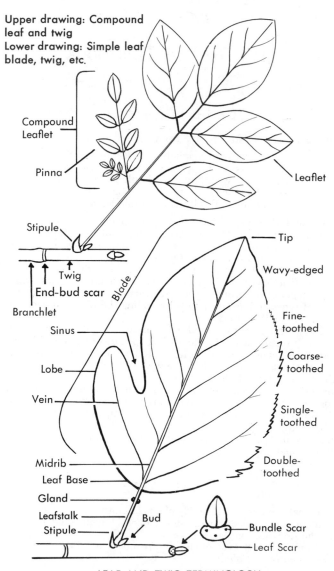

Upper drawing: Compound leaf and twig
Lower drawing: Simple leaf blade, twig, etc.

Compound
Leaflet

Pinna

Leaflet

Stipule

Tip

Wavy-edged

Twig

End-bud scar

Blade

Branchlet

Fine-toothed

Sinus

Coarse-toothed

Lobe

Vein

Single-toothed

Double-toothed

Midrib
Leaf Base

Gland

Leafstalk

Bud

Stipule

Bundle Scar

Leaf Scar

LEAF AND TWIG TERMINOLOGY

Compound leaves are those divided into three (rarely two) to several dozen *leaflets*. The leaflet of a compound leaf is attached by its stalk to a midrib, or rachis, which is not especially woody, and there is only an indefinite mark on the midrib when the leaflet is plucked. The midrib is attached to the woody twig and leaves a definite *leaf scar* (see drawing, p. xxiv) on it when picked.

A *simple leaf* has only a single leaf blade and is joined by its stalk to a woody *twig*. It leaves a distinct leaf scar when plucked.

Both compound and simple leaves may vary in shape, size, texture, and other characteristics, but despite all variations, these two main leaf types are fundamental.

Opposite leaves are of either compound or simple type and occur in opposing pairs along the twigs. Less frequently, *whorled leaves* may occur where three or more leaves arise together and their attachments tend to encircle the twigs at intervals. Plants with opposite and whorled leaves are grouped together in this volume.

Alternate leaves are arranged singly at intervals along the twigs. One should be cautious of misidentifying the opposite leaflets of some compound leaves, even of alternate compound leaves, as opposite simple leaves. Also, some alternate-leaved plants bear *spur branches,* on which leaves are densely clustered (see p. 310). These can be mistaken for opposite or whorled leaves if one is not careful to select strong-growing specimen twigs for study (see "Identifying Unknown Plants").

Leaflets of compound leaves and simple leaves both have essentially the same parts. Similarly, the various leaf shapes may occur in both. Leaf shape within each species usually varies considerably. Fewer major shapes are named in this book than in most technical manuals. The comparative drawings, page xxii, illustrate common leaf shapes.

Other leaf characteristics are described or illustrated where encountered in the book.

TWIG AND BUD TYPES

A *twig* is not just any small division of a branch. It is only the end portion, the part that constitutes the newest growth. It is separated from the *branchlet,* which is the previous year's growth, by a series of encircling *end-bud scars.*

In winter, *nonevergreen* broad-leaved plants make up two main groups: (1) those of Sections II and III, with leaf scars arranged on the twigs in opposing pairs, or, much less commonly, in whorls of three or four, and (2) those of Sections IV and V, with leaf scars arranged singly on the twigs in a more or less scattered pattern. These positions are illustrated on pages xxiv and xvii. Some alternate-leaved plants have spur branches on which leaf scars are densely crowded, appearing opposite or

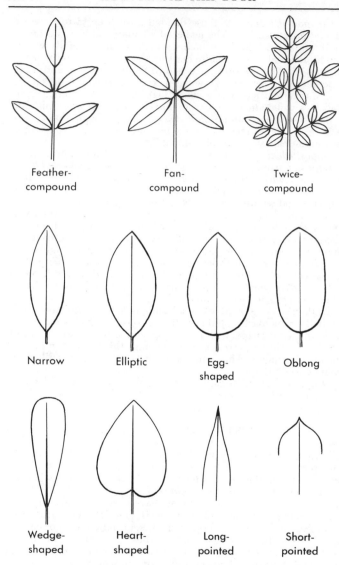

Feather-compound

Fan-compound

Twice-compound

Narrow

Elliptic

Egg-shaped

Oblong

Wedge-shaped

Heart-shaped

Long-pointed

Short-pointed

LEAF SHAPES

whorled. Spur branches can be recognized as such or avoided by selecting quick-growing twigs for study (see "Identifying Unknown Plants," p. xxvii).

It is not always possible to distinguish between leaf scars of compound leaves and those of simple leaves, though often those of compound leaves are larger and have more than three bundle scars. Further subdivisions within the opposite or alternate-leaved groups depend on the number of bundle scars, occurrence of true or false end buds, type of buds, type of pith, presence of milky sap, and other characters. True end buds and clear sap may be considered to be present unless statements are made to the contrary (alternate references to end buds present or absent correspond with end buds true or false, respectively). Central end buds are lacking in several species with opposite buds (as shown on Plate 8). Bud descriptions apply to mature winter buds. The term *pith chambered* is used here to include all types of segmented, transversely divided pith, including those diaphragmed and partitioned. The main characteristics of winter twigs and buds are shown on page xxiv. Unless otherwise specified, references to bark characteristics apply to the trunk bark.

DRAWINGS

The plates are located at the end of each Section for convenient use with the text descriptions in the five main parts of the book. They are diagrammatic illustrations, indicating the principal identification points of most species. The diagrammatic form avoids the possibility of minor individual differences in specimens being interpreted by the reader as identification points. Occasional dotted lines indicate varying leaf shapes in some species. The reader will recognize that not all specimens will look precisely like the drawings, but they will possess the designated critical points of identification as well as unpredictable irregularities not necessarily of value in identification. Stipules (p. xx) are illustrated only where they are of diagnostic value, since they often drop off easily. The green color was provided to aid identification by emphasizing leaf shape; it does not represent the shade of green of the plants.

Each plate attempts to show those plants that most resemble each other in leaf and twig characteristics. Often these are related plants; frequently, however, they are not. Wherever possible, related species are shown on plates as close to one another in sequence as is otherwise consistent with the main objective of grouping plants similar in appearance. Family relationships are indicated briefly in Appendix E. Because of great variation in leaf size no attempt has been made, except in a general way, to draw the plants to scale. Leaf and plant sizes are given in the text.

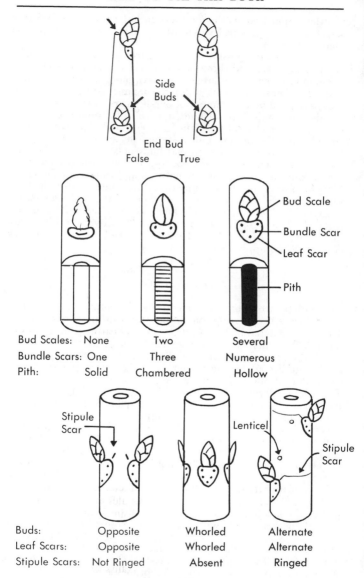

TWIG AND BUD TERMINOLOGY

SYMBOLS

For convenience in quick reference the following symbols are employed on the legend pages opposite the plates:

⚹ **Tree.** A large woody plant having one (rarely several) self-supporting stems or trunks and numerous branches, the whole ranging from about 20 feet to a considerable height.

Ѱ **Shrub.** Most plants in this *Field Guide* fall into this category. A shrub, or bush, is a woody plant, smaller than a tree, which consists of a number of small stems from the ground or small branches from near the ground.

⚹Ѱ **Small tree or shrub** (usually not exceeding 25 feet). These borderline plants may assume either form.

Ƨ **Vine.** A climbing or sprawling woody plant without self-supporting upright stem.

SPECIES DESCRIPTIONS

Where both italic and boldface page references occur at the beginning of the species descriptions, the italic numbers refer to the silhouettes, the boldface numbers to the plates.

Plant names. Both common and scientific names are given for each species. Although for many species common names are well established, these or similar names are sometimes also applied to different, even unrelated species. For instance, Purple Honeysuckle frequently is given as the common name of an azalea. Other species may have no well-known common name. For the most part, one of the names given by Fernald (see my Preface) — usually the one considered to be most widely used — has been chosen for use in this book. But for tree species reference was made to the U.S. Forest Service *Check List of Native and Naturalized Trees of the United States* by Elbert L. Little, Jr. (Washington, D.C.: Govt. Printing Office, 1953). An effort was made to use the preferred common name given there; in some cases, where confusion seemed likely, alternates were chosen. The work of Kelsey and Dayton° was consulted on occasion. For some species, especially shrubs, in cases where no common names were known, or where it seemed preferable to avoid undesirable connotations, liberties were taken in modifying or assigning names. It is hoped that the names selected will be acceptable.

Scientific names have three essential parts: the name of the *genus* (plural, *genera*), the name of the *species* (plural, *species*), and the name or names, commonly abbreviated, of the botanist(s) who assigned the scientific names. Example: *Quercus rubra* L.,

---

° *Standardized Plant Names*, 2nd ed., by Harlan P. Kelsey and William A. Dayton (Harrisburg, Pa.: McFarland, 1942) for the American Joint Committee on Horticultural Nomenclature.

where the initial stands for Linnaeus, the "father of systematic botany." Where the varieties (or, less frequently, forms) of species are named, the varietal name and the name or names of the authority or authorities responsible for them is placed after the scientific name of the species. Example: *Quercus rubra* var. *borealis* (Michx. f.) Farw.

A main purpose of scientific nomenclature is standardization, permitting botanists anywhere to discuss a plant with the assurance that they are indeed all talking about the same species. It is an international cataloguing system that also indicates, within limits, plant relationships. Scientific names are not constant, however, but may change as authorities decide that a species has closer relationships in a different genus than that first assigned, that what once were considered two species should only be termed two varieties of a single species, that a species described as new already had a name. The rules of botanical nomenclature are much too involved to go into here. To the reader the principal value of scientific names probably will be in looking up the same species in several reference books. As stated previously, the names used here are the same as those in the 8th edition of *Gray's Manual of Botany* (see my Preface). Following the example of Little (1953), however, none of the Latin species names are capitalized.

Incidentally, no one need hesitate to attempt pronunciations of scientific names. In the United States and Canada nowadays such names tend to be anglicized and most pronunciations are acceptable. If one can say *Hibiscus* or *Hydrangea*, he already uses scientific names. In speech, the authors' names are usually omitted.

Recognition. Plant descriptions are limited largely to identification characteristics. A statement of the general growth habits of the species is followed by characteristics of foliage, twigs, and bark. Invariably there is variation between individual specimens of a species. Where such individual variation may cause confusion in identification, its extent is indicated in the text. Attempts to describe degrees of "hairiness" are made where possible, but the exact extent of hairiness in leaves and twigs is sometimes difficult to describe. Nearly all leaves will show some fine hairs if examined closely under a hand lens. Plants described in the text or on the plates as being hairy are usually markedly so. "Hairless" plants are those in which hairiness is not conspicuous. A hand lens should be used in ascertaining the abundance of hairlike structures. Reference to bark is to the mature bark of large stems unless otherwise indicated.

The few measurements given are in the following order: leaf lengths, plant heights, and, for trees, trunk diameters. Minimum and maximum leaf lengths are generalizations for normal leaves and include the length of the leafstalk unless stated otherwise. Sprouts of some species bear abnormally huge leaves. The heights of shrubs are given as the usual maximums. For trees, the common minimum height and diameter for mature specimens are each followed by the common maximum for each measurement and, in parentheses, the exceptional maximum. Diameters are given for tree species and are trunk diameters at breast height (about 4½ feet above the ground; the foresters' d.b.h.). All these figures are given only as general guides. The several maximum measurements usually are not all possessed by a single specimen. The "largest" Jack Pine recorded by the American Forestry Association, for example, is only 27 feet tall, though 42 inches in circumference. All measurements are given in feet ('), inches ("), and fractions rather than in metric-system units, because the English units are more widely familiar in our area.

Flower and fruit data are limited to those general identification characteristics that might be useful in supplementing vegetative characteristics. Further details are provided only for those species not easily recognized by leaf and twig characteristics alone. Types of fruit cluster, though not given, are the same as for the flowers. The extreme dates of flowering and fruiting given may have to be modified by a month or so, according to locality. Where fruiting dates are lacking, those of the flowers will indicate at least the earliest possible for fruits. Fruit colors apply to ripe fruits. General statements regarding the distinctiveness of certain species apply to the geographic area of the book.

Similar species. Critical differences are discussed for species that most closely resemble one another, either when in foliage or in leafless condition.

Where found. General habitat and limits of distribution are given for the area north of Mexico, range limits reading from northeast to northwest and southeast to southwest. These are taken mainly from Fernald (1950); Little (1953) scarcely differs. For illustrated plants geographic ranges are opposite the plates and for nonillustrated or partially illustrated, in the text; sometimes, however, the range is duplicated on the legend page to aid identification of certain species.

Remarks. General observations are provided on those plants that serve as sources of lumber, fuel, medicine, food, drink, poison, fiber, ornament, tannin, and Christmas trees, or are of especial value in soil and wildlife management. References to wildlife usually are limited to game birds and to mammals of chipmunk size or larger. Most of such references are taken from William R. Van Dersal's *Native Woody Plants of the United States: Their Erosion Control and Wildlife Values* (U.S. Dept. of Agriculture Misc. Publ. 303, 1938).

IDENTIFYING UNKNOWN PLANTS

Before attempting to identify unknown plants, one should first learn the general appearance of Poison-ivy, Poison-oak, and

Poison Sumac (Plates 25 and 26). Once their main characteristics are learned, the plants are easily avoided.

Rather than collecting specimens for later identification at home, it is highly preferable that identifications be made in the field, where additional materials are available and growth habits are evident. If this cannot be done, then twig specimens, with leaves when available, may be collected and either carried fresh or pressed. *Good specimens are essential to easy identification.* Dwarfed, twisted, gnarled twigs should be avoided. Except for abnormally large sucker shoots, strong quick-growing twigs should be collected for study. On such twigs, the leaves and leaf scars are larger and all details are more evident.

In summer, the first step in identifying an unknown plant is to place it in one of the five main groups (see drawings, pp. xvi–xvii) according to leaf type and arrangement:

1. Leaves needlelike or scalelike   Section I, p. 15
1. Leaves broad:
    2. Leaves opposite or whorled:
        3. Leaves compound   Section II, p. 46
        3. Leaves simple   Section III, p. 66
    2. Leaves alternate:
        4. Leaves compound   Section IV, p. 122
        4. Leaves simple   Section V, p. 168

Turning to the proper Section, one follows the key given there.

Keys to plant identification may look formidable at first but should be regarded as something like a book's table of contents. They merely divide the subject matter, in this case plant species, into subsections, further sub-subsections, and eventually species or groups of species. For the most part keys attempt to divide the many species into two groups. Then each group in turn is divided into two. This is repeated again and again until finally species or groups of species are named. In such a key, as in the short one of the preceding paragraph, the person seeking identification of a tree or shrub chooses first between the two number 1's, then between the two number 2's, and in that case finally decides between either of the two number 3's or the two number 4's. It is only a matter of following a trail that forks repeatedly but rarely offers more than two paths at any single point. The seeker continues to make choices between the options which bear the same number, making certain at each point that the choice made fits the plant being identified, until an end point is reached.

After following the sectional key, the plate (or plates) finally arrived at are then scanned and the species most like the unknown one is selected. It is important to take the next step and *read the text description* of the species. Agreement should be reached between the specimen and its description and range, or else another attempt should be made to "run it down." The text portion on "Similar species" also may disclose errors in interpreting identification marks.

It is possible, of course, to disregard the sectional leaf keys and rely upon spotting the proper diagram, for the plates in themselves are a pictorial key. This often is possible if the species falls in Sections I through IV. There are relatively few plants with needelike, compound, or opposite leaves. But unless the specimen has quite distinctive characteristics, in Section V one should follow the keys.

In winter, unless the plant is evergreen, one must either find leaf remains on or under the specimen (and run some risk of picking up a wrong one) or rely on twig and other winter characteristics. If dried leaves are found, one can attempt to proceed as in summer. If not, then it is suggested that good twig specimens be secured and the Winter Keys used as follows:

Leaf scars opposite or whorled — Appendix A
Leaf scars alternate — Appendix B.

The most difficult time for woody plant identification usually is early spring, when buds have burst but leaves are small and new twigs soft. Some plants then may not be easily identifiable for a month or so.

Where one wishes to identify a plant that is definitely a tree (plants smaller than 25 feet or so might be either shrubs or small trees), another approach is available through the keys to tree identification supplied as appendixes. Appendix C is for trees in summer leafy condition and Appendix D for use in winter. These two keys supplement the others given throughout the book and need not be used unless one wishes to.

Everyone likes to feel that he has discovered a rare specimen. But when one identifies a species outside its usual range or thinks he has something entirely new to science it would be well to recheck carefully to make certain that no error in identification has been made. If something unusual still seems likely, a specimen could be collected (with flowers or fruits, if possible, and always with notes on the exact location, date of collection, and collector's name and address), carefully pressed, dried, and forwarded to the department of botany at one's state or provincial university or agricultural college with a request for confirmation of identification.

EQUIPMENT

Fortunately, plant identification requires little paraphernalia. Only two items are essential: a field guide or manual and a hand lens. Some progress can be made without the latter, but a good hand lens is especially helpful in ascertaining twig characteristics.

Furthermore, it discloses hidden beauty in small tree blossoms and in other plant parts. Lenses for general use should magnify 6× to 10×. Those manufactured by well-known optical companies generally are worth the slightly higher price usually asked for them. Hand lenses sell for from $8 to $15 and are practically indestructible. Often secondhand ones can be procured very cheaply, especially in university towns.

It is strongly suggested that, when possible, identifications be made in the field where additional specimens and supplementary data are available. Where there is need for collecting specimens, however, one can secure a vasculum (a metal container to keep specimens fresh in the field) and plant press from any biological supply house. Two large firms are: General Biological Supply House, Inc., 8200 South Hoyne Avenue, Chicago, Illinois 60620, and Ward's Natural Science Establishment, Inc., P.O. Box 1712, Rochester, New York 14603.

One can substitute any fairly airtight bag or box for the vasculum and make the press of scrap wood (two frames of light slats; about 1′ × 1½′) and blotters tied by straps. A roll of newspapers held by a strap, or even a large magazine, often does well as a field carrier if specimens are merely being carried for early identification.

PLANT SUCCESSION

Each plant species, through evolutionary processes, has become something of a specialist. Each lives in a certain type of place, the *habitat,* and each thrives under a particular set of climatic, soil, and water conditions. On a newly available site local conditions are varied and usually seeds or other reproductive parts of several species manage to be present. This results in the establishment of a *plant community* composed of several species. Once established, most plants and plant communities alter their sites so that the longer they persist in a spot the less suitable it becomes for them. Increasing fertility due to root decay and leaf fall, for example, may permit competition from species originally unable to become established on the site; or increasing shade may prevent survival of seedlings even though they are adjacent to or even surrounded by their parents. These factors and others result in the phenomenon of *succession,* wherein plant communities and the soils they occupy pass through succeeding stages until finally a stable community of plants and a mature soil structure are developed. This final relatively permanent community is the *climax* plant association.

Primary plant succession occurs when community development begins and develops from a bare surface or in open water. Primary succession may begin on such areas as cliff faces, rockslides, gravel slopes, road cuts, sand dunes, lava flows, peat deposits, gully sides, or on shallow lake bottoms, in bogs, or on river bars and deltas. In such places *pioneer* plant communities become established which eventually are succeeded by others, each of which tends to be more intermediate in its moisture requirements than the community it replaced. That is, within the limits set by climate, succeeding communities beginning in a wet environment live on drier sites than do their predecessors, while those in a dry environment live on moister sites, with the climax community occurring on neither wet nor dry, but upon intermediate, moist sites.

Secondary plant succession occurs when a plant community is entirely or partly killed or removed, exposing a soil that has already advanced to some degree toward maturity. Such plant destruction might be accomplished by light fires, trampling, drainage, windthrow, lumbering, cultivation, or otherwise. The secondary plant community series that follows a change in the original vegetation is generally different from that of the primary succession.

Species in developmental stages of plant succession may be more widespread than those of the climax stage. They may even take a part in succession in regions with different climax types. Some species may occupy slightly different habitats and successional stages in different portions of their ranges, whereas others are restricted to only a portion of a single climax area.

Knowledge of local successional stages is very important in studies of land use, soil conservation, forestry, wildlife management, and outdoor recreation. An interesting and valuable project for the amateur botanist is the preparation of a plant succession chart for his locality (see H. J. Oosting's *The Study of Plant Communities*, San Francisco, Freeman and Co., 1956).

CLIMAX VEGETATION TYPES

From north to south and from east to west in our area, major changes in the character of the climax vegetation are evident. These major units are mostly characterized by distinctive vegetative *life forms* (evergreen trees, deciduous trees, grasses, etc.) and are termed *plant formations*. The *tundra* of the Far North and of the mountaintops of eastern Canada and New England is vegetated with sedges, grasses, lichens, herbs, and low and creeping shrubs. The northern evergreen or *boreal forest* that covers most of Canada and part of the northern United States is dominated by White Spruce and Balsam Fir, although American Larch becomes prominent along its northern edge. The *hemlock-hardwood* forest of the Great Lakes area — a formation of mixed conifers and broad-leaved trees — sometimes is also designated as the *lake forest*. Its dominant species include Hemlock, Beech, Sugar Maple, Yellow Birch, and White Pine.

Over most of our area is the broad-leaved or *deciduous forest.* Several principal climax associations occur in this formation: (1) Mixed Mesophytic (Beech–Sugar Maple–Tulip-tree–Sweet Buckeye–White Oak–Red Oak–Hemlock) in southern mountain valleys and some lowlands, (2) Beech–Sugar Maple in moist deep soils, (3) Oak–Hickory or Oak–Pine (and formerly Oak–Chestnut) mostly in drier areas, and (4) Sugar Maple–Basswood in parts of Wisconsin and Minnesota. On the flat coastal plain in the southeast of our area is a portion of the *southeastern evergreen forest,* principally of Loblolly and Shortleaf Pines. *Prairie* formations occur in the western part of our area, with woody species important only in valley bottoms.

A Field Guide
to Trees and Shrubs

Tree Silhouettes

(by R.T.P.)

AN EXPERT bird-watcher can often identify a bird by its silhouette alone. Birds are dependable: a grackle always is shaped precisely like a grackle, and one starling invariably resembles another starling. Trees, on the other hand, are not so consistent. The beginner, learning his trees, yearns for a book that will give him shapes and field marks by which he can make snap identifications from a moving car. But it isn't that easy. True, an elm somehow always looks like an elm, but many trees assume a variety of shapes. A young tree might look entirely unlike a grizzled veteran of the same species. And a forest-grown tree, reaching for the light, might be tall, slender, and restricted in its branching compared to a field-grown example where plenty of sun, soil, and moisture have enabled it to develop a maximum crown.

But within limits one can, with a little practice, recognize by shape and manner of growth quite a few of the trees and also some of the shrubs. On the following pages are presented some silhouettes of a selection of trees (and one or two shrubs). Not all examples will look like these, but they are, on the whole, typical. They represent open-grown specimens, not those of crowded woodland situations. If in doubt check the leaf and twig characters. Silhouette page numbers appear in italic at the beginning of the descriptions in the text.

1

WHITE PINE
Tall dark trunk; spreading horizontal limbs; delicate spraylike foliage

LOBLOLLY PINE
Tall, clean cinnamon trunk; open crown, drooping lower limbs

RED PINE

Tall, erect trunk; stout right-angle branches, symmetrical crown; long dark green foliage, ascending tips

PITCH PINE

Usually low, irregular, scraggly; many dead branches; coarse foliage in rigid tufts

WHITE SPRUCE
Pyramidal; upper branches ascending, lower nearly horizontal; foliage bluish green

RED SPRUCE
Rather open-branched, tips upcurved; foliage yellowish green

BLACK SPRUCE
Slender; short branches; foliage bluish green

NORWAY SPRUCE
Usually near houses; pyramidal; strongly drooping lateral branchlets

3

BALSAM FIR
Conical; branches ascending;
erect cones; flat needles

HEMLOCK
Loose, irregular, feathery;
short flat needles

RED CEDAR
Conical head (wider with age);
short stem

NORTHERN WHITE CEDAR
Dense conical head clothed almost
to base; flat sprays

COMMON COTTONWOOD

Wide-spreading open crown
(shaggier than Elm)

AMERICAN LARCH

Pyramidal (when young); short
needles in tufts (shed in winter)

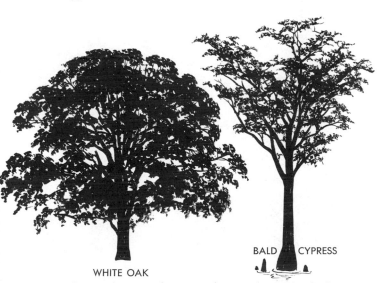

WHITE OAK

Short trunk; crown often
much wider than high

BALD CYPRESS

Flat-topped; irregular, feathery;
buttressed; "knees" often protrude
from water

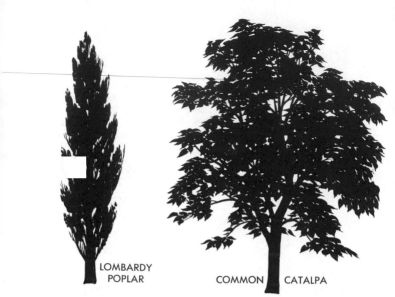

LOMBARDY POPLAR

Tall, slender; trunk continuous;
many hugging branches

COMMON CATALPA

Round-topped; large heart-shaped
leaves; long beanlike pods

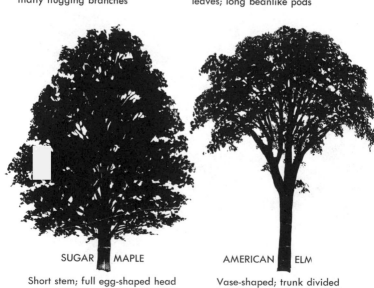

SUGAR MAPLE

Short stem; full egg-shaped head

AMERICAN ELM

Vase-shaped; trunk divided
into large outspreading limbs

6

SUGAR MAPLE

Short trunk; many ascending
branches; symmetrical oval head;
dark flaky bark

RED MAPLE

Short trunk; broad oval head
(sometimes broader at top);
gray beechlike upper branches

WHITE ASH

Trunk often divided low down;
oval head; cross-shaped branching;
diamond-ridged bark

TULIP- TREE

Upright trunk; branches often
angle upward; erect dry seed cones

7

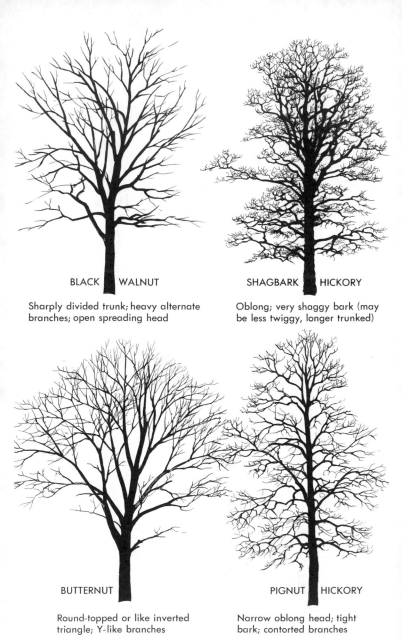

BLACK WALNUT

Sharply divided trunk; heavy alternate branches; open spreading head

SHAGBARK HICKORY

Oblong; very shaggy bark (may be less twiggy, longer trunked)

BUTTERNUT

Round-topped or like inverted triangle; Y-like branches

PIGNUT HICKORY

Narrow oblong head; tight bark; contorted branches

8

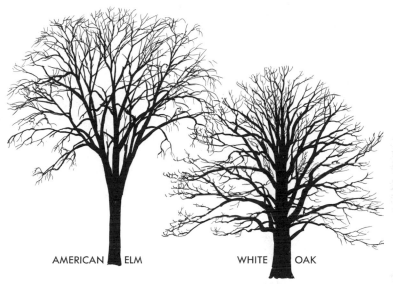

AMERICAN ELM

Vase-shaped; trunk divided into
large outspreading branches

WHITE OAK

Broader than tall; short trunk;
branches gnarled

MOSSYCUP OAK

Broad round top; spreading;
lower limbs often drooping

PIN OAK

Upper branches ascending;
lower branches drooping

9

SYCAMORE

Large, open, irregular;
bark in patches revealing
whitish under bark

QUAKING ASPEN

Upper bark whitish with dark
blotches; reddish-brown twigs

BEECH

Smooth light gray bark;
dense ovate head; often a few
persistent leaves

GRAY BIRCH

Often clumped; chalky bark
(not peeling) with dark triangular
patches; slender twigs

FLOWERING DOGWOOD

Spreading bushy head; conspicuous erect flower buds at ends of twigs

BLACK WILLOW

Disheveled-looking; much branched, often many shoots and suckers

WEEPING WILLOW

Drooping twigs and branches

PUSSY WILLOW

Clumped; catkins evident in early spring

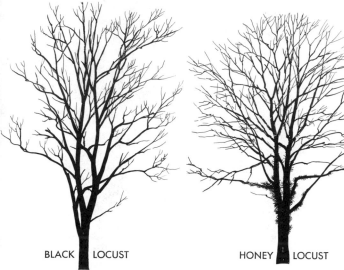

BLACK LOCUST

Trunk usually divided; oblong
head, scraggly branches

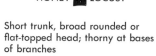

HONEY LOCUST

Short trunk, broad rounded or
flat-topped head; thorny at bases
of branches

TREE-OF-HEAVEN

Flat-topped; branches without
sprays; clusters of winged seeds

STAGHORN SUMAC

Small, straggling, forked, flat-
topped; erect red fruit clusters

SASSAFRAS

Oblong or flat-topped head;
side branches at right angles,
contorted, ending in bushy spray

SWEETGUM

Symmetrical; conical or flat-
topped; twigs with corky wings;
hanging seedballs

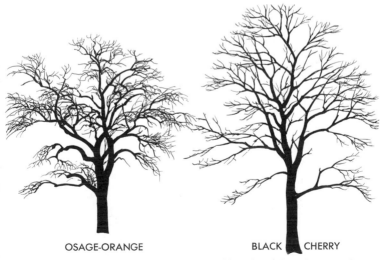

OSAGE-ORANGE

Low ragged crown; gnarled,
thorny; often in hedges

BLACK CHERRY

Oblong head; branches irregular
spreading, often zigzag

Plants with Needlelike or Scalelike Leaves; Mostly Evergreens

THE CONE-BEARING plants and a few evergreen nonconiferous plants with narrow pointed leaves make up this well-defined group.

For the most part, these needle-bearing plants are conifers of the pine family. Exceptions are: related yews and junipers with peculiar berrylike fruits; a miscellaneous group of flowering plants whose showy blossoms often contrast with their needle- or scalelike leaves. Leaves of the last group are not indicative of relationship to the more primitive cone-producing clan.

Though most needle-leaved plants carry evergreen leaves throughout the year, needles are continually dropping and being replaced by new springtime growth. Exceptions are the larches and the Baldcypress, cone-bearers that shed their needles annually. The term evergreen also is often applied to those broad-leaved plants, such as some hollies and rhododendrons, which retain green foliage throughout the year.

A number of needle-bearing species that normally are trees in size and form become dwarfed and sprawling at timberline and in other situations exposed to extreme cold or wind.

Identify unknown plants in this Section by looking through Plates 1–6 (pp. 34–45), or by first tracing down a definite plate number according to the guide below. The few nonevergreen species also are included in the Winter Key in Appendix B.

	Name	*Plate*
1. Erect trees and shrubs, usually neither creeping nor forming mats; seeds borne in woody cones (yews have red and junipers have bluish berries):		
2. Leaves long, needlelike:		
3. Needles occurring in bundles or groups along the twigs	**PINES, LARCHES**	1, 2
3. Needles occurring singly:		
4. Needles blunt, flat	**FIRS, etc.**	3
4. Needles sharp:		
5. Needles more or less 4-sided, neither in opposing pairs nor in whorls of 3	**SPRUCES**	4
5. Needles 3-sided, either in opposing pairs or in whorls of 3	**JUNIPERS**	5
5. Needles thornlike	**GORSE**	6

  2. Leaves very small and scalelike, hugging the twigs:
     6. Leaves blunt; conifers   **WHITE CEDARS,**
                                   JUNIPERS   5
     6. Leaves sharp; a flowering tree   **TAMARISK**   6
1. Plants creeping or forming low mats over the ground
(in much exposed locations or mountains and in the
Far North, see also White Pine (Plate 1), Red Pine
(Plate 2), Balsam Fir, Eastern Hemlock, and Yew
(Plate 3), Black and White Spruces (Plate 4):
     7. Nonflowering plants, seeds borne in woody cones
or hard bluish berries; at least some needles either
small and scalelike, hugging twigs tightly, or
strongly whitened   **WHITE CEDARS,**
                                   JUNIPERS   5
     7. Flowering plants, fruits not cones; needles various   **NON-CONE-BEARERS**   6

Conifers with Needles in Clusters (1): Pines

(Plates 1 and 2, pp. 34, 36)

The pines are cone-bearing evergreen trees with slender needles occurring in groups of 2 to 5 along the twigs. The needle groups are bound in bundles at the base. Only the White Pine has 5 needles per cluster. All the remaining species, generally known as the yellow pines, have 2 or 3 needles per bundle. The cones described are the mature woody female cones. Male cones are small pollen-producing organs that are obvious only during the early flowering period. Female cones usually take two years to mature. If not present on the tree, frequently old ones can be found on the ground nearby. The mature bark of the White Pine is dark and furrowed but that of other pines usually is divided into more or less rectangular plates. Pine branches usually occur in whorls about the trunks; normally 1 whorl is added each year. Only a few pine species occur in any one state; they are more numerous to the south and east. The distribution limits often will assist in identification.

The pines are probably the most important timber trees in the world. Growing principally on dry, sandy soils of little value, they yield not only lumber, but also turpentine, tar, pitch, and a medicinal oil. In Germany and Sweden pine needles are treated to remove the resin and loosen the fibers and are made into "forest wool." This material is used to stuff cushions and mattresses, and blankets and garments woven of it are said to be warm and durable. Several western pines produce edible seeds; those of the pinyon pines (*Pinus edulis* and *P. monophylla*) of the Great Basin region are especially delicious. Seeds of many species rank high among the foods of nearly all game birds, rabbits, hares, squirrels, and chipmunks, and are also eaten by coyote and black bear. The twigs and needles serve as food for deer, moose, and other browsing animals, but mostly under near-starvation conditions.

WHITE PINE *Pinus strobus* L. **pp. 2, 34**
  Recognition: A tall tree with relatively few and horizontal large limbs. Needles 2"–4" long, slender, and occurring 5 *to the bundle.* Cones slender; tapering, thornless, 3"–10" long. Bark not scaly as in other pines but dark with deep furrows. A dwarf matted form occurs in windswept northern areas. Height 80'–110'; diameter 2'–3' (6').
  Similar species: This is our only 5-needled pine.
  Remarks: One of the most important and tallest timber trees in Northeast. So extensively lumbered that few virgin trees, which once grew to heights of 200' to 220', remain. In some areas reforestation is considerable. Wood light, soft, straight-grained, and generally not as resinous as in other pines; of great value for house construction. Plagued by white pine blister rust, a fungus attacking the inner bark, and white pine weevil, an insect that kills the topmost shoot, deforming the tree and limiting its value. The rust can be controlled by removal of currants and gooseberries (Plates 40 and 41) — upon which the fungus spends a portion of its life cycle — from within a quarter-mile of the pines.

PITCH PINE *Pinus rigida* Mill. **pp. 2, 34**
  Recognition: A medium-sized tree with needles 1½"–5" long, *3 per cluster.* Needles coarse, stiff, *mostly twisted,* ⅟₁₆" or more wide. Needle sheaths ⅛"–⅝" long. Cones stout, 1"–3" long, often remaining long on tree; scales tipped with thorns up to ⅛" long. Height 40'–60' (70'); diameter 1'–2' (3').
  Similar species: When (1) Shortleaf or (2) Mountain Pines have needles in 3's the Shortleaf may be identified by whitened twigs, slender untwisted needles, and weak cone prickles and Mountain by the shorter needles and cone prickles over ⅛" long.

SWAMP PINE *Pinus serotina* Michx. f. **p. 34**
  Recognition: Similar to Pitch Pine but needles 5"–11" long. Needle sheaths ⅜"–1" long. Cones 2"–2½", opening late, and with prickles weak or absent. Height to 80'; diameter to 2'.

LOBLOLLY PINE   *Pinus taeda* L.   **pp.** 2, 34
  Recognition: A tall *southern* tree with needles 5″–10″ long and
  3, or sometimes 2, needles per cluster. Needles less than ¹⁄₁₆″
  across. Cones stout, more or less cylindrical, 2½″–5″ long; scales
  mostly under ½″ wide, and when caught by hand the thorn-
  tipped scales hurt. Height 80′–100′ (115′); diameter 1′–2′ (5′).
  Similar species: (1) Pitch Pine has much shorter needles and
  cones; (2) Longleaf Pine, longer needles and cones, much stouter
  twigs. (3) Swamp Pine has coarser needles and shorter, less
  thorny cones. (4) Shortleaf Pine may have some needles in 3's
  but needles shorter, prickles over ⅛″ long. (5) Red Pine occurs
  northward.
  Remarks: An important lumber tree. Invades old fields.

LONGLEAF PINE   *Pinus australis* Michx. f.   **p.** 34
  Recognition: A beautiful straight *southern* tree with *very long
  needles* grouped in 3's. Needles 8″–18″, mostly over 11″, long
  and less than ¹⁄₁₆″ across. Twigs *stout*, diameter ½″ or more.
  Cones stout, conical, 6″–10″ long; scales over ½″ wide. Thrown
  cones hardly prickle when caught by hand. Height 60′–70′ (85′);
  diameter 1′–2′ (3′ 6″).
  Similar species: No other pine has such long needles.
  Remarks: The most important turpentine pine and most valuable timber pine in South. Quick-growing and fire-resistant.

Plate 2
(p. 36)

SHORTLEAF PINE   *Pinus echinata* Mill.   **p.** 36
  Recognition: A tall *southern* tree with 3″–5″ needles in bundles
  of 2's or sometimes 3's. Needles less than ¹⁄₁₆″ across, mostly
  straight and untwisted. Twigs *whitened* with a powdery covering. Cones 1½″–3″ long; scales tipped with a short weak
  prickle. Height 90′–100′ (150′); diameter 3′–4′.
  Similar species: (1) Of 2-needled pines only Red Pine has needles
  as long, but it has pointless cone scales and occurs mostly north
  of this species. (2) Loblolly may have 2-clustered needles but
  they are longer, and cones strongly thorny. (3) When needles
  occur in 3's, Shortleaf Pine resembles Pitch Pine, but that tree
  has twisted needles, unwhitened twigs, and stoutly thorny cones.
  Remarks: An important timber species.

RED PINE   *Pinus resinosa* Ait.   **pp.** 2, 36
  Recognition: A tall *northern* tree with 3″–8″ needles in 2's.
  Needles less than ¹⁄₁₆″ across. Twigs not whitened. Cones
  1½″–2½″ long; scales thornless. Bark plates somewhat red-

dish. A dwarf form is rare. Height 50'–80' (85'); diameter 1'–2' (3').

Similar species: Only (1) Loblolly and (2) Shortleaf Pines may have paired needles of similar length. Both are more southerly, overlapping of ranges being likely only for the Shortleaf, which is differentiated by whitened twigs and somewhat prickly cones.

Remarks: A beautiful tree widely used in reforestation. Often called Norway Pine, but native only to N. America.

JACK PINE   *Pinus banksiana* Lamb.   **p. 36**

Recognition: A scrubby small or medium-sized *northern* tree with *very short* 2-needled clusters. Needles only ¾"–1⅜" long and more than ¹⁄₁₆" across. Cones usually curved or bulging on one side, 1¼"–2" long; scales either thornless or with tiny weak prickles. Height 15'–40'; diameter 9"–15".

Similar species: No other pine in our area has such short needles or curved cones.

Remarks: Produces poor timber, but widespread in some northern areas that otherwise would support no tree growth.

SCRUB PINE   *Pinus virginiana* Mill.   **p. 36**

Recognition: A mostly small or medium-sized southern tree with 1½"–3" needles in 2's. Needles ¹⁄₁₆" or less across. Twigs yellowish or somewhat purplish and *whitened*. Cones somewhat egg-shaped, 1½"–2½", numerous, remaining on tree for many years; scales tipped by ¹⁄₁₆"–⅛" thorns. Height 30'–40' (60'); diameter 1' 2' (3').

Similar species: (1) Scotch and (2) Mountain Pines have needles of this length in 2's but twigs are not whitened. (3) Cones of Scotch Pine are thornless, whereas those of (4) Mountain Pine have sharp thorns of ³⁄₁₆" or more. Scotch Pine spreads from plantings mostly north of Scrub Pine ranges.

SCOTCH PINE   *Pinus sylvestris* L.   **p. 36**

Recognition: A medium-sized to tall northern tree with 1½"–3" needles in 2's. Needles up to ¹⁄₁₆" across. Twigs only slightly or not whitened. Cones 1¼"–2½"; scales with raised more or less sharp point but actually thornless. Higher trunk and branches *bright orange color*. Height 60'–90'; diameter 1'–2'.

Similiar species: (1) Scrub Pine has whitened twigs and thorny cones. (2) Mountain Pine has coarser needles and heavy, long-thorny cones. Neither of these species has the upper bark bright orange.

Remarks: Imported from Europe for forest and Christmas tree plantings.

MOUNTAIN PINE   *Pinus pungens* Lamb.   **p. 36**

Recognition: A small to medium-sized tree with 1½"–3" needles in 2's or, less commonly, in 3's. Needles usually ¹⁄₁₆" or more across. Twigs not whitened. Cones 2″–3½″ long, unusually heavy, woody, opening late; scales tipped by *exceptionally long thorns*, over ³⁄₁₆″. Height to 60′; diameter to 2′. **Similar species:** Cones are distinctive and limited range is helpful. Pitch Pine has longer needles, in 3's and shorter cone thorns. See under Scrub and Scotch Pines.

Conifers with Needles in Clusters (2): Larches

(Plate 2 contd., p. 36)

The larches and Baldcypress (Plate 3) are our only conifers that *drop their leaves* in autumn, leaving conspicuous *warty "spurs"* on the twigs. Needles are clustered at the ends of these spurs. Leaf scars have 1 bundle scar. Cones have relatively few scales, thinner than in pines. Larches are frequently called tamaracks.

AMERICAN LARCH (TAMARACK)   **pp. 5, 36**
Larix laricina (Du Roi) K. Koch.
 Recognition: A medium-sized to large pointed-top tree with slender needles ³⁄₈″–1″ long, on short spurs; needles *many on short spurs*. On longer shoots needles are single. Branchlets not drooping. Cones ½″–1³⁄₁₆″ long. Trunk bark dark, flakes off in small scales. An uncommon form is low, with branches flattened on ground. Height 40′–80′ (90′); diameter 1′–2′ (3′).
 Similar species: (1) European Larch has longer needles and cones, drooping branchlets, and bark with large plates. (2) Baldcypress is southern, and flat needles not clustered.
 Remarks: An important northern timber tree (poles, posts, railroad ties). Seeds, needles, or inner bark eaten by ruffed and sharptail grouse, snowshoe hare, red squirrel, porcupine, and deer.

EUROPEAN LARCH   *Larix decidua* Mill.   **p. 36**
 Recognition: This European form sometimes spreads from plantings. Needles 1″–1¼″ long; branchlets may droop. Cones ¹³⁄₁₆″–1⅜″ in length. Red-brown trunk bark divided into large plates. This is more of an upland species.

Conifers with Flat Needles

(Plate 3, p. 38)

Unlike the pines and spruces, this is a group that for the most part is not closely related. They are alike in having flat needles arranged on the twigs in flat foliage sprays. Plants with flat needles which are low or creeping also should be compared with the plants of Plate 6.

BALSAM FIR *Abies balsamea* (L.) Mill. **pp.** *4*, **38**
  Recognition: A steeple-shaped evergreen tree with needles ⅜″–1¼″ long and *whitened beneath*. Needles have a *broad circular base;* twigs rather *smooth* after needles are removed. Cones 1″–3″ long, *upright and fleshy*, falling apart upon ripening and often leaving erect slender central cores. They are purplish to green, no bracts visible between scales. The plant may grow as a low matlike shrub at timberline. Bark rather smooth, with resin blisters. Height 40′–60′ (75′); diameter 1′–2′ (3′).
  Similar species: Upright cones distinctive when present. Hemlocks have stalked needles and rough twigs. (1) American Yew is shrubby and has smooth twigs. (2) See also Fraser Fir.
  Remarks: A good Christmas tree that holds its needles. Soft, perishable wood of less value than spruce as lumber or pulp. Canada balsam is obtained from bark blisters, a gum used by woodsmen as a wound plaster and waterproof cement; sold in stores as a confection before advent of chicle chewing gum. Formerly used in cementing lenses and in mounting specimens on microscope slides. Fire-by-friction sets are often made of this wood, and resinous fir knots once were used as torches. Seeds are eaten by ruffed, spruce, and sharptail grouse; twigs eaten by snowshoe hare, whitetail deer, and moose; bark gnawed by porcupine.

FRASER FIR *Abies fraseri* (Pursh) Poir. **Not illus.**
  Recognition: Differs from Balsam Fir in cone scale structure and distribution. Cones adorned with bracts whose 3-parted tips *project obviously* from between the scales. Foliage occurs less frequently in flattened sprays. Mostly above 4000′ altitude in mountains of sw. Virginia, w. N. Carolina, and e. Tennessee.

EASTERN HEMLOCK *Tsuga canadensis* (L.) Carr. **pp.** *4*, **38**
  Recognition: Frequently a more round-topped tree than the spruces or firs. Twigs and branchlets more flexible than in those groups; they "ride with the wind." Needles ⁵⁄₁₆″–⁹⁄₁₆″ long, *whitened* beneath, attached to the twigs *by slender stalks*. Twigs *rough* when leaves are removed. Cones only ⅝″–1″ long, brown, few-scaled, pendent. A matlike form occurs in exposed places in n. New England and e. Canada. Bark dark and rough. Height 60′–70′ (100′); diameter 2′–3′ (6′).
  Similar species: Firs have circular needle bases, smooth twigs.
  Remarks: The delicate silvery foliage and small, pendent, perfectly formed brown cones of the hemlock make this one of

our most beautiful forest trees. The fact that the leaves fall upon drying makes it a poor Christmas tree. Formerly spared the ax because of poor quality of wood and stonelike hardness of the knots, which will chip steel blades, but the dearth of timber and tanbark has recently doomed most virgin stands. Lumber taken for pulp but particularly useful for railroad ties, since it holds spikes exceptionally well. Bark rich in tannin; a tea was once made from leaves and twigs by woodsmen and Indians. As fuel, the wood throws sparks. Seeds and needles eaten by ruffed and sharptail grouse; twigs browsed by deer, red squirrel, snowshoe hare, and cottontail rabbit.

CAROLINA HEMLOCK   Not illus.
Tsuga caroliniana Engelm.
Recognition: Like Eastern Hemlock but with needles ⅝″–¾″ long and cones ¾″–1⅜″ long. Occurs in mountains from w. Virginia to w. S. Carolina, n. Georgia, and e. Tennessee.

AMERICAN YEW   *Taxus canadensis* Marsh.   p. 38
Recognition: An evergreen shrub with needles ⅜″–1″ long, pointed, *green on both sides.* Needles stalked, stalks following down twig for a distance below needle. Twigs *smooth.* On female plants, fruits juicy, red, *berrylike,* about ½″ in diameter, single hard seeds visible from beneath. Height to 3′ (6′).
Similar species: No other plants have such fruits. (1) See Balsam Fir. (2) The very low Mountain-heath (Plate 6) or flattened forms of firs or hemlocks might occasionally be confusing, but Mountain-heath has short blunt needles and firs and hemlocks blunt whitened needles.
Remarks: Despite reports that twigs, foliage, and seeds may be poisonous to livestock, the berries are eaten by birds and foliage is a preferred food of deer and moose. Wood is hard, close-grained, and strong. Before the advent of firearms the European species was used in manufacture of bows; the name *Taxus* is from the ancient Greek word meaning bow.

BALDCYPRESS   *Taxodium distichum* (L.) Richard.   pp. 5, 38
Recognition: A majestic *non*evergreen tall tree of *southern swamps.* Needles ¼″–⅞″ long, green on both sides, mostly flat but sometimes somewhat 3-sided; clustered along slender greenish twigs. Needles and most twigs *drop in winter,* leaving branchlets roughened by small few-scaled buds. Leaf scars lacking but areas similar to leaf scars present although without bundle scars. Bark brown and rather smooth but fibrous, and trunk base often deeply ridged. In deep water, *peculiar root growths* called "knees" come upward to surface. Cones *ball-shaped,* about 1″ in diameter, with thick scales. Height 80′–120′ (140′); diameter 3′–4′ (20′).

Similar species: Larches (northern), the only other nonevergreen conifers, have needles in clusters and single bundle scars.

Remarks: Once seen, a mature stand of this majestic relative of the Redwood is not soon forgotten. One of the most valuable lumber trees; used for construction work, railroad ties, posts, shingles. Wood is soft, light, straight-grained, very durable, and does not warp easily. Only distantly related to true cypresses such as famed Monterey Cypress of California. Seeds eaten by cranes and some songbirds. Grows on uplands if planted.

Conifers with 4-sided Needles: Spruces

(Plate 4, p. 40)

Spruces are ornamental, sharply steeple-shaped evergreen trees of cold climates whose needlelike leaves are somewhat 4-angled, short, stiff, and sharp. They tend to grow all around the twigs. When these needles are removed, the twigs and branchlets remain rough from the persistent needle bases. Like firs and yews, spruce branchlets are tipped with twigs arranged in the shape of Christian crosses. Spruce cones are brown and woody when mature and, unlike the firs, are not erect and do not fall apart on the tree. Their scales are thin, not heavy or thorny as in the pines. The bark is rough and dark.

Spruces grow north to the limit of trees, forests thinning down to dwarf specimens extending far into the tundra. One species persists on mountaintops as far south as Georgia. Low matted specimens should be compared with the plants of Plate 6.

Spruces often are used as Christmas trees, but their needles fall quickly upon drying out. The wood is soft, light, resinous, and straight-grained. It provides a principal source of pulp for paper and is valuable for sounding boards in pianos and in construction work, interior finishing, and boatbuilding. Tannin and "burgundy pitch," used in varnishes and medicinal compounds, come from the bark of certain species. In Europe some spruces are tapped for turpentine, and in times of food shortage the inner bark has been ground and added to flour. Spruce beer, it is reported, is made from the fermented leaves and twigs of Red or Black Spruces after being boiled with honey. Several spruces are of great value in landscaping. Their immaculate appearance doubtless provides the basis for the term "spruced."

RED SPRUCE   *Picea rubens* Sarg.   **pp. 3, 40**
   Recognition: Twigs and buds typically *hairy;* needles *dark or yellow-green,* ½"–⅝" long and often curved upward. Cones

1¼″–1⅝″ long, more or less reddish brown with scale edges smooth. They fall soon after maturity. Height 60′–70′ (75′); diameter 1′–2′ (3′).
Similar species: Black Spruce has shorter needles and cones; occurs on moist sites.

BLACK SPRUCE   *Picea mariana* (Mill.) BSP.   **pp.** 3, **40**
Recognition: Twigs and buds *hairy*. Needles *short*. Needles mostly ¼″–⁷⁄₁₆″ long, sometimes blue-green with a white powder. Cones only ¾″–1¼″ long, somewhat gray-brown, with scale edges rather ragged. Cones usually remain on tree for several years. Low matlike forms are known from northern mountains, especially where exposed to severe winds and cold. Height 25′–30′; diameter 1′–2′.
Similar species: (1) Red and (2) White Spruces have longer needles and cones and occur mostly on uplands. White Spruce has hairless twigs.

NORWAY SPRUCE   *Picea abies* (L.) Karst.   **pp.** 3, **40**
Recognition: Twigs are *hairless* or nearly so. Needles *dark green*, mostly ½″–1″ long. The twigs and *branchlets hang downward*. Cones 4″–6″ *long*, falling soon after maturing; scales stiff. Height 60′–90′; diameter 1′–3′.
Similar species: Only spruce with drooping branchlets and only one with large cones.

WHITE SPRUCE   *Picea glauca* (Moench) Voss   **pp.** 3, **40**
Recognition: Twigs and buds are *hairless;* needles *blue-green*, ⅜″–¾″ long. Branchlets do not droop. Cones 1″–2″ long; scales flexible, dropping soon after maturing. In Far North and on high mountains a low matlike form occurs in exposed locations. Height 50′–60′; diameter 1′–2′.
Similar species: Black Spruce has shorter needles, hairy twigs, and occurs more abundantly in swamps.

Conifers with Scalelike or 3-sided Leaves
(Plate 5, p. 42)

Differing from all other cone-bearing trees, these related species possess very small, peculiarly flattened leaves that form scaly coverings for at least some twigs. *Juniperus* fruits, though technically similar to cones, are berrylike.
  The white cedars possess only scalelike, flattened needles; the junipers (including the Red Cedar) may bear either scaly or hollowed 3-sided needles, or both. Occasionally, some leaves of

the Baldcypress are 3-sided rather than flat but they are more fernlike and not whitened (see Plate 3).

The 3-sided type of leaf is only approximately triangular in cross section, but is easily recognized by the concave whitish inside surface. These needles may occur in pairs of 3's but are never bound at the base in bundles as are pine and larch needles. It may be necessary to use a magnifying glass to determine arrangements of scaly leaves, but usually more easily determined characteristics are available. Seedlings may be impossible to identify. The fruiting structures are quite diverse (see p. 42).

Although several of these are popularly known as cedars, only members of the Old World genus *Cedrus*, including the cedars of Lebanon, N. Africa, and the Himalayas, are true cedars. They may be seen in this country only where planted for decorative purposes. True cedars have larchlike clusters of needles that remain evergreen.

NORTHERN WHITE CEDAR (ARBOR VITAE) pp. 4, 42
Thuja occidentalis L.

Recognition: A medium-sized tree with leaves nearly all scalelike and $\frac{1}{16}''$–$\frac{1}{8}''$ long. They occur in 4 rows around twigs but are flattened from the sides. Central leaves show tiny glands. Twigs and leaves occur *in flattened sprays* that typically are aligned vertically. Heartwood light-colored. Cones more or less bell-shaped, about $\frac{1}{2}''$ long. A prostrate, carpetlike form occurs in Quebec. Bark is fibrous with numerous cross-thatched ridges. Height 40′–50′ (125′); diameter 2′–3′ (5′).

Similar species: (1) Atlantic White Cedar has different range, less flattened leaves and leaf sprays, globular cones. (2) See Tamarisk (p. 28).

Remarks: An earlier, widely used name is Arbor Vitae, a latinized French name meaning "tree-of-life." It was so named after it cured the men of Jacques Cartier's Canadian expedition of a disease, probably scurvy. The incident resulted in this being the first tree to be imported from America into Europe. Over 50 varieties now in cultivation. Known also as Canoe-wood, it was used by the Indians. Thin slabs of the wood were prepared by pounding the ends of short logs until they separated along the annual rings. Wood is soft, light-colored, durable, and used for shingles and fire-by-friction sets. Outer bark supplies tinder. Cedar swamps provide favorite winter quarters and food for deer. Moose, snowshoe hares, and cottontail rabbits also eat the twigs and foliage; red squirrels and many songbirds consume the seeds.

ATLANTIC WHITE CEDAR p. 42
Chamaecyparis thyoides (L.) BSP.

Recognition: Similar to Northern White Cedar but with the scalelike leaves *narrower*, less distinct, and not so much flattened on the twigs. The foliage sprays not flattened. Cones *globular*, ¼″–½″ in diameter. Height 40′–60′; diameter 1′–2′ (3′).

Similar species: See Tamarisk (p. 28).

Remarks: Both the lumber and crushed foliage are aromatic. Wood is soft, durable, very light. The lumber, used in ship-building, construction work, and as shingles, is of such value that large logs buried in prehistoric times have been mined in New Jersey bogs. Formerly, organ pipes were made of this resonant wood. White cedar charcoal was used in making gunpowder during American Revolution. Their beauty and resistance to insects and disease have caused a number of horticultural varieties of this tree and its oriental relatives to be used in landscaping. A native species also known as Arbor Vitae. It is browsed by deer.

DWARF JUNIPER   *Juniperus communis* L.   **p. 42**

Recognition: A tree, or more commonly a shrub, with sharp, hollowed, 3-sided needles or scalelike leaves that occur in *whorls of 3, whitened above* and ¼″–⅞″ long. Twigs, or at least branchlets, are *3-sided*. Fruits are berries, rather hard, blue-black, with a white powder, and are ball-shaped. In our area, 3 varieties (especially var. *depressa* Pursh) of low, creeping, mat-forming habit are more widespread than the upright form. Height 1′–4′ (35′); diameter 1″–6″ (1′).

Similar species: Only juniper with needles in 3's and strongly whitened. (1) Trailing Juniper has paired green needles. (2) Heather (Plate 6) has 4-sided leafy twigs. (3) Tamarisk (p. 28) is taller, with flowers and fruit capsules.

Remarks: Oil from leaves and wood is used in perfumery, and the aromatic foliage is burned as an incense in India. The plant supplies food for ruffed and sharptail grouse, bobwhite, "Hungarian" partridge, pheasant, whitetail deer, moose, and smaller birds and mammals.

RED CEDAR   *Juniperus virginiana* L.   **pp. 4, 42**

Recognition: A medium-sized tree usually with both scalelike and longer, sharply 3-sided, needlelike leaves. Leaves ¹⁄₁₆″–¾″, entirely green, in pairs in 4 rows along *4-sided twigs* and branchlets. Heartwood reddish. Fruits more or less *globular*, hard, whitish- to blackish-green berries about ¼″ in diameter, 1–2 seeds. Bark dry, shreddy, not ridged. Rarely — in wind-swept locations — shrubby and creeping. Height 40′–50′ (62′); diameter 1′–2′ (4′).

Similar species: (1) Mexican Juniper has no central trunk and barely enters our area. (2) Tamarisk (p. 28) has alternate needles, flowers, and fruit capsules.

Remarks: Birds pass the seeds through their digestive tracts undamaged, dropping them particularly along fences. The Red Cedar acts as alternate host to the apple rust. During half its life cycle this fungus spots apples and their leaves; during the other half, it forms ball-shaped brown galls on cedar twigs. After heavy rains these galls extrude numerous hanging brown gelatinous threads. Do not confuse with cedar fruits, which are hard but berrylike.

Heartwood is aromatic and of rose-brown color. It is light, strong, durable, and widely used for cedar chests, cabinets, lead pencils, fuel, and fence posts. The dry outer bark, when stripped and rubbed between the hands, provides excellent tinder and is used in flint-and-steel and sunglass fire sets. A volatile oil derived from juniper leaves is used in perfumes and a flavoring may be derived from the berries. The fruits are consumed by well over 50 species of birds, including bobwhite, sharptail grouse, pheasant, and mourning dove, and also by opossum.

MEXICAN JUNIPER   Not illus.
Juniperus mexicana Spreng.
  Recognition: A round-topped shrub or tree that, unlike other upright junipers, has *no central trunk*. Unlike Red Cedar and Trailing Juniper, the seeds (not fruits) are over 3/16" long. There is usually 1 seed per fruit, but there may be 2–3. Sw. Missouri and w. Texas westward.

TRAILING JUNIPER   p. 42
Juniperus horizontalis Moench
  Recognition: Like the preceding 2 species in needle arrangement but more northerly and *prostrate*, mat-forming, and often trailing. Fruits may be up to 3/8" in diameter, containing 3–5 seeds. Foliage or fruits eaten by sharptail grouse, whitetail deer, and moose. Dwarf Juniper has whitened needles in whorls of 3. Heather (Plate 6) has 4-sided, rather leafy twigs. Tamarisk (p. 28) is taller, with flowers and fruit capsules.

Needle-bearing, Non-Cone-bearing Evergreens
(Plate 6, p. 44)

In addition to the cone-bearers, a few flowering plants have needlelike and sometimes also scalelike leaves. Nearly all such plants have colorful blossoms. In general, they are creeping in habit, forming dense, matted, sometimes mosslike, growths.

Tamarisk, however, is an erect shrub or tree and Gorse is an upright shrub. Dwarf Mistletoe is parasitic on conifer branches. Of the plants discussed in the following accounts only Tamarisk, Heather, and Mountain-heath conceivably might be confused with any other members of the needle-bearing group. Alpine-azalea and Sandmyrtle, whose small opposite leaves are too broad to be considered needlelike, are shown on Plates 12 and 17. Some plants of this plate are of value in the control of soil erosion or in the anchoring of dunes.

Nearly all the conifers that grow in the Far North and on high mountains may grow in a dwarf or matted manner in exposed locations. This is true of White and Red Pines (Plates 1 and 2), Balsam Fir, Eastern Hemlock, and American Yew (Plate 3). Black and White Spruces (Plate 4), Northern White Cedar, Red Cedar, and Dwarf and Trailing Junipers (Plate 5). When identifications are attempted in such locations, the accounts of those conifers also should be consulted.

DOWNY HUDSONIA   *Hudsonia ericoides* L.   **p. 44**
Recognition: A *mosslike* shrub with the needlelike leaves somewhat hairy but greenish, spreading, sharp, and ⅛″–³⁄₁₆″ long. Older bark flaking. Flowers small, clustered, yellow, or rarely white, May–June. Fruits small, dry, 1-parted capsules.
Similar species: (1) Woolly Hudsonia also hairy but has shorter and more matted-hairy needlelike leaves. (2) Purple Crowberry has fleshy fruits and blunt-tipped leaves.

WOOLLY HUDSONIA   *Hudsonia tomentosa* Nutt.   **p. 44**
Recognition: Similar to preceding species but with ¹⁄₁₆″–⅛″ needles enmeshed in *thick whitish hair* and hugging the twigs. A form intermediate between the two species may be a hybrid.

TAMARISK   *Tamarix gallica* L.   **Not illus.**
Recognition: An importation from Eurasia, this upright shrub or tree is becoming established in the Northeast. In some localities called Salt-cedar. Pale green leaves less than ¹⁄₁₆″ long, scalelike, on long, slender, often drooping twigs. Numerous slender spikes of pink, or sometimes whitish, flowers usually present from May to Sept. Fruits small dry capsules. Roadsides and thickets; Massachusetts, Indiana, and Kansas to Florida, s. Texas, and s. California.

HEATHER   *Calluna vulgaris* (L.) Hull   **p. 44**
Recognition: A low *fernlike* shrub with *sharp* green needles ¹⁄₃₂″–¹⁄₁₆″ long, crowded in 4 rows along twigs. Bare portions of twigs or branchlets evident. Older bark smooth. Height 5″–15″. Flowers small, clustered, pink, or less commonly white, July–Nov. Fruits small, dry, 4-parted capsules.

Similar species: The junipers are low and bushy but do not have needles in 4 dense rows.

CASSIOPE   *Cassiope hypnoides* (L.) D. Don   **p. 44**
Recognition: A tufted *mosslike* creeping shrub with *blunt* green needles ⅟₁₆″–³⁄₁₆″ long, crowded in 4 rows along twigs. Bare portions of twigs or branchlets usually hidden on upright portions of plant. Older outer bark smooth. Height 1″–5″. Flowers small, single, pink or white, on long stalks, June–Aug. Fruits small, dry, 4- to 5-parted capsules.

CROSSLEAF HEATH   *Erica tetralix* L.   **Not illus.**
Recognition: Like Cassiope, a creeping shrub with needles ⅟₁₆″–³⁄₁₆″ long in 4 rows on twigs. Leaves less densely crowded, with *knob-tipped hairs* visible to the eye and readily apparent under hand lens. Bare portions of twigs readily evident. Height to 10″–12″. Flowers small, pink, vase-shaped, clustered at twig tips, July–Oct. Fruits small, dry, 4-parted capsules. European plant established in acid soils; scattered localities in Maine, e. Massachusetts, and W. Virginia.

CORNISH HEATH   *Erica vagans* L.   **Not illus.**
Recognition: Similar to Crossleaf Heath but with needles *hairless*, in 3's and 4's. Flowers occur in side rather than end clusters. Established locally on Nantucket I., Massachusetts.

SCOTCH HEATH   *Erica cinerea* L.   **Not illus.**
Recognition: A low creeping shrub with needles ⅛″–¼″ long *in whorls of 3* with numerous additional and smaller needles clustered in the angles of longer needles; not hairy. Flowers vase-shaped, purple, at twig tips or in side clusters, July–Oct. Fruits small, dry, 4-parted capsules. A European introduction established locally on Nantucket I., Massachusetts.

BROOM-CROWBERRY   *Corema conradii* Torr.   **p. 44**
Recognition: A spreading low shrub with very narrow green needles ⅛″–³⁄₁₆″ long. Leaves may be in 4's but are staggered on twigs to form 8 rows or a scattered pattern. Older bark flaky. Height 6″–24″. Flowers without petals; male blossoms purplish, in heads at ends of twigs, March–May. Fruits small, rather *dry* brown berries with 3, or less commonly 4–5, seeds, July–Aug.
Similar species: True crowberries are lower, have wider needles, scattered flowers, and juicy fruits with more numerous seeds.

BLACK CROWBERRY   *Empetrum nigrum* L.   **p. 44**
Recognition: A ground-hugging, spreading shrub with narrow or somewhat elliptic, sharp-tipped, green needles ⅛″–¼″ long.

Leaves dense, not regularly in 4 rows. Twigs hairless or somewhat long-hairy. Older bark flaky. Height 2″–3″. Flowers
without petals, scattered, June–July. Fruits pea-sized, *juicy*,
black, rarely white, with 6–9 seeds, July–Nov. or longer.
Similar species: (1) Purple and (2) Rock Crowberries have hairy
leaves. (3) See also Broom-crowberry.
Remarks: Over 40 birds, including ruffed grouse and ptarmigan,
are known to eat the fruits.

PURPLE CROWBERRY   Not illus.
Empetrum atropurpureum Fern. & Wieg.
  Recognition: Similar to Black Crowberry but with *white-woolly*
  leaves and twigs. Leaves of growing shoots blunt-tipped,
  ³⁄₁₆″–¼″ long. Fruits red to purple, ³⁄₁₆″–⅝″ across. Rock
  Crowberry has shorter leaves. Downy Hudsonia has longer,
  sharp-tipped leaves. Sandy and rocky soils; s. Labrador and
  Quebec to s. Nova Scotia and n. New England.

ROCK CROWBERRY   Not illus.
Empetrum eamesii Fern. & Wieg.
  Recognition: Like Purple Crowberry but with needles of grow-
  ing shoots ⅛″–³⁄₁₆″ long. Fruits pink to light red, ⅛″–³⁄₁₆″ across.
  Sandy and rocky soils; se. Labrador and Newfoundland to Nova
  Scotia.

DWARF MISTLETOE   Not illus.
Arceuthobium pusillum Peck
  Recognition: An *inconspicuous parasitic shrub* with tiny opposite scalelike leaves. Stems rectangular in cross section, less than
  1″ long. Fruits small, dry. Only other mistletoe (p. 69) has wide,
  opposite, leathery leaves. This plant often causes "witches
  brooms" among branches of host plant, but such dense tangles
  also may be caused by bacteria, fungi, or other organisms.
  Grows mostly on Spruce but also on Larch and White Pine
  branches. Newfoundland, Ontario, and Minnesota to n. New
  Jersey, n. Pennsylvania, and Michigan.

MOUNTAIN-HEATH *Phyllodoce caerulea* (L.) Bab.   **p. 44**
  Recognition: A low shrub with *blunt flat needles* ³⁄₁₆″–⅜″ long.
  Needle bases appear to follow along twigs for a short distance,
  as in American Yew (Plate 3). Older bark flaky. Height to 8″.
  Flowers small, cup-shaped, purplish, scattered, June–Aug.
  Fruits small, dry, 5-parted capsules.
  Similar species: Seedling American Yews (Plate 3) have longer
  pointed needles and red fleshy fruits.

GORSE *Ulex europaeus* L.   **p. 44**
  Recognition: A *very spiny* low dense shrub with sharp triangular

spinelike leaves ¼″–2″ long. Twigs and branchlets are somewhat hairy and are marked by distinct lengthwise *ridges*. Buds
small; no leaf scars. Height to 4′. Flowers large, yellow,
May–Sept. Fruits short pods, Aug.–Oct.

Remarks: A European importation of some use as a sand binder.
Reportedly very flammable when dry.

FRUITS OF CONIFERS

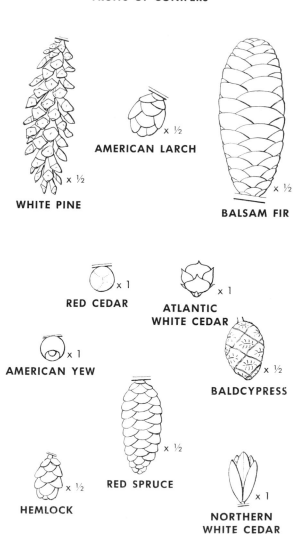

WHITE PINE × ½

AMERICAN LARCH × ½

BALSAM FIR × ½

RED CEDAR × 1

ATLANTIC WHITE CEDAR × 1

AMERICAN YEW × 1

BALDCYPRESS × ½

RED SPRUCE × ½

HEMLOCK × ½

NORTHERN WHITE CEDAR × 1

Plants with Needlelike or Scalelike Leaves

(Key, pages 15–16; text, pages 15–31)

FRUITS OF CONIFERS *(opposite)*

THOUGH the fruits of the yews and junipers are fleshy and bear little resemblance to the usual cones of members of the pine family, all are alike in having developed from naked ovules. Higher flowering plants have their ovules enclosed in ovaries.

Each yew fruit consists of a single bony seed partially surrounded by reddish pulp.

Juniper (including Red Cedar) "berries" are bluish black and covered with a whitish powder. In most junipers, they completely enclose several seeds.

Variously shaped cones are borne by the other conifers. Their seeds are developed at the bases of the cone scales.

CONIFERS WITH NEEDLES IN CLUSTERS (1): PINES

Needles 2–5 in bundles, evergreen

(3- and 5-leaved pines on this plate,
2-leaved pines on next plate)

♠ WHITE PINE, *Pinus strobus*   p. 17
   Uplands; Newfoundland, centr. Ontario and sw. Manitoba to
   e. Maryland, w. N. Carolina, n. Georgia, e. Tennessee, and
   ne. Iowa.

♠ PITCH PINE, *Pinus rigida*   p. 17
   Sterile soils; Maine, se. Ontario and e. Ohio south to w.
   S. Carolina, and in mts. to nw. Georgia and e. Tennessee.

♠ SWAMP PINE, *Pinus serotina*   p. 17
   Coastal Plain swamps and woods; s. New Jersey to Florida
   and Alabama. Uncommon in our portion of range.

♠ LOBLOLLY PINE, *Pinus taeda*   p. 18
   Coastal Plain and Piedmont Plateau; s. New Jersey to Florida,
   west to e. Texas and north in Mississippi Valley to sw. Tennessee, Arkansas, and e. Oklahoma.

♠ LONGLEAF PINE, *Pinus australis*   p. 18
   Sandy soils; Coastal Plain from se. Virginia to Florida and
   west to e. Texas.

5-LEAVED PINE

WHITE PINE
Needles 2″–4″, slender.
Cones 3″–10″, thornless.

3-LEAVED PINES

PITCH PINE
Needles 2″–5″, stout.
Cones 1″–3″, with stout thorns.

SWAMP PINE
Needles 5″–11″, stout.
Cones 2″–2½″, with weak prickles.

LOBLOLLY PINE*
Needles 5″–10″, slender.
Cones 2½″–5″, with stout thorns.

LONGLEAF PINE
Needles 8″–18″, slender.
Cones 6″–10″, with weak prickles.

*Some specimens of Loblolly may bear
both 2- and 3-needle clusters.

PITCH

SWAMP

LOBLOLLY

LONGLEAF

CONIFERS WITH NEEDLES IN CLUSTERS (2): PINES AND LARCHES

PINES: **Needles 2–5 in bunches, evergreen**

(2-leaved pines on this plate,
3- and 5-leaved pines on preceding plate)

LARCHES: **Needles numerous at the ends of warty spur branches; drop in autumn**

⁜ SHORTLEAF PINE, *Pinus echinata*   p. 18
   Dry soils; se. New York, New Jersey, Pennsylvania, s. Ohio, s. Illinois, s. Missouri, and e. Oklahoma to n. Florida and ne. Texas.

⁜ RED PINE, *Pinus resinosa*   p. 18
   Dry soils; Newfoundland, Ontario, and se. Manitoba to n. New Jersey, n. Pennsylvania, Michigan, and Minnesota; locally in e. W. Virginia.

⁜ JACK PINE, *Pinus banksiana*   p. 19
   Poor dry soils; Nova Scotia, n. Quebec, Northwest Territories and n. British Columbia to n. New England, n. New York, nw. Indiana, n. Illinois, Minnesota, s. Manitoba, and centr. Alberta.

⁜ SCRUB PINE, *Pinus virginiana*   p. 19
   Poor soils; se. New York, Pennsylvania, and s. Indiana to n. Georgia, Alabama, and Mississippi.

⁜ SCOTCH PINE, *Pinus sylvestris*   p. 19
   Spreading from plantings; New England, Ontario, and Michigan to Delaware and Iowa.

⁜ MOUNTAIN PINE, *Pinus pungens*   p. 19
   Appalachians and foothills; local, New Jersey and Pennsylvania to S. Carolina, Georgia, and Tennessee.

⁜ AMERICAN LARCH (TAMARACK), *Larix laricina*   p. 20
   Wooded swamps and bogs; Newfoundland, Labrador, and Alaska to n. New Jersey, n. Maryland, n. W. Virginia, ne. Illinois, Minnesota, and nw. British Columbia.

⁜ EUROPEAN LARCH, *Larix decidua*   p. 20
   European; mostly uplands; sometimes spreads from plantings.

2-LEAVED PINES
Needles 3"–8", slender
SHORTLEAF PINE*
  Southern distribution, twigs whitish.
  Cones 1½"–3", usually weakly thorny.
RED PINE
  Northern distribution, twigs brown.
  Cones 1½"–2½", thornless.

Needles ½"–3", usually stout
JACK PINE
  Needles usually very short, ¾"–1⅝".
  Cones 1¼"–2", lopsided, thornless.
SCRUB PINE
  Needles longer, 1½"–3". Twigs whitish.
  Cones 1½"–2½", thorny.
SCOTCH PINE
  Needles 1½"–3". Twigs yellow to brown.
  Cones 1¼"–2½", thornless.
MOUNTAIN PINE*
  Needles 1½"–3". Twigs yellow to brown.
  Cones 2"–3½", very thorny.

*Some specimens may bear both 2- and 3-needle clusters (most
bundles, however, have 2 needles).

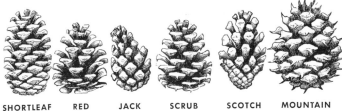

SHORTLEAF   RED   JACK   SCRUB   SCOTCH   MOUNTAIN

LARCHES
Needles mainly numerous on spurs, dropping in autumn

AMERICAN LARCH (Tamarack)
  Needles ⅜"–1" long; cones less than 1³⁄₁₆";
  lateral branchlets not drooping; bark shedding
  in small pieces; mostly swamps.
EUROPEAN LARCH
  Needles mostly more than 1"; cones more than
  1³⁄₁₆"; lateral branchlets drooping; bark shedding in large plates; mostly uplands.

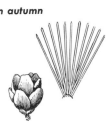

CONIFERS WITH FLAT NEEDLES

Needles attached singly; needles and twigs arranged
in flat sprays.

⬆ BALSAM FIR, *Abies balsamea*   p. 21
   Bottomland and moist woods; Newfoundland, Labrador, and
   ne. Alberta to New England, w. Virginia, e. W. Virginia, ne.
   Ohio, ne. Iowa, and Minnesota.
   ⬆ FRASER FIR, *A. fraseri* (not illus.)   p. 21
   Mostly above 4000 ft. in mts.; sw. Virginia, w. N. Carolina,
   and e. Tennessee.

⬆ EASTERN HEMLOCK, *Tsuga canadensis*   p. 21
   Well-drained or moist woods; Nova Scotia, s. Ontario, n.
   Michigan, e. Minnesota to Maryland, Kentucky, and Indiana,
   and in mts. to n. Georgia and n. Alabama.
   ⬆ CAROLINA HEMLOCK, *T. caroliniana* (not illus.)   p. 22
   Mountains; from W. Virginia to w. S. Carolina, n. Georgia,
   and e. Tennessee.

⬇ AMERICAN YEW, *Taxus canadensis*   p. 22
   Moist woods; Newfoundland and Manitoba to New England,
   w. Virginia, ne. Kentucky, and ne. Iowa.

⬆ BALDCYPRESS, *Taxodium distichum*   p. 22
   Flooded swamps and along streambanks; Coastal Plain from
   s. New Jersey to Florida, west to Texas, and north in Mississippi Valley to sw. Indiana, s. Illinois, w. Kentucky, and
   se. Missouri.

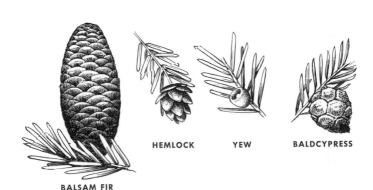

HEMLOCK   YEW   BALDCYPRESS

BALSAM FIR

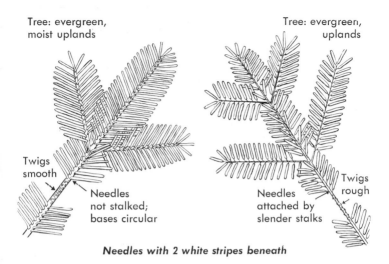

Tree: evergreen, moist uplands

Twigs smooth

Needles not stalked; bases circular

Tree: evergreen, uplands

Needles attached by slender stalks

Twigs rough

Needles with 2 white stripes beneath

BALSAM FIR

EASTERN HEMLOCK

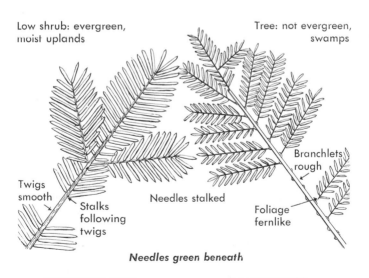

Low shrub: evergreen, moist uplands

Tree: not evergreen, swamps

Twigs smooth

Stalks following twigs

Needles stalked

Branchlets rough

Foliage fernlike

Needles green beneath

AMERICAN YEW

BALDCYPRESS

CONIFERS WITH MOSTLY 4-SIDED NEEDLES: SPRUCES

Needles square in cross section, stiff, sharp, attached singly. Branchlets rough when needles removed. Cones hang pendently; brown, woody.

♦ RED SPRUCE, *Picea rubens*   p. 23
   Well-drained soils; Nova Scotia and s. Quebec to n. New Jersey, ne. Pennsylvania, and e. New York; also in mts. from w. Maryland and W. Virginia to w. N. Carolina and e. Tennessee.

♦ BLACK SPRUCE, *Picea mariana*   p. 24
   Bogs and wet soils; Newfoundland, Labrador, and Alaska to n. New Jersey, n. Pennsylvania, Michigan, n. Minnesota, s. Manitoba, and British Columbia.

♦ NORWAY SPRUCE, *Picea abies*   p. 24
   European; occasionally spreading from plantings, on uplands.

♦ WHITE SPRUCE, *Picea glauca*   p. 24
   Upland soils; Newfoundland, Labrador, and Alaska to Maine, nw. Massachusetts, n. New York, Michigan, Minnesota, w. S. Dakota, and Wyoming.

BLACK	RED	WHITE	NORWAY
Under 1¼″ long; scales stiff; old cones remain on tree for years.	Over 1¼″ long; scales stiff; mostly falling upon ripening.	1″–2″ long; scales flexible; mostly falling upon ripening.	4″–6″ long; scales stiff; mostly falling upon ripening.

CONES OF SPRUCES

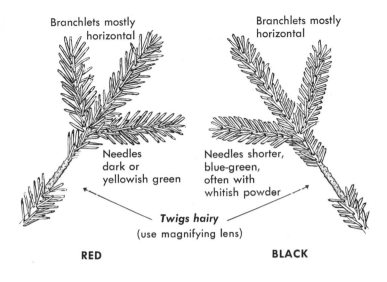

Branchlets mostly horizontal

Branchlets mostly horizontal

Needles dark or yellowish green

Needles shorter, blue-green, often with whitish powder

Twigs hairy
(use magnifying lens)

RED

BLACK

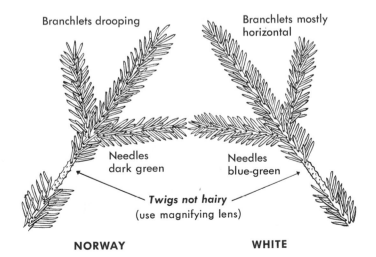

Branchlets drooping

Branchlets mostly horizontal

Needles dark green

Needles blue-green

Twigs not hairy
(use magnifying lens)

NORWAY

WHITE

CONIFERS WITH SCALELIKE OR 3-SIDED HOLLOWED LEAVES

Leaves in pairs or whorls and of 2 types, either or both of which may be present as indicated on opposite page.

⬧ NORTHERN WHITE CEDAR (ARBOR VITAE)   p. 25
   Thuja occidentalis
       Swamps and limestone soils; Nova Scotia, Quebec, n. Ontario and s. Manitoba to s. New York, s. Ohio, n. Illinois and e. Minnesota; in mts. to w. N. Carolina and e. Tennessee.

⬧ ATLANTIC WHITE CEDAR   p. 25
   Chamaecyparis thyoides
       Swamps near coast; s. Maine to n. Florida and west to Mississippi.

⬧V DWARF JUNIPER, *Juniperus communis*   p. 26
       Rocky infertile soils; Greenland and Alaska to Virginia, w. Illinois, Minnesota, New Mexico, and California; in mts. to w. S. Carolina, n. Georgia, and e. Tennessee.

⬧ RED CEDAR, *Juniperus virginiana*   p. 26
       Dry soils, old fields; sw. Maine, s. Quebec, s. Ontario, s. Michigan, s. Minnesota, and sw. N. Dakota to Georgia and Texas.
   ⬧V MEXICAN JUNIPER, *J. mexicana* (not illus.)   p. 27
       Sw. Missouri and w. Texas westward.

V TRAILING JUNIPER, *Juniperus horizontalis* p. 27
       Dry, mostly sandy soils; Newfoundland and Alaska to Maine, nw. New York, n. Illinois, Nebraska, and Wyoming.

NORTHERN   **ATLANTIC**   **RED CEDAR**
WHITE CEDAR   **WHITE CEDAR**   **(AND JUNIPERS)**

Leaves scalelike, hugging the twigs and branchlets

Trees

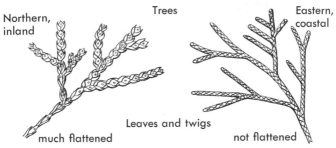

Northern, inland

much flattened

Eastern, coastal

Leaves and twigs

not flattened

NORTHERN WHITE CEDAR

ATLANTIC WHITE CEDAR

Leaves scalelike, hugging twigs and branchlets, or 3-sided hollow needles, or mixed,
with scales on older branches, needles on twigs

Fruits, bluish berries

Low shrub, some varieties matlike; rarely a small tree

Needles in whorls of 3, one side white

Branchlets 3-sided

DWARF JUNIPER

Tree

Scalelike foliage

Needlelike foliage

Low, creeping, mat-forming shrub

Needles mostly opposite, entirely green. Scale-covered branchlets 4-sided

RED CEDAR

TRAILING JUNIPER

NEEDLE-BEARING, NON-CONE-BEARING EVERGREENS

Flowering plants that, excepting Tamarisk, Gorse, and Dwarf Mistletoe, are creeping, mat-forming. Dry fruit capsules, pods, or berries often present.

Ⅴ DOWNY HUDSONIA, *Hudsonia ericoides*   p. 28
   Sands and poor soils near the coast; Newfoundland and Prince Edward I. to New Jersey and Delaware.

Ⅴ WOOLLY HUDSONIA, *Hudsonia tomentosa*   p. 28
   Sands, especially along coast and Great Lakes; Prince Edward I., s. Labrador, and n. Alberta to N. Carolina, n. Indiana, Illinois, and Saskatchewan.

   ♦Ⅴ TAMARISK, *Tamarix gallica* (not illus.)   p. 28
Ⅴ HEATHER, *Calluna vulgaris*   p. 28
   European; established on sandy or acid soils; local, Newfoundland and Michigan to New Jersey and W. Virginia.

Ⅴ CASSIOPE, *Cassiope hypnoides*   p. 29
   Tundras and mountaintops; from the Far North to Maine, New Hampshire and New York.

   Ⅴ CROSSLEAF HEATH, *Erica tetralix* (not illus.)   p. 29
   Ⅴ CORNISH HEATH, *E. vagans* (not illus.)   p. 29
   Ⅴ SCOTCH HEATH, *E. cinerea* (not illus.)   p. 29

Ⅴ BROOM-CROWBERRY, *Corema conradii*   p. 29
   Sandy and rocky places near coast; Newfoundland to New Jersey.

Ⅴ BLACK CROWBERRY, *Empetrum nigrum*   p. 29
   Acid and sandy soils; Arctic to n. New England, n. Michigan, n. Minnesota, s. Alberta, and n. California and on e. Long Island.

   Ⅴ PURPLE CROWBERRY   p. 30
   E. atropurpureum (not illus.)

   Ⅴ ROCK CROWBERRY, *E. eamesii* (not illus.)   p. 30

   Ⅴ DWARF MISTLETOE   p. 30
   Arceuthobium pusillum (not illus.)
   Parasitic mostly on Spruce, but also on Larch and White Pine branches; Newfoundland, Ontario, and Minnesota to n. New Jersey, n. Pennsylvania, and Michigan.

Ⅴ MOUNTAIN-HEATH, *Phyllodoce caerulea*   p. 30
   Tundras and bogs; south to Newfoundland, Quebec, Maine, and New Hampshire.

Ⅴ GORSE, *Ulex europaeus*   p. 30
   European; sandy areas; escape from se. Massachusetts to Virginia and W. Virginia and on the West Coast.

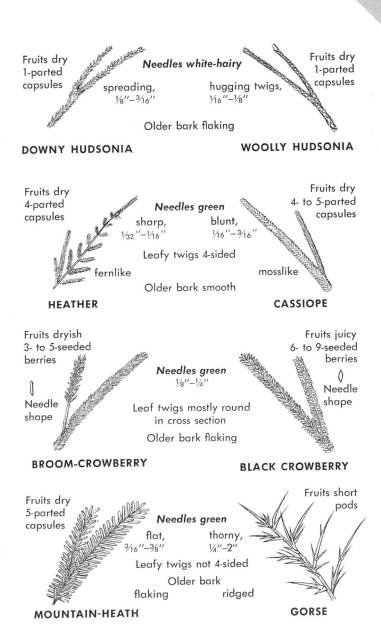

Fruits dry
1-parted
capsules

Needles white-hairy

spreading,
1/8″–3/16″

hugging twigs,
1/16″–1/8″

Fruits dry
1-parted
capsules

Older bark flaking

DOWNY HUDSONIA

WOOLLY HUDSONIA

Fruits dry
4-parted
capsules

Needles green

sharp,
1/32″–1/16″

blunt,
1/16″–3/16″

Leafy twigs 4-sided

fernlike

mosslike

Older bark smooth

Fruits dry
4- to 5-parted
capsules

HEATHER

CASSIOPE

Fruits dryish
3- to 5-seeded
berries

Needle
shape

Needles green
1/8″–1/4″

Leaf twigs mostly round
in cross section

Older bark flaking

Fruits juicy
6- to 9-seeded
berries

Needle
shape

BROOM-CROWBERRY

BLACK CROWBERRY

Fruits dry
5-parted
capsules

Needles green

flat,
3/16″–3/8″

thorny,
1/4″–2″

Leafy twigs not 4-sided

Older bark

flaking   ridged

Fruits short
pods

MOUNTAIN-HEATH

GORSE

SECTION II

Broad-leaved Plants with Opposite Compound Leaves

ONLY a few plants bear leaves of this type. Their identification, therefore, is comparatively simple when foliage is present. In winter, however, unless dead or evergreen leaves are attached to the twigs, there are no certain clues to indicate whether the plant once bore compound or simple leaves. Then, this Section must be grouped with the next, whose twigs also bear opposite (occasionally whorled) leaf scars and buds. The twigs of a leafless unknown plant with opposite leaf scars may be compared with the drawings in Sections II and III.

Some alternate-leaved plants bear stubby, scarred, leaf-crowded spur branches (see p. 310). Care should be taken that their leaves and leaf scars are not assumed to be opposite or whorled because of this crowding. None of the plants in our area with true opposite or whorled leaf scars ever develop spur branches. Select twigs with uncrowded leaves or leaf scars for identification.

		Name	Plate
1. Vines		**CLEMATIS, etc.**	7
1. Erect plants:			
2. Leaflets 3:			
3. End buds false; all leaves with 3 leaflets		**BLADDERNUT**	8
3. End buds true; at least some leaves with 5–7 leaflets		**ASHLEAF MAPLE**	10
2. Leaflets 5–11:			
4. Leaves feather-compound:			
5. Shrubs; twigs rarely stout and pithy		**ELDERBERRIES**	8
5. Trees; twigs rarely stout and not pithy:			
6. Twigs hairless and not white-powdered		**ASHES (1)**	9
6. Twigs either velvety-hairy or white-powdered		**ASHES (2), etc.**	10
4. Leaves fan-compound		**BUCKEYES**	11

Vines with Opposite Compound Leaves
(Plate 7, p. 56)

Few in number, these climbing shrubs are easy to recognize at any time of year. Even in winter, those vines that have shed their opposite simple leaves (Plate 13) cause no confusion, since with the exception of Decumaria (see under Trumpet Creeeper below) they climb by means of twining stems.

PURPLE CLEMATIS   *Clematis verticillaris* DC.   **p. 56**
    Recognition: Only vine climbing by *twining leafstalks.* Leaves divided into 3 egg- to heart-shaped leaflets; occasionally in whorls of 3. Twigs angled. Leaves 3″–7″. Flowers purplish, 2″–3″ across, May–June. Fruits feathery, July–Aug.
    Remarks: Genus *Clematis* comprises 14 wild species in our area. Purple Clematis is the most woody; the remainder are not considered shrubby. All have general characteristics of this species, though 5–9 leaflets may occur and blossoms may be white. All have alternate name of Virgin's Bower. Two cultivated woody Asiatic species occasionally escape: *C. orientalis* L., with much divided leaflets and yellow blossoms; and *C. viticella* L., with 3–7 narrow egg-shaped leaflets and pink to purple flowers.

CROSS VINE   *Bignonia capreolata* L.   **p. 56**
    Recognition: Only vine with leaves divided into 2 *leaflets and a tendril* and only vine whose stem in cross section shows *a cross.* High-climbing; leaflets *evergreen,* narrowly heart-shaped. Flowers 2″, orange to red, rather bell-like, April–June. Fruits 4″–8″, dry, podlike, containing many small winged seeds, Aug.–Oct.

TRUMPET CREEPER   *Campsis radicans* (L.) Seem   **p. 56**
    Recognition: A vine climbing high by *aerial rootlets* in double rows along twigs. Leaflets 7–11 egg-shaped, toothed. Buds green, smooth. Leaves 3″–12″. Flowers 2″–3″, orange-red, tubular or funnel-shaped, clustered, July–Sept. Fruits 4″–8″, dry, podlike, containing many small winged seeds, Aug.–Oct., or longer.
    Similar species: (1) Decumaria (p. 70) also has opposite leaves, aerial rootlets, but barely enters our area in se. Virginia; it has simple leaves and in winter red, hairy buds. (2) See Cross Vine.
    Remarks: Sometimes cultivated. Hummingbirds visit blossoms.

Plants with Opposite Compound Leaves
(*Plate 8, p. 58*)

Only these 4 erect shrubs (or small trees) bear opposite feather-compound leaves. Their twigs lack central end buds at the tips. The other nonclimbing plants with opposite compound leaves have true end buds present. Bladdernut and European Elderberry may attain small-tree size but usually are smaller.

BLADDERNUT   *Staphylea trifolia* L.   **p. 58**
   Recognition: A shrub or small tree whose leaves have 3 (rarely 5) fine-toothed, elliptic leaflets. Twigs slender with few small wartlike lenticels or none. Pith white, narrow. Buds brown, 2–4 scaled, small. Leaf scars small, without connecting lines between. Bundle scars 3–7. Bark of older branches greenish or gray streaked with white. Leaves 2″–6″. Height 5′–15′ (25′); diameter 1″–2″ (6″). Flowers whitish, clustered, drooping, April–June. Fruits inflated papery capsules, 1″–2″, Aug.–Oct.
   Similar species: No other woody species has such fruits. The only shrub with all leaflets usually in 3's. Ashes and Ashleaf Maple (p. 51) may have some 3-parted leaves but normally leaves with 5–11 leaflets are present.

COMMON ELDERBERRY   *Sambucus canadensis* L.   **p. 58**
   Recognition: A shrub with large leaves composed of 5–11 coarse-toothed, elliptic leaflets. Twigs stout with *large white pith.* Small wartlike lenticels common. Leaf scars large, with connecting lines between; 5–7 bundle scars. Buds small, green or brown. Bark brownish. Leaves 4″–11″. Height 3′–13′; diameter ¾″–1″ (3″). Flowers small, white, in dense *flat-topped* clusters, June–July. Fruits small (mostly less than ³⁄₁₆″ in diameter), juicy, *purple-black,* rarely bright red, yellow, or orange, Aug.–Oct.
   Similar species: (1) Red Elderberry, more of a forest species, has brown pith, larger purplish buds and cone-shaped heads of red fruits. (2) European Elderberry has larger fruits, may grow to tree size.
   Remarks: All parts of plant reported to yield hydrocyanic acid. Regardless, fruits are used in making jam, jelly, wine, pies. Ripe fruits are eaten by 43 species of birds, including pheasant, mourning dove, and wild turkey.

EUROPEAN ELDERBERRY   *Sambucus nigra* L.   **Not illus.**
   Recognition: Similar to Common Elderberry but branchlets have more numerous lenticels. Leaflets mostly 5–7. Fruits shiny

black, ¼″–⁵⁄₁₆″ across. Plant grows to 30′. European; occasionally escaped from cultivation; New England to Virginia.

RED ELDERBERRY   *Sambucus pubens* Michx.   **p. 58**
   Recognition: Like Common Elderberry but with *brown* pith, larger purplish buds, 5–7 leaflets, and *cone-shaped* flower and fruit clusters. Flowers April–July. Fruits *brilliant red* or (uncommonly) white or yellow, June–Sept.

Trees with Opposite Feather-compound Leaves: Ashes, Ashleaf Maple, and Corktree
(*Plates 9 and 10, pp. 60, 62*)

The ashes and the Ashleaf Maple, or Box Elder, are our only native trees with opposite feather-compound leaves. All are tall trees. Young trees may be distinguished from shrubs with similar leaves by the presence of true end buds. These are lacking in the shrubby species (see Plate 8). In winter, ashes are the only plants having: 4 or more bundle scars per leaf scar, central end buds present (but not exceptionally large), and opposing leaf scars that do not meet. At that season, Ashleaf Maple has green or purplish, smooth, hairless, often white-powdered, twigs whose opposite leaf scars meet at raised points. See Japanese Corktree (p. 52).

   Identification of ash species is never simple except for a few well-marked forms. If the winged fruits, which look like the blades of canoe paddles, are present they may be useful. The leaflets may be variably toothed or not within a single species (except as noted, Plates 9-10). Though found most frequently as shown in the drawings, slight variations from this shape are common. Usually the twigs of the 3 hairy types are obviously velvety; only rarely is it necessary to use a lens. The flowers are dark, clustered but without petals and inconspicuous. Leaf scars are large, shield-shaped, with numerous bundle scars; buds have a somewhat granular surface texture.

   The ashes yield quality lumber for furniture, tool handles, baseball bats, baskets, and many special purposes. The twigs serve as deer food; the flowers provide pollen for bees. Indians once made a dark bitter sugar from the sap.

BLUE ASH   *Fraxinus quadrangulata* Michx.   **p. 60**
   Recognition: A tree of high ground with vigorous twigs often *square* in cross section. Twigs hairless, with long lines leading from leaf scars. Leaflets 7–11, green beneath, stalked and

always toothed. Upper edges of leaf scars only shallowly notched. Trunk bark whitish and somewhat scaly. Leaves 8″–12″. Height 60′–70′ (115′); diameter 2′–3′ (3½′). Flowers April–May. Fruits with *broad squared tips*, June–Oct.

Similar species: No other opposite-leaved plant has such squarish twigs and shield-shaped leaf scars. Where twigs are not sharply angled, the long lines along them are distinctive.

Remarks: Inner bark yields a blue dye.

WHITE ASH   *Fraxinus americana* L.   **pp. 7, 60**
Recognition: An upland tree with twigs that have the brown side buds usually set in deep *U- or V-shaped notches* in upper edges of leaf scars. Twigs round and hairless. Leaflets 5–9, stalked (sometimes short-stalked), usually *white* or pale beneath and either toothed or not. Trunk bark rather dark and tight with rigid interwoven pattern of shallow ridges and furrows. Leaves 8″–12″. Height 70′–80′ (100′); diameter 2′–3′ (7′). Flowers April–June. Fruits *narrow*, Oct.–Nov.

Similar species: When present, very deeply notched leaf scars are a good field mark among ashes with hairless twigs. Unfortunately, there is some variation in depth of notch in this and other species. Doubtful cases must be identified by fruits. Biltmore Ash, a variety, has hairy twigs.

Remarks: Most valuable and largest native ash, providing hard, strong, durable timber for furniture, interior decorating, agricultural implements, tool handles, oars, tennis rackets, musical instruments, baseball bats, snowshoes, and skis. As a campfire fuel, it ranks with oak and hickory.

BLACK ASH   *Fraxinus nigra* Marsh.   **p. 60**
Recognition: A tree of swamps and bottomlands whose leaflets are *not stalked.* The 7–11 leaflets always toothed. Twigs round, hairless, rather dull. Leaf scars not deeply notched. Buds *very dark*, nearly black. Trunk bark generally rather tight and furrowed but may be somewhat scaly. Leaves 12″–16″. Height 40′–80′; diameter 1′–2′. Flowers April–May. Fruits *blunt at both ends*, June–Sept.

Similar species: Both (1) White and (2) Green Ashes may have short-stalked leaflets but they lack dark buds and blunt fruits of this species.

Remarks: Known also as Hoop or Basket Ash. Short logs or planks when hammered repeatedly on the ends split along the annual growth rings into thin sheets that can be cut into strips for weaving pack baskets, chair seats, barrel hoops, etc. Knotty burls of the trunk are made into veneers and furniture.

GREEN ASH   **p. 60**
Fraxinus pennsylvanica var. *subintegerrima* (Vahl) Fern.
Recognition: A lowland tree whose leaflets are stalked (some-

times short-stalked. Leaflets 5–9, green on both sides, toothed or not. Twigs hairless, mostly *shiny* and buds *brownish*. Trunk bark tight and closely furrowed. Leaves 10″–12″. Height 60′–70′; diameter 2′–3′ (4′). Flowers April–May. Fruits wedge-shaped, Sept.–Oct.
Similar species: A hairless variety of (1) Red Ash; intermediate specimens occur. (2) See also Black Ash. (3) Water Ash may have hairless twigs but has scaly bark, wider fruit, usually swollen trunk base.

Plate 10
(*p. 62*)

RED ASH *Fraxinus pennsylvanica* Marsh.   **p. 62**
  Recognition: A tree of low grounds with *velvety-hairy* twigs and leafstalks. Leaflets 5–9, stalked, green on both sides, toothed or not. Twigs gray or brownish. Trunk bark tight, furrowed, with inner surface of outer bark reddish. Trunk base not swollen. Leaves 10″–12″. Height 40′–60′ (85′); diameter 2′–3′ (4′). Flowers April–May. Fruits with long *tapering seeds,* Sept.–Oct.
  Similar species: (1) Forms intermediate with its variety the Green Ash may occur. (2) Biltmore Ash has leaflets whitened beneath. (3) Pumpkin and (4) Water Ashes have swollen trunk bases and often grow in standing water. Water Ash barely enters our area.

BILTMORE ASH   **p. 62**
Fraxinus americana var. *biltmoreana* (Beadle) J. Wright
  Recognition: Similar to Red Ash but with leaflets *whitened beneath,* inner bark surface not reddish and fruit seeds *stout* and *blunt.* Leaf scars not notched (see related White Ash).

PUMPKIN ASH *Fraxinus tomentosa* Michx. f.   **p. 62**
  Recognition: A small to large tree of swamps and bottomlands, with *velvety-hairy* twigs and leafstalks. The leaves are *large, shiny above,* and sometimes leathery. The 7–9 *long-pointed* leaflets are *not toothed* but are sometimes wavy-edged; they vary from red-brown hairy to nearly hairless beneath. Trunk bark is tight (with shallow furrows) to somewhat scaly. Trunk base usually swollen on wet sites. Leaves 4″–18″. Height to 125′. Flowers April–May. Fruits *long,* 1½″–3″, seeds not stout, Sept.–Oct.
  Similar species: Water Ash is strictly southern and its leaves are neither leathery nor rusty-hairy and are more likely to be toothed.

WATER ASH   **Fruit illus., p. 62**
Fraxinus caroliniana Mill.
   Recognition: A small tree of *southern swamps* with twigs usually
   velvety-hairy. Leaflets and twigs generally as in Red Ash, but
   may be hairless in this species. Trunk bark tight and somewhat
   scaly. Trunk base usually *swollen* when growing in water.
   Leaves 7″–12″. Height to 35′; diameter 10″–12″. Flowers
   April–May. Fruits to 2″; broad-winged with narrow bases.
   Similar species: See under (1) Red Ash and (2) Green Ash.

ASHLEAF MAPLE (BOX ELDER)   *Acer negundo* L.   **p. 62**
   Recognition: A medium-sized tree of moist fertile soils with
   green or purplish, glossy, frequently white-powdered or, rarely,
   slightly hairy twigs. Leaflets 3–5 (uncommonly 7) with few
   coarse teeth or none. End leaflet often 3-pointed and somewhat
   lobed. Narrow leaf scars *meet in raised points* on opposite sides
   of twigs. Bundle scars 3 (or 5); buds white-hairy. Trunk bark
   furrowed. Leaves 4″–10″. Height 50′–75′; diameter 2′–4′.
   Flowers April–May. Fruits paired "keys," Sept.–Oct.
   Similar species: Only ashlike tree with leaf scars meeting in
   raised points. (1) When only 3 leaflets present, they often
   resemble those of Poison-ivy (Plate 25), whose leaves are alternate. (2) Other maples (Plate 22) have simple leaves and dissimilar winter characteristics.
   Remarks: Box Elder, a widely used common name, fails to
   indicate proper relationships. Soft white wood is used for boxes,
   etc. Syrup can be made from the sap. Squirrels and songbirds
   eat the seeds.

JAPANESE CORKTREE   **Not. illus.**
Phellodendron japonicum Maxim.
   Recognition: Oriental; occasionally escapes to the wild. Identified easily as the only nonclimbing plant with *toothless leaflets*
   among those with opposite compound leaves. Leaflets 5–13,
   egg- to heart-shaped, white-hairy beneath, with long tips. Twigs
   reddish, with buds small, hairy, with 2 obscure scales and
   hidden beneath base of leafstalk. Leaf scars deeply U-shaped,
   with 3 groups of bundle scars; partially enclosing bud. Height
   to 35′. Flowers small, greenish, clustered, May–July. Fruits
   black, fleshy, 5-seeded, Sept.–Oct.

Trees with Opposite Fan-compound Leaves: Buckeyes

(Plate 11, p. 64)

Buckeyes are the only plants with opposite leaves whose leaflets
are arranged like spokes of a wheel. In winter, a combination of

characteristics will identify the group: leaf scars have 5 or more bundle scars, twigs and end buds are large, and side buds have 4 or more pairs of scales. The flowers are in large showy upright spikes and the fruits have 3-parted husks that contain 1–3 large shiny brown nuts.

The native Ohio and Sweet Buckeyes may be large and important trees in forests west of the Appalachian Mountains. There they are sometimes dominant with the White Oak in the few areas of virgin timber remaining. Hybrids are known. To the eastward an imported relative, the Horsechestnut, common in shade-tree plantings, occasionally escapes to grow wild.

Seeds, young twigs, and leaves of all buckeyes sometimes are toxic to livestock. Crushed fruits and branches have been used to kill fish for food but this practice is now illegal.

HORSECHESTNUT   *Aesculus hippocastanum* L.   **p. 61**
Recognition: A large imported tree with 7–9 wedge-shaped toothed leaflets. End buds large, very *sticky*. Broken twigs have no decidedly disagreeable odor. Trunk bark somewhat scaly. Leaves 4″–15″. Height 60′–75′ (80′); diameter 1′–2′ (3′). Flowers white, May. Fruits with *strongly thorny husks*, Sept.–Oct.
Similar species: Only buckeye with sticky end buds and strongly thorny fruit husks. The chestnuts (Plate 57) have large brown nuts but are otherwise dissimilar.

SWEET BUCKEYE   *Aesculus octandra* Marsh.   **p. 64**
Recognition: Similar to Horsechestnut but with usually 5 (4–7) leaflets and *nonsticky* buds. Bud scales not ridged. Trunk bark fairly smooth or broken with large plates. The rare form *vestita* (Sarg.) Fern. has leaves hairy beneath. Leaves 4″–15″. Height to 90′; diameter to 3′. Flowers yellow, bell-shaped, May–June. Fruits with *smooth husks*, Sept.–Oct.
Similar species: Ohio Buckeye has ridged end-bud scales.
Remarks: Fruits, unlike those of other buckeyes, sometimes are eaten by cattle and hogs. They are said also to make an excellent paste when powdered and mixed with water. Wood is light and tough.

OHIO BUCKEYE   *Aesculus glabra* Willd.   **p. 64**
Recognition: A smaller tree than Sweet Buckeye and with prominently *ridged* bud scales on end buds. Twigs emit a *foul odor* when broken. Trunk bark scaly. Leaflets may be hairy in forma *pallida* (K. Koch) Fern., or unusually narrow and long-pointed in var. *sargentii* Rehd. Var. *leucodermis* Sarg. has whitened bark and leaf undersides. Leaves 4″–15″. Height to 40′; diameter to 2′. Flowers yellow, bell-shaped, April–May. Fruit husks with *weak thorns*, fruits Sept.–Oct.
Similar species: (1) Sweet Buckeye has scales of end buds not ridged. (2) Dwarf Buckeye has fruit husks without prickles.

DWARF BUCKEYE   *Aesculus sylvatica* Bartr.   **Not. illus.**
 Recognition: A thicket-forming shrub barely entering our area.
Flowers *bell-shaped* like Ohio Buckeye and unlike next 2 species;
they are yellow or cream-colored. Leaves 5-parted and fruits
not prickly. Mostly Coastal Plain and Piedmont Plateau bottomlands; se. Virginia to Florida and Alabama.

RED BUCKEYE   *Aesculus pavia* L.   **Not. illus.**
 Recognition: A shrub or small tree with 5 leaflets that are
narrow to elliptic and hairless when mature. Flowers bright red
and tubular, the stamens hidden within tube unlike preceding
buckeyes. Fruits not prickly. Coastal Plain woods; se. Virginia
to Florida, west to centr. Texas, and north in Mississippi Valley
to s. Illinois, se. Missouri, and se. Oklahoma.

PARTICOLORED BUCKEYE   **Not. illus.**
Aesculus discolor Pursh
 Recognition: Similar to Red Buckeye and considered by some
botanists to be synonymous with it. Leaflets *broader and hairy
beneath.* Flowers red, yellow-green, or both. Woods; N. Carolina, Kentucky, and Missouri to Georgia and Texas.

Broad-leaved Plants with Opposite Compound Leaves

(Key, page 46; text, pages 46–54)

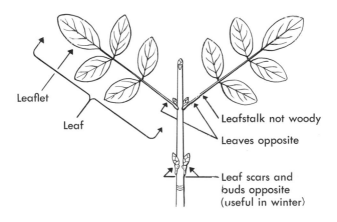

ONLY a few plants bear leaves of this type. Their identification, therefore, is comparatively simple when foliage is present. In winter, however, unless dead or evergreen leaves are attached to the twigs, there are no certain clues to indicate whether the plant once bore compound or simple leaves. Then, this Section must be grouped with the next, whose twigs also bear opposite (occasionally whorled) leaf scars and buds. The twigs of a leafless unknown plant with opposite leaf scars may be compared with the drawings in Sections II and III.

Some alternate-leaved plants bear stubby, scarred, leaf-crowded spur branches. Care should be taken that their leaves and leaf scars are not assumed to be opposite or whorled because of this crowding. None of the plants in our area with true opposite or whorled leaf scars ever develop spur branches. Twigs with un-crowded leaves or leaf scars should be selected for identification.

VINES WITH OPPOSITE COMPOUND LEAVES

All other vines have either alternate compound leaves or simple leaves.

⸹ PURPLE CLEMATIS, *Clematis verticillaris*   p. 47
    Woods and rocky places; e. Quebec and Manitoba to Delaware, W. Virginia, Michigan, and ne. Iowa.

⸹ CROSS VINE, *Bignonia capreolata*   p. 47
    Floodplains and swamp forests; e. Maryland, W. Virginia, s. Ohio, Indiana, Illinois, and Missouri.

⸹ TRUMPET CREEPER, *Campsis radicans*   p. 47
    Thickets; Connecticut, e. Pennsylvania, W. Virginia, Michigan, and se. Iowa to Florida and Texas.

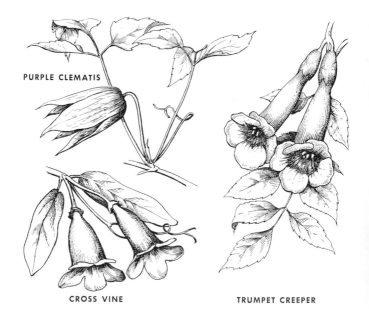

PURPLE CLEMATIS

CROSS VINE   TRUMPET CREEPER

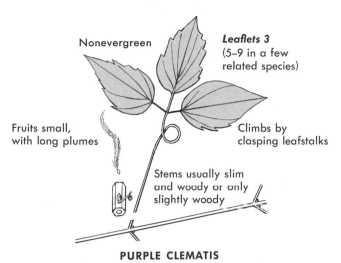

Nonevergreen

Leaflets 3
(5–9 in a few
related species)

Fruits small,
with long plumes

Climbs by
clasping leafstalks

Stems usually slim
and woody or only
slightly woody

PURPLE CLEMATIS

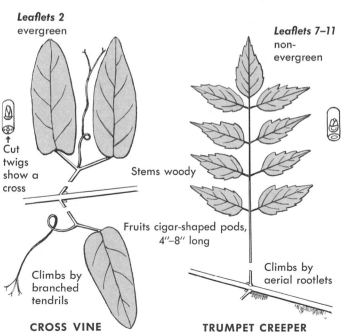

Leaflets 2
evergreen

↑
Cut
twigs
show a
cross

Leaflets 7–11
non-
evergreen

Stems woody

Fruits cigar-shaped pods,
4''–8'' long

Climbs by
branched
tendrils

Climbs by
aerial rootlets

CROSS VINE

TRUMPET CREEPER

PLANTS WITH OPPOSITE COMPOUND LEAVES

The only upright shrubs (or small trees) with
paired, feather-compound leaves.

↑⋎ BLADDERNUT, *Staphylea trifolia*   p. 48
     Bottomlands and fertile soils; Massachusetts, sw. Quebec, s.
     Ontario, n. Michigan, and s. Minnesota to Georgia, Alabama,
     se. Oklahoma, and se. Nebraska.

⋎ COMMON ELDERBERRY, *Sambucus canadensis*   p. 48
     Thickets; Nova Scotia and Manitoba to Georgia and Texas.
↑⋎ EUROPEAN ELDERBERRY, *S. nigra* (not illus.)   p. 48
     European; occasional escape from New England to Virginia.

⋎ RED ELDERBERRY, *Sambucus pubens*   p. 49
     Forest openings; Newfoundland and Alaska to New Jersey,
     W. Virginia, Illinois, ne. Iowa, Colorado, and Oregon; in
     Appalachians to Georgia.

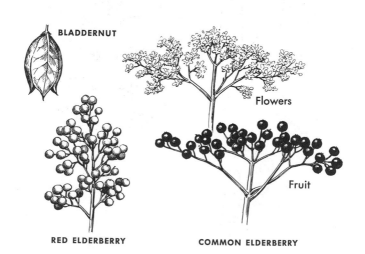

BLADDERNUT

Flowers

Fruit

RED ELDERBERRY   COMMON ELDERBERRY

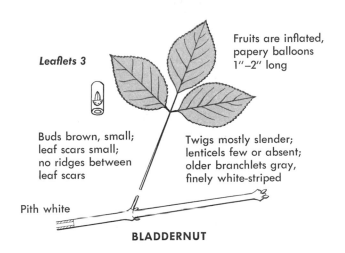

Leaflets 3

Fruits are inflated, papery balloons 1″–2″ long

Buds brown, small; leaf scars small; no ridges between leaf scars

Twigs mostly slender; lenticels few or absent; older branchlets gray, finely white-striped

Pith white

BLADDERNUT

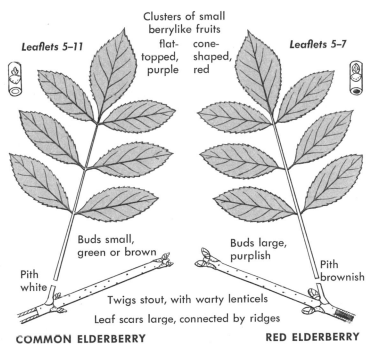

Leaflets 5–11

Clusters of small berrylike fruits

flat-topped, purple

cone-shaped, red

Leaflets 5–7

Buds small, green or brown

Buds large, purplish

Pith white

Pith brownish

Twigs stout, with warty lenticels

Leaf scars large, connected by ridges

COMMON ELDERBERRY

RED ELDERBERRY

ASHES (1)

The ashes (and Ashleaf Maple and Japanese Corktree, see also Plate 10) are our only trees with opposite feather-compound leaves. The following 4 species have twigs that are neither velvety nor white-powdered.

♦ BLUE ASH, *Fraxinus quadrangulata*   p. 49
     Upland woods; s. Ontario and s. Wisconsin to W. Virginia, Alabama, Arkansas, and ne. Oklahoma.

♦ WHITE ASH, *Fraxinus americana*   p. 50
     Upland forests; Nova Scotia, s. Quebec, s. Ontario, n. Michigan, and se. Minnesota to Florida and e. Texas.

♦ BLACK ASH, *Fraxinus nigra*   p. 50
     Floodplains and swamps; Newfoundland and Manitoba to n. Virginia, W. Virginia, Illinois, Iowa, and ne. N. Dakota.

♦ GREEN ASH   p. 50
     Fraxinus pennsylvanica var. *subintegerrima*
     Streambanks and floodplains; Nova Scotia, Quebec, s. Ontario, Saskatchewan, and se. Alberta to Georgia and Texas.

BLUE	WHITE	BLACK	GREEN
(Square or notched tip)	(Pointed at both ends)	(Blunt at both ends)	(Wedge-shaped)

FRUITS OF ASHES

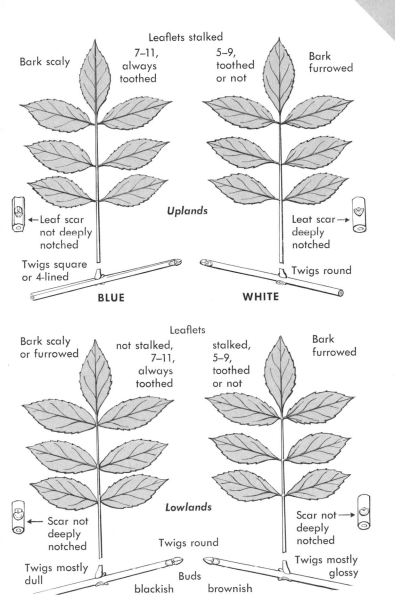

Leaflets stalked

Bark scaly

7–11, always toothed

5–9, toothed or not

Bark furrowed

Uplands

←Leaf scar not deeply notched

Leaf scar→ deeply notched

Twigs square or 4-lined

Twigs round

BLUE

WHITE

Leaflets

Bark scaly or furrowed

not stalked, 7–11, always toothed

stalked, 5–9, toothed or not

Bark furrowed

Lowlands

←Scar not deeply notched

Scar not→ deeply notched

Twigs mostly dull

Twigs round

Buds blackish

Buds brownish

Twigs mostly glossy

BLACK

GREEN

ASHES (2) AND ASHLEAF MAPLE, ETC.

The only trees with opposite feather-compound leaves
(see also Plate 9). The species of this group have
velvety-hairy or bright green and usually white-powdered
round twigs.

⬩ RED ASH, *Fraxinus pennsylvanica*   p. 51
   Damp soils; sw. Quebec and s. Ontario and Manitoba to
   Alabama, Louisiana, and Iowa.

⬩ BILTMORE ASH   p. 51
   Fraxinus americana var. *biltmoreana*
   Woods; New Jersey, s. Illinois, and Missouri to Georgia and
   Alabama.

⬩ PUMPKIN ASH, *Fraxinus tomentosa*   p. 51
   Floodplains and swamps; se. and sw. New York to nw. Florida
   and Louisiana.
   ⬩ WATER ASH, *F. caroliniana* (fruit illus.)   p. 52
      Coastal Plain swamps and shorelines; e. Virginia to Florida,
      west to e. Texas, and north in Mississippi Valley to Arkansas.

⬩ ASHLEAF MAPLE (BOX ELDER), *Acer negundo*   p. 52
   Riverbanks, floodplains, and fertile uplands; Nova Scotia,
   centr. Manitoba, and s. Alberta to Florida, Texas, and California.
   ⬩ JAPANESE CORKTREE   p. 52
      Phellodendron japonicum (not illus.)
      Oriental; occasionally escapes to the wild.

RED
(Fruits with
tapering seeds)

BILTMORE
(Fruits with
blunt seeds)

PUMPKIN
(Fruits large,
to 3")

WATER
(Rather diamond-
shaped)

ASHLEAF
MAPLE
(Fruits paired)

FRUITS

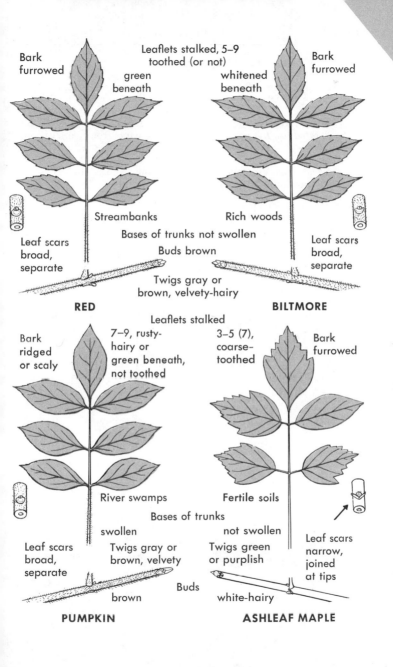

Leaflets stalked, 5–9 toothed (or not)

Bark furrowed

green beneath

whitened beneath

Bark furrowed

Streambanks

Rich woods

Bases of trunks not swollen

Buds brown

Leaf scars broad, separate

Leaf scars broad, separate

Twigs gray or brown, velvety-hairy

RED

BILTMORE

Leaflets stalked

Bark ridged or scaly

7–9, rusty-hairy or green beneath, not toothed

3–5 (7), coarse-toothed

Bark furrowed

River swamps

Fertile soils

Bases of trunks

swollen

Twigs gray or brown, velvety

not swollen

Twigs green or purplish

Leaf scars broad, separate

Leaf scars narrow, joined at tips

Buds brown

white-hairy

PUMPKIN

ASHLEAF MAPLE

BUCKEYES

The only trees or shrubs with opposite compound leaves
whose leaflets are arranged like the spokes of a wheel.

⧹ HORSECHESTNUT, *Aesculus hippocastanum*   p. 53
  Planted in towns; an occasional escape from cultivation.

⧹ SWEET BUCKEYE, *Aesculus octandra*   p. 53
  Woods; W. Virginia, sw. Pennsylvania, and s. Illinois to w.
  N. Carolina and n. Georgia.

⧹ OHIO BUCKEYE, *Aesculus glabra*   p. 53
  Moist woods; W. Virginia, w. Pennsylvania, Iowa, and se.
  Nebraska to e. Tennessee, centr. Alabama, and centr. Okla-
  homa.
  Ⓥ DWARF BUCKEYE, *A. sylvatica* (not illus.)   p. 54
  Coastal Plain and Piedmont Plateau bottomlands; se. Virginia
  to Florida and Alabama.
  ⧹Ⓥ RED BUCKEYE, *A. pavia* (not illus.)   p. 54
  Coastal Plain woods; se. Virginia to Florida, west to centr.
  Texas, and north in Mississippi Valley to s. Illinois, se. Mis-
  souri, and se. Oklahoma.
  ⧹Ⓥ PARTICOLORED BUCKEYE   p. 54
  A. discolor. (not illus.)
  Woods; N. Carolina, Kentucky, and Missouri to Georgia and
  Texas.

Blossoms

Nut

HORSECHESTNUT
(Fruit husk thorny)

SWEET BUCKEYE
(Fruit husk smooth)

OHIO BUCKEYE
(Fruit husk weakly
thorny when young
or warty when old)

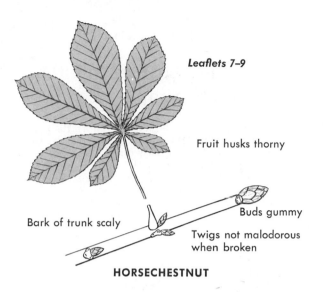

Leaflets 7–9

Fruit husks thorny

Buds gummy

Bark of trunk scaly

Twigs not malodorous
when broken

HORSECHESTNUT

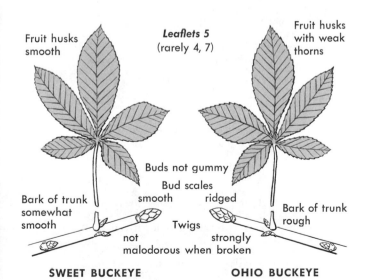

Fruit husks
smooth

Leaflets 5
(rarely 4, 7)

Fruit husks
with weak
thorns

Buds not gummy

Bark of trunk
somewhat
smooth

Bud scales
smooth   ridged

Bark of trunk
rough

Twigs
not   strongly
malodorous when broken

SWEET BUCKEYE   **OHIO BUCKEYE**

Broad-leaved Plants with Opposite Simple Leaves

THOUGH more numerous than those of Section II, the plants with opposite simple leaves are still so few as to be rather easily identified. In winter, of course, plants with opposite leaf scars may be members of either Section II or III and the drawings in both Sections must be reviewed. Care should be taken that the leaves or leaf scars on the stubby, scar-crowded spur branches of some alternate-leaved plants are not thought to be opposite or whorled. No opposite-leaved plants have spur branches (see p. 310).

When opposite simple leaves are present, the plants bearing them may be identified as follows:

	Name	Plate
1. Low creeping or trailing shrubs (plus the parasitic Mistletoe)	**CREEPING SHRUBS**	12
1. Climbing vines	**HONEYSUCKLES (1)**	13
1. Erect trees and shrubs:		
2. Leaves not toothed, although sometimes wavy-edged:		
3. Leaves not heart-shaped:		
4. Several papery scales present at twig bases (see Plate 14):		
5. Bundle scars 3	**HONEYSUCKLES (2)**	14
5. Bundle scars 1	**CORALBERRY, etc.**	17
4. Papery scales not present at twig bases:		
6. Leaves with veins that strongly tend to follow the leaf edges (see Plate 15):		
7. Bundle scars 3; uplands, or if bottomlands then only seasonally wet:		
8. Bud scales caplike, single	**BASKET WILLOW**	56
8. Bud scales 2	**DOGWOODS**	15
7. Bundle scars 1; plants always in or beside water	**BUTTONBUSH**	16
6. Leaves with veins only slightly, if at all, following the leaf edges:		
9. Buds long, slender, with 2 scales; bundle scars 3; plants not evergreen	**VIBURNUMS (1)**	20

                                              Name   *Plate*
     9. Buds otherwise; bundle scars 1–3; ever-
          green or not   **MISCELLANEOUS**   16, 17
  3. Leaves more or less heart-shaped, especially at
       the base   **LILAC, etc.**   18
2. Leaves definitely toothed:
     10. Toothed leaves not lobed:
          11. Leaves fine-toothed:
               12. Fruits various   **MISCELLANEOUS**   19
               12. Fruits fleshy with single flat seeds
                                         VIBURNUMS (1)   20
          11. Leaves coarse-toothed:
               13. Bark thin and papery; flat-topped clus-
                    ters of small dry fruits often present
                                         WILD HYDRANGEA 19
               13. Bark thicker; fruits fleshy
                                         VIBURNUMS (2)   21
     10. Toothed leaves lobed:
          14. Twigs very red-hairy; leaves oaklike
                                    OAKLEAF HYDRANGEA   19
          14. Twigs not red-hairy; leaves not oaklike
                         VIBURNUMS (2); MAPLES   21, 22

Low Creeping and Trailing Shrubs (and American Mistletoe)

(Plate 12, p. 100)

These are opposite-leaved sprawling shrubs or running vines, none of which climb or stand erect. (As a matter of convenience, a parasitic shrub of deciduous tree branches, American Mistletoe, is added here.) The group is readily recognizable by growth habits, both in summer and winter. The nonevergreen plants have single bundle scars.

The only other opposite-leaved plants of this type are one form of Red-osier Dogwood (Plate 15), which has toothless leaves whose veins strongly tend to follow the leaf edges, and Sandmyrtle (Plate 17), which is low but usually upright with shreddy bark. Pipsissewa leaves may be whorled, see page 179.

ST. ANDREW'S CROSS   *Ascyrum hypericoides* L.   **p. 100**
   Recognition: A small, barely woody shrub whose leaves have numerous tiny *transparent dots* visible when held up to light (use lens). Leaves *narrowed at base,* not clasping, not toothed. Leafy appendages may occur in leaf angles. Foliage often remains on plant all winter. Twigs slender, round, *ridged;* larger branches *shreddy.* Buds small; 2 scales. Leaves ¼″–1″.

Height to 24″. Flowers with 4 petals and 4 sepals, yellow, July–Sept. Fruits small 2- or 4-parted capsules, Sept.–Oct.
Similar species: St. Johnsworts (Plate 17) are more upright and have 5-parted flowers. St. Peterswort has wider-based clasping leaves.

ST. PETERSWORT *Ascyrum stans* Michx.   p. 100
Recognition: Similar to preceding species but with leaves longer and *upper leaves heart-shaped.* Twigs more stout. Leaves 1¼″–1½″.

AMERICAN STRAWBERRY-BUSH   p. 100
Euonymus americanus L.
Recognition: A semi-upright or sprawling shrub with distinctive *green, squarish,* 4-lined twigs. Leaves narrow, fine-toothed, short-stalked, somewhat long-pointed and thin or only slightly thickened; they drop in winter. Leaves 2″–4″. Height 2′–7′. Flowers not obvious, greenish purple, May–June. Fruits *orange-red and warty,* beneath attractive *5-parted pinkish* "husks," Sept.–Oct.
Similar species: (1) Burningbush (Plate 19) is more upright, with longer leafstalks, 4-lined but not squared twigs, smooth fruits and fewer-scaled buds. (2) Running Strawberry-bush is less upright, with wider leaves. The bittersweets (Plate 37) have similar fruits but they are more orange and leaves and buds are alternate.

RUNNING STRAWBERRY-BUSH   p. 100
Euonymus obovatus Nutt.
Recognition: Similar to American Strawberry-bush but *trailing* over ground; branches occasionally taking root. Leaves *wider,* somewhat egg-shaped. Height to 1′.
Similar species: Japanese Honeysuckle (Plate 13) has nontoothed hairy leaves and brownish twigs.

PARTRIDGEBERRY *Mitchella repens* L.   p. 100
Recognition: A delicate barely woody *trailing* plant. Leaves small egg- to heart-shaped, *evergreen, not toothed.* Leaves ¼″–1″. Flowers small, paired, tubular, white, fragrant, June–July. Fruits bright red, rarely white, edible, July–winter.
Similar species: Twinflower is more northern and has toothed leaves.
Remarks: A good indicator of acid soils. Fruits eaten by ruffed, spruce, and sharptail grouse, prairie chicken, bobwhite, raccoon, and red fox.

TWINFLOWER   p. 100
Linnaea borealis var. *americana* (Forbes) Rehd.
Recognition: A slender barely woody *trailing* plant with small

broad *evergreen* leaves and *hairy* stems. Leaves rounded and most *few-toothed* near tips. Leaves ¼″–¾″. Flowers in pairs, small, drooping, white with purplish stripes, fragrant, June–Aug. Fruits small dry capsules.

Similar species: Partridgeberry leaves are not toothed.

ALPINE-AZALEA *Loiseleuria procumbens* (L.) Desv.   **p. 100**
  Recognition: A *northern*, low, gnarled *mat-forming* shrub. Leaves *evergreen*, small, leathery, *without teeth* and mostly elliptic, with edges much curled. Twigs smooth. Leaves ⅛″–⅜″. Height to 1′. Flowers small, white or pink, several per cluster, June–July. Fruits 2- or 3-valved, dry capsules.
  Similar species: (1) Pachistima only other matlike evergreen with opposite leaves, and its leaves are fine-toothed. (2) Sandmyrtle (Plate 17) is taller.

PACHISTIMA *Pachistima canbyi* Gray   **p. 100**
  Recognition: An Appalachian *mat-forming* shrub with small, leathery, *fine-toothed*, narrow to wedge-shaped *evergreen* leaves. Twigs indistinctly 4-sided, often ringed with numerous stipule scars. Leaves ½″–1″. Height to 8″. Flowers small, brown or green, in angles of leaves, April–May. Fruits small capsules, Aug.–Sept.
  Similar species: (1) Alpine-azalea has leaves without teeth. (2) Sandmyrtle (Plate 17) is taller, with shreddy older bark.

AMERICAN MISTLETOE   **Not illus.**
Phoradendron flavescens (Pursh) Nutt.
  Recognition: The only shrub *parasitic on* the *branches* of broad-leaved trees. The thick green leathery leaves are evergreen and wedge- to egg-shaped. Stems jointed. Leaves 1″–2″. Flowers small, Oct., Nov. Fruits, whitish, pulpy, globular, Nov. There is nothing else like it. Dwarf Mistletoe (p. 30) is very small; it has tiny needlelike leaves and occurs only on conifers. American Mistletoe grows on branches of deciduous trees; New Jersey, e. Pennsylvania, W. Virginia, s. Ohio, s. Illinois, and se. Kansas to Florida and e. Texas.
  Remarks: Fruits eaten by many birds and mammals; apparently the plant is spread principally by birds.

Vines with Opposite Simple Leaves
(*including HONEYSUCKLES 1, Plate 13, p. 102*)

In addition to the climbing honeysuckles, 2 European and 2 native vines have opposite simple leaves. Two are escapes from cultivation; the others barely enter southeastern Virginia.

CLIMBING EUONYMUS   Not illus.
Euonymus fortunei (Turcz.) Hand.-Maz.
> **Recognition:** This and the next are the only vines of this group which climb by means of *aerial rootlets* like the Trumpet Creeper (Plate 7). Leaves elliptic, thick, *evergreen* and toothed. Twigs *green* and squarish. Leaves 1″–3″. Fruits reddish, beneath woody bracts. Sometimes spreads from plantings.

DECUMARIA   *Decumaria barbara* L.   Not illus.
> **Recognition:** Like Climbing Euonymus and Trumpet Creeper (Plate 7), this native vine climbs by aerial rootlets. Leaves thin, *not evergreen*, egg-shaped, toothed or not. Twigs brown. Buds *red-hairy*, unlike those of Trumpet Creeper (p. 47), which are greenish, smooth, and scaly. Leaves 1½″–7″. Flowers white, clustered, fragrant, May–June. Fruits many-seeded capsules, July–Aug. Damp woods; se. Virginia and Tennessee to Florida and Louisiana.

FALSE JESSAMINE   Not illus.
Gelsemium sempervirens (L.) Ait. f.
> **Recognition:** A twining vine with narrow to egg-shaped evergreen, somewhat leathery leaves that are not toothed. Unlike honeysuckles, *no persistent scales* remain at twig bases. Twigs hairless, with *solid pith* (all vine honeysuckles have hollow pith). Leaves sharp-tipped and *separate* (see honeysuckles). Leaves 1″–2½″. Flowers yellow, bell-shaped, clustered, very fragrant, March–May. Fruits capsules. Woods; se. Virginia and Arkansas to Florida and Texas.

SILKVINE   *Periploca graeca* L.   Not illus.
> **Recognition:** Twining vine with *hollow pith, milky sap,* and small buds *nearly hidden* by much raised leaf scars. Flowers dark, June–Sept. Fruits milkweedlike pods. European escape, New England and Kansas to Florida and Oklahoma. See following.

Honeysuckles (1): Climbing Vines
(*Plate 13, p. 102*)

These 8 forms are the only climbing vines with opposite leaves which ascend by twining stems, without benefit of tendrils, aerial rootlets, clasping leafstalks, or other secondary aids (except see False Jessamine and Silkvine, above). The pith of all vine honeysuckles is hollow (lacking). The twig bases are marked by persistent scales where they join the older branchlets. The opposing leaf scars are connected by lines and the bark is papery. The tubular flowers of all species except the Trumpet Honeysuckle have a single lower and 4 upper lobes at the mouth of the tube

(Type A). Those of that species have starlike regularly distributed lobes at the tube mouth (Type B).

Unfortunately, the members of this group with few exceptions are inconsistent in hairiness and in leaf and bud characteristics. The leaves are *never toothed* but their shapes vary considerably. The upper 1 to 4 pairs of leaves may be fused. Winter characteristics are not well known.

JAPANESE HONEYSUCKLE   p. 102
Lonicera japonica Thunb.

Recognition: An aggressive imported vine forming *dense tangles* climbing over underbrush or sprawling over open ground. Twigs and leaves *densely hairy,* green on both sides, or purplish beneath. Upper leaves *not united;* lower leaves often lobed in the White Oak manner. Foliage often *evergreen,* or nearly so. Leaves 1½″–3½″. Flowers ½″–1″, mostly single, white or yellowish, sometimes tinged with red or purple, hairy inside, April–July. Fruits *black* berries, Sept.–Nov.

Similar species: Only vine honeysuckle with berries not red. Among climbing honeysuckles, only this and (1) Woodbine Honeysuckle have end leaves not united. (2) Running Strawberry-bush (Plate 12) has green 4-lined stems.

Remarks: Fruits eaten by many birds and mammals and the dense cover is much used, but generally speaking it is a weed.

WOODBINE HONEYSUCKLE   Not illus.
Lonicera periclymenum L.

Recognition: Similar to Japanese Honeysuckle but less hairy, with *red berries* and flowers ⅞″–1⅛″ long, in dense circular clusters. Of European origin. Thickets; Newfoundland to Nova Scotia.

HAIRY HONEYSUCKLE   *Lonicera hirsuta* Eat.   p. 102
Recognition: Somewhat like Japanese Honeysuckle but more *high-climbing* and with *united upper leaves.* Foliage *not evergreen.* Flowers orange-yellow and sticky-hairy. Fruits *red.*

MOUNTAIN HONEYSUCKLE   *Lonicera dioica* L.   p. 102
Recognition: A low-climbing vine whose leaves are green above and *whitened beneath.* Upper *united* leaves usually are *pointed.* Leaves typically hairless but var. *glaucescens* (Rydb.) Butters is white-hairy beneath. Lower leaves *narrow.* Twigs *hairless.* Leaves 1½″–3½″. Flowers ½″–1″, in crowded whorls, greenish yellow to red or purple, hairy inside, base obviously swollen on one side, May–July. Fruits red, July–Sept.

Similar species: (1) Trumpet Honeysuckle also has leaves distinctly whitened beneath, but narrower. (2–4) The next 3 species have flower-tube base not much swollen.

ROCK HONEYSUCKLE   **p. 102**
Lonicera prolifera (Kirchn.) Rehd.
  Recognition: Somewhat similar to Mountain Honeysuckle but
  more coarse, with top *united leaves circular*, or nearly so, and
  much whitened above as well as below. Lower leaves too are
  mostly *rounded*. Sometimes foliage is slightly hairy beneath.
  Flowers pale yellow, not much swollen at base, May–June.
  Fruits July–Oct.
  Similar species: Only one of this group with the leaves distinctly
  and obviously whitened above.

YELLOW HONEYSUCKLE   *Lonicera flava* Sims   **p. 102**
  Recognition: *Southern,* and unlike preceding 2 species the leaves
  are *merely grayish* beneath. Leaves just below united leaves
  have no stalks. Leaves 1½″–3½″. Flowers about 1³⁄₁₆″ long,
  orange-yellow, tubes hairless or slightly hairy *within,* April–
  May. Fruits red, Aug.–Sept.
  Similar species: See Pale Honeysuckle.

PALE HONEYSUCKLE   **Not illus.**
Lonicera flavida Cockerell
  Recognition: Like Yellow Honeysuckle but leaves just below the
  united leaves have *short stalks.* Flowers ¾″–1″, pale yellow,
  very hairy within tube. Limestone areas; w. S. Carolina and
  Kentucky to Tennessee and Missouri.

TRUMPET HONEYSUCKLE   *Lonicera sempervirens* L. **p. 102**
  Recognition: A climbing vine with long *slender blossoms* unlike
  other climbing honeysuckles. Leaves *whitened beneath* and
  those not united often are slender but may be elliptic. More
  or less evergreen. Leaves 1½″–3½″. Flowers long, *reddish,*
  vaselike, with lobes at mouth evenly spaced, April–Sept.
  Fruits red, Aug.–Oct.
  Similar species: Mountain Honeysuckle is only other of this
  group with leaves green above and much whitened beneath.

Honeysuckles (2): Erect Shrubs
(*Plate 14, p. 104*)

Honeysuckles are among the few shrubs having scales that
remain at the bases of the twigs, marking the boundaries between
the twigs of the present season and the branchlets of the previous
year (see Plate 14). Other woody plants with this characteristic are the hydrangeas and Bush-honeysuckle (Plate 19), which
have leaves that are more heart-shaped and toothed, and the

Coralberry and Snowberry (Plate 17), which have only 1, rather than 3, bundle scars per leaf scar. In winter, hydrangeas usually bear umbrellalike clusters of dried fruit capsules in contrast to the berries of honeysuckles; their twigs too are usually more shiny and stout. The ridged twigs of the Bush-honeysuckle are distinctive. The prominent fruits of the Coralberry and Snowberry frequently are present in winter. Occasionally honeysuckles bear several buds, one above the other, where 1 normally grows. When present, this definitely separates them from the other plants mentioned. Honeysuckle leaves are not toothed, and the bark of twigs and branchlets, at least, is papery. Opposing leaf scars are connected by lines. The bundle scars are 3. In contrast to the climbing honeysuckles, these bushy plants, which rarely exceed 10 feet, may be identified by both leaf and twig characteristics. When present, the white, pink, or yellowish flowers are aids. The blossoms mostly are of 2 types, as diagrammed. One group of species has the petal lobes arranged unevenly in 2 sections (Type A), while the other has rather regularly spaced petal lobes at the mouth of the tube (Type C). The Northern Honeysuckle has short petal lobes but generally resembles the Type C pattern.

The erect honeysuckles do not have united upper leaves as in some vine species. The upright honeysuckles that have hollow pith (pith lacking) are of Eurasian origin. Those with solid pith are native species. (One Asiatic importation with solid pith has very limited American range as an escape.)

TARTARIAN HONEYSUCKLE *Lonicera tatarica* L.   **p. 104**
   Recognition: A shrubby honeysuckle with *hollow branchlets.* Leaves elliptic to heart-shaped and nearly hairless. Buds *short and blunt.* Leaves 1½″–2½″. Height to 10′. Flowers Type C, pink, rarely white, ⅝″–⅞″, stalks longer than flowers, May–June. Fruits red, rarely yellow, berries, June–Aug.
   Similar species: Four shrub honeysuckles, one a hybrid, have hollow piths: (1) European and (2) Morrow Honeysuckles are hairy; (3) hybrid Bella Honeysuckle is similar but flower stalks are shorter than the flowers; (4) see also Snowberry (Plate 17).

EUROPEAN HONEYSUCKLE *Lonicera xylosteum* L.   **p. 104**
   Recognition: Similar to Tartarian Honeysuckle but twigs and leaf undersides, at least, usually *gray-hairy.* Buds *long and sharp.* Flowers Type A, pink, yellowish, or white, about ⅜″ long, stalks of variable length. Fruits red.

MORROW HONEYSUCKLE   **Not illus.**
Lonicera morrowi Gray
   Recognition: Similar to European Honeysuckle, but has narrow or oblong leaves that are gray-hairy beneath. Buds short and conical. Flowers about ⅞″ long, white to yellow. Fruits red

or yellow. Leaves 1″–2″. Eurasian; escaped to thickets; Maine and Michigan to New Jersey and Pennsylvania.

BELLA HONEYSUCKLE   Not illus.
Lonicera morrowi Gray × *L. bella* Zabel

Recognition: An Asiatic hybrid having characteristics appearing as intermediate between Tartarian and Morrow Honeysuckles. Leaves elliptic or egg-shaped. Twigs and foliage hairless or nearly so. Flower stalks shorter than the pink to yellow Type C flowers. Escape; Maine and New York to New Jersey and Pennsylvania.

FOUR-LINED HONEYSUCKLE   p. 104
Lonicera involucrata (Richards.) Banks

Recognition: An upright shrub with solid white pith and *4-lined* and squarish twigs. Twigs and foliage *hairless* or nearly so and leaves elliptic or somewhat oblong. Lower bud scales as long as buds; more than 2 evident. Leaves 2″–5″. Height to 10′. Flowers yellowish, unlike others of this group in that they are *cylindrical for most of their ⅜″–⅝″ length*, with quite short petal lobes and located above 4 conspicuous green to purplish leaflike bracts (the involucre), June–July. Fruits black, July–Aug.

Similar species: Only honeysuckle with 4-lined twigs. Also has unique flowers and black berries.

SWAMP HONEYSUCKLE   p. 104
Lonicera oblongifolia (Goldie) Hook.

Recognition: A more or less *hairless* honeysuckle with solid pith. Twigs and leaf undersides finely hairy to hairless. Leaves somewhat oblong to egg-shaped. Bud scales several, lower ones as long as bud. Leaves 1″–3½″. Height to 5′. Flowers Type A, yellowish, rarely white, ⅜″–⅝″, stalks longer than blossoms, May–June. Fruits *orange to red*, July–Aug.

Similar species: (1) Northern Honeysuckle is hairy, has 2-scaled buds, blue fruits. (2) Canada Honeysuckle has shorter outer bud scales. Both have more rounded leaves, Type C flowers. (3) Standish Honeysuckle has very long-pointed leaves.

NORTHERN HONEYSUCKLE   p. 104
Lonicera villosa (Michx.) R. & S.

Recognition: A small *hairy* honeysuckle with solid pith and 2 bud scales that cover buds like a pea pod. Twigs and both leaf surfaces *densely hairy*, but some varieties hairless or nearly so. Leaf edges typically *fringed* with fine hairs. Leaves 1″–2½″. Height to 3½′. Flowers Type C, yellowish, about ⅝″, stalks much shorter than flowers, April–July. Fruits *blue*, May–Aug.

Similar species: Bud type and fruit color are distinctive, whether plant is hairy or not.

CANADA HONEYSUCKLE   *Lonicera canadensis* Bartr. **p. 104**
  Recognition: A mostly *hairless* honeysuckle with solid pith and lower bud scales shorter than buds. Twigs generally *hairless* as are egg- to heart-shaped leaves, except that leaf edges are *fringed* with fine hairs. Leaves 1″–3′. Height to 6′. Flowers Type C, yellowish or yellowish green, about ¾″, stalks longer than blossoms, April–July. Fruits *red,* June–Aug.
  Similar species: See Swamp Honeysuckle.

STANDISH HONEYSUCKLE   **Not illus.**
Lonicera standishii Jacq.
  Recognition: Escaped from gardens on Long Island, New York, this Asiatic resembles the last in having solid pith, fringed leaves, red berries. It is nearly evergreen, however, and the leaves are much *long-pointed.* Twigs somewhat bristly-hairy. See Swamp Honeysuckle. Height to 8′. Flowers Type A, white, short-stalked, April.

Dogwoods
(*Plate 15, p. 106*)

In addition to the Flowering Dogwood, which grows to tree size, there are 9 species that have less conspicuous blossoms. These usually are shrubs but some rarely grow to small tree size. One of these shrubs has alternate leaves (see Plate 59). All species have leaf veins that strongly tend to follow the leaf edges toward the leaf tips. The buds have 1 pair of scales and the bundle scars are 3. Twigs, branchlets, and pith often are distinctively colored. Flowers and fruits of the shrubby species are in umbrella-shaped clusters. The fleshy fruits (drupes) have a single stony seed.
  In winter the dogwoods may resemble some viburnums (Plates 20 and 21) or maples (Plate 22), but the leaf scars on the new twigs are raised in the dogwoods.

ROUNDLEAF DOGWOOD   *Cornus rugosa* Lam.   **p. 106**
  Recognition: A medium-sized shrub usually with broadly egg-shaped to *nearly round* leaves. Some plants may have narrower leaves. Twigs *greenish* or red-brown, marked with *purplish blotches.* Leaves have 5–9 *pairs of veins* and are woolly to hairless beneath. Leaves 2″–5″. Height to 10′. Flowers in flat-topped clusters, May–July. Fruits *light blue,* rarely white, Aug.–Oct.
  Similar species: No other dogwood has purple-blotched greenish twigs.
  Remarks: Fruits eaten by ruffed and sharptail grouse. Twigs are consumed by cottontail, moose, and are a favorite of white-tail deer.

FLOWERING DOGWOOD   *Cornus florida* L.   **pp.** *11*, **106**
Recognition: A small to medium-sized tree with hidden side
buds and *stalked* flower buds. Leaves hairless or nearly so,
elliptic to egg- or wedge-shaped, *5–6 pairs* of veins. Twigs and
branchlets sometimes green, *mostly dark purple,* often swollen
from insect attacks. Pith white. Trunk bark dark, *deeply checkered* in an alligator-hide-like pattern. Leaves 2″–5″. Height
10′–40′; diameter 12″–18″. Flowers small, clustered, each cluster with 4 (rarely 6–8) *large white or seldomly pink bracts* (not
true petals), March–June. Fruits *red* or rarely yellow, Aug.–Nov.
Similar species: Only dogwood with showy white bracts, hidden
side buds, and stalked flower buds. Checkered bark less corky
than similar barks of blackhaw viburnums (Plate 20) or (1)
Persimmon (Plate 68). (2) Common Mock-orange (Plate 19) has
leaf scars not raised and bark of branchlets thin and papery.
Remarks: Powdered bark is reported to have been made into
a toothpaste, a black ink (when mixed with iron sulphate), and
a quinine substitute. Bark of the roots yields a scarlet dye.
Shuttles, bobbins, tool handles, mallets, and golf club heads are
manufactured from the hard close-grained wood. Humans find
the bitter red fruits inedible, but with twigs they are important
foods of numerous song and game birds, skunks, deer, rabbits,
and squirrels.

RED-PANICLE DOGWOOD   *Cornus racemosa* Lam.   **p. 106**
Recognition: A small or medium-sized shrub with light gray
branchlets and *clusters* (*panicles*) *of white fruits supported by
red stems.* Leaves elliptic to egg-shaped, usually with 3–5 pairs
of veins, somewhat whitened, hairless or slightly hairy beneath.
Twigs brownish; pith light brown. Leaves 1″–5″. Height to 10′.
Flowers small, whitish, in long *cone-shaped clusters,* June–July.
Fruits white, red-stemmed, July–Oct.
Similar species: (1) Roughleaf and (2) Price Dogwoods have
sandpapery, woolly foliage and twigs, round-topped fruit clusters. (3) Stiff Dogwood has reddish twigs, white pith, and bluish
fruits.
Remarks: Fruits eaten by pheasant and ruffed and sharptail
grouse.

RED-OSIER DOGWOOD   *Cornus stolonifera* Michx.   **p. 106**
Recognition: A small to medium-sized shrub with *bright red* or,
less commonly, green twigs and branchlets and *white pith.* A
rare form (*repens* Vict.) is creeping and carpet-forming, with
small leaves. Leaves elliptic with 3–5 (less commonly 6–7) pairs
of veins, *whitened,* hairless or somewhat silky beneath. Var.
baileyi (Coult. and Evans) Drescher has brownish-red hairy
twigs and leaves densely woolly beneath. Leaves 2″–5″.

Height to 10′. Flowers small, whitish, *in flat-topped clusters,* May–Aug. Fruits *white,* July–Oct.
Similar species: Only Stiff Dogwood also may have red twigs and white pith, but leaves not whitened beneath and fruits are blue and in round-topped clusters.
Remarks: Fruits much sought after by songbirds, ruffed and sharptail grouse, bobwhite, and European partridge. Twigs eaten by deer, elk, moose, cottontail, and snowshoe hare.

STIFF DOGWOOD   *Cornus foemina* Mill.   **Not illus.**
Recognition: Similar to Red-osier Dogwood and, like it, with white pith. Stiff Dogwood more *southern;* twigs and branchlets may be reddish or *brownish.* Leaves green on both sides, slightly paler but *not whitened* beneath, somewhat long-tipped, 4–5 pairs of veins. Leaves 2″–5″. Height to 15′. Flowers small, whitish, in somewhat *round-topped clusters,* May–June. Fruits *blue,* Aug.–Oct. See Red-osier Dogwood and Red-panicle Dogwood. Wet places; e. Virginia, s. Indiana, se. Missouri to Florida and Texas.

SILKY DOGWOOD   *Cornus amomum* Mill.   **p. 106**
Recognition: A small to medium-sized shrub with dull-*purple silky-hairy twigs and brown pith.* Leaves broadly egg-shaped, less than twice as long as broad, with wide *rounded bases* and 3–5 pairs of veins, smooth above and hairless or somewhat brown- or gray-hairy beneath. Branchlets as well as twigs dull purple. Leaves 2″–4″. Height to 10′. Flowers small, whitish, in flat-topped clusters, June–July. Fruits *bluish,* Aug. Oct.
Similar species: (1) Narrowleaf Dogwood has narrower leaves, tapering leaf bases; probably these 2 cannot be separated in winter, unless dead leaves can be located. (2) Roughleaf and (3) Price Dogwoods have "sandpapery" upper leaf surfaces and rough-hairy twigs.

NARROWLEAF DOGWOOD   *Cornus obliqua* Raf.   **Not illus.**
Recognition: Like Silky Dogwood but leaves narrower, with *tapered bases,* whitened or white-hairy beneath. Leaves *twice as long as broad,* or longer. Wet places; New Brunswick and N. Dakota to New Jersey, W. Virginia, Kentucky, Oklahoma.

ROUGHLEAF DOGWOOD   **p. 106**
Cornus drummondi Meyer
Recognition: A midwestern shrub or in South a medium-sized tree. Leaves *sandpapery above, woolly beneath,* egg-shaped or elliptic with 3–5 pairs of veins. Twigs *red-brown* or brownish; branchlets brown or gray. Pith *brown,* rarely white. Leaves 2″–5″. Height 4′–15′ (50′); diameter 2″–8″ (10″). Flowers small, whitish, in round-topped clusters, petals ³⁄₁₆″–¼″, May–June. Fruits white, ³⁄₁₆″–¼″, Aug.–Oct.

Similar species: (1) Price Dogwood the only other dogwood with rough leaves and rough-hairy twigs. (2) Red-panicle Dogwood has brownish twigs but they are not sandpapery as in this species.
Remarks: Fruits eaten by many songbirds and by prairie chicken, sharptail and ruffed grouse, bobwhite, wild turkey, pheasant.

PRICE DOGWOOD   *Cornus priceae* Small   **Not illus.**
Recognition: Nearly identical with Roughleaf Dogwood, sometimes considered same species. Leaves broader. Fruits *less than* ³⁄₁₆″ *in diameter.* River bluffs; Kentucky and Tennessee.

Miscellaneous Plants with Opposite Leaves Not Toothed (1) and (2)
(*Plates 16 and 17, pp. 108, 110*)

Among the upright woody plants with opposite (or whorled) leaves that are not toothed are the honeysuckles and dogwoods, previously discussed. There are a number, however, of miscellaneous additional species. Those with heart-shaped leaves are given on Plate 18. Those miscellaneous species with leaves not heart-shaped are shown on Plates 16 and 17.

1. Plate 16
(*p. 108*)

Some of these plants may have leaves and leaf scars in whorls of 3. Only 1, the Fringe-tree, may grow to tree size.

SHEEP LAUREL   *Kalmia angustifolia* L.   **p. 108**
Recognition: A small shrub with *leathery, evergreen,* narrow to oblong leaves. Leaves *flat,* opposite or in whorls of 3. Mostly less than 2½″ long; sometimes rust-colored beneath when young but *green or pale green* beneath when mature. A southern variety that occurs north to Virginia has leaves pale and fine-hairy beneath. Twigs round in cross section and hairless. Leaves 1½″–2″. Height to 3′. Flowers cuplike, ⅜″–½″ across, with pollen-bearing anthers of stamens tucked in pockets near the border and springing out suddenly when center of flower is probed; pink, red, or rarely white, in clusters *along sides* of twigs, May–Aug. Fruits 5-parted capsules; all winter.
Similar species: (1) Pale Laurel has whitened leaf undersides, rolled leaf edges, and 2-edged twigs. (2) Mountain Laurel (Plate 65) has larger, mostly alternate leaves. (3) Sandmyrtle (Plate 17) has smaller crowded leaves.

Remarks: Though normally shunned by livestock, foliage may be poisonous, hence such names as Sheepkill, Lambkill, Calfkill. Peculiar action of stamens forces nectar-seeking insects to carry pollen.

PALE LAUREL   Kalmia polifolia Wang.   p. 108

Recognition: Differs from Sheep Laurel in having leaves *strongly whitened beneath*, leaf edges *rolled*, leafstalks *lacking*, or nearly so, twigs 2-edged, and flower clusters at *twig tips*. Leaves seldom occur in 3's. Height to 2'. Flowers ½"–⅞" across, May–July.

DEVILWOOD   Not illus.
Osmanthus americanus (L.) Gray

Recognition: The only *tree* with *opposite* leathery leaves. Leaves evergreen, shiny, thick, narrow, and green or pale beneath. They somewhat resemble Mountain Laurel (Plate 65), whose leaves occasionally are opposite but more narrow (see also Southern Wild-raisin, Plate 20). Twigs hairless, stout, *whitish*. Leaves 2"–6". Height to 50'. Flowers small, white, clustered on twigs, April–May. Fruits purplish, fleshy, 1-seeded, about ⅜" long, June. Swamps; se. Virginia to Florida and se. Louisiana.

COMMON PRIVET   Ligustrum vulgare L.   p. 108

Recognition: A tall European shrub escaping from plantings. Leaves firm but not tough and leathery, not evergreen, slightly less than 2½" long, never in 3's, not aromatic, elliptic, and hairless. Twigs slender (1/16" or less thick), barely fine-hairy or hairless. Central end bud present; buds have 4 or more blunt scales; bundle scar single. Leaf scars much raised. Leaves 1"–2¼". Height to 15'. Flowers small, white, in cone-shaped clusters at twig ends, June–July. Fruits small black berries, Sept.–Oct., or longer.

Similar species: (1–3) Next 3 privets are less common and have pointed bud scales or very hairy twigs. (4) In winter, Fringe-tree also has true end buds present, but twigs are stouter, over 1/16" thick, and leaf scars not raised.

Remarks: Fruits eaten by some song and game birds.

CALIFORNIA PRIVET   Not illus.
Ligustrum ovalifolium Hassk.

Recognition: Similar to Common Privet in having hairless twigs, but leaves are shiny, more leathery, and may be evergreen. Bud scales *long-pointed*. Occasionally escapes from cultivation, especially toward the South.

AMUR PRIVET   Ligustrum amurense Carr.   Not illus.

Recognition: Resembles Common Privet in general appearance but is like Regal Privet in having twigs *densely hairy* and bud *scales blunt.* Leaves hairy beneath, at least along midrib, and usually tips pointed. Escaped cultivation; se. Virginia southward.

REGAL PRIVET   Not illus.
Ligustrum obtusifolium Sieb. & Zucc.
  Recognition: Like Amur Privet but leaves mostly *blunt-tipped.* Escaped from cultivation; e. Pennsylvania southward.

BUCKLEYA   *Buckleya distichophylla* Torr.   Not illus.
  Recognition: A shrub that grows as a *parasite* attached to *hemlock roots.* Leaves rounded at base but with long-pointed tips. Twigs slightly hairy; twigs and branchlets pale brown. Buds have 6–7 scales, pointed. Central end bud lacking; leaf scars with 1 bundle scar. Leaves 1″–2½″. Height to 12′. Flowers greenish, clustered, May. Fruits 1-seeded, somewhat elongate. Scarce; w. Virginia to w. N. Carolina and e. Tennessee.

NESTRONIA   *Nestronia umbellula* Raf.   Not illus.
  Recognition: Somewhat like Buckleya but smaller, *parasitic on roots of broad-leaved trees.* Most leaves pointed at both ends; some may be blunt-tipped. Twigs hairless; branchlets dark gray. Buds small. Leaves 1″–2½″. Height to 3′. Flowers May–June. Fruits ball-shaped. Mountains; w. Virginia to Georgia and Alabama.

BUTTONBUSH   *Cephalanthus occidentalis* L.   p. 108
  Recognition: An *aquatic* shrub with leaves over 2½″ long, often occurring in 3's and 4's, elliptic and short-pointed. Leafstalks often red. Side buds imbedded in bark; end buds false. Twigs round, with single bundle scar. Var. *pubescens* Raf. has velvety-hairy twigs and leaf undersides (typical plant is hairless). The rare forma *lanceolatus* Fern. has narrow leaves. Leaves 3″–6″. Height 3′–8′ (18′). Flowers small, white, tubular, densely clustered in *ball-like heads,* May–Aug. Fruits small, dry, Sept.–Dec., or later.
  Similar species: Swamp Loosestrife has ridged twigs.
  Remarks: Honey plant. Wilted leaves may poison stock.

SWAMP LOOSESTRIFE   Not illus.
Decodon verticillatus (L.) Ell.
  Recognition: A shrub that is woody principally at the stem base. Like Buttonbush, the leaves occur in pairs or in 3's and plant grows in or near ponds. Leaves narrow, short-stalked, and hairy or hairless beneath. Twigs *angular* with 4–6 prominent lengthwise ridges. Stems often spongy near base; twig tips usually bend downward and older bark light brown and flaky. Leaves 2″–5″. Height to 4′. Flowers showy, magenta. Pond edges and wet ground; centr. Maine, s. Ontario, s. Michigan, and Minnesota to Virginia and Tennessee.

SEA-OXEYE *Borrichia frutescens* (L.) DC.   **Not illus.**
  Recognition: Low finely gray-hairy shrub with *narrow leaf scar pairs encircling branchlets.* Leaves somewhat leathery, either without teeth or spiny-toothed. Twigs with fine lengthwise lines. Flowers yellow, sunflowerlike, July–Oct. Salt marshes, District of Columbia to Florida and Texas.

SMOOTH ALLSPICE *Calycanthus fertilis* Walt.   **p. 108**
  Recognition: A woodland shrub with leaves and twigs that are hairless and *spicy-scented* when crushed. Leaves thin, nonevergreen, over 2½", somewhat rough above, generally egg-shaped, with blunt or sharp tips. Foliage sometimes whitened beneath. Twigs swollen at leaf scars and hairless or barely fine-hairy; buds hairy without evident scales, leaf scar U-shaped with 3 bundle scars. Central end bud is lacking. Leaves 2½"–7". Height to 6'. Flowers brownish, without much odor, May–Aug. Fruits fleshy, Sept.–winter.
  Similar species: Only the 2 allspices are opposite-leaved and aromatic.
  Remarks: Seeds reported to be poisonous.

HAIRY ALLSPICE *Calycanthus floridus* L.   **Not illus.**
  Recognition: Similar to Smooth Allspice but more southern, with twigs and leaf undersides *soft-hairy.* Flowers very fragrant, giving off a strawberrylike odor. Flowers April–Aug. Woods; Virginia and s. W. Virginia to Florida and Mississippi.

FRINGE TREE *Chionanthus virginicus* L.   **p. 108**
  Recognition: A shrub or small tree with leaves over 2½" long and true end buds present. Leaves moderately large, nonevergreen, nonaromatic and hairless or nearly so, narrow egg-shaped to elliptic. Twigs moderately stout, over ⅟₁₆" thick, slightly hairy or hairless. Buds scaly, bundle scar 1. Leaves 3"–8". Height 8'–18' (35'); diameter 1"–4" (8"). Flowers white in drooping clusters, petals very slender, May–June. Fruits purple, ball-shaped, fleshy, Sept.–Oct.
  Similar species: The privets have twigs under ⅟₁₆" thick and raised leaf scars. In winter, lilac (Plate 18) buds are thick and fleshy rather than papery. Northern Wild-raisin (Plate 20) has only 2 bud scales. Ashes (Plates 9, 10) have more bundle scars.

Miscellaneous Plants with
Opposite Leaves Not Toothed (2)
(2. Plate 17, p. 110)

All of these plants are shrubby. None have whorled leaves (but the St. Johnsworts may have leafy shoots clustered in the angles of the larger paired leaves). Bundle scars are single.

CORALBERRY   *Symphoricarpos orbiculatus* Moench   **p. 110**
Recognition: A shrub with scales present where twigs *meet the branchlets.* Leaves elliptic to nearly circular, sometimes wavy-edged, no transparent dots. Twigs and leaf undersides barely or quite hairy. Twigs and branchlets round, with *papery* bark. Pith solid, white. Leaves 1"–2". Height to 6'. Flowers greenish to purple, *bell*-shaped, clustered, less than 3/16", July–Aug. Fruits berrylike, *coral to purple,* less than 3/8", Sept.–winter.
Similar species: Shrubby honeysuckles (Plate 14) and hydrangeas (Plate 19) have scales at twig bases but have 3 bundle scars. (1) Snowberry and (2) Wolfberry have hollow pith, white fruits.
Remarks: Numerous songbirds, bobwhite, ruffed grouse, prairie chicken, pheasant, "Hungarian" partridge, and wild turkey occasionally eat the fruits.

SNOWBERRY   *Symphoricarpos albus* (L.) Blake   **p. 110**
Recognition: Somewhat similar to Coralberry but pith *hollow.* Leaves and twigs hairless or barely hairy. Leaves 1"–2". Height 1'–3' (6'). Flowers pink, 1/4"–3/8" long, short-stalked, May–July. Fruits *white,* 1/4"–5/8", seeds 3/16"–1/4", Aug.–May.
Similar species: (1) See Wolfberry. (2) Tartarian Honeysuckle (Plate 14) is more eastern and has 3 bundle scars.

WOLFBERRY   **Not illus.**
Symphoricarpos occidentalis Hook.
Recognition: Like Snowberry but with leaves larger and somewhat leathery, often wavy-edged. Twigs usually slightly hairy. Flowers *without stalks.* Fruits greenish white, becoming dark; seeds less than 3/16" long. Plains and rocky places; Ontario and British Columbia to New England, Pennsylvania, n. Illinois, Missouri, Kansas, and New Mexico.

KALM ST. JOHNSWORT   *Hypericum kalmianum* L.   **p. 110**
Recognition: A small shrub whose leaves have *many tiny transparent dots* when held up to light and viewed through a hand lens. *Clusters of leafy shoots* often present in leaf-angles. Leaves more or less hairless, somewhat oblong. Branchlets *4-edged,* twigs *2-edged.* Twigs angled at leaf scars. No scales present at twig bases. Older bark *papery* and shreddy. Buds very small, with 2 scales. Leaves 1"–2". Height to 3'. Flowers bright yellow, with 5 petals and 5 sepals, clustered at twig ends, July–Sept. Fruits small, dry 5-parted (rarely 3, 4, or 6) capsules, 5/16"–7/16" long (not counting slender projecting tips), Sept.–Oct.
Similar species: Related (1) St. Andrew's Cross and (2) St. Peterswort (Plate 12) also have dotted leaves but are lower creeping or reclining shrubs, with only 4 petals and sepals. (3–5) The next 3 St. Johnsworts have 2-angled branchlets. Single bundle scars,

papery bark, and tiny buds are helpful in winter in separating St. Johnsworts from other plants with opposite leaf scars.

SHRUBBY ST. JOHNSWORT   p. 110
Hypericum spathulatum (Spach) Steud.

Recognition: Similar to Kalm St. Johnswort but more widespread and with 2-*angled* branchlets and twigs. Leaves narrowly oblong, 1″–3″. Height to 7′. Flowers ⅝″–1″, in clusters at twig ends and in upper-leaf angles. The 5 green sepals underlying the 5 yellow petals are *shorter than petals* (¼″–1¼″). Fruits 3-parted, ⅜″–⅝″.

Similar species: (1) Golden St. Johnswort has larger flowers, longer sepals. (2) Dense St. Johnswort has smaller flowers, shorter sepals and fruits.

GOLDEN ST. JOHNSWORT   Not illus.
Hypericum frondosum Michx.

Recognition: Resembles Shrubby St. Johnswort but south-midwestern. Flowers 1″–1⅝″. Green sepals underlying yellow petals are *longer* than the petals (⅞″–1⅜″). Fruit capsules ⁵⁄₁₆″–⅝″. Limestone soils; S. Carolina, Kentucky, and s. Indiana to Alabama and Texas.

DENSE ST. JOHNSWORT   Leaf illus., p. 110
Hypericum densiflorum Pursh

Recognition: Like Shrubby St. Johnswort but with *narrow* or oblong leaves, and flowers ½″–1¹⁄₁₆″, in *side clusters*. Green sepals underlying yellow petals are *shorter* than the petals (less than ¼″). Fruits ¼″ or less. Var. *lobocarpum* (Gattinger) Svenson has 4- to 5-parted fruits but reaches our area only in se. Missouri. Height to 6′. Wet areas; se. New York, West Virginia, s. Indiana, and s. Missouri to Florida and Texas.

CANADA BUFFALOBERRY   p. 110
Shepherdia canadensis (L.) Nutt.

Recognition: A northern shrub with twigs and leaf undersides covered with *mixed brown and silver or white scales.* Leaves elliptic, green above, not leathery, often somewhat hairy. Small leaves may be present at bases of leafstalks. Twigs and branchlets not angled, no scales present at twig bases, bark *not papery.* Buds 2-scaled, with narrowed bases. Leaves 1″–1½″. Height 3′–7′. Flowers small, greenish yellow, bell-shaped, clustered, April–June. Fruits yellow or reddish, berrylike, July–Sept.

Similar species: Only opposite-leaved plant with brown and silver scales. (1) Silver Buffaloberry has only silver scales. (2) Beautyberry (p. 89) has gray-scaly twigs. Silverberries (Plate 68) have brown and silver scales but leaves are alternate.

Remarks: Fruits, sometimes known as soapberries, contain bitter substance that foams in water. Indians are said to have

enjoyed sweetened "soapberry" suds. Fruits eaten by several
songbirds. Nitrogen-fixing bacterial root nodules present, contrary to pattern for most plants that are not members of the
pea family.

SILVER BUFFALOBERRY   Not illus.
Shepherdia argentea Nutt.

Recognition: Similar to Canada Buffaloberry but more western
and with *silver scales only.* Leaves somewhat wedge-shaped,
silvery on *both sides.* Plant may be rather thorny. Fruits *bright
red,* edible. Streambanks; Manitoba and Alberta to Iowa, w.
Kansas, and n. New Mexico.

SANDMYRTLE   *Leiophyllum buxifolium* (Berg.) Ell.   **p. 110**

Recognition: A low but upright shrub of limited range. Leaves
small, elliptic, leathery, *evergreen.* Most leaves opposite, some
may be alternate. Older bark papery and *shreddy.* Twigs and
branchlets not angled, no scales present at twig bases. Leaves
¼″–½″. Height to 2½′. Flowers small, white, clustered, petal
entirely separate, April–June. Fruits dry, 2- to 3-parted capsules.

Similar species: (1) Alpine-azalea and (2) Pachistima (Plate 12)
have smaller leaves and are mat-forming, not upright. (3) Sheep
and (4) Pale Laurels (Plate 16) have larger, less crowded leaves.

Plants with Opposite or Whorled
Heart-shaped Leaves That Are Not Toothed
(Plate 18, p. 112)

With the exception of 1 or 2 honeysuckles (Plate 14) that may
bear a few leaves of this type, only these woody plants in our range
have opposite or whorled heart-shaped leaves that are not toothed.
The twigs of these plants lack central end buds but the tree species
are even more easily differentiated in winter from all others with
opposite leaf scars by the elliptical series of tiny bundle scars
within each circular leaf scar. The lilac is a shrub. The other
species here discussed are the only plants with opposite simple
leaves of any type which grow to tall tree size. Flowering Dogwood (Plate 15) and blackhaw viburnums (Plate 20) are smaller
in size. Two shrubby viburnums (Plate 20) bear leaves regularly
triangular or heart-shaped and a 3rd species is somewhat heart-
shaped (Plate 21), but they are toothed. The leaves of the
toothed hydrangeas are rarely heart-shaped.

COMMON LILAC   *Syringa vulgaris* L.   **p. 112**

Recognition: A hairless European shrub with leaves *heart-*

shaped and long-pointed. Buds stout, green or reddish with 2–3 thick scales. Twigs rather slender, rarely moderately stout. Leaf scars have single bundle scars. Leaves 2″–3½″. Height to 10′. Flowers small, *densely clustered, purple or white,* May–June. Fruits small capsules.

Similar species: No other shrub has heart-shaped leaves and single bundle scars. In winter see Fringe-tree (Plate 16).

PERSIAN LILAC   *Syringa persica* L.   **Not illus.**
   Recognition: Similar to Common Lilac but with slender, long-pointed leaves tapering at the base. Escapes rarely from cultivation.

PRINCESS-TREE   *Paulownia tomentosa* (Thunb.) Steud. **p. 112**
   Recognition: A medium-sized oriental tree with *large paired heart-shaped* leaves, chambered or hollow pith, and *clusters of large nutlike fruits or husks.* Leaves velvety-hairy beneath, usually short-pointed, sometimes only with shallowly heart-shaped bases, not whorled. Twigs stout, leaf scars circular, bundle scars numerous. Trunk bark rough with interlaced, smooth, often shiny, areas. Leaves 6″–13″. Height 30′–60′; diameter 1′–2′. Flowers about 2″, purplish with yellow stripes inside, in large clusters, buffy spikes of next years' flowers present after autumn, April–May. Fruits 1¼″–1¾″, somewhat *pecan-shaped woody capsules* containing many small winged seeds; husks present all winter.
   Similar species: Catalpas have solid white pith, sometimes whorled leaves, and long slender fruit capsules.

COMMON CATALPA   *Catalpa bignonioides* Walt.   **pp. 6, 112**
   Recognition: Similar to Princess-tree but with solid whitish pith and *cigar-shaped* fruits. Leaves paired or in whorls of 3, hairy beneath; have somewhat foul odor when crushed. Trunk bark scaly. Leaves 6″–13″. Height 50′–60′; diameter 1′–4′. Flowers 1″–1⅝″, white with yellow and purple spots, clustered, lower petal not notched, May–July. Fruits long slender pods containing many small seeds, Sept.–winter.
   Similar species: (1) Princess-tree has chambered pith. (2) Catawba-tree has more long-pointed leaves and flowers with lower petal notched. (3) Chinese Catalpa has hairless short-pointed leaves, yellow blossoms.
   Remarks: Once widely planted for fence posts, its rapid growth unfortunately is often counteracted by insect, storm, and frost damage. Often highly productive of "catawba worms" for fish bait.

CATAWBA-TREE   *Catalpa speciosa* Warder   **Not illus.**
   Recognition: Resembles Common Catalpa but larger, with *long-pointed* leaves that are not foul-odored when crushed. Trunk bark deeply ridged. Height 50′–70′ (120′); diameter 2′–4′ (5′).

Flowers 1⅜"–2", lower petal notched, May–June. Wet woods; e. Virginia, Ohio, s. Illinois, and Kansas to Louisiana and e. Texas.

CHINESE CATALPA   *Catalpa ovata* G. Don   **Not illus.**
Recognition: A shrub or small tree generally like preceding 2 species but with leaves *hairless*, or quickly becoming so, and short-pointed. Twigs and fruits more slender. Flowers yellow, marked with orange and purple, June–Aug. Escaped from cultivation; Connecticut and s. Ontario to Maryland and Ohio.

Miscellaneous Shrubs with Opposite Toothed Leaves
(*Plate 19, p. 114*)

Surprisingly few plants have opposite simple leaves that are toothed. Several nonerect species are on Plate 12. The maples (Plate 22) have toothed leaves but these are also deeply lobed. Only some viburnums (Plates 20 and 21) and plants of this plate have leaves of this type. Many species have only limited northern ranges. Oakleaf Hydrangea (not illustrated) is discussed here with its relatives even though its leaves are lobed.

NORTHERN BUSH-HONEYSUCKLE   p. 114
Diervilla lonicera Mill.
Recognition: A low shrub with *slender ridged* twigs and scales present at the *twig bases*. Leaves more or less egg-shaped, *long-pointed*, fine-toothed. Typically nearly hairless but a north-western variety (*hypomalaca* Fern.) has leaves densely hairy beneath. Leaves distinctly stalked. Twigs have slender ridges running downward from lines connecting leaf scars. Buds have 4 or more pairs of scales; bundle scars 3. Leaves 2"–5". Height to 4'. Flowers yellow to crimson, tubular with spreading petal tips, ⅜"–⅝", June–Aug. Fruits long-pointed dry capsules.
Similar species: Though honeysuckles (Plate 14), Coralberry and relatives (Plate 17), and hydrangeas (below) also have scales present at twig bases, the ridged twigs of this species are distinctive. Southern Bush-honeysuckle has short leafstalks. True honeysuckles have leaves not toothed, fleshy fruits. Certain of the unrelated and dissimilar azaleas (Plate 64) sometimes are called bush-honeysuckles.

SOUTHERN BUSH-HONEYSUCKLE   **Not illus.**
Diervilla sessilifolia Buckl.
Recognition: Like the preceding but leafstalks *extremely short*

and twigs distinctly *4-sided*. Mountains; w. Virginia and e. Tennessee to nw. Georgia and n. Alabama.

WILD HYDRANGEA   *Hydrangea arborescens* L.   p. 114
Recognition: A low to medium-sized shrub with smooth and medium-stout twigs that are not ridged but have scales *present* where they meet branchlets. Leaves large-toothed, very variable. They may be pale green and hairless or fine white-hairy beneath; nearly circular, heart-shaped, egg-shaped, elliptic, or long-pointed. Leaves and leaf scars may be in whorls of 3. Buds have 4 or more pairs of scales; bundle scars 3. Bark of branchlets thin, papery, glossy. Leaves 5″–15″. Height to 6′ (10′). Flowers whitish, small, in *flat-topped umbrella-shaped clusters,* outer flowers larger but sterile, June–July. Fruits small dry capsules, Oct–Dec., or longer.
Similar species: (1) Asiatic Hydrangea has cone-shaped flower and fruit clusters, hairy twigs. (2) Oakleaf Hydrangea has lobed leaves. Upright honeysuckles (Plate 14) have fleshy fruits, more slender twigs, less papery bark on branchlets. Bush-honeysuckles are more northern, have ridged twigs.
Remarks: Twigs recorded as poisonous to livestock, yet sometimes eaten by whitetail deer. Wild turkey eat fruits.

ASIATIC HYDRANGEA   Not illus.
Hydrangea paniculata Sieb.
Recognition: Similar to Wild Hydrangea but with restricted range, hairy twigs, smaller leaves, cone-shaped flower and fruit clusters. Leaves 2″–5″. Swamps; scattered localities from Massachusetts southward.

OAKLEAF HYDRANGEA   Not illus.
Hydrangea quercifolia Bartr.
Recognition: A southern species similar in some twig characteristics to the Wild Hydrangea but with deeply lobed, somewhat oaklike leaves that are white-hairy beneath. Twigs *very red-hairy.* Bark extremely flaky. Leaves 6″–8″. Flowers in cone-shaped clusters. Escaped from cultivation; north to Connecticut.

BURNINGBUSH   *Euonymus atropurpureus* Jacq.   p. 114
Recognition: A shrub or small tree with *green 4-lined* twigs. Leaves egg-shaped or elliptic, short-pointed, fine-toothed, somewhat hairy beneath. Twigs nearly round, buds scaly, bundle scars single, leaf scars not connected by lines. Leaves 2″–6″. Height 6′–12′ (25′). Flowers purple, clustered, June–July. Fruits *reddish and berrylike,* beneath *woody purplish* bracts, Aug.–Nov.
Similar species: Among opposite-leaved plants with single bundle scars only members of this genus have 4-lined twigs.

(1) Strawberry-bushes (Plate 12) are not erect, twigs are more square in cross section. (2) European Spindletree has hairless, smaller leaves, orange and pink fruits.
Remarks: Fruits reported to be poisonous to children. Recorded as eaten by only a few birds.

EUROPEAN SPINDLETREE   Not illus.
Euonymus europaeus L.
  Recognition: Similar to Burningbush but leaves smaller (1″–4″), undersides *hairless*. Fruits orange beneath pinkish bracts. Escape; waste places; north to Massachusetts and Wisconsin.

COMMON BUCKTHORN   *Rhamnus cathartica* L.   p. 114
  Recognition: A European medium-sized to large shrub with twigs ending in *sharp spines*. Leaves elliptic, hairless, fine-toothed. A few may be alternate rather than opposite. Twigs dark and unlined, buds have several scales. Bundle scars 3, less commonly fused and single. No scales present at twig bases, leaf scars not connected by lines. Inner bark *yellow*. Leaves 1½″–2″. Height to 16′ (26′). Flowers small, greenish, clustered, May–June. Fruits dark and berrylike.
  Similar species: Combination of thorn-tipped twigs and yellow inner bark is distinctive. Other buckthorns (Plate 58) have alternate leaves. The only other thorny opposite-leaved plants in our area are (1) Silver Buffaloberry (p. 84) and (2) Swamp Forestiera.

SWAMP FORESTIERA   p. 114
Forestiera acuminata (Michx.) Poir.
  Recognition: An occasionally thorny shrub or small tree. Buds *globular*, often more than 1 above each leaf scar. Leaves long-pointed at *both ends*, fine-toothed, often clustered. Leaf scars not connected by lines. Twigs hairless or slightly hairy; bundle scars single. Leaves 1½″–3″. Height to 12′ (25′). Flowers small, March–May. Fruits small, fleshy, May–Oct.
  Similar species: (1) Only other plant with globose buds and single bundle scars is Buttonbush (Plate 16), which has leaves often whorled, leaf scars connected by lines, and buds single above leaf scars. Leaf shape of this species unique among shrubs with opposite toothed leaves. See (2) Upland Forestiera and, when thorniness is found, (3) Common Buckthorn.
  Remarks: Fruits eaten by wood ducks, mallards, other waterfowl.

UPLAND FORESTIERA   Not illus.
Forestiera ligustrina (Michx.) Poir.
  Recognition: A species related to Swamp Forestiera that barely enters our area. Leaves somewhat egg-shaped, blunt-tipped,

rather hairy beneath. Flowers in Aug. Dry and rocky soils; Georgia and Kentucky to Florida and Alabama.

BEAUTYBERRY   *Callicarpa americana* L.   **Not illus.**
Recognition: A southern shrub with *gray-scaly* or gray-hairy twigs, *white-woolly* leaf undersides, and *violet-colored* fruit clusters. Leaves taper at both ends; buds silky-hairy with scales absent or smaller buds may have 2 scales. Buds have narrowed bases. Bundle scars single. Leaf scars not connected by lines. Leaves 3″–6″. Height to 5′. Flowers small, tubular, bluish, clustered, June–Aug. Fruits small, bright, purple, Aug.–Nov. In this group, only the buffaloberries (Plate 17) also have conspicuously scaly twigs. Their twigs are covered with silver and brown scales and bud scales are present on all buds. Woods; Maryland, Tennessee, Arkansas, and Oklahoma to Florida and Texas.

COMMON MOCK-ORANGE   *Philadelphus inodorus* L. **p. 114**
Recognition: A southern shrub with buds small or hidden beneath leaf scars. Leaves egg-shaped, somewhat long-pointed, hairless or slightly long-hairy, have from a few tiny to many larger teeth. Leaf veins tend to parallel leaf edges. Bundle scars 3; leaf scars *connected by lines.* Twigs hairless, tips not thorny. Bark of branchlets papery. Leaves 2″–4″. Height to 10′. Flowers 1–4, white, to 2″ across, at twig ends, petals ¾″–1″, May–June. Fruits dry 3- to 4-parted capsules.
Similar species: (1) Only Flowering Dogwood also has 3 bundle scars and hidden buds. It, however, has raised leaf scars, tight bark. (2) Hairy Mock-orange has hairy twigs; other mock-oranges have 5–7 flowers in cluster.

HAIRY MOCK-ORANGE   **Not illus.**
Philadelphus hirsutus Nutt.
Recognition: A similar but smaller species than Common Mock-orange with *hairy* twigs and *woolly* leaf undersides. Twigs red or straw-colored; older branchlets have flaking papery bark. Leaf scars narrower; buds *fully exposed.* Flower petals ⅜″–¾″. Rocky areas and streambanks; N. Carolina and Kentucky to Georgia and Alabama.

GARDEN MOCK-ORANGE   **Not illus.**
Philadelphus coronarius L.
Recognition: Similar to Common Mock-orange but flowers 5–7 in clusters. Leaves *hairless* except on veins beneath. Flowers 1″–1⅜″ across and very fragrant, petals ⅜″–¾″. They are the "orange blossoms" frequently used ornamentally in the North. A European species, sometimes spreading from cultivation.

GRAY MOCK-ORANGE   **Not illus.**
Philadelphus pubescens Loisel.
  Recognition: Unlike other mock-oranges, the bark of branchlets
  of this species *tight*, not flaky. Furthermore, this bark is *gray*,
  not straw-colored or reddish. Leaves *gray-hairy beneath*.
  Flowers 5–7, but barely fragrant. Bluffs and riverbanks; Tennessee and s. Illinois to Alabama and Arkansas.

MARSH-ELDER   *Iva frutescens* L.   **Not illus.**
  Recognition: A partly woody plant that grows on *sea beaches*
  and *salt marshes*. Leaves somewhat *thickened* and at least upper
  ones narrow to elliptic. Foliage hairless or fine-hairy, with 6–15
  pairs of large coarse teeth. Twigs branched (see Sassafras, Plate
  43), with fine lines running lengthwise. Buds hidden in bark.
  Leaves 3″–4″. Height to 11′. Flowers small, greenish white,
  in end clusters, Aug.–Oct. Fruits small, dry. Coastal saline soils;
  w. Novia Scotia to Florida and Texas.

Viburnums (1) and (2)
(*Plates 20 and 21, pp. 116, 118*)

Though widespread and common in eastern United States,
viburnums are difficult to identify as a group. Few of the common
names ordinarily include the word viburnum and no all-inclusive
vegetative characteristics define the group. All viburnums, however, have small fleshy fruits containing single flat seeds. Usually
the flowers are small and white. They and the fruits occur in
mostly flat-topped clusters 3″–5″ across. Siebold Viburnum and
a variety of Guelder-rose have round-topped flower heads.
Hobblebush, Cranberry Viburnum, and Guelder-rose have some
blossoms larger, more showy, and sterile. The bundle scars are 3.
  The viburnums are readily divisible into 4 main groups according to bud and leaf type:

1. Leaves finely toothed or wavy-edged, not lobed (Plate 20):
    2. Buds without scales; leaves somewhat heart-shaped; leaf
       scars triangular   **WAYFARING-TREE GROUP**
    2. Buds with 2 scales; leaves egg-shaped to elliptic; leaf
       scars narrow   **BLACKHAW GROUP**
1. Leaves coarsely toothed, sometimes lobed; leaf scars narrow (Plate 21):
    3. Leaves with a single main midrib, not lobed; bud scales
       several   **ARROWWOOD GROUP**
    3. Leaves with 3–5 main veins meeting near the base, often
       lobed; bud scales 2 or several   **MAPLELEAF GROUP**

The true haws, or hawthorns (Plate 39), and the Deciduous Holly, or Possum-haw (Plate 61), should not be confused with the blackhaw viburnums.

Viburnums (1)
(Plate 20, p. 116)

WAYFARING-TREE   *Viburnum lantana* L.   **p. 116**
   Recognition: An upright European shrub or small tree with egg- to heart-shaped fine-toothed leaves and naked buds. Leaf undersides, twigs, and buds covered with fine gray hair. Leaf scars broadly triangular. Leaves 2"–5". Height to 12' (20'). Flowers small, white, all alike, May–June. Fruits red to black, seeds have 3 grooves, Aug.–Sept.
   Similar species: Hobblebush has larger leaves, rusty hair, and blossoms of 2 sizes. All other viburnums have scaly buds, larger leaf scars, and leaves not heart-shaped.

HOBBLEBUSH   *Viburnum alnifolium* Marsh.   **p. 116**
   Recognition: Similar to but more straggling than Wayfaring-tree; *rusty-hairy* and with *larger* leaves. Branches reclining, often rooted near tips. Leaves may become less hairy with age. Leaves 4"–8". Height to 10'. Flowers white or pink, *marginal ones large-petaled*, showy, and sterile; seeds have a single groove. Fruits Aug.–Sept., or longer.

SMOOTH BLACKHAW   *Viburnum prunifolium* L.   **p. 116**
   Recognition: A shrub or small tree with short, stiff side twigs. Leaves elliptic to egg-shaped, with blunt or somewhat pointed (but not long-pointed) tips, sharply fine-toothed, dull-surfaced, hairless or slightly scaly beneath. Leafstalks not winged or with very narrow "wings." Foliage may become somewhat leathery. Buds 2-scaled, powder-covered, or brown-hairy. Leaf scars narrow. Trunk bark dark, divided into many small squarish blocks. Var. *bushii* (Ashe) P. & S., ranging from s. Illinois to Arkansas, has narrower leaves, winged leafstalks. Leaves 1"–3". Height 6'–15' (30'); diameter 2"–6" (10"). Flowers small, clusters *without stalks*, April–May. Fruits blackish, Sept.–Oct.
   Similar species: Five viburnums have 2-scaled hairy or powdery buds and leaves more or less elliptic and fine-toothed or not toothed: Smooth and (1) Rusty Blackhaws and (2) Nannyberry regularly have fine-toothed leaves; Rusty Blackhaw has red-hairy leaves and buds; Nannyberry has long-pointed leaves and large flower buds; (3) Northern and (4) Southern Wild-raisins have leaves often wavy-toothed or without teeth, large flower buds with scales not entirely covering the buds, and stalked

flower clusters. (5) Cranberry Viburnum and (6) Squashberry (Plate 21) have hairless buds with 2 scales. (7) For bark similarities, see Persimmon (Plate 68).
Remarks: Fruits eaten by foxes, bobwhites, and several songbirds. Some people also like them.

RUSTY BLACKHAW   *Viburnum rufidulum* Raf.   **p. 116**
Recognition: More southern and differing from Smooth Blackhaw in having side branches somewhat more *flexible.* Leaf undersides, leafstalks, buds, and often twigs *densely red-hairy.* Upper leaf surfaces *shiny* and foliage more leathery. Leafstalks *winged.* Leaves 1″–4″. Height 6′–18′ (40′); diameter 2″–10″ (18″).

NANNYBERRY   *Viburnum lentago* L.   **p. 116**
Recognition: A northern shrub or small tree with sharply fine-toothed and short- to rather long-pointed leaves. Leaves hairless or nearly so and somewhat egg-shaped to narrowly elliptic. Leafstalks winged. The brown or gray buds have rough-granular scales and are of 2 sizes; larger flower buds are *completely covered by the 2 scales.* Twigs rough-granular and side twigs flexible. Leaves 2″–5″. Height 9′–18′ (30′); diameter 1″–3″ (10″). Flowers small, clusters *not stalked,* May–June. Fruits blue-black, Aug.–Sept.
Similar species: Only viburnum with 2 bud scales whose leaves are regularly long-pointed. (1) Northern and (2) Southern Wild-raisins have larger buds not completely covered by scales.

NORTHERN WILD-RAISIN   *Viburnum cassinoides* L.   **p. 116**
Recognition: A northern shrub with leaves often not toothed and larger flower buds only partly covered by the 2 scales. Leaves narrow to egg-shaped and either fine-toothed or somewhat wavy-edged. Leaves *dull above,* not leathery, and may have short prolonged tip. Leafstalks winged. The larger flower buds have 2 rough-granular yellowish to brownish scales whose edges do not quite meet in centers. Twigs dull, somewhat scaly and flexible. Leaves 2″–5″. Height to 12′. Flowers small, clusters *stalked,* June–Aug. Fruits yellowish to blue-black, white-powdered, pulp sweet, Sept.–Oct.
Similar species: (1) Leaves of Nannyberry are always toothed and more long-pointed. (2) Southern Wild-raisin has more glossy leaves and twigs. (3) See also Smooth Blackhaw.
Remarks: Fruits edible. Dried leaves have been used as tea. Fruits eaten by ruffed and sharptail grouse, pheasant, European partridge, and several songbirds. Deer and rabbits browse twigs.

SOUTHERN WILD-RAISIN   *Viburnum nudum* L.   **p. 116**
Recognition: Differs from Northern Wild-raisin in being more

southern and in having *glossy, leathery* (but *nonevergreen*) leaves, *glossy* twigs, and *brown to reddish* buds. Leaves regularly wavy-edged, rarely fine-toothed, rounded or merely pointed at the tip. Height to 20'. Flowers May–July. Fruits with pulp often bitter, July–Oct.

Similar species: Devilwood (p. 79) has evergreen foliage with leafstalks not winged.

Viburnums (2)
(*Plate 21, p. 118*)

These viburnums may be divided into 2 groups: (1) the arrowwood viburnums, with rather egg-shaped coarse-toothed leaves whose buds have several scales (usually 2 pairs), and (2) the mapleleaf viburnums, with lobed, rather maplelike leaves whose buds either have 2 or several scales. All have narrow leaf scars.

NORTHERN ARROWWOOD   p. 118
Viburnum recognitum Fern.
Recognition: A shrub with egg-shaped to round leaves that are *hairless* (or hairy only on veins beneath), with 4–22 pairs of coarse teeth. Leaves rounded or slightly heart-shaped at base and leafstalks mostly without stipules. Twigs *hairless*, often somewhat 6-sided and ridged. Buds have several scales. Leaves 2"–3". Height to 15'. Flowers May–July. Fruits blackish, seed with a *shallow broad* groove, July–Sept.
Similar species: (1) Southern Arrowwood has hairy twigs; (2) Shortstalk and (3) Softleaf Arrowwoods have velvety leaves and twigs not ridged. (4) In winter, Mapleleaf Viburnum has non-ridged twigs.
Remarks: Fruits eaten by ruffed grouse and chipmunks. Shoots once used by Indians for arrow shafts.

SOUTHERN ARROWWOOD   *Viburnum dentatum* L.   p. 118
Recognition: Similar to the preceding but twigs *velvety-hairy* and leaves occasionally velvety-hairy beneath. From w. Pennsylvania and Tennessee to e. Missouri, var. *deamii* (Rehd.) Fern. has nearly hairless twigs. Seed has *deep narrow* groove. Height to 10'. Flowers June–Aug. Fruits Aug.–Nov.
Similar species: Hairy ridged twigs characterize the typical form. Hairless variety can best be distinguished from Northern Arrowwood by seed structure and locality.

SHORTSTALK ARROWWOOD   p. 118
Viburnum rafinesquianum Schultes
Recognition: A low midwestern shrub. Leaves have *only 4–10 pairs* of coarse teeth, velvety-hairy beneath, at least when young,

heart-shaped at base. Leafstalks, at least those near flowers, usually less than ¼″, short stipules near base. Twigs *hairless,* not ridged. Bark of stems dark gray, does not flake. Leaves 1″–3″. Height to 7′. Flowers May–June. Fruits purplish, seeds mostly with pair of shallow grooves, July–Sept.

Similar species: In summer the few-toothed leaves are unique among arrowwood viburnums. In winter the darker, nonpeeling bark will distinguish it from next species.

SOFTLEAF ARROWWOOD   *Viburnum molle* Michx.   **p. 118**
Recognition: A shrub with *light gray, flaking* older bark. Leaves broadly egg- to heart-shaped, short-pointed, *soft-hairy beneath, 20–30 pairs* of teeth. Small stipules may be present early in year on bases of leafstalks. Twigs *hairless* and not ridged. Leaves 1″–3″. Height to 13′. Flowers May–June. Fruits dark blue, the seeds with a single deep groove, June–Aug.
Similar species: No other arrowwood has hairy heart-shaped many-toothed leaves and none has older bark of this type.

SIEBOLD VIBURNUM   **Not illus.**
Viburnum sieboldii Miq.
Recognition: A Japanese tree or shrub that has escaped from cultivation, Connecticut to e. Pennsylvania. Twigs *ashy-woolly.* Leaves shiny, *wedge-shaped,* and coarse-toothed. The only viburnum with *opposite-branched, round-topped* flower clusters, but see text p. 90 and under Guelder-rose (p. 95). Seeds have 1 deep groove.

CRANBERRY VIBURNUM (HIGHBUSH-CRANBERRY)
Viburnum trilobum Marsh.   **p. 118**
Recognition: A tall shrub with *3-lobed* leaves that are variably hairy or hairless on both surfaces. Lobes tend to be long-pointed. Leafstalks bear *tiny dome-shaped glands* (use lens) near leaf base and small, somewhat blunt, paired stipules near the twigs. Twigs hairless. Bud scales 2. Leaves 2″–4″. Height to 17′. Flowers white, with those of outer border of cluster sterile and larger, cluster 1⅝″–3″ across, May–July. Fruits red, tart but edible, seed not grooved, Sept.–Oct.
Similar species: Long-pointed leaf lobes are distinctive. (1) Guelder-rose also has glands on leafstalk but these have concave surfaces (use lens). (2) Squashberry has short-lobed leaves that usually do not bear glands; in winter, Squashberry may be separated on basis of smaller size and more straggling growth. Other viburnums with 2 bud scales have hairy or powdery buds. Maples (Plate 22) lack leafstalk glands. True cranberries are low and creeping (Plate 32).
Remarks: People sometimes use the fruits as a substitute for true cranberries. Eaten by ruffed and sharptail grouse, pheas-

ant, and songbirds. Extract of the bark used medicinally. Though usually called Highbush-cranberry, it seems desirable to use a common name showing proper relationship.

GUELDER-ROSE *Viburnum opulus* L. **Not illus.**
Recognition: European, frequently cultivated and sometimes escaping to the wild. Similar to Cranberry Viburnum but glands of leafstalks concave on top; leaf lobes less long-pointed. Stipules more slender and pointed and fruits more bitter. Snowballtree, a variety of this species (var. *roseum* L.), has a round-topped flower cluster, like Siebold Viburnum. *All* flowers are showy but sterile. A viburnum, not a rose.

SQUASHBERRY *Viburnum edule* (Michx.) Raf. **p. 118**
Recognition: A northern straggling shrub. Leaves with *3 short, often uneven lobes* or sometimes not lobed. Leaf teeth coarse and irregular. Leafstalks without stipules and generally without glands; if present, more likely to be on leaf base than on leafstalk. Twigs hairless. Bud scales 2. Leaves 2″–4″. Height 2′–5′. Flowers all fertile, cluster up to 1½″ across, May–Aug. Fruits yellow to red, seed not grooved, Aug.–Oct.
Similar species: See Cranberry Viburnum.
Remarks: Fruits make excellent jam. Also, are eaten by grouse and squirrels. Twigs browsed by moose and woodland caribou.

MAPLELEAF VIBURNUM *Viburnum acerifolium* L. **p. 118**
Recognition: A shrub. Leaves *3-lobed, velvety-hairy beneath,* yellow and black dots on undersides. Leaf bases and stalks without glands, but leafstalks do have small paired stipules. Twigs velvety. Bud scales several. The hairless variety *glabrescens* Rehd. occurs from Kentucky southward. Leaves 2″–5″. Height to 7′. Flowers all fertile, May–Aug. Fruits red, turning black or purple, rarely white, seed barely or not grooved, July–Oct.
Similar species: Only lobed-leaf viburnum with more than 2 bud scales per bud. (1) In winter, separated from Southern Arrowwood by lack of twig ridges. The southern hairless form distinguished in winter from (2) Softleaf Arrowwood by lack of gray flaking bark; from (3) Shortstalk Arrowwood by lack of grooved seeds.
Remarks: Twigs eaten by deer and rabbits, fruits by grouse.

Maples
(Plate 22, p. 120)

Maples are our only trees with opposite, fan-lobed leaves. Though the leaves of the lobed-leaved viburnums (Plate 21) somewhat resemble those of some small maples, viburnum leaves are either velvety-hairy or equipped with tiny warty glands on the stalks, or both. One maple, the Ashleaf Maple, bears opposite compound leaves and is pictured with the ashes (Plate 10). Maple flowers mostly are greenish, small, and clustered. The dry, double-winged fruits, known as "keys," are eaten by many birds and by squirrels.

The native maples are of great value for shade, ornament, lumber, and sugar. Porcupines sometimes eat the inner bark, and the twigs are a staple food of cottontail rabbit, snowshoe hare, whitetail deer, and moose.

STRIPED MAPLE (MOOSEWOOD)   p. 120
Acer pensylvanicum L.

Recognition: A small slender northern tree with *green* bark vertically marked with *white stripes.* Leaves *3-lobed*, sometimes with 2 additional small lobes near base, lobes somewhat long-pointed. Foliage double-toothed, hairless, green on both sides. paler beneath. Twigs hairless, mostly greenish. Buds stalked, with 2 scales. Leaves 2"–10". Height 5'–15' (35'); diameter 1"–2" (9"). Flowers in long clusters, May–June. Fruits June–Sept.

Similar species: (1) Mountain Maple has darker, unstriped bark, hairy twigs. (2) Cranberry Viburnum (Plate 21) is lower, with fleshy fruits and without greenish white-striped bark.

MOUNTAIN MAPLE   *Acer spicatum* Lam.   p. 120
Recognition: A small northern tree with bark dark or somewhat greenish, but *not* white-striped. Leaves 3- to 5-lobed, coarsely toothed, hairless or slightly hairy beneath. Twigs *velvety-hairy,* mostly greenish. Buds stalked and have 2 scales. Leaves 2"–10". Height mostly under 20'. Flowers in long clusters, May–Aug. Fruits July–Oct.

Similar species: See Striped Maple.

SIBERIAN MAPLE   *Acer ginnala* Maxim.   Not illus.
Recognition: An Asiatic shrub or small tree; escaped locally from Maine and Connecticut to w. New York. Leaves 3-lobed, but buds not stalked and covered by several scales. Buds brown. Twigs hairless. Flowers and fruits in lengthened clusters.

RED MAPLE   *Acer rubrum* L.   pp. 7, 120
Recognition: A medium-sized tree with *smooth gray* young trunk bark and broken darker older bark. Leaves 3- to 5-lobed, *much whitened* and hairless or hairy *beneath.* Notches between leaf lobes relatively *shallow,* base of terminal lobe *wide.* Var. *trilobum* K. Koch has only 3-lobed or unlobed, rounded to wedge-shaped leaves. Twigs and buds *reddish,* the latter blunt

and several-scaled. Extra buds may be present above some side leaf scars. Broken twigs do not have unpleasant odor. Leaves 2″–8″. Height 20′–40′ (100′); diameter 1′–2′ (4′). Flowers red, rarely yellow, in short clusters, March–May. Fruits reddish, May–July.

Similar species: Though variable, distinguished from (1) Silver Maple by shallow leaf notches, wide base of end leaf lobe, nonodorous twigs, and smoother trunk bark. Both Red and Silver Maples differ from (2) Sycamore Maple in having red buds and more coarsely toothed leaves. (3) A form of the Sugar Maple with whitened leaf undersides can be recognized by slender, pointed, brown buds. (4) Norway Maple has milky sap evident in broken leafstalk.

Remarks: Wood sometimes used for furniture.

SILVER MAPLE *Acer saccharinum* L.   **p. 120**
Recognition: A tall tree with *greyish* older bark that tends to *flake*, leaving *brown spots*. Leaves *deeply 5-lobed* with base of terminal leaf lobe *narrowed*. Foliage *whitened*, sometimes hairy beneath. Twigs and buds as in Red Maple but broken twigs have *unpleasant odor*. Leaves 2″–10″. Height 40′–60′ (120′); diameter 1′–3′ (5′). Flowers greenish or reddish, short-clustered, Feb.–May. Fruits greenish or reddish, April–June.
Similar species: See Red Maple.
Remarks: Sap sweet but less sugary than that of Sugar Maple.

SYCAMORE MAPLE *Acer pseudo-platanus* L.   **Not illus.**
Recognition: Like preceding 2 species, this European tree has leaves *5-lobed and whitened beneath.* Unlike these native species, however, Sycamore Maple leaves are more *wavy-edged* than sharply toothed. Furthermore, buds are *green* rather than red and only single buds occur above leafstalk or leaf scar. In winter, it most resembles Norway Maple but edges of opposing leaf scars *do not meet.* Sycamore Maple resembles Striped and Mountain Maples in having elongate flower and fruit clusters. Occasionally escapes from cultivation; open upland areas.

SUGAR MAPLE *Acer saccharum* Marsh.   **pp. 6, 7, 120**
Recognition: A large tree with dark brown trunk bark marked with rough vertical grooves and ridges. Leaves mostly *5-lobed* with moderately deep notches between lobes. Foliage *pale green beneath* but an uncommon form has whitened leaf undersides. Leaves usually hairless but leaf undersides velvety in a s. Indiana, Illinois, and Missouri variety. Leaf edges firm and not drooping. Leafstalk bases not much enlarged, no stipules, or small ones that do not cover buds. Buds slender, sharp-pointed, brown. Side buds occur singly. Twigs glossy and reddish brown. Leaves 2″–10″. Height 40′–60′ (80′); diameter

1'-2' (3'). Flowers yellowish, April–June. Fruits June–Sept.
Similar species: (1) Black Maple has shallowly lobed leaves
with drooping edges, larger stipules and leafstalk bases, and
dull orange-tinged twigs. (2) Florida Maple has whitish-gray
bark and often hairy twigs and leaf undersides. (3) See Norway
Maple.
Remarks: One of our most valuable hardwood trees. Neither
sap nor wood is separated commercially from those of Black
Maple; both species supply maple syrup as well as birds-
eye, curly, blister, and plain lumber. Wood much used for furniture.

FLORIDA MAPLE *Acer barbatum* Michx. **Not illus.**
Recognition: Much like Sugar Maple but with *light gray* bark
on younger trunks and branches which resembles that of Beech
or Red Maple. Twigs and leaf undersides *velvety-hairy* but may
sometimes be hairless. Stalks of male flowers only ⅝"–1" rather
than 1"–2" as in Sugar and Black Maples. Bottomlands and
slopes of Coastal Plain and Piedmont sections from se. Virginia
to centr. Florida, west to e. Texas, and north in Mississippi Valley
to se. Missouri.

BLACK MAPLE *Acer nigrum* Michx. f. **p. 120**
Recognition: Similar to Sugar Maple but with darker older bark
and mostly *shallowly 3-lobed* leaves darker green and more
hairy; edges tend to *droop.* Leafstalks enlarge abruptly at base
and usually bear stipules large enough to enclose buds. Twigs
duller, somewhat orange-brown. Wings of paired fruits more
widely separated.

NORWAY MAPLE *Acer platanoides* L. **Fruit illus., p. 120**
Recognition: European; resembles Sugar Maple but has more
leaf teeth. Its best field mark is *milky juice* of broken leafstalk
(see also next species). Buds large (over 3/16"), green or reddish,
and blunt. In winter, resembles Sycamore Maple but edges of
opposing leaf scars meet on Norway Maple twigs. Buds of Red
and Silver Maples are smaller and, unlike this maple, extra buds
may be present above some leaf scars. Leaves 2"–8". Height
40'–70'; diameter 1'–2'. Occasionally spreading from plantings
to upland fields and hedgerows.

HEDGE MAPLE *Acer campestre* L. **Not illus.**
Recognition: Rarely found in wild, this European shrub or small
tree has small leaves which have 3–5 rounded lobes that are
not toothed. Sap of broken leafstalk *milky.* Leaf undersides,
small gray buds, and twigs somewhat hairy. Branchlets may have
corky ridges. See Norway Maple.

Broad-leaved Plants with Opposite Simple Leaves

(Key, pages 66–67; text, pages 66–98)

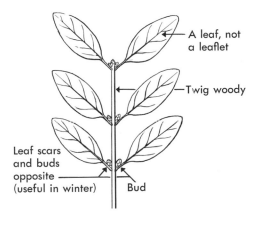

THOUGH more numerous than those of Section II, the plants with opposite simple leaves are still so few as to be rather easily identified. In winter, of course, plants with opposite leaf scars may be members of either Section II or III and the drawings in both Sections must be reviewed. Care should be taken that the leaves or leaf scars on the stubby, scar-crowded spur branches of some alternate-leaved plants are not thought to be opposite or whorled. No opposite-leaved plants have spur branches.

LOW CREEPING AND TRAILING SHRUBS

as distinguished from climbing vines and erect woody plants.
The creeping stems often take root. American Mistletoe (a parasite on branches of broad-leaved trees), p. 69, is included here.

Ѵ ST. ANDREW'S CROSS, *Ascyrum hypericoides*   p. 67
     Sandy and rocky fields and woods; se. Massachusetts, Penn-
     sylvania, Kentucky, s. Indiana, s. Illinois, and Kansas to
     Florida and Texas.

Ѵ ST. PETERSWORT, *Ascyrum stans*   p. 68
     Dry to moist woods and fields; se. New York, e. Pennsylvania,
     and Kentucky to Florida and Texas.

Ѵ AMERICAN STRAWBERRY-BUSH   p. 68
     Euonymus americanus
     Fertile woods; se. New York, Pennsylvania, s. Illinois, Missouri,
     and Oklahoma to Florida and Texas.

Ѵ RUNNING STRAWBERRY-BUSH, *Euonymus obovatus* p. 68
     Damp woods and thickets; w. New York, s. Ontario, and s.
     Michigan to Tennessee and Missouri.

Ѵ PARTRIDGEBERRY, *Mitchella repens*   p. 68
     Forest floors; sw. Newfoundland, s. Quebec, and Minnesota
     to Florida and Texas.

Ѵ TWINFLOWER, *Linnaea borealis* var. *americana*   p. 68
     Tundras, bogs, cool swamps; w. Greenland and Alaska to se.
     New York, w. Maryland, W. Virginia, ne. Ohio, n. Indiana,
     S. Dakota, Colorado, and n. California.

Ѵ ALPINE-AZALEA, *Loiseleuria procumbens*   p. 69
     Tundras and bogs; Greenland and Alaska to mts. of Maine,
     New Hampshire, and Alberta.

Ѵ PACHISTIMA, *Pachistima canbyi*   p. 69
     Rocky slopes; w. Virginia, W. Virginia, and se. Ohio.

  Ѵ AMERICAN MISTLETOE   p. 69
     Phoradendron flavescens (not illus.)

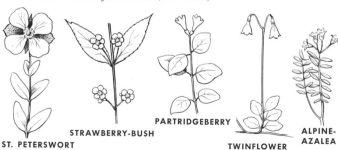

PARTRIDGEBERRY

STRAWBERRY-BUSH

ST. PETERSWORT

TWINFLOWER

ALPINE-AZALEA

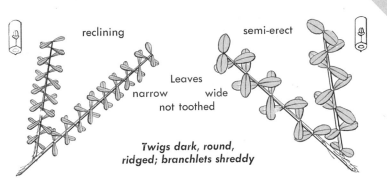

reclining

semi-erect

Leaves

narrow   wide

not toothed

*Twigs dark, round,
ridged; branchlets shreddy*

ST. ANDREW'S CROSS   **ST. PETERSWORT**

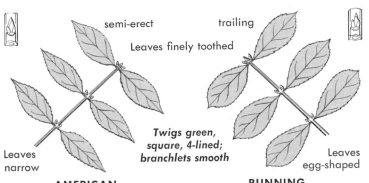

semi-erect   trailing

Leaves finely toothed

*Twigs green,
square, 4-lined;
branchlets smooth*

Leaves
narrow   Leaves
                                    egg-shaped

**AMERICAN   RUNNING
STRAWBERRY-BUSH**   **STRAWBERRY-BUSH**

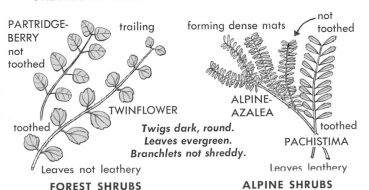

PARTRIDGE-   trailing   not
BERRY   toothed
not
toothed   forming dense mats

                                     ALPINE-
toothed   AZALEA
              TWINFLOWER   toothed
Twigs dark, round.   PACHISTIMA
Leaves evergreen.
Branchlets not shreddy.
Leaves not leathery   Leaves leathery
FOREST SHRUBS   **ALPINE SHRUBS**

HONEYSUCKLES (1) — VINES*

Climbing by twining stems only and leaves not toothed (but see Japanese Honeysuckle); bark papery; branchlets hollow; scales present at twig bases; opposing leaf scars connected by lines.

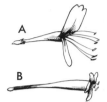

Flowers of these vines are of Type A, except for Trumpet Honeysuckle (B).

ʃ JAPANESE HONEYSUCKLE, *Lonicera japonica*   p. 71
  Woods and fields; Massachusetts, Ohio, Missouri, and Kansas to Florida and Texas.
ʃ WOODBINE HONEYSUCKLE   p. 71
  L. periclymenum (not illus.)

ʃ HAIRY HONEYSUCKLE, *Lonicera hirsuta*   p. 71
  Thickets and rocky soils; w. England, w. Quebec, and Saskatchewan to Pennsylvania, Ohio, Michigan, Minnesota, and Nebraska.

ʃ MOUNTAIN HONEYSUCKLE, *Lonicera dioica*   p. 71
  Dry thickets and woods; sw. Maine, s. Quebec, Manitoba, and British Columbia to Georgia and ne. Kansas.

ʃ ROCK HONEYSUCKLE, *Lonicera prolifera*   p. 72
  Rocky areas; e. Massachusetts, s. Ontario, and se. Manitoba to Tennessee, Arkansas, and e. Kansas.

ʃ YELLOW HONEYSUCKLE, *Lonicera flava*   p. 72
  Rocky areas; N. Carolina and Missouri to Georgia, Alabama, and Oklahoma.
ʃ PALE HONEYSUCKLE, *L. flavida* (not illus.)   p. 72

ʃ TRUMPET HONEYSUCKLE, *Lonicera sempervirens*   p. 72
  Woods; s. Maine, Iowa, and Nebraska to Florida and Texas.

° *Four other vines* with opposite simple leaves, not honeysuckles, are treated in the text only. See Climbing Euonymus, Decumaria, False Jessamine, and Silkvine on page 70.

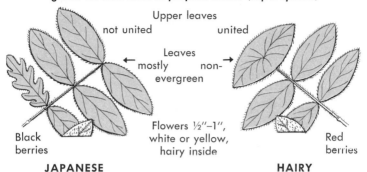

**Twigs densely hairy; leaves hairy,
green on both sides or purplish below (top 2 species)**

Upper leaves
not united   united

← Leaves
mostly non- →
evergreen

Flowers ½″–1″,
white or yellow,
hairy inside

Black
berries

Red
berries

JAPANESE   **HAIRY**

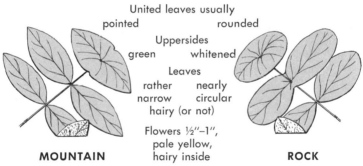

**Twigs nearly hairless; leaves whitish beneath;
upper leaves united; berries red (lower 4 species)**

United leaves usually
pointed   rounded

Uppersides
green   whitened

Leaves
rather   nearly
narrow   circular
hairy (or not)

Flowers ½″–1″,
pale yellow,
hairy inside

MOUNTAIN   **ROCK**

Tips of united leaves
somewhat   rounded or
pointed   pointed

Leaves hairless

Flowers 1¼″–2″,
not trumpet-   trumpet-
shaped,   shaped,
orange-   coral-
yellow   red

not
ever-
green

often
ever-
green

YELLOW   **TRUMPET**

HONEYSUCKLES (2) — ERECT SHRUBS

Erect shrubs; leaves not toothed; bark papery; papery scales present at twig bases (see arrows); opposing leaf scars connected by lines.

Flowers

Type A   Type C

ᕓ TARTARIAN HONEYSUCKLE, *Lonicera tatarica*   p. 73
   Woods borders and thickets; New England, Quebec, and Ontario to New Jersey, Kentucky, and Iowa.

ᕓ EUROPEAN HONEYSUCKLE, *Lonicera xylosteum*   p. 73
   Escaped to thickets; New England and Michigan to New Jersey and Ohio.
   ᕓ MORROW HONEYSUCKLE, *L. morrowi* (not illus.)   p. 73
   ᕓ BELLA HONEYSUCKLE   p. 74
   L. morrowi Gray × *L. bella* Zabel (not illus.)

ᕓ FOUR-LINED HONEYSUCKLE, *Lonicera involucrata*   p. 74
   Moist woods; e. Quebec, w. Ontario, and Alaska to New Brunswick, Michigan, Wisconsin, and in the West.

ᕓ SWAMP HONEYSUCKLE, *Lonicera oblongifolia*   p. 74
   Acid bogs and white cedar swamps; New Brunswick, se. Quebec, and Manitoba to e. Maine, w. Pennsylvania, Michigan, and Minnesota.

ᕓ NORTHERN HONEYSUCKLE, *Lonicera villosa*   p. 74
   Rocky or peaty soils, often swamps and bogs; Newfoundland, s. Labrador, and Manitoba to New England, Pennsylvania, Michigan, and Minnesota.

ᕓ CANADA HONEYSUCKLE, *Lonicera canadensis*   p. 75
   Woods; Nova Scotia, ne. Quebec, and Saskatchewan to n. New Jersey, Pennsylvania, w. N. Carolina, W. Virginia, Indiana, and ne. Iowa.
   ᕓ STANDISH HONEYSUCKLE, *L. standishii* (not illus.) p. 75

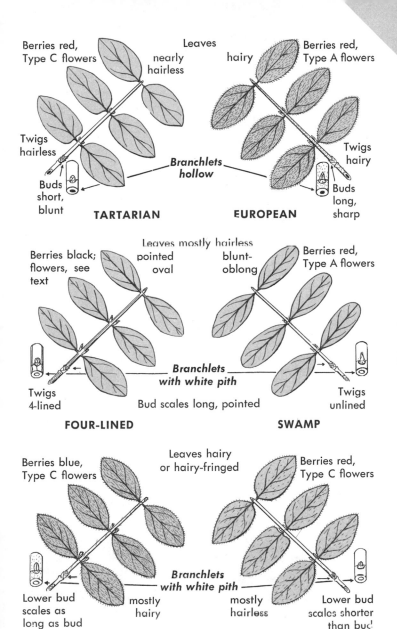

Berries red,
Type C flowers

Leaves
nearly
hairless

Twigs
hairless

Buds
short,
blunt

TARTARIAN

Berries red,
Type A flowers

hairy

Twigs
hairy

*Branchlets
hollow*

Buds
long,
sharp

EUROPEAN

Berries black;
flowers, see
text

Leaves mostly hairless
pointed
oval

*Branchlets
with white pith*

Twigs
4-lined

Bud scales long, pointed

FOUR-LINED

blunt-
oblong

Berries red,
Type A flowers

Twigs
unlined

SWAMP

Berries blue,
Type C flowers

Leaves hairy
or hairy-fringed

Lower bud
scales as
long as bud

mostly
hairy

*Branchlets
with white pith*

NORTHERN

Berries red,
Type C flowers

mostly
hairless

Lower bud
scales shorter
than bud

CANADA

DOGWOODS

Erect shrubs or trees; leaves not toothed; leaf veins follow the smooth leaf edges toward the tips; twigs often reddish or purple; leaf buds with only 1 pair of scales.

Typical bud shown at right.

Ⅴ ROUNDLEAF DOGWOOD, *Cornus rugosa*   p. 75
    Woods and thickets; Nova Scotia, e. Quebec, and Manitoba to New England, w. Virginia, W. Virginia, Indiana, and ne. Iowa.

⩗ FLOWERING DOGWOOD, *Cornus florida*   p. 76
    Woodlands; sw. Maine, s. Vermont, s. Ontario, s. Michigan, and e. Kansas to Florida and e. Texas.

Ⅴ RED-PANICLE DOGWOOD, *Cornus racemosa*   p. 76
    Hedgerows and thickets; centr. Maine, s. Ontario, and Minnesota to Delaware, W. Virginia, Kentucky, and Oklahoma.

Ⅴ RED-OSIER DOGWOOD, *Cornus stolonifera*   p. 76
    Wet places; Newfoundland, s. Labrador, and Alaska to New York, w. Maryland, W. Virginia, Indiana, Nebraska, New Mexico, and California.
    Ⅴ STIFF DOGWOOD, *C. foemina* (not illus.)   p. 77

Ⅴ SILKY DOGWOOD, *Cornus amomum*   p. 77
    Wet places; s. Maine and Indiana to s. New England, Georgia, and Alabama.
    Ⅴ NARROWLEAF DOGWOOD, *C. obliqua* (not illus.) p. 77

⩗Ⅴ ROUGHLEAF DOGWOOD, *Cornus drummondi*   p. 77
    Wet places; s. Ontario, Illinois, and Nebraska to Mississippi and e. Texas.
    ⩗Ⅴ PRICE DOGWOOD, *C. priceae* (not illus.)   p. 78

FLOWERING DOGWOOD   **OTHER DOGWOODS**

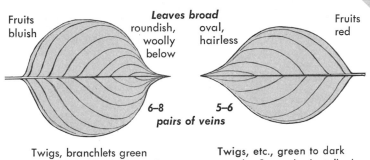

Fruits bluish

Leaves broad
roundish, woolly below

oval, hairless

Fruits red

6–8   5–6
pairs of veins

Twigs, branchlets green or reddish, blotched purple

Twigs, etc., green to dark purple; flower buds stalked

ROUNDLEAF

FLOWERING

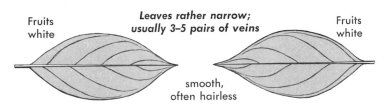

Fruits white

**Leaves rather narrow;
usually 3–5 pairs of veins**

Fruits white

smooth, often hairless

Twigs brown, branchlets gray, hairless; pith brownish

Twigs, branchlets bright red, typically hairless; pith white

RED-PANICLE

RED-OSIER

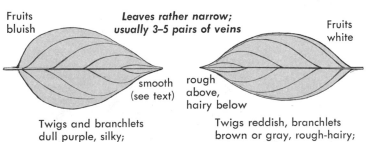

Fruits bluish

**Leaves rather narrow;
usually 3–5 pairs of veins**

Fruits white

smooth (see text)

rough above, hairy below

Twigs and branchlets dull purple, silky; pith brown

Twigs reddish, branchlets brown or gray, rough-hairy; pith usually brown

SILKY

ROUGHLEAF

PLANTS WITH OPPOSITE LEAVES
NOT TOOTHED (1)

Erect woody plants with leaves paired or whorled.

V SHEEP LAUREL, *Kalmia angustifolia*   p. 78
　　Moist open areas, often bogs; Newfoundland, Labrador, and
　　Manitoba to S. Carolina, nw. Georgia, and Tennessee.
V PALE LAUREL, *Kalmia polifolia*   p. 79
　　Bogs and peat soils; Newfoundland, Labrador, and Alaska to
　　New Jersey, Pennsylvania, Michigan, and Oregon.
V COMMON PRIVET, *Ligustrum vulgare*   p. 79
　　Thickets, field borders and open woods; s. Maine and s.
　　Ontario to N. Carolina, Ohio, and Michigan.
　V CALIFORNIA PRIVET, *L. ovalifolium* (not illus.)   p. 79
　V AMUR PRIVET, *L. amurense* (not illus.)   p. 79
　V REGAL PRIVET, *L. obtusifolium* (not illus.)   p. 80
V BUTTONBUSH, *Cephalanthus occidentalis*   p. 80
　　Shallow ponds and wet shores; w. Nova Scotia, sw. Quebec,
　　s. Ontario, s. Michigan, and se. Minnesota to Florida, Texas,
　　and California.
　V SEA-OXEYE, *Borrichia frutescens* (not illus.)   p. 81
V SMOOTH ALLSPICE, *Calycanthus fertilis*   p. 81
　　Mountain forests; s. Pennsylvania and s. Ohio to Georgia and
　　Alabama.
　V HAIRY ALLSPICE, *C. floridus* (not illus.)   p. 81
⬧V FRINGE-TREE, *Chionanthus virginicus*   p. 81
　　Floodplains; New Jersey, W. Virginia, s. Ohio, s. Missouri,
　　and se. Oklahoma to centr. Florida, e. Texas.
　　For the following species not illustrated, see text:
　⬧ DEVILWOOD, *Osmanthus americanus*   p. 79
　V BUCKLEYA, *Buckleya distichophylla*   p. 80
　V NESTRONIA, *Nestronia umbellula*   p. 80
　V SWAMP LOOSESTRIFE, *Decodon verticillatus*   p. 80

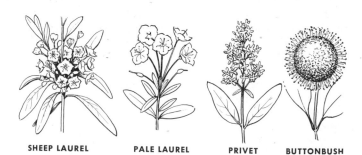

SHEEP LAUREL　　**PALE LAUREL**　　**PRIVET**　**BUTTONBUSH**

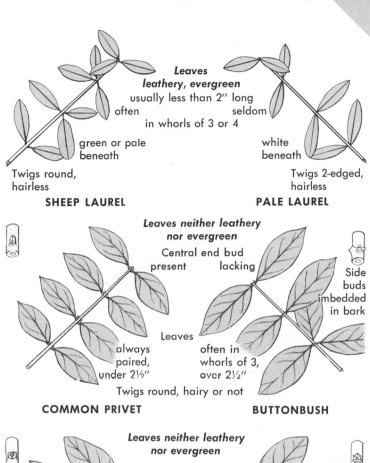

**Leaves
leathery, evergreen**
usually less than 2" long
often   seldom
in whorls of 3 or 4

green or pale
beneath

white
beneath

Twigs round,
hairless

Twigs 2-edged,
hairless

SHEEP LAUREL   **PALE LAUREL**

*Leaves neither leathery
nor evergreen*
Central end bud
present   lacking

Side
buds
imbedded
in bark

Leaves

always
paired,
under 2½"

often in
whorls of 3,
over 2½"

Twigs round, hairy or not

COMMON PRIVET   **BUTTONBUSH**

*Leaves neither leathery
nor evergreen*
Central end bud
lacking   present

Leaves paired,
over 2½"

spicy odor
when crushed

Twigs round,
hairy or not

not
aromatic

SMOOTH ALLSPICE   **FRINGE-TREE**

PLANTS WITH OPPOSITE LEAVES
NOT TOOTHED (2)

Erect woody plants with leaves always paired.

Ⅴ CORALBERRY, *Symphoricarpos orbiculatus*   p. 82
   Old fields and open woods; New England, Ohio, Illinois,
   Minnesota, S. Dakota, and Colorado to Florida and Texas.

Ⅴ SNOWBERRY, *Symphoricarpos albus*   p. 82
   Dry and rocky soils; e. Quebec and British Columbia to
   Massachusetts, w. Virginia, W. Virginia, Michigan, Wisconsin,
   Nebraska, and Colorado.
   Ⅴ WOLFBERRY, *S. occidentalis* (not illus.)   p. 82

Ⅴ KALM ST. JOHNSWORT, *Hypericum kalmianum*   p. 82
   Dry or sandy soils; mostly near Great Lakes, w. New York,
   w. Quebec, and w. Ontario to Ohio and Illinois.

Ⅴ SHRUBBY ST. JOHNSWORT, *Hypericum spathulatum* p. 83
   Open areas; Massachusetts, Ontario, and Minnesota to
   Georgia, Alabama, and Arkansas.
   Ⅴ GOLDEN ST. JOHNSWORT   p. 83
   H. frondosum (not illus.)
   Ⅴ DENSE ST. JOHNSWORT   p. 83
   H. densiflorum (leaf illus.)
Ⅴ CANADA BUFFALOBERRY, *Shepherdia canadensis*   p. 83
   Rocky and sandy soils; Newfoundland and Alaska to Maine,
   n. Ohio, n. Illinois, S. Dakota, and New Mexico.
   Ⅴ SILVER BUFFALOBERRY, *S. argentea* (not illus.)   p. 84

Ⅴ SANDMYRTLE, *Leiophyllum buxifolium*   p. 84
   Sandy pinelands in separated areas; New Jersey, the Caro-
   linas, and in e. Kentucky.

CORALBERRY   **SNOWBERRY**   **KALM ST. JOHNSWORT**   **SHRUBBY ST. JOHNSWORT**

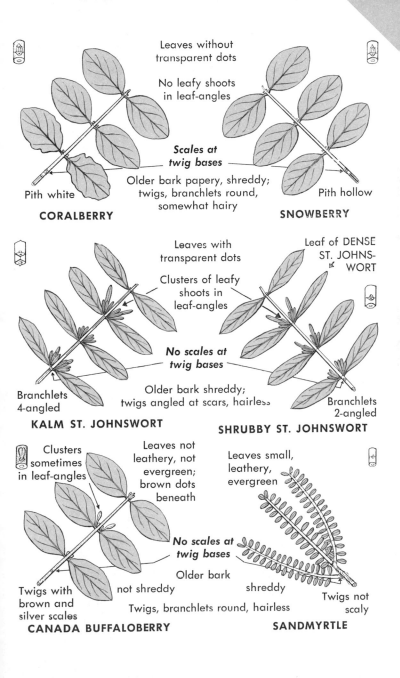

Leaves without transparent dots

No leafy shoots in leaf-angles

Scales at twig bases

Older bark papery, shreddy; twigs, branchlets round, somewhat hairy

Pith white

CORALBERRY

Pith hollow

SNOWBERRY

Leaves with transparent dots

Clusters of leafy shoots in leaf-angles

Leaf of DENSE ST. JOHNS-WORT

No scales at twig bases

Older bark shreddy; twigs angled at scars, hairless

Branchlets 4-angled

KALM ST. JOHNSWORT

Branchlets 2-angled

SHRUBBY ST. JOHNSWORT

Clusters sometimes in leaf-angles

Leaves not leathery, not evergreen; brown dots beneath

Leaves small, leathery, evergreen

No scales at twig bases

Older bark not shreddy

shreddy

Twigs, branchlets round, hairless

Twigs with brown and silver scales

CANADA BUFFALOBERRY

Twigs not scaly

SANDMYRTLE

PLANTS WITH OPPOSITE HEART-SHAPED LEAVES

The Princess-tree and the catalpas are the only large trees with opposite or whorled simple leaves. The lilacs are the only shrubs with opposite leaves that are mostly heart-shaped and not toothed. Central end buds are lacking.

⋎ COMMON LILAC, *Syringa vulgaris*   p. 84
    Escaped from cultivation.
  ⋎ PERSIAN LILAC, *S. persica* (not illus.)   p. 85

⭡ PRINCESS-TREE, *Paulownia tomentosa*   p. 85
    Oriental; waste places; s. New York, W. Virginia, and e. Missouri to n. Florida and s. Texas.

⭡ COMMON CATALPA, *Catalpa bignonioides*   p. 85
    Gulf Coast; but escaped from cultivation from s. New England, Ohio, and Michigan to Florida and Texas.
  ⭡ CATAWBA-TREE, *C. speciosa* (not illus.)   p. 85
    Wet woods; e. Virginia, Ohio, s. Illinois, and Kansas to Louisiana and e. Texas.
  ⭡⋎ CHINESE CATALPA, *C. ovata* (not illus.)   p. 86

PRINCESS-TREE

COMMON CATALPA

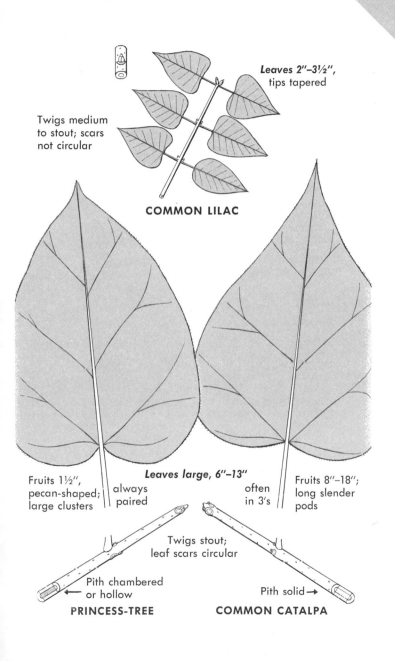

Twigs medium to stout; scars not circular

Leaves 2″–3½″, tips tapered

COMMON LILAC

Fruits 1½″, pecan-shaped; large clusters

always paired

Leaves large, 6″–13″

often in 3's

Fruits 8″–18″; long slender pods

Twigs stout; leaf scars circular

Pith chambered or hollow ←

Pith solid →

PRINCESS-TREE

COMMON CATALPA

SHRUBS WITH OPPOSITE TOOTHED LEAVES

Along with the viburnums (Plate 20), the only erect plants with
unlobed leaves of this type. Several are of limited distribution.

Ⅴ NORTHERN BUSH-HONEYSUCKLE　　　　　　　p. 86
　　Diervilla lonicera
　　　　Woods openings, dry soils; Newfoundland and Manitoba to
　　　　Delaware, w. N. Carolina, Ohio, and Iowa.
Ⅴ SOUTHERN BUSH-HONEYSUCKLE　　　　　　　p. 86
　　D. sessilifolia (not illus.)

Ⅴ WILD HYDRANGEA, *Hydrangea arborescens*　　　　p. 87
　　Damp woods; s. New York, Ohio, and Missouri to n. Florida,
　　Louisiana, and Oklahoma.
　Ⅴ ASIATIC HYDRANGEA, *H. paniculata* (not illus.)　　p. 87
　Ⅴ OAKLEAF HYDRANGEA, *H. quercifolia* (not illus.)　p. 87

♦Ⅴ BURNINGBUSH, *Euonymus atropurpureus*　　　　p. 87
　　Damp woods; w. New York, s. Ontario, s. Michigan, centr.
　　Minnesota, and Montana to e. Virginia, n. Alabama, Arkansas,
　　and Oklahoma.
　♦Ⅴ EUROPEAN SPINDLETREE　　　　　　　　p. 88
　　E. europaeus (not illus.)

Ⅴ COMMON BUCKTHORN, *Rhamnus cathartica*　　　p. 88
　　Hedgerows, thickets; Nova Scotia, s. Quebec, s. Ontario, s.
　　Wisconsin, and e. N. Dakota to Virginia, Ohio, and Missouri.

♦Ⅴ SWAMP FORESTIERA, *Forestiera acuminata*　　　p. 88
　　Coastal Plain swamps and riverbanks; S. Carolina and n.
　　Florida, west to e. Texas, and north in Mississippi Valley to
　　s. Indiana, centr. Illinois, se. Kansas, and s. Oklahoma.
　Ⅴ UPLAND FORESTIERA, *F. ligustrina* (not illus.)　　p. 88

Ⅴ BEAUTYBERRY, *Callicarpa americana* (not illus.)　　p. 89

Ⅴ COMMON MOCK-ORANGE, *Philadelphus inodorus*　p. 89
　　Streambanks and thickets; Virginia and Tennessee to Florida
　　and Alabama, occasionally spreading from cultivation to the
　　North.
　Ⅴ HAIRY MOCK-ORANGE, *P. hirsutus* (not illus.)　　p. 89
　Ⅴ GARDEN MOCK-ORANGE
　　P. coronarius (not illus.)　　　　　　　　　　p. 89
　Ⅴ GRAY MOCK-ORANGE, *P. pubescens* (not illus.)　p. 90

Ⅴ MARSH-ELDER, *Iva frutescens* (not illus.)　　　　p. 90

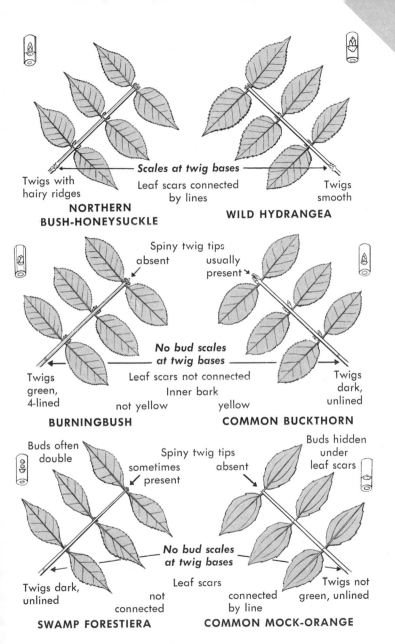

Twigs with hairy ridges

Scales at twig bases

Leaf scars connected by lines

Twigs smooth

NORTHERN BUSH-HONEYSUCKLE

WILD HYDRANGEA

Spiny twig tips absent

Spiny twig tips usually present

No bud scales at twig bases

Leaf scars not connected

Twigs green, 4-lined

Inner bark not yellow

yellow

Twigs dark, unlined

BURNINGBUSH

COMMON BUCKTHORN

Buds often double

Spiny twig tips sometimes present

Buds hidden under leaf scars

No bud scales at twig bases

Twigs dark, unlined

Leaf scars not connected

connected by line

Twigs not green, unlined

SWAMP FORESTIERA

COMMON MOCK-ORANGE

VIBURNUMS (1)

Identify by subgroups (opposite and on Plate 21). All species
except top 2 have very narrow, opposite leaf scars.

♦ⱴ WAYFARING-TREE, *Viburnum lantana*   p. 91
     Escaped from cultivation; Connecticut to s. Ontario.

ⱴ HOBBLEBUSH, *Viburnum alnifolium*   p. 91
     Moist woods; Prince Edward I. and Ontario to n. New Jersey,
     Pennsylvania, and ne. Ohio, and in mts. to Tennessee and
     Georgia.

♦ⱴ SMOOTH BLACKHAW, *Viburnum prunifolium*   p. 91
     Woods and hedgerows; Connecticut, s. Michigan, Iowa, and
     e. Kansas to n. Florida and Texas.

♦ⱴ RUSTY BLACKHAW, *Viburnum rufidulum*   p. 92
     Woods and thickets; Virginia, s. Ohio, s. Illinois, Missouri, and
     se. Kansas to Florida and Texas.

♦ⱴ NANNYBERRY, *Viburnum lentago*   p. 92
     Woods; New England, w. Quebec, and Manitoba to New
     Jersey, Ohio, ne. Missouri, and Colorado; in Appalachians to
     N. Carolina and Georgia.

ⱴ NORTHERN WILD-RAISIN, *Viburnum cassinoides*   p. 92
     Swamps and thickets; Newfoundland and w. Ontario to
     Delaware, Maryland, Ohio, n. Indiana, and Wisconsin; in mts.
     to Alabama.

♦ⱴ SOUTHERN WILD-RAISIN, *Viburnum nudum*   p. 92
     Coastal Plain wet woods and bogs; s. Connecticut to Florida,
     west to e. Texas, and north in the Mississippi Valley to
     Kentucky and Arkansas.

HOBBLEBUSH

OTHER VIBURNUMS
on this plate have flower
clusters of this type

Leaves finely toothed, heart-shaped; buds without scales

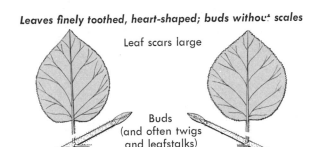

Leaf scars large

Buds
(and often twigs
and leafstalks)

gray-hairy · rusty-hairy

WAYFARING-TREE · **HOBBLEBUSH**

Leaves oval, finely toothed or not; buds with 2 scales

Side twigs mostly short and stiff; leaves often wide

Leaves

dull above, · shiny above,
never · often
red-hairy beneath

Stalks of upper leaves

not winged, · winged,
hairless · hairy

Buds

powdery or · very
brown-hairy · red-hairy

SMOOTH BLACKHAW · **RUSTY BLACKHAW**

Side twigs long and flexible; leaves rarely wide.
Buds hairy or powdery; stalks of upper leaves "winged"

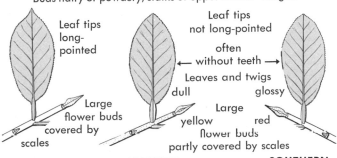

Leaf tips
long-
pointed

Leaf tips
not long-pointed

often
← without teeth →

Leaves and twigs
dull · glossy

Large
flower buds
covered by
scales

Large
yellow · red
flower buds
partly covered by scales

NANNYBERRY · **NORTHERN WILD-RAISIN** · **SOUTHERN WILD-RAISIN**

VIBURNUMS (2)

Identify by subgroups (opposite and on Plate 20).

ⱴ NORTHERN ARROWWOOD, *Viburnum recognitum*   p. 93
   Woods; New Brunswick and s. Ontario to se. New York, n.
   Ohio, and Michigan.

ⱴ SOUTHERN ARROWWOOD, *Viburnum dentatum*   p. 93
   Woods and thickets; se. Massachusetts, Pennsylvania, and e.
   Missouri to Florida and Texas.

ⱴ SHORTSTALK ARROWWOOD   p. 93
   Viburnum rafinesquianum
      Woods; sw. Quebec and Manitoba to Georgia, Kentucky, and
      Missouri.

ⱴ SOFTLEAF ARROWWOOD, *Viburnum molle*   p. 94
   Rocky woods; Indiana and Missouri to Kentucky and Arkansas.
   ⱴ SIEBOLD VIBURNUM, *V. sieboldii* (not illus.)   p. 94

ⱴ CRANBERRY VIBURNUM   p. 94
   (HIGHBUSH-CRANBERRY) *Viburnum trilobum*
      Woods and low places; Newfoundland and British Columbia
      to New England, Pennsylvania, n. Ohio, n. Illinois, ne. Iowa,
      sw. S. Dakota, se. Wyoming, and Washington.
   ⱴ GUELDER-ROSE, *V. opulus* (not illus.)   p. 95

ⱴ SQUASHBERRY, *Viburnum edule*   p. 95
   Woods; Newfoundland, Labrador, and Alaska to n. New
   England, w. Pennsylvania, n. Michigan, n. Wisconsin, n.
   Minnesota, Colorado, and Oregon.

ⱴ MAPLELEAF VIBURNUM, *Viburnum acerifolium*   p. 95
   Woods; sw. Quebec and Minnesota to New England, Georgia,
   and Tennessee.

Leaves with a single main midrib, not lobed

Bud scales several

a. Leaves hairless or slightly hairy beneath; twigs often ridged

Leaves with 4–22 pairs of teeth

Leaf bases rounded or slightly heart-shaped

Twigs

hairless   velvety-hairy

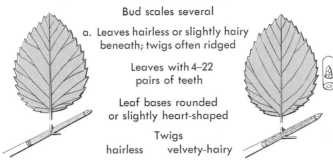

NORTHERN ARROWWOOD   **SOUTHERN ARROWWOOD**

b. Leaves velvety-hairy beneath; twigs not ridged

Leaves with

4–10   20–30 pairs of teeth

Leaf bases heart-shaped

Twigs hairless

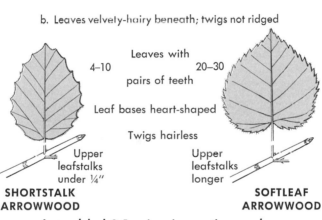

Upper leafstalks under ¼"

Upper leafstalks longer

SHORTSTALK ARROWWOOD

SOFTLEAF ARROWWOOD

Leaves lobed, 3–5 main veins meeting near base

hairy or hairless beneath

hairless beneath

hairy beneath

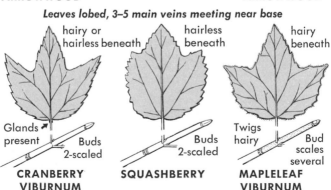

Glands present

Buds 2-scaled

Buds 2-scaled

Twigs hairy

Bud scales several

CRANBERRY VIBURNUM

SQUASHBERRY

MAPLELEAF VIBURNUM

MAPLES

The only trees with opposite 3- to 5-lobed leaves. See also Plate
21 (Viburnums 2).

⬧ STRIPED MAPLE (MOOSEWOOD)   p. 96
  Acer pensylvanicum
      Woods; Nova Scotia, Quebec, centr. Michigan, and Manitoba
      to New England, Pennsylvania, and Ohio; in mts. to Ten-
      nessee and n. Georgia.

⬧ MOUNTAIN MAPLE, *Acer spicatum*   p. 96
      Woods; Newfoundland and e. Saskatchewan to n. New Jersey,
      Pennsylvania, n. Ohio, Michigan, ne. Iowa, and Minnesota;
      in mts. to n. Georgia and Tennessee.
  ⬧∨ SIBERIAN MAPLE, *A. ginnala* (not illus.)   p. 96

⬧ RED MAPLE, *Acer rubrum*   p. 96
      Wet woods and second growth; Newfoundland, Ontario, and
      se. Manitoba to Florida and e. Texas.

⬧ SILVER MAPLE, *Acer saccharinum*   p. 97
      Riverbanks and floodplains; New Brunswick, s. Ontario, and
      Minnesota to nw. Florida and e. Oklahoma.
  ⬧ SYCAMORE MAPLE
    A. pseudo-platanus (not illus.)   p. 97

⬧ SUGAR MAPLE, *Acer saccharum*   p. 97
      Mature upland forests; Newfoundland, Nova Scotia, Quebec,
      and sw. Manitoba to Virginia, n. Georgia, and e. Texas.
  ⬧ FLORIDA MAPLE, *A. barbatum* (not illus.)   p. 98

⬧ BLACK MAPLE, *Acer nigrum*   p. 98
      Mature upland woods; sw. Quebec, Vermont, s. Ontario, se.
      Minnesota, and ne. S. Dakota to New Jersey, w. Virginia, w.
      N. Carolina, Kentucky, and ne. Kansas.
  ⬧ NORWAY MAPLE, *A. platanoides* (fruit illus.)   p. 98
  ⬧∨ HEDGE MAPLE, *A. campestre* (not illus.)   p. 98

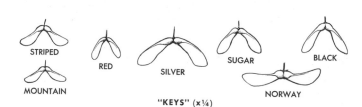

STRIPED   RED   SILVER   SUGAR   BLACK   NORWAY
MOUNTAIN   "KEYS" (x¼)

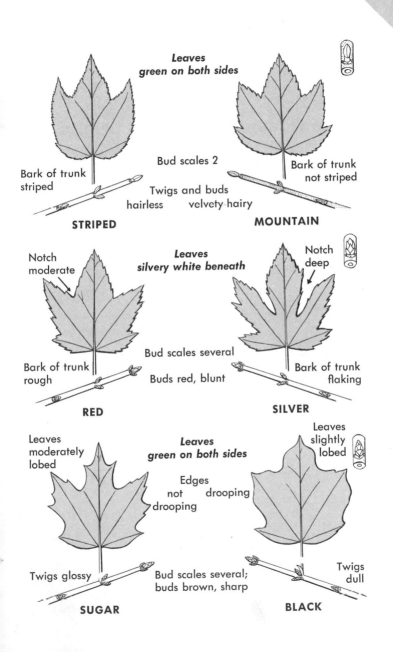

Leaves
green on both sides

Bark of trunk striped

Bud scales 2

Bark of trunk not striped

Twigs and buds
hairless   velvety-hairy

STRIPED

MOUNTAIN

Notch moderate

Leaves
silvery white beneath

Notch deep

Bark of trunk rough

Bud scales several

Buds red, blunt

Bark of trunk flaking

RED

SILVER

Leaves moderately lobed

Leaves
green on both sides

Edges not drooping

drooping

Leaves slightly lobed

Twigs glossy

Bud scales several;
buds brown, sharp

Twigs dull

SUGAR

BLACK

SECTION IV

Broad-leaved Plants with Alternate Compound Leaves

RELATIVELY few plants have compound leaves. Those with oppo-site leaves were presented in Section II (Plates 7–11, pp. 56–65). The rest are in this Section. In winter, the alternate leaf scars may sometimes indicate by their large size the former presence of compound leaves. Where there is doubt, however, the twigs of a leafless unknown plant with alternate leaf scars will have to be compared with the drawings of *both* Sections IV and V or identified by means of the Winter Key in Appendix B. **Warning:** Poison-ivy (Plate 25) and Poison Sumac (Plate 26) are in this group. Do not handle them. Be careful of unknown plants of this type.

		Name	Plate
1. Plants prickly or thorny:			
2. Arching brambles or climbing vines		**BLACKBERRIES, ROSES, etc.**	23
2. Erect plants:			
3. Leaf scars narrow, half-encircling twigs		**ROSES**	23
3. Leaf scars otherwise		**LOCUSTS, etc.**	24
1. Plants without prickles or thorns:			
4. Leaves only once-compound:			
5. Vines		**MISCELLANEOUS**	25, 30
5. Erect trees and shrubs:			
6. Leaf scars narrow, half encircling twigs		**ROSES**	23
6. Leaf scars otherwise:			
7. Leaflets 3		**POISON-IVY, etc.**	25
7. Leaflets more than 3:			
8. Leaflets toothed (though in Tree-of-Heaven with only 1 basal pair of glandular teeth):			
9. Leaflets mostly 11–14 (rarely 7 or 9):			
10. Buds nearly hidden beneath the leafstalk bases; sap often milky; mostly shrubs		**SUMACS**	26
10. Buds easily visible (somewhat hidden in Tree-of-Heaven); trees, shrubs, or vines:			
11. Buds white-woolly, brown-woolly, or red-gummy		**WALNUTS, etc.**	27
11. Buds yellow-hairy or brown-hairless		**PECAN, WATER HICKORY**	28

                                            Name   *Plate*
9. Leaflets 5–9:
    12. Leaflets mostly 5–7:
        13. Wood not yellow   **HICKORIES (1)**   28
        13. Wood bright yellow   **YELLOWROOT**   31
    12. Leaflets mostly 7–9   **HICKORIES (2)**   29
8. Leaflets not toothed:
    14. Bundle scars more than 5   **SUMACS** 26
    14. Bundle scars 1 to 5   **MISCELLANEOUS**   30
4. Leaves twice- or thrice-compound (lea*flets* as well as
   leaves compound)   **COFFEE-TREE, etc.** 31

Prickly Brambles

(Plate 23, p. 150)

The raspberries, dewberries, and blackberries (all in the genus
Rubus), and the roses are the only compound-leaved, rambling or
arching, mostly nonclimbing, usually prickly or bristly shrubs in
our area. The woody species of *Rubus* are all normally prickly
except the flowering raspberries, which have simple leaves (Plate
42). A few roses are without prickles or may climb by means of
twining stems. The twigs of brambles usually are green or red
and both the stems and leafstalks are prickly. Except for the nearly
flat-on-the-ground dewberries, they mostly grow in vaselike
clumps with the stems arching back toward the ground. The
only other plants at all likely to be confused with the brambles are
the prickly greenbriers (Plate 33), which are simple-leaved green-
stemmed vines climbing or scrambling over neighboring plants by
means of tendrils.

In plants of the genus *Rubus*, new canes (stems) normally are
produced each year. Each lives a year and a half or so, generally
flowering and fruiting in the second season. The roots live on from
year to year. The stems of roses are perennial, like most woody
plants.

The leaves of all groups are toothed and divided into 3 or
more leaflets. Where there are more than 3 leaflets, their arrangement differs by groups and species. In the Red Raspberry and
the roses, the leaflets are feather-compound, that is, placed at
right angles to the central leafstalk. In the Black Raspberry,
dewberries, and blackberries, the leaflets are arranged like the
spokes of a wheel. Winglike stipules are attached to the bases of
the leafstalks in the roses and the leaf scars are narrow, half
encircling the twigs. Stipules are absent and the leafstalk bases
remain attached to the stems all winter in the other brambles.
Raspberry fruits differ from those of dewberries and blackberries
in that when ripe they separate from the fleshy stalks upon which

they are borne, forming hollow shells. Rose fruits are seed-filled organs called "hips."

Both the genera *Rubus* (blackberries and relatives) and *Rosa* (roses) are extremely complex. Many specimens are encountered representing numerous varieties and hybrids that are puzzling even to professional botanists. Even disregarding the multitude of minor forms, there are over 200 species of *Rubus* and 23 species of *Rosa* listed for our region by Fernald.° Because of the difficulty of identifying the various species (and not all botanists agree there are so many), only representatives of the outstanding groups are illustrated and discussed here.

Several subgroups can be separated easily:

Stems round, usually *white-powdered,* arching; leafstalk
     bases not winged   **RASPBERRIES**
Stems round or angular, not white-powdered, *trailing;*
     leafstalk bases not winged   **DEWBERRIES**
Stems *angular,* not white-powdered, arching; leafstalk
     bases not winged   **BLACKBERRIES**
Stems round, not white-powdered, mostly arching; *leaf-
     stalk bases winged*   **ROSES**

All brambles are of value in soil-erosion control and wildlife management. They grow even on barren soils and reproduce by seeds, often dropped by animals, and in many *Rubus* species by rooting branches. These plants provide cover for wildlife and have been recorded as being eaten by over 150 birds and mammals (including nearly all the game birds and big-game animals on the continent). Rabbits, skunks, opossums, foxes, beavers, porcupines, and chipmunks are among other eastern mammals eating twigs or fruits. Raspberry, dewberry, and blackberry fruits are made into jam and desserts, leaves of some species occasionally are dried as tea, and peeled young sprouts are eaten raw in some localities. The petals of rose flowers have been candied as a confection and also have been eaten in salads. Rose fruits can be used in making jelly.

RED RASPBERRY   *Rubus idaeus* L.   **p. 150**
Recognition: An *arching* shrub with *round, bristly* stems, some-what white-powdered when young. Canes do not root at tips. In a few localities either without bristles or with strong prickles. Leaves may consist of 3–7 elliptic leaflets, but on older fruiting canes 3 are usual. When 5- to 7-parted the leaves are *feather-compound.* Leaflets *whitened* beneath; side ones without stalks. Number of varieties and forms are recognized. Leaves 3″–10″. Height to 6′. Flowers white, May–July. Fruits *red,* June–Oct.

° Merritt Lyndon Fernald, *Gray's Manual of Botany,* 8th ed. (New York: American Book Co., 1950).

Similar species: There are only 3 perennial raspberries in our area. (1) Canes of Wine Raspberry root at tips and are covered with long gland-tipped reddish hairs. (2) Black Raspberry has strong hooked prickles.

WINE RASPBERRY *Rubus phoenicolasius* Maxim. **Not illus.**
Recognition: Similar to preceding species but end leaflet somewhat *heart-shaped. Canes root at tips* and are covered by long gland-tipped reddish hairs. Introduced from e. Asia. Thickets; Massachusetts and Indiana to Virginia and Kentucky.

BLACK RASPBERRY *Rubus occidentalis* L. **p. 150**
Recognition: Differs from Red Raspberry in having *strong hooked prickles.* Canes longer (to 12'), more strongly whitened, and may root at tips. Leaves 5-parted, *fan-compound.* Leaves 2″–8″. Height to 6'. Flowers white, April–July. Fruits *black,* June–Aug.

BRISTLY DEWBERRY *Rubus hispidus* L. **p. 150**
Recognition: A *trailing* shrub with densely glandular-*bristly round stems.* Leaves shiny, leathery, often evergreen, with 3, less commonly 5, *fan-compound,* blunt-toothed leaflets. Leaves 3″–7″. Height to 12″. Flowers white, June–Sept. Fruits black, Aug.–Oct.
Similar species: Dewberries are divided primarily into 2 groups: those bristly and those prickly. Fernald lists 24 species of bristly dewberries for our area. Some blackberries are bristly but are relatively upright.

PRICKLY DEWBERRY *Rubus flagellaris* Willd. **p. 150**
Recognition: A *flattened* shrub with stems mostly round and with scattered but *stout curved prickles.* Leaves dull, thin, light green, sometimes slightly hairy with 3–5 sharp-toothed leaflets. Leaves 5-parted, *fan-compound.* Leaves 2″–7″. Height to 12″. Flowers white, May–June. Fruits black, June–Aug.
Similar species: Fernald lists 44 species of prickly dewberries.

BLACKBERRY *Rubus allegheniensis* Porter **p. 150**
Recognition: An upright or *arching* shrub; stems strongly *angular,* with *stout prickles.* Leaves have 3–7, mostly 5, leaflets, woolly or velvety beneath, at least when young; when 5- to 7-parted, the leaves are *fan-compound.* Young stems and left undersides glandular-hairy. Var. *gravesii* Fern. (w. Maine and ne. New York to Maryland) may be thornless, with round stems. Leaves 3″–8″. Height to 10'. Flowers white, May–July. Fruits black, July–Sept.
Similar species: Blackberries are the most complex category of

the genus. Fernald records 122 species. They are grouped as: (1) plants rooting at stem tips, (2) stems bristly rather than prickly, (3) stems gray-woolly when young and leaves white- or gray-woolly on undersides, (4) young stems not gray-hairy but glandular-hairy, (5) young stems otherwise hairy, and (6) stems hairless with prickles few or even absent. This species is a well-marked one of the 4th group.

ROSES   *Rosa* spp.   **p. 150**
  Recognition: Some of the characteristics of roses have been listed above. Briefly, roses are usually *prickly or bristly arching* shrubs with 3–11 leaflets per leaf, varying with the species. Leaves 5- to 11-parted and *feather-compound.* They have long *leafy stipules* attached to lower portions of leafstalks. These leafstalk "wings" may vary. In some species they are partially free of the leafstalk; in others they may be either thick, thin, wide, narrow, hairy, toothed, or comblike. Leaf scars are *narrow, half encircling the twigs,* and contain 3 bundle scars. Twigs and stems mostly are green or red. Rose fruits, known as "hips," are fleshy, covering numerous small seeds. They usually are red and remain on the plants all winter. They are eaten by many wild animals, but mostly incidentally or where preferred foods are lacking.
  A few imported escaped species and the Prairie Rose (*R. setigera* Michx.), the latter distinctive with only 3 leaflets among these, may climb by twining stems. The Multiflora Rose (*R. multiflora* Thunb.), now being planted widely for erosion control and wildlife benefits, can be distinguished from other roses with 7–9 leaflets by fringed or comblike stipules extending about half the length of leafstalks.

Erect Thorny Trees and Shrubs
(*Plate 24, p. 152*)

With the brambles, the following few species are the only thorny or prickly woody plants with compound leaves (whether alternate or opposite). The only other upright thorny plants are those with simple leaves on Plates 37–40. The locusts and Trifoliate Orange have smooth-edged or fine-toothed leaflets whose leafstalks never bear thorns; the other plants of this group have more coarsely toothed leaflets and often thorny leafstalks.

HONEY LOCUST   *Gleditsia triacanthos* L.   **pp. *12*, 152**
  Recognition: A tall tree with *feather-compound* or *twice-compound* leaves. Bark dark, somewhat scaly, adorned with numerous stout *branched thorns,* each *several inches* long. Leaves

divided into numerous narrow leaflets, which may be slightly toothed. These leaflets, in turn, frequently are subdivided. Hairless buds, hidden by the leafstalk bases in summer, are surrounded by leaf scars when twigs are leafless and may be supplemented by smaller buds located just above them. End buds false. Twigs stout; bundle scars 3. Leaves 6″–15″. Height 70′–80′ (140′); diameter 2′–3′ (6′). Flowers small, greenish, clustered May–July. Fruits *8″–18″ long*, flattened twisted pods with sweet pulp between numerous oval seeds, Sept.–Feb.

Similar species: (1) Only Water Locust also has such long thorns. (2) Black Locust has small paired thorns.

Remarks: Honey Locust, believed originally to have been restricted to Mississippi Valley, is now common eastward. The thorns have been used by woodsmen for pins, spear points, and animal traps. Heavy, durable wood used for railroad ties, fence posts, and agricultural implements. The tree does not harbor root bacteria capable of fixing nitrogen as do most legumes. Fruits eaten by cattle, deer, rabbits, squirrels, and bobwhite. A thornless variety is sometimes cultivated.

WATER LOCUST   Thorn illus., p. 152
Gleditsia aquatica Marsh.

Recognition: Similar to Honey Locust but smaller, with leaflets somewhat wider, thorns of branches mostly *unbranched* and fruit pods *only 2″ long*, pulpless, containing only 1–3 seeds. Coastal Plain swamps; e. N. Carolina to centr. Florida, west to e. Texas, and north in the Mississippi Valley to sw. Indiana, s. Illinois, and se. Missouri.

BLACK LOCUST *Robinia pseudo-acacia* L.   pp. *12*, **152**

Recognition: A medium-sized tree with *once-compound* leaves. Leaflets 6–20, egg-shaped. Strong ½″–1″ *paired thorns* flank nearly circular leaf scars. White-hairy buds burst through leaf scars upon enlargement. Twigs moderately stout, hairless; bundle scars 3. End buds false. Bark on old trunks dark, deeply ridged, and crosshatched. Leaves 6″–12″. Height 70′–80′ (100′); diameter 2′–3′ (6′). Flowers medium-sized, white, clustered, fragrant, May–June. Fruits 2″–6″ long, flat pods, Sept.–April.

Similar species: Other *Robinia* locusts have bristly, glandular or hairy twigs. (1) Prickly-ash is smaller and has reddish exposed buds, toothed leaflets, and usually thorny leafstalks. (2) Honey Locust has large branched unpaired thorns.

Remarks: Black Locusts often planted for fence posts. Wood strong, hard, and durable in the soil. Young shoots and bark sometimes poisonous to livestock but seeds eaten by bobwhite, pheasant, mourning dove, cottontail rabbit, snowshoe hare, and deer.

CLAMMY LOCUST *Robinia viscosa* Vent. **Twig illus., p. 152**
Recognition: A shrub or small tree; leaves similar to Black Locust. Thorns paired, *weak*, usually not over 1/4"; twigs covered with *sticky glands*. Bark smooth, light brown, marked with short horizontal streaks. Leaves 6"–12". Height 5'–20' (40'); diameter 1"–3" (6"). Flowers pink, not fragrant, May. Fruits sticky pods, 2"–3", Aug.–Sept. Mountain woods; Pennsylvania and W. Virginia to Georgia and Alabama; occasionally escaped from cultivation northward to Nova Scotia and Quebec.

BRISTLY LOCUST *Robinia hispida* L. **Twig illus., p. 152**
Recognition: Similar to Clammy Locust but shrubby and twigs covered with *bristly hairs* almost as long as the paired thorns. Leaflets bristle-tipped; buds visible in winter. Height 2'–10'. Flowers rose-colored (often called Rose-acacia), not fragrant, May–June. Fruits bristly, Sept. Mountains from Virginia and Tennessee to Georgia and Alabama; escaped from cultivation northward to Connecticut.

DOWNY LOCUST **Not illus.**
Robinia elliottii (Chapm.) Ashe
Recognition: Similar to Black Locust but a low shrub with gray-hairy twigs, small thorns, and 5–7 leaflets that are somewhat hairy beneath. Height to 6'. Flowers purplish, May. Fruits hairy. Thickets and woods; N. Carolina and Georgia; escaped from cultivation in ne. Maryland.

HERCULES-CLUB *Aralia spinosa* L. **p. 152**
Recognition: A *very spiny* shrub or small tree with *very large twice- or even thrice-compound* leaves. Trunk and twigs stout, with numerous coarse prickles. Leaflets toothed, pointed; leafstalks thorny. Long, narrow leaf scars have about 20 bundle scars. End buds may be false. Leaves 2'–4'. Height 5'–15' (35'); diameter 1"–4" (9"). Flowers white, in flat-topped clusters, July–Sept. Fruits black, fleshy, 1-seeded, Aug.–Nov.
Similar species: Prickly stout stems and V-shaped leaf scars with numerous bundle scars are distinctive at all seasons. (1) Bristly Sarsaparilla is smaller, bristly rather than prickly. (2) Devil's-club (p. 197) has simple leaves and northwestern range.

BRISTLY SARSAPARILLA **Twig illus., p. 152**
Aralia hispida Vent.
Recognition: Similar to Hercules-club but smaller and woody only at stem base, with once- or twice-compound leaves. Twigs and leafstalks bristly-hairy. Leaves 4"–12". Height 6"–36". Flowers June–Aug. Fruits blue-black, Aug.–Sept. Poor soils;

Newfoundland, s. Labrador, and Manitoba to w. N. Carolina,
West Virginia, Illinois, and Minnesota.

NORTHERN PRICKLY-ASH   p. 152
Xanthoxylum americanum Mill.

Recognition: A shrub, often thicket-forming, with *paired prickles*
flanking leaf scars and buds. Leaves once-compound with 5–11
toothed egg-shaped leaflets and often *prickly* leafstalks. Foliage
has lemonlike odor when crushed and is hairy when young. Buds
red-hairy, located above leaf scars. Bundle scars 3. True end
buds present. Specimens without prickles are encountered
rarely. Leaves 3"–10". Height 4'–10' (25'). Flowers small,
greenish, clustered, April–May. Fruits small, dry, reddish-brown,
1- to 2-seeded pods, Aug.–Oct.

Similar species: (1) Black Locust grows to tree size, has hidden
buds, leaflets not toothed, leafstalks not prickly. (2) See Southern
Prickly-ash.

Remarks: Chewing leaves, fruits, or bark was once popular as
a toothache cure. Known as Toothache-tree in some places.

SOUTHERN PRICKLY-ASH   Leaflet illus., p. 152
Xanthoxylum clava-herculis L.

Recognition: This southern shrub or tree is larger than the
northern species. Has a peculiar smooth gray trunk bark decorated with scattered *large corky knobs*, often prickle-tipped.
Leaflets hairless, shiny, somewhat curved and unsymmetrical.
Leaves 8"–16". Height 10'–20' (50'); diameter 4"–8" (18"). Poor
Coastal Plain soils; se. Virginia to s. Florida and west to e. Texas,
north in Mississippi Valley to s. Arkansas and se. Oklahoma.

TRIFOLIATE ORANGE   Not illus.
Poncirus trifoliata (L.) Raf.

Recognition: An imported shrub often planted as a hedge in
South. Easily identified by stiff green stems that bear many stout
green thorns. Buds bright red, ball-like; end buds false; leaf scars
very small, with 1 scarcely visible bundle scar. Leaves divided
into 3 small wavy-edged leaflets. Leafstalks "winged." Small
citrus fruits are bitter. Height rarely to 20'. Flowers white,
April–May. Fruits Sept.–Oct. Thickets; e. Virginia to Florida
and Texas.

Thornless Trifoliates
(Plate 25, p. 154)

Relatively few plants bear 3-parted compound leaves. Several opposite-leaved species and the prickly brambles are in this category. In addition, a blackberry (*Rubus canadensis* L.) and a rose (*Rosa blanda* Ait.) may lack prickles and also bear 3-parted leaves. They more closely resemble the species drawn on Plate 23 than they do these thornless trifoliates. The following thornless plants are those outside the genera *Rubus* and *Rosa* which have alternate trifoliate leaves. See also Boston Ivy (p. 188).

POISON-IVY   *Rhus radicans* L.   **p. 154**
   Recognition: DANGER: DO NOT TOUCH THIS PLANT. All parts contain a dangerous skin irritant. Grows as *an erect shrub, trailing vine, or climber.* Leaves *3-parted* and long-stalked but otherwise variable. They may be stiff and leathery or merely thin, somewhat hairy beneath or not, shiny or dull, coarse-toothed and wavy-edged, or neither. Poison-ivy leaves may be somewhat reddish but this occurs only in young or in dying leaves. End leaflet has *longer stalk* than side ones and has pointed tip. Twigs are brown and, if climbing, have many short aerial rootlets. Old stems of climbing vines densely covered with dark fibers. Aerial rootlets and fibrous coverings lacking in upright specimens. Buds visible, hairy, without scales, pinched at base. Leaf scars large, with a half-dozen or so bundle scars. Upright plants usually are branches of underground stems and occur in thickets. Leaves 4″–14″. Height 2′–5′ (10′) when not climbing. Flowers small, yellowish, May–July. Fruits small, smooth, *white*, ball-shaped, clustered, Aug.–Nov. or longer.
   Similar species: Poison-ivy and (1) Poison-oak (see next) are the only common thornless alternate-leaved woody plants with 3-parted leaves and visible buds. In winter, even upright form can be distinguished by numerous bundle scars and stalked hairy buds. Long stalks of end leaflets and white fruits are additional, though seasonal, field marks. Poison-ivy is the only alternate-leaved vine climbing by aerial rootlets and the only one with fiber-hairy stems. Both (2) Fragrant Sumac and (3) Hoptree have hidden buds and short-stalked end leaflets; (4) Cissus (p. 132) and (5) Boston Ivy (p. 188) climb by tendrils. (6) "Five-leaved Poison-ivy" is an unsuitable name sometimes used for the pretty and harmless Virginia Creeper. (7) See also Ashleaf Maple (p. 52).
   Remarks: All parts of the plant contain a heavy nonvolatile oil that causes inflammation of the skin, with blisters and swelling, in susceptible persons. Individuals vary in reaction but the

skin must come in direct contact with the dangerous oil or with the smoke from burning Poison-ivy in order to be irritated. *Anyone who learns to recognize the plant and avoids it and anything that comes in contact with it will not be affected.* The old saying "leaflets three, let it be" provides adequate warning when the plant is in leaf.

Contact with the plant usually results in itching and other symptoms within a few hours. Washing the exposed parts of the body with a thick lather of yellow laundry soap is of value soon after exposure. Water alone, unless in large amounts, may only serve to spread the oil. Mild irritations may be treated with mild astringent lotions but cases of ivy poisoning involving the eyes or genitals and widespread irritations of other parts of the body should be treated promptly by a physician. The merits of taking injections for the prevention of ivy poisoning is a matter for medical opinion.

Despite poisonous effects of the plant on humans, the fruits are relished by over 60 species of birds, including the bobwhite, pheasant, prairie chicken, ruffed and sharptail grouse. Many seeds are passed undamaged through their digestive systems and distribution of Poison-ivy is thus aided.

POISON-OAK   *Rhus toxicodendron* L.   **Not illus.**
Recognition: DANGER: A southern species generally similar to Poison-ivy but *always erect.* Leaflets varied, *blunt-tipped,* obviously *hairy on both sides.* They may be lobed somewhat like oak leaves. Fruits usually hairy. Some authorities believe differences between the several forms of Poison-oak and Poison-ivy are inconsequential and that all probably should be grouped under one name. The irritating effects of Poison-oak are similar to those of Poison-ivy. Height to 10'. Flowers May–June. Fruits Aug.–Nov. or longer. Sandy and gravelly soils of Coastal Plain, New Jersey, and Maryland to Florida and e. Texas, and s. Missouri, e. Oklahoma, and Tennessee to Texas.

FRAGRANT SUMAC   *Rhus aromatica* Ait.   **p. 154**
Recognition: A low bush or rambling shrub with *3-parted* large-toothed leaves that have a pleasant odor when crushed. End leaflet *short-stalked.* Twigs brown, bark smooth; aerial rootlets and fibrous coverings not present. Leaf buds hidden beneath round leaf scars; end buds false. Bundle scars numerous. Flower buds clustered in dense spikes, present at twig tips from late summer to spring. Leaves 4"–6". Height to 7'. Flowers small, greenish, April–July. Fruits *small, hairy, red,* ball-shaped, clustered, May–July.
Similar species: Aromatic leaves, hidden buds, circular leaf scars, and winter flower spikes are distinctive at all seasons.

132 IV. THORNLESS TRIFOLIATES

Remarks: Fruits eaten by ruffed grouse and wild turkey. Twigs browsed by whitetail deer.

CISSUS *Cissus incisa* (Nutt.) Des Moulins   Not illus.
Recognition: A stout, sometimes evergreen climbing vine with deeply 3-lobed or 3-parted thick leaves. *Tendrils* (see grapes, Plate 34) that do not have disks at the tips, occur opposite most leaf scars. Even when bearing 3-lobed leaves, it is distinct from the true grapes in that the bark is tight rather than shreddy and the pith is white, not brown. Poison-ivy climbs by aerial rootlets. Found primarily in sandy and rocky areas; se. Kansas and Missouri to Texas and Florida.

HOPTREE *Ptelea trifoliata* L.   p. 154
Recognition: An upright shrub or small tree with *3-parted leaves* that usually are hairless but may be hairy beneath. Leaflets usually without teeth, end leaflet *short-stalked.* Twigs brownish and round; buds hairy and hidden in summer by leafstalk; leaf scars U-shaped; bundle scars 3. End buds false. Trunk bark rather smooth, light colored, shallowly grooved. Var. *mollis* T. & G., occurring only on Lake Michigan sand dunes, has velvety twigs and leaves. Leaves 4″–10″. Height 10′–20′ (25′); diameter 2″–10″ (16″). Flowers greenish, small, clustered, May–July. Fruits flat, circular, papery, 2-seeded, Sept.–spring.
Similar species: (1) Often mistaken for Poison-ivy (p. 130). (2) See Fragrant Sumac (p. 131).

SCOTCH BROOM *Cytisus scoparius* (L.) Link   p. 154
Recognition: A dense *stiff-branched,* hairless, *evergreen* shrub. Leaves small, some not divided, but trifoliate compound leaves most abundant. Twigs slender, *angular,* grooved, greenish, often withered at tips. Leaf scars round; bundle scars single. Buds small but visible, flanked by slender stipules. Leaves ½″–1″. Height to 10′. Flowers large, yellow, May–June. Fruits pods, ¾″–1½″ long, July–Sept.
Similar species: Small leaves and green ridged twigs of this European importation are unique among thornless woody trifoliates except for (1) Bicolor Lespedeza, which is less bushy, not evergreen, and has smaller fruits. (2) Matrimony-vines (Plate 37) usually thorny and twigs not green. (3) Shrubby Cinquefoil (Plate 30) lower and has 5-parted leaves. (4) See also Gorse (Plate 6).

BICOLOR LESPEDEZA *Lespedeza bicolor* Turcz.   Not illus.
Recognition: In many places this slender and weak shrub is planted as food for the bobwhite quail. Although not reported as spreading, it may be encountered under conditions appearing to be wild. Usually grows in patches or stands.

Leaves shaped like those of Scotch Broom but all leaves are 3-parted. Leaflets blunt-tipped, with midrib usually extending *slightly beyond leaflet tip.* Twigs very slender, brownish or greenish, with 8–12 fine lines and grooves running lengthwise. Buds very small, flanked by slender stipules. Weak stems mostly end in upright cluster of purplish flowers or small dry fruit pods ⅛″–¼″. Leaves 1″–3″. Height 4′–6′ (10′). Fields; north to New York, Michigan, and Minnesota.

Sumacs

(*Plate 26, p. 156*)

Strictly speaking, the sumacs as a genus (*Rhus*) also include Poison-ivy, Poison-oak, and Fragrant Sumac (Plate 25). The sumacs considered on this plate, however, are distinctive in having more than 3 leaflets per feather-compound leaf, in being upright shrubs, and in having stout, more pithy twigs. Leaflets occur in opposing pairs except for end one. Side buds are mostly hidden by bases of the leafstalks and end buds are false. Bundle scars are numerous. Milky sap occurs in all on this plate except Poison Sumac. The flowers are small, greenish, and clustered. The fruits of Poison Sumac are greenish white like those of Poison-ivy. The other species bear dense spikes of small, dry, red, hairy fruits, which usually remain on the plants all winter and provide an apparently little-relished but available food supply for wildlife.

A number of plants of Plates 26–30 are similar in being upright and nonthorny with alternate once-compound leaves of more than 3 leaflets. Of these, the Tree-of-Heaven, Yellowwood, indigo-bushes, and Western Soapberry are the only ones with false end buds. The hairy twigs, toothed leaflets, hidden buds, and milky sap will separate three of these sumacs from those plants. To distinguish the Poison Sumac, see under that species.

WINGED SUMAC *Rhus copallina* L.   **p. 156**
  Recognition: A shrub or, in South, rarely a small tree. Leaves large, divided into 11–23 narrow, *smooth-edged shiny* leaflets, midrib bordered by *thin "wings."* Twigs and leafstalks *velvety,* round, and marked with obviously raised dots. Buds hairy, surrounded by U-shaped leaf scars. Trunk is dark and smooth, with numerous raised cross streaks (lenticels). Leaves 6″–14″. Height 4′–10′ (30′); diameter 1″–3″ (10″). Flowers July–Sept. Fruits red, short-hairy.
  Similar species: Winged midribs and dotted twigs distinctive.
  Remarks: Twigs are cropped by deer.

STAGHORN SUMAC   *Rhus typhina* L.   **pp.** *12,* **156**
   Recognition: A shrub or small tree with *very hairy* twigs and
   leafstalks. Leaves large, made up of 11–31 *toothed* leaflets.
   Twigs round, no obvious dots. Buds hairy, surrounded by
   U-shaped leaf scars. Bark dark and smooth, with numerous raised cross streaks. Leaves 12″–24″. Height 4′–15′ (50′);
   diameter 2″–4″ (15″). Flowers June–July. Fruits red, long-
   hairy.
   Similar species: (1) Lack of winged midribs and twig dots
   separates this from Winged Sumac. (2) Hybridization with
   Smooth Sumac sometimes occurs, and intermediate characteristics result.
   Remarks: Aptly named, this shrub's branches bear a marked
   resemblance to the antlers of a deer "in velvet." It is cultivated
   in Europe. Bark and leaves rich in tannin; it is reported that
   a black ink can be made by boiling leaves and fruit. The
   long-haired fruits have been found in stomachs of many songbirds, ruffed and sharptail grouse, bobwhite, pheasant, mourning
   dove, and skunk. Twigs cropped by moose, whitetail deer, and
   cottontail rabbit.

POISON SUMAC   *Rhus vernix* L.   **p. 156**
   Recognition: DANGER: DO NOT TOUCH ANY PART OF
   THIS PLANT. All parts contain a dangerous skin irritant. Shrub
   or small tree with large leaves composed of 7–13 pointed leaflets
   not toothed. Twigs and buds round, *hairless;* leaf scars crescent-
   or shield-shaped, do not surround buds. Bark smooth and dark
   with numerous narrow cross streaks often tending to encircle
   trunk. Leaves 6″–12″. Height 6′–20′ (30′); diameter 3″–8″
   (10″). Flowers May–July. Fruits *white,* Aug.–spring.
   Similar species: Over most of our area the only shrub with
   hairless buds and twigs and *once-compound* leaves that are *not*
   toothed. Its *swampy* habitat is a clue. Most similar are (1)
   Yellowwood (Plate 30), with blunt-tipped leaflets, and (2) Western Soapberry (p. 145), with greater height and only 3 bundle
   scars.
   Remarks: Though more virulent than Poison-ivy, this species is
   generally uncommon; largely confined to swamps. Few people
   are likely to come in contact with it. Medical symptoms and
   treatment similar to those for Poison-ivy (see p. 130). Poison-ivy
   (with Poison-oak) and Poison Sumac are the only plants in our
   area that for most people are dangerous to touch. Names in
   common use, such as Poison-elder or Poison-dogwood, usually refer to Poison Sumac. Fruits eaten by numerous birds,
   including bobwhite, pheasant, and ruffed grouse. Twigs
   browsed by cottontail rabbit. Foliage may turn yellow or red
   in autumn.

SMOOTH SUMAC *Rhus glabra* L.   **p. 156**
   Recognition: Similar to Staghorn Sumac, but with twigs and
   leafstalks *hairless.* Twigs somewhat flat-sided. A variety with
   short-hairy twigs is believed to be a hybrid between this and
   Staghorn Sumac. Fruits red, short-hairy.

Walnuts and Similar Trees

(*Plate 27, p. 158*)

These are trees with alternate feather-compound leaves. The
leaflets are numerous and toothed, although the Tree-of-Heaven
often has only 1 pair of gland-bearing teeth at the bases of the
leaflets. They are best distinguished from the sumacs and hickories
as indicated later.

BLACK WALNUT *Juglans nigra* L.   **pp. 8, 158**
   Recognition: A tall tree whose large leaves have 7–17 narrow,
   toothed leaflets slightly hairy beneath. Often end leaflet is
   lacking. Crushed leaves are spicy-scented. Twigs hairless, stout,
   pith light brown and chambered by woody partitions (pith of
   branchlets usually better developed than that of twigs). Buds
   whitish woolly; leaf scars large, *without hairy fringe;* bundle
   scars in 3 groups. True end buds present. Bark dark and deeply
   grooved; ridges not shiny. Leaves 12″–24″. Height 70′–100′
   (150′); diameter 2′–4′ (6′). Flowers catkins, April–June. Fruits
   large spherical nuts with husks of 1 piece, Oct.–Nov.
   Similar species: Black Walnut and Butternut only plants with
   compound leaves that have chambered piths. Butternut has
   hairy ridge above leaf scar, darker pith, end leaflet present, bark
   shiny-ridged.
   Remarks: One of the most valuable and beautiful native trees.
   Heavy, strong, durable heartwood easily worked, in great demand for veneers, cabinetmaking, interior finishing, and gunstocks. Bark is used in tanning; yellow-brown dye can be made
   from nut husks. Nuts eaten by humans, squirrels, and mice; twigs
   by deer. Large trees have been almost exterminated in some
   regions. The bruised nut husks once were used to kill fish for
   food but this is now illegal. Tomatoes, apples, and other species
   may not survive near large walnut trees.

BUTTERNUT *Juglans cinerea* L.   **pp. 8, 158**
   Recognition: Similar to Black Walnut but with prominent
   hairy fringe above leaf scar. Pith dark brown; end leaflet
   normally present. The wider bark ridges are smooth-topped,

making a *shiny*, interlaced gray network superimposed upon the black fissures. Number of leaflets varies between 7 and 17. Twigs and leafstalk bases somewhat hairy. Height 40′–80′ (100′); diameter 1′–2′ (3′). Fruits are somewhat *oblong and sticky;* nuts with 1-piece husks, Oct.–Nov.

Remarks: Also known as White Walnut, wood lighter in color than that of its more valuable relative. Lumber is light, soft, and weak, but easily worked and polished; darkens upon exposure to air. Though not an important timber species, used for interiors, cabinetwork, furniture, and instrument cases. The early colonists are reported to have prepared a yellow-brown stain by boiling the soft, half-ripe fruits. They also pickled the boiled nuts and made a dark stain from the husks and inner bark to dye uniforms. Indians are said to have boiled the nuts to obtain oil that came to top for use as butter. The nutmeats then were collected and dried. In spring, sap was boiled down to make syrup. The crushed fruits also were once used to poison fish. Bark yields useful drugs and nuts are eaten by many wild animals.

TREE-OF-HEAVEN (AILANTHUS)   **pp.** *12*, **158**
Ailanthus altissima (Mill.) Swingle

Recognition: A fast-growing small to large tree with very large leaves having 11–41 leaflets. Leaflets *not toothed* except for pair of *gland-tipped teeth near bases.* Twigs hairless, yellow-brown, stout, with continuous yellowish pith. Buds small, brown-woolly; end buds false. Leaf scars *very large*, somewhat triangular, with numerous bundle scars. Bark gray-brown, smooth, or with narrow light-colored grooves. Leaves 12″–24″ or more. Height 80′–100′; diameter 1′–2′. Flowers small, yellowish, clustered, male blossoms with foul odor, June–July. Fruits dry, narrow, 1-seeded, winged, Sept.–winter.

Similar species: No other tree has such gland-tipped leaflet lobes. In winter, stout twigs, false end buds, large leaf scars, and numerous bundle scars are distinctive. The Coffee-tree (Plate 31) has large leaf scars but fewer bundle scars. It has twice-compound leaves and salmon-colored pith.

Remarks: An oriental species; has become a weed here. Imported by way of England, where first planted in 1751. Most rapid growing woody plant in our area. Will thrive under extremely adverse conditions, growing as much as 8′ in a year. Annual sprouts 12′ long not uncommon where a tree has been cut down. Since it is adapted to disturbed sites, even a crack between bricks in an alleyway may provide a seedbed for this plant. Immune to dust and smoke and may grow to a large size. Though soft, wood has some lumber and fuel values. The common name is supposed to be of Asiatic or Australian origin, alluding to its height.

AMERICAN MOUNTAIN-ASH   p. 158
Pyrus americana (Marsh.) DC.

Recognition: A shrub or small tree. Compound leaves have 11–17 long, narrow, toothed, *long-pointed* leaflets; leaflets over 3 times as long as broad. Leaves and twigs hairless. Buds *reddish, sticky, and hairless;* leaf scars narrow, with 5 bundle scars. End buds true. Spur branches may be present; bark rather smooth and gray-brown. Leaves 6″–9″. Height to 40′; diameter to 12″. Flowers small, about ¼″, clustered, May–June. Fruits *small, reddish, clustered, about ¼″,* Aug.–March.

Similar species: (1) Northern Mountain-ash has wider leaflets, flowers, and fruits. (2) European Mountain-ash has woolly buds.

Remarks: This member of the rose family is one of most ornamental northern trees. Fleshy red fruits often remain on tree late in winter and are eaten by many birds and mammals, including ruffed and sharptail grouse, ptarmigan, fisher, and marten. Deer and moose browse twigs.

NORTHERN MOUNTAIN-ASH   Leaflet illus., p. 158
Pyrus decora (Sarg.) Hyland

Recognition: Like American Mountain-ash but leaflets *less than 3 times* as long as broad and somewhat whitened beneath. Flowers about ⅜″ across and *fruits over ⁵⁄₁₆″.* Var. *groenlandica* (Schneid.) Fern. has long-pointed leaflets not whitened beneath; their wider portions are relatively wider than in American Mountain-ash. See also next species. Var. *groenlandica* is limited to area from s. Greenland and Labrador to mountains of Newfoundland, e. Quebec, and n. New England. Flowers June–July. Fruits Sept.–winter. Woods and rocky places; Greenland, Labrador, n. Ontario, and Minnesota to Maine, nw. Massachusetts, n. Ohio, n. Indiana, and Iowa.

EUROPEAN MOUNTAIN-ASH   Not illus.
Pyrus aucuparia (L.) Gaertn.

Recognition: Widely cultivated and occasionally escapes. Resembles previous 2 species except that leaflets are smaller and somewhat hairy beneath; buds white-woolly and not sticky. Leaflets short-pointed as in American Mountain-ash; flowers and fruits more closely resemble Northern Mountain-ash. Local; Newfoundland, s. Canada, and se. Alaska to Maine, Pennsylvania, Iowa, and Washington.

Hickories (1) and (2)

(Plates 28 and 29, pp. 160, 162)

The hickories are trees with feather-compound leaves whose leaflets are toothed and mostly long-pointed. Twigs are stout, tough, and flexible, pith solid. Buds and leaf scars are large and conspicuous. True end buds are present; bundle scars numerous. The male flowers are in prominent catkins, occurring in spring. Husks of hickory nuts characteristically break into 4 rather separate parts upon ripening; those of walnuts and other similar nut-bearing species remain entire.

Most other nonthorny plants with alternate compound leaves have false end buds. Among those that resemble the hickories in having true end buds, Poison-ivy (Plate 25) has slender twigs and nonscaly buds, Black Walnut and Butternut (Plate 27) have chambered piths, and the mountain-ashes (Plate 27) and Yellowroot (Plate 31) have narrow leaf scars. In winter the hickories may be distinguished by the occurrence of true end buds, large leaf scars, and solid pith.

Fruits of several hickories, especially Pecan and Shagbark, are edible and have commercial value. They usually fall in September

Brief Guide to Identification of Hickories Species	Number of leaflets	Bud scales paired	End buds large°	Twigs hairy	Mature bark shaggy	Outer bud scales fall early†	*Further notes*
Pecan	9–17	yes	no	no	no	no	buds yellow, hairy
Bitternut	5–11	yes	no	no	no	no	buds yellow, hairless
Water	9–17	yes	no	no	yes	yes	buds brown with yellow glands
Shagbark	5–7	no	yes	var.	yes	no	twigs red-brown
Shellbark	7–9	no	yes	no?	yes	no	twigs light tan
Mockernut	7–9	no	yes	yes	no	yes	
Pignut	5–7	no	no	no	no	yes	nut husks split partly
Sweet Pignut	5–7	no	no	no	var.	yes	nut husks split to base
Black	5–7	no	no	var.	no	yes	twigs, buds rusty-hairy
Pale	7–9	no	no	var.	no	yes	end buds to ¼″

° End buds mostly over ½″ long. Associated characteristics: twigs stout and nut husks over ⅛″ thick.

† Such buds look quite smooth.

and October. Nuts of most species are eaten by domestic swine, squirrels, opossums, wild turkey, and occasionally by ducks. Twigs are browsed by rabbits and deer. Crushed green nut husks formerly were used to poison fish for food, but fortunately this is now illegal.

Hickory wood is strong, heavy, tough, and elastic but decays on contact with moisture and is subject to insect attacks. It is of value in the manufacture of skis, tool handles, agricultural implements, wagons, gunstocks, axletrees, chair backs, and baskets, and once was important as best American wood for barrel hoops. As fuel it is excellent, producing great heat and high-grade charcoal.

The hickories may be divided into 3 groups: *pecans*, with paired and usually yellow bud scales; *shagbarks*, with mature trunk bark that peels in strips, large end buds (over ½″ long), stout twigs (over ⅛″ diameter), and thick nut husks (over ⅛″); and *pignuts*, with tight bark, small end buds, slender twigs, and thin nut husks.

PECAN *Carya illinoensis* (Wang.) K. Koch   **p. 160**
  Recognition: A tall tree with 9–17 leaflets per leaf. Buds have 2–3 pairs of nonoverlapping *yellow-hairy* bud scales. Twigs hairless; bark closely ridged, *not peeling*. Nuts edible; considerably longer than wide. Husks *thin*, ridged along 4 joint lines. Bark medium dark, with numerous vertical ridges. Leaves 12″–20″. Height 100′–120′ (160′); diameter 3′–4′ (6′).
  Similar species: Two other hickories have bud scales paired with edges meeting: (1) Water Hickory has brownish buds with yellowish glands that soon fall off; (2) Bitternut has permanently yellow hairless bud scales and 7–9 leaflets.
  Remarks: About 100 varieties of this tallest hickory are cultivated in Southeast for their delicious nuts. Fruits of orchard trees have thinner husks than those of wild specimens. Although principally a southern species of river bottoms, it will grow on uplands as far north as Massachusetts (in sheltered places). Fruits rarely mature in North, where pecans are mostly planted for ornament. In South, opossum, wild turkey, and squirrels feed on nuts.

WATER HICKORY (BITTER PECAN)   **p. 160**
Carya aquatica (Michx. f.) Nutt.
  Recognition: Similar to Pecan but more southern and smaller. Buds *red-brown* with yellowish gland spots, which soon disappear; bark *shaggy*. Nuts bitter, egg- or *ball-shaped*. Husks wrinkled, not splitting to base. Leaves 8″–18″. Height 50′–70′ (100′); diameter 12″–24″ (30″).

SHAGBARK HICKORY   **pp. 8, 160**
Carya ovata (Mill.) K. Koch
  Recognition: A tall tree with leaves with 5–7 (usually 5)

hairless leaflets. When present, dense tufts of hair on leaflet teeth (use lens) are field marks. Buds covered by many
overlapping scales; end buds over ½″. Twigs *stout, red-brown*,
slightly hairy to shiny. Bark light-colored, *very shaggy*, in long,
loose strips. Nuts *egg-shaped*, 1⅜″–3″, edible, 4-angled, not
ridged. Nut husk yellowish, thick, splitting to base. Var. *pubescens* Sarg. (sw. New Hampshire to Georgia and Mississippi) has
hairy twigs and leaf undersides. Var. *nuttallii* Sarg. (Massachusetts and Pennsylvania to Missouri) has nuts less than ⅞″ long.
Var. *fraxinifolia* Sarg. (w. New York, w. Ontario, and Iowa to
Ohio and Oklahoma) has narrow, ashlike leaflets. Leaves 8″–14″;
height 60′–90′ (120′); diameter 2′–3′ (4′).
Similar species: This is the only one of the shagbark group with
so few leaflets; the 3 other hickories with 5–7 leaflets all have
small end buds. (1) Shellbark Hickory has, and (2) Sweet Pignut
may have, shaggy trunk bark; Shellbark has 7–9 leaflets, soft-
hairy beneath, plus light tan or orange twigs; Sweet Pignut has
small end buds and slender twigs. (3) Mockernut Hickory also
has large end buds, but its 7–9 leaflets, tight trunk bark, early-
falling outer bud scales, and its woolly twigs and foliage
distinguish it.

PIGNUT HICKORY *Carya glabra* (Mill.) Sweet   **pp. 8, 160**
  Recognition: A tall tree with leaves of 5 (less commonly 7)
  hairless leaflets. Buds have overlapping scales; end bud ⅜″–½″,
  silky-hairy after outer scales drop in autumn. Twigs *slender*,
  red-brown, and hairless. Bark dark, *tight* and smooth-ridged.
  Nuts egg-shaped, ⅝″–1⅜″, hard-shelled, sometimes sweet. Nut
  husks thin, brown, usually *not* splitting to the base. Var.
  megacarpa Sarg. has longer leaves and fruits, thicker nut husks.
  Leaves 6″–12″. Height 80′–90′ (120′); diameter 2′–3′ (4′).
  Similar species: (1) Also with 5–7 leaflets, Shagbark has loose
  bark, large end buds and end leaflets; (2) Pale Hickory has end
  buds less than ¼″; (3) Sweet Pignut has leaflets somewhat
  yellowish beneath. Two others may have tight bark and overlapping bud scales: (4) Mockernut has large end buds, hairy twigs
  and leaflets; (5) Black Hickory has rusty-hairy twigs and leaves;
  both have 7–9 leaflets.

SWEET PIGNUT HICKORY   **Fruit illus., p. 160**
Carya ovalis (Wang.) Sarg.
  Recognition: Similar to Pignut Hickory and considered by some
  botanists as a variation of that species. Leaflets usually 7, less
  commonly 5; yellow-powdery beneath when young. Bark variously ridged, *scaly* or *shaggy*. Thin-husked fruits regularly split
  to the base, nuts always sweet. Twigs mostly hairless. Varieties
  with different characteristics of leaf undersides are known: hairy,
  hirsuta (Ashe) Sarg.; sticky, *odorata* (Marsh.) Sarg. Leaves

6"–12". Height 50'–80' (100'); diameter 2'–3'. Moist or dry woods; sw. New Hampshire, s. Ontario, Wisconsin, and Iowa to Georgia, Mississippi, and Arkansas.
Similar species: Looser bark, more readily splitting nut husks, and consistently sweet nuts distinguish this species in winter from Pignut Hickory.

BLACK HICKORY *Carya texana* Buckl.   **Not illus.**
  Recognition: Like Pignut Hickory, a large close-barked, small-budded tree with 5–7 leaflets. Unlike all other hickories, however, twigs, buds, and leaf undersides are *rusty-hairy*. Nut edible, ball- to egg-shaped, husk yellow-scaly and up to ³⁄₁₆" thick. Dry woods; s. Indiana, s. Illinois, Missouri and e. Kansas, to Louisiana, and s. Texas.

Hickories (2)
(*Plate 29, p. 162*)

These species have leaves mostly with 7–9 leaflets.

BITTERNUT HICKORY   p. 162
Carya cordiformis (Wang.) K. Koch
  Recognition: A medium-sized to tall tree. Leaflets 5–11, somewhat hairy beneath. Buds *bright yellow-powdery* with scales in *pairs*, not overlapping. End buds under ½", sometimes more than 2 scales exposed. Twigs *slender*, mostly hairless. Bark *tight* with network of fine smooth ridges. Nuts cylindrical, smooth and bitter; husks *thin*, ridged toward outer end. Hybrids with Pecan and Shagbark Hickory sometimes occur. Leaves 6"–12". Height 50'–60' (100'); diameter 18"–24" (36").
  Similar species: See Pecan (Plate 28).

PALE HICKORY   p. 162
Carya pallida (Ashe) Eng. & Graebn.
  Recognition: A tree with pale to dark gray, smooth to furrowed, sometimes shaggy bark. End buds *mostly* ¼" or less. Leafstalks usually long-hairy. Twigs fine-hairy or not. Fruit husks thin, yellow-powdery, ridged, typically split to the base. Nuts sweet. Height 40'–50'; diameter 18"–20".
  Similar species: Very small end buds tend to be distinctive. See under Pignut Hickory (p. 140).

MOCKERNUT HICKORY *Carya tomentosa* Nutt.   p. 162
  Recognition: A medium-sized to tall tree with 7–9 leaflets; leaf undersides and twigs *matted-woolly*. Hairs curly and clustered. Leaves fragrant when crushed, pale or orange-brown beneath.

Buds have overlapping scales. End buds ⅝"–1"; *outer scales fall* in autumn. Twigs stout. Bark *tight* and deeply furrowed. Nuts ball- to egg-shaped, edible, with *thick husk* not splitting to base. Bark tight with network of smooth ridges. Leaves 8"–15". Height 50'–80' (100'); diameter 18"–24" (36").
Similar species: Three hickories have end buds over ½". This the only one with tight bark, end buds dropping the outer scales in autumn, and with matted-woolly twigs and foliage.

SHELLBARK HICKORY   **p. 162**
Carya laciniosa (Michx.) Loud.
Recognition: A tall tree. Leaflets 7–9, hairless or short-hairy beneath. Buds have overlapping scales; end buds ½"–1", somewhat hairy, darker *outer scales present.* Twigs *stout, orange-brown, hairless* or slightly hairy. Bark *very shaggy,* loosening in *long strips.* Nuts egg-shaped, 1⅛"–2⅜", edible, angled but not ridged. Husks thick, splitting to base. Leaves 15"–22". Height 80'–100' (120'); diameter 3'–4'.
Similar species: See Shagbark Hickory (Plate 28).

Miscellaneous Species with Alternate Once-compound Leaves
(*Plate 30, p. 164*)

Except for Poison-ivy (Plate 25), the Virginia creepers and wisterias are the only vines with leaves of this type. The other species discussed here are upright shrubs or trees. They (and some sumacs, Plate 26) are the only plants with alternate once-compound leaves that have more than 3 leaflets and no leaf teeth.

YELLOWWOOD   *Cladrastis lutea* (Michx. f.) K. Koch   **p. 164**
Recognition: A medium-sized tree with 7–11 *smooth-edged,* sometimes silky leaflets, 2"–4" long, arranged alternately along midrib. Buds hairy, often several, one above the other, hidden beneath hollow leafstalk bases or, in winter, surrounded by U-shaped leaf scars. Twigs brownish, stout, end buds false; bundle scars 5. Bark smooth, gray; wood *yellow.* Leaves 5"–8". Height to 60'; diameter to 3'. Flowers white, clustered, May–June. Fruits pealike pods, Sept.–Oct.
Similar species: Only other thornless species with alternate once-compound toothless leaves of more than 3 leaflets are: (1) Poison Sumac (Plate 26), which usually is shrubbier and has more or less visible buds; (2) Winged Sumac (Plate 26), with winged midribs and velvety twigs; and (3) Western Soapberry

(p. 145), with narrow leaflets, visible buds, and 3 bundle scars. (4) Yellowroot (Plate 31) has toothed leaflets, long narrow leaf scars. (5) In winter, Beech (Plate 57) has similar bark but has long slim hairless buds.

BLADDER-SENNA   *Colutea arborescens* L.   **Not illus.**
Recognition: Shrub with leaves of 9–13 elliptic, sometimes notch-tipped, leaflets, each ¾″–1¼″ long. Triangular stipules flank much raised leaf scars. Buds with 2–4 scales, often clustered; bundle scars 1 or 3. Leaves 2″–4″. Height to 12′. Flowers yellow, in leaf angles, June–Sept. Fruits papery, inflated, pods. Occasional escape from cultivation. See next.

SHRUBBY CINQUEFOIL   *Potentilla fruticosa* L.   **p. 164**
Recognition: A low shrub, sometimes somewhat flattened on ground on exposed northern sites. Small leaves have 5, less commonly 7, narrow, hairless to white-silky leaflets. Leaflets less than 1″ long, edges sometimes curled over. Bark *shreddy*, buds hairless and visible, leaf scars much raised and, with pointed stipules, somewhat clasp bases of buds. Bundle scars single. Leaves ½″–1½″. Height to 3′. Flowers yellow, up to 1⅛″ across, June–Oct. Fruits small, dry, hairy, in a head.
Similar species: This species and some indigobushes are the only low shrubs with small compound leaves. In summer the fewer leaflets identify this species. In winter shreddy bark and clasping leaf scars and stipules are distinctive. Scotch Broom (Plate 25) is taller, with 3-parted leaves, green ridged twigs.

DULL-LEAF INDIGOBUSH   *Amorpha fruticosa* L.   **p. 164**
Recognition: A variable, medium-sized shrub with numerous leaflets. Both leaves and leaflets have *obvious stalks;* leaflets thick, *dull-surfaced,* ¾″–1½″, blunt or sometimes somewhat pointed, hairless or fine gray- or brown-hairy, resin-dots visible through a lens. Twigs round or finely grooved, hairless or very fine-hairy. Buds hairless, visible, sometimes several above each other; end one false. Leaf scars somewhat raised; bundle scars 3; bark smooth. Leaves 3″–9″. Height to 13′. Flowers purplish spikes, May–June. Fruits small pods, resin-dotted, Aug.
Similar species: (1) Shrubby Cinquefoil is lower, has shreddy bark and fewer leaflets. (2) Shining Indigobush has shiny leaves; lower indigobushes have stalkless leaves and leaflets.

SHINING INDIGOBUSH   **Not illus.**
Amorpha nitens F. E. Boynt.
Recognition: Differs from Dull-leaf in having thin *glossy leaflets* and fruit pods that lack dots when viewed through hand lens. Twigs and leaves almost hairless. Flowers May–June. Height to 10′. Floodplains; s. Illinois to Georgia and Arkansas.

DOWNY INDIGOBUSH   Leaflet illus., p. 164
Amorpha canescens Pursh
   Recognition: Buds, fruits, and half-inch-long leaflets of this low
   shrub typically are *white-hairy*, rarely nearly hairless. Leaflets
   15–51, *nearly lacking stalks*, narrow or oblong, usually with blunt
   tips. Called Leadplant, it once was thought to indicate presence
   of lead. Leaves 1″–4″. Height to 4′. Flowers June–Aug. Fruits
   Aug.–Sept. Dry open places; s. Michigan and Saskatchewan to
   Indiana, Arkansas, Texas, and New Mexico.

FRAGRANT INDIGOBUSH   Leaflet illus., p. 164
Amorpha nana Nutt.
   Recognition: Similar to Downy Indigobush but nearly *hairless;*
   with leafstalks very *short or lacking.* Flower clusters *mostly
   single, unbranched,* less than 4″. Height to 3′. Flowers June–
   July. Fruits July–Aug. Grasslands; Manitoba and Saskatchewan
   to Iowa and Kansas.

MISSOURI INDIGOBUSH   Not illus.
Amorpha brachycarpa Palmer
   Recognition: Differing from Fragrant Indigobush principally in
   having *branched* flower-bearing stalks 4″–10″ long. Height to
   3′. Flowers May–Aug. Open areas; Missouri.

VIRGINIA CREEPER   p. 164
Parthenocissus quinquefolia (L.) Planch.
   Recognition: A climbing vine with tendrils and *fan-compound*
   leaves. Leaflets 5 (rarely 3 or 7), toothed, arranged like *spokes
   of wheel,* hairy or hairless, dull above. Tendrils rather long,
   slender, *disk-tipped,* with several branches. Buds scale-covered,
   twigs hairless, pith white and continuous. Bundle scars numerous; tendrils absent opposite every 3rd leaf. Bark tight,
   often dotted. Leaves 3″–8″. Flowers small, greenish, clustered,
   June–Aug. Fruits blue berries, ³⁄₁₆″–⁵⁄₁₆″, Aug.–Feb.
   Similar species: This and (1) Thicket Creeper only vines with
   fan-compound leaves and slender-tipped tendrils. (2) Boston Ivy
   (p. 187) only other vine with tendrils disk-tipped, has simple
   evergreen leaves, very short tendrils, and short distances between leaves and tendrils. (3) Poison-ivy (Plate 25) has 3-parted
   leaves and climbs by aerial rootlets.
   Remarks: Blue fruits eagerly consumed by numerous birds,
   including all game species within area; also eaten by mice,
   chipmunks, and skunks. Foliage and twigs cropped by whitetail
   deer.

THICKET CREEPER   Tendrils illus., p. 164
Parthenocissus inserta (Kerner) K. Fritsch
   Recognition: Similar to Virginia Creeper, but tendril tips *with-*

out adhesive disks. Leaves shiny; fruits ⁵⁄₁₆″–⁷⁄₁₆″. Slender-tipped branched tendrils, tight bark, and white pith distinguish it in winter. Flowers June–July. Fruits Aug.–Oct. Woods and thickets; Nova Scotia, Quebec, Manitoba, and Montana to Florida, Texas, and California.

AMERICAN WISTERIA *Wisteria frutescens* (L.) Poir. **p. 164**
  Recognition: A high-climbing vine with *feather-compound toothless* leaves, twining branches, smooth tight bark, sometimes slightly ridged twigs, silky buds, single bundle scars, beautiful flower clusters, and *hairless* knobby beanlike fruit pods. Leaflets 9–15, elliptic, ½″–¾″ wide. Flower clusters less than 4½″ long. Small raised knobs adjoin leaf scars. Leaves 3″–8″. Flowers showy clusters, purplish or white, April–June. Fruits Sept.–Nov., or longer.
  Similar species: American, (1) Kentucky, (2) Chinese, and (3) Japanese Wisterias are the only vines with feather-compound leaves not toothed; also only vines climbing by twining stems that have single bundle scars and leaf scars with flanking warty knobs. *Wisteria* species difficult to separate unless flowers or fruits are present.

KENTUCKY WISTERIA   Not illus.
Wisteria macrostachya Nutt.
  Recognition: Fruit pods *hairless.* Leaflets 9–15, somewhat rounded at base, *long-pointed* and ⅞″–1⅞″ wide. Flower clusters 6″–12″ long. Floodplains of Mississippi drainage; Kentucky, s. Illinois, and Missouri to Louisiana and Texas.

CHINESE WISTERIA *Wisteria sinensis* Sweet   Not illus.
  Recognition: Fruit pods *velvety-hairy.* Leaflets silky or hairless, 7–13. Flower clusters 6″–8″ long, all blossoms opening at once, slightly fragrant. *Northeastern;* escaped to thickets and woods; s. New England to Virginia and Illinois.

JAPANESE WISTERIA   Not illus.
Wisteria floribunda (Willd.) DC.
  Recognition: Similar to Chinese Wisteria but leaflets *13–19* and flower clusters 8″–20″ long, blossoms opening successively, starting at base, very fragrant. Locally escaped; Massachusetts to Louisiana.

WESTERN SOAPBERRY   Not illus.
Sapindus drummondi H. & A.
  Recognition: This medium-sized plains tree has feather-compound leaves with *8–18 narrow, sharply pointed,* somewhat

leathery leaflets not toothed. End leaflets usually lacking. Buds small, fuzzy, globular, with 2 visible scales; may occur one above the other; end one false. Leaf scars triangular, with 3 large indistinct bundle scars. Bark light gray, scaly. Pulp of clustered fruits reportedly poisonous and forms lather in water. Flowers white, clustered, May–June. Fruits ball-shaped, white, Sept.–Oct. or longer. Leaves 4″–15″. Height 20′–50′ (75′); diameter 10″–18″ (24″). Bottomlands; sw. Missouri, Kansas, s. Colorado, and Arizona to w. Louisiana and s. Texas.

Thornless Plants
with Leaves Twice-compound
(*Plate 31, p. 166*)

Only these few plants and 2 thorny ones (Honey Locust and Hercules-club, Plate 24) have leaves in which leaflets, as well as leaves, are divided into smaller leaflets. Of those considered here, Yellowroot frequently bears leaves only once compound.

YELLOWROOT   *Xanthorhiza simplicissima* Marsh   **p. 166**
Recognition: A low shrub with once- or, less commonly, twice-compound leaves. Leaflets pointed and deeply toothed. Wood of both roots and upper parts bright *yellow*. Leaf scars narrow, more than half encircling twig; bundle scars numerous. Side buds small, blunt, and few-scaled; end bud much larger, with about 5 scales. Leaves 4″–10″. Height to 3′. Flowers purplish, in drooping clusters, April–May. Fruits small, dry.
Similar species: Yellow wood and nearly encircling leaf scars are certain identification marks. Yellowwood (Plate 30) is taller, has leaflets not toothed, and leaf scars U-shaped.

PEPPER VINE   *Ampelopsis arborea* (L.) Koehne   **p. 166**
Recognition: Either bushy and somewhat upright or a climbing vine with *twice- or even thrice-compound* leaves. Climbs by means of slender *branched* tendrils that are mostly present opposite upper leaves. Leaflets large-toothed. Twigs hairless or nearly so; buds small. Pith white and continuous. Leaves 2″–8″. Flowers small, greenish, clustered, June–July. Fruits black berries, bitter, inedible, Aug.–Nov.
Similar species: Grapes (Plates 34 and 35) have simple leaves and brown, mostly partitioned pith. (1) American and (2) Asiatic Ampelopsis (Plate 35) have simple leaves and unbranched tendrils.

CHINABERRY   *Melia azedarach* L.   **Not illus.**
Recognition: An oriental tree widely planted in dooryards in South and often escaped to the wild. Leaves twice-compound (roughly resembling those of Pepper Vine), with toothed leaflets. Twigs stout and hairless. Buds small, nearly spherical, fuzzy. Leaf scars large, somewhat 3-lobed, with 3 groups of scattered bundle scars. End buds false. Pith white. Leaves 4″–12″. Height to 40′. Flowers purplish with unpleasant odor, clustered, May–June. Fruits *yellowish, ball-like,* usually present. E. Virginia and se. Oklahoma to Florida and centr. Texas.

COFFEE-TREE   *Gymnocladus dioica* (L.) K. Koch   **p. 166**
Recognition: A tall tree with *very large twice-compound* leaves. Leaflets *very numerous,* pointed, *not toothed.* Twigs very stout, somewhat whitened; leaf scars large, 3–5 bundle scars. Buds silky, sunk in bark, often one above the other. End buds false; pith pinkish. Bark dark and scaly. Leaves 17″–36″. Height 40′–60′ (100′); diameter 1′–2′ (3′). Flowers whitish, clustered, May–June. Fruits 2″–10″ brown pods, Sept.–winter.
Similar species: Only other thornless trees with twice-compound leaves are (1) Albizzia and (2) Prairie Acacia, with fernlike leaves, and (3) Chinaberry, with toothed leaflets. In winter the combination of false end buds and sunken lateral buds is distinctive among species with double characteristic of many bundle scars and large leaf scars.
Remarks: As a shade tree, often planted in city parks along eastern seaboard; sometimes escapes. Native mostly west of Appalachians. One of few members of pea family which do not grow bacterial root nodules capable of fixing nitrogen. Seeds were roasted and used as coffee in some areas during Civil War. Indians are supposed to have roasted seeds, but they ate them as nuts. Pulp between seeds, however, reported to be poisonous and cattle have been made sick by leaves or fruits dropping into their drinking water. Reddish wood is strong and coarse but takes a good polish. Useful in cabinetwork and for fence posts and railroad ties.

ALBIZZIA   *Albizzia julibrissin* Durazzini   **p. 166**
Recognition: A small tree with feathery, *fernlike twice-compound* leaves. On being handled, leaflets *close like pages of a book.* Twigs hairless, slender, leaf scars small, with 3 bundle scars. Buds few-scaled, small, blunt, not sunk in bark, sometimes occur one above the other; end buds false. Pith whitish. Bark smooth, light brownish. Leaves 5″–8″. Height 20′–40′; diameter 6″–12″. Flowers powder-puff-like, pink, June–Aug. Fruits beanlike pods 2″–3″.
Similar species: Prairie Acacia has hairy twigs.

PRAIRIE ACACIA   Not illus.
Acacia angustissima var. *hirta* (Nutt.) Robins.

Recognition: A *thornless* member of the large group of tropical and subtropical acacias. Foliage somewhat resembles that of Albizzia but twigs *quite hairy*. Leaf scars have single bundle scars; end buds false. Height to 6'. Flowers yellow or pink, in heads, June–Oct. Fruits pods, 2″–4″ long, flat. Dry soils; sw. Missouri and s. Kansas to Arkansas and Texas.

PLATES FOR SECTION IV

Broad-leaved Plants with Alternate Compound Leaves

(Key, pages 122–123; text, pages 122–148)

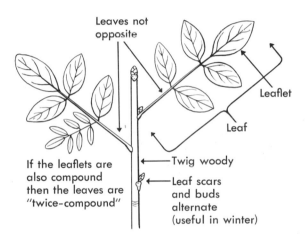

RELATIVELY few plants have compound leaves. Those with opposite leaves were presented in Section II (Plates 7–11). The remainder are in this Section. In winter, the alternate leaf scars may sometimes indicate by their large size the former presence of compound leaves. In case of doubt, however, the twigs of a leafless unknown plant with alternate leaf scars will have to be compared with the drawings of *both* Sections IV and V. **Warning:** Poison-ivy and Poison Sumac are in this group. Do not handle them. Be careful of unknown plants of this type.

PRICKLY BRAMBLES

The only groups of prickly rambling shrubs that have alternate compound leaves. Leaflets 3–11.

Ⅴ RED RASPBERRY, *Rubus idaeus*   p. 124
    Thickets; Newfoundland, Labrador, and British Columbia to s. New England, w. Virginia, w. N. Carolina, Ohio, Indiana, Nebraska, and Wyoming.
    Ⅴ WINE RASPBERRY, *R. phoenicolasius* (not illus.)   p. 125

Ⅴ BLACK RASPBERRY, *Rubus occidentalis*   p. 125
    Thickets; Quebec and Minnesota to the southern states.

Ⅴ BRISTLY DEWBERRY,° *Rubus hispidus*   p. 125
    Thickets; Prince Edward I. and centr. Ontario to Maryland, w. N. Carolina, Ohio, Illinois, and Wisconsin.

Ⅴ PRICKLY DEWBERRY,° *Rubus flagellaris*   p. 125
    Thickets; Maine, sw. Quebec, s. Ontario, and Minnesota to the southern states.

Ⅴ BLACKBERRY,° *Rubus allegheniensis*   p. 125
    Thickets; New Brunswick, Nova Scotia, s. Quebec, and Minnesota to Maryland, N. Carolina, Tennessee, Indiana, and Michigan.

Ⅴ ROSES,° *Rosa* spp.   p. 126

    ° There are many related species. See text.

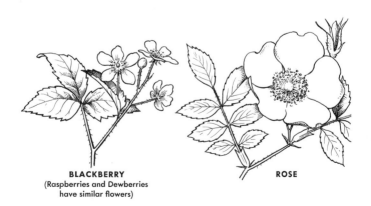

BLACKBERRY
(Raspberries and Dewberries
have similar flowers)

ROSE

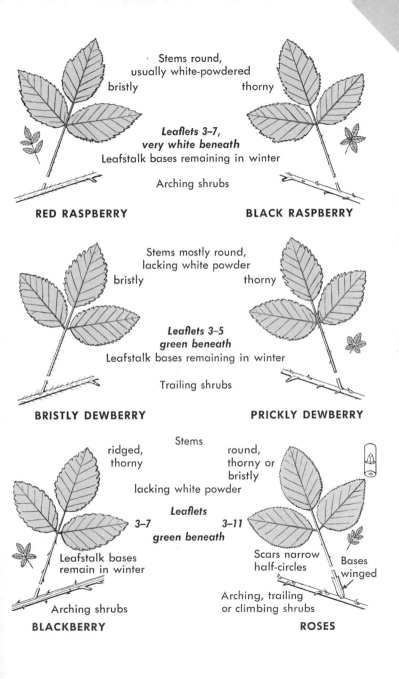

Stems round,
usually white-powdered

bristly   thorny

*Leaflets 3–7,
very white beneath*
Leafstalk bases remaining in winter

Arching shrubs

RED RASPBERRY   **BLACK RASPBERRY**

Stems mostly round,
lacking white powder

bristly   thorny

*Leaflets 3–5
green beneath*
Leafstalk bases remaining in winter

Trailing shrubs

BRISTLY DEWBERRY   **PRICKLY DEWBERRY**

Stems

ridged,   round,
thorny   thorny or
                                       bristly
           lacking white powder

Leaflets

*3–7   3–11
green beneath*

Leafstalk bases   Scars narrow   Bases
remain in winter   half-circles   winged

                                       Arching, trailing
Arching shrubs   or climbing shrubs

BLACKBERRY   **ROSES**

ERECT THORNY TREES AND SHRUBS

The only such plants with alternate compound leaves.

↟ HONEY LOCUST, *Gleditsia triacanthos*   p. 126
    Woods and fields; Nova Scotia, s. Ontario, s. Michigan, and
    se. S. Dakota to nw. Florida, e. Texas, and w. Oklahoma.
   ↟ WATER LOCUST, *G. aquatica* (thorn illus.)   p. 127

↟ BLACK LOCUST, *Robinia pseudo-acacia*   p. 127
    Woods and fields; Nova Scotia, Quebec, and Ontario to
    Georgia and Louisiana and e. Oklahoma.
  ↟Ѵ CLAMMY LOCUST, *R. viscosa* (twig illus.)   p. 128
  Ѵ BRISTLY LOCUST, *R. hispida* (twig illus.)   p. 128
  Ѵ DOWNY LOCUST, *R. elliottii* (not illus.)   p. 128

↟Ѵ HERCULES-CLUB, *Aralia spinosa*   p. 128
    Woods and riverbanks; s. New England, centr. New York,
    Michigan, and Iowa to n. Florida and e. Texas.
  Ѵ BRISTLY SARSAPARILLA, *A. hispida* (twig illus.)   p. 128

Ѵ NORTHERN PRICKLY-ASH   p. 129
  Xanthoxylum americanum
    Old fields, fertile woods, and riverbanks; w. Quebec, Ontario,
    and s. N. Dakota to sw. Virginia, Georgia, Alabama, and ne.
    Oklahoma.
↟Ѵ SOUTHERN PRICKLY-ASH   p. 129
  X. clava-herculis (leaflet illus.)

Ѵ TRIFOLIATE ORANGE, *Poncirus trifoliata* (not illus.) p. 129

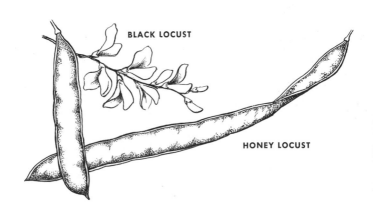

BLACK LOCUST

HONEY LOCUST

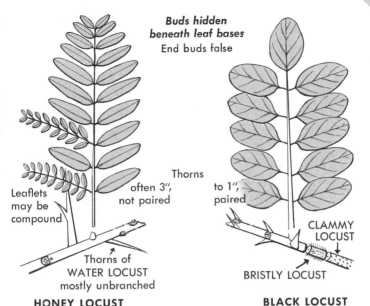

Buds hidden beneath leaf bases
End buds false

Leaflets may be compound

Thorns often 3", not paired

Thorns of WATER LOCUST mostly unbranched

HONEY LOCUST

Thorns to 1", paired

CLAMMY LOCUST

BRISTLY LOCUST

BLACK LOCUST

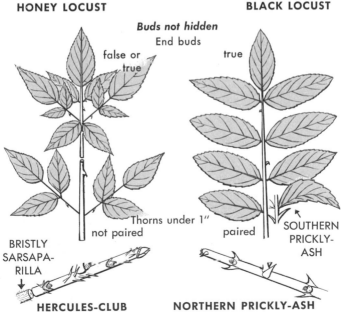

Buds not hidden
End buds false or true

End buds true

Thorns under 1" not paired

BRISTLY SARSAPARILLA

HERCULES-CLUB

paired

SOUTHERN PRICKLY-ASH

NORTHERN PRICKLY-ASH

THORNLESS TRIFOLIATES

Thornless plants whose compound leaves
are divided into only 3 leaflets.

ʃ POISON-IVY,° *Rhus radicans*   p. 130
    Woods and thickets; Quebec and s. British Columbia to
    Florida, Texas, and Arizona.
Ѵ POISON-OAK, *R. toxicodendron* (not illus.)   p. 131

Ѵ FRAGRANT SUMAC, *Rhus aromatica*   p. 131
    Sandy and rocky soils; sw. Quebec, w. Vermont, n. Indiana,
    ne. Kansas, Nebraska, and Oklahoma to nw. Florida and e.
    Texas.

  ʃ CISSUS, *Cissus incisa* (not illus.)   p. 132

↟Ѵ HOPTREE, *Ptelea trifoliata*   p. 132
    Woods; Connecticut, sw. Quebec, s. Ontario, s. Michigan,
    and e. Kansas to n. Florida and s. Texas.

Ѵ SCOTCH BROOM, *Cytisus scoparius*   p. 132
    Thickets; locally in the East from Nova Scotia and w. New
    York to Georgia and W. Virginia.

  Ѵ BICOLOR LESPEDEZA   p. 132
    Lespedeza bicolor (not illus.)

  ° May grow either as a vine or an erect shrub.

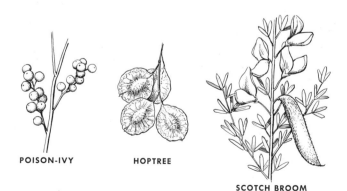

POISON-IVY   HOPTREE

SCOTCH BROOM

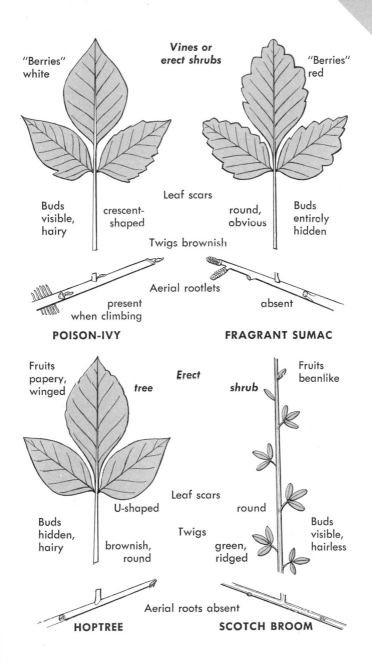

Vines or erect shrubs

"Berries" white

"Berries" red

Buds visible, hairy

crescent-shaped

Leaf scars

round, obvious

Buds entirely hidden

Twigs brownish

Aerial rootlets

present when climbing

absent

POISON-IVY

FRAGRANT SUMAC

Erect

Fruits papery, winged

tree

shrub

Fruits beanlike

Buds hidden, hairy

U-shaped

Leaf scars

round

Buds visible, hairless

Twigs

brownish, round

green, ridged

Aerial roots absent

HOPTREE

SCOTCH BROOM

SUMACS

Shrubs or small trees. Feather-compound leaves
with 7–31 leaflets. Buds mostly hidden when
leaves present. Sap often milky.

♦W WINGED SUMAC, *Rhus copallina*   p. 133
    Upland fields and openings; s. Maine, se. New York, Michigan,
    centr. Wisconsin, and e. Kansas to Florida and e. Texas.

♦W STAGHORN SUMAC, *Rhus typhina*   p. 134
    Upland fields and openings; Nova Scotia, e. Quebec, s.
    Ontario, and Minnesota to Maryland, n. Georgia, centr.
    Tennessee, Illinois, and ne. Iowa.

♦W POISON SUMAC, *Rhus vernix*   p. 134
    Partly wooded swamps; sw. Maine, sw. Quebec, s. Ontario,
    and se. Minnesota to Florida and Texas.

♦W SMOOTH SUMAC, *Rhus glabra*   p. 135
    Fields and openings; centr. Maine, sw. Quebec, and s. British
    Columbia to nw. Florida and s. California.

STAGHORN   POISON   SMOOTH
(Red)   (White)   (Red)

FRUITS OF SUMAC

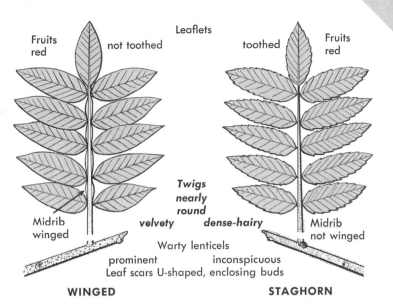

Leaflets

Fruits red — not toothed

Fruits red — toothed

Midrib winged

Twigs nearly round

velvety

dense-hairy

Midrib not winged

Warty lenticels
prominent — inconspicuous
Leaf scars U-shaped, enclosing buds

WINGED

STAGHORN

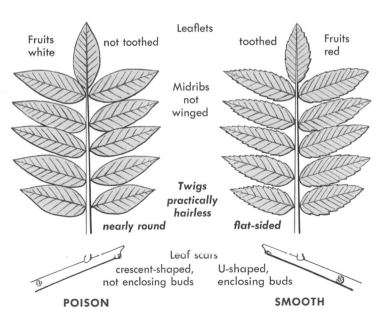

Leaflets

Fruits white — not toothed

toothed — Fruits red

Midribs not winged

Twigs practically hairless

nearly round

flat-sided

Leaf scars
crescent-shaped, not enclosing buds

U-shaped, enclosing buds

POISON

SMOOTH

WALNUTS AND SIMILAR TREES

Leaves feather-compound with 7–41 toothed
or glandular leaflets. Buds visible.

⬧ BLACK WALNUT, *Juglans nigra*   p. 135
  Woods; w. Massachusetts, s. Ontario, s. Minnesota, and se.
  S. Dakota to nw. Florida, e. Texas, and w. Oklahoma.

⬧ BUTTERNUT, *Juglans cinerea*   p. 135
  Fertile woods; w. New Brunswick, s. Ontario, and se. Minnesota to w. S. Carolina, w. Georgia, n. Mississippi, and
  n. Arkansas.

⬧ TREE-OF-HEAVEN (AILANTHUS)   p. 136
  Ailanthus altissima
  Imported; waste places, woods, and fields; Massachusetts, s.
  Ontario, Iowa, and Kansas to Florida and Texas. Local in
  the West.

⬧Ⅴ AMERICAN MOUNTAIN-ASH, *Pyrus americana*   p. 137
  Woods and openings; Newfoundland, e. Quebec, n. Michigan,
  and se. Manitoba to n. New Jersey and n. Illinois; in mts.
  to w. N. Carolina, e. Tennessee, and n. Georgia.
⬧Ⅴ NORTHERN MOUNTAIN-ASH   p. 137
  P. decora (leaflet illus.)
⬧Ⅴ EUROPEAN MOUNTAIN-ASH   p. 137
  P. aucuparia (not illus.)

WALNUT

BUTTERNUT

TREE-OF-HEAVEN
(Large clusters of
winged seeds)

MOUNTAIN-ASH
(Red berries)

Husks of Walnut and Butternut
in one piece (unlike hickories)

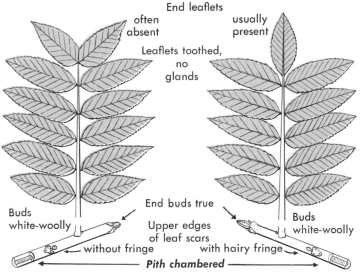

End leaflets
often absent

End leaflets
usually present

Leaflets toothed,
no glands

Buds white-woolly

Buds white-woolly

End buds true

Upper edges
of leaf scars

without fringe

with hairy fringe

Pith chambered

BLACK WALNUT

BUTTERNUT

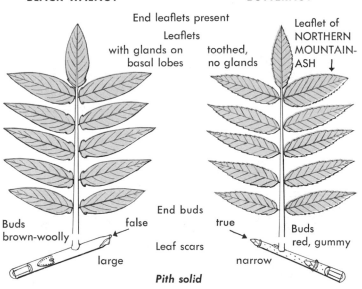

End leaflets present

Leaflets
with glands on
basal lobes

toothed,
no glands

Leaflet of
NORTHERN
MOUNTAIN-
ASH ↓

Buds brown-woolly

false

large

End buds
true

Leaf scars
narrow

Pith solid

Buds red, gummy

TREE-OF-HEAVEN

AMERICAN MOUNTAIN-ASH

HICKORIES (1)

Trees with feather-compound leaves. Husks of nuts 4-parted.

↟ PECAN, *Carya illinoensis*   p. 139
    Floodplains; Indiana and Iowa to Alabama and centr. Texas.

↟ WATER HICKORY (BITTER PECAN)   p. 139
    Carya aquatica
    River swamps of Coastal Plain; se. Virginia to s. Florida, west
    to e. Texas, and north in Mississippi Valley to sw. Illinois,
    se. Missouri, and se. Oklahoma.

↟ SHAGBARK HICKORY, *Carya ovata*   p. 139
    Mature woods and fencerows; sw. Maine, sw. Quebec, s.
    Ontario, centr. Michigan, se. Minnesota, and se. Nebraska
    to nw. Florida and e. Texas.

↟ PIGNUT HICKORY, *Carya glabra*   p. 140
    Dry woods; s. New Hampshire, New York, s. Ontario, s.
    Michigan, Illinois, and ne. Kansas to Florida, Louisiana, and
    Arkansas.
   ↟ SWEET PIGNUT HICKORY, *C. ovalis* (fruit illus.) p. 140
    Moist or dry woods; sw. New Hampshire, s. Ontario, Wis-
    consin, and Iowa to Georgia, Mississippi, and Arkansas.
   ↟ BLACK HICKORY, *C. texana* (not illus.)   p. 141
    Dry woods; s. Indiana, s. Illinois, Missouri, and e. Kansas to
    Louisiana and s. Texas.

WATER
(Thin husk, bitter
soft-shelled nut)

SHAGBARK
(Thick-walled
husk)

PECAN
(Thin oval husk,
smooth brown nut)

SWEET PIGNUT
(Thin husk,
sweet kernels)

PIGNUT
(Thin husk may
not split to base)

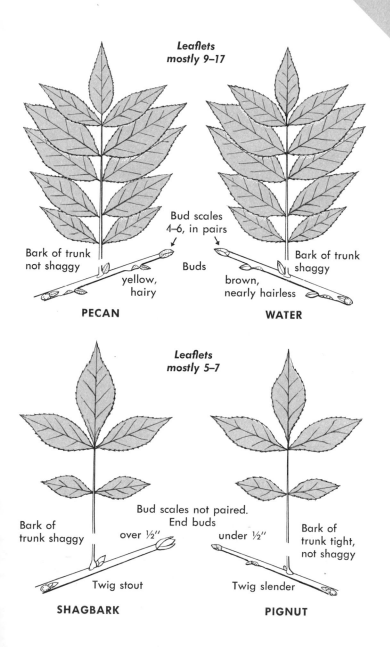

*Leaflets
mostly 9–17*

Bark of trunk
not shaggy

Bud scales
4–6, in pairs

Buds

Bark of trunk
shaggy

yellow,
hairy

brown,
nearly hairless

PECAN

WATER

*Leaflets
mostly 5–7*

Bark of
trunk shaggy

Bud scales not paired.
End buds

over ½″

under ½″

Bark of
trunk tight,
not shaggy

Twig stout

Twig slender

SHAGBARK

PIGNUT

HICKORIES (2)

Trees with feather-compound leaves. Husks of nuts 4-parted.

⚹ BITTERNUT HICKORY, *Carya cordiformis*   p. 141
    Woods; New Hampshire, sw. Quebec, s. Ontario, Michigan,
    Minnesota, and se. Nebraska to nw. Florida and Texas.

⚹ PALE HICKORY, *Carya pallida*   p. 141
    Coastal Plain woods; s. New Jersey, N. Carolina, and Ten-
    nessee to Florida and Louisiana.

⚹ MOCKERNUT HICKORY, *Carya tomentosa*   p. 141
    Upland woods; s. New Hampshire, New York, s. Ontario,
    s. Michigan, se. Iowa, and Nebraska to n. Florida and e.
    Texas.

⚹ SHELLBARK HICKORY, *Carya laciniosa*   p. 142
    Bottomlands and rich soils; w. New York, s. Ontario, s.
    Michigan, s. Iowa, and e. Kansas to Virginia, w. N. Carolina,
    n. Georgia, Alabama, Louisiana, and e. Kansas.

BITTERNUT   **PALE**   **MOCKERNUT**   **SHELLBARK**
(Bitter kernels) (Sweet kernels) (Fruits large,   (Fruits large, husks
                                   husks not splitting splitting to base)
                                   to base)

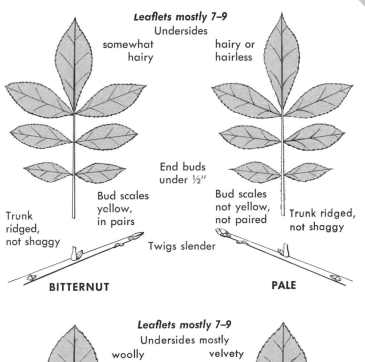

Leaflets mostly 7–9
Undersides
somewhat hairy — hairy or hairless

End buds under ½"

Bud scales yellow, in pairs

Bud scales not yellow, not paired

Trunk ridged, not shaggy

Trunk ridged, not shaggy

Twigs slender

BITTERNUT

PALE

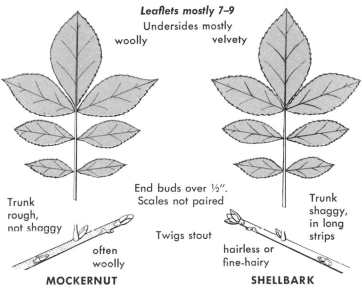

Leaflets mostly 7–9
Undersides mostly
woolly — velvety

End buds over ½".
Scales not paired

Trunk rough, not shaggy

Trunk shaggy, in long strips

Twigs stout

often woolly

hairless or fine-hairy

MOCKERNUT

SHELLBARK

IV. PLATE 30

MISCELLANEOUS SPECIES

with alternate once-compound leaves.

⚶ YELLOWWOOD, *Cladrastis lutea*   p. 142
    Rich soils; w. N. Carolina, s. Indiana, and s. Illinois to n.
    Georgia and n. Alabama, also in sw. Missouri, nw. Arkansas,
    and ne. Oklahoma; sometimes spreading from cultivation
    farther north.

  Ⅴ BLADDER-SENNA, *Colutea arborescens* (not illus.)   p. 143

  Ⅴ SHRUBBY CINQUEFOIL, *Potentilla fruticosa*   p. 143
    Meadows and bogs; Newfoundland, s. Labrador, and Alaska
    to n. New Jersey, n. Pennsylvania, n. Illinois, n. Iowa, S.
    Dakota, New Mexico, and California.

  Ⅴ DULL-LEAF INDIGOBUSH, *Amorpha fruticosa*   p. 143
    Fertile soils; New England, New York, s. Michigan, Manitoba,
    and Saskatchewan to n. Florida, Mexico, and Arizona.
  Ⅴ DOWNY INDIGOBUSH, *A. canesceas* (leaflet illus.)   p. 144
  Ⅴ FRAGRANT INDIGOBUSH, *A. nana* (leaflet illus.)   p. 144
    For other indigobushes see pages 143–44.

  Ƨ VIRGINIA CREEPER, *Parthenocissus quinquefolia*   p. 144
    Woods and thickets; se. Maine, sw. Quebec, and Minnesota
    to Florida and Mexico.
  Ƨ THICKET CREEPER, *P. inserta* (tendrils illus.)   p. 144

  Ƨ AMERICAN WISTERIA, *Wisteria frutescens*   p. 145
    Floodplains and streambanks; e. Maryland and se. Virginia
    to Florida and Alabama.
    For other wisterias see page 145.

  ⚶ WESTERN SOAPBERRY   p. 145
    Sapindus drummondi (not illus.)

SHRUBBY CINQUEFOIL

INDIGOBUSH

VIRGINIA CREEPER

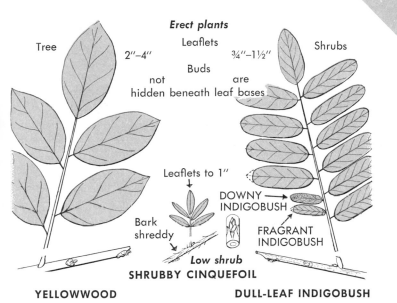

Erect plants

Tree

Leaflets

2"–4"

Shrubs

¾"–1½"

Buds
not   are
hidden beneath leaf bases

Leaflets to 1"

DOWNY →
INDIGOBUSH

Bark
shreddy

FRAGRANT
INDIGOBUSH

Low shrub
SHRUBBY CINQUEFOIL

YELLOWWOOD

DULL-LEAF INDIGOBUSH

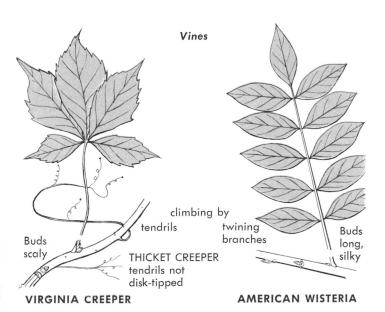

Vines

climbing by
tendrils

Buds
scaly

THICKET CREEPER
tendrils not
disk-tipped

twining
branches

Buds
long,
silky

VIRGINIA CREEPER

AMERICAN WISTERIA

THORNLESS PLANTS WITH LEAVES TWICE-COMPOUND

Only these thornless plants and 2 spiny species on Plate 24 have compound leaves whose *leaflets* are also compound.

Ѵ YELLOWROOT, *Xanthorhiza simplicissima*   p. 146
    Floodplains and wet woods; sw. New York to Florida and Alabama.

Ƨ PEPPER VINE,° *Ampelopsis arborea*   p. 146
    Wet woods; e. Maryland, W. Virginia, s. Illinois, Missouri, and Oklahoma to Florida and Texas.

   ⫯ CHINABERRY, *Melia azedarach* (not illus.)   p. 147
     Oriental; planted e. Virginia and se. Oklahoma to Florida and centr. Texas.

⫯ COFFEE-TREE, *Gymnocladus dioica*   p. 147
    Fertile woods; centr. New York, s. Ontario, s. Michigan, and se. S. Dakota to Virginia, Tennessee, and w. Oklahoma.

⫯ ALBIZZIA, *Albizzia julibrissin*   p. 147
    Asiatic; escaped to woods and thickets; Maryland and Indiana to Florida and Louisiana.

  Ѵ PRAIRIE ACACIA   p. 148
    Acacia angustissima var. *hirta* (not illus.)

° May be either a vine or a shrub.

COFFEE-TREE   **ALBIZZIA**

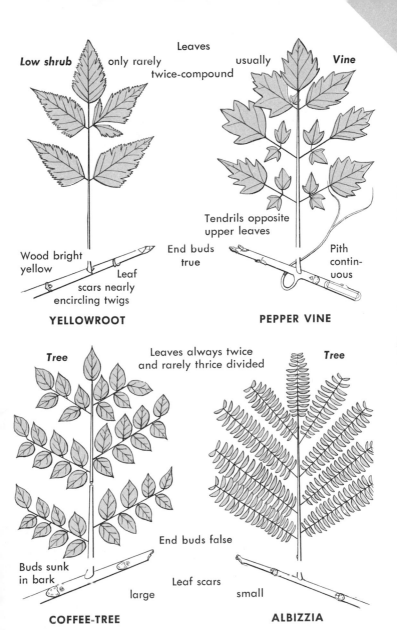

Low shrub   only rarely

Leaves

twice-compound   usually   **Vine**

Wood bright
yellow

Leaf
scars nearly
encircling twigs

Tendrils opposite
upper leaves

End buds
true

Pith
contin-
uous

YELLOWROOT

PEPPER VINE

Tree

Leaves always twice
and rarely thrice divided

Tree

End buds false

Buds sunk
in bark

Leaf scars

large   small

COFFEE-TREE

ALBIZZIA

Broad-leaved Plants with Alternate Simple Leaves

OVER HALF of our woody plants fall in this category. Although a number of species therefore resemble one another in having alternate simple leaves, the separation of the group into subdivisions aids in their identification. The outline below indicates the major characteristics used in subdividing the group. It may be used as a general guide to identification. More detailed keys (A–F) follow it. (If in doubt about number of bundle scars, try both keys E and F.) A Winter Key to nonevergreen plants with alternate leaf scars is given in Appendix B, p. 378.

Major Subdivisions of Broad-leaved Plants with Alternate Simple Leaves

	Plate	Key Sub-division
1. Creeping, trailing or otherwise flattened shrubs	32	A
1. Climbing or sprawling vines	33–37	B
1. Erect trees and shrubs:		
2. Thorny plants	37–40	C
2. Thornless plants:		
3. Leaves lobed (see also Sweetfern, Plate 57; Groundsel-tree, Plate 58)	41–46	D
3. Leaves not lobed:		
4. Leaves fan-veined (with 3–5 main veins meeting near the leaf base) or leaf scars with 3 or more bundle scars	43–59	E
4. Leaves not fan-veined and leaf scars with 1 bundle scar	60–68	F

Subdivision A
Creeping, Trailing, or Otherwise Flattened Shrubs

These plants do not climb. They creep, trail, or become matted on the ground. All are grouped on Plate 32.

Subdivision B
Climbing or Sprawling Vines

	Name	Plate

5. Tendrils present:
    6. Prickly or green-stemmed   **GREENBRIERS**   33
    6. Without prickles, brown-stemmed
                         GRAPES (1), (2), etc.   34, 35
5. Tendrils lacking:
    7. Leaves finely toothed and somewhat heart-shaped   **GRAPES** (1), (2), **AMPELOPSIS**   34, 35
    7. Leaves not toothed or if so not heart-shaped:
        8. Leaf scars with more than 3 bundle scars; seeds crescent- or cup-shaped **MOONSEEDS, etc.**   36
        8. Leaf scars with 1 or 3 bundle scars; seeds neither crescent- nor cup-shaped
                         MISCELLANEOUS   37

Subdivision C
Erect Plants with Thorny or Prickly Twigs

9. Leaves not lobed:
    10. Thorns less than 1″ long or, if longer, then the buds not ball-shaped:
        11. Stems ridged; usually somewhat vinelike
                      MATRIMONY-VINES   37
        11. Stems not ridged; never vinelike
                      OSAGE-ORANGE   38
    10. Thorns mostly over 1″ long; buds ball-shaped
                      HAWTHORNS   39
9. Leaves lobed:
    12. Thorns equipped with buds or leaves
                      CRABAPPLES   38
    12. Thorns without buds or leaves:
        13. Leaves mostly over 6″; leaf veins prickly
                      DEVIL'S-CLUB   38
        13. Leaves mostly under 6″; leaf veins not prickly:
             14. Thorns mostly over 1″ long; buds ball-shaped   **HAWTHORNS**   39
             14. Thorns under 1″ long; buds long
                      GOOSEBERRIES   40

Subdivision D
Erect Plants with Thornless Twigs and Deeply Lobed Leaves

15. Leaves fan-lobed, with 3–5 main veins meeting near the leaf base:
    16. Plants usually somewhat vinelike; pith with a solid partition near each leaf base **SAND GRAPE**   34

Name   Plate

16. Plants upright, not vinelike; pith not as above
    or if so then the leaf surface very sandpaper-
    like:
    17. Twigs with 2 long lines descending from
        each leaf scar; if 3 such lines are present
        then leaves and twigs are yellow-dotted
        (use lens); leaf scars narrow   **CURRANTS**   **41**
    17. Twigs without such lines, or if present
        they are quite short; yellow resin-dots are
        lacking (use lens); leaf scars variable:
        18. Plants with all leaves lobed
                                MISCELLANEOUS   **42**
        18. Plants usually with some leaves not
            lobed   **MULBERRIES, etc.**   **43**
15. Leaves feather-lobed, with single midvein, other
    veins more or less at right angles to midvein:
    19. Leaves wide, not at all fernlike   **OAKS (1), (2)**   **45, 46**
    19. Leaves long, narrow, quite fernlike **SWEETFERN**   **57**

Subdivision E
Erect Plants with Twigs Thornless and Leaves Not Lobed.
Either Leaves Fan-veined or Leaf Scars Contain
More Than 1 Bundle Scar

20. Leaves mostly heart-shaped or triangular, with
    3–5 stout veins meeting near the leaf base:
    21. Bundle scars 3; leaves toothed; bark of upper
        branches and young trunks usually smooth
        whitish- or greenish-yellow; lowermost bud
        scale in the outside position squarely above
        the leaf scar; pith continuous   **POPLARS**   **44**
    21. Bundle scars 1 to many, or if 3 then leaflets
        not toothed or pith usually chambered; bud
        scales not as above   **MISCELLANEOUS**   **43**
20. Leaves neither heart-shaped nor triangular, or if
    so with only a single main midvein:
    22. Twigs with clustered end buds:
        23. Acorns or their cups present on the twigs
            or on the ground beneath the plant;
            bundle scars 4 or more   **OAKS (3), (4)**   **47, 48**
        23. Acorns absent; bundle scars 3:
            24. Leafstalks with glands; broken twigs
                with a peculiar sour odor; trunk bark
                often with narrow cross stripes
                                FIRE CHERRY   **53**
            24. Without such characteristics; swamps
                from sw. Mo. south   **CORKWOOD**   **59**
    22. Twigs with single end buds:

Name   *Plate*

25. Twigs with completely encircling lines or rings (stipule scars) beneath the leaf scars:
    26. Leaves not toothed   **MAGNOLIAS**   49
    26. Leaves toothed   **BEECH**   57
25. Twigs without completely encircling lines (stipule scars):
    27. Leaves not toothed and not definitely wavy-edged:
        28. Buds with a single scale; leaves mostly narrow   **WILLOWS** (1), (2)   **55, 56**
        28. Buds without scales or with more than 1 scale; leaves various:
            29. Buds without scales:
                30. Leaves usually under 6″ long, more or less elliptic or egg-shaped   **BUCKTHORNS**   58
                30. Leaves usually over 6″ long, wedge-shaped   **PAWPAWS**   59
            29. Buds with 2 or more scales:
                31. Leaf bases uneven   **UPLAND HACKBERRY**   43
                31. Leaf bases even   **MISCELLANEOUS**   59
    27. Leaves with definite teeth or distinctly wavy-edged:
        32. Leaves with distinct double teeth:
            33. Leaf bases mostly uneven, one side being much lower than the other (see plates); buds many-scaled, the scales in 2 even rows:
                34. Leaves quite long-pointed, usually triangular   **HACKBERRIES**   43
                34. Leaves not long-pointed, mostly egg-shaped   **ELMS**   50
            33. Leaf bases mostly even, both sides similar or only slightly uneven:
                35. Buds with 2–3 scales, neither hairy nor narrowed at the base; if a tree, the older bark often conspicuously streaked horizontally   **BIRCHES**   52
                35. Buds with 2 or more scales, hairy or narrowed at the base:
                    36. Leafstalks without glands near the leaf base; the older bark not streaked or slightly streaked   **IRONWOOD**, etc.   51

Name   Plate

36. Leafstalks with small paired glands near the leaf base; if a tree, the older bark usually streaked horizontally   **CHERRIES**   53

32. Leaves with single teeth or definite wavy edges:

  37. Bark of upper branches and young trunks often smooth and whitish- or greenish-yellow; lowermost bud scales located in the outside position squarely above the leaf scar; leafstalk often much flattened   **POPLARS**   44

  37. Bark not of this type; bud scales, if present, not as above; leafstalks not much flattened:

    38. Leafstalks mostly with a pair of small swollen glands near the leaf bases; broken twigs with a unique, strong, nonspicy odor; older bark often striped horizontally   **CHERRIES**   53

    38. Leafstalks without glands; twigs without peculiar "cherry" odor; older bark striped or not:

      39. Buds long, slender, reddish, the several scales with tiny dark tips and often twisted; trunk bark smooth and often twisted   **JUNEBERRIES**   54

      39. Buds with a single scale; leaves usually long and slender   **WILLOWS** (1), (2)   55, 56

      39. Buds otherwise:

        40. Leaves spicy-scented when crushed and yellow resin-dotted (use lens)   **BAYBERRIES**   57

        40. Leaves otherwise:

          41. Pith chambered (see plate)   **SWEET-SPIRES**   59

          41. Pith not chambered:

            42. Leaves toothed, tips sharply pointed; leaf bases uneven; southern swamps   **WATER-ELM**   50

            42. Leaves toothed, tips blunt; leaf bases even; northern bogs and barrens   **BIRCHES**   52

            42. Leaves toothed or wavy-edged, tips pointed or not; leaf bases even or uneven   **MISCELLANEOUS** (1), (2)   57, 58

Subdivision F

Erect Plants with Thornless Twigs and Leaves Not Lobed. Leaves Not Fan-veined and Leaf Scars Containing only 1 Bundle Scar

	Name	Plate

43. Shrubs with numerous tiny raised dots on the twigs (use lens):

    44. Twig dots merely raised; twigs greenish or reddish; leaves and buds small; fruits many-seeded blue berries   **BLUEBERRIES**   62

    44. Twig dots brown or silver scales; twigs brownish; leaves and buds small to medium-sized; fruits brownish, 1-seeded, fleshy   **SILVERBERRY, etc.**   68

43. Trees and shrubs with twigs not dotted:

    45. Leaf undersides with tiny bright yellow resin-dots (use lens)   **HUCKLEBERRIES**   63

    45. Resin-dots absent:

        46. End buds clustered at twig tips, often large; leaves not toothed, edges with a hairy fringe (use lens):

            47. Branchlets with tight bark   **AZALEAS**   64

            47. Branchlets with shreddy bark   **MINNIEBUSH**   68

        46. End buds not clustered at twig tips (though sometimes crowded toward the tip and sometimes large), or if so then leaves toothed; leaves toothed or not, edges not hairy-fringed:

            48. Leaves evergreen, mostly leathery:

                49. Spur branches usually present; tiny black thornlike stipules flanking each leaf scar (use lens); end buds true   **HOLLIES**   61

                49. Spur branches and stipules of the above type absent:

                    50. Fruits fleshy berries; end buds false   **BILBERRIES, etc.**   63

                    50. Fruits dry capsules; end buds true or false   **EVERGREEN HEATHS**   65

            48. Leaves thin, not evergreen:

                51. Leaf scars conspicuously raised, often with descending lines at the sides; twigs very long and slender; clustered small dry fruits commonly at twig tips; leaves toothed except occasionally in 1 species   **SPIREAS**   60

Name   *Plate*

51. Leaf scars not conspicuously raised; without lines
at sides; twigs less wandlike; fruits, leaves various:
  52. Spur branches usually present; tiny black
  thornlike stipules flanking the leaf scars (use
  lens); end buds true; fruits fleshy; leaves
  toothed   **HOLLIES**   61
  52. Spur branches and stipules of above type
  absent; end buds, fruits, and leaves variable:
    53. Pith chambered or buds without scales
                          MISCELLANEOUS (1)   67
    53. Pith not chambered and buds scaly:
      54. Fruits small, fleshy, many-seeded and
      blue to black (red in 1 species)
                          BILBERRIES, etc.   63
      54. Fruits dry, or if fleshy then not both
      dark-colored and many-seeded:
        55. Leaves toothed:
          56. End buds false:
            57. Fruits fleshy, red
  SOUTHERN MOUNTAIN-CRANBERRY   63
            57. Fruits small dry capsules
                  NONEVERGREEN HEATHS   66
          56. End buds true:
            58. End buds much longer
            than side buds:
              59. Outer bud scales not
              as long as the buds
                  TOOTHED AZALEA   64
              59. Outer bud scales as
              long as buds
                  PEPPERBUSHES   66
            58. End buds about size of
            side buds
                  SILKY-CAMELLIAS   67
        55. Leaves not toothed:
          60. Fruits small, fleshy, blue to
          black, many-seeded berries
                  BILBERRIES, etc.   63
          60. Fruits dry capsules or pods,
          or if fleshy, then either not
          dark-colored or not many-
          seeded   **MISCELLANEOUS (2)**   68

Low Creeping or Trailing Shrubs
(*Plate 32, p. 298*)

Unlike the climbing or even sprawling vines of Plate 33 and elsewhere in the book, these plants largely creep, trail, or become

matted on the ground. For the most part this group is of northern, often circumpolar, distribution. All on this plate except Alpine and Red Bearberries, Sand Cherry, and dwarf willows have leathery evergreen leaves. The flowers, except in Sand Cherry and dwarf willows, are vase-shaped.

In addition to the plants on this plate, there are a few others that occasionally are low-growing and thus subject to confusion. Among plants with small leathery leaves, Alpine-azalea and Pachistima (Plate 12) and Sandmyrtle (Plate 17) have mostly opposite leaves. Dwarf Bilberry (Plate 63) has flat elliptic leaves, shreddy older bark; Bog Rosemary (Plate 65) has curled leaves much whitened beneath. The matted evergreen plants of Plate 6 and other northern evergreens of Plates 3–5 have needlelike leaves.

Among nonevergreen plants with alternate simple leaves, Garden Red Currant, and especially Skunk Currant and Swamp Red Currant (Plate 41) may have reclining or sprawling branches. Northern Birch, Tundra Dwarf Birch, and Minor Birch (pp. 234–35) vary in growth from mats to erect shrubs; Newfoundland Dwarf Birch (p. 234) has creeping stems but erect branches. Beach Plum (Plate 53) and Graves Plum (p. 239) are often somewhat straggling. On sites exposed to severe weather, American Larch (Plate 2) and Mountain Alder (p. 230) form prostrate mats. Dewberries (Plate 23) and Shrubby Cinquefoil (Plate 30) may grow close to the ground but they have compound leaves. The nonevergreen simple-leaved plants that may grow in a creeping, trailing, or matted manner are all included in this key:

	Name	Plate
1. Twigs with warty spurs	**AMERICAN LARCH**	2
1. Twigs without warty growths:		
2. Buds covered by a single scale		
	DWARF WILLOWS	32
2. Buds covered by several scales:		
3. Leaves fan-lobed, maplelike	**CURRANTS**	40, 41
3. Leaves more or less egg-shaped:		
4. Leaf teeth rounded, wavy-toothed		
	BEARBERRIES	32
4. Leaf teeth sharp:		
5. End buds false	**PLUMS**	53
5. End buds true:		
6. Buds with 2–3 scales	**BIRCHES**	52
6. Buds with 4 or more scales:		
7. Twigs speckled; broken twigs with sour odor	**SAND CHERRY**	32
7. Twigs not speckled; broken twigs without sour odor		
	MOUNTAIN ALDER	51

CRANBERRIES and Close Relatives *Vaccinium* spp. **p. 298**
  Recognition: Cranberries, mountain-cranberries, and Creeping

Blueberry are closely related members of same genus. Trailing plants with smooth, *hairless, odorless, evergreen* leaves. Stems neither hairy nor scaly. Flowers are small and bell-shaped and the fruits are many-seeded, globular, and edible either raw or cooked. The several species may be separated easily:

1. Leaves black-dotted beneath (use lens), with edges smooth
                    NORTHERN MOUNTAIN-CRANBERRY
1. Leaves green beneath, wavy-edged
                         CREEPING BLUEBERRY
1. Leaves whitened beneath, with edges smooth:
    2. Leaves very white beneath, tips pointed, edges rolled
                           SMALL CRANBERRY
    2. Leaves pale beneath, tips blunt, edges not rolled
                           LARGE CRANBERRY

Southern Mountain-cranberry (p. 282) is more erect and is discussed with the blueberries.

NORTHERN MOUNTAIN-CRANBERRY   **p. 298**
Vaccinium vitis-idaea var. *minus* Lodd.
   Recognition: A creeping mat-forming shrub with small egg-shaped, leathery, evergreen leaves *dotted beneath* with tiny black points (use lens). Stems slender. Leaves ¼″–¾″. Height to 7″. Flowers pink or red, June–July. Fruits red, Aug.–Oct. No other creeping shrub has black-dotted foliage. Southern Mountain-cranberry (p. 282) is an upright shrub. Rocky areas and bogs; subarctic south to Newfoundland, New England, sw. Ontario, n. Minnesota, Manitoba, and British Columbia.

CREEPING BLUEBERRY   **p. 298**
Vaccinium crassifolium Andr.
   Recognition: A scarce prostrate mat-forming shrub with small elliptic evergreen leaves. Leaves have *rolled wavy-toothed edges;* stems *slender,* rising from thickened base. Leaves ³⁄₁₆″–⅝″. Flowers white or pink, June–Aug. Fruits black, shiny, sweet, Aug.–Oct. Other blueberries often are not tall but, though low, generally on upright stems. Sandy or acid soils; se. Virginia and e. S. Carolina.

SMALL CRANBERRY   *Vaccinium oxycoccus* L.   **p. 298**
   Recognition: A creeping shrub. Leaves small, egg-shaped or triangular, *pointed,* evergreen. They have *rolled edges* and are *white beneath.* Stems *very slender.* Typically, leaves are less than ⅜″ long and fruits less than ⅜″, but var. *ovalifolium* Michx. has leaves as large as those of Large Cranberry and fruits may be as big, up to ⁷⁄₁₆″. Leaves ³⁄₁₆″–⅝″. Flowers pink, May–July. Fruits red or dark red, rarely white, Aug.–Oct. Leaves of Large Cranberry blunt, larger, and pale white beneath. Those of Bog Rosemary (Plate 65) white beneath, pointed, and with rolled edges, but much larger and the

fruits are dry capsules. Bogs; Greenland, Labrador, and Alaska to Newfoundland, New Jersey, Pennsylvania, mountains of Virginia, W. Virginia, and N. Carolina, n. Ohio, Michigan, Minnesota, Manitoba, Saskatchewan, and Oregon.

Remarks: Chipmunks, sharptail grouse, pheasant eat fruits.

LARGE CRANBERRY   *Vaccinium macrocarpon* Ait.   **p. 298**
Recognition: A creeping shrub. Leaves small, wedge-shaped to round, *blunt-tipped,* evergreen, flat or with slightly rolled edges, *slightly whitened or pale beneath.* Stems slender. Leaves ¼″–⅝″. Flowers pinkish, June–Aug. Fruits red or dark red, ⁷⁄₁₆″–1³⁄₁₆″ across, Sept.–Nov. See Small Cranberry. Boggy places; Newfoundland and Minnesota to Long Island; mountains to N. Carolina, W. Virginia, Ohio, Illinois, and Arkansas.
Remarks: Many varieties grown commercially. Ruffed and sharptail grouse, bobwhite, mourning dove, and several songbirds may include Large Cranberry in their diets.

SNOWBERRY WINTERGREEN (CREEPING SNOWBERRY)
Gaultheria hispidula (L.) Bigel.   **p. 298**
Recognition: A mat-forming evergreen. Leaves small, pointed, *brown-hairy* beneath; have rolled edges and *spicy odor* when crushed. Slender stems, too, are *brown-hairy.* Leaves ¼″–½″. Flowers small, white, May–June. Fruits small white berries, Aug.–Sept.
Remarks: Fruits eaten by ruffed and spruce grouse, thrushes.

SMOOTHLEAF DRYAS   *Dryas integrifolia* Vahl   **Not illus.**
Recognition: An arctic trailing or matted shrub with leathery foliage. Leaves narrowly heart-shaped or triangular to elliptic, *whitened beneath,* short-stalked, with prominent sunken veins, *toothless* or with a few teeth near base; edges rolled. One form has foliage hairy or whitened above. Stems have *shreddy bark* and buds have several scales. Leaves ¼″–⅞″. Flowers white, June–July. Fruits small, with a feathery plume. Cranberries also have leaf undersides whitened but stems are not shreddy. Toothleaf Dryas has toothed leaves. Tundras and stony barrens; n. Canada and Alaska to w. Newfoundland, e. Quebec, Hudson Bay, and Alberta.

TOOTHLEAF DRYAS   **Not illus.**
Dryas drummondii Richards.
Recognition: Generally like Smoothleaf Dryas but more southern. Leaves elliptic to egg-shaped, *toothed.* Twigs and stems *white-hairy.* Foliage may be sparsely hairy. Stony ground; w. Newfoundland and Alaska to e. Quebec, s. and centr. Ontario, Montana, and Oregon.

RHODODENDRON ROSEBAY   **p. 298**
Rhododendron lapponicum (L.) Wahlenb.
Recognition: A gnarled mat-forming evergreen. Leaves narrow

to wide-elliptic, somewhat *wrinked above, yellow-brown scaly beneath.* Twigs similarly scaly. Leaves ¼″–¾″. Flowers *attractive, purple,* ⅜″–⅞″ across, June–July. Fruits small dry capsules on upright stalks, usually present.

Similar species: The taller azaleas and rhododendrons are on Plates 64 and 65. Leatherleaf, with yellow-brown scaly evergreen leaves, also is taller (see Plate 65).

EVERGREEN BEARBERRY   p. 298
Arctostaphylos uva-ursi (L.) Spreng.

Recognition: A trailing shrub. Leaves wedge-based to elliptic, *evergreen,* hairless, smooth-edged, and *green on both sides.* Twigs variously sticky fine-hairy, finely white-woolly, black-dotted, sticky-hairy, or (after late summer) hairless. Leaves ¾″–1¼″. Flowers small, pink or white, May–July (and Oct.–Nov. in a form found in extreme e. Massachusetts). Fruits red, fleshy but dry, ball-shaped, often present through winter.

Similar species: (1) Alpine and (2) Red Bearberries, northeastern forms, have wavy-edged leaves that either drop off or become withered in winter.

Remarks: Related manzanitas, common in western N. America, represented in East only by this and next 2 inconspicuous species. Evergreen Bearberry fruits important food for grouse and bears. Deer occasionally browse foliage.

ALPINE BEARBERRY   Not illus.
Arctostaphylos alpina (L.) Spreng.

Recognition: Similar to the Evergreen Bearberry but with leaves only thin-leathery, *withering* but usually remaining attached in winter, more egg-shaped, wrinkled, net-veined, and *wavy-toothed.* Lower portions of leaves and leafstalks have bristly hairs along margins. Inner bud scales have rounded tips. Twigs hairless; branches have papery bark; bundle scars single. Leaves to 1½″. Fruits dark, juicy, somewhat edible. Poor soils; Arctic to Newfoundland and mountains of Quebec, Maine, and New Hampshire.

RED BEARBERRY   Not illus.
Arctostaphylos rubra (Rehd. & Wils.) Fern.

Recognition: Like Alpine Bearberry but leaves not leathery, and much wrinkled; do not usually drop in winter. Leaves lack bristly hairs. Inner bud scales pointed at tips. Stems mostly underground. Leaves to 3″. Fruits scarlet and juicy. See under Evergreen Bearberry. Rocky areas; nw. Newfoundland and Alaska to e. Quebec and Alberta.

REDBERRY WINTERGREEN   p. 298
Gaultheria procumbens L.

Recognition: A creeping shrub with elliptic to nearly circular *evergreen* leaves. Foliage hairless and *spicy-scented* when crushed. Stems and twigs hairless. Leaves 1"–2". Flowers small, white, July–Aug. Fruits red, pea-shaped, edible, Aug.–June. **Remarks:** Leaves sometimes used as tea (also called Teaberry). Foliage yields oil of wintergreen. Fruits eaten by many wild animals, including bobwhite, ruffed and sharptail grouse, and pheasant. Deer take both fruits and leaves.

COMMON PIPSISSEWA   **Not illus.**
Chimaphila umbellata (L.) Bart.
   Recognition: Creeping evergreen, hardly woody, with short *upright* stems. Leaves alternate or whorled, leathery, shiny, green, *wedge-shaped*, coarse-toothed, not aromatic. Leaves 1"–3". Height to 10". Flowers white to pink, clustered, July–Aug. Fruits dry capsules. Forests, Nova Scotia and Alaska to Georgia, ne. Illinois, Minnesota, and California.

MOTTLED PIPSISSEWA (SPOTTED WINTERGREEN)
Chimaphila maculata (L.) Pursh.   **Not illus.**
   Recognition: Similar to Common Pipsissewa but leaves broader, widest below the middle, *variegated* whitish. Flowers white, June–Aug. Forests, s. New Hampshire and Michigan to Georgia, Alabama, Tennessee.

TRAILING ARBUTUS   *Epigaea repens* L.   **p. 298**
   Recognition: A trailing shrub with wide, *heart-shaped*, usually hairy-edged leaves. Leaves vary from rough and hairy on both surfaces to hairless. Twigs normally *brown hairy*. Leaves 1"–5". Flowers white or pink, delicately fragrant, March–July. Fruits dry capsules, May–Aug., or longer.

SAND CHERRY   *Prunus depressa* Pursh   **p. 298**
   Recognition: A prostrate shrub. Leaves narrow, wedge-based, green above, pale or whitish beneath, shallowly toothed and thin, not evergreen. The pair of tiny glands present on leafstalks of most cherries occurs on some leaves here. Twigs *reddish, speckled, with lines* leading from leaf scars; sour odor when broken. Older bark somewhat speckled. Buds many-scaled; bundle scars 3. Leaves 1"–3". Flowers white, ½" across, April–May. Fruits purplish, pea-sized, bitter, June–Aug.
   Similar species: Other cherries are on Plate 53.

DWARF WILLOWS   *Salix* spp.   **p. 298**
   Recognition: At high altitudes and at northern latitudes, several willows occur as creeping shrubs. All have characteristic *single bud scale* of willows. None are evergreen. Bundle scars 3; bark not speckled. Catkins of inconspicuous flowers may be present; small dry fruits fall quickly. Other willows on Plates 55, 56, more truly dwarf willows listed below.

WIDELEAF DWARF WILLOW   Leaf illus., p. 298
Salix herbacea L.
Recognition: A tiny shrub with main branches underground and, like next 3 species, aboveground branches *rooting*. Leaves broad, usually heart-shaped, hairless, shiny, *green on both sides*, wavy-toothed, and with *netted veins* obvious beneath. Leaves ½″–1¼″. Flowers June–July. Arctic tundras south to mountains of Newfoundland, e. Quebec, Maine, New Hampshire, and New York.

NETVEIN DWARF WILLOW   *Salix reticulata* L.   Not illus.
Recognition: Similar to Wideleaf Dwarf Willow. Leaves oval to nearly circular, pale, and *much net-veined beneath*, edges rolled, teeth small or lacking. Leafstalks reddish, over ¼″. Buds hairless, somewhat sticky. See Wideleaf Dwarf Willow. Leaves ½″–2″. Flowers June–July. Barren areas; Labrador to n. and nw. Newfoundland.

BELLE ISLE DWARF WILLOW   Not illus.
Salix jejuna Fern.
Recognition: Like preceding but leafstalks *only* ¼″ or shorter. Leaves smaller (¼″–1″), *somewhat pointed, not toothed*. See Wideleaf Dwarf Willow. Rocky places; se. Labrador and n. Newfoundland.

SMOOTH DWARF WILLOW   Not illus.
Salix leiolepis Fern.
Recognition: Similar to Belle Isle Dwarf Willow but leaves *round-tipped and wavy-toothed*. See Wideleaf Dwarf Willow. Mossy limestone soils; local, se. Newfoundland.

BEARBERRY DWARF WILLOW   Leaf illus. p. 298
Salix uva-ursi Pursh
Recognition: This and the following 3 species have branches aboveground which *do not take root*. Leaves of this species narrow, *wedge-based* with *sharply fine-toothed* margins, usually shiny and hairless but woolly above in 1 uncommon form. Foliage not obviously net-veined beneath. Twigs hairless. A hybrid with Wideleaf Dwarf Willow occurs on Mount Adams, New Hampshire, and near Hudson Bay. See also Taller Willows (opposite). Leaves ¼″–1″. Flowers June–July. Tundras; Greenland and eastern arctic archipelago to Newfoundland, Nova Scotia, and mountains of Quebec, n. New England, and n. New York.

TUNDRA DWARF WILLOW   Not illus.
Salix arctophila Cockerell
Recognition: Similar to Bearberry Dwarf Willow but leaves *not toothed*. Foliage *dark green, shiny* above and wider than in

Bearberry Dwarf Willow. Twigs brittle when dry. Leaves ½"–2". Tundras of Greenland, eastern Arctic, and n. Quebec to Newfoundland; mountains of e. Quebec and Maine.

ARCTIC DWARF WILLOW *Salix arctica* Pallas   **Not illus.**
   Recognition: Like Tundra Dwarf Willow but leaves *pale green*, barely shiny. Foliage quite variable, with leaves narrow to nearly heart-shaped or circular, hairless to hairy, thick or thin. Twigs *flexible*. Leaves 1"–3". See also Taller Willows (below). Tundras of arctic coastal areas south to mountains of Newfoundland, and e. Quebec; also mountains of Alberta and British Columbia.

WIEGAND DWARF WILLOW   **Not illus.**
Salix wiegandii Fern.
   Recognition: A mat-forming shrub with *white-woolly* twigs and buds. Leaves elliptic, *leathery, somewhat white-woolly* on both surfaces; edges slightly rolled. Branches do not root. Unlike other dwarf willows with such branches, *large leafy* stipules occur where leaves are attached to twigs. See also Taller Willows, next. Leaves ½"–2". Limestone soils; nw. Newfoundland.

TALLER WILLOWS sometimes flattened or mat-forming
   Recognition: Several willows sometimes grow flat on ground, yet at other times are somewhat more erect. They include: Bluntleaf Willow (p. 257), which resembles Bearberry Dwarf Willow but has larger coarse-toothed leaves; Ungava Willow (p. 252), which is like Arctic Dwarf Willow and similarly variable but leaves often heart-shaped at base and both leaves and twigs usually gray-hairy; Roundleaf Willow (p. 259), which also is similar to Arctic Dwarf Willow but has egg-shaped to circular leaves dark green above, twigs and leaf undersides shiny white-hairy, and branches sharply angled; Limestone Willow (p. 253), which resembles Wiegand Dwarf Willow in possessing stipules but differs in having hairless, more circular leaves. See also the quite local Newfoundland, Mount Albert, and Spreading Willows (pp. 253–54) and nonwidespread Myrtleleaf Willow (p. 257).

Greenbriers
(Plate 33, p. 300)

These are some of the few woody members of the lily family. Greenbriers are green-stemmed vines climbing by tendrils attached to bases of leafstalks, which remain after leaves drop. Stems have no central pith and leaves are parallel-veined. Most are prickly and some retain foliage in winter, particularly in the South.

Flowers are small and greenish. In our area, no other tendril-equipped vines are green-stemmed and, except for a few roses (Plate 23), no other climbing vines are prickly. Boston Ivy (p. 188) has shiny evergreen leaves but these are 3-lobed or 3-parted. All of our vines except greenbriers have central piths and nonparallel leaf veins. Some greenbriers are herbaceous; only those with woody stems are considered here.

Greenbrier fruits are small berries with 1 to several large seeds. They are eaten by songbirds, bobwhite, ruffed grouse, and wild turkey. Stems browsed by cottontail and marsh rabbits.

Hellfetter, Blasphemy-vine, and Tramps' Troubles are realistic colloquial names.

LAUREL GREENBRIER *Smilax laurifolia* L.   **p. 300**
Recognition: A high-climbing vine with *leathery evergreen* leaves. Leaves elliptic, green on both sides; many lack tendrils. Stems round with prickles *absent or present on vigorous shoots* and near stem bases. Leaves 2″–5″. Flowers July–Aug. Fruits black, Aug.–Sept.
Similar species: Only truly evergreen greenbrier. (1) Redberry Greenbrier mostly without prickles but has thinner, wider leaves, and red fruits. (2) Hellfetter Greenbrier has some fiddle-shaped leaves present. (3) Bullbrier Greenbrier has 4-angled stems.

REDBERRY GREENBRIER *Smilax walteri* Pursh   **p. 300**
Recognition: A low vine, sprawling over bushes. Leaves neither leathery nor evergreen, broadly *heart-shaped*, and green beneath. Tendrils plentiful. Stems round, lower half with scattered slender prickles. Branches and twigs *without prickles*. Leaves 2″–5″. Flowers April–June. Fruits *red*, Sept.–Oct., or longer.
Similar species: Our only red-berried greenbrier. (1) Laurel and (2) Hellfetter Greenbriers also may be separated from this species by leaf shape.

BRISTLY GREENBRIER   **p. 300**
Smilax tamnoides var. *hispida* (Muhl.) Fern.
Recognition: A high-climbing vine. Leaves nonleathery, green beneath, egg- to heart-shaped. Stems round, *weak bristles.* Leaves 2″–5″. Flowers May–July. Fruits Sept.–Nov., or longer.
Similar species: Among greenbriers with weak prickles, (1) Hellfetter Greenbrier differs in being only sparsely prickly on upper parts; (2) Glaucous Greenbrier has whitened leaf undersides.

HELLFETTER GREENBRIER   **Not illus.**
Smilax tamnoides L.
Recognition: The typical form of species (Bristly Greenbrier a variety). Similar to its variety except that upper twigs, branches,

and stem mostly without prickles and some leaves fiddle-shaped (see Bullbrier Greenbrier). Mostly Coastal Plain; e. Virginia to Florida, west to e. Texas, and north in Mississippi Valley to Kansas.

GLAUCOUS GREENBRIER *Smilax glauca* Walt.   **p. 300**
  Recognition: A high-climbing vine. Leaves nonleathery, *whitened*, hairy or hairless beneath, narrowly to broadly heart-shaped. Stems round, often whitened, with many or scattered *weak prickles*. Leaves 2″–5″. Flowers May–June. Fruits blue or black, with white powdery surface, Sept.–Oct., or longer.
  Similar species: Only greenbrier with whitened leaf undersides.

BULLBRIER GREENBRIER *Smilax bona-nox* L.   **p. 300**
  Recognition: A highly variable species; has been separated into 3 varieties in addition to typical form. Typical form a widespread shrub that rarely climbs high. Leaves *leathery, triangular* (see dotted lines in drawing) to *fiddle-shaped*, with bases heart-shaped, green beneath but often mottled with white. Leaves have *bristly edges* and quite prominent veins. Two southern varieties have similar habits but foliage differs: var. *exauriculata* Fern. has narrow leaves with heart-shaped bases; var. *hastata* (Willd.) A. DC. has leaves with narrow tips and enlarged heart-shaped bases. These varieties are confined to se. Virginia and southward. Only other widespread form is var. *hederaefolia* (Beyrich) Fern., a high-climbing vine with leaves variable in shape, seldom mottled, and sometimes lacking hairy fringe. Stems of all are *4-angled* with *many stout prickles;* bases somewhat scaly. Some twigs may be without prickles. Rootstocks (underground) are thick and knobby. Leaves 2″–5″. Flowers May–June. Fruits black, 1-seeded, Oct.–spring.
  Similar species: This and Common Greenbrier are only greenbriers with angled stems. Leaves in Common Greenbrier lack fringed edges.

COMMON GREENBRIER *Smilax rotundifolia* L.   **p. 300**
  Recognition: Similar to Bullbrier Greenbrier but leaves *broadly rounded* or heart-shaped, less thick, with less prominent veins and *no fringe* on edges; green on both sides. Stems either angled or rounded, with many strong prickles; bases smooth, not scaly. Rootstocks long and slender. Leaves 2″–5″. Flowers April–Aug. Fruits blue-black, with powdery bloom, mostly 2-seeded, Sept.–spring.

Grapes
(and Ampelopsis and Boston Ivy)
(Plates 34 and 35, pp. 302, 304)

The grapes are thornless, dark-stemmed, green-flowered, mostly shreddy-barked, and high-climbing vines that climb by means of tendrils. Leaves are toothed, heart-shaped, especially at base, and often lobed (see Cat Grape, Plate 35). In most species the pith is brown and not continuous (see Winter Grape, Plate 35), interrupted by partitions across twig centers near each leaf scar. Only other native vines climbing by tendrils are Cross Vine (Plate 7), which has opposite compound leaves, Virginia creepers (Plate 30), which have compound leaves and continuous pith, and greenbriers (Plate 33), which have persistent leaf bases, green stems, and usually thorns. Boston Ivy (p. 188) occasionally escapes from cultivation. Its leaves, however, are shiny and sometimes evergreen and tendrils are disk-tipped. Cissus (p. 132) also has 3-parted leaves and white pith. Winter specimens of Muscadine Grape and Ampelopsis can be distinguished from Virginia creepers by unbranched tendrils. Not all grape species can be readily identified in winter condition. The woody pith diaphragms are evident in the drawings of Winter and Cat Grape. Buds short, with 2 scales.

A number of cultivated varieties have been developed from wild grapes. During warm months, sap from grape stems can provide a cool drink, but the plant is destroyed in the process. A 6-foot section from a vine 2 inches in diameter will yield a pint of pure fluid. Upper cut must be made first.

Almost 100 species of songbirds have been recorded eating grapes. Animals utilizing these fruits include ruffed and sharptail grouse, prairie chicken, bobwhite, "Hungarian" partridge, pheasant, wild turkey, mourning dove, striped skunk, gray fox, red fox, coyote, raccoon, cottontail rabbit, red squirrel, and opossum.

Ampelopsis is a related vine with bluish inedible berries.

FOX GRAPE *Vitis labrusca* L.   p. 302
Recognition: Leaf undersides and twigs densely covered with *red-woolly felt.* Leaf uppersides dark green, somewhat leathery. Tendrils or fruit clusters *opposite nearly every leaf.* Though typically with large leaf teeth, 1 variety (*subedentata* Fern., New York to S. Carolina) has few, poorly developed teeth. Leaves 3″–9″. Flowers May–July. Fruits black, purple, or amber, sweet, ½″–1″, Aug.–Oct.
Similar species: Most grapes regularly have tendrils absent from opposite every 3rd leaf. This and (1) New England Grape are only ones consistently to have more tendrils present. (2) Excep-

tional specimens of Dune Grape have more tendrils but leaf hairiness is not red. (3) New England Grape has leaves that soon lose hairiness; older leaves and twigs nearly hairless. (4) Summer Grape and (5) Winter Grape (Plate 35) are woolly but tendrils are absent opposite every 3rd leaf.
Remarks: Concord and other cultivated grapes have been derived from Fox Grape.

NEW ENGLAND GRAPE   Not illus.
Vitis novae-angliae Fern.
  Recognition: Resembles Fox Grape in having tendrils opposite most leaves and red-hairy leaves and twigs, but leaves soon lose hairiness. Older leaves and twigs hairless or with sparse loose patches of cottony hair. Winter Grape (Plate 35) has angled twigs and fewer tendrils. Flowers June–July. Fruits purple-black and shining, bitter, ½″–¾″, Sept. Fertile soils; New England, e. New York, New Jersey, and Pennsylvania.

SUMMER GRAPE   *Vitis aestivalis* Michx.   p. 302
  Recognition: Leaf undersides and twigs *loosely red-woolly*, at least on new growth and on leafstalks and veins. Tendrils lacking opposite every 3rd leaf. Woody partitions across pith ⅛″–³⁄₁₆″ thick. Leaves 2″–9″. Flowers May–July. Fruits black, ³⁄₁₆″–½″, seeds less than ³⁄₁₆″, Sept.–Oct., or longer.
  Similar species: (1) Silverleaf Grape is only a variety of this species; intermediate specimens are found. (2) Fox Grape differs in tendril arrangement. (3) Postoak Grape has thinner pith partitions; (4) Winter Grape (Plate 35) has angled twigs.

SILVERLEAF GRAPE   p. 302
Vitis aestivalis var. *argentifolia* (Munson) Fern.
  Recognition: Classified as a variety of Summer Grape, this form may be quite distinctive. Hairless leaf undersides and often twigs *white with powdery bloom.*
  Similar species: A variety of Postoak Grape is similar but has thinner pith diaphragms and larger fruits and seeds.

POSTOAK GRAPE   *Vitis lincecumii* Buckl.   Not illus.
  Recognition: This south-central species resembles Summer Grape, even to extent of having a hairless, pale-leaved variety (*glauca* Munson) similar to Silverleaf Grape. Red-hairiness on lower surfaces of leaves of typical form is less dense than in Summer Grape. Diaphragms dividing pith are only ¹⁄₁₆″–⅛″ thick. Flowers May–June. Fruits purple-black, ⅜″–1″, seeds more than ³⁄₁₆″, July–Sept. Woods and thickets; s. Indiana, Missouri, and se. Kansas to Mississippi and Texas.

FROST GRAPE   *Vitis vulpina* L.   p. 302
  Recognition: Leaves shiny above, *hairless*, green beneath, and

seldom deeply lobed, longer than broad; teeth broad. Twigs *hairless* or nearly so. Tendrils lacking opposite every 3rd leaf. Diaphragms across pith 1/8"–1/4" thick. Leaves 2"–9". Flowers May–June. Fruits black, shining, sweet, 1/8"–3/8", Sept.–Oct. **Similar species:** Three grapes are high-climbing with hairless twigs and hairless leaves green beneath. This species differs from (1) Riverbank Grape in leaf tooth shape and thicker pith diaphragms; from (2) Cat Grape (Plate 35) in having brown twigs and usually unlobed leaves.

RIVERBANK GRAPE   *Vitis riparia* Michx.   **p. 302**
Recognition: Leaves shiny, green beneath, hairless except for occasional indistinct fringe of fine hairs; often deeply lobed (as in Cat Grape). Leaf tips and teeth somewhat *long-pointed.* Twigs brownish, green, or red, hairless or nearly so. Pith diaphragms woody, only 1/32"–3/32" thick. Tendrils normally absent opposite every 3rd leaf (but see Dune Grape, next). Leaves 2"–9". Flowers May–July. Fruits blue-black, with whitish powder, bitter (may be without powder and sweet in sw. Illinois and ne. Missouri), 5/16"–1/2", Aug.–Sept.
Similar species: Both (1) Frost Grape and (2) Cat Grape (Plate 35) have thicker pith diaphragms. (3) Dune Grape has hairy leaf undersides.

DUNE GRAPE   **Not illus.**
Vitis riparia var. *syrticola* (Fern. & Wieg.) Fern.
Recognition: Like typical Riverbank Grape but with leaf undersides very soft-hairy and tendrils sometimes more numerous. Differs from Fox Grape in that the hairiness is not reddish; from Winter Grape (Plate 35) in lacking ridged twigs. Great Lakes sand dunes; New York to Michigan and Indiana.

SAND GRAPE   *Vitis rupestris* Scheele   **p. 302**
Recognition: A low bushy grape with tendrils *absent,* or present only near the tips of twigs. Leaves shiny, broader than long even though leaf tips may be somewhat long-pointed. One form has much-lobed leaves. Leaves and brown twigs hairless. Pith diaphragms 1/16"–1/8" thick. Leaves 2"–9". Flowers May. Fruits black, with or without powdery surface, sweet, about 3/8", July–Aug.
Similar species: Bush Grape is of similar growth habits but is hairy and more western.

BUSH GRAPE   *Vitis acerifolia* Raf.   **Not illus.**
Recognition: Similar to Sand Grape, but twigs and leaves densely hairy. Flowers May. Fruits July–Aug. Dry places; sw. Missouri and se. Colorado to Texas.

Plate 35
(p. 304)

MUSCADINE GRAPE   *Vitis rotundifolia* Michx.   **p. 304**
  Recognition: Unique among grapes in usually having smooth dark bark marked with small dots, *no woody pith partitions*, and tendrils *not forked*. Twigs crowded with tiny white, often raised dots. Pith *brown;* leaves thick, shiny. Leaves 2″–9″. Flowers June. Fruits purple-black, thick-skinned, sweet, ½″–1″, Sept.–Oct.
  Similar species: See American Ampelopsis.

AMERICAN AMPELOPSIS   *Ampelopsis cordata* Michx. **p. 304**
  Recognition: Similar to Muscadine Grape but with pith *white* and leaves regularly heart-shaped. Leaves more finely toothed and bases not so deeply cut. Plant often bushy, not high-climbing. Tendrils may be scarce or lacking. Leaves 3″–6″. Flowers May–June. Fruits bluish, pea-sized, dry, inedible, Aug.–Nov.
  Similar species: This and the next are the only white-pithed vines with nonforked tendrils.
  Remarks: Sometimes cultivated for colorful fruits, which are eaten by several songbirds and bobwhite.

ASIATIC AMPELOPSIS   **Not illus.**
Ampelopsis brevipedunculata (Maxim.) Trautv.
  Recognition: Similar to American Ampelopsis but with hairy, longer-pointed, 3-lobed leaves. Fruits blue to purple. Escaped from cultivation; New England and Ohio southward.

CAT GRAPE   *Vitis palmata* Vahl   **p. 304**
  Recognition: Leaves hairless, green beneath, somewhat long-pointed, *usually deeply lobed*. Twigs *hairless, generally red*. Woody pith partitions about ³⁄₁₆″ thick. Tendrils absent opposite every 3rd leaf. Leaves 2″–9″. Flowers June–July. Fruits black, without powdery bloom, sweet, ³⁄₁₆″–⁵⁄₁₆″, Oct.
  Similar species: (1) Frost Grape has brown twigs and mostly unlobed leaves; (2) Riverbank Grape has thinner pith partitions (both on Plate 34).

WINTER GRAPE   *Vitis cinerea* Engelm.   **p. 304**
  Recognition: Leaves *gray-hairy* or (less commonly) white hairy on both surfaces, but upper surface becomes hairless. Foliage rarely deeply lobed. Twigs are *ridged and gray-hairy*. Var. *floridana* Munson is red-hairy but occurs north only to e. Virginia and Arkansas. Tendrils absent opposite every 3rd leaf.

Leaves 2″–9″. Flowers June–July. Fruits black, sweet when ripe, ³⁄₁₆″–½″, Sept.–Oct.

Similar species: Typical form is only grape with gray-hairy twigs and leaves. Red-hairy form is distinct from (1) Summer and (2) Postoak Grapes in having angled twigs; from (3) Fox and (4) New England Grapes in twig shape and tendril arrangement (see Plate 34). (5) See also Possum Grape.

POSSUM GRAPE *Vitis baileyana* Munson   **Not illus.**
Recognition: Resembles Winter Grape except that hairiness, especially on leaves, is loose, not close-matted. Fruits ripen earlier. Flowers May–June. Fruits black, sweet, ⅛″–⅜″, Aug.–Oct. Bottomlands; e. Virginia, Kentucky, and Missouri to Alabama and Arkansas.

BOSTON IVY   **Not illus.**
Parthenocissus tricuspidata (Sieb. & Zucc.) Planch.
Recognition: A high-climbing vine often occurring on buildings and trees; occasionally escapes from cultivation. Leaves *shiny,* toothed, *3-lobed,* with heart-shaped bases. Some lower leaves may be divided into 3 leaflets. Distances between leaves very short. Climbs by means of *short disk-tipped* tendrils. Only Virginia Creeper (Plate 30) also has disk-tipped tendrils, but its leaves are 5-parted. See English Ivy (opposite) and Cissus (p. 132). Asiatic origin; local, Massachusetts to Ohio.

Moonseeds
(*Plate 36, p. 306*)

These represent a family mostly tropical in distribution. They are thornless, nonevergreen vines that climb by green twining stems. Leaves are fan-veined, usually lobed. Buds small, hairy. The soft fruits contain single crescent- or cup-shaped seeds.

Moonseeds differ from other twining vines in having *more than 3 bundle scars* per leaf scar. Leaf shapes and unusual seeds are diagnostic.

REDBERRY MOONSEED *Cocculus carolinus* (L.) DC. **p. 306**
Recognition: A scrambling vine, partly evergreen in southern parts of range. Leaves variable; egg-, triangular-, or heart-shaped and may be lobed. Leafstalks under 2″. Leaves and twigs fine-hairy. Leaves 2″–8″. Flowers green, July–Aug. Fruits *red*, pea-sized, with crescent-shaped ridged seeds, Sept.–Oct., or longer.

CUPSEED *Calycocarpum lyoni* (Pursh) Gray   **p. 306**
Recognition: A nearly hairless, high-climbing southern vine.

Leaves large, deeply 3- to 5-*lobed*, bases of leaf blades joined to 2″–6″ leafstalks. Stems stout. Leaves 5″–11″. Flowers greenish, May–June. Fruits black, to 1″, with cuplike seeds, Aug.–Oct.

CANADA MOONSEED *Menispermum canadense* L.   **p. 306**
  Recognition: A nearly hairless scrambling vine with *large shallowly lobed* leaves. Leaf bases *not attached* to 2″–6″ stalks. Stems slender. Leaves 5″–11″. Flowers white, May–July. Fruits black, with whitish powder, size of small grapes, Sept.–Oct.
  Remarks: Fruits probably among those responsible for reports of poisoning by "wild grapes." They should not be eaten.

Miscellaneous Vines
Climbing without Tendrils
(*Plate 37, p. 308*)

False Jessamine, and Silkvine (p. 70), honeysuckles (Plate 13), a few roses (Plate 23), wisterias (Plate 30), moonseeds (Plate 36), and most plants of this plate climb or scramble over other vegetation or objects by twining stems. No tendrils, aerial roots, twining leafstalks, or other climbing accessories occur except in English Ivy.
  False Jessamine, Silkvine, honeysuckles have opposite leaves; roses are thorny; moonseeds have more than 3 bundle scars. Wisterias have compound leaves and long, silky buds.

ENGLISH IVY *Hedera helix* L.   **Not illus.**
  Recognition: The only alternate-leaved vine climbing with *aerial rootlets.* Evergreen with dark green *leathery* leaves, mostly fan-lobed. Common on buildings; escaped to woods, Virginia southward. See Boston Ivy (opposite).

AMERICAN BITTERSWEET *Celastrus scandens* L.   **p. 308**
  Recognition: A tangled or high-climbing vine with egg- to wedge-shaped, somewhat long-pointed, finely wavy-toothed leaves. Buds small, pointed, sharply set *nearly at right angles* to stems. Stems round, hairless, thornless, brown. Leaf scars not raised; bundle scar single. Leaves 2″–5″. Climbs to 60′. Flowers small, green, clustered, May–June. Fruits ornamental clustered orange-colored pods that open to reveal scarlet seed-coverings, Sept.–Dec., or longer.
  Similar species: Fruits distinctive, if present. Strawberry-bushes (Plate 12) have similar fruits; may trail, resembling vines, but have opposite leaves and green twigs. No other vine has buds arranged as in Bittersweet. See Asiatic Bittersweet.

Remarks: Collection of Bittersweet for commercial sale has much reduced or exterminated it in many areas. Fruits eaten by songbirds, ruffed grouse, pheasant, bobwhite, and fox squirrel. Cottontail eats twigs and bark.

ASIATIC BITTERSWEET   Not illus.
Celastrus orbiculatus Thunb.

Recognition: Similar to American Bittersweet but with leaves nearly circular. Escaped from cultivation; New York southward.

SUPPLEJACK   *Berchemia scandens* (Hill) K. Koch   p. 308
Recognition: A southern high-climbing vine, often large. Elliptic leaves have distinctively straight, *parallel side-veins.* Fine leaf teeth may be present or lacking. Leaf scars much raised; bundle scar single. Buds sharp, hug twigs. Leaves 1″–4″. Flowers greenish white, April–June. Fruits blue, single-seeded, July–Oct.

Remarks: Fruits eaten by numerous birds, including wood duck, mallard, bobwhite, and wild turkey.

EUROPEAN MATRIMONY-VINE   p. 308
Lycium halimifolium Mill.

Recognition: A low scrambling vine or upright shrub. Stems *ridged* and usually somewhat *thorny.* Leaves gray-green, narrow or wedge-shaped, not toothed, often in small clusters. Pith solid; stems and buds hairless. Buds have 2–3 scales; bundle scar single. Leaves ½″–2″. Flowers small, greenish purple, June–Sept. Fruits red berries, ⅜″–3⁄16″, Aug.–May.

Similar species: Some greenbriers (Plate 33) conceivably might be confused with this thorny species but they have tendrils and climb high. (1) Scotch Broom (Plate 25) has mostly trifoliate leaves; it is not thorny and twigs are green. (2) See next species.

Remarks: Leaves and young shoots of this European introduction contain an alkaloid reportedly dangerous to sheep and cattle.

CHINESE MATRIMONY-VINE   Not illus.
Lycium chinense Mill.

Recognition: Similar to the European species but less thorny; leaves dark green, wider, and less often clustered. Fruits usually larger. Flowers June–Oct. Whin (p. 295) has more finely lined stems and yellow blossoms. Waste places; Massachusetts and Michigan to Virginia, Louisiana, and Oklahoma.

BITTER NIGHTSHADE   *Solanum dulcamara* L.   p. 308
Recognition: A low scrambling or climbing vine with ridged stems and hollow pith. Leaves *long-pointed* and either *with or without basal lobes.* Typically hairless. The widespread variety

villosissimum Desv. has hairy stems and leaves. Bundle scar single. Leaves 1"–5". Flowers purple, rarely white, May–Sept. Fruits red berries, Aug.–May.
Similar species: Only other twining vines with hollow pith are the opposite-leaved honeysuckles (Plate 13).
Remarks: This relative of the potato, tomato, and eggplant sometimes transmits diseases and insect pests of those plants. Fruits eaten' by birds including ruffed grouse, pheasant, bob-white, and black duck. Stems browsed by cottontail rabbit. Livestock have been poisoned, however, upon eating foliage.

DUTCHMAN'S-PIPE   *Aristolochia durior* Hill   **p. 308**
   Recognition: A high climbing vine with large *hairless heart-shaped* leaves and round green stems. Buds woolly, often in groups above leaf scars; hidden by leafstalks during warm months. Bundle scars 3 per leaf scar. Leaves 4"–10". Flowers long, curved, pipelike, brownish purple, May–June. Fruits dry capsules, 2"–3", Sept.
   Similar species: Clustered woolly buds and large heart-shaped leaves distinguish pipe-vines. Next species is hairy.

WOOLLY PIPE-VINE   *Aristolochia tomentosa* Sims   **p. 308**
   Recognition: Somewhat more southern and western than Dutchman's-pipe. Leaf undersides, twigs, and flowers *hairy;* leaf tips more blunt. Flowers yellow and purple, May–June. Fruits all year.

Miscellaneous Upright Thorny Plants
(Plate 38, p. 310)

The only other thorny or prickly upright woody plants with alternate leaves are the hawthorns (Plate 39), the gooseberries and a currant (Plate 40), which follow this account, and the compound-leaved species given earlier (Plates 23 and 24). The only opposite-leaved thorny plant is the Common Buckthorn (Plate 19). Spur branches, present in all members of this group except Fire-thorn and Devil's-club, are stubby, leaf-scar-crowded offshoots of the older branches. They may bear dense clusters of leaves in summer. Bundle scars are 3 per leaf scar except in Osage-orange.

OSAGE-ORANGE   **pp.** *13,* **310**
Maclura pomifera (Raf.) Schneid.
   Recognition: A medium-sized tree. Leaves egg-shaped, some-what *long-pointed, not toothed.* Strong unbranched thorns at each leaf scar. Sap *milky* (Caution: it causes a rash in some people). Wood *yellow.* Buds nearly ball-shaped; end ones false.

Bundle scars 1 to more than 3. Bark orange-brown, furrowed, tight, fibrous. Spur branches of clustered leaves often present. Leaves 1"–8". Height 50'–60'; diameter 18"–36". Flowers May–June. Fruits green, *wrinkled, grapefruit-sized*, Oct.

Similar species: This species and the bumelias are the only thorny plants with milky sap. Small specimens differ from bumelias in having false end buds and in leaf shape. Barberries have yellow wood but thorns are mostly branched; shrubby, with sap not milky, and fruits are red berries.

Remarks: Once native in northern Texas, se. Oklahoma, and nearby Arkansas, home of Osage Indians, this species was widely planted for living fences before invention of barbed wire. Because of its use in making bows, French name *bois d'arc* (colloquially Bodarc, Bodock) is still heard. Bark yields tannin; boiled wood chips yield yellow dye.

EASTERN BUMELIA *Bumelia lycioides* (L.) Gaertn. f. **p. 310**
 Recognition: A shrub to small tree with sharp thorns at buds. Leaves narrow to elliptic or even parallel-sided or egg-shaped, *without teeth*, tips *short-pointed* or rounded, either hairless or somewhat silky. Spur branches with crowded leaves; leaf scars often present. Sap *milky*. Buds ball-like; true end buds present. Leaf blades 2½"–6". Height to 30'. Flowers small, white, clustered, June–July. Fruits small, cherrylike, black, Sept.–Nov.
 Similar species: (1) See Osage-orange. (2) Small Bumelia is lower, with smaller, more leathery leaves. (3) Woolly Bumelia has hairy leaves.
 Remarks: Frequently used name Buckthorn may be confused with buckthorns of genus *Rhamnus* (Plates 19 and 58).

SMALL BUMELIA *Bumelia smallii* R. B. Clark **Not illus.**
 Recognition: Similar to Eastern Bumelia but shrubbier, with leathery leaves having blades not more than 2½". Sometimes considered merely a variant of Eastern Bumelia. Bottomlands; se. Missouri to Louisiana and e. Texas.

WOOLLY BUMELIA **Not illus.**
Bumelia lanuginosa (Michx.) Pers.
 Recognition: Similar to Eastern Bumelia but wedge-shaped or parallel-sided leaves *rusty-hairy* beneath. Twigs and buds *woolly*. Leaves 1"–4". Height to 50' but usually shrubby. Sandy soils; s. Illinois, centr. Missouri, se. Kansas to n. Florida, Texas, and s. Arizona.

FIRETHORN *Cotoneaster pyracantha* (L.) Spach **p. 310**
 Recognition: A European shrub with narrow, *wavy-edged* leaves that have wedge-shaped bases and rounded tips. Leaves thick, usually evergreen. Spur branches lacking, short thorns *not*

branched, sap not milky. End buds true. Leaves ½″–2″. Height to 10′. Flowers small, white, clustered, May–June. Fruits small, *bright orange*, clustered, usually present all winter.

Similar species: Evergreen wavy-edged leaves and colorful fruits are distinctive. Hawthorns, if evergreen, have much longer thorns, usually sharply toothed leaves, and larger fruits.

Remarks: Fruits regularly eaten by many birds and mammals.

AMERICAN BARBERRY *Berberis canadensis* Mill. **p. 310**
  Recognition: A low shrub whose wedge-shaped leaves are sharply but *widely toothed*. Twigs brown and rough-warty; thorns usually with *2 side branches* as long as central spine. Inner bark and wood *yellow;* spur branches may be present. Sap not milky. Leaves 1½″–3″. Height to 5′. Flowers yellow, May–June. Fruits red, ball-like, Sept.–winter.
  Similar species: (1) Only other native thorny plant with yellow wood is much taller Osage-orange, which has milky sap and unbranched thorns. (2) European Barberry has closer bristle-tipped teeth. (3) Japanese Barberry leaves not toothed.
  Remarks: Although named *canadensis*, does not occur naturally in Canada. An alternate host for the wheat black stem rust.

EUROPEAN BARBERRY *Berberis vulgaris* L. **Not illus.**
  Recognition: Has escaped in some areas. Leaves more *closely bristle-toothed* than in American Barberry. Thorns *branched* like those of American Barberry. Taller, looser arrangement of branches helps in winter to separate this from Japanese species. Twigs *gray*, not roughened by numerous fine warts as in American Barberry. Inner bark and wood yellow. The most susceptible of all barberries to black stem rust of wheat. Leaves ½″–3″. Height to 10′. Flowers yellow, May–June. Fruits red, longer than broad, Aug.–spring. Thickets; Nova Scotia and Minnesota to Delaware and Missouri.
  Remarks: Birds including ruffed grouse, bobwhite, and pheasant eat fruits.

JAPANESE BARBERRY *Berberis thunbergii* DC. **Not illus.**
  Recognition: A low compact oriental shrub with wedge-shaped leaves that are *not toothed*. Twigs *brown*, somewhat ridged; thorns either *unbranched* or with 2 small side branches; inner bark and wood yellow. Only barberry in this area which does not transmit stem rust of grains. See American Barberry. Leaves ½″–1½″. Height to 5′. Flowers yellow, April–May. Fruits red, long or globular, often present through winter. Escaped from cultivation to pastures, open habitats; Nova Scotia and Michigan to N. Carolina and Missouri.
  Remarks: Fruits eaten by many birds, including ruffed grouse, bobwhite, and pheasant.

WILD PLUMS *Prunus* spp. **p. 310**
  Recognition: Though the cherries, also in the genus *Prunus*, are never spiny, the plums are variously thorny or not. Alleghany Plum (p. 240), for example, sometimes has spine-tipped twigs. For upright cherries and such usually thornless plums see Plate 53. Some spines of plums may be simple spikes, but most are short, stiff, bud-bearing branches with sharpened tips. Thorns are generally absent from young twigs. Like other species of *Prunus*, leafstalks of most plums (but see American Plum) bear paired small glands. Sap clear and spur branches often present. Bark often marked with horizontal line-like lenticels. Unlike cherries, the end buds are false in plums. Wild plum fruits are small, ball-shaped, with single large seeds.
  The several plums that regularly bear thorns usually may be separated by the following key, but also see species accounts:

1. Twigs hairless or nearly so:
    2. Leaf scars raised but not hiding any large part of the buds:
        3. Buds red-brown, mostly about ⅛″ long
            AMERICAN PLUM
        3. Buds gray or blackish, mostly ³⁄₁₆″ long
            CANADA PLUM
    2. Leaf scars raised, hiding the lower half of the buds
            CHICKASAW PLUM
1. Twigs velvety-hairy or woolly:
    4. Buds longer than broad:
        5. Leaf teeth rounded   **BULLACE PLUM**
        5. Leaf teeth sharp   **AMERICAN PLUM**
    4. Buds shorter than broad   **SLOE PLUM**

AMERICAN PLUM *Prunus americana* Marsh. **p. 310**
  Recognition: A shrub or small tree with *shaggy bark*. Leaves narrow to wedge-shaped, hairless or nearly so (except in var. *lanata*), somewhat long-pointed, sharply and often doubly toothed. Usually no glands on leafstalks. Twigs typically hairless but var. *lanata* Sudw. (Indiana and Iowa to Tennessee, Arkansas, and Texas) has hairy twigs and leaf undersides. Buds *red-brown*, mostly about ⅛″. Leaf scars not abnormally enlarged. Leaves 1″–5″. Height 15′–30′ (35′); diameter 5″–10″ (14″). Flowers white, 3–5 in clusters, April–June. Fruits red or yellow, ⅞″–1¼″, seed somewhat flattened, Aug.–Oct.
  Similar species: Only thorny plum to have sharp leaf teeth and regularly to lack glands on leafstalks.
  Remarks: Several hundred varieties have been named. Some are cultivated.

CANADA PLUM   *Prunus nigra* Ait.   **Leaf edge illus., p. 310**
 Recognition: Similar to American Plum but leaf teeth *rounded* and *glands* on leafstalks usually present. Twigs hairless; buds *gray* or blackish, about ³⁄₁₆″. Numerous strains known and several cultivated. Leaf scars not abnormally enlarged. Bullace Plum is similar but hairy. Leaves 1″–5″. Height 6′–20′ (25′); diameter 4″–10″ (12″). Flowers white to pink, April–June. Fruits yellow to reddish, slightly elongate, Aug.–Oct. Thickets; Nova Scotia, s. Quebec, s. Ontario, n. Michigan, and s. Manitoba to Virginia, W. Virginia, Ohio, n. Illinois, and Iowa; in mountains to Georgia.

CHICKASAW PLUM   **Not illus.**
Prunus angustifolia Marsh.
 Recognition: A southern shrub or small tree with hairless narrow leaves with fine, gland-tipped, rounded teeth. Toward southwest, leaves become wider and somewhat leathery. Leafstalks bear glands. Twigs hairless, *reddish*. Leaf scars *raised* to such an extent that lower halves of buds are hidden. Leaves 1″–3″. Height to 20′; diameter to 10″. Flowers white, clustered, March–April. Fruits red or yellow, seeds nearly spherical, July–Aug. Thickets; New Jersey, Maryland, Kentucky, s. Illinois, and s. Nebraska to centr. Florida and centr. Texas.

BULLACE PLUM   *Prunus insititia* L.   **Not illus.**
 Recognition: European; similar to Canada Plum but with *velvety* leaf undersides, twigs, and flower and fruit stalks. Leaf bases somewhat wedge-shaped. Buds longer than broad. Sloe Plum has shorter buds, single blossoms. Leaves 2″–4″. Height to 20′. Flowers mostly in pairs, white, over ⅞″ across, April–May. Fruits blue-black, with a bloom, spherical, Aug.–Sept. Escaped from cultivation; local in se. Canada and ne. U.S.

SLOE PLUM   *Prunus spinosa* L.   **Not illus.**
 Recognition: Similar to Bullace Plum but more spiny and with smaller leaves. Buds shorter than broad. Flowers mostly single and only ⅜″–⅝″ across. Flower and fruit stalks hairless. Eurasian; occasionally spreading from cultivation; se. Canada and ne. U.S.

NATIVE CRABAPPLES   *Pyrus* spp.   **p. 310**
 Recognition: The apples differ from the plums in having true end buds, no glands on leafstalks, scaly nonstriped bark, and several-seeded fruits. Some hawthorns (Plate 39) have thorns, leaves, and fruits resembling those of apples but their thorns never bear buds or leaves and their thorns occur on the twigs, not on older wood as in apples (or plums). Spur branches occur in all 3 groups.

Some apples are more regularly spiny than others. These are the ones discussed here. They are the only apples native to our area. The imported crabapples, apples, and pears are less likely to be thorny and are given on Plate 58. Since they may be spiny, however, the text discussion also should be seen in identifying members of the group. Hybrids between species are frequent and usually have intermediate characteristics.

The related mountain-ashes (Plate 27) and chokeberries (Plate 58) are also included in the genus *Pyrus* but are quite distinctive. Identification of the apples and pears, including those on Plate 58 (marked °), may be made as follows:

1. Twigs and leaf undersides usually hairy to woolly:
    2. Leaf teeth rounded; leaves never deeply cut
                                                  DOMESTIC APPLE°
    2. Leaf teeth sharp; leaves on vigorous shoots often deeply toothed or lobed:
        3. Leaf bases rounded:
            4. Northeast area; leaves barely hairy; fruits without grit cells   **CHINESE APPLE°**
            4. Midwest area; leaves densely woolly; fruits without grit cells   **PRAIRIE CRABAPPLE**
            4. Southeast area; leaves often densely woolly; fruits with grit cells   **CHINESE PEAR°**
        3. Leaf bases wedge-shaped; southeast area; a variety of the   **NARROWLEAF CRABAPPLE**
1. Twigs and leaf undersides usually hairless or nearly so:
    5. Leaf teeth rounded; leaves never deeply cut
                                                  DOMESTIC PEAR°
    5. Leaf teeth sharp:
        6. Leaves long-pointed:
            7. Leaves not deeply cut
                                                  SIBERIAN CRABAPPLE°
            7. Leaves on vigorous shoots often deeply toothed or lobed; a variety of **AMERICAN CRABAPPLE**
        6. Leaves not long-pointed, often deeply toothed or lobed:
            8. Leaf bases wedge-shaped, tips blunt; southeastern   **NARROWLEAF CRABAPPLE**
            8. Leaf bases rounded, tips sharp, north-central
                                                  AMERICAN CRABAPPLE

AMERICAN CRABAPPLE *Pyrus coronaria* L.   **p. 310**
Recognition: A thicket-forming shrub or small tree with hairless twigs and leaves. Leaves have *round bases,* sharp tips. Those on vigorous shoots deeply toothed to somewhat lobed. Though usually heart-shaped to triangular, foliage of var. *lancifolia* (Rehd.) Fern. (Pennsylvania and Illinois to w. N. Caro-

lina, Tennessee, and Missouri) is narrowly long-pointed. Buds sharp-pointed. Bark gray, rough, cracked vertically. Leaves 1"–5". Height 15'–30'; diameter 6"–14". Flowers pink or white, highly fragrant, March–May. Fruits yellow-green, 1"–2", bitter, Sept.–Nov.

Similar species: (1) Narrowleaf Crabapple has leaves more elliptic. (2) Prairie Crabapple is woolly.

Remarks: Widely planted for ornament. Fruits used in preserves and vinegar; trunks used as stock on which to graft less hardy cultivated apples.

NARROWLEAF CRABAPPLE   Not illus.
Pyrus angustifolia Ait.

   Recognition: Similar to American Crabapple but with elliptic leaves, leaf bases more wedge-shaped and tapering, and leaf tips usually rather blunt. Leaves tend to be evergreen in some areas, but even where this is not true dead leaves often can be found to assist in winter identification. Fruits 1"–1½", bitter, but used for preserves and cider. Widespread variety *spinosa* (Rehd.) Bailey is quite woolly. Coastal Plain woods and thickets; Maryland to Florida, west to Louisiana; and north in Mississippi Valley to s. Illinois and Arkansas.

PRAIRIE CRABAPPLE   Not illus.
Pyrus ioensis (Wood) Bailey

   Recognition: Midwestern. Similar to American Crabapple but twigs and leaf undersurfaces densely woolly. Flowers April–May. Thickets and open places; Indiana, se. Minnesota, and se. Nebraska to Louisiana and centr. Texas.

DEVIL'S-CLUB   *Oplopanax horridus* (Sm.) Miq.   Not illus.
   Recognition: Related to Hercules-club (Plate 24). Twigs, branches, stems, and leafstalks of this straggling shrub *covered with slender thorns.* Leaves 4"–12" across, fan-lobed, with 3–11 toothed lobes. Leaf veins prickly beneath. Nothing else like it. Flowers July–Aug. Fruits red, Aug.–Oct. Rocky places; from Alaska to w. Ontario, Isle Royale (Michigan), Montana, and California.

Hawthorns
(*Plate 39, p. 312*)

HAWTHORNS   *Crataegus* spp.   p. 312
   Recognition: These plants, distinctive though they are as a group, are virtually indistinguishable as species except by the few botanists who have given the genus special study. Frequent hybridization complicated by great individual variation con-

founds accurate identification. Even the specialists vary greatly in their decisions as to the validity of many forms. The number of species of *Crataegus* in this country has been variously determined as over a thousand and as less than a hundred. In this volume, therefore, no attempt is made to differentiate between the many species. The drawings serve only to indicate major leaf types as an aid to identification of the genus. Thornless hawthorns occasionally are encountered.

In general, the hawthorns are a widespread group of very dense shrubs or small trees with long thorns and smooth or scaly bark. Bundle scars 3. Buds nearly spherical; end buds true. Hawthorn spines are without buds or leaves. The fruits are small, yellow to red, and applelike. They often remain on the plants all winter, providing food for numerous birds and mammals, including bobwhite, partridge, pheasant, ruffed and sharptail grouse, gray fox, cottontail rabbit, and whitetail deer. Hawthorns are greatly preferred for nesting by many songbirds, apparently because of their density. They are important honey plants, but are pests in pastures. Formerly were widely used for fences in England. Many varieties are used in landscaping. The name "haw" comes from the same root as "hedge."

Some crabapples may have long thorns but usually some or all of those thorns carry buds or leaves on them. Plums (Plate 53) have false end buds. Deciduous Holly (Plate 61) sometimes is called Possum-haw but is not thorny and has only 1 bundle scar.

The hawthorns illustrated are: Cockspur (*Crataegus crus-galli* L.), Dotted (*C. punctata* Jacq.), Thicket (*C. pedicellata* Sarg.), Margaret (*C. margaretta* Ashe), Frosted (*C. pruinosa* (Wendl.) K. Koch), Spike (*C. succulenta* Link), and Washington (*C. phaenopyrum* (L. f.) Medic.).

Thorny Currant and Gooseberries
(*Plate 40, p. 314*)

When foliage is present, these shrubs are quite distinctive in possessing 3- to 5-lobed maplelike leaves, which, unlike maples, however, are alternate rather than opposite. Often they are small. In winter this group can be identified by the rather long papery-scaled brown buds, very narrow leaf scars, lines on twigs which descend on either side of leaf scars, and the papery, often shreddy bark. Gooseberry plants bear 1–3 thorns at bases of leafstalks; currants are usually thornless. Fruits of both groups are nearly ball-shaped and often bristly. Gooseberries have flowers and fruits in short clusters of 1–5; currants have lengthened clusters of numerous flowers and fruits. The only other thorny shrubs with maplelike leaves are the coarse Devil's-club (p. 197), with thorny leaf ribs, and a few hawthorns (Plate 39), with ball-shaped buds.

Gooseberries and currants act as intermediate hosts in transmitting blister rust disease from one 5-needled pine to another. They have been instrumental in causing extensive forest damage by this disease and have been eradicated from some areas.

As food, the fleshy berries are enjoyed by nearly all birds and mammals that are not strictly carnivorous. Aside from numerous songbirds, they have been recorded in our area as eaten by mourning dove, spruce, ruffed, and sharptail grouse, bobwhite, pheasant, coyote, skunk, cottontail rabbit, red squirrel, and several chipmunks and ground squirrels. Twigs and bark are eaten by whitetail deer, moose, and porcupine. Jams and jellies are commonly made from wild fruits for human consumption.

Characteristics are not available for naming all species in winter, but the restricted geographic ranges of some are of assistance.

BRISTLY BLACK CURRANT   p. 314
Ribes lacustre (Pers.) Poir.

Recognition: A bristly shrub with *many prickles* as long (about ¼″) as the weak thorns. Leaves nearly hairless; lobes *more deeply cut* than in most other *Ribes*. Twigs red-brown, usually have *foul odor* when broken. Leaves ½″–4″. Height to 5′. Flowers small, green or purple, May–Aug. Fruits purplish, bristly, foul-smelling when broken, hardly edible, July–Sept.

Similar species: (1–3) The next 3 frequently have prickles as well as thorns. However, they have either hairy leaves or long thorns and may have red fruits. (4) See Smooth Gooseberry.

CANADA GOOSEBERRY   Not illus.
Ribes oxyacanthoides L.

Recognition: A low northern species with many weak prickles on the twigs between the slightly longer (⅛″–⁵⁄₁₆″) and stouter thorns. Leaves somewhat glandular-hairy, at least beneath. Rock Gooseberry has longer thorns. A hairy variety of Smooth Gooseberry lacks glands. Leaves ½″–4″. Height to 3′. Flowers purple, May–July. Fruits purplish, smooth, tasty, June–Sept. Woods and wet places; n. Ontario and Yukon to n. Michigan, n. Minnesota, S. Dakota, and Montana.

ROCK GOOSEBERRY *Ribes setosum* Lindl.   Not illus.
Recognition: Bristly like Canada Gooseberry but with thorns, if present, up to ¹³⁄₁₆″. See Smooth Gooseberry. Flowers white. Fruits red or black, sometimes glandular-hairy. Rocky soils; n.-centr. Ontario, Manitoba, and Alberta to n. Michigan, Wisconsin, Nebraska.

PASTURE GOOSEBERRY *Ribes cynosbati* L.   **p. 314**
  Recognition: A variable shrub normally *without bristles* between
  thorns but occasionally with them (var. *atrox* Fern.), especially
  on Manitoulin I., Ontario. Thorns ¼″–⅜″ but rarely (forma
  inerma Rehd.) both thorns and prickles lacking. Leaves *soft-
  hairy* except in a hairless variety—*glabratum* Fern. (Ohio and
  Michigan to w. Virginia and N. Carolina). Twigs *gray to dark
  brown.* Leaves ½″–4″. Height to 5′. Flowers greenish, May–
  June. Fruits red-purple, covered with long spines, sweet, July–
  Sept.
  Similar species: Where prickles are lacking, short thorns, hairy
  leaves, and reddish fruits are distinctive. Hairless and thornless
  varieties difficult to identify unless fruits present. See Smooth
  Gooseberry.

MISSOURI GOOSEBERRY *Ribes missouriense* Nutt.   **p. 314**
  Recognition: A stout-thorned shrub. Thorns ⁵⁄₁₆″–1¹⁄₁₆″, *strong*
  and *usually red.* Leaves hairless or nearly so. Leaves 2″–4″.
  Height to 7′. Flowers whitish, April–May. Fruits black, smooth,
  June–Sept.
  Similar species: No other nonbristly gooseberry has such large
  thorns.

EUROPEAN GOOSEBERRY *Ribes grossularia* L.   **p. 314**
  Recognition: Similar to Missouri Gooseberry but thorns ⅜″–⅝″,
  flowers green, and fruits green or red and hairy or somewhat
  bristly. Escaped from gardens in scattered localities.

ROUNDLEAF GOOSEBERRY   **p. 314**
Ribes rotundifolium Michx.
  Recognition: An eastern short-thorned shrub with somewhat
  round-lobed leaves hairless or less commonly slightly hairy
  beneath. Thorns ¹⁄₁₆″–¼″. Leafstalks have *unbranched* hairs
  (use lens); buds mostly under ⅛″. Leaves ½″–4″. Height to
  3′. Flowers green to purple, April–June. Fruits blackish,
  smooth, tasty, June–Sept.
  Similar species: The next has branched hairs on leafstalks, longer
  buds, more pointed leaf lobes, more northern distribution.

SMOOTH GOOSEBERRY *Ribes hirtellum* Michx.   **p. 314**
  Recognition: A northern short-thorned shrub with rather
  pointed leaf lobes. Thorns ⅛″–⁵⁄₁₆″; new shoots may be prickly
  between thorns. Leaves typically hairless but var. *calcicola*
  Fern. has foliage velvety beneath. Leafstalks have *branched*
  hairs (use lens); buds mostly over ³⁄₁₆″. Leaves ½″–4″. Height
  to 3′. Flowers green to purple, April–July. Fruits blackish,
  smooth, tasty, June–Sept.
  Similar species: When prickles are present between thorns
  this may resemble (1) Bristly Black Currant, (2) Canada, (3)

Rock, and (4) Pasture Gooseberries. Differs from Bristly Black
Currant in that broken twigs and fruits do not have foul odor
and fruits are not bristly. Canada Gooseberry has hairy leaves
and is not easily distinguishable from hairy variety of this species
when it also is prickly, but Smooth Gooseberry lacks glands
mixed in hair of leaves. Rock Gooseberry has longer thorns or
none, and red fruits. (5) Roundleaf Gooseberry has unbranched
hairs on leafstalks. (6) American Black Currant (Plate 41) is
resin-dotted. (7) Golden Currant has hairy twigs (Plate 41).

Thornless Currants
(*Plate 41, p. 316*)

These differ from the *Ribes* of Plate 40 in being thornless. The
group may be identified by the characteristics mentioned on
page 198. Short spur branches with clustered leaves and leaf scars
also may be useful in identification.

AMERICAN BLACK CURRANT   p. 316
Ribes americanum Mill.
   Recognition: An upright shrub with both leaf surfaces, twigs,
   buds, flower ovaries, and fruits *resin-dotted.* These dots appear
   as tiny bright yellow droplets when viewed through hand lens.
   Leaves double-toothed, somewhat hairy beneath. Twigs not
   foul-smelling when broken; marked with *ridges* leading down
   from centers of leaf scars, and hairless or nearly so. Leaves
   ½″–4″. Height to 5′. Flowers yellow or white, clusters drooping, April–June. Fruits black, smooth, resin-dotted, June–Sept.
   Similar species: (1) European and (2) Canadian Black Currants
   also have resin-dotted foliage but these dots are lacking on upper
   leaf surface. Their twigs are not ridged. (3) Smooth Gooseberry
   (Plate 40) in thornless condition lacks resin-dots.

EUROPEAN BLACK CURRANT   *Ribes nigrum* L.   p. 316
   Recognition: Like American Black Currant but resin-dots *absent*
   from *upper* leaf surface and fewer on twigs and buds. Broken
   twigs have *strong unpleasant odor.* No lines from leaf scars.
   Twigs somewhat hairy. Leaves ½″–4″. Height to 5′. Flowers
   yellow, white, or purplish, clusters drooping.
   Similar species: See next species.

CANADIAN BLACK CURRANT   Not illus.
Ribes hudsonianum Richards.
   Recognition: Like European Black Currant but more northern
   and western. Flowers always white. Flower and fruit clusters
   more or less upright. Leaves ½″–6″. Height to 3′. Flowers

May–July. Fruits July–Aug. Wet places; n. Quebec and Alaska to Michigan, ne. Iowa, s. Manitoba, Saskatchewan, Wyoming, Utah, and Oregon.

GOLDEN CURRANT *Ribes odoratum* Wendland f.   **p. 316**
Recognition: A rather tall western currant *without* resin-dots. Leaves *rarely* heart-shaped at base; either hairy or hairless beneath. Twigs *hairy* without foul odor when broken. Leaves ½″–4″. Height to 10′. Flowers *golden yellow*, spicy-scented, April–June. Fruits *black*, rarely yellow, smooth, June–Aug.
Similar species: Only 2 currants are thornless, upright, and lack resin-dots: this and Garden Red Currant. Differs from next in having hairy twigs, yellow flowers, and nonred fruits.

GARDEN RED CURRANT *Ribes sativum* Syme   **p. 316**
Recognition: An upright or sometimes somewhat reclining shrub *without* resin-dots; leaves *usually* heart-shaped at base, not deeply lobed, either hairy or hairless beneath. Twigs *hairless*, without foul odor when broken. Leaves ½″–4″. Height to 5′. Flowers *yellow-green*, not spicy-scented, May. Fruits red, smooth, juicy, June–July.
Similar species: (1) See Golden Currant. (2) Swamp Red Currant has rooting branches and small fruits.

SKUNK CURRANT *Ribes glandulosum* Grauer   **p. 316**
Recognition: A low spreading or sprawling shrub with all parts giving off a *skunklike odor* when crushed. Leaves rather deeply divided with 5–7 *lobes*, double-toothed and hairless. Twigs pale brown, hairless; buds green or purplish. Leaves ½″–4″. Height to 6′. Flowers white or pink, May–Aug. Fruits red, sticky-bristly, June–Sept.
Similar species: (1) Swamp Red Currant also is a straggling swamp currant but lacks foul odor and has hairy leaves averaging fewer lobes, gray-brown buds, and smooth fruits. (2) Garden Red Currant occurs on drier soils and lacks skunky odor.

SWAMP RED CURRANT *Ribes triste* Pall.   **p. 316**
Recognition: A straggly shrub with branches often along ground and taking root. Leaves 3- to 5-*lobed*, double-toothed, *usually hairy* beneath, varying from white-woolly to hairless. Twigs grayish and hairless; buds brownish. Leaves ½″–6″. Height to 3′. Flowers gray to purplish, April–July. Fruits red, smooth, small, hard, June–Aug.
Similar species: (1) Skunk Currant is foul-smelling. (2) Garden Red Currant occasionally not upright but its branches do not take root, fruits are large and juicy, and it occurs in fields, openings.

Miscellaneous Plants with Fan-lobed Leaves

(*Plate 42, p. 318*)

The mulberries and Sassafras (Plate 43) possess leaves frequently deeply lobed, but they also usually carry some unlobed foliage. White Poplar (Plate 44) has leaves rarely lobed but white-woolly. Sand and Bush Grapes (Plate 34) have lobed leaves and may be bushy, but they usually look somewhat vinelike and their stem pith is divided by partitions near the places of leaf attachment. These species, most currants (Plate 41), and the following few plants are the only alternate-leaved trees and shrubs that are thornless and possess leaves fan-lobed. The species of this plate lack the long lines descending from leaf scars which are present in the currants. Maples (Plate 22) and some viburnums (Plates 20 and 21) have fan-lobed leaves but these are opposite, not alternate.

TULIP-TREE *Liriodendron tulipifera* L. **pp. 7, 318**
  Recognition: A straight tall tree with peculiar *notched-tip, 4-pointed* hairless leaves. Pairs of large leafy stipules attach to twigs and enclose buds. Twigs hairless with *completely encircling lines* (stipule scars) at leaf scars. Pith chambered. Only 2 bud scales cover each end bud; side buds small or indistinct. Crushed buds and leaves spicy-aromatic; bundle scars more than 3. Bark light gray, *often whitened* in grooves and in patches on younger bark. Leaves 6″–10″. Height 50′–100′ (190′); diameter 2′–6′ (10′). Flowers large, *tuliplike*, orange and green, May–June. Fruits slim, winged, whitish, 1″–2″, clustered upright in conelike structure about 3″ long, Sept.–Nov., or longer; often central stalks of cones remain throughout winter and are evident on higher limbs.
  Similar species: None; distinctive at all seasons.
  Remarks: Tallest and in many ways handsomest eastern forest tree. Second only to Sycamore in trunk diameter. Wood straight-grained, fine, soft, resistant to splitting and easily worked. Used for furniture, interiors, shingles, boats, implements, boxes, toys, pulp, and fuel. Indians made trunks into dugout canoes. Seeds eaten by squirrels and songbirds. Though widely known as Yellow Poplar and Tulip Poplar, this relative of magnolias (Plate 49) is not closely related to true poplars (Plate 44).

SWEETGUM *Liquidambar styraciflua* L. **pp. 13, 318**
  Recognition: A tall tree with peculiar *star-shaped*, toothed

hairless leaves. Leaves may be 5- or 7-*lobed;* pleasantly fragrant when crushed. Twigs not ringed; branchlets often corky-
winged. Stubby "spur" branches densely covered by leaf
scars or crowded leaves. Bud scales numerous and hairy-fringed;
bundle scars 3; pith continuous. Mature bark grayish, regularly
grooved. Leaves 5″–8″. Height 50′–120′ (140′); diameter 3′–4′
(5′). Flowers in spherical heads, April–May. Fruits in brown,
dry, somewhat *prickly, long-stemmed, hanging balls,* Sept.–Nov.,
or longer.

Similar species: None in summer. In winter some elm twigs
may have corky wings present but those species have false end
buds and their bud scales have dark borders without a hairy
fringe.

Remarks: Both common and scientific names allude to the sap
that exudes from wounds. Hardened clumps of this gum are
chewed by some people. Because Sweetgum veneer takes a
high polish, it is widely used for furniture. Lumber also used
for interiors, woodenware, boats, toys, boxes, and fuel. Seeds
eaten by songbirds, bobwhite, wild turkey, chipmunks, and gray
squirrel.

SYCAMORE   *Platanus occidentalis* L.   pp. *10,* **318**
Recognition: A very large lowland tree with distinctive mottled
brown *bark* that flakes off in jigsaw-puzzle-like pieces, exposing
yellowish and whitish underbark. Leaves nearly hairless, 3- *to*
5-*lobed,* edged with large teeth. Leafstalk bases hollow, covering buds; leaf scars *surround* buds. Single saucerlike, leafy,
toothed stipules *clasp and encircle twigs* at points of leaf attachment; stipule scars ring winter twigs. Buds covered by a
single scale; end buds false. Bundle scars many. Leaves 6″–10″.
Height 50′–130′ (175′); diameter 3′–8′ (14′). Flowers small, in
globose heads, April–June. Fruits small and hairy, in tight,
brown, long-stalked hanging balls ¾″–1½″ in diameter, Oct.,
often through winter.

Similar species: Old World Sycamores, often planted in our
cities, are called Plane-trees. They usually have 2 or more fruit
"balls" per stalk rather than 1 and have more yellowish underbark.

Remarks: Tulip-tree occasionally may be taller, but Sycamore
is generally conceded to be the most massive tree of eastern
U.S. Attains greatest size in Ohio and Mississippi river basins,
but, unlike Sequoias and Redwoods of California, is old at
500–600 years. Hard coarse-grained wood used for boxes,
barrels, butchers' blocks, cabinetwork, and furniture. Indians
used trunks for dugouts. One such canoe reported to have been
65′ long and to have weighed 9000 pounds. Twigs eaten by
deer and muskrats. Cavities sought for nests and shelter by
wood duck, opposum, and raccoon.

ROSE-OF-SHARON *Hibiscus syriacus* L. **p. 318**
Recognition: Shrub with *3-lobed, round-toothed* leaves hairy beneath. Twigs often somewhat hairy, with tips expanded. Buds very small, white-hairy, clustered toward twig tips. End buds true; bundle scars more than 3. Tiny pointed stipules flank bases of leafstalks. Leaves 2″–6″. Height to 18′. Flowers large, hollyhocklike, pink, July–Sept.
Similar species: Ninebark has visible buds, twig tips not expanded, and shreddy older bark.

FLOWERING RASPBERRY *Rubus odoratus* L. **p. 318**
Recognition: A thornless rambling shrub. Leaves *maplelike,* but alternate, 3- to 5-lobed, toothed, varying from nearly hairless to velvety-hairy. Leaves in autumn break off above leaf bases, which remain on twig. No bundle scars evident unless leaf base is sharply cut across, whereupon 3 bundle scars can be discerned. Twigs usually quite hairy but occasionally nearly hairless. Hairs on leaves, twigs, and flowers often *clammy-tipped* (use lens). Twig tips usually wither back in winter; no end buds apparent. Older bark papery. Leaves 4″–15″. Height to 5′. Flowers *rose-purple,* rarely white, 1″–2″, June–Sept. Fruits red, rather *dry* and tasteless, July–Sept.
Similar species: Thimbleberry is more western, has white flowers. Only other shrubs with leaves distinctly maplelike but alternate are currants and gooseberries (Plates 40 and 41), which have obvious buds, less sharp leaf teeth, and often bear thorns. In winter no other shrubs, except prickly brambles (Plate 23), have persistent leaf bases without readily evident bundle scars.
Remarks: Fruits are eaten by great variety of wild animals.

THIMBLEBERRY *Rubus parviflorus* Nutt. **Not illus.**
Recognition: Similar to Flowering Raspberry but more western and with white blossoms. Twigs and flower parts are rarely clammy. Fruits *juicy,* used in making jelly, but not particularly tasty raw. Woods and thickets; w. Ontario, n. Michigan, Minnesota, sw. S. Dakota, and s. Alaska to Mexico, Arizona, and California.

NINEBARK *Physocarpus opulifolius* (L.) Maxim. **p. 318**
Recognition: A shrub with *3-lobed,* round-toothed, hairless leaves. Twigs hairless; buds many-scaled. Bundle scars 3–5; leaf scar distinctly raised, with 3 descending lines. Bark of older branches *papery* and shreddy. Leaves 1″–5″. Height to 10′. Flowers small, white, in umbrellalike clusters, May–July. Fruits small dry bladders, Sept.–often through winter.
Similar species: Twigs and papery bark of some currants (Plate 41) similar in winter but their leaf scars more narrow,

less raised, and mostly without a 3rd center line descending from the leaf scars. Currant fruits, furthermore, are fleshy. See Rose-of-Sharon (p. 205).

Plants with Leaves Fan-lobed or Fan-veined

(*Plate 43, p. 320*)

These plants have leaves that are either lobed or not. Usually, when in leaf both lobed and unlobed foliage is present at the same time. When unlobed, the leaves generally are heart-shaped. All these species have distinctly fan-veined leaves, with 3–5 main veins meeting near the ends of the leafstalks. The number of bundle scars per leaf scar varies by species.

PAPER-MULBERRY   **p. 320**
Broussonetia papyrifera (L.) Vent.
   Recognition: A medium-sized Asiatic tree with *sandpaper-textured* leaves and twigs. Leaves fine-toothed, varying from heart-shaped to deeply and intricately lobed, "sandpapery" above and velvety below. Twigs *rough-hairy;* buds have only 2–3 visible scales. Sap *milky* (not always evident in winter). Bundle scars more than 3 per leaf scar. Pith blocked by a woody partition near each bud. End buds false. Bark a *yellow-brown* smooth network of fine ridges. Leaves 4"–11". Height to 50'; diameter to 4'. Flowers April–May. Fruits red, fleshy, barely edible, Sept.
   Similar species: No other plant has such rough leaves and twigs.
   Remarks: Fibrous inner bark, especially of roots, can be twisted into improvised ropes and lines in this and next several species.

RED MULBERRY   *Morus rubra* L.   **p. 320**
   Recognition: A native tree whose fine-toothed leaves are some-what *"sandpapery"* above and *hairy* beneath. Foliage often lobed. Twigs *hairless* or slightly hairy. Buds have 5–6 visible scales, greenish brown with darker scale borders; end buds false. Sap of twigs and leafstalks *milky.* Bundle scars more than 3 per leaf scar. Pith continuous. Trunk bark *red-brown* with smooth ridges. Leaves 3"–10". Height 30'–60' (80'); diameter 1'–3' (4'). Flowers April–June. Fruits red-black, blackberrylike, tasty, June–July.
   Similar species: White Mulberry is quite similar in winter but may be separated by its red-brown buds and yellow-brown bark.
   Remarks: Delicious fruits eaten by squirrels and numerous song and game birds, as well as by humans.

WHITE MULBERRY   *Morus alba* L.   **p. 320**
Recognition: An Asiatic tree similar to Red Mulberry but leaves *hairless;* buds *red-brown,* mostly without darker scale borders; bark *yellow-brown.* Fruits *whitish,* rather tasteless.
Remarks: Introduced by the British before the Revolution in an unsuccessful attempt to establish a silkworm industry.

BASSWOODS   *Tilia* spp.   **p. 320**
Recognition: The basswoods, or lindens, make up a small but complex group of trees. As a genus, characterized by more or less *heart-shaped, fine-toothed* leaves with *uneven* bases. Buds green to bright red and have only 2–3 visible bud scales. End buds false; bundle scars more than 3 per leaf scar. Pith continuous and sap clear. Bark dark and shallowly grooved when mature but often smooth grayish on the upper parts. Leaves 5″–10″. Height 50′–80′ (125′); diameter 2′–3′ (4′). Flowers yellow, fragrant, June–Aug. Fruits small nutlets clustered beneath large leafy wings that act as spinning parachutes upon ripening, Aug.–Oct.

The species of *Tilia* are difficult to separate. Fernald (*Gray's Manual of Botany,* 8th ed.) states that "the genus demands careful restudy." He provides, however, a tentative basis for identification, from which the following key is derived. In addition to these species, occasionally European and Asiatic species escape from cultivation.

1. Grown leaves hairless:
    2. Flower stalks hairless; New Brunswick and s. Manitoba to Florida and Texas.   **AMERICAN BASSWOOD** *T. americana* L.
    2. Flower stalks hairy; Coastal Plain, se. Virginia to Florida, west to Texas and north in the Mississippi Valley to Missouri and e. Oklahoma.   **FLORIDA BASSWOOD** *T. floridana* (V. Engler) Small
1. Grown leaves hairy beneath:
    3. Leaf undersides green, hairs loose; sw. Quebec and Minnesota to N. Carolina, s. Illinois, and Missouri.   **HOARY BASSWOOD** *T. neglecta* Spach
    3. Leaf undersides white-velvety; New York, s. Illinois, and e. Missouri to Alabama.   **WHITE BASSWOOD** *T. heterophylla* Vent.

Similar species: In winter, the Chestnut (Plate 57) sometimes has more than 3 bundle scars per leaf scar and 2–3 bud scales per bud. Nowadays, it rarely reaches tree size and the buds are brown and the pith is irregular rather than round in cross section. Occurs typically on dry rather than moist sites.

Where found: The several basswoods occur mostly in moist woods, New Brunswick, s. Quebec, and Manitoba to Florida and Texas.

Remarks: As with the mulberries, inner bark, especially of roots, is tough and fibrous and can be twisted into cords, mats, and lines. Buds and fruits eaten by ruffed grouse, prairie chickens, quails, squirrels, and chipmunks; twigs eaten by deer and cottontails. Important honey plants.

SASSAFRAS   *Sassafras albidum* (Nutt.) Nees   **pp.** *13*, **320**

Recognition: A medium-sized to large tree. Leaves untoothed, lobed or not, in *3 patterns* (3 "fingers," a "thumb and mitten" outline, or smooth egg-shape), usually all present. Leaves hairless to velvety-hairy beneath. Twigs *green*, often *branched*, sometimes hairy. Only 1 bundle scar per leaf scar; true end buds present. Crushed leaves, twigs, and bark *spicy-fragrant*. Mature bark *red-brown* and furrowed. Leaves 2″–9″. Height 10′–50′ (90′); diameter 2″–12″ (6′). Flowers greenish yellow, April–June. Fruits blue, fleshy, 1-seeded, Aug.–Oct.

Similar species: Green forked twigs, peculiar leaf outlines, and aromatic odor distinctive. (1) Only other spicy-scented species with 1 bundle scar is Pondspice (Plate 68), which has unbranched twigs, a southern range, and occurs in swamps. (2) Spicebush (Plate 59) has a similar odor but has unbranched brownish twigs and 3 bundle scars.

Remarks: The durable coarse lumber was once used for barrels, buckets, posts, small boats, dugout canoes, and fuel. A pleasant tea may be made by boiling pieces of outer bark of roots. Sassafras oil used in some soaps; a bark extract can be used to dye wool orange. Fruits eaten by songbirds, bobwhite, wild turkey, and black bear. Twigs browsed by marsh and cottontail rabbits and whitetail deer.

REDBUD   *Cercis canadensis* L.   **p. 320**

Recognition: A small tree with *showy reddish* springtime flowers that appear before the leaves. Leaves smoothly *heart-shaped*, hairless, or slightly hairy beneath. Twigs hairless; buds mostly more than 1 per leaf scar, covered by a number of scales. Bundle scars 3 per leaf scar; end buds false. Most leaf scars fringed with hairs at top, with 2 or sometimes 3 lines descending from them on twigs. Bark dark with fine grooves. Leaves 2″–6″. Height 40′–50′; diameter 10″–12″. Flowers *red-purple* (rarely white), in showy clusters, March–May. Fruits dry pods, July–Aug., or longer.

Similar species: Leaves distinctive. In winter, combination of 3 bundle scars, raised and fringed leaf scars, false end buds,

and buds with many scales separates it from other species.
Remarks: Blossoms, not buds, reddish. Flowers sometimes eaten
in salads; red roots yield a dye. Wood of commercial value
in some areas. Though a member of the pea family, Redbud exceptional in not growing nitrogen-fixing root nodules.
Only bobwhite and a few songbirds are known to eat the
seeds.

AMERICAN HACKBERRY   *Celtis occidentalis* L.   **p. 320**
Recognition: A small to large tree with long-pointed, coarse-
toothed leaves; bases mostly uneven. Typically, foliage is
rough-hairy above but is smooth in 2 widespread varieties,
pumila (Pursh) Gray and *canina* (Raf.) Sarg. Twigs hairless; *pith
usually chambered* throughout, or only near the leaf scars. Bud
scales hairy; end buds false. Bundle scars 3 (rarely more). Bark
basically light gray, rather smooth, but becomes covered with
dark warty knobs and ridges. Leaves 3″–7″. Height 20′–70′
(100′); diameter 1′–3′ (4′). Flowers greenish, April–May. Fruits
spherical, ⁵⁄₁₆″–⁷⁄₁₆″, 1-seeded, dry, Oct.–Nov., or longer.
Similar species: Other hackberries have leaves toothed only
slightly, if at all; bud scales barely hairy; fruits smaller. All 3
species are highly variable and, furthermore, may hybridize.
Whether all are valid species even seems in doubt. (1) Sour-gum
and (2) Tupelo (Plate 59) have similar winter twigs but have
true end buds and fleshy fruits.
Remarks: Wood similar to ash; of commercial value. Fruits
("sugarberries") eaten by numerous birds, including bobwhite,
lesser prairie chicken, sharptail grouse, pheasant, and wild
turkey.

UPLAND HACKBERRY   *Celtis tenuifolia* Nutt.   **Not illus.**
Recognition: A smaller upland species. Leaves on fruiting twigs
not toothed and ½ to ¾ as broad as long. *Not* usually long-
pointed; may be sandpapery or not. Fruits ³⁄₁₆″–⁵⁄₁₆″, Sept.–Oct.
Height to 25′. Dry situations; Pennsylvania, Indiana, Missouri,
and e. Kansas to n. Florida, Louisiana, and Oklahoma.

LOWLAND HACKBERRY   *Celtis laevigata* Willd.   **Not illus.**
Recognition: Like the last but leaves *narrower*, either toothed
or not and often with very long-pointed tips. Leaves *less than
½ as broad as long*. A taller tree of *lowlands* (to 100′). Fruits
³⁄₁₆″–⁵⁄₁₆″, Oct.–Nov. Mostly Coastal Plain bottomlands; se.
Virginia to s. Florida, west to Texas, and north in Mississippi
Valley to centr. Kentucky, s. Indiana, s. Illinois, s. Kansas, and
w. Oklahoma.

NEW JERSEY TEA   *Ceanothus americanus* L.   **p. 320**
Recognition: A low shrub. Leaves egg-shaped to triangular,
sharp-tipped, toothed, typically smooth above and somewhat

velvety beneath. One variety (*pitcheri* T. & G.) has blunt-tipped leaves, woolly above and velvety beneath. Twigs and slender buds somewhat hairy; bundle scar single (rarely 3). Sometimes twigs are branched. Leaves 2″–4″. Height to 4′. Flowers white in dense heads, May–Sept. Fruits 3-lobed dry capsules in clusters, *mostly in angles* of leaves, Sept.–Nov., saucerlike capsule bases often present longer.

Similar species: The fruit remnants usually will identify the genus in absence of fan-veined leaves. Redroot has blunt-tipped leaves and flower and fruit heads at ends of branches.

Remarks: One of few nonlegumes to grow nitrogen-fixing nodules on roots. Leaves used for tea during American Revolution. A few birds, including bobwhite and wild turkey, eat fruits.

REDROOT   *Ceanothus ovatus* Desf.   **Leaf illus. p. 320**
Recognition: Similar to New Jersey Tea but leaves smaller, *blunt-tipped.* Flowers and fruits borne at *tips* of branches. Leaves 1″–2½″. Flowers April–July. Dry soils; w. Maine, w. Quebec, and Manitoba to w. Georgia and Texas.

WILD-LILAC   *Ceanothus sanguineus* Pursh   **Not illus.**
Recognition: A larger western shrub reported from our area only on Keewenaw Peninsula of northern Michigan. Not a true lilac. Leaves more or less egg-shaped, rounded at tips, wavy-toothed, and sometimes hairy beneath. Flowers and fruits occur on older wood, below twigs and foliage of current year, in contrast to preceding 2 *Ceanothus* species, which bear flowers on the current season's growth. Height to 14′. Flowers white, May–June. Upper Peninsula of Michigan, sw. S. Dakota, and from Montana and s. British Columbia to n. California.

Poplars
(*Plate 44, p. 322*)

The poplars, aspens, and cottonwoods are all members of the same genus. The leaves are mostly toothed and somewhat triangular, with 3–5 main veins meeting near the leaf base. The leafstalks of all poplars are unusually long; the drawings do not show the entire stalks. In some species the leafstalks are flattened and the leaves flutter even in a slight breeze. Poplar buds are unique among plants with 3 bundle scars in that the lowermost bud scale of side buds is always in the outside position directly above the leaf scar. In other plants the lowermost bud scales are lateral. The true end buds may have more scales than the side buds. The bark of most species is distinctively smooth and green-ish white when young and dark-furrowed when older. The twigs are often sharply angled. Fruits of poplars are in long, clustered, caterpillarlike catkins, which often release "cottony" seeds. The sexes are separate in poplars. Male plants of White Poplar, Gray Poplar, and Balm-of-Gilead are unknown in our area.

Distributed widely in the Northern Hemisphere, trees of the poplar group may form extensive forests on barren, burned, or cleared areas. Rapid-growing, short-lived species, they are of most value for paper pulp, though some of the soft lumber is used in construction work and in the manufacture of boxes and wooden-ware. Some kinds are of value as ornamentals and windbreaks. Seeds, buds, and twigs are important foods of numerous birds and mammals, including ruffed, spruce, and sharptail grouse, prairie chicken, whitetail deer, moose, beaver, porcupine, snowshoe hare, cottontail rabbit, and black bear.

WHITE POPLAR *Populus alba* L. **p. 322**
Recognition: European. A tall tree with *white-woolly* leaves, twigs, and buds. Leaves somewhat leathery, with a few large blunt teeth (or shallow lobes). Leafstalks round. Bark smooth and whitish above, often thick and dark at base. Spreads by means of sucker shoots. Leaves 2″–6″. Height 60′–80′ (100′); diameter 2′–3′ (4′).
Similar species: No other tree is as silvery white in all aspects. (1) Gray Poplar has gray-hairy, sharply toothed leaves. (2) Bigtooth Aspen has wide-toothed leaves.

GRAY POPLAR *Populus canescens* (Ait.) Sm. **Not illus.**
Recognition: Similar to White Poplar but leaf undersurfaces and twigs gray-hairy. Leaves never lobed, but rather sharply toothed. A European tree that has spread from cultivation; New England and Minnesota southward.

BIGTOOTH ASPEN *Populus grandidentata* Michx. **p. 322**
Recognition: A small to medium-sized tree with 5–15 pairs of *large* leaf teeth *and flattened* leafstalks. Leaves white-woolly beneath when young. Twigs hairless or slightly gray-silky; buds decidedly gray-hairy. Bark mostly *smooth yellow-green.* Leaves 2″–6″. Height 30′–40′ (80′); diameter 1′–2′.
Similar species: (1) White Poplar has distinctively white-hairy leaves, twigs, and buds. (2) Quaking Aspen is similar in general aspect but has fine-toothed leaves, hairless buds, and often more whitish mature bark.

COMMON COTTONWOOD **pp. 5, 322**
Populus deltoides Marsh.
Recognition: A tall tree with *coarse-toothed* leaves which have 2–3 small but obvious *glands* (use lens) at top of *flattened*

leafstalks. Twigs usually hairless, yellowish, sometimes 4-angled on vigorous shoots. End buds ⅝″–1″; quite *gummy*. They have 6–7 scales and are not spicy-fragrant when crushed. Side buds usually hug twig. Bark smooth, yellow-green when young but on mature trees dark and ridged. Leaves 2″–3″. Height 40′–80′ (100′); diameter 1′–2′ (3½′).

Similar species: Of the 4 poplars with flattened leafstalks, only this has glands on stalks. In winter large gummy end buds when crushed lack the firlike fragrance of the more northern (1) Balsam Poplar and (2) Balm-of-Gilead. End buds of Common Cottonwood also have more than 5 scales. Leaf teeth larger and twigs more yellowish than in (3) Quaking Aspen.

LOMBARDY POPLAR   pp. *6*, 322
Populus nigra var. *italica* Muenchh.

Recognition: An imported tall, thin, *steeplelike* tree much used for windbreaks. Leaves *fine-toothed;* flattened leafstalks *lack* glands. Twigs hairless, yellowish; end buds under ⅜″, not gummy; side buds not usually pressed against twigs. Bark furrowed, rather dark. Leaves 2″–8″. Height 30′–70′ (100′); diameter 1′–2′ (3′).

Similar species: (1) Typical Black Poplar (*P. nigra* L.) may occur locally; lacks peculiar thin spirelike shape but has same leaf, twig, and bud characteristics as var. *italica.* In *P. nigra* form, it is unlike (2) Quaking Aspen in having dark bark, yellow twigs, and much more sharply triangular or even heart-shaped leaves.

QUAKING ASPEN   *Populus tremuloides* Michx.   pp. *10*, 322

Recognition: A medium-sized tree; leaves with flattened leafstalks and edged with 20–40 pairs of *fine teeth.* Twigs hairless and dark brown; end buds shiny, ¼″–⅜″. Mature bark mostly *smooth, chalk-white to yellow-green.* Var. *magnifica* Vict. has leathery leaves and brittle twigs swollen at leaf scars. Leaves 2″–6″, appearing earlier in spring than leaves of Bigtooth Aspen. Height 20′–50′ (75′); diameter 1′–2′ (3′).

Similar species: (1) Bigtooth Aspen has fewer and larger leaf teeth, hairy buds, and more yellowish bark. (2) Lombardy (and its parent form, the Black) Poplar has dark bark, yellow twigs, and more heart-shaped or triangular leaves. (3) See also Common Cottonwood (p. 211).

SWAMP COTTONWOOD   *Populus heterophylla* L.   p. 322

Recognition: A southern tree with *fine-toothed* leaves and *rounded* leafstalks. Leaves and dark brown twigs *white-woolly* or hairless; end buds ⅜″–⅝″, hairless or white-hairy toward base and *somewhat gummy.* Bark dark and deeply ridged. Leaves 2″–8″. Height 40′–60′ (90′); diameter 1′–2′ (3′).

Similar species: Only poplar with end buds gummy yet under ⅝″.

BALSAM POPLAR *Populus balsamifera* L. **p. 322**
Recognition: A northern tree with *fine-toothed* leaves and *rounded* (or occasionally slightly flattened) leafstalks. Leaves usually hairless but may be slightly hairy on veins beneath. Twigs dark brown and hairless. End buds *more than* ⅝″, *gummy, spicy-fragrant* when crushed; 5 bud scales. Side buds have 2 visible scales. Mature bark dark and grooved; gray-green and smooth on younger parts. Leaves 3″–8″. Height 30′–80′ (100′); diameter 1′–3′ (6′).
Similar species: (1) Balm-of-Gilead is more hairy and has 3 exposed scales on the side buds. See (2) Common and (3) Swamp Cottonwoods.
Remarks: Frequently called Balm-of-Gilead (see also next species).

BALM-OF-GILEAD *Populus gileadensis* Rouleau **p. 322**
Recognition: A large sterile tree that may be only a variety of Balsam Poplar, but leaf undersides, leafstalks, and twigs somewhat *hairy.* Side buds have 3 visible scales. Leaves 3″–8″. Height 50′–70′ (80′); diameter 1′–3′ (6′). Reproduces by sprouts.

Oaks (1), (2), (3), and (4)
(Plates 45–48, pp. 324–330)

The oaks are usually tall trees and have great and diversified values. Group identification points are: true end buds clustered at tips of twigs, more than 3 bundle scars per leaf scar, and presence of acorns. Only a very few other plants have clustered end buds (principally Rose-of-Sharon, Plate 42, Corkwood, Plate 59, some cherries, Plate 53, and azaleas, Plate 64) and they lack the other characteristics. Male flowers appear in May and early June as slender drooping clusters of long catkins. Female blossoms are inconspicuous.

The genus *Quercus* is generally divided into 2 sections: the red (or black) oaks and the white oaks. Red oaks differ from the white in that (1) leaf lobes or teeth have hairlike bristle-tips, (2) broken brown acorn shells (not the cups) have hairy inner surfaces, and (3) acorns require 2 years to mature, so both tiny 1st-year and larger 2nd-year acorns usually are present on mature trees in summer. White oaks have leaves that lack bristle-tips and have hairless inner acorn shells and acorns that mature in 1 year. Acorns of red oaks are yellow, bitter, and usually inedible; those of some white oaks are white and relatively sweet and edible. The barks of many red oaks are dark in color; those of white oaks are mostly light. Within the white oak group, however, the Chestnut Oaks are a distinctive subdivision. They have wavy-edged or toothed leaves, mostly inedible acorns, and often dark, frequently deeply ridged barks. Oaks (1), (3), and Live Oak of (4) are white oaks. The others are of the red oak subdivision.

To provide for more simple identification, the oaks are here divided into groups primarily according to whether the leaves are lobed or not. Though variable, most oaks can be identified in season by their leaf shapes alone, as shown on the plates. Exceptions are the Scarlet-Pin Oak group and apparent hybrids between species. Additional foliage data are given beyond for each species. As an aid to winter identification, the drawings, with their natural-size sketches of single end buds, are supplemented (p. 215) by a table. In this table, where a species is listed as having hairy twigs, the degree of hairiness often is slight. A magnifying lens should be used to determine whether twigs or buds are hairy. Buds taken for identification from unknown specimens should be carefully selected for their full, mature growth. Acorns are necessary aids in some identifications. If none are growing, look for old ones on the ground. Acorns always grow partly enclosed in basal growths universally called "cups," but despite this the "cups" are nearly as universally described as "saucerlike," "goblet-shaped," or otherwise treated as uncuplike. Acorns and their cups often provide the most certain means for identifying oak species.

Not every oak specimen can be definitely identified by the amateur. Even professional botanists frequently are puzzled by apparent hybrids and variants. Winter identifications often are especially difficult.

Oaks provide about half the annual production of hardwood lumber in the United States. They are slow-growing, long-lived, and relatively disease- and insect-resistant, although the oak wilt disease currently is causing concern. Bark of several oaks is rich in tannin used in curing leather. By boiling out the tannic acid, the Indians converted into staple articles of diet even the acorns of red oaks. During the Anglo-Saxon rule in England oak forests were valued highly for fattening swine, and laws provided that anyone wantonly injuring or destroying an oak should be fined according to size of tree and its ability to bear fruits.

Extensive browsing on early spring foliage by cattle occasionally results in poisoning. Twigs and fruits of oaks form a large portion of the food consumed by many game birds and mammals. Acorns are eaten by nearly all herbivorous birds and mammals. List of species eating these nuts in our area includes many songbirds as well as the ruffed and sharptail grouse, prairie chicken, bobwhite, wild turkey, pheasant, mourning dove, wood duck,

Brief Guide to Winter Identification of Oaks — Non-evergreen oaks	Twigs hairless or nearly so	End buds under 3/16''	End buds narrow, sharp	End buds hairy	End buds angled	Further notes
Post	no	no	no	yes	no	
Blackjack	no	no	yes	yes	yes	
Scrub	no	yes	no	no	no	
Spanish	no	yes	yes	yes	no	acorn cup saucer-shaped
Sand	no	var.	yes	yes	no	acorn cup goblet-shaped
White	yes	yes	no	no	no	acorn short-stalked, cup bowl-shaped
Swamp	yes	yes	no	no	no	acorn long-stalked, cup bowl-shaped
Overcup	yes	yes	no	no	no	acorn cup unique; see text
Dwarf	yes	yes	no	no	no	shrub
Mossycup	yes	yes	no	yes	no	
Pin	yes	yes	yes	no	no	many stubby pinlike branches
Jack	yes	yes	yes	no	no	northern; acorn cup deep conical
Shumard	yes	yes	yes	no	no	southern; acorn cup shallow
Willow	yes	yes	yes	no	yes	uplands
Laurel	yes	yes	yes	no	yes	lowlands
Water	yes	yes	yes	yes	no	buds almost woolly
Shingle	yes	yes	yes	yes	yes	bud scales with hairy edges
Scarlet	yes	no	no	yes	no	apex of bud white-hairy
Red	yes	no	yes	no	no	bark dark, usually with flat shiny ridges
Chestnut	yes	no	yes	no	no	bark dark, with sharp dull ridges
Chinquapin	yes	no	yes	no	no	bark light gray; acorn cup scales tight
Basket	yes	no	yes	no	no	bark light gray; acorn cup scales free
Nuttall	yes	no	yes	yes	no	Mississippi valley
Turkey	yes	no	yes	yes	no	southern Coastal Plain
Black	yes	no	yes	yes	yes	bark dark, blocky

whitetail deer, black bear, red fox, gray fox, raccoon, opossum, gray squirrel, fox squirrel, red squirrel, and several chipmunks and ground squirrels. Deer, cottontail, and snowshoe hare browse twigs; porcupine eats the growing layer beneath bark. Many Indians ate acorns; acids of Red Oak acorns were removed by grinding and washing with hot water.

Oaks (1): Leaves Lobed
without Bristle-tips
(*Plate 45, p. 324*)

WHITE OAK   *Quercus alba* L.   **pp. 5, 9, 324**
   Recognition: A tall tree with rather *evenly lobed* hairless leaves that may be somewhat whitened beneath. Twigs hairless; end buds red-brown, small, blunt, and hairless. Acorn cup bowl-shaped, covering ⅓ or less of acorn. Bark whitish, slightly furrowed to scaly. Leaves 2″–9″. Height 60′–80′ (150′); diameter 2′–3′ (5′).
   Similar species: (1) Overcup and (2) Mossycup Oak leaves usually have deeper divisions. (3) Swamp Oak (Plate 47) leaves may have shallow lobes.

OVERCUP OAK   *Quercus lyrata* Walt.   **p. 324**
   Recognition: A moderate-sized tree of southern bottomlands. Leaves vary (may even resemble White Oak somewhat), but generally with *deep indentation* near base and narrow basal lobes; *fine-hairy* and often whitened beneath. Twigs and end buds as in White Oak except that buds are chestnut-brown. Rough acorn cup is unique, *enclosing nearly all of globular nut;* only very tip visible. Twigs somewhat hairy when very young but soon become hairless. Bark whitish, broken by shallow cracks. Leaves 3″–10″. Height 60′–80′ (100′); diameter 2′–3′ (4′).
   Similar species: (1) Mossycup Oak leaves have deep sinuses more centrally located. Acorn cups of both species distinctive. (2) White Oak has shallower leaf sinuses and wider basal lobes.

POST OAK   *Quercus stellata* Wang.   **p. 324**
   Recognition: A small tree with often *leathery* leaves usually lobed so as to resemble a *cross*. Leaves gray or *brown-hairy beneath* except in uncommon hairless shrubby variety *margaretta* (Ashe) Sarg. Twigs somewhat gray-hairy; end buds over ³⁄₁₆″, blunt and rather hairy. Bowl-shaped acorn cups cover ⅓–½ of acorn. Bark brownish, broken by long shallow cracks and often divided into rectangular blocks. Leaves 3″–8″. Height 50′–60′ (100′); diameter 1′–2′ (3′).

Similar species: Blackjack Oak (Plate 46) frequently grows with this species but its leaves lobed and bristle-tipped.

MOSSYCUP OAK (BUR OAK)   **pp. 9, 324**
Quercus macrocarpa Michx.
   Recognition: A tall tree with variable leaves usually marked by at least *1 deep pair* of identations which divide leaves *into 2* or more portions. Leaves usually somewhat *hairy and whitish beneath*. Twigs yellow-brown, variably hairless to rather hairy; end buds as in Post Oak. Acorn cups bowl-shaped with peculiar *"mossy" fringe* of elongate scales. Bark light gray, shallowly grooved. Branchlets sometimes have *corky wings* like those of Sweetgum (Plate 42). Leaves 4″–10″. Height 70′–80′ (170′); diameter 2′–3′ (7′).
   Similar species: See (1) Overcup and (2) White Oaks.

Oaks (2): Leaves Lobed with Bristle-tips
(*Plate 46, p. 326*)

SCARLET OAK   *Quercus coccinea* Muenchh.   **p. 326**
   Recognition: A medium-sized tree of the red oak group. Leaves *deeply lobed*, either hairless or with tufts of hair in angles of veins beneath. Twigs hairless; end buds scraggly-hairy, over ³⁄₁₆″, and blunt. Acorn cup brownish, hairless or nearly so (use lens), over ¼″ deep, bowl-like, and ⅝″ to ⅞″ in diameter. Bark dark and finely grooved. Leaves 3″–6″. Height 40′–50′ (80′); diameter 1′–2′ (3′).
   Similar species: This and next 4 species have similar foliage; best identified by acorn cups. Pin Oak occurs on moister sites.

PIN OAK   *Quercus palustris* Muenchh.   **pp. 9, 326**
   Recognition: Similar to Scarlet Oak but end buds small, *hairless*, sharp. Twigs hairless. Acorn cup brownish and hairless but *shallow*, saucerlike, and only ⅜″–⅝″ in diameter and less than ¼″ high. Lower branches characteristically point downward; many stubby pinlike branches usually present. Leaves 3″–7″. Height 70′–80′ (110′); diameter 2′–3′ (5′).
   Similar species: Jack Oak occurs on uplands and has deeper-tapering acorn cups.

JACK OAK   *Quercus ellipsoidalis* E. J. Hill   **p. 326**
   Recognition: Similar to Pin Oak but growing on uplands. Acorn cup somewhat *conical*, with sides sloping gradually to stalk. Cups finely *gray-hairy;* mostly under ½″ across. Buds red-

brown. Leaves 3″–7″. Height 60′–70′; diameter 2′–3′.
Similar species: (1) Nuttall and (2) Shumard Oaks also have
gray-hairy acorn cups. Nuttall Oak occupies a more southern
range and acorn cups, if cone-shaped, have a basal constriction.
Shumard Oak more southern; leaves and acorns generally
larger.

NUTTALL OAK   *Quercus nuttallii* E. J. Palmer   **p. 326**
Recognition: Similar to the more northern Jack Oak but with
acorn cup usually constricted to form a definitely distinct basal
portion. Acorn cup varies from cone- to saucer-shaped, is
⅝″–¾″ across, and has a contracted scaly basal portion ¹⁄₁₆″–¼″
long. End buds over ³⁄₁₆″ long.

SHUMARD OAK   *Quercus shumardii* Buckl.   **p. 326**
Recognition: Resembles Scarlet Oak but mature leaves mostly
over 6″ long. Buds clay- or straw-colored and hairless. Acorn
cup *gray, fine-hairy, shallow,* saucerlike, ¾″–1½″ in diameter.
Var. *schneckii* (Britt.) Sarg. has deeper acorn cups, covering
about ⅓ of nut. Leaves 6″–8″. Height 70′–100′ (120′); diameter
2′–3′ (6′).
Similar species: (1) Red and (2) Black Oak leaves not so deeply
lobed. (3) Scarlet, (4) Pin, (5) Jack, and (6) Nuttall Oaks have
smaller leaves and either hairless or deep acorn cups.

BLACK OAK   *Quercus velutina* Lam.   **p. 326**
Recognition: A large tree. Leaves moderately lobed, usually
somewhat hairy beneath, somewhat thickened and generally
glossy above. Twigs hairless; end buds ¼″–½″, densely *gray-
hairy* and *sharply angled.* Acorn cup bowl-shaped and finely
gray-hairy; edge rough with fringelike scales. Bark dark, blocky,
usually but not always without shiny ridges. Leaves 4″–10″.
Height 70′–80′ (100′); diameter 3′–4′ (5′).
Similar species: (1) Best separation point between this and Red
Oak is the buds, which are hairless and smaller in Red Oak.
Mature buds usually not available between May and Aug., at
which time leaf textures (and acorn cups, if available) are
helpful. Orange inner bark, often relied upon as an identification mark of Black Oak, frequently seems to be similar to that
of Red Oak. (2) Shumard Oak has leaves more deeply lobed
and acorn cups shallow, not fringed.

RED OAK   *Quercus rubra* L.   **p. 326**
Recognition: Similar to Black Oak but leaves *hairless, thin,* and
dull above. End buds ³⁄₁₆″–⁵⁄₁₆″, *hairless, and not angled.* Acorn
cup flat and saucerlike; bark dark, furrowed, often laced with
broad shiny strips. Northern variety *borealis* (Michx. f.) Farw.
has deeper acorn cup covering about ⅓ of nut and has smoother,
grayer upper bark. It may be more common than typical form

southward to n. New England, n. Pennsylvania, n. Michigan,
Iowa, and in mountains to N. Carolina. Leaves 4″–10″. Height
70′–80′ (150′); diameter 3′–4′ (5′).

SPANISH OAK   *Quercus falcata* Michx.   **p. 326**
  Recognition: A moderate-sized to tall tree; leaves *variable*,
  usually with *prominent pair of narrow lobes* toward tip. Var.
  triloba (Michx.) Nutt. lacks lower leaf lobes. Leafstalks over
  ¾″. Leaf undersides and twigs gray-hairy. End buds small,
  hairy, sharp-pointed but not angled. Acorn cup flat, gray-hairy,
  saucerlike. Bark dark, somewhat furrowed. Leaves 4″–12″.
  Height 70′–80′ (100′); diameter 2′–3′ (5′).
  Similar species: Three-pronged leaf tips are distinctive. (1)
  Turkey Oak has more prominent basal leaf lobes. (2) A form
  of Water Oak has 3-parted leaf tips but they are not so sharp-
  pointed and are nearly hairless beneath.

TURKEY OAK   *Quercus laevis* Walt.   **Not illus.**
  Recognition: Leaves and twigs of this small southern tree most
  closely resemble Spanish Oak. Lower lobes of leaves *longer* than
  upper ones. Leaves often 3-lobed, with central and lower lobes
  all narrow, resembling turkey tracks in outline. End buds
  ⅜″–½″, somewhat fine-hairy. Acorn cups ¾″–1″ in diameter,
  deeply bowl-shaped, gray-hairy. Trunk bark *blue-gray*, furrowed. Sandy Coastal Plain soils; se. Virginia to centr. Florida
  and se. Louisiana.

BLACKJACK OAK   *Quercus marilandica* Muenchh.   **p. 326**
  Recognition: A low to medium-sized tree. Leaves thick, *leathery, shallow-lobed, brownish-scaly* or hairy beneath. Twigs
  hairy; end buds large, red-hairy, sharp-pointed, angled. Acorn
  cup somewhat hairy, shaped like a shallow goblet. Cup scales
  appear loosely attached. Dark bark broken into *squarish blocks*.
  Leaves 4″–8″. Height 40′–50′ (70′); diameter 1′–2′ (4′).
  Similar species: Post Oak (Plate 45) also has leathery foliage;
  often grows with Blackjack but leaves more deeply lobed and
  not bristle-tipped.

SCRUB OAK   *Quercus ilicifolia* Wang.   **p. 326**
  Recognition: A thicket-forming shrub to small tree with *small*
  leaves *white-woolly* beneath. Twigs hairy; end buds small,
  blunt, hairless. Acorn less than ⅜″ long and cup is bowl-shaped.
  Bark dark. Leaves 2″–5″. Height 3′–9′ (18′).
  Similar species: Dwarf Oak (Plate 47) also shrubby but leaves
  toothed rather than lobed.

Oaks (3): Leaves Toothed or Wavy-edged
(*Plate 47, p. 328*)

SWAMP OAK   *Quercus bicolor* Willd.   **p. 328**
Recognition: A bottomland tree. Leaves mostly have 4–6 pairs of *large rounded teeth* (occasionally sharp-toothed and sometimes forming shallow lobes), *wedge-shaped* at base and usually *white-hairy* beneath. Twigs hairless. Chestnut-brown end buds small, blunt, hairless. Acorn cup bowl-shaped with stalks 1″–2½″, *longer* than leafstalks. Bark *light gray*, ridged or flaky. Leaves 4″–9″. Height 60′–70′ (100′); diameter 2′–3′ (8′).
Similar species: No other oak has acorn stalks much longer than its leafstalks. White Oak leaves much more deeply lobed.
Remarks: Also known as Swamp White Oak. The lumber not distinguished from White Oak.

CHESTNUT OAK   *Quercus prinus* L.   **p. 328**
Recognition: An upland tree whose leaves have 7–16 pairs of *rounded teeth* (sometimes sharp). Foliage often somewhat leathery; leaves may be slightly hairy beneath. Twigs hairless. End buds narrow, sharp, and mostly over ³⁄₁₆″. Acorn cup bowl-shaped, less than 1″ across, with tight scales free only at the tips. Trunk bark *dark, deeply ridged*, quite distinctive. Leaves 4″–9″. Height 60′–70′ (100′); diameter 3′–4′ (7′).
Similar species: (1) Basket Oak has light-colored bark, more scaly and larger acorns. (2) Chinquapin Oak has sharp leaf teeth. (3) Chestnut (Plate 57) lacks clustered end buds.

BASKET OAK   **Leaf edge illus., p. 328**
Quercus michauxii Nutt.
Recognition: Leaves similar in outline to Chestnut Oak but typically more deeply and sometimes more sharply toothed; often white-hairy beneath. Trunk bark *light gray*, rough, and flaky like Chinquapin. Acorn cup similar to that of Chestnut Oak but 1″–1¼″ in diameter, bowl-shaped, with scales attached *only at base.* Leaves 4″–8″. Height to 100′; diameter to 4′. Coastal Plain bottomlands; New Jersey to centr. Florida, west to e. Texas, north in Mississippi Valley to e. Kentucky, sw. Ohio, centr. Illinois, and se. Missouri.

CHINQUAPIN OAK   **p. 328**
Quercus muehlenbergii Engelm.
Recognition: A medium-sized tree whose leaves have 8–13 pairs of *sharp teeth*. Twigs, buds, and acorn cups resemble those of Chestnut Oak but bark *light gray* and often flaky, not ridged. Leaves 4″–9″. Height 20′–50′ (160′); diameter 6″–24″ (4′).
Similar species: (1) Dwarf Oak also has sharp-toothed leaves

but teeth are fewer and leaves smaller. (2) Live and (3) Darlington Oaks (Plate 48) may have some leaves with sharp teeth but foliage is leathery and evergreen.

DWARF OAK   *Quercus prinoides* Willd.   **p. 328**
Recognition: A shrubby oak. Leaves *small, sharply toothed*, 3–7 pairs of teeth, white-hairy beneath. Twigs and buds resemble Swamp Oak but smaller. Acorn cup ⅜″–⅞″ across, with tight scales. Var. *rufescens* Rehd. of several Atlantic coastal places has reddish-hairy twigs and leaf undersides. Leaves 2″–5″. Height 2′–10′ (18′); diameter 1″–4″ (10″).
Similar species: See (1) Chinquapin Oak; also (2) Scrub Oak (Plate 46).
Remarks: The name Dwarf Chinquapin Oak also used.

Oaks (4): Leaves Not Lobed, Toothed, or Wavy-edged

(Plate 48, p. 330)

SHINGLE OAK   *Quercus imbricaria* Michx.   **p. 330**
Recognition: A tree whose leaves *lack* either teeth or lobes but whose single bristle-tips indicate it to be one of red oak group. Foliage densely *hairy beneath*. Twigs hairless; end buds more or less *silky* and angular; bud-scale edges hairy. Acorn cup bowl-shaped, covering ⅓–½ of acorn and ⁹⁄₁₆″–1³⁄₁₆″ across. Bark dark, irregularly grooved. Leaves 3″–7″. Height 50′–60′ (100′); diameter 2′–3′ (4′).
Similar species: Four other oaks have thin, nonleathery leaves neither toothed nor lobed. All are red oaks. (1) Laurel Oak has narrower hairless leaves, deeply saucer-shaped acorn cups, gray bark. (2) Willow Oak has still narrower leaves, hairless or, less commonly, silky beneath; acorn cups shallowly saucer-like; and the bark is dark. (3) Water Oak has unique wedge-shaped foliage. (4) Sand Oak has somewhat leathery leaves, white-woolly beneath.

LAUREL OAK   *Quercus laurifolia* Michx.   **Not illus.**
Recognition: A large nonevergreen tree whose *nonleathery* leaves are intermediate in shape between Shingle and Willow Oaks. *Hairless* except for tufts in angles of veins beneath. Twigs hairless or slightly hairy. End buds angled, sharp, hairless, often over ⅛″. Acorn cups vary from deep saucer shape to bowl shape, ⅝″–⅞″ across. Cup scales have free tips. Bark *gray*, scaly. Darlington Oak has similar but leathery leaves. Coastal Plain swamps; s. New Jersey to centr. Florida, west to e. Texas.

WILLOW OAK   *Quercus phellos* L.   **p. 330**
  Recognition: A tall tree with *narrow, bristle-tipped* leaves that
  are hairless or, in form *intonsa* Fern., white-silky beneath.
  Twigs hairless; end buds narrow, sharp, hairless, mostly under
  ⅛″. Acorn cups *very shallow* and saucerlike, ⅜″–½″ across.
  Bark dark and shallowly grooved. Leaves 2″–5″. Height 70′–80′
  (100′); diameter 2′–3′ (4′).
  Similar species: (1) Shingle Oak has wider leaves and deeper
  acorn cups; (2) Sand Oak has leaf undersides and twigs woolly.

SAND OAK   *Quercus incana* Bartr.   **Not illus.**
  Recognition: A small tree with somewhat *leathery but not
  evergreen* leaves shaped like those of Willow Oak but occasionally wavy-edged. Foliage with *fine, whitish woolliness* beneath. Twigs densely woolly to nearly hairless; buds variable
  in length. Acorn cup goblet-shaped, ⅜″–⅝″ across. Bark black
  or gray, dividing into squarish blocks. Shingle Oak is less hairy
  and has smaller acorns. Coastal Plain soils; se. Virginia to s.
  Florida, west to centr. Texas and se. Oklahoma.

WATER OAK   *Quercus nigra* L.   **p. 330**
  Recognition: A southern tree with wedge-shaped hairless leaves
  broadest near tip. Leaves may be bristle-tipped. Tips deeply
  3-parted in uncommon form *tridentifera* (Sarg.) Trel. Twigs
  hairless but narrow end buds quite hairy. Acorn cup flat,
  saucer-shaped, ⅜″–⅝″ across. Bark dark and rather smooth.
  Leaves 2″–5″. Height 50′–60′ (80′); diameter 2′–3′ (4′).
  Similar species: (1) See Shingle Oak (p. 221). (2) If leaves are
  deeply 3-parted at tips, see Spanish Oak (Plate 46).

LIVE OAK   *Quercus virginiana* Mill.   **p. 330**
  Recognition: A spreading southern evergreen tree or shrub of
  the white oak group, with *leathery* leaves. Leaves usually have
  rolled edges; mostly gray or white-hairy beneath. Some may
  be sharply toothed in part. Leaves *not* bristle-tipped. Twigs
  gray-hairy; end buds small, hairless, blunt. Acorn cup is cup-
  shaped. Bark dark, somewhat broken into squares. Trees often
  draped with Spanish "moss." Shrubby variety *maritima*
  (Chapm.) Sarg. occurs on sand dunes. Leaves 1″–4″. Height
  to 60′; diameter to 8′.
  Similar species: Only this and next species have thick, leathery,
  evergreen unlobed leaves. Darlington Oak has saucer-shaped
  acorn cups and characteristics of red oak group. Rare toothed
  Live Oak leaves are nevertheless distinctively leathery.

DARLINGTON OAK   **Not illus.**
Quercus hemisphaerica Bartr.
  Recognition: A somewhat evergreen tree with narrow unlobed

leathery leaves whose edges may be rolled. They are widest near tips and many have wavy or even toothed edges. Leaf tips bear bristles characteristic of red oak group. Some strong shoots may bear toothed leaves but leathery leaves are unlike Chinquapin (Plate 47) or similar oaks. Acorn cups saucerlike; scales have free tips. Some consider this plant to be only a variant of Laurel Oak. Coastal Plain; se. Virginia and Florida to e. Texas.

Magnolias
(*Plate 49, p. 332*)

The magnolias are distinctively marked plants of tropical appearance and southern relationships. The ranges of a number extend into the northern states, especially in the Appalachians. The leaves are smooth-edged and often large; the twigs are ringed by stipule scars; the buds are covered by a single scale; the true end buds usually are especially large; and the bundle scars are many. All magnolias are frequently cultivated for their large leaves and showy white flowers. Their large brownish conelike fruit clusters are frequently ornamental when ripe. They release bright red seeds on silklike threads from many slitlike openings.

Only the magnolias, Tulip-tree, and Sycamore have more than 3 bundle scars per leaf scar and ringed twigs. Sycamore (Plate 42) has peculiar mottled bark and buds surrounded by leaf scar; Tulip-tree (Plate 42) has notched leaves, buds spicy when crushed, and chambered pith; it is a member of the magnolia family. Beech (Plate 57) has ringed twigs but the leaves are toothed and the bundle scars only 3. Tall Pawpaw (Plate 59) has similar foliage but lacks stipular rings and has only 3 bundle scars.

SWEETBAY MAGNOLIA *Magnolia virginiana* L. **p. 332**
Recognition: A large shrub or small tree with thick, rather *leathery*, elliptic leaves that are evergreen, especially in South. Foliage *spicy* when crushed; *white beneath*. Leaves hairless except in var. *australis* Sarg. (north only to Arkansas and se. Virginia). Buds hairy and green but twigs generally hairless. Pith *chambered*. Leaves 4"–7". Height to 50' (rarely 70'); diameter to 2' (rarely 3'). Flowers white, large, fragrant, May–July. Fruits 1"–2", Sept.–Oct.
Similar species: No other wild magnolia in our area has both thick leathery leaves and chambered pith.

CUCUMBER MAGNOLIA *Magnolia acuminata* L. **p. 332**
Recognition: A hardy magnolia of tree size with large, thin, egg-shaped leaves *green* and slightly hairy beneath. Twigs

brown, hairless; pith not chambered. Buds *hairy;* end buds whitish and up to ¾". Trunk bark dark, furrowed much like that of ashes (Plate 9 and 10). Leaves 4"–10". Height 40'–70' (90'); diameter 1'–2' (3'). Flowers green or green and yellow, May–June. Fruits dark red, but cucumberlike when young, 2"–3", Aug.–Oct.
Similar species: Bigleaf Magnolia also has hairy buds but leaves and end buds are larger.
Remarks: Wood is of some commercial value for interiors, cabinetmaking, and woodenware. Twigs eaten by deer.

BIGLEAF MAGNOLIA   *Magnolia macrophylla* Michx.   **p. 332**
Recognition: A southern small tree with *largest leaves* of any in our area. Leaves often clustered near twig tips; *white and hairy* beneath, bases often shallowly heart-shaped. Twigs and buds greenish, hairy; end buds 1"–2"; pith not chambered. Trunk bark smooth, grayish. Leaves 12"–36". Height 20'–30' (50'); diameter 12"–18" (24"). Flowers white with purple spots, often 10" across, May–June. Fruits globular, 2"–3", Sept.–Oct.
Similar species: See Cucumber Magnolia.

EARLEAF MAGNOLIA   *Magnolia fraseri* Walt.   **p. 332**
Recognition: The only magnolia with leaf bases *deeply heart-shaped.* Leaves usually large and crowded near twig tips. Buds and slender twigs hairless. Purplish end buds less than 1⅛". Pith often somewhat chambered. Trunk bark smooth, *gray.* Leaves 8"–18". Height 20'–30' (40'); diameter 10"–12" (18"). Flowers white, May. Fruits cylindrical, 3"–4", Sept.–Oct.

UMBRELLA MAGNOLIA   *Magnolia tripetala* L.   **p. 332**
Recognition: Similar to Earleaf Magnolia but leaf bases *not* "eared." End buds purplish; *over* 1⅛". Twigs *stout;* pith not chambered. Trunk bark *brown* and smooth. Leaves 8"–27". Height 20'–30' (40'); diameter 10"–12" (18"). Flowers white, May. Fruits cylindrical, 3"–4", Sept.–Oct.

Elms and Water-elm
(*Plate 50, p. 334*)

The true elms are trees with double-toothed (except Siberian Elm and Water-elm), feather-veined leaves that have uneven or often somewhat heart-shaped bases. Buds are many-scaled, with scales in 2 vertical rows; end buds false. Leaf scars are unusually smooth; the 3 bundle scars sunken. Trunk bark is grayish, with vertical, often cross-thatched ridges. Flowers are inconspicuous and give rise to small, flat, papery-winged, oval to circular fruits. The several plants of Plate 51 can be separated from elms by their distinctive buds and other characteristics.

Water-elm, or Planer-tree, is included as a close relative of the true elms, although it is in a different genus. It differs in having fruits which are small, wingless, soft-spiny nuts. Leaves are single-toothed.

Most elms are ornamental and the strong timber is valuable. Inner bark, particularly of roots, generally tough and fibrous, and can be twisted into improvised rope, fishline, nets, or snares. Fruits are eaten by many game and song birds and squirrels. Twigs and foliage are consumed by rabbits, deer, and muskrats.

WINGED ELM   *Ulmus alata* Michx.   **p. 334**
Recognition: A small single- or divided-trunk tree usually bearing some branchlets with *wide corky "wings."* Leaves small, hairy beneath, smooth above. Leafstalks so short as to be nearly lacking. Twigs and buds hairless or nearly so; buds less than ³⁄₁₆″; bud scales have dark borders. Leaves 1″–4″. Height 40′–50′ (60′); diameter 1′–2′. Flowers March. Fruits less than ¼″ broad, hairy or not, with fringed edges and pointed tips, long-stemmed, March–April.
Similar species: (1) Sweetgum (Plate 42) is the only alternate-leaved woody plant besides several elms which regularly possess corky "wings." It has star-shaped leaves and true end buds. (2) Rock Elm has larger leaves, with longer stalks, larger buds, and hairy twigs. (3) September Elm has flowers in fall. (4) English Elm has dark buds.

SEPTEMBER ELM   *Ulmus serotina* Sarg.   **Not illus.**
Recognition: A rare southern species very similar to Winged Elm but with flowers and fruits appearing in autumn. Fruits notch-tipped. Flowers Sept.–Oct. Limestone soils; s. Kentucky and s. Illinois to nw. Georgia, n. Alabama, Arkansas, and e. Oklahoma.

ROCK ELM   *Ulmus thomasi* Sarg.   **p. 334**
Recognition: A single-trunked tree usually with *corky "wings"* on some branchlets and often with strongly drooping lower branches. Leaves hairless; leafstalks ⅛″–⅜″. Twigs and buds somewhat hairy; buds over ¼″, with dark scale edges. Leaves 2″–7″. Height 60′–80′ (100′); diameter 2′–3′ (4′). Flowers April–May. Fruits ⅜″–⅝″ broad, pointed-tipped, hairy, with fringed margins, long-stemmed, May.
Similar species: (1) When corky wings are present see Winged Elm. (2) When wings are lacking, hairy twigs and buds, columnar trunk, and upland habitat distinguish it from American Elm.

AMERICAN ELM   *Ulmus americana* L.   **pp.** *6, 9,* **334**
Recognition: When growing in the open as a large tree, trunk divides near the ground into large limbs, giving a *unique vase-shaped form*. Leaves variable, smooth or sandpapery above, hairless or hairy beneath. Twigs hairless or barely hairy; branchlets without corky "wings." Buds over ¼", with light brown but dark-edged scales. Leaves 2"–6". Height 80'–100' (125'); diameter 2'–5' (10'). Flowers March–May. Fruits about ⅜" broad, hairless except for hairy margin, long-stemmed, April–May.
Similar species: Other elms have distinctive buds, but Rock Elm without corky wings may be confusing (see preceding species).
Remarks: Seeds eaten by bobwhite, "Hungarian" partridge, ruffed grouse, prairie chicken, gray and fox squirrels, and opossum. Cottontail rabbit, snowshoe hare, and whitetail deer browse twigs. Like the Chestnut (p. 264) in an earlier generation, this beloved species is rapidly being decimated by disease. Stands of dead trees occupy lowland sites in many places. Full-sized trees are becoming scarce. "Dutch" elm disease is a fungus spread by a beetle.

ENGLISH ELM   *Ulmus procera* Salisb.   **p. 334**
Recognition: An introduced tree, usually with several large branches mostly at right angles to upright trunk. Leaves moderate-sized, slightly sandpapery above, nearly hairless beneath. Branchlets *often corky-winged;* buds a uniform dark color. Leaves 1½"–3". Height 80'–100' (125'); diameter 2'–3' (5'). Flowers April. Fruits ⅜"–½" broad, base narrow, entirely hairless, short-stemmed, April–May.
Similar species: Dark buds rather distinctive, but see Witch Elm.

WITCH ELM   *Ulmus glabra* Huds.   **Not illus.**
Recognition: Similar to the English Elm but twigs *hairy* and leaves sandpapery above and hairy beneath. Sometimes spreads from plantings.

SLIPPERY ELM   *Ulmus rubra* Muhl.   **p. 334**
Recognition: A medium-sized tree with single or divided trunk. Leaves very rough and sandpapery above and hairy beneath. Twigs *rough-hairy;* buds prominently *red-hairy* and over ⅛". Leaves 5"–9". Height 40'–60' (70'); diameter 1'–2' (3'). Flowers March–May. Fruits ⅜"–⅞" broad, hairless except for centers of each side, short-stemmed, May–June.
Similar species: No other elm has rough-hairy twigs and red-hairy buds.
Remarks: Common name of this rough-textured tree comes from the slimy inner bark, once well known as a scurvy preventive. It was ground into flour or chewed piecemeal. Cottontail rabbits and deer eat twigs. Porcupines may eat the growing layer beneath bark.

SIBERIAN ELM   *Ulmus pumila* L.   **Not illus.**
   Recognition: A shrub or small tree introduced from Asia, and
   established at least from Minnesota to Kansas. The 1″–3″ leaves
   mostly are narrow and only *singly toothed.* Twigs and buds
   nearly hairless; buds small and *blunt.* Fruits hairless, ⅜″–⅝″
   broad and shorter than broad. Water-elm occurs eastward.

WATER-ELM   *Planera aquatica* (Walt.) J. F. Gmel.   **p. 334**
   Recognition: A small southern tree with egg-shaped, *single-
   toothed,* nearly hairless leaves. Twigs and buds *hairless,* the
   latter mostly less than ⅛″ but *pointed.* Trunk bark more scaly
   than in true elms. Leaves 2″–3″. Height 30′–40′; diameter
   18″–20″. Flowers April. Fruits wingless nuts covered with
   irregular protuberances, April–May.
   Similar species: Only this and Siberian Elm have single-toothed
   leaves. Ranges, fruit and bud shapes, however, are dissimilar.
   Remarks: Fruits eaten by mallard, black, and ringneck ducks
   and squirrels.

Ironwood, Hornbeam, Hazelnuts, and Alders
(*Plate 51, p. 336*)

These species and the birches (Plate 52) make up a family related
to the willows, poplars, oaks, and other plants whose flowers occur
in catkins. Catkins are usually dangling strands of small flowers
but may be short and inconspicuous.
   Elms and birches and plants of this plate mostly have double-
toothed leaves (see Speckled Alder) and 3 bundle scars per leaf
scar (see hazelnuts). Elms have leaves uneven-based, end buds
false, and bud scales in 2 rows. Birches have leaves even-based,
true end buds, and only 2–3 bud scales per bud. Those plants
on Plates 50 and 51 which have false end buds also have leaves
(and buds and leaf scars) arranged in 2 opposing rows along twigs.

IRONWOOD   *Carpinus caroliniana* Walt.   **p. 336**
   Recognition: A small tree with distinctive *muscular-appearing,
   smooth, dark gray* bark. Trunk has a deeply rippled and sinewy
   look. Leaves egg-shaped, double-toothed, and in North sometimes long-pointed. Twigs variably hairy or not. Buds brown,
   somewhat square in cross section, with scales in 4 rows; end
   buds false. Leaves 1″–5″. Height 20′–40′; diameter 10″–24″.
   Flowers April, male catkins not present in winter. Fruits tiny
   nuts attached to 3 pointed leafy bracts, Aug.–Oct.
   Similar species: Trunk and bark are unique. Angled buds help
   separate small specimens from those of Hornbeam.

Remarks: Nearly all botany books published during the past generation name this plant Blue Beech and the next one Ironwood. However, *Carpinus* (which is not in the same family as the true Beech) is still commonly called Ironwood in many areas because of the strong muscular appearance of trunk. Conversely, *Ostrya* appears no stronger than most small trees. This results in a confusion of 2 "ironwoods" and is further complicated by the alternate names of American Hornbeam and Hop Hornbeam applied to these 2 species respectively.

Wood of this tree is heavy and tough but, surprisingly, decays rapidly upon contact with the ground. Charcoal made from Ironwood reportedly once used in manufacture of gunpowder. Fruits eaten by many birds, including ruffed grouse, bobwhite, pheasant, and wild turkey and by gray squirrels. Cottontail rabbit and whitetail deer nip the shoots.

HORNBEAM   *Ostrya virginiana* (Mill.) K. Koch   **p. 336**
Recognition: A small tree with foliage and twigs much as in Ironwood but bark brownish, grooved, and shreddy. Buds *round* in cross section and pointed; end buds false. Bud scales finely grooved (use lens) and not arranged in rows. Leaves 1″–5″. Height 20′–30′ (40′); diameter 6″–12″ (24″). Flowers April–May, male catkins usually present in winter. Fruits small bladder-enclosed nuts, Aug.–Oct.
Similar species: (1) Ironwood has squarish buds and (2) American Hazelnut has blunt buds.
Remarks: Related European trees were originally used in yoking oxen and were known as Yoke-elms or Hornbeams. Seeds eaten by ruffed and sharptail grouse, bobwhite, pheasant, and ptarmigan. Deer and cottontail rabbit browse twigs.

AMERICAN HAZELNUT   *Corylus americana* Walt.   **p. 336**
Recognition: A shrub with broad, somewhat *heart-shaped, double-toothed* leaves. Twigs and leafstalks with *stiff hairs.* Buds blunt, with several evident bud scales; end buds false. Bundle scars 3 or sometimes more. Leaves 2″–5″. Height to 10′. Flowers April–May. Fruit edible nuts enclosed in thin flattened hairy *ragged-edged* husks, July–Sept.
Similar species: (1) Beaked Hazelnut has nearly hairless twigs, fewer bud scales, beaked fruits. (2) Hornbeam has pointed buds, narrower leaves.
Remarks: Anyone who has tried to collect these nuts (also called filberts) in late summer has found that he is not alone in appreciation of them. Squirrels, chipmunks, jays, deer, grouse, quail, and pheasant usually get there first.

BEAKED HAZELNUT   **Fruit illus., p. 336**
Corylus cornuta Marsh.
Recognition: Similar to American Hazelnut but twigs usually

hairless. Buds less blunt, with several scales, lowermost scales large and paired. Edible nuts enclosed in bristly husks, which are *prolonged to form a beak*, Aug.–Sept. Thickets and woods borders; Newfoundland and British Columbia to Georgia, e. Kansas, and Colorado.

EUROPEAN BLACK ALDER   p. 336
Alnus glutinosa (L.) Gaertn.

Recognition: An upright tree with *wide, blunt-tipped,* usually double-toothed leaves. Twigs and young leaves *gummy.* Buds, as in most alders, smooth, few-scaled, reddish, narrow-based. Bundle scars 3. Bark of stout trunk *dark,* with numerous short warty stripes. Leaves 2″–5″. Height 20′–50′ (70′); diameter 1′–2′. Flowers March–May. Fruits small *pine-cone-like catkins* on long slender stalks, usually present.

Similar species: Alders are unique in having stalked buds covered by 2–3 (3–4 in Mountain Alder) smooth, usually reddish scales and in having peculiar small "cones." This and (1) Seaside Alder only alders that regularly grow as trees. This species larger, leaves are blunt, cones long-stalked. Flowers appear in spring and the range is more northern. (2) See European White Alder. (3) Common Winterberry Holly (Plate 61) often called Black Alder.

EUROPEAN WHITE ALDER   Not illus.
Alnus incana (L.) Moench

Recognition: Similar to European Black Alder but leaves pointed, hairy beneath. Bark whitish gray; cones short-stalked. Rarely escapes from cultivation.

SEASIDE ALDER   Twig illus., p. 336
Alnus maritima (Marsh.) Nutt.

Recognition: A shrub or tree of restricted coastal distribution. Leaves egg-shaped to elliptic, with bases either narrow or broad, upper surfaces *glossy.* Bud scales narrow and distinct. Stem bark smooth. Leaves 2″–5″. Height to 30′; diameter to 6″. Flowers in *late summer,* Aug.–Sept. Fruits require 2 years to mature. See other alders. Pond and streambanks; coastal districts of Maryland and Delaware, also reported from the Red River, Oklahoma.

SMOOTH ALDER   *Alnus serrulata* (Ait.) Willd.   p. 336
Recognition: A shrub or, rarely, small tree forming thickets along watercourses. Leaves variably hairless or velvety beneath, bases wedge-shaped or only slightly rounded. Leaf edges double-toothed and somewhat wavy. A round-leaved variety sometimes found east of Appalachians; some forms of this variety have notched or rounded leaf tips. Dark stem

bark *lacks* speckles or may have some white barlike markings of Speckled Alder, but these are shorter and fewer. Leaves 2″–5″. Height 6′–12′ (25′); diameter 1″–2″ (4″). Flowers Feb.–May, only slender male catkins drooping. Fruits woody *"cones,"* usually present, do not droop.

Similar species: Wedge-shaped leaf bases, nondrooping "cones," and relatively unspeckled bark distinguish this species from Speckled Alder, only other common shrubby alder with stalked reddish buds.

Remarks: Inner bark can be ground into a crude flour in an emergency. Deer eat twigs but not a favorite food.

SPECKLED ALDER *Alnus rugosa* (Du Roi) Spreng.   **p. 336**
Recognition: Similar to Smooth Alder but more northern. Leaves egg-shaped, edges often *single-toothed*, and not wavy. Leaf bases rounded to somewhat heart-shaped. Leaf undersurfaces typically green and hairless but may be whitened or velvety. A rare cut-leaved form (forma *tomophylla* Fern.) occurs in Newfoundland and Maine. Dark bark plentifully *speckled* with transverse white warty lenticels. Leaves 2″–5″. Height 6′–12′ (25′); diameter 1″–2″ (4″).

Similar species: (1) See Smooth Alder. (2) Unlike Mountain Alder in having buds 2-scaled and blunt, and leaf undersides dull.

Remarks: Ptarmigan and sharptail grouse feed on buds; muskrats, cottontail rabbits, deer, and moose browse twigs. Sometimes plant called Black Alder and then should not be confused with Common Winterberry Holly (Plate 61), also sometimes given that name.

MOUNTAIN ALDER   **Twig illus., p. 336**
Alnus crispa (Ait.) Pursh
Recognition: A northern shrub with leaves shaped like those of Speckled Alder and often double-toothed. Leaves typically hairless and somewhat *shiny beneath,* but in var. *mollis* Fern. (lowland sites) have velvety undersides. Twigs similarly are hairless or not. Buds 3- *to 4-scaled,* reddish or greenish, somewhat stalked, *long-pointed.* Leaf scars triangular; bundle scars 3. Stem bark *smooth,* not speckled. Leaves 2″–5″. Height to 12′. A prostrate creeping form occurs in very exposed locations. Flowers June–Aug. Differs from other alders in bud type, having 3- to 4-scaled pointed buds; from Speckled Alder by shiny leaf undersides. Where "cones" are lacking, may be distinguished from birches and hazelnuts by leaf shape and bud type; from Ironwood and Hornbeam by size, bark type, and presence of true end buds. Not confined to wet sites but forming thickets also on rocky slopes; Newfoundland, Labrador, and Alaska to n. New England, n. New York, Ontario, n. Michigan, Minnesota, and Alberta; also in w. N. Carolina.

Birches
(Plate 52, p. 338)

Birches are trees and shrubs of northern distribution. The leaves
are mostly double-toothed and more or less egg-shaped or triangular, with blunt bases. Bark of most species is marked by numerous
cross streaks and tends to separate into papery sheets. Buds are
2- to 3-scaled and bundle scars are 3. Short spur branches of
densely clustered leaves and leaf scars may be present.

Native birches that possess dark bark might be confused with
some cherries (Plate 53). Birches differ in that (1) bud scales are
fewer, (2) leafstalks do not have glands, (3) broken twigs may have
a strong wintergreen odor, rather than sour smell of cherry twigs,
(4) bark of many species can be separated into papery sheets,
and (5) leaves are double-toothed and usually do not taper at base.
The flowers of birches are in catkins; these become long clusters of small dry fruits.

Birch lumber is of value in cabinetmaking and interior finishing.
It is also used in the manufacture of agricultural implements,
spools, clothespins, etc. The bark of some species once was used
in making canoes. In several birches the curling older bark is
highly flammable; even when damp it provides excellent tinder.
The fermented sap of several birches has been used in beverages.
Seeds and buds are eaten by numerous song and game birds.
Several mammals consume the twigs and bark.

AMERICAN WHITE BIRCH   p. 338
Betula papyrifera Marsh.

Recognition: White birches grow from small brownish-barked
saplings to be white-trunked small to medium-sized trees. This,
and less common similar species (see below), are our only trees
with *clear white peeling bark* marked by narrow *horizontal
stripes*. Varieties occurring locally: with brown bark in maturity, *commutata* (Regel) Fern.; with drooping twigs, *pensilis*
Fern.; and with heart-shaped leaves, *cordifolia* (Regel) Fern.
Leaf blades 1″–4″. Height 70′–80′ (120′); diameter 1″–2″ (4″).
Flowers spring. Fruits Aug.–Sept.

Similar species: (1) See Gray Birch. (2–4) 3 other species of
birches have white peeling bark. Although this one will be
most frequently encountered, it may be separated from the
others as follows:

1. Twigs and leaf undersides (at least at angles of the veins)
   hairy:
   2. Buds not covered with resin
                                    AMERICAN WHITE BIRCH
   2. Buds shiny with a sticky resin
                                    EUROPEAN WHITE BIRCH

   1. Twigs and leaves not hairy:
      3. Twigs long, drooping, not gummy; leaf bases not
         toothed   **EUROPEAN WEEPING BIRCH**
      3. Twigs not "weeping," often gummy; leaf bases
         toothed   **BLUELEAF BIRCH**

Remarks: The various layers of bark have been used for canoe and wigwam coverings (tied in place with spruce rootlets), boxes, cups, makeshift shoes, and emergency snow goggles. Leaves have been used for tea, but are not as good as those of Black and Yellow Birches. White Birch lumber used for woodenware, pulp, and fuel. Seeds and buds eaten by ruffed and sharptail grouse. Twigs are cropped by moose, deer, and snowshoe hare.

EUROPEAN WHITE BIRCH   *Betula alba* L.   **Not illus.**
Recognition: This Old World tree has spread from Newfoundland and New England to Michigan. Twigs densely hairy and leaf blades shorter (1″–2″), not so long-tipped as in native white birch. Buds shiny with a gummy substance.

EUROPEAN WEEPING BIRCH   **Not illus.**
Betula pendula Roth
   Recognition: This second European birch with white bark occurs only occasionally from Nova Scotia and Wisconsin to New England and Iowa. Mature trees are small, with long, drooping, hairless twigs. Leaf blades 1″–3″, with bases not toothed.

BLUELEAF BIRCH   **Not illus.**
Betula caerulea-grandis Blanch.
   Recognition: A large tree. Twigs hairless and sometimes gummy. Leaf blades somewhat bluish, long-pointed, 2″–4″; bases toothed except near leafstalk. Bark white. Occurs from Nova Scotia and n. Quebec to n. New England and e. New York.

GRAY BIRCH   *Betula populifolia* Marsh.   **pp.** *10,* **338**
   Recognition: A 1- to many-stemmed small tree with *chalky-white* bark and *triangular long-pointed* leaves. Trunks are marked by many *dark chevrons* at bases of branches as well as by narrow horizontal marks characteristic of all birches (and most cherries). Bark does not readily separate into layers. Leaves 1″–4″. Height 20′–30′ (40′); diameter 10″–18″. Flowers April–May. Fruits Sept.
   Similar species: Preceding 4 white-barked birches may have some inverted V-shaped marks, but they are neither so strong nor so numerous as in this species. Long-pointed leaves, hairless rough-warty twigs, and chalky-white (not creamy) nonpeeling bark distinctive.

Remarks: Gray Birch used mainly for fuel and charcoal, but may be made into small woodenware. Seeds and buds eaten by ruffed grouse and several songbirds. Twigs browsed by whitetail deer.

BLACK BIRCH *Betula lenta* L. p. 338
Recognition: A tall, straight, brown- or *black-barked* tree of Great Lakes area and Appalachian forests. Young trunk bark tight, marked by thin horizontal stripes. Main side veins of leaves mostly *branched*. Broken twigs have delightful spicy *wintergreen* odor. Buds and twigs *hairless*, or with only lower bud scale fringed with sparse hairs. Leaves 1″–6″. Height 50′–70′ (80′); diameter 2′–3′ (5′). Flowers April–May. Fruits Aug.–Oct.
Similar species: (1) Mature Yellow Birches normally have distinctive yellow- to silver-gray bark, but small Yellow and Black Birches may grow side by side and look and smell alike. Branched leaf veins and hairless twigs and buds help identify this species. (2) See Virginia Birch.
Remarks: Black Birch wood, hard and heavy, is frequently made into furniture. Rare "curly" and "wavy" grain woods are especially valuable. Oil of wintergreen is obtainable from sap and leaves. Fermented sap may be an ingredient of birch beer. Buds and seeds eaten by ruffed and sharptail grouse; twigs browsed by whitetail deer, moose, and cottontail rabbit.

VIRGINIA BIRCH *Betula uber* (Ashe) Fern. **Not illus.**
Recognition: A small birch with dark bark, hairless twigs and foliage, and nearly circular, 1″-long, toothed leaves described from mountains of Smyth County, Virginia. Growing 30′ tall, the species is little known and may be only a variety of the Black Birch.

YELLOW BIRCH *Betula lutea* Michx. f. p. 338
Recognition: A tall tree often associated with Black Birch and Hemlock. Bark *shiny yellow or silver-gray* with narrow horizontal lines, and peeling in small thin curls (except in uncommon dark-barked form *fallax* Fassett). Like Black Birch, but unlike all other birches, broken twigs give off *wintergreen* odor. Main side veins of leaves mostly *unbranched;* twigs and buds (at least scale edges) somewhat *hairy*. Shrubby hybrids with Swamp Birch occur uncommonly in larch swamps. These have either wintergreen odor or rusty-hairy twigs. Leaves 1″–5″. Height 70′–80′ (100′); diameter 2′–3′ (4′). Flowers spring. Fruits Aug.–Oct.
Similar species: Mature Yellow Birch is usually distinctive, but see Black Birch.

Remarks: Oil of wintergreen occurs in sap and leaves. Wood important in commerce; often stained for cherry or mahogany finishes. Wildlife utilizing the plant for food includes ruffed and sharptail grouse, prairie chicken, whitetail deer, moose, cottontail rabbit, and red squirrel.

RIVER BIRCH *Betula nigra* L.   p. 338
Recognition: A *shaggy-barked* tree of streambanks; most southern of our birches. Bark varies from smooth red-brown on youngest branches to rough near-black plates on trunk. Undersides of leaves whitish and sometimes velvety. Leafstalks and buds hairy. Leaves 1″–5″. Height 60′–80′ (90′); diameter 2′–3′ (5′). Flowers April–May. Fruits June–Sept.
Similar species: (1) Only other streamside tree birches have white bark. (2) Swamp Birch is shrubby, with single-toothed leaves.
Remarks: Ruffed grouse and wild turkey sometimes eat the seeds.

SWAMP BIRCH *Betula pumila* L.   p. 338
Recognition: A low but upright bog-inhabiting birch. Only *shrubby* birch occurring in much of our U.S. area. Typical specimens have soft-hairy twigs and egg-shaped single-toothed leaves *pale green to white beneath.* Hairless variety *glabra* Regel occurs in Michigan and n. Indiana. The low, spreading, hairy variety *renifolia* Fern., with darker kidney-shaped leaves, occurs in Canadian Maritime Provinces. Var. *glandulifera* Regel is more or less hairless, with somewhat warty twigs and lower leaf surfaces. Leaves ½″–4″. Height to 9′. Flowers May–June. Fruits Aug.–Sept.
Similar species: Following 4 are also shrubby but only next 2 may have hairy twigs. (1) Northern Birch has double-toothed leaves; (2) Newfoundland Dwarf Birch may be differentiated by leathery leaves. (3) See Yellow Birch hybrids.

NORTHERN BIRCH *Betula borealis* Spach   Not illus.
Recognition: Growing variously as a flattened shrub, erect shrub, or small tree, this species has densely *white-hairy* twigs, and double-toothed leaves ½″–3″ long and not conspicuously lightened beneath. See Swamp Birch. Poor soils; Newfoundland, Labrador, and Ungava to Nova Scotia, centr. Maine, and n. Vermont.

NEWFOUNDLAND DWARF BIRCH   Not illus.
Betula michauxii Spach
Recognition: A very small shrub that creeps by means of underground stems much like dwarf willows (Plate 32). The 4″ to 24″ branches are erect, however, and have brownish-woolly twigs. Leaves hairless, leathery, only ¼″–½″ long and about

as broad. See Swamp Birch. Acid soils; se. Labrador, n. Quebec, and Newfoundland.

TUNDRA DWARF BIRCH   Twig illus., p. 338
Betula glandulosa Michx.
  Recognition: A matted to erect shrub. Twigs hairless, or very nearly so, roughened with resinous *wartlike dots*. Leaves *leathery*, egg-shaped to nearly circular. Leaves ¼″–1½″. Height to 7′. Flowers June–July. Fruits Aug.–Sept. The following is the only other shrubby birch with hairless warty twigs. Its leaves are not leathery. Mostly tundra and alpine areas; Newfoundland, centr. Maine, mountains of New Hampshire, n. New York, n. Ontario, and sw. S. Dakota northward.
  Remarks: Ptarmigan, sharptail grouse, and prairie chicken have been recorded as eating seeds, buds, or foliage.

MINOR BIRCH   *Betula minor* (Tuckerm.) Fern.   **Not illus.**
  Recognition: Shrubby, with hairless warty twigs and growth habits varying from low and sprawling to erect and 6′ tall. Leaves ½″–2″, not leathery. See Tundra Dwarf Birch. Arctic and alpine areas; from Newfoundland and mountains of New England, New York, and Quebec northward.

Cherries and Thornless Plums
(Plate 53, p. 340)

The cherries, plums, and peach are all members of the genus *Prunus*, in the rose family. Only some of the first 2 groups are native to the United States. Those discussed here are upright thornless species. The low Sand Cherry is on Plate 32 and the thorny plums are on Plate 38. The cherries, plums, and peach are alike in having: bark marked with numerous cross streaks, leafstalks usually bearing glands, leaves single-toothed, narrow-based (except Mahaleb Cherry) and frequently with long-pointed tips, twigs when broken possessing a peculiar odor, and buds with more than 3 scales. Short spur branches (drawing, p. 310) may be present. The "almond" scent of the broken twigs is difficult to describe but is a reliable aid to the identification of the genus. Though many plums bear thorns (see Plate 38), several species do not. Fruits of plums are covered with whitish powder; they are encircled about the long axis by a line, and the stones mostly are somewhat flattened. Cherries are always thornless, their fruits lack powdery bloom and encircling lines, and the seeds are nearly spherical. Plums and peach also differ from cherries in that the twigs lack true end buds.
  Despite the edible fruits of most cherries, the leaves, twigs, and seeds frequently contain hydrocyanic acid, believed to lend the

characteristic odor to crushed *Prunus* twigs. Depending, apparently, upon the reaction of the stomach juices, the kind of feed previously consumed, and the condition of the plant when eaten, horses and cattle are variously killed, made ill, or remain unaffected by browsing the potentially dangerous foliage of cherries. No plums have been listed as dangerous to stock.

Wood of the larger cherries is of commercial value. Fruits of all species are eaten by a large number of birds and mammals. Cherries and plums are among the most widely eaten of all wildlife food plants. Plums and other thicket-forming species provide excellent escape cover.

BLACK CHERRY   *Prunus serotina* Ehrh.   **pp. *13*, 340**
   Recognition: A small to large tree whose mature trunk has a *rough dark* outer bark, often exposing red-brown underbark where cracked. Reddish bark is characteristic of smaller branches. Bark marked with short horizontal lines. Leaves long, narrow, blunt-toothed; distinctive among cherries in nearly always having midrib *prominently fringed beneath* with white to brown hair. Only this cherry and next 2 have blossoms and fruits in *long clusters* and spur branches lacking. Buds *less than* ³⁄₁₆″, hairless; bud scales pointed. Leaves 2″–6″. Height 60′–80′ (100′); diameter 2′–3′ (5′). Flowers white, May–June. Fruits blackish, June–Oct.
   Similar species: (1) Only other tree cherry with regularly narrow leaves is Fire Cherry; it, however, has nonhairy leaves, spur branches, short-clustered fruits, and buds clustered at twig tips. (2) Choke Cherry leaves are hairless and sharp-toothed; buds have rounded scale tips and are somewhat longer.
   Remarks: One of the largest cherries, this species is of value for lumber and as food for humans and wildlife. Wood hard and close-grained; used for furniture and interior finishing. Cherries bitter but often used for jelly. Bark has been used as flavoring. A great number of songbirds and ruffed and sharptail grouse, prairie chicken, bobwhite, pheasant, raccoon, black bear, red fox, whitetail deer, cottontail rabbit, and gray squirrel regularly consume the fruits.

CHOKE CHERRY   *Prunus virginiana* L.   **p. 340**
   Recognition: Similar to Black Cherry but smaller. A shrub or small tree with egg-shaped, *sharp-toothed* leaves with *hairless* midribs. Bark gray-brown and *smooth.* Winter buds *over* ³⁄₁₆″; bud scales rounded at tips. Leaves 2″–5″. Height 6′–20′ (30′); diameter 2″–6″ (8″). Flowers white, April–July. Fruits purplish, July–Oct.
   Similar species: See (1) Black Cherry and also (2) European Bird Cherry. (3) Sweet, (4) Sour, and (5) Mahaleb Cherries have spur branches and short-clustered fruits. Common names are similar,

but chokeberries (Plate 58) have glandular midribs and notched bud-scale tips.

Remarks: The tart fruits can be made into delicious jellies and are used for pies. Fruits and twigs eaten by much the same animals as listed for Black Cherry.

EUROPEAN BIRD CHERRY   *Prunus padus* L.   **Not illus.**
Recognition: Similar to Choke Cherry and has elongate flower clusters like preceding 2, but seeds *irregularly grooved* and blossoms larger. Se. Canada and ne. U.S. Ornamental; rarely escapes to wild.

FIRE CHERRY (PIN CHERRY)   **p. 340**
Prunus pensylvanica L.
Recognition: Growing either as a shrub or small tree, this cherry has *narrow* leaves and *clusters of buds* at or near ends of red twig tips (as well as on spur branches, which may be present). Short white flower clusters are *umbrellalike,* as in all remaining species. Bark red-brown and smooth, though marked with crossbars of all cherries. Leaves 2″–5″. Height 10′–30′ (40′); diameter 2″–10″ (12″). Flowers March–July. Fruits red, ¼″ across, July–Sept.
Similar species: (1) Only other native cherry with narrow leaves is Black Cherry; but that species has leaves with hairy midribs beneath and lacks clustered buds and red fruits and twigs of Fire Cherry. (2) See Peach. See also (3) Sweet and (4) Sour Cherries.
Remarks: Known also as Bird Cherry. Especially common following burns or clearings. Sour fruits are eaten raw or used in jellies and cough mixtures. Consumed by bobwhite, ruffed and sharptail grouse, ptarmigan, prairie chicken. Deer, moose, cottontail rabbit, beaver, and chipmunk browse the twigs.

PEACH   *Prunus persica* (L.) Batsch   **Twig illus., p. 340**
Recognition: Occasionally the cultivated peach, a native of Asia, escapes to thickets. Very long, narrow, toothed leaves, hairy buds and fruits, false end buds, hairless twigs, pitted seeds, and pink flowers help to identify it. Buds are not clustered at twig tips. See Fire Cherry. New York and s. Ontario to Florida and e. Texas.

EASTERN DWARF CHERRY   **p. 340**
Prunus susquehanae Willd.
Recognition: Of dwarf but upright shrubby cherries, the only one with *nonleathery* leaves. Leaves narrowly wedge-shaped to elliptic; tips *not* prolonged. Leafstalks mostly under ⅜″. Leaves have few teeth and are *not toothed near base.* Leaves

1″–3½″ long and ½″–1½″ wide. Height to 3′. Flowers in short clusters May–June. Fruits blackish, July–Sept.
Similar species: Only widespread dwarf cherry in our area. (1) Northern and (2) Western Dwarf Cherries both have leathery leaves; Northern is taller. (3) Sand Cherry (Plate 32) grows as a low mat.

NORTHERN DWARF CHERRY   Not illus.
Prunus pumila L.
   Recognition: Similar to Eastern Dwarf Cherry but with *leathery* leaves widest toward tips and tapering toward base. Leaf tips somewhat long-pointed; leafstalks mostly ⅜″–⅝″. Leaves green beneath, 1″–3½″ long and ¼″–⁷⁄₁₆″ wide. Height to 8′. Flowers May–June. Fruits blackish, July–Sept. Sandy and rocky soils; Ontario and Great Lakes–St. Lawrence River drainage from New York to e. Minnesota.

WESTERN DWARF CHERRY   Not illus.
Prunus besseyi Bailey
   Recognition: Although like Eastern Dwarf Cherry in size and leaf shape, leaves of this western species are *leathery and smaller.* Leaves 1″–2″ long and ⅜″–1″ wide. Height to 3′. Flowers April–May. Fruits blackish, July–Oct. Sandy and rocky soils; Minnesota and Manitoba to Kansas and Colorado.

SWEET CHERRY   *Prunus avium* L.   p. 340
   Recognition: A rather tall tree with single main trunk; red-brown *smooth* bark prominently marked with horizontal stripes and often peeling. Leaves egg-shaped, frequently double-toothed; *10–14 pairs* of veins, which are hairy beneath. Buds slender, light brown. Flowers or fruits may be clustered on *leafless spur branches.* Leaves 2″–6″. Height 30′–50′ (75′); diameter 1′–2′ (3′). Flowers April–May. Fruits red to black, sweet, June–July.
   Similar species: (1) Sour and (2) Mahaleb Cherries also have egg-shaped leaves and spur branches. Sour Cherry has fewer (6–8) pairs of leaf veins, rougher bark, and leafy fruiting spurs. Mahaleb Cherry has hairy twigs. (3) Choke Cherry has long flower clusters and lacks spur branches. (4) Fire Cherry has much narrower leaves.
   Remarks: Imported from Europe, this species, known also as Mazzard Cherry, is the parent of many of the sweeter garden cherries. A few ornamental varieties possess variegated foliage. Escapes to wild. Fruits attractive to many songbirds and to squirrels.

SOUR CHERRY   *Prunus cerasus* L.   p. 340
   Recognition: A shrub or small tree often lacking a central trunk.

Grayish bark, at least of older trunks, much cracked and broken, sometimes scaly. Leaves egg-shaped, often double-toothed, with 6–8 pairs of veins that are hairless beneath. Buds stout and dark brown. Flowers or fruits may be clustered on *leafy spur branches*. Leaves 2″–5″. Height 20′–30′; diameter 10″–12″. Flowers May–June. Fruits red, sour, June–July.

Similar species: See Sweet Cherry.

Remarks: Believed to have originated in western Asia. Many cultivated varieties, principally those with tart flavor, are derived from this stock.

MAHALEB CHERRY   Twig illus., p. 340
Prunus mahaleb L.

Recognition: Similar to Sour Cherry but with *hairy* twigs and small but wide, *almost circular, hairless* leaves, which may be heart-shaped at base. Leaves 1″–3″. Height 20′–25′; diameter 8″–10″. Flowers April–May. Fruits July. Only cherry with velvety twigs. Beach Plum has such twigs but the end buds are false. Established locally; New England and s. Ontario southward.

Remarks: The Mahaleb, or Perfumed, Cherry was imported from Europe and the Caucasus for grafting stock. The fruits are inedible but yield a violet dye. Oil from seeds is used to fix perfumes. Aromatic wood is fashioned into pipes and walking sticks.

BEACH PLUM   *Prunus maritima* Marsh.   p. 340

Recognition: *Velvety* twigs and *hairy* buds mark this coastal, straggling, shrubby plum. Leaves egg-shaped, *hairy* beneath. Leaves 2″–3″. Height to 8′. Flowers white, April–June. Fruit purplish, Sept.–Oct.

Similar species: (1) Graves Plum has more circular leaves. (2) Alleghany Plum (p. 240) has long-pointed leaves and less bushy growth form.

Remarks: Edible fruits used in sauces, preserves, jellies, and pies.

GRAVES PLUM   *Prunus gravesii* Small   Not illus.

Recognition: Similar to Beach Plum but with somewhat wider, nearly circular leaves, lower growth, and more restricted range. Height to 4′. Flowers white, May. Fruits blackish, Sept. Sandy areas; Long Island and se. Connecticut.

GOOSE PLUM   *Prunus hortulana* Bailey   p. 340

Recognition: A shrub or small tree with narrow to egg-shaped and usually *flat* leaves that are hairless or nearly so. Stones of fruit *pointed at both ends*. Leaves 3″–6″. Height 10′–20′ (30′);

diameter 4″–10″ (12″). Flowers March–May. Fruits yellow or red, Aug.–Oct.

Similar species: Munson Plum has leaves that are not flat but tend to fold lengthwise; stones not pointed at both ends.

Remarks: Grown by horticulturists, this native species has given rise to numerous orchard varieties.

MUNSON PLUM   Not illus.
Prunus munsoniana Wight & Hedrick

Recognition: A close relative of the Goose Plum. Has longer, quite narrow leaves, which tend to fold lengthwise. Teeth on leaves may bear tiny reddish glands. Stones of fruits pointed *at one end.* It too is parent of horticultural varieties. Thickets; s. Ohio, Missouri, and se. Kansas to Georgia, n. Mississippi, and centr. Texas.

ALLEGHANY PLUM   Not illus.
Prunus alleghaniensis Porter

Recognition: An eastern shrub or small tree with *hairy* twigs and narrow to egg-shaped finely-toothed and gradually long-pointed leaves that may be somewhat hairy beneath. Occasionally twig tips are spiny. Leaves 2″–5″. Height to 17′; diameter to 8″. Flowers April–May. Fruits purple, about ⁷⁄₁₆″ in diameter, stone less flattened than in other plums, Aug.–Sept. See Beach Plum (p. 239). Thickets; Connecticut and w. Pennsylvania to nw. N. Carolina and ne. Tennessee. Reported also from Michigan.

Juneberries
(*Plate 54, p. 342*)

The juneberries are shrubs or small trees with the leaves toothed and often blunt-tipped. The buds are different from those of other plants in being pink to reddish, slender, with scales that are dark-tipped and usually somewhat twisted. Bundle scars are 3 per leaf scar. The trunk bark is usually tight and rather dark, with low vertical twisting ridges. A number of the lower clumped species spread by horizontal stems on or just beneath the ground surface.

Known variously as serviceberries, shadbushes, shadblows, and sarvis, the amelanchiers make up one of the "difficult" groups within the rose family. Whether there are few or many species depends upon the botanist consulted. The species are quite variable and some apparently hybridize. Marks of identification in winter have not been determined for all juneberries. The better-known species are illustrated.

Because a number of the juneberries are not illustrated, a pre-
liminary tabulation is presented here. Reference to the drawings
and to these lists and then to the text may simplify identification
of unknown juneberries. Those marked ° have limited distribution
in our area.

Fine-toothed juneberries (14–30 teeth per inch):

Long-pointed leaves	Short-pointed leaves	Blunt-tipped leaves
Downy	Inland°	Running
Smooth	Swamp	Coastal
	Bartram	Nantucket°
		Nova Scotia°
		Fernald°
		Oblongleaf

Coarse-toothed juneberries (6–12 teeth per inch):

Short-pointed leaves	Blunt-tipped leaves
Wiegand	Low
Minnesota°	Alderleaf°
	Gaspé
	Roundleaf
	Large-flowered°
	Huron

Though the group is composed mostly of shrubs, small-tree
juneberries often are prominent in the forest understory. In the
early spring, before the leaves develop, the drooping white flower
clusters are quite attractive. In the eastern states, near tidal rivers,
the name shadbush is a result of the flowers appearing when the
shad ascend coastal streams to spawn.

The small applelike fruits of the juneberries are esteemed by
humans. Heavy crops are rare because numerous birds and mammals are quick to take advantage of whatever fruits mature. When
available, they are delicious in jams, jellies, and pies. They are
eaten by many songbirds, wild turkey, ruffed and sharptail grouse,
bobwhite, mourning dove, striped skunk, red fox, raccoon, black
bear, red and gray squirrels, and chipmunks. Cottontail rabbit,
beaver, whitetail deer, and moose browse the twigs.

Juneberry Holly (p. 275) has only 1 bundle scar per leaf scar.

DOWNY JUNEBERRY   p. 342
Amelanchier arborea (Michx. f.) Fern.
  Recognition: One of the taller juneberries, often growing to tree
height. Leaves fine-toothed, usually *heart-shaped at base*, somewhat *long-pointed,* white-hairy beneath, at least along veins and
leafstalk. Leaves 3″–5″. Height 20′–40′ (50′); diameter

8″–16″ (24″). Flowers March–June. Fruits reddish purple, *dryish, not tasty,* June–Aug.
Similar species: All fine-toothed juneberries are similar. Of those approaching tree size, only Smooth Juneberry also has long-pointed leaves but these are hairless.
Remarks: Wood heavy, hard, close-grained. Sometimes used for tool handles.

SMOOTH JUNEBERRY *Amelanchier laevis* Wieg.   p. 342
Recognition: Similar to Downy Juneberry but with *hairless* leaves, less commonly heart-shaped at base. In spring and fall, leaves may have distinctive purplish cast, most evident at a distance. Leaves 3″–5″. Height 15′–30′ (40′); diameter 6″–12″ (18″). Flowers March–June. Fruits dark purple, *juicy, tasty,* June–Aug.
Similar species: See Inland Juneberry.

INLAND JUNEBERRY   **Not illus.**
Amelanchier interior Nielsen
Recognition: Much like Smooth Juneberry, having fine-toothed hairless leaves with heart-shaped bases, but these are *short-pointed.* Separated with certainty only by examining the ovary (of flower) or fruits; upper portions of those structures are hairy in this species, hairless in Smooth Juneberry. Inland Juneberry may usually be identified by location. Leaves 2″–3″. Height to 30′. Flowers June. Fruits July. Woods; n. Michigan, Wisconsin, s. Minnesota, and s. S. Dakota to ne. Iowa.

SWAMP JUNEBERRY *Amelanchier intermedia* Spach   p. 342
Recognition: A rather tall shrub growing in clumps. Leaves fine-toothed, slightly *hairy* beneath, short-pointed; normal-length leafstalks. Leaves 2″–3″. Height to 25′. Flowers May–June. Fruits blackish, July–Aug.
Similar species: Smaller Bartram Juneberry has shorter leafstalks and peculiar few-flowered, scattered flower clusters.

BARTRAM JUNEBERRY   p. 342
Amelanchier bartramiana (Tausch) Roemer
Recognition: Instead of having long clusters of flowers, this species is alone among juneberries in having small *groups of 1 to 4* flowers scattered in angles of leaves. Fine-toothed leaves unlike all other juneberries in that they have *very short* stalks and leaf blades tend to be pointed *at both ends.* Leaves 2″–3″. Height to 9′. Flowers May–Aug. Fruits blackish, July–Sept.

RUNNING JUNEBERRY   p. 342
Amelanchier stolonifera Wieg.
Recognition: A low shrub with blunt-tipped and often *almost*

circular fine-toothed leaves *not toothed* on the *lower* portions. Expanding leaves may be white-woolly but this down soon disappears. Spreads by underground runners. Leaves 1″–3″. Height to 5′. Flowers May–June. Fruits blackish, July–Aug. **Similar species:** Next 4 species are low, fine-toothed, and grow in patches like this one, but their leaves are toothed to the base and either somewhat oblong in shape or leathery in texture.

COASTAL JUNEBERRY   Not illus.
Amelanchier obovalis (Michx.) Ashe

Recognition: Like Running Juneberry but southern. Leaves *oblong-shaped, dull-surfaced,* toothed nearly to base. They remain somewhat hairy after losing their original white-woolliness. Leafstalks *woolly.* Leaves 2″–3″. Height to 5′. Flowers March–April. Fruits purplish, May–June. Nantucket Juneberry has small leaves. Foliage of Nova Scotia Juneberry is leathery. Fernald Juneberry leaves are hairless. Oblongleaf Juneberry is taller and lacks underground runners. Running Juneberry has almost circular leaves. Mostly Coastal Plain woods; s. New Jersey, se. Pennsylvania, and centr. Virginia to Georgia and Alabama.

NANTUCKET JUNEBERRY   Not illus.
Amelanchier nantucketensis Bickn.

Recognition: Like Coastal Juneberry but with *small, hairless, shiny* leaves with hairy leafstalks. Leaves 1″–1½″. Height to 5′. Flowers May–June. Fruits June–July. Nantucket I. and Martha's Vineyard, Massachusetts.

NOVA SCOTIA JUNEBERRY   Not illus.
Amelanchier lucida Fern.

Recognition: Like Coastal Juneberry but with *leathery, shiny, often nearly circular* leaves with leafstalks hairless. Leaves 1″–4″. Height to 5′. Flowers June. Fruits July–Aug. Dry or peaty soils; Nova Scotia.

FERNALD JUNEBERRY   Not illus.
Amelanchier fernaldii Wieg.

Recognition: Like Coastal Juneberry but with *hairless, thin, egg-shaped* or *oblong* leaves. Leaves 2″–4″. Height to 4′. Flowers June–July. Fruits dark purplish, Aug.–Sept. Thickets and shores; Newfoundland and e. Quebec to Cape Breton I. and Prince Edward I.

OBLONGLEAF JUNEBERRY   p. 342
Amelanchier canadensis (L.) Medic.

Recognition: An upright tall shrub or small tree growing in clumps. Leaves *oblong, fine-toothed,* mostly rounded at tips,

and toothed nearly to base. Although white-woolly when growing, leaves soon become nearly hairless. A form with leaves
lacking teeth occurs in se. Virginia. Leaves 1″–3″. Height to
25′. Flowers March–June. Fruits blackish, June–July.
Similar species: Coastal Juneberry has similar foliage but is
lower, with underground runners.

LOW JUNEBERRY *Amelanchier humilis* Wieg.   **p. 342**
Recognition: A clumped upright shrub with coarse-toothed
leaves that are white- or gray-hairy when young but nearly
hairless or with hairy leafstalks when mature. Leaves variable;
typically either oblong or egg-shaped, blunt-tipped, sometimes
heart-shaped at base, mostly toothed *above the middle* (or lacking teeth in var. *exserrata* Nielsen, from se. Minnesota). Clumps
usually in groups, *spreading by underground runners.* Leaves
1″–3″. Height mostly low but to 25′. Flowers May–June. Fruits
black with white powder, July–Aug.
Similar species: Among juneberries with coarse-toothed, blunt-
tipped leaves, this species distinctive because leaves are not
toothed near base.

ALDERLEAF JUNEBERRY   **Not illus.**
Amelanchier alnifolia Nutt.
Recognition: A clumped upright shrub. Leaves *coarse-toothed,
blunt-tipped,* yellow-hairy when young but nearly hairless when
mature; *nearly circular,* heart-shaped at base, and toothed well
below the middle. A Great Plains species that has underground runners. Leaves 1″–3″. Height to 22′. Flowers May.
Fruits bluish purple (rarely white), July–Aug. No other coarse-
leaved juneberry may have nearly circular leaves except the
Roundleaf and Large-flowered, which have arched or straggling stems. See also Gaspé Juneberry. Thickets; w. Ontario,
s. Manitoba, and Yukon to nw. Iowa, Nebraska, Colorado, and
Oregon.

GASPE JUNEBERRY   **Not illus.**
Amelanchier gaspensis (Wieg.) Fern. & Weath.
Recognition: A very low, clumped, upright shrub. Leaves
coarse-toothed, blunt-tipped, hairless or slightly hairy beneath.
They vary from egg-shaped to nearly circular and are toothed
nearly to the base. Spreads by underground runners. Leaves
1″–3″. Height to 4′. Flowers June–Aug. Fruits black, July–
Sept. Only other low juneberries with blunt-tipped coarse-
toothed leaves which are clumped, spreading by underground
runners, are the Roundleaf and Alderleaf. Rocky soils; e.
Quebec, and ne. Ontario, to New Brunswick, n. Maine, n.
Michigan, and ne. Minnesota.

ROUNDLEAF JUNEBERRY p. 342
Amelanchier sanguinea (Pursh) DC.
Recognition: A rather low shrub with arching or straggling stems. Leaves coarse-toothed, blunt-tipped, toothed to base or nearly so, hairy beneath when young but soon hairless except for leafstalk; shape somewhat oblong to nearly circular. Clumped or not, sometimes spreading by underground stems. Winter buds dull, not shiny. Leaves 1″–3″. Height to 9′ (23′). Flowers May–June. Fruits purple, July–Aug.
Similar species: Among coarse-toothed juneberries, only (1) Alderleaf and (2) Gaspé are clumped and have leaves blunt-tipped and toothed nearly to base. They are more western and northern and have less arched or straggling stems. When not clumped, this species can be separated from (3) Large-flowered by its green leaves and from (4) Huron Juneberry by dull, nongummy buds.

LARGE-FLOWERED JUNEBERRY Not illus.
Amelanchier amabilis Wieg.
Recognition: Like the Roundleaf but with leaves covered with *whitish bloom* or powder. Flower petals somewhat broader than in other juneberries. Does not spread by underground shoots to form clumps. Woods and thickets; sw. Quebec and s. Ontario to New York.

HURON JUNEBERRY Not illus.
Amelanchier huronensis Wieg.
Recognition: Somewhat resembling Roundleaf Juneberry and sometimes considered identical. Typically upright, *not clumped,* and with *shiny, gummy winter buds.* Leaves 1″–4″. Height to 21′. Flowers May–July. Fruits July–Aug. Rocky soils; centr. and w. Ontario to n. Michigan, Wisconsin, and Minnesota.

WIEGAND JUNEBERRY Not illus.
Amelanchier wiegandii Nielsen
Recognition: Of coarse-toothed juneberries only this and the next have *short-pointed* leaf tips. This species is taller, does not occur in clumps, and is more widespread. Leaves 1″–3″. Height to 21′. Flowers May–July. Fruits July–Aug. Newfoundland and Ontario to Nova Scotia, n. New England, New York, n. Michigan, n. Wisconsin, and n. Minnesota.

MINNESOTA JUNEBERRY Not illus.
Amelanchier mucronata Nielsen
Recognition: Differs from the last in being *low, clumped,* and of

limited distribution. Leaves short-pointed or with short bristle-tip. Leaves 1″–3″. Height to 4′. Flowers June. Fruits Aug. Non-acid soils; n. Minnesota and se. Manitoba.

Willows

(Plates 55 and 56, pp. 344, 346)

Many willows, but not all, are easily recognized as such by the long narrow leaves. The single scale of the willow bud, however, forms a hoodlike complete covering and, although not obvious except on close examination, is absolutely distinctive among plants with 3 bundle scars. Some species, indicated below, have small and somewhat leaflike stipules on the twigs at bases of the leaf-stalks. The stipules are useful in identification but may be dropped early. They are most obvious on vigorous shoots. When stated to be large, they are reasonably leafy; when reported to be small, they are not evident except upon close examination. The bark of tree species is mostly yellow-ridged. Frequently galls that resemble pine cones grow on the twigs.

Identifying willows often is a difficult task even for the professional botanist. Individual variation, minute identification marks, and hybridization are complicating factors. Because of the great number of species, only the more distinctive and widespread of the upright species are pictured. The species not illustrated are inserted in the text near those they most resemble. Many have only a limited distribution. Winter characteristics are incompletely known. Since final identification of willows frequently depends on examination of the tiny flowers and fruits, some uncertain specimens may have to be identified professionally or accepted merely as willows. Creeping and sprawling willows are referred to on Plate 32 and are treated more fully in the text relating to that plate. Willow Oak (Plate 48) has clustered, scaly end buds and bears acorns.

Probably willows are most valuable in controlling streambank and mountainside erosion. Stakes of green branches often will sprout if merely driven into damp ground. Several willows provide long twigs used in basketmaking. A great many are valued as ornamental plants. The wood of tree species is of some commercial value but is generally used only for fuel, charcoal, and posts. Their bark provides tannin and a medicinal substance, salicin.

Willow leaves, twigs, and buds are of importance as browse for livestock. Among the many birds and mammals eating willow twigs, buds, leaves, or fruits are ruffed and sharptail grouse, willow and rock ptarmigan, elk, whitetail deer, moose, beaver, muskrat, snowshoe hare, and porcupine.

A Key to the Willows

Name   Page

1. Plants creeping and very low, often with underground
   stems   **DWARF WILLOWS** 179-81
1. Plants upright:
   2. Leaves not toothed, though sometimes wavy-edged:
      3. Leaves hairy, silky, or woolly beneath:
         4. Leaf undersides and twigs bearing loose
            white wool   **HOARY**   254
         4. Leaf undersides and twigs not bearing loose
            white wool:
            5. Leaf undersides and twigs gray-hairy:
               6. Leaf bases wedge-shaped:
                  7. Leaves up to 5″ long; plant height
                     to 13′   **TALL PRAIRIE** 250
                  7. Leaves under 3″ long; plant height
                     to 4′   **DWARF PRAIRIE** 251
               6. Leaf bases U- to heart-shaped:
                  8. Leaves over 2″ long, tips sharp;
                     plant to 17′ tall   **QUEBEC**   251
                  8. Leaves under 2″ long, tips blunt;
                     plant to 1½′ tall   **CANADA**   251
            5. Leaf undersides whitish-silky:
               9. Twigs not coated with a white powder:
                  10. Leaves shiny above; stipules con-
                      spicuous   **QUEBEC**   251
                  10. Leaves dull above; stipules small
                      or absent:
                      11. Leaves under 4″ long; plants
                          to 6′ tall:
                          12. Leaves quite narrow
                                                  SILVERLEAF 252
                          12. Leaves wider, egg-shaped
                              to circular   **UNGAVA**   252
                      11. Leaves 6″–10″ long; plants to
                          25′ tall   **OSIER**   252
               9. Twigs coated with a white powder:
                  13. Leaves strongly whitened beneath,
                      somewhat leathery   **ONTARIO**   252
                  13. Leaves only pale beneath, thin
                                                  FLATLEAF   253
      3. Leaves essentially hairless beneath:
         14. Leaves mostly somewhat paired   **BASKET**   258
         14. Leaves definitely alternate:
            15. Leaves thin, not leathery; plants to 10′
                tall:
                16. Leaf edges rolled   **TALL PRAIRIE** 250

Name   *Page*

16. Leaf edges not rolled:
    17. Widespread in North; catkins
        stalkless   **FLATLEAF**   **253**
    17. Known only from Newfound-
        land; catkins with stalks
                NEWFOUNDLAND   **253**
15. Leaves thicker, somewhat leathery;
    plants under 3′ tall:
    18. Plants not spreading by underground
        stems; leaf edges not rolled:
        19. Twigs and buds hairy; leaves
            quite leathery, nearly circular;
            stipules obvious   **LIMESTONE**   **253**
        19. Twigs and buds hairless; leaves
            somewhat leathery, more or less
            egg-shaped; stipules small or
            lacking   **MOUNT ALBERT**   **253**
    18. Plants spreading by underground
        stems; leaf edges rolled:
        20. Branches upright; bogs at low
            elevations   **BOG**   **254**
        20. Branches spreading; mountain
            areas   **SPREADING**   **254**
2. Leaves toothed:
    21. Leaves green and mostly hairless, not gray-hairy,
        whitened, or white-hairy beneath:
        22. Leaf tips pointed:
            23. Leaves very narrow, not long-pointed,
                leathery, or aromatic:
                24. Leaf teeth widely spaced; leaf bases
                    tapered   **SANDBAR**   **255**
                24. Leaf teeth closely spaced:
                    25. Leaf bases tapered; stipules small
                        or lacking   **CRACK**   **256**
                  25. Leaf bases rounded; stipules con-
                        spicuous   **BLACK**   **256**
            23. Leaves wider and either long-pointed,
                leathery or aromatic:
                26. Leaves not spicy-scented when
                  crushed; leaves quite long-pointed;
                  stipules usually conspicuous:
                  27. Leaves thick, rather leathery;
                    leafstalks with glands near or on
                    the leaf base:
                    28. Leaves with very long, tail-
                        like tips   **SHINING**   **256**
                    28. Leaves with only moder-
                      ately long tips   **BAYLEAF**   **256**

Name   *Page*

27. Leaves thin, not leathery; leafstalks without glands:
   29. Twigs gray-hairy
         HEARTLEAF 256
   29. Twigs hairless   **RIGID** 257
  26. Leaves spicy-scented when crushed;
   stipules small or lacking   **BALSAM** 257
22. Leaf tips blunt; stipules usually obvious:
  30. Leafstalks short; stipules broad
         MYRTLELEAF 257
  30. Leafstalks long; stipules heart-shaped
         BLUNTLEAF 257
21. Leaves gray-hairy, whitened or white-hairy beneath:
 31. Leaves gray-hairy at least beneath:
  32. Leaves wide, more or less egg-shaped:
   33. Leaves with long-pointed tips, bases
sometimes heart-shaped; twigs gray-
hairy   **HEARTLEAF** 256
   33. Leaves with short-pointed tips:
    34. Leaves without heart-shaped bases:
     35. Twigs densely gray-woolly;
leaves dull above   **BEBB** 254
     35. Twigs hairless or nearly so;
leaves shiny above   **GOAT** 255
    34. Leaves with heart-shaped bases,
often short-stalked   **SANDDUNE** 255
  32. Leaves narrow, canoe-shaped:
   36. Leaves hairy on both surfaces
         EUROPEAN GRAY 255
   36. Leaves not hairy above
         NORTHERN GRAY 255
 31. Leaves whitened or white-hairy beneath:
  37. Leaves usually opposite or nearly opposite;
leaves narrow with teeth only near the tips
         BASKET 258
  37. Leaves alternate:
   38. Leaves toothed mostly above the middle; teeth rather coarse:
    39. Leaves wide, elliptic; stipules often
large and obvious   **PUSSY** 258
    39. Leaves narrower; stipules small or
lacking   **MEADOW** 260
   38. Leaves toothed to the base or nearly so:
    40. Leaves with the tips long-pointed:
     41. Stipules small or lacking:
      42. Twigs very long, drooping;
leaves hairless or silky
         WEEPING 259

                                                    Name   *Page*
  42. Twigs droop only moderately; leaves hairless
                                              PEACHLEAF   **258**
 41. Stipules usually large and conspicuous:
    43. Twigs reddish; trunk bark gray   **WARD**   **258**
    43. Twigs white-woolly; trunk bark black
                                              MISSOURI   **259**
40. Leaves without long-pointed tips:
  44. Leaves silky, white-hairy, or woolly at least
    beneath:
    45. Leaves densely white-hairy above   **WHITE**   **260**
    45. Leaves not densely white-hairy above:
      46. Leaves merely silky beneath:
        47. Leaves narrow   **SILKY**   **259**
        47. Leaves wide, nearly circular
                                             ROUNDLEAF   **259**
      46. Leaves densely hairy to woolly beneath:
        48. Leaves with coarse, obvious teeth
                                                FELTED   **260**
        48. Leaves with small teeth:
          49. Leaf teeth rounded, indefinite
                                                WOOLLY   **260**
          49. Leaf teeth fine, sharp
                                             BROADLEAF   **261**
  44. Leaves hairless, though whitened beneath:
    50. Leaves leathery; leafstalks with glands
                                                AUTUMN   **261**
    50. Leaves thin, not leathery; leafstalks without
      glands:
      51. Stipules small or lacking:
        52. Tree; leaves usually at least slightly
          silky and dull above   **WHITE**   **260**
        52. Shrub; leaves hairless and shiny
          above   **MEADOW**   **260**
      51. Stipules usually conspicuous:
        53. Leaves dark green above; twigs dark
                                             BROADLEAF   **261**
        53. Leaves yellow-green above; twigs
          yellowish   **YELLOW**   **261**

Willows with Leaves Not Toothed

(*Plate 55, first part, p. 344*)

TALL PRAIRIE WILLOW *Salix humilis* Marsh.   **p. 344**
  Recognition: A shrub with leaves *wavy-edged*, dull gray-green
above (except in forma *festiva* Fern. from Cape Cod) and typi-

cally *gray-hairy* beneath. From n. New York and n. Michigan southward, however, var. *hyporhysa* Fern. has leaves hairless or nearly so beneath. Leaves widest above middle, edges rolled slightly and base *wedge-shaped*. Twigs usually gray-hairy but sometimes hairless. Stipules small or lacking. Leaves 1″–5″. Height to 13′. Flowers March–June.

Similar species: Of upright willows whose leaves are not toothed, this species, (1) Quebec, (2) Dwarf Prairie, and (3) Canada Willows have densely gray-hairy twigs and leaf undersides. Gray-green color and wedge-shaped leaf bases distinguish the 2 prairie willows from the others. Small size of Dwarf Prairie Willow and Canada Willow (below) usually separate them from Tall Prairie Willow. (4) Basket Willow (Plate 56) sometimes has leaves similar to hairless form but purplish twigs are distinctive. (5) Flatleaf Willow (p. 253) lacks rolled leaf edges.

DWARF PRAIRIE WILLOW   p. 344
Salix humilis var. *microphylla* (Anderss.) Fern.
    Recognition: Now classified (by Fernald but not by all botanists) as a dwarf variety of Tall Prairie Willow. It is distinctive, though variable. A low shrub with small leaves; leaf undersides and twigs *densely gray-hairy*. Leaf bases wedge-shaped. Leaf-stalks much longer than side buds. Leaves ½″–3″. Height to 4′. Flowers March–June.
    Similar species: (1) See Tall Prairie Willow. (2) Canada Willow has broader leaf bases, longer leafstalks.

CANADA WILLOW   *Salix brachycarpa* Nutt.   Not illus.
    Recognition: A very low shrub like Dwarf Prairie Willow but leaf undersides *white- or gray-hairy* to woolly. Leaves toothless, small, oblong-shaped, blunt-tipped, and strongly overlap each other. Leaf bases U-shaped; leafstalks shorter than the very hairy buds. Leaves ½″–1½″. Height to 1½′. Flowers June–Aug. Dry soils; e. Quebec, n. Quebec, and British Columbia to Manitoba, Colorado, Utah, and Oregon.

QUEBEC WILLOW   *Salix laurentiana* Fern.   Not illus.
    Recognition: A shrub or small tree. Leaves dark green and *shining* above and *white- or gray-hairy* beneath, bases wide, sometimes heart-shaped, tips slightly extended, edges wavy-edged or not toothed. Leafstalks and twigs densely gray-hairy. Stipules usually conspicuous. Leaves 2″–8″. Height to 17′. Flowers June. Only willow with leaf edges wavy-toothed or not toothed and with leaves hairy beneath and shining above. Sometimes considered a hybrid involving the Broadleaf Willow. Gulf of St. Lawrence, n. Quebec, and James Bay to e. Quebec, and nearby islands.

SILVERLEAF WILLOW   **Not illus.**
Salix argyrocarpa Anderss.
   Recognition: A low shrub with small leaves. Leaves wavy-
edged, usually shaped like those of Dwarf Prairie Willow and
sometimes blunt-tipped, but quite *silvery-silky* beneath. Leaves
1″–2½″. Height to 5′. Stipules small or lacking. Flowers
June–Aug. Of upright willows whose leaves are not toothed
and twigs not white-coated, only 4 are whitish-silky beneath.
The others are either gray-hairy, white-woolly, or hairless. This
species may be distinguished from Ungava Willow by its narrower leaves and from Osier and Ontario Willows by its
shorter leaves, height, and arctic-alpine distribution. Arctic
tundras and barrens; Labrador to the mountains of e. Quebec
and New Hampshire.

UNGAVA WILLOW   *Salix cordifolia* Pursh   **Not illus.**
   Recognition: A variable low arctic-alpine shrub. Leaves *wide*,
from shape of Bebb Willow to nearly circular, *densely silky*,
but *wavy-edged* or *not toothed.* Twigs quite silky. Leaves typically heart-shaped at base but 4 varieties with rounded leaf bases
are known; a 5th is hairless. Recognizable with certainty only
from minute characteristics of reproductive parts, unless leaf
bases are heart-shaped; then its toothless leaves are distinctive.
Stipules lacking. Leaves ½″–4″. Height to 6′. Flowers June–
July. Silverleaf Willow has narrower leaves with wedge-shaped
bases. Osier Willow has longer, narrower leaves. Ontario Willow has twigs covered with white powder. See Taller Willows
(p. 181). Rocky soils; Greenland and e. Arctic to Newfoundland,
Nova Scotia, and e. Quebec.

OSIER WILLOW   *Salix viminalis* L.   **Not illus.**
   Recognition: A shrub or small tree with distinctive leaves that
are *very long, narrow*, pointed, *toothless*, and *silvery-hairy* beneath. Twigs and branches very long and flexible. Stipules small
or lacking. Leaves 6″–10″. Height to 25′. Flowers April–June.
Among willows with toothless leaves white-hairy beneath, this
is the only one with long narrow leaves. Escaped from cultivation; Newfoundland and Quebec to Nova Scotia and New
England.

ONTARIO WILLOW   *Salix pellita* Anderss.   **Not illus.**
   Recognition: A large shrub to small tree with thick, *toothless*
leaves narrow like those of Hoary Willow. Foliage *whitened
beneath*, often silky-hairy and somewhat *long-pointed.* Twigs
covered with *white powder.* Stipules small or lacking. Leaves
2″–5″. Height to 30′. Flowers May–June. When leaves
are hairy, whitened twigs distinguish this species from preceding 2. Of following several species with toothless hairless leaves, only Flatleaf also has white-powdered twigs. Its

leaves are wider and not long-pointed. Damp thickets; Newfoundland, s. Labrador, and n. Ontario to Nova Scotia, n. New
England, n. Michigan, and westward.

FLATLEAF WILLOW   Salix planifolia Pursh   Not illus.
Recognition: A variable low shrub with leaves elliptic, hairless,
dark green above, whitened beneath, essentially toothless,
though sometimes with a few tiny teeth. Hairless twigs sometimes covered with whitish powder. Stipules small or lacking.
Catkins without stalks. Leaves 1″–3″. Height to 10′. Flowers
June–Aug. Of 8 upright willows that may have hairless, toothless leaves, this species is distinctive when twigs have whitish
coating. Otherwise, the group is divided into those with leaves
thickened and generally short with rolled margins (see Limestone Willow) and those with longer thinner leaves. In latter
group, this species very similar to 3 little-known Newfoundland willows (next), except that its catkins have no stalks.
Basket Willow (p. 258), usually with toothed leaves, can be
distinguished by nearly opposite leaves when leaf teeth are lacking. See also Tall Prairie and Northern Gray Willows (pp. 250,
255). Tundras and damp thickets; Newfoundland and Labrador
to mountains of e. Quebec and n. New England and westward
to Alberta.

NEWFOUNDLAND WILLOWS   Not illus.
Salix pedunculata Fern., S. *amoena* Fern., S. *ancorifera* Fern.
Recognition: Similar to Flatleaf but with stalks of catkins leafy.
The several species are separable principally by minute floral
characteristics. Stipules small or lacking. Local; Newfound-
land.

LIMESTONE WILLOW   Not illus.
Salix calcicola Fern. & Wieg.
Recognition: A ground-hugging or very low gnarled shrub with
egg-shaped to nearly circular hairless leaves and hairy twigs
and buds. Leaves leathery and short-stalked, edges not rolled.
Stipules usually obvious. Does not spread by underground
stems. Leaves ½″–2½″. Height to 1½′. Flowers June. Mount
Albert Willow also low with leathery leaves and does not spread
by underground stems, but its twigs are hairless. See Taller
Willows (p. 181). Limestone and other rocky soils; Newfoundland, Baffin I., and Keewatin to e. Quebec and ne.
Ontario.

MOUNT ALBERT WILLOW   Not illus.
Salix chlorolepis Fern.
Recognition: Another very low shrub with short, egg-shaped,
hairless, and somewhat leathery leaves. Twigs hairless. Leaf

edges not rolled. Stipules small or lacking. Leaves to 1″. Height to 7″. Mount Albert, Quebec. See Taller Willows (p. 181) and next 2 species.

BOG WILLOW *Salix pedicellaris* Pursh **Not illus.**
Recognition: A low, clumped plant, spreading by underground stems. Leaves more or less elliptic, leathery, hairless, with rolled edges. Branches erect. Stipules small or lacking. Leaves ½″–2″. Height to 3′. Flowers May–July. Spreading Willow also is low, with leathery leaves, and spreads by underground stems. It has more spreading branches and grows on uplands. Bog Willow grows in acid bogs at low elevations; Newfoundland, Labrador, and British Columbia to n. New Jersey, Pennsylvania, Indiana, n. Iowa, Manitoba, and Oregon.

SPREADING WILLOW *Salix hebecarpa* Fern. **Not illus.**
Recognition: Very similar to Bog Willow (sometimes interpreted as a hybrid of it) but branches less upright and stalks of catkins thick and hairy rather than thin and hairless. Known only from rocky soils on Mount Albert, Quebec. See also Taller Willows (p. 181).

HOARY WILLOW *Salix candida* Flügge **p. 344**
Recognition: A medium-sized shrub with narrow leaves with rolled edges. Our only upright willow with leaves lacking teeth and with leaf undersides and twigs bearing *loose white wool*. Stipules usually conspicuous. Leaves 1½″–5″. Height to 7′. Flowers April–June.

Willows with Toothed Leaves, Gray-hairy At Least Beneath
(*Plate 55 contd., p. 344*)

BEBB WILLOW *Salix bebbiana* Sarg. **p. 344**
Recognition: A variable shrub or small tree. Leaves wide, coarse-toothed, less commonly nearly without teeth. Foliage dull above, *grayish-woolly* and veiny beneath. Twigs gray-woolly. Stipules small or lacking. Leaves 2″–5″. Height to 25′; diameter to 8″. Flowers April–June.
Similar species: Only upright species with wide, coarse-toothed and gray-hairy leaves with tapered tips and bases. Broad leaves and moderate plant size help separate it from other willows with gray-hairy leaves, even when teeth of leaves are obscure. Goat Willow has nonwoolly twigs and shining upper leaf surfaces.

GOAT WILLOW   *Salix caprea* L.   **Not illus.**
Recognition: Like Bebb Willow with *wide*, more or less egg-shaped leaves, but these may bear only inconspicuous teeth above middle. Moderately gray-hairy beneath; hairless and shining above. Leafstalks mostly ⅜″–¾″. Twigs hairless or slightly hairy. Stipules small. Leaves 1″–5″. Height to 25′. Flowers March–April. See Bebb Willow. Sanddune Willow has heart-shaped, short-stalked leaves. Early leaves of Pussy Willow (Plate 56) resemble those of this species but leaf teeth and stipules are more conspicuous in Pussy Willow. European; escaped from plantings; New England to Ohio and Maryland.

SANDDUNE WILLOW   *Salix syrticola* Fern.   **Not illus.**
Recognition: Like Goat Willow in having wide fine-toothed leaves gray-hairy beneath, but leaves more or less *heart-shaped* at base and stalks usually only ⅛″–⅜″. Twigs gray-hairy or -woolly. Stipules usually large. Leaves 1½″–4″. Height to 10′. Flowers May–June. See Heartleaf Willow, p. 256 (usually hairless). Sanddune and Heartleaf Willows are considered identical by some botanists. Great Lakes dunes; w. Ontario, Michigan, Indiana, ne. Illinois, and e. Wisconsin.

EUROPEAN GRAY WILLOW   *Salix cinerea* L.   **Not illus.**
Recognition: An Old World shrub or small tree. Leaves wedge-shaped like Tall Prairie Willow but distinctly though *finely toothed.* Both leaf surfaces and twigs densely gray-hairy. Stipules small or lacking. Leaves 1″–4″. Flowers April–May. Escaped; Nova Scotia and Massachusetts.

NORTHERN GRAY WILLOW   **Not illus.**
Salix paraleuca Fern.
Recognition: Similar to European Gray Willow but gray-hairy leaves dull and not hairy above. Leaves 1″–4″. Height to 13′. Flowers June. Considered by some botanists to be a hybrid involving Flatleaf Willow, which is not toothed. E. and ne. Quebec.

Willows with Toothed, Mostly Hairless Leaves, Green on Both Sides
(*Plate 55 contd., p. 344*)

SANDBAR WILLOW   *Salix interior* Rowlee   **p. 344**
Recognition: A shrub or small tree with long, quite narrow, hairless or rarely silky, short-stalked leaves. Teeth small but widely spaced; leaf bases tapered. Twigs hairless. Stipules small or lacking. Leaves 2″–6″. Height to 20′. Flowers May–June.

Similar species: Of willows that have toothed, hairless, point-tipped leaves green on both sides, only 3 have leaves also very narrow. In contrast to (1) Crack and (2) Black Willows, leaves of this species have widely spaced teeth.

BLACK WILLOW   *Salix nigra* Marsh.   **pp. *11*, 344**
Recognition: A shrub or tree with long narrow leaves but with bases *rounded*. Leaves fine-toothed, hairless except for hairy glandless stalks. Twigs hairless. Stipules usually conspicuous. Leaves 1″–6″. Height 10′–40′ (120′); diameter 2″–24″ (96″). Flowers April–June.
Similar species: See (1) Sandbar and (2) Crack Willows.

CRACK WILLOW   *Salix fragilis* L.   **Not illus.**
Recognition: This European tree has leaves like Black Willow but with *tapering* bases. Leafstalks may bear glands. Buds somewhat sticky; twigs hairless, very brittle at base. Stipules small or lacking. Leaves 1″–7″. Height 50′–70′ (80′); diameter 2′–3′ (4′). Flowers April–June. See Black Willow. Spread from cultivation; Newfoundland, Ontario, and Minnesota to Virginia, Kentucky, Kansas.

SHINING WILLOW   *Salix lucida* Muhl.   **p. 344**
Recognition: The *extremely long-pointed* leaves are distinctive. They are hairless, fine-toothed, and usually rather leathery. Leafstalks have heavy *glands* near or at leaf bases. Twigs hairless; stipules usually large. Var. *intonsa* Fern. (Newfoundland and Ontario to Maine and n. Indiana) has hairy leaf undersides and twigs. Leaves 2″–7″. Height 10′–15′ (25′); diameter 1″–6″ (12″). Flowers April–June.
Similar species: This and (1) Bayleaf, (2) Heartleaf, and (3) Rigid Willows have toothed leaves, green on both sides, which might be considered long-pointed. This species and Bayleaf Willow have leathery leaves with glandular leafstalks; this one is unique in having very long tail-like leaf tips.

BAYLEAF WILLOW   *Salix pentandra* L.   **Not illus.**
Recognition: Like Shining Willow in having toothed, hairless, leathery leaves with glandular leafstalks; but leaves of this European species only *moderately long-pointed*. Twigs hairless. Leaves 1″–4″. Height to 25′. Flowers May–June. Shining Willow has longer leaf tips; Heartleaf has nonleathery leaves. Spread from cultivation; Nova Scotia and Ontario to Maryland, Ohio, and Iowa.

HEARTLEAF WILLOW   *Salix cordata* Michx.   **p. 344**
Recognition: Differing from Bayleaf Willow in having leaves *not leathery* and sometimes barely heart-shaped at base.

Though usually hairless at maturity, young leaves, and sometimes mature ones, may be gray-hairy on both surfaces. They have long-pointed tips. Leafstalks long-hairy; twigs densely gray-hairy. Stipules usually conspicuous. Leaves 1″–5″. Height to 5′. Flowers May–June.
Similar species: Only this and (1) Rigid Willow regularly have nonleathery toothed leaves, green beneath, with moderately long-pointed tips. Rigid Willow has hairless twigs. When gray-hairy beneath, Heartleaf Willow is the only species so marked which also has prolonged leaf tips. (2) Balsam Willow leaves may have heart-shaped bases, but when crushed have firlike fragrance.
Remarks: Sanddune Willow (p. 255) is considered by some botanists to be only a hairy form of this species.

RIGID WILLOW   *Salix rigida* Muhl.   **Not illus.**
    Recognition: Very similar to Heartleaf Willow but with more narrow, pointed leaves and usually with hairless leaves and twigs. Leaves 1″–5″. Height to 10′. Flowers April–June. Damp soils; s. Newfoundland and Ontario to N. Carolina, Mississippi, Arkansas, and Kansas.

BALSAM WILLOW   *Salix pyrifolia* Anderss.   **Not illus.**
    Recognition: A shrub or small tree with fine-toothed, hairless, broad, thin, egg-shaped to heart-shaped, point-tipped leaves on long slender stalks. Foliage has a pleasant firlike *aromatic* odor when crushed. Twigs hairless. Stipules small or lacking. Leaves 1″–5″. Height to 20′. Flowers May–Aug. Woods and thickets; Newfoundland, s. Labrador, and n. British Columbia to Maine, n. New York, Michigan, Wisconsin, Minnesota, and Saskatchewan.

MYRTLELEAF WILLOW   **Not illus.**
Salix myrtillifolia Anderss.
    Recognition: A low, sometimes creeping, shrub with blunt-tipped oblong leaves that are rather large-toothed, hairless, and green on both sides. Leaf bases rounded; leafstalks short and stout. Broad stipules often obvious. Leaves 1″–3½″. Height to 3′. Flowers June–July. Only this and Bluntleaf Willow have toothed, hairless leaves green on both sides and with rounded tips. See dwarf willows (pp. 179–81). Damp soils; Newfoundland, se. Labrador, and Alaska to e. Quebec, n. Ontario, Manitoba, and s. British Columbia.

BLUNTLEAF WILLOW   *Salix obtusata* Fern.   **Not illus.**
    Recognition: Similar to the more widespread Myrtleleaf Willow (and sometimes considered a variety of it), but with long and slender leafstalks and obvious *heart-shaped stipules.*

Some leaves may be nearly circular and occasionally young leaves are somewhat woolly. See Taller Willows (p. 181). Leaves 1″–2″. Height to 3′. Flowers June. Gravelly soils; local; Quebec.

Willows with Toothed Leaves, Whitened or White-hairy Beneath
(*Plate 56, p. 346*)

BASKET WILLOW   *Salix purpurea* L.   **p. 346**
Recognition: A tall shrub with narrow leaves that have small teeth only near tips, or these lacking. Leaves usually opposite or nearly opposite each other, hairless, and whitened beneath. Twigs purplish and hairless. Leaves 1″–5″. Height to 20′. Flowers April–May.
Similar species: Leaf type and nearly opposite leaves and buds are distinctive. Flatleaf Willow has similar but always toothless and alternate leaves.
Remarks: A European import; twigs used to make baskets.

PUSSY WILLOW   *Salix discolor* Muhl.   **pp. 11, 346**
Recognition: A shrub or tree. Leaves elliptic, whitened beneath, hairless, except immediately upon unfolding, or more rarely rusty-hairy beneath, toothed *mostly above middle*. Twigs either hairless or somewhat long-hairy. Stipules often large. Leaves 2″–5″. Height to 30′. Flowers Feb.–May.
Similar species: Except when leaves are hairy, the leaf-tooth pattern is rather distinctive. (1) When hairy, it most resembles Goat Willow (p. 255) but leaves have more prominent teeth. (2) One variety of Meadow Willow has similar but narrower leaves; stipules are small or lacking.
Remarks: Furry flower catkins are a symbol of spring.

PEACHLEAF WILLOW   *Salix amygdaloides* Anderss.   **p. 346**
Recognition: A shrub or small tree. Leaves *long-pointed*, fine-toothed, hairless, somewhat leathery, whitened beneath. The hairless, yellow, flexible twigs *droop moderately*. Stipules *small or lacking*. Leaves 3″–7″. Height to 40′. Flowers April–June.
Similar species: (1) Ward and (2) Missouri Willows also have long-pointed leaves, but their stipules are large and leafy. (3) Weeping Willow has longer, more flexible twigs and may have silky leaf undersides.

WARD WILLOW   *Salix caroliniana* Michx.   **Not illus.**
Recognition: A small southern tree. Leaves very narrow, *long-pointed*, hairless, whitened or white-hairy beneath. Twigs

hairless or somewhat hairy, reddish, brittle at base. They do not droop. *Conspicuous* leafy stipules. Trunk bark gray. Leaves 2″–7″. Height to 35″. Flowers May–June. Missouri Willow also has long-pointed leaves and large stipules but has more woolly twigs, black bark, and a more western range. Mostly floodplains; Maryland, W. Virginia, sw. Pennsylvania, s. Illinois, Missouri, and e. Kansas, to Florida and Texas.

MISSOURI WILLOW *Salix eriocephala* Michx. **Not illus.**
Recognition: The only willow with *long-pointed* leaves that are *white-woolly* at least on veins beneath. Twigs densely *white hairy*. Stipules usually conspicuous. Trunk bark black. Leaves 3″–7″. Height 20′–50′ (60′); diameter 4″–10″ (14″). Flowers March–April. Ward Willow has reddish and sometimes hairy (but not white-hairy) twigs. Floodplains and shorelines; sw. Indiana, Minnesota, and S. Dakota to Kentucky, Missouri, and Nebraska.

WEEPING WILLOW *Salix babylonica* L. **pp. *11*, 346**
Recognition: An Old World Tree with *extremely long*, brittle-based, *drooping* twigs and branchlets, often overhanging a lake or stream. Leaves thin, narrow, hairless or silky, often long-pointed, whitened beneath. Stipules small or lacking. Leaves 1″–5″. Height 30′–50′ (60′); diameter 1′–3′ (5′).
Similar species: Extreme weeping characteristics of this willow rarely seen in other species. (1) The sometimes slightly pendent White Willow has leaves silky on both sides and nonbrittle twigs. (2) See also Peachleaf Willow (opposite).

SILKY WILLOW *Salix sericea* Marsh. **p. 346**
Recognition: A shrub with narrow, fine-toothed leaves, dark green above and very *white-silky* beneath. Twigs brown, hairless or nearly so, and brittle at base. Stipules usually obvious on vigorous shoots. Leaves 2″–5″. Height to 15′ (24′). Flowers March–May.
Similar species: Six willows may have short-pointed, toothed leaves that are obviously white-hairy beneath. Only this species, however, and (1) Roundleaf Willow are merely silky beneath. (2) Felted, (3) Woolly, (4) White, and (5) Broadleaf Willows have densely white-hairy or white-woolly leaf undersides. Roundleaf Willow has nearly circular leaves. (6) Missouri Willow has long-pointed leaves.

ROUNDLEAF WILLOW *Salix vestita* Pursh **Not illus.**
Recognition: A low, even creeping shrub. Leaves *leathery*, egg-shaped to circular, fine-toothed, blunt-tipped or nearly so, wrinkled above and slightly to densely white silky-hairy beneath. Twigs dark; branches usually angled. Buds hairy.

Leaves ½"–4". Height to 4'. Flowers June–Aug. See Taller Willows (p. 181). Rocky soils; Labrador and n. Quebec to Newfoundland and e. Quebec, and in Montana, Alberta, Oregon, and British Columbia.

FELTED WILLOW   *Salix coactilis* Fern.   **Not illus.**
Recognition: Leaves shaped like Silky and Meadow Willows but slightly wider and *densely white-hairy* beneath. They have *coarse* teeth like those pictured for Bebb Willow. Stipules usually obvious on vigorous shoots; twigs brittle at base. Leaves 2"–6". Height to 12'. Flowers May. The only coarse-toothed willow with leaves densely white-hairy beneath. Damp soils; w. New Brunswick and s. Quebec to centr. Maine.

WOOLLY WILLOW   *Salix cryptodonta* Fern.   **Not illus.**
Recognition: Similar to Felted Willow but leaves with obscure, *tiny, rounded* teeth, rolled edges, and loosely white-woolly beneath. Stipules usually conspicuous. Height to 13'. Flowers May–June, catkins expanding before leaves unfold. Var. *albo-vestita* (C. R. Ball) Fern. of Broadleaf Willow is very much like this species but occurs on sand dunes near Great Lakes. Its catkins come out with leaves or afterwards. Woolly Willow grows on wet soils; Newfoundland and e. Quebec.

WHITE WILLOW   *Salix alba* L.   **p. 346**
Recognition: This European tree is the only willow with leaves white-hairy *above and below*. Twigs silky, not brittle at base and sometimes slightly drooping. Common varieties, *calva* C. F. W. Mey. and *vitellina* (L.) Stokes, and some hybrids, however, are hairless. Stipules mostly lacking. Leaves 2"–6". Height to 80'. Flowers April–May.
Similar species: When hairless, similar to the remaining willows that have fine-toothed leaves with whitish, hairless undersides, but may be separated from (1) Broadleaf and (2) Yellow Willows by absence of stipules; from (3) Autumn Willow also by narrower nonleathery leaves and lack of glands on leafstalks; from (4) Meadow Willow by taller size and firmer foliage. (5) When drooping, nonbrittle twigs distinguish it from Weeping Willow.

MEADOW WILLOW   *Salix gracilis* Anderss.   **p. 346**
Recognition: A shrub. Leaves narrow, nonleathery, shiny green above, whitish beneath, hairless or white- to rusty-silky beneath, toothed mostly *above middle*. Var. *textoris* Fern. has coarse-toothed leaves. Twigs hairless, sometimes whitened, not brittle at base. Stipules *absent* or very small. Leaves 1"–4". Height to 10'. Flowers May–June.
Similar species: Limited leaf teeth and lack of obvious stipules distinguish this species even when silky leaf undersides are present. (1) Occasional coarse-toothed specimens have narrower

leaves than Pussy Willow, which also has obvious stipules on vigorous shoots. (2) Variants of White Willow are taller, leaves at least slightly silky and dull above.

BROADLEAF WILLOW   Not illus.
Salix glaucophylloides Fern.
Recognition: A northeastern shrub or small tree. Leaves narrow to almost egg-shaped, semileathery, fine-toothed, shiny dark green above, whitened beneath; bases tapering to heart-shaped. Twigs dark and hairless except in uncommon form *lasioclada* Fern., which has gray-hairy twigs. Var. *glaucophylla* (Bebb) Schneid., of Great Lakes dunes from New York to Ontario and Michigan, has white-woolly twigs and leaves. Stipules usually present and conspicuous. Leaves 1″–6″. Height to 17′. Flowers May–June. Typical form resembles Yellow Willow. Var. *glaucophylla* is most like Felted Willow, but has fine-toothed leaves. White Willow has leaves hairy also above. Quebec Willow is sometimes considered to be a hybrid involving this species but its leaves are gray-hairy beneath. Rocky and sandy soils; Newfoundland, n. Ontario, and Wisconsin to n. Maine, Ohio, and Illinois.

YELLOW WILLOW   *Salix lutea* Nutt.   Not illus.
Recognition: Similar to Broadleaf Willow, but leaves *yellow-green above* and twigs *yellow*. Streamsides, n. Ontario, Northwest Territories, and British Columbia to nw. Iowa, Nebraska, Utah, and California

AUTUMN WILLOW   *Salix serissima* (Bailey) Fern.   **p. 346**
Recognition: A shrub with rather narrow leaves hairless, green above, white beneath, and *quite leathery*. Leafstalks carry large *glands* at or on leaf bases. Fruits released in late summer or in autumn. Twigs hairless. Leaves 2″–5″. Height to 15′. Flowers May–July.
Similar species: Among the species with hairless but whitened leaves, the only one with leathery leaves and with glands on leafstalks.

Miscellaneous Plants
with 3 Bundle Scars (1)
(Plate 57, p. 348)

Of the several plants of this group, the first 6 are related species of the waxmyrtle family. These plants are among the few outside the pea (legume) family which enrich the soil through nitrogen-fixing bacteria contained in root nodules. The crushed foliage has a pleasant aroma, and the short-stalked leaves and usually the twigs are marked with tiny yellow resin-dots. The dots, ordinarily not visible except when magnified, are good identification marks. The flowers and fruits are small and clustered.

Beech, Chestnut, and Chinquapin are members of the oak family, to which the bayberry group also shows relationship by similarly having flowers in catkins. Witch-hazels are related to the Sweetgum (Plate 42).

SWEETGALE   *Myrica gale* L.   **p. 348**
   Recognition: A *northern* shrub with *thin, nonevergreen,* blunt-tipped, wedge-shaped, *nonleathery* leaves. Leaves toothed at tip; slightly hairy beneath or hairless. Twigs hairless, with false end buds. Buds whitish, oval. Resin-dots *prominent* beneath or on both surfaces. Leaves 1″–3″. Height to 6′. Flowers April–June. Fruits small nuts, not wax-covered, July.
   Similar species: Aromatic, resin-dotted foliage and twigs distinctive. Of the 5 species of *Myrica,* only Northern Bayberry also has nonleathery leaves. It has hairy twigs and true end buds.
   Remarks: Leaves have been used to flavor meat and scent clothes. Deer browse foliage and twigs; sharptail grouse eat buds and leaves.

COMMON WAXMYRTLE   *Myrica cerifera* L.   **p. 348**
   Recognition: An evergreen, *southern* shrub or tree. Leaves often leathery, *wedge-shaped,* toothed or not toward tip, hairless, with *resin-dots* on both surfaces. Twigs sparsely hairy or hairless. Buds yellowish and globular; true end buds present. Leaves 1½″–3″. Height 10′–30′ (40′); diameter 3″–10″ (12″). Flowers April–June. Fruits small wax-covered nuts, Aug.–Oct.
   Similar species: Of the 3 evergreen Myricas, this the only one with wedge-shaped leaves. See (1) Dwarf Waxmyrtle and (2) Black Bayberry.
   Remarks: The wax is collected for making scented candles. A pound of nutlets immersed in hot water yields 4 ounces of wax. Fruits are eaten by many birds, including bobwhite and wild turkey.

DWARF WAXMYRTLE   *Myrica pusilla* Raf.   **Not illus.**
   Recognition: Similar to Common Waxmyrtle but lower, spreads by underground runners, and grows in clumps. Leaves smaller, more or less egg-shaped. Leaves ½″–1½″. Height to 6′. Flowers April–June. Fruits May–Oct. Woods; s. Delaware to Florida, Texas, and Arkansas.

NORTHERN BAYBERRY   *Myrica pensylvanica* Loisel.   **p. 348**
   Recognition: *Nonevergreen,* like Sweetgale, but with much

larger, more egg-shaped, point-tipped, thin leaves. Resin-dots few or lacking on the often somewhat hairy upper surface. Twigs gray-hairy; buds whitish; true end buds present. Leaves 1″–5″. Usually shrubby, but height to 35′; diameter to 6″. Flowers May–July. Fruits hairy, June–April.

Similar species: See (1) Sweetgale and (2) Black Bayberry.

Remarks: Many songbirds (notably myrtle warbler) and also ruffed grouse, bobwhite, and pheasant eat the fruits.

BLACK BAYBERRY   *Myrica heterophylla* Raf.   **Not illus.**

Recognition: Somewhat similar to Northern Bayberry, but with leathery, *evergreen* leaves and *black-hairy* twigs. Flowers April–June. Coastal Plain; s. New Jersey to Florida and Louisiana.

SWEETFERN   *Comptonia peregrina* (L.) Coult.   **p. 348**

Recognition: Any time a "fern" is found growing in our part of the world as a low bush with woody stem and branches, the observer is viewing this plant. Foliage *fernlike*. Twigs *aromatic* when crushed; usually hairy. Buds have 4 or more scales; end buds false. Leaves 3″–6″. Height to 5′. Flowers April–June. Fruits small nuts, not waxy, Sept.–Oct.

Similar species: Unique when in leaf. In winter, the only aromatic plant among those with 3 bundle scars, false end buds, and buds with more than 4 scales.

Remarks: Ruffed and sharptail grouse and whitetail deer feed on plant.

BEECH   *Fagus grandifolia* Ehrh.   **pp. *10*, 348**

Recognition: A tall tree with distinctive *smooth gray bark*, *slender many-scaled buds*, and elliptic or egg-shaped, *coarse-toothed* leaves. Twigs hairless or somewhat long-hairy, encircled or almost encircled by stipule scars at each leaf scar. Leaves 1″–5″. Height 60′–80′ (120′); diameter 2′–3′ (4′). Flowers April–May. Fruits small *triangular nuts*, edible, Sept.–Oct.

Similar species: Combination of bark, twig, bud, and leaf characteristics is unique. (1) Yellowwood (Plate 30) has similar bark but compound leaves; not common. (2) See Chestnut (p. 264). Several oaks (Plate 47) have similar leaves but buds and leaves are clustered at twig tips.

Remarks: An important timber species. Quality of wood only fair but used for cheap furniture, tool handles, veneer, shoe lasts, and fuel. Beeches are planted widely for ornament. Fruits eaten by ruffed grouse, wild turkey, bobwhite, pheasant, black bear, raccoon, red and gray foxes, whitetail deer, cottontail rabbit, gray, red, and flying squirrels, porcupine, and opossum.

COMMON WITCH-HAZEL   *Hamamelis virginiana* L.   **p. 348**

Recognition: A shrub or small tree with *wavy-toothed, uneven-*

based leaves, and hairy buds somewhat stalked at the base and without scales. Leaves and twigs typically hairless, but in var. *parvifolia* Nutt. (Ohio and Louisiana eastward) they may be very hairy and leathery. Some pairs or tight groups of stubby 4-parted seed pods usually can be found at any time of year. Bark smooth or rough in patches, often with some cross stripes. Leaves 2″–7″. Height 10′–25′ (30′); diameter 2″–10″ (14″). Flowers yellow, Sept.–Nov. Fruits Aug.–Oct.

Similar species: Only other species with naked buds and 3 bundle scars are the buckthorns (Plates 19 and 58). They have more egg-shaped leaves and buds without narrowed bases. (1) Springtime Witch-hazel and (2) Witch-alder quite hairy and restricted to southern ranges.

Remarks: Colloquial names Winter-bloom and Snapping-alder indicate peculiarities of this plant. In late autumn, after the leaves drop and the old fruit pods "pop out" their seeds for distances up to 20′ — and sometimes even after snow is on the ground — the straggly blossoms appear. An extract of the bark has long been used for medicinal purposes. Branches are used as "divining rods" in attempts to indicate, in some mysterious way, the presence of underground water. Witch-hazel seeds, buds, or twigs are dietary items of pheasant, bobwhite, ruffed grouse, whitetail deer, cottontail rabbit, and beaver.

SPRINGTIME WITCH-HAZEL   Not illus.
Hamamelis vernalis Sarg.

Recognition: Somewhat similar to Common Witch-hazel but flowering in late winter or spring and twigs and leaves *woolly*. Leaf bases wedge-shaped or rounded. Height to 10′. Flowers Jan.–April. Streamsides; s. Missouri and Oklahoma to Alabama and Louisiana.

WITCH-ALDER   *Fothergilla gardeni* Murr.   Not illus.

Recognition: This southern relative of the witch-hazels has leaves of similar shape but they are toothed, somewhat sharply, *only above the middle,* and are woolly beneath. Flowers are white, and appear in spring. Blossoms and fruits in long clusters unlike short-pod groups of witch-hazels. Leaves 1″–3″. Height to 3′. Flowers April–May. Fruits July–Aug. Streamsides; Virginia to Georgia and Alabama.

CHESTNUT   *Castanea dentata* (Marsh.) Borkh.   p. 348

Recognition: Originally a large tree but now existing primarily as sprouts from old stumps. Leaves *large but narrow,* hairless, *coarse-toothed.* Buds blunt, few-scaled; twigs brownish, hairless. End buds false. Bundle scars 3, occasionally more. Mature bark dark, with numerous wide-topped shiny ridges. Leaves 4″–8″. Height 60′–80′ (100′), now mostly under 15′; diameter 2′–4′ (17′). Flowers June–Aug. Fruits nuts, *several* to each spiny husk, each nut *flattened* on 1 or more sides, edible, Sept.–Oct.

Similar species: (1) Species name is not be confused with the compound-leaved Horsechestnut (Plate 11). (2) Chestnut Oak (Plate 47) has leaves and buds clustered at twig tips; buds have more scales. (3) Beech has shorter leaves and long slender buds. See (4) Eastern and (6) Ozark Chinquapins. In winter, basswoods (Plate 43) have tough inner bark on branchlets and branches; twigs mostly red or green.

Remarks: The Chestnut not so long ago was a dominant tree in dry forests throughout much of our region. Soon after 1900, however, a fungus bark disease, believed to be of Asiatic origin, became epidemic and in less than a human generation completely eliminated the Chestnut as an important forest tree. Sprouts may continue from some old stumps, and these flower and produce fruits. As soon as these shoots attain a moderate size, the bark-shattering blight usually girdles them near their bases. Someday a blight-resistant specimen may occur, from which a new strain could be developed.

Chestnut lumber was quite valuable. It was used for furniture, musical instruments, interiors, caskets, and fences. Tannin was derived from the bark and the nuts were marketed. Bobwhite, wild turkey, squirrels, and whitetail deer are among the many forms of wildlife that once fed on the nuts.

EASTERN CHINQUAPIN   Not illus.
Castanea pumila (L.) Mill.
   Recognition: Similar to Chestnut but rarely growing to tree size and with leaves *white-hairy* beneath. Leaf teeth coarse; shorter than ⅛″. Twigs and buds somewhat hairy. The edible nuts *occur singly* in husks decorated with hairy spines ½″ or shorter. Nuts *not flattened.* Leaves 3″–5″. Height 10′-15′ (50′); diameter 1″–2″ (36″). Both the last and next species are taller and have more hairy leaves. Dry woods; Massachusetts (local), New Jersey, e. Pennsylvania, Tennessee, and Arkansas to Florida and e. Texas.

OZARK CHINQUAPIN   Not illus.
Castanea ozarkensis Ashe
   Recognition: Similar to Eastern Chinquapin but taller and with *white-downy* leaf undersides. Coarse leaf teeth ½″–⅜″. Twigs *hairless.* Hairy spines of fruit husks longer than ⅜″. Leaves 3″–5″. Height to 65′. Flowers June. Dry woods; s. Missouri and Oklahoma to Mississippi and Louisiana.

Miscellaneous Plants
with 3 Bundle Scars (2)
(*Plate 58, p. 350*)

With the exception of the apples and pears, plants on this plate are mainly shrubs.

RED CHOKEBERRY   *Pyrus arbutifolia* (L.) L. f.   **p. 350**
   Recognition: A clumped shrub or small tree with fine-toothed, elliptic leaves, densely hairy beneath, hairless above; midrib bears tiny *raised glands* on top, easily visible with hand lens (or, upon careful examination, even without lens). Twigs and buds white- or *gray-woolly.* Buds reddish; scales minutely notched at tips. Leaves 2″–5″. Height to 20′. Flowers April–July. Fruits small, fleshy, red, Aug.–Nov.
   Similar species: Glands of midrib in summer and notched tips of reddish bud scales in winter identify the group. (1) Only Purple Chokeberry also is hairy. The 2 species sometimes interbreed, producing confusing specimens. (2) Choke Cherry (Plate 53) is similar in name only.
   Remarks: Fruits eaten by ruffed grouse, pheasant, and songbirds.

PURPLE CHOKEBERRY   *Pyrus floribunda* Lindl.   **Not illus.**
   Recognition: Similar to Red Chokeberry but leaves, twigs, and especially buds less hairy. Fruits purple. Height to 10′. Wet or dry thickets; Newfoundland, s. Labrador, and s.-centr. Ontario to Virginia and Indiana.

BLACK CHOKEBERRY   **p. 350**
Pyrus melanocarpa (Michx.) Willd.
   Recognition: Similar to other chokeberries but *hairless;* fruits *black.* Height to 10′.
   Remarks: Ruffed and sharptail grouse and prairie chicken eat fruits.

ALDERLEAF BUCKTHORN   **p. 350**
Rhamnus alnifolia L'Hér.
   Recognition: A low shrub with fine-toothed, elliptic, hairless leaves whose veins tend to *follow leaf edges.* Twigs hairless; inner bark of older stems yellowish. Buds covered with several dark scales; end buds false. Fruit small, fleshy; seeds 2–4, flat, and barely grooved on back. Leaves 2″–6″. Height to 3′. Flowers May–July. Fruits black, Aug.-Sept.
   Similar species: (1) Only Common Buckthorn (Plate 19) is thorny. Thornless buckthorns have few easily recognizable features. Dark bud scales are helpful in winter identification.

(2) Lanceleaf Buckthorn differs principally in leaf shape, hairiness, and seed number and structure. Bumelias (Plate 38), sometimes called buckthorns, are spiny and have milky sap.

LANCELEAF BUCKTHORN   p. 350
Rhamnus lanceolata Pursh
Recognition: Similar to Alderleaf Buckthorn but *taller* and leaves *narrow*. Twigs and leaf undersides typically hairy but, particularly in South, hairless variety *glabrata* Gleason occurs. Seeds 2 per fruit, not flat and deeply grooved on back. Leaves 2″–6″. Height to 6′. Flowers May. Fruits July–Sept.

CAROLINA BUCKTHORN   p. 350
Rhamnus caroliniana Walt.
Recognition: This and European Buckthorn are the only plants with alternate simple leaves and 3 bundle scars to have *long naked buds* that are *not stalked*. This species taller. Leaves similar in shape to Alderleaf Buckthorn and bear very fine teeth. Though usually hairless, a form with velvety leaves occurs from s. Indiana and Tennessee to Missouri and Texas. Twigs *fine-hairy;* fruits 3-seeded, not grooved on back; flower stalks hairy. Leaves 2″–6″. Height to 35′. Flowers May–June. Fruits black, Aug.–Oct.
Similar species: Witch-hazel and relatives (Plate 57) also have naked buds, but they are much narrower at base.

EUROPEAN BUCKTHORN   *Rhamnus frangula* L.   p. 350
Recognition: Escaped from cultivation. Similar to Carolina Buckthorn but less tall and leaves smaller, not toothed, and hairy beneath. Twigs hairy but fruits 2-seeded, not grooved on back. Flower stalks hairless or nearly so. Leaves 1½″–3″. Height to 20′. Flowers May–July. Fruits black.
Remarks: Sometimes known as Alder Buckthorn (see Alderleaf Buckthorn, opposite). Common Buckthorn (Plate 19) may be called European Buckthorn. Both Alderleaf and Common Buckthorns have scaly buds.

DOMESTIC APPLE   *Pyrus malus* L.   p. 350
Recognition: The apples are the only species of this plate which usually have short spur branches of crowded leaves and leaf scars. A round-topped small tree. Leaves egg-shaped, more or less round-toothed, usually somewhat white- or *gray-woolly beneath;* may be heart-shaped at base. Twigs short, stiff, sometimes with thorny tips; usually somewhat woolly. Leaf scars somewhat raised; short lines leading downward at sides. Buds usually blunt and woolly. Bark scaly and brownish. Leaves 1″–4″. Height 20′–30′ (50′); diameter 6″–24″. Flowers April–June. Fruits more than 1″ across, Sept.–Nov.

Similar species: The apple group is a collection of 6 species. The 3 native species are almost always thorny, have sharp buds, and are discussed on pages 195–97. The 3 imported species below occasionally may be somewhat thorny. This species is unlike other apples in lacking sharp leaf teeth. Domestic Pear is mostly hairless, more often thorny, usually has long, not round, fruits and has 1 or several strong upright branches, giving the tree a pointed rather than round-topped crown shape. In winter this apple has hairier twigs, blunter buds, and more-raised leaf scars than the pear.

Remarks: The exact origin is lost in antiquity but the etymology of the name indicates that it originated in the western Himalayas and traveled westward by way of northern Persia, Asia Minor, the Caucasus, and the Mediterranean countries. The apple of the Bible is believed to have been not our northern fruit but the apricot, still common in the Holy Land. The Domestic Apple locally gone wild is an important wildlife food eaten by deer, pheasant, mourning dove, gray fox, and many other animals.

CHINESE APPLE   *Pyrus prunifolia* Willd.   **Not illus.**
Recognition: Asiatic, similar to Domestic Apple but leaves wider, sharp-toothed, hairless except on veins. Twigs somewhat hairy but not woolly. Flowers May–June. Fruits about ¾" across. Escaped; Nova Scotia and New Brunswick to New England and Pennsylvania.

SIBERIAN CRABAPPLE   *Pyrus baccata* L.   **Not illus.**
Recognition: Another Asiatic; similar to Chinese Apple but with long-pointed, sharp-toothed, hairless leaves. Twigs hairless, at least after early summer. Fruits usually less than ½" across. Spread from cultivation; local.

DOMESTIC PEAR   *Pyrus communis* L.   **p. 350**
Recognition: Similar to Domestic Apple but nearly hairless, more often thorny, with *elongate fleshy fruits*, and usually with several strong upright branches, making a narrow-topped tree. Leaves 1"–3". Height 20'–35' (60'); diameter 6"–24". Twigs of Chinese Pear are more hairy.

CHINESE PEAR   **Not illus.**
Pyrus pyrifolia (Burm. f.) Nakai
Recognition: Similar to Domestic Pear but young leaves, at least, woolly and finely sharp-toothed. Fruits nearly round. Escaped; se. Virginia.

GROUNDSEL-TREE   *Baccharis halimifolia* L.   **p. 350**
Recognition: A shrub with *green angled twigs*. Wedge-shaped

leaves of lower portions of plant have large and often deep teeth; those of upper portions often lack teeth. Buds 2- to 3-scaled; true end buds lacking. Leaves 1″–2½″. Height to 9′. Flowers Aug.–Sept. Fruits small, dry, white, silky, Sept.–Dec.
Similar species: No other plant with 3 bundle scars has green angled twigs.

Miscellaneous Plants with 3 (or more) Bundle Scars (3)

(*Plate 59, p. 352*)

These are the remaining woody plants that are upright (neither creeping nor climbing), nonthorny, and have 3 or more bundle scars and leaves that are not lobed.

All except Sweet-spires have leaves not toothed. The first 3 (2 illustrated) have more than 3 bundle scars per leaf scar. When leaves are present they resemble some magnolias (Plate 49) and oaks (Plate 48), but lack the "ringed" twigs of the former and clustered end buds of the latter group. Sweet-spires is distinctive among woody plants with similar leaves in having the pith divided by woody plates.

LEATHERWOOD *Dirca palustris* L. **p. 352**
  Recognition: A distinctive shrub with elliptic leaves that are not toothed. Very short leafstalks *entirely covering* brown velvety buds. In winter, buds are encircled by leaf scars; bundle scars 5. Twig ends swollen; end buds false. Bark pliant and so *tough* that it can hardly be broken by hand. Leaves 2″–3″. Height to 10′. Flowers yellow, April–May. Fruits fleshy, green to red, May–June.
  Similar species: Combined bark and bud characteristics distinctive, although related Daphne (Plate 68) has similarly tough bark. Daphne has only 1 bundle scar per leaf scar.
  Remarks: Bark once was used by Indians for making bowstrings, fishlines, and baskets. Foliage and twigs eaten by deer and moose.

TALL PAWPAW *Asimina triloba* (L.) Dunal **p. 352**
  Recognition: Usually a shrub or small tree with *large toothless* leaves and *long, naked, deep brown-hairy or reddish-hairy* end buds. Side buds shorter, also hairy. Twigs and young leaves often hairy like buds. Pith usually, but not always, partitioned by transverse woody diaphragms. Bark dark, smooth or somewhat broken. Leaves 6″–12″. Height 6′–20′ (40′). Flowers

purplish, over 1″ broad, April–May. Fruits large, fleshy, green, *somewhat bananalike*, Aug.–Oct.

Similar species: Magnolias (Plate 49) have similar leaves but twigs are encircled by stipule scars at each leaf scar. Dark naked end buds and (usually) chambered pith are unique among plants with more than 3 bundle scars (see next species).

Remarks: Also known as Common Pawpaw; a northern representative of the tropical custard-apple family. Fully ripened fruits difficult to find, since they are eaten by opossum, squirrels, raccoon, foxes, etc. They can be eaten raw or made into desserts.

DWARF PAWPAW   **Not illus.**
Asimina parviflora (Michx.) Dunal
    Recognition: Similar to Tall Pawpaw but not over 4′ tall, with leaves less than 7″ long and flowers under 1″ across. Dry woods; se. Virginia to n. Florida and Mississippi.

SOUR-GUM   *Nyssa sylvatica* Marsh.   **p. 352**
    Recognition: A tree with dark, deeply grooved and checkered bark. Leaves shiny, hairless or nearly so, egg-shaped to elliptic (less commonly roundish), often somewhat leathery; scarlet in autumn. Pith distinctly chambered. Buds stand out from twigs. In southern swamps, trunks growing in water are swollen at base. Leaves 3″–6″. Height 40′–60′ (125′); diameter 1′–2′ (5′). Flowers greenish, April–June. Fruits less than ¾″, bluish, berrylike, Aug.–Oct.
    Similar species: (1) Plain foliage and checkered bark are most like Persimmon (Plate 68) but chambered rather than solid pith, triple rather than single bundle scars, and lowland rather than upland habitat separate the two. (2) In winter this and Tupelo are the only alternate-leaved species with chambered pith and slender brown twigs that have end buds true and with several scales. See also the hackberries (Plate 43).
    Remarks: Lumber of Sour-gum, or Black Gum, is useful for furniture, boxes, crates, veneer, and paper pulp. Fleshy bitter fruits relished by black bear and by over 30 species of birds, including ruffed grouse, prairie chicken, pheasant, and wild turkey.

TUPELO   *Nyssa aquatica* L.   **Not illus.**
    Recognition: Similar to Sour-gum but leaves larger, frequently with 1 to 3 or more large teeth, sometimes somewhat hairy beneath; rarely heart-shaped at base. Buds broad and pressed against twigs. Leaves 4″–13″. Height to 100′; diameter to 4′. Flowers greenish, April–May. Fruits more than ¾″, bluish. See Sour-gum. Southern Coastal Plain swamps; se. Virginia to Florida and e. Texas, and north in Mississippi Valley to s. Indiana, s. Illinois, and se. Missouri.

SWEET-SPIRES *Itea virginica* L.   **p. 352**
  Recognition: A shrub with fine-toothed, elliptic leaves, buds
  occurring more than 1 above each leaf scar, *green twigs*, and
  pith chambered (sometimes faintly). Flower spears (hence the
  name) give rise to clusters of tiny dry fruits, frequently present.
  Leaves 1″–4″. Height to 10′. Flowers white, May–June. Fruits
  July–winter.
  Similar species: No other species with 3 bundle scars has combination of chambered pith and green twigs.

COMMON SPICEBUSH   *Lindera benzoin* (L.) Blume   **p. 352**
  Recognition: A *spicy-scented* shrub. Leaves elliptic, not
  toothed, hairless or nearly so. Stalked flower buds may flank
  stalkless 2- to 3-scaled leaf buds. End buds false. Red (rarely
  yellow) berries aromatic when crushed, as are leaves, twigs, and
  buds. Leaves 2″–6″. Height to 12′. Flowers yellow, March–
  May. Fruits July–Sept.
  Similar species: Spicebush scent is distinctive once learned.
  (1) Sassafras (Plate 43) has a somewhat similar odor but has
  green, often forked twigs, 1 bundle scar, and, frequently, lobed
  leaves. (2) Pondspice (Plate 68) has only 1 bundle scar. (3)
  Sweetfern (Plate 57) has a less spicy odor, more than 3 bud
  scales, a more open habitat, and distinctive foliage. (4) Hairy
  Spicebush is hairy and more southern.
  Remarks: Early land surveyors regarded this as an indicator of
  good agricultural land. The strongly aromatic twigs and leaves
  have been used for tea and dried berries have been powdered
  as a spice. Whitetail deer, cottontail rabbit, opossum, pheasant,
  bobwhite, ruffed grouse, and numerous songbirds eat twigs or
  fruits.

HAIRY SPICEBUSH   Not illus.
Lindera melissaefolium (Walt.) Blume
  Recognition: Similar to Common Spicebush but with *hairy* twigs
  and buds and narrow leaves that are *rounded* at the base and
  hairy at least beneath. Leaves 2″–6″. Height to 6′. Flowers
  Feb.–March. Fruits Sept.–Oct. Swamps; uncommon; Florida
  and Louisiana north to N. Carolina and s. Missouri.

ALTERNATE-LEAF DOGWOOD   **p. 352**
Cornus alternifolia L. f.
  Recognition: Among the many dogwoods (Plate 15) only this
  shrub or small tree does not have opposite leaves. Leaf veins
  tend to follow *leaf edges to tip*. Leaves have 1″–2″ stalks;
  often crowded (some may be opposite or whorled) toward tips
  of *greenish* twigs. Side twigs clustered near ends of central
  stem. Pith white. Buds have only 2 scales. Leaf scars narrow
  and raised; bundle scars 3. Hybrids with Red-osier Dogwood

(Plate 15) have intermediate characteristics. Leaves 2″–5″. Height to 25′. Flowers May–July. Fruits blue-black with red stems, July–Sept.
Remarks: Fruits eaten by many birds, including ruffed grouse. Twigs browsed by deer and rabbits.

SMOKETREE   *Cotinus obovatus* Raf.   p. 352
Recognition: One of the rarest American trees, this relative of the sumacs is found in only a few spots (see range opposite Plate 59). Wood yellow and odorous. Leaves wide, usually blunt-tipped; side buds with 2–4 scales and somewhat long-pointed. Name alludes to foot-long hazy sprays of small feathery fruits that resemble puffs of smoke. Foliage becomes a brilliant red in autumn. A European relative (*C. coggygria* Scop.) is used in landscaping. Leaves 3″–6″. Height 6′–25′ (35′); diameter 1″–12″ (14″). Flowers April–May. Fruits June–Sept.

CORKWOOD   *Leitneria floridana* Chapm.   p. 352
Recognition: A shrub or small tree related to poplars and other catkin-bearing plants but peculiar enough to be classified in a family by itself. Leaves narrow to elliptic, gray-hairy beneath. End buds clustered; much larger than some of side ones. The swamp habitat and 3 bundle scars separate this species from the oaks, which also have clustered buds at twig tips. Bark smooth and, like many other swamp trees, trunk swollen at base. Wood more buoyant than cork; local fishermen are said to use Corkwood blocks for net floats. Leaves 3″–6″. Height to 25′. Flowers March. Fruits May.

Spireas
(*Plate 60, p. 354*)

Spireas are shrubs with slender wandlike twigs, narrow-based and mostly toothed leaves, papery bark that often flakes off, and raised leaf scars with only 1 bundle scar. Leafstalks characteristically are short. Twig ends often wither in winter; some twigs may retain scales at their bases as in the honeysuckles (Plate 14) and some other opposite-leaved plants. Clusters of tiny dry 5-parted fruits often are present at twig tips following white or pink flowers.
    On Plate 66 are several plants also with toothed leaves, 1 bundle scar, and small dry fruits. Sourwood and the sweetbells have raised leaf scars. Maleberry has smaller buds with more than

2 scales. Pepperbushes have true end buds smaller or lacking. The New Jersey teas (Plate 43) have only saucer-shaped remnants of fruit present in winter, and Sweet-spires (Plate 59) has 3 bundle scars and chambered pith.

Spirea buds are eaten by ruffed and sharptail grouse and twigs by rabbits and deer.

STEEPLEBUSH SPIREA Spiraea tomentosa L. **p. 354**
   Recognition: No other spirea has *woolly* twigs and leaf undersides. Leaves coarse-toothed, egg-shaped to elliptic. Leaves 1″–3″. Height to 5′. Flowers pinkish, less commonly white, in slender pointed "steeples," June–Sept. Fruits Aug.–Dec.

NARROWLEAF SPIREA (MEADOWSWEET) **p. 354**
Spiraea alba Du Roi
   Recognition: The only spirea with *narrow fine-toothed* leaves. Twigs sometimes somewhat yellow-hairy. Buds long-pointed and silky. Flower and fruit clusters long and slender. Leaves 2″–3″. Height to 4′. Flowers white, June–Sept.

BROADLEAF SPIREA (MEADOWSWEET) **p. 354**
Spiraea latifolia (Ait.) Borkh.
   Recognition: Like Narrowleaf in the type of flowering structure, but with *wider, elliptic, coarse-toothed* leaves, hairless and reddish twigs, and short, hairless buds. Leaves 2″–3″. Height to 6′. Flowers white or pale pink, June–Sept.

DWARF SPIREA Spiraea corymbosa Raf. **p. 354**
   Recognition: A low Appalachian species with wide, elliptic leaves, coarse-toothed *only above the middle*, purplish twigs, and short hairless buds. This spirea, like the next 2, has *flat-topped* flower and fruit clusters. Leaves 1″–3″. Height to 3′. Flowers white, June–July.

VIRGINIA SPIREA Spiraea virginiana Britt. **p. 354**
   Recognition: The only *narrow-leaved* spirea with leaf margins bearing *a few coarse teeth or none*. Otherwise much like Dwarf Spirea. Leaves 1″–2″. Height to 5′.

JAPANESE SPIREA Spiraea japonica L. f. **Not illus.**
   Recognition: Similar to Virginia Spirea but with *gray-hairy* twigs and long-pointed, narrow, *many toothed*, coarse-toothed leaves. Leaves 1″–3″. Height to 5′. Flowers pink to rose, July–Aug. Escaped from cultivation; New England and Indiana to Tennessee.

Hollies

(Plate 61, p. 356)

Hollies as a group are difficult to identify. No easily apparent characteristic occurs throughout. Nonevergreen species are particularly nondescript. When present, *minute* black stipules that flank the leaf scars are diagnostic. They are difficult to see, however, and may drop off with age. When shed, stipule scars marking their former location are very minute. Bundle scars, however, are single and true end buds are present. Furthermore, bud scales are paired, usually with 2, but sometimes with 4–6, apparent.

Hollies frequently develop short, stubby spur branches crowded with leaf scars or, in season, terminated by a whorl of leaves. Leaf blades of most hollies are toothed and wedge-shaped at the bottom. Buds commonly are more numerous near tips of the twigs; often they are clustered here. There may be more than 1 bud above each leaf scar. In general, holly bark is smooth. Male and female flowers may occur on different plants. The small nutlets in the fleshy red or dark fruits are smooth or grooved on the outside surface.

When in fruit, hollies most closely resemble Daphne and Mountain-holly (Plate 68), which also bear red fruits. The leaves of those plants, however, are not toothed.

AMERICAN HOLLY   *Ilex opaca* Ait.   **p. 356**
   Recognition: One of the most universally recognized eastern trees. The *prickly evergreen* leaves are distinctive. Buds minute. Fruits *red* or, rarely, yellow; nutlets grooved. Leaves 2″–4″. Height 10′–40′ (100′); diameter 6″–24″ (48″). Flowers May–June. Fruits Aug.–June.
   Remarks: This is the Christmas holly. The collection of foliage sprays has become a sizable business and, because of over-harvesting, this decorative plant is less common than formerly in some areas. Holly lumber, peculiarly ivory-white, is in demand for special products such as piano keys, ship models, and inlays. Though reported to be somewhat toxic to some animals, the fruits are eaten by numerous songbirds, bobwhite, and wild turkey.

LOW GALLBERRY HOLLY   *Ilex glabra* (L.) Gray   **p. 356**
   Recognition: An evergreen holly. Leaves usually blunt-tipped, *leathery, notched near tip*, toothless or with a few wavy-edged teeth above middle. Twigs finely gray-hairy; nutlets smooth. Leaves 1″–3″. Height to 10′. Flowers May–Aug. Fruits black, June–July.
   Remarks: Though grown as a garden shrub in England, Low Gallberry Holly is little cultivated here. Leaves are reported

to make a good tea. Fruits are food for many songbirds, bob-white, and wild turkey. Another common name, Inkberry, may cause it to be confused with Pokeweed (*Phytolacca*), a nonwoody perennial also sometimes known by that name.

TALL GALLBERRY HOLLY   Leaf illus., p. 356
Ilex coriacea (Pursh) Chapm.
   Recognition: A southern evergreen shrub whose leaves some-what resemble those of Low Gallberry Holly. They may have sharp teeth near the pointed tips or may lack teeth. Leaves often marked with fine black dots beneath. Twigs hairless or sticky; nutlets smooth. Leaves 2″–3″. Height to 15′; diameter 2″–3″. Flowers May. Fruits dark, Sept.–Oct. Swamps and sandy soils; Florida and Louisiana to se. Virginia.

YAUPON HOLLY   *Ilex vomitoria* Ait.   Leaf illus., p. 356
   Recognition: A distinctive plant whose branches with red ber-ries are often gathered for decorative purposes. Evergreen leaves small and wavy-edged; nutlets grooved. A strong me-dicinal "black drink" once brewed by Indians is believed to have been of Yaupon leaves. The caffeine-containing dried leaves reportedly make a desirable tea. Leaves ½″–2″. Height 5′–15′ (30′); diameter 2″–4″ (12″). Flowers May–June. Fruits red, Sept.–Oct. Sandy Coastal Plain; se. Virginia to centr. Florida, west to s. Texas, and north in Mississippi Valley to n. Arkansas and se. Oklahoma.

DECIDUOUS HOLLY   *Ilex decidua* Walt.   p. 356
   Recognition: Shrubby or growing to small-tree size, this *non-evergreen* holly has variable narrow to egg-shaped leaves, gen-erally thin but sometimes may be somewhat thickened. Leaf edges wavy- to blunt-toothed; twigs often stiff and buds some-what pointed. Nutlets grooved. Leaves 2″–3″. Height 10′–20′ (30′); diameter 2″–6″ (10″). Flowers April–May. Fruits shiny red, Sept.–March.
   Similar species: (1) Yaupon leaves are smaller and evergreen. (2) Juneberry Holly is rare and has fine-toothed leaves.
   Remarks: Fruits eaten by several birds, including bobwhite. Sometimes called Possum-haw (see p. 198).

JUNEBERRY HOLLY   Not illus.
Ilex amelanchier M. A. Curtis
   Recognition: A rare low *nonevergreen* shrub of southern swamps with foliage resembling that of some juneberries (Plate 54). Leaves *fine-toothed*, somewhat oblong, leathery and veiny, and slightly hairy beneath. Nutlets grooved. Fruits dull red and on stalks ¼″–⅞″ long. Leaves 1″–2″. Height to 7′. See Decid-uous Holly and Georgia Holly (p. 276). Local; Louisiana to Georgia and se. Virginia.

LARGELEAF HOLLY *Ilex montana* T. & G. **p. 356**
Recognition: A tall shrub or tree with *large* leaves for a holly. Leaves thin, narrow to elliptic, long-pointed, sharply *fine-toothed;* somewhat hairy beneath in var. *mollis* (Gray) Britt. Side twigs not especially stiff. Twigs green to reddish; buds somewhat *pointed;* nutlets grooved. Leaves 2½″–6″. Height 6′–20′ (40′); diameter 2″–10″ (12″). Flowers June. Fruits short-stalked (under ½″), red, Oct.–Nov.
Similar species: (1) Georgia Holly and (2) Common Winterberry Holly most closely resemble this species. Both are coarse-toothed, however, and have blunt buds. The former has long-stalked fruits and the latter less prolonged leaf tips and smooth nutlets. (3) Juneberry Holly is lower, with smaller leaves which are not long-pointed, and often has long-stalked fruits.
Remarks: An alternate name, Mountain Holly, should not be confused with the nontoothed Mountain-holly, *Nemopanthus* (Plate 68).

GEORGIA HOLLY *Ilex longipes* Chapm. **Not illus.**
Recognition: A large shrub with leaves similar to Largeleaf Holly but with fewer, coarser teeth. Leaf tips and bases both usually are sharp-pointed. Buds *blunt;* nutlets grooved. All other hollies except the fine-toothed Juneberry Holly have short-stalked fruits. Fruit stalks slender, *up to 1″ long.* Leaves ½″–4″. Height to 15′. Flowers May–June. Fruits red, rarely yellow, Oct. Streamsides and wooded slopes; N. Carolina, W. Virginia, and Tennessee to Florida and Louisiana.

COMMON WINTERBERRY HOLLY **p. 356**
Ilex verticillata (L.) Gray
Recognition: A variable small to large shrub whose leaves usually are wide but vary from narrow to nearly circular. Leaves *dull* above, with distinct coarse teeth; may be thin or thickish and somewhat hairy beneath or not. In some varieties, tiny transparent dots can be seen in leaves when a lens is used. Buds *blunt* with broadly pointed scales; nutlets *smooth.* Leaves 2″–4″. Height to 15′. Flowers June–Aug. Fruits red, rarely yellow, Sept.–Oct., or later.
Similar species: Dull upper leaf surfaces, shallow leaf teeth, and less pointed bud scales separate this species from the next. Largeleaf Holly has long-pointed leaves and grooved nutlets.
Remarks: Sometimes called Black Alder (see *Alnus*, Plate 51).

SMOOTH WINTERBERRY HOLLY **p. 356**
Ilex laevigata (Pursh) Gray
Recognition: Similar to but less variable than the preceding; foliage nevertheless may be narrow to elliptic. Leaves *shiny* above, hairless or nearly so beneath, and fine-toothed. Buds

blunt but with *sharp-pointed* scales. Leaves ½″–4″. Height to 20′. Flowers May–July. Fruits red, rarely yellow, Sept.–Jan.

Blueberries

(*Plate 62, p. 358*)

Blueberries, huckleberries, bilberries, deerberries, and cranberries all are included in the genus *Vaccinium,* a large and complex series of acid-soil plants of the heath family. They often resemble one another closely and many hybridize. Small specimens in particular are frequently difficult to identify. Winter identification characteristics are not always available. Cranberries are shown on Plate 32; other vacciniums on Plates 62 and 63.

Blueberries have small, mostly elliptic, short-stalked leaves. Twigs are slender, green or reddish, and often zigzag, covered with very numerous raised, granular speckles, or warts, usually visible to the eye but better seen under a lens. Two types of buds are commonly present: slim leaf buds and swollen flower buds, though both are small. The tiny bud scales frequently have long tapered tips. The end buds are false. There is 1 bundle scar per leaf scar. The small, whitish, bell-like blossoms are very ornamental. The blue or black fruits of blueberries contain many small seeds, in contrast to the huckleberries, which regularly have 10 nutlets per fruit. All have edible fruits; some are very tasty.

VELVETLEAF BLUEBERRY p. 358
Vaccinium myrtilloides Michx.

Recognition: The only low blueberry with leaves that are *not toothed* and are *velvety* and whitened beneath and often hairy also above. Twigs densely velvety-hairy. Leaves 1″–2″, mostly less than 1⅝″ long and ¾″ wide. Height to nearly 3′. Flowers May–June. Fruits blue with white powder (rarely white), sour, July–Sept.

Similar species: Black Highbush Blueberry has similar foliage and twigs but leaves usually longer and wider, fruits black, and full-size plants taller; it is more southern.

Remarks: Fruits eaten by sharptail and ruffed grouse.

BLACK HIGHBUSH BLUEBERRY p. 358
Vaccinium atrococcum (Gray) Heller

Recognition: *The only tall woolly-leaved blueberry.* Leaves not toothed; twigs hairy. Leaves 1⅝″–3¼″. Height to 12′. Flowers as leaves come out, May–June. Fruits black without whitish powder, rarely white, sweet, June–Aug.

Similar species: Velvetleaf Blueberry is much lower, with smaller leaves and blue fruits.

COASTAL HIGHBUSH BLUEBERRY   Not illus.
Vaccinium caesariense Mackenz.
   Recognition: Like Black Highbush in lacking leaf teeth, but somewhat lower and with *smaller hairless* leaves that are always *whitened* beneath. Twig speckles less numerous. A variety of Common Highbush Blueberry has whitened leaf undersides but has toothed leaves. Leaves 1″–2″ (3″). Height to 10′. Flowers May. Fruits dark blue with white powder. Mostly Coastal Plain; s. Maine and centr. New York to Florida.

COMMON HIGHBUSH BLUEBERRY   p. 358
Vaccinium corymbosum L.
   Recognition: A tall shrub. Leaves elliptic, slightly hairy or hairless, usually without teeth, and *green* beneath, but one variety, *albiflorum* (Hook.) Fern., has very fine teeth and green leaf undersides; another (var. *glabrum* Gray) has larger bristle-teeth and whitened lower leaf surfaces. Leaves 1⅝″–3¼″. Height to 12′. Flowers after leaves expand, May–June. Fruits blue to blue-black with whitish powder, sweet, June–Aug.
   Similar species: (1) Coastal Highbush and (2) Elliott Blueberries have smaller leaves. The former has leaf undersides whitened and the latter has them shiny.
   Remarks: This species is the basic stock of many cultivated varieties. Fruits taken by mourning dove, ruffed grouse, pheasant, and many songbirds.

ELLIOTT BLUEBERRY   Not illus.
Vaccinium elliottii Chapm.
   Recognition: A tall southern shrub. Leaves small, either wavy-edged or fine-toothed, *shiny green on both surfaces*. Twigs hairless or slightly hairy. Leaves ½″–1½″. Height to 12′. Flowers March–May. Fruits long-stemmed, black, dry, June–July. Thickets; Florida and Louisiana n. to se. Virginia and Arkansas.

EARLY LOW BLUEBERRY   p. 358
Vaccinium vacillans Torr.
   Recognition: A low hairless shrub. Egg-shaped to elliptic leaves may have a few bristle-tipped teeth or teeth may be lacking. Foliage *dull above, whitish beneath;* may become somewhat leathery with age. Leaves ⅝″–2″ long and ⅝″–1⅜″ wide. Height to 3′. Flowers April–June. Fruits dark blue with white powder (or, toward the West, black and powderless), sweet, June–Sept.
   Similar species: (1) Late Low Blueberry has narrower, thinner leaves with full sets of teeth. (2) Elliott and (3) Slender

Blueberries have leaves shiny above and fruits black. It may be difficult to separate small highbush blueberries without teeth from Early Low Blueberry.

Remarks: Fruits eaten by wild turkey, ruffed grouse, and gray fox. Whitetail deer and cottontail browse twigs.

SLENDER BLUEBERRY   *Vaccinium tenellum* Ait.   **Not illus.**
Recognition: A clumped low southern shrub. Leaves small and somewhat wedge-shaped, with a few teeth or none, shiny above; undersides usually somewhat hairy, with scattered red glandular hairs. Branches very few. Leaves ½″–1¼″. Height to 1½′. Flowers April–May. Fruits black, dryish, June–July. Mostly sandy soils; se. Virginia and Tennessee to Florida and Mississippi.

LATE LOW BLUEBERRY   **p. 358**
Vaccinium angustifolium Ait.
Recognition: A low, much branched shrub that forms clumps, spreading by underground stems. Leaves mostly *narrow* and always *finely toothed*, each tooth bristle-tipped; dull above and green on both sides, though lighter beneath. Foliage and twigs may be somewhat hairy or not. Leaves ¼″–1⅜″ long and ⅛″–⅝″ wide. Height to 2′. Flowers April–June. Fruits blue with white powder—black without powder in var. *nigrum* (Wood) Dole—sweet, over ¼″, Aug.–Sept.
Similar species: (1) Southern Low Blueberry has larger leaves; (2) Slender Blueberry has shiny foliage. (3) Early Low Blueberry has wider leaves.
Remarks: Fruits eaten by bobwhite, prairie chicken, and ruffed grouse.

SOUTHERN LOW BLUEBERRY   **p. 358**
Vaccinium pallidum Ait.
Recognition: Similar to preceding but leaves *larger;* berries mostly smaller, dry to the taste. Leaves hairless, except often for leafstalk. Twigs hairless or hairy in lines. Leaves 1¼″–2″ long and ⅝″–1″ broad. Height to 2′. Fruits blue, under ⁵⁄₁₆″.

Huckleberries, Bilberries, and Relatives
(*Plate 63, p. 360*)

These plants are similar to the closely related blueberries in lacking true end buds and in having small, short-stalked leaves that are mostly elliptic. Also, the twigs are slender, often green or red, and the flowers are small and mostly whitish. The fruits (10 to many seeds) are small blue to black berries (red in 1 species), generally in lengthened clusters, and usually edible. None of these species, however, have twigs densely covered with fine warty speckles as in the true blueberries (p. 277).

DWARF HUCKLEBERRY   p. 360
Gaylussacia dumosa (Andr.) T. & G.

Recognition: A low shrub. Leaves wedge-shaped at base, rounded and bristle-tipped on outer portion, *not toothed*, shiny above, somewhat hairy, covered with yellow resin-dots *beneath and often above* (use lens), somewhat leathery, though not evergreen. Flower buds larger than leaf buds. The latter have 4–5 scales. Twigs usually *hairy*. Leaves 1″–2″. Height to 20″. Flowers clustered, white or pink, May–June. Fruits black, hairy, June–Oct.

Similar species: Of this group, Dwarf, (1) Tall, and (2) Black Huckleberries have resin-dotted foliage (Box Huckleberry, though related, does not); Tall Huckleberry is taller, with whitish-hairy leaf undersides; Dwarf Bilberry has toothed, undotted leaves.

TALL HUCKLEBERRY   Not illus.
Gaylussacia frondosa (L.) T. & G.

Recognition: Somewhat like the last but leaves more egg-shaped, quite *whitish-hairy* and veiny beneath and with resin-dots *only beneath*. Twigs mostly hairy; leaf buds have 4–5 scales. Known also as Dangleberry. Height to 6′. Fruits dark blue with white powder, June–Sept. Upland woods; Massachusetts and s. New Hampshire to Florida and Louisiana.

BLACK HUCKLEBERRY   p. 360
Gaylussacia baccata (Wang.) K. Koch

Recognition: A shrub with leaves egg-shaped or elliptic, dull above, not toothed and covered on *both surfaces* with yellow *resin-dots*. Leaf undersides often yellowish. Twigs hairy. Buds of 2 types; leaf buds smaller, with 2–3 *scales*. Leaves 1″–3″. Height to 3′. Flowers clustered, greenish white or greenish red, May–June. Fruits black, less commonly blue or even whitish, July–Sept.

Similar species: (1) Tall Huckleberry has resin-dots only on leaf undersides and it and (2) Dwarf Huckleberry have 4–5 bud scales. In winter, deerberries have buds all of 1 size.

Remarks: The most widespread and frequently the most common huckleberry. Ruffed and sharptail grouse, prairie chicken, bobwhite, wild turkey, and mourning dove eat fruits. Jellies, marmalades, and desserts can be made from fruits.

TALL DEERBERRY   *Vaccinium stamineum* L.   p. 360
Recognition: A tall shrub with variable foliage, mostly egg-shaped to elliptic. Leaves thin, *not toothed*, typically whitish and hairy *beneath*. Two southern varieties, *interius* (Ashe)

Palmer & Steyerm. and *neglectum* (Small) Deam, have hairless foliage. Twigs hairy. Buds of *1 type*, long-pointed, 2–3 scales. Leaves 1″–4″. Height to 10′. Flowers May–June. Fruits greenish to purple, sometimes white-powdered, July–Sept.

Similar species: (1) Tall, (2) Dwarf, and (3) Black Huckleberries have resin-dotted foliage. Bilberries have either toothed or leathery leaves except for (4) Tundra and (5) Ovalleaf Bilberries, which are more northern; Tundra Bilberry is lower and Ovalleaf has angled twigs. (6) See Low Deerberry.

Remarks: Stewed and sweetened fruits are said to be good when served cold. Ruffed grouse, bobwhite, and gray fox eat wild fruits.

LOW DEERBERRY   *Vaccinium caesium* Greene   **Not illus.**
Recognition: Similar to Tall Deerberry but lower. Leaves thin, mostly under 2″, *blunt-tipped*, whitened or green beneath. Twigs may or may not be hairy. Height to 20″ (rarely 3′). Dry soils; mountains of w. Pennsylvania and W. Virginia to Florida and Louisiana.

TUNDRA BILBERRY   *Vaccinium uliginosum* L.   **p. 360**
Recognition: A somewhat leaning or upright low shrub. Leaves small, usually hairless, more or less elliptic, *smooth-edged*, somewhat pale beneath. Older branchlets have shreddy bark. Leaves ³⁄₁₆″–1″. Height to 2′. Flowers June–July. Fruits blue to black, sweet, July–Sept.

Similar species: (1) Box Huckleberry has wavy-toothed leaves and occurs only in southern areas. (2) Labrador Tea, (3) Leatherleaf, and (4) Bog Rosemary (Plate 65) have distinctive leaf undersides. (5) Dwarf Bilberry has toothed, wedge-shaped leaves.

Remarks: Spruce grouse and ptarmigan feed on fruits.

OVALLEAF BILBERRY   *Vaccinium ovalifolium* Sm. **Not illus.**
Recognition: Like the preceding 2 species in having leaves *not toothed* but otherwise resembles the Square-twig Bilberry. Leaves sometimes slightly wavy-edged. Leaves 1″–2″. Height to 5′. Flowers June. Fruits blue with white powder. Thickets; Newfoundland and se. Labrador to w. Ontario and n. Michigan; Alaska to Idaho and Oregon.

SQUARE-TWIG BILBERRY   **p. 360**
Vaccinium membranaceum Dougl.
   Recognition: A low to medium-sized shrub with *4-angled* or 4-lined twigs and peeling older bark. Leaves elliptic and always *toothed.* Leaves 1″–3″. Height to 4½′. Flowers June–July. Fruits purple or black, sometimes with slight bloom, Aug.–Sept.

Similar species: (1) Ovalleaf Bilberry has leaves not toothed. (2) Box Huckleberry has leathery foliage. (3) Newfoundland Bilberry has twigs not angled.

NEWFOUNDLAND BILBERRY   Not illus.
Vaccinium nubigenum Fern.

Recognition: Much like Square-twig Bilberry but twigs *not angled* and leaves smaller. Leaves hairless, ½″–1⅜″. Fruits blue-black with white powder, sweet, Aug.–Sept. Rocky and acid soils; n. Newfoundland and e. Quebec mountains.

DWARF BILBERRY   *Vaccinium cespitosum* Michx.   p. 360
Recognition: A very low clumped shrub. Leaves shiny, *toothed, wedge-shaped,* less commonly egg-shaped. Leaves ½″–1⅜″. Height to 1′. Flowers June–July. Fruits light blue with whitish powder, July–Aug.

Similar species: (1) Tundra Bilberry has leaves not toothed and not regularly wedge-shaped. (2) Box Huckleberry is more southern and has wavy-toothed leaf edges. Dwarf Huckleberry has resin-dotted foliage.

SOUTHERN MOUNTAIN-CRANBERRY   Not illus.
Vaccinium erythrocarpum Michx.

Recognition: Though the true cranberries and Northern Mountain-cranberry (Plate 32) creep or run prostrate, this southern species is *upright* and often rather tall. Leaves more or less egg-shaped but *long-pointed.* Leaf edges *bristle-toothed.* Twigs and leaf undersides slightly hairy. Leaves 1″–3″. Height to 8′. Flowers May–June. Fruits *red,* tasteless, single, June–Aug. Mountain forests; W. Virginia and w. Virginia to Georgia and Tennessee.

BOX HUCKLEBERRY   p. 360
Gaylussacia brachycera (Michx.) Gray

Recognition: A southern low shrub with *thick leathery evergreen* foliage. Branches from creeping underground stems. Leaves 1″ long or less, oval, green beneath, more or less finely round-toothed. Twigs *sharply angled.* Leaves ¼″–1″. Height to 15″. Flowers May–June. Fruits July–Aug.

Similar species: (1) Tundra and (2) Dwarf Bilberries are more northern. (3) Labrador Tea, (4) Leatherleaf, and (5) Bog Rosemary (Plate 65) all lack green leaf undersides. (6) See Farkleberry. Bilberries with angled twigs have thin leaves.

Remarks: Ruffed grouse eats fruits.

FARKLEBERRY   *Vaccinium arboreum* Marsh.   p. 360
Recognition: Largely southern; the only *Vaccinium* occasionally to grow to tree size. A large shrub or small tree. Leaves egg-shaped, *thick, and leathery,* toothed or not. Evergreen in

South. Leaves 1"–2". Height to 30'; diameter to 6". Flowers July–Aug. Fruits black, dry, Aug.–Oct.

Similar species: Thick leathery leaves and large size are rather distinctive. Mountain Laurel (Plate 65) has dry fruits and longer leaves clustered at twig tips.

Remarks: Fruits are eaten by bobwhite and numerous songbirds.

Azaleas
(Plate 64, p. 362)

Azaleas are small to large shrubs whose leaves and buds are clustered near the twig tips. Furthermore, the twigs also are clustered and typically radiate out from the ends of the older branchlets. The true end buds usually are flower buds much larger than the lateral leaf buds. Azaleas are the only nonevergreen species with 1 bundle scar which have large end buds and clustered leaves, buds, and twigs. The leaves are not toothed (except see Toothed Azalea) but have hairy edges, seen under magnification. The flowers fundamentally are vaselike, with long stamens protruding from the mouth of the tubular basal portion. Some often are improperly called wild honeysuckle or bush-honeysuckle. Fruits are dry, brown, slender vaselike capsules, often present in winter.

The azaleas, which are deciduous, and the evergreen rhododendrons (Plates 32, 65) constitute the genus *Rhododendron* in our area. Other species found elsewhere in the world connect these 2 sections of the genus within the heath family. Azaleas do not occur in the northwestern portion of our area. Alpine-azalea (Plate 12) is neither similar nor closely related but Rhododendron Rosebay (Plate 32) is a matted evergreen.

Like the evergreen rhododendrons, the shrubby azaleas are highly prized for their beautiful clusters of large and colorful blossoms. Many native species, as well as Asiatic and hybrid forms, are commonly planted in gardens. In the wild they are often locally rare because of picking.

SMOOTH AZALEA p. 362
Rhododendron arborescens (Pursh) Torr.
    Recognition: A shrub of eastern mountains. Unlike all other native azaleas, both the leaf undersides (even midribs) and twigs *lack hairs.* Leaves elliptic, relatively wider than those of other azaleas. Leaves 1"–3". Height to 20'. Flowers pink, sometimes white, appearing after the leaves, June–July.

PINKSHELL AZALEA *Rhododendron vaseyi* Gray **Not illus.**
    Recognition: In Massachusetts this cultivated azalea is reported

to have escaped. The pointed leaves are hairless and the flowers, which appear before the leaves, are rose-colored.

RHODORA AZALEA   p. 362
Rhododendron canadense (L.) Torr.

Recognition: A low shrub with *blunt-tipped* somewhat hairy leaves and hairless twigs. Buds *hairy;* large flower buds have only a few scales, which drop early. Unlike other azaleas, flowers have a very short tube. Leaves ½″–2½″. Height to 3′. Flowers purplish, rarely white, usually appearing *before leaves,* March–July.

Similar species: The flower type, blunt leaves, and combination of hairy buds, hairless twigs, and few-scaled flower buds set this species aside from our other azaleas. See next species.

JAPANESE AZALEA   Not illus.
Rhododendron japonicum (Gray) Suringar

Recognition: The only other regularly *blunt-leaved* azalea is Rhodora, but leaves of Japanese Azalea are *hairless.* Some leaves of other species may be blunt-tipped, but usually most are of the typical pointed type. Escaped from cultivation; Connecticut and n. New Jersey.

EARLY AZALEA   p. 362
Rhododendron roseum (Loisel.) Rehd.

Recognition: A northern shrub with narrow (as illustrated) to wide leaves that are *woolly beneath.* Both twigs and buds woolly. Leaves 1″–4½″. Height to 10′. Flowers white or pink, appearing before or with leaves, May–June. Flower tube only *about as long* as petal lobes.

Similar species: Separable from (1) Woolly Azalea mostly by more northern upland range and shorter flower tubes; from (2) Flame Azalea by hairy buds and less colorful blossoms.

WOOLLY AZALEA   Not illus.
Rhododendron canescens (Michx.) Sweet

Recognition: Very similar to Early Azalea but leaves typically narrow. Most certain identification is by flower-tube length, which is *twice as long* as petal lobes. Swamps and woods; Florida and e. Texas, north to e. Delaware and ne. Maryland and to s. Illinois and s. Ohio.

FLAME AZALEA   p. 362
Rhododendron calendulaceum (Michx.) Torr.

Recognition: A sometimes tall shrub with beautiful *orange or scarlet* blossoms. Leaves narrow to wide; woolly, with short hairs beneath. Twigs densely hairy or sparsely long-hairy but buds hairless. Leaves 1″–3″. Height to 17′. Flowers appear before or with leaves, May–June.

Similar species: (1) Early Azalea has hairy buds and white or pink flowers. (2) Cumberland Azalea has hairless twigs.

CUMBERLAND AZALEA   Not illus.
Rhododendron cumberlandense E. L. Br.
   Recognition: Similar to Flame Azalea in color of blossoms but these do not appear until after leaves have matured. Furthermore, twigs are hairless and flower-bud scales are bristle-tipped. Flowers June–July. Oak forests; Kentucky and W. Virginia.

SWAMP AZALEA *Rhododendron viscosum* (L.) Torr.   p. 362
   Recognition: A medium-sized to tall shrub with leaves *glossy* above and green to white beneath; midrib beneath bristly-hairy. Twigs sometimes densely bristly-hairy; buds also somewhat hairy. Winter flower buds have 8–12 scales that are rounded or have short bristle-tips. Leaves ⅝″–2½″. Height to 17′. Flowers white, rarely pink-striped or reddish, appearing after leaves have grown, June–Sept.
   Similar species: Four azaleas have leaves of this shape and hairiness. This species differs from (1) Toothed Azalea in having fewer flower-bud scales, toothless leaves, and northern range; from (2) Pink Azalea in whiter blossoms, which appear after leaves, glossy leaf uppersides, and usually more hairy buds. (3) Dwarf Azalea has a lower, clumped form and Coastal Plain habitat.

TOOTHED AZALEA   Not illus.
Rhododendron serrulatum (Small) Millais
   Recognition: A southern plant; resembles Swamp Azalea but leaves larger, *very finely toothed*, and always green on both sides. Winter flower buds have 15–20 bristle-tipped dark-bordered scales. Leaves 1″–3¼″. Height to 22′. Flowers white, appearing after leaves, June–July. Low woods; Mississippi to Florida and north to se. Virginia.

PINK AZALEA *Rhododendron nudiflorum* (L.) Torr.   p. 362
   Recognition: Much like Swamp Azalea but leaves *dull* above and green beneath. Twigs bristly-hairy; buds usually nearly *hairless* but may be somewhat hairy. Leaves 1″–3¼″. Height to 10′. Flowers pink, rarely white or purplish, appearing before or with leaves, March–May.
   Remarks: Succulent green leaf galls, though abnormalities, frequently occur. These are edible raw or, reportedly, pickled.

DWARF AZALEA   Not illus.
Rhododendron atlanticum (Ashe) Rehd.
   Recognition: A low Coastal Plain shrub growing in *dense colonies* and spreading by underground runners. Leaves wedge-shaped

to elliptic. Twigs both bristly and soft-hairy. Leaves 1″–2″. Height to 2′ or 3′. Flowers purple to pink, less commonly white, appearing before or with leaves. April–May. See Swamp Azalea. Sandy woods; Delaware and ne. Maryland to S. Carolina.

Evergreen Heaths
(*Plate 65, p. 364*)

These are the only upright broad-leaved evergreen members of the heath family which have mostly alternate leaves and small dry woody fruit structures, the last being present over long periods. Some leaves of rhododendrons and Mountain Laurel may be opposite, and some leaves of Sandmyrtle (Plate 17) may be alternate but most are opposite. Box Huckleberry and Farkleberry (Plate 63) are evergreen heaths with fleshy fruits. Rhododendron Rosebay (Plate 32) is an evergreen rhododendron but lies flat on the ground.

GREAT RHODODENDRON p. 364
Rhododendron maximum L.
  Recognition: A dense thicket-forming evergreen shrub or small tree, mostly of the mountains. Leaves *large, leathery,* toothless, tapered at base, edges *rolled;* usually somewhat *hairy and whitish beneath.* Twigs hairy. Large flower buds have long thin bracts. Leaves 3″–8″. Height to 30′ or 40′; diameter to 10′ or 12′. Flowers large, pink to purple (1 variety white), in large clusters, June–July. Fruits elongate capsules, not rusty-hairy.
  Similar species: The 2 rhododendrons and Mountain Laurel form almost impenetrable tangles on many mountain slopes. The next 2 species have hairless leaves. (1) Catawba Rhododendron has wider leaf bases. (2) Mountain Laurel has smaller leaves without rolled edges. (3) Fetterbush has triangular twigs.
  Remarks: When in full bloom, a rhododendron-covered slope is beautiful. Frequently cultivated for ornament. The hard wood may be used for tool handles, decorative objects, and fuel. Leaves sometimes poisonous to cattle and deer but usually avoided by them.

CATAWBA RHODODENDRON Leaf illus., p. 364
Rhododendron catawbiense Michx.
  Recognition: Like the preceding but more southern and with *wider hairless leaves.* Leaf bases and tips *rounded.* Leaves lighter beneath, and flower buds lack bracts. Leaves 3″–8″. Height to 20′. Flowers large, rose-purple, clustered, May–June. Fruits elongate rusty-hairy capsules. Both the last

species and the next have leaf bases and tips pointed. Damp slopes and streamsides; Virginia, W. Virginia, and se. Kentucky to w. S. Carolina, n. Georgia, and n. Alabama.

MOUNTAIN LAUREL *Kalmia latifolia* L. p. 364
Recognition: A gnarled evergreen shrub or small tree. Leaves *hairless, flat,* leathery, pointed, toothless, *light green beneath.* A rare form has blunt leaves. Twigs hairless. Large flower buds of rhododendron type lacking. Leaves 2″–5″. Height to 10′, rarely to 35′. Flowers medium-sized, white to purple, clustered, May–July. Fruits rounded capsules.
Similar species: (1) See Great Rhododendron. (2) Sheep Laurel (Plate 16) and relatives are lower and have opposite leaves. (3) Devilwood (p. 79) has regularly opposite leaves.
Remarks: Leaves poisonous to cattle, sheep, and deer but eaten only when better foods are lacking.

FETTERBUSH Leaf illus., p. 364
Lyonia lucida (Lam.) K. Koch
Recognition: A southern evergreen shrub with leathery toothless leaves that have a *conspicuous vein* paralleling the rolled edges. Twigs somewhat *triangular* in cross section at the leaf bases. Leaves 1″–3″. Height to 5′. Flowers small, white to pink, bell-like, in clusters in angles of leaves, April–May. See Great Rhododendron. Woods and thickets; Virginia to Florida and se. Louisiana.

LABRADOR TEA *Ledum groenlandicum* Oeder p. 364
Recognition: A low northern shrub with leathery evergreen leaves that have *rolled edges.* Leaves narrow, toothless, fragrant when crushed, and except in one uncommon form (*denudatum* Vict. & Rousseau), densely *white- or rusty-hairy beneath.* Twigs hairy. Leaves ½″–2″. Height to 3′. Flowers small, white, in end clusters, May–June, or later.
Similar species: (1) Labrador Tea, (2) Leatherleaf, and (3) Bog Rosemary are often associated in northern bogs. Leaf undersides of Labrador Tea are woolly; those of Leatherleaf hairless and yellow-scaly; those of Bog Rosemary hairless or slightly hairy and white. (4) Tundra Bilberry and (5) Box Huckleberry (Plate 63) have green leaf undersides.
Remarks: The dried leaves have been used for tea.

LEATHERLEAF p. 364
Chamaedaphne calyculata (L.) Moench
Recognition: A low northern shrub. Leaves leathery, narrow to elliptic, toothless, evergreen, scaly (use lens), and usually somewhat *yellowish* beneath. Crushed foliage not especially scented. Twigs mostly hairless. Leaves 1″–2″. Height to 4′.

Flowers small, white, bell-like, in clusters in angles of upper leaves, March–July.
Similar species: (1) See Labrador Tea. (2) Rhododendron Rosebay (Plate 32) is lower, with scaly leaves and twigs.
Remarks: Fruits and buds sometimes eaten by sharptail grouse. Twigs browsed by snowshoe hare.

PIERIS *Pieris floribunda* (Pursh) B. & H. **p. 364**
Recognition: A shrub of southern mountains. Leaves leathery, evergreen, *hairy and black-dotted* beneath, *fine-toothed,* and somewhat long-pointed. Twigs hairy and end buds false. Leaves 1½″–2½″. Height to 5′. Flowers small, white, bell-like, in clusters at twig ends, May.
Similar species: Among those with 1 bundle scar, only this species and (1) Coastal and (2) Upland Sweetbells have leathery evergreen leaves that are toothed. This species, however, is hairy.

COASTAL SWEETBELLS Not illus.
Leucothoë axillaris (Lam.) D. Don
Recognition: A shrub with *shiny,* evergreen leaves, hairless and usually toothed, at least near tip. Typical leaves are elliptic but var. *ambigens* Fern. is long-pointed like next species. Leafstalks *less than ⅜″.* Twigs green. End buds false. Leaves 1½″–6″. Height to 7′. Flowers small, white, bell-like, in clusters in leaf-angles, Feb.–May. Pieris has hairy leaves and twigs. Damp woods; Mississippi to Florida and north to se. Virginia.
Remarks: Similar in appearance to related species (Plate 66).

UPLAND SWEETBELLS Not illus.
Leucothoë editorum Fern. & Schub.
Recognition: Similar to Coastal Sweetbells but leaves always *long-pointed* and toothed. Leafstalks ⅜″–⅝″. Flowers May. Mountain forests; Virginia and Tennessee to Georgia.

BOG ROSEMARY *Andromeda glaucophylla* Link **p. 364**
Recognition: A low northern shrub with unique *toothless,* leathery, evergreen, narrow leaves, *much whitened beneath* by tiny hairs. Leaf edges *rolled.* Twigs hairless. Leaves 1″–1½″. Height to 2′. Flowers small, pink or white, bell-like, in end clusters, May–July, or longer.
Similar species: The small and large cranberries (Plate 32) have similar but much smaller leaves and are creeping plants with red berries. See under Labrador Tea.

Nonevergreen Heaths with Toothed Leaves

(*Plate 66, p. 366*)

These species are alike in that their fruits are small dry capsules that occur in clusters and split open when ripe. These fruits often are present during much of the year. Leaves are deciduous and toothed; leaf scars contain only 1 bundle scar. All these species often are placed in the heath family, but pepperbushes sometimes are assigned to a family by themselves. The flowers of all are small, white, bell-like, and clustered mostly at ends of twigs. All species are rare or absent west of the Appalachians except Sourwood, which reaches Indiana, and Maleberry, reported as rare in Michigan.

Three other related nonevergreen heaths whose leaves are wavy-edged or not toothed are on Plate 68. See also spireas (Plate 60).

SOURWOOD   *Oxydendrum arboreum* (L.) DC.   **p. 366**
  Recognition: The only full-size tree with flower and fruit clusters of the heath type. Leaves narrow to egg-shaped and have a sour taste. Twigs hairless. Buds small with end buds false. Bark dark and furrowed. Leaves 4″–8″. Height 20′–50′ (70′); diameter 18″–20″. Flowers in *1-sided clusters,* June–July. Fruits 5-parted.
  Similar species: The only tall nonevergreen tree with 1 bundle scar and toothed simple leaves. See also Persimmon (Plate 68).
  Remarks: Highly ornamental at all seasons but especially so when in flower or in crimson autumn color. Deer eat twigs.

MALEBERRY   *Lyonia ligustrina* (L.) DC.   **p. 366**
  Recognition: A shrub usually with thickish narrow to egg-shaped leaves. Leaves typically hairy beneath but may be hairless, fine-toothed or not, thin or thickened, point-tipped, or, more rarely, blunt-tipped. Slender buds have only 2 bud scales; end buds false. Twigs may be hairy near tips. Leaves 1″–4″. Height to 13′. Flowers in clusters that are not 1-sided, May–July. Fruits 5-parted.
  Similar species: The 2-scaled buds often will serve to identify the species in leaf, whether the leaves are toothed or not.

MOUNTAIN PEPPERBUSH   **p. 366**
Clethra acuminata Michx.
  Recognition: A shrub of southern mountains with usually *hairy* twigs, *large* end buds with loose or shedding hairy outer scales, and long-pointed fine-toothed leaves. Outer bark red-brown, separating into loose strips. Leaves 3″–6″. Height to 18′.

Flowers in dense spikes that are not 1-sided, July–Aug. Fruits 3-parted.

Similar species: Pepperbushes are the only plants with 1 bundle scar which have large end buds (much bigger than side buds) whose outer scales are as long as the buds. They are the only upright nonevergreen heathlike plants with dry fruits and true end buds present which also have hairy twigs. Leaves of this species larger and more long-pointed than those of the next.

COAST PEPPERBUSH *Clethra alnifolia* L.   **p. 366**
Recognition: Similar to preceding but with smaller, more wedge-shaped, *short-pointed* leaves. Older bark grayish and flaking. Leaves 1½″–3″. Height to 10′. Flowers, July–Sept.

SWAMP SWEETBELLS *Leucothoë racemosa* (L.) Gray **p. 366**
Recognition: A shrub with upright branches. Leaves rather *narrow, long-pointed,* fine-toothed, sometimes slightly hairy. Twigs often reddish, usually hairless; may have small catkinlike flower-bud clusters present in winter. Small buds have several visible bud scales. End buds false. Leaves 2″–4″. Height to 13′. Flowers very fragrant, in *1-sided clusters,* May–June. Fruits 5-parted.
Similar species: Others of this group have wider leaves and, where end buds are lacking, ball-like or 2-scaled buds. Mountain Sweetbells differs in leaf shape, has more wide-spreading branches and mountain habitat.
Remarks: Reportedly poisonous to livestock.

MOUNTAIN SWEETBELLS   **p. 366**
Leucothoë recurva (Buckley) Gray
Recognition: Similar to Swamp Sweetbells but smaller and of more spreading growth. Leaves narrow to egg-shaped and long-pointed. Leaves 2″–5″. Height to 10′. Flowers April.

Miscellaneous Plants
with 1 Bundle Scar (1)
(*Plate 67, p. 368*)

The limited distributions of these mostly southern species will eliminate them from consideration in many localities. They are among the relatively few alternate-leaved species whose leaf scars contain only single bundle traces. Species with leaves usually or commonly toothed are considered here; those whose leaves are not toothed (but see Mountain-holly, Plate 68) are on the next plate.

SWEETLEAF   *Symplocos tinctoria* (L.) L'Hér.   **p. 368**
Recognition: A large shrub or small tree of the Coastal Plain. Leaves narrow to egg-shaped, usually at least partially toothed and semileathery, often remaining until spring; *sweet* to the taste. Buds dark with several scales. Pith *chambered*. Bark grayish-smooth, often with shallow vertical cracks. Leaves 3"–7". Height to 40'; diameter to 10". A pine-woods variety in se. Virginia grows only to 4' or less. Flowers white, April–May. Fruits fleshy, reddish, single-seeded, about ⅜", Aug.–Sept.
Similar species: Only 3 species with single bundle scars have chambered piths. (1) Silverbell-tree has reddish buds, and (2) the buds of Persimmon (Plate 68) are dark, with only 2 scales.

SILVERBELL-TREE   *Halesia carolina* L.   **p. 368**
Recognition: A shrub or small tree with somewhat white-striped bark. Leaves toothed, egg-shaped, somewhat hairy beneath. Twigs hairless to hairy. Buds *reddish;* pith *chambered*. Leaves 2"–7". Height 10'–20' (90'); diameter 6"–12" (3'). Flowers *showy, white 4-petaled,* May. Fruits dry, *4-winged,* 1"–1¾".
Similar species: See Sweetleaf.

AMERICAN SNOWBELL   *Styrax americana* Lam.   **p. 368**
Recognition: A shrub with elliptic leaves usually nearly hairless; few teeth or none. (Var. *pulverulenta* (Michx.) Perkins with leaves sometimes egg-shaped and hairy or scaly beneath occurs north to s. Virginia and Arkansas.) Twigs hairless or nearly so. Buds have *no scales*, blunt and brown-hairy, often one above another; end buds false. Single bundle scar, sometimes somewhat broken. Leaves 1"–4". Height to 14'. Flowers white, showy, in 1"–2" elongate clusters, May. Fruits dry, 1-seeded, Sept.–Oct.
Similar species: Snowbells are our only species with naked buds and single bundle scars. Bigleaf Snowbell has wider-based, more hairy leaves and very hairy or scaly twigs.

BIGLEAF SNOWBELL   *Styrax grandifolia* Ait.   **p. 368**
Recognition: Similar to American Snowbell but with egg-shaped leaves *white-hairy* beneath. Twigs very hairy or scaly. Leaves 2"–8". Height to 12' (40'). Flowers in 2"–6" clusters.

SILKY-CAMELLIA   *Stewartia malachodendron* L.   **p. 368**
Recognition: A shrub with elliptic toothed leaves, soft-hairy beneath. Buds slender, under ⅛", often slightly hairy. Twigs may be fine-hairy. Leaves 2"–4". Height to 15'. Flowers white,

2″–3″, June. Fruits dry, 5- to 10-seeded, round, and blunt.
Similar species: Among 1-bundle-scar plants with true end buds present and about the size of the side buds, this and Mountain-camellia are the only ones with 2–3 visible and hairy bud scales. Mountain Camellia has larger leaves and buds.
Remarks: Closely related to cultivated camellias.

MOUNTAIN-CAMELLIA   **p. 368**
Stewartia ovata (Cav.) Weath.
    Recognition: Similar to Silky-Camellia but leaves 5″–6″ long and buds over ⅛″. Flowers May–Aug.

Miscellaneous Plants
with 1 Bundle Scar (2)
(*Plate 68, p. 370*)

Of the plants whose leaf scars contain but 1 bundle scar, only some of the blueberries (Plate 62), huckleberries (Plate 63), azaleas (Plate 64), and this group regularly have leaves that are not toothed. American Silverberry and Zenobia, however, may have wavy-edged leaves and the leaves of Mountain-holly are very rarely few-toothed. Some hollies (Plate 61), Maleberry (Plate 66), and Sweetleaf and Snowbells (Plate 67) also have leaves sometimes not toothed. European Matrimony-vine (Plate 37) usually is thorny and vinelike, but sometimes neither; Chinese Matrimony-vine (p. 190) is thornless and bushy rather than vinelike. But both have ridged twigs.

PERSIMMON   *Diospyros virginiana* L.   **p. 370**
    Recognition: A tree with distinctive dark thick bark typically broken into *small squarish blocks.* Leaves somewhat thickened, egg-shaped, and *not toothed.* Buds *very dark with 2 scales.* End buds false. Pith sometimes divided into chambers by weak partitions. Var. *pubescens* (Pursh) Dippel (found south from Virginia, s. Illinois, and s. Iowa) has hairy twigs and leaf under-sides. Leaves 2″–5″. Height 30′–50′ (130′); diameter 10″–12″ (7′). Flowers yellowish, May–June. Fruits slightly larger than cultivated cherries, orange-colored, edible when ripe, Aug.–Oct., or later.
    Similar species: No other tree has the combination of toothless leaves, dark buds, and regularly cracked bark. Barks of (1) Flowering Dogwood (Plate 15) and blackhaw viburnums (Plate 20) are similar, but those plants have opposite leaves. (2) Sourwood (Plate 66) bark is vaguely like it but leaves are toothed. (3)

Sweetleaf (Plate 67) has chambered pith and dark bark but there are more than 2 bud scales. (4) See Sour-gum (p. 270). **Remarks:** The green fruit causes the mouth to "pucker up" for some time after being tasted. However, cool, ripe Persimmons that are soft and fully colored are delicious. They are eaten by nearly all birds and mammals, from songbirds to turkeys and from dogs to deer. The Persimmon, a member of the ebony family, has strong, heavy, close-grained wood, occasionally used as shoe lasts and shuttles.

AMERICAN SILVERBERRY   **p. 370**
Elaeagnus commutata Bernh.
    Recognition: A shrub marked with distinctive *rusty and silvery* scales. Leaves egg-shaped to elliptic, silver-brown and scaly on both sides; smooth- to wavy-edged. A pair of small leaves may be present at leaf angles. Twigs marked with *brown* and usually also *silver* scales. Leaves 1″–5″. Height to 12′. Flowers silvery yellow, fragrant, June–July. Fruits silvery, small, elliptic, fleshy and edible, but dry, July–Oct.
    Similar species: (1) Autumn-olive may be somewhat spiny and has leaves green above and fruits reddish and juicy. Several Asiatic relatives are just becoming established and are merely listed here. (2) Russian-olive (*E. angustifolia* L.), locally spreading, has only silvery scales and leaves are long and narrow. It may be somewhat thorny. (3) Many-flowered Silverberry (*E. multiflora* Thunb.) has only brown scales. Only other plants with silver-brown scales are the related buffaloberries (Plate 17), which have opposite leaves. (4) Minniebush has glands, not scales, on leaf midrib.
    Remarks: *Elaeagnus* species are among the few nonlegumes that fix nitrogen in the soil by means of bacterial root nodules.

AUTUMN-OLIVE   *Elaeagnus umbellata* Thunb.   **Not illus.**
    Recognition: Similar to American Silverberry but often *somewhat thorny*. Leaves green above; fruits reddish, juicy. Sometimes planted for erosion control and ornament. Of oriental origin, it may be known as Japanese or Asiatic Silverberry. Spread from cultivation; Maine to New Jersey and Pennsylvania.

DAPHNE   *Daphne mezereum* L.   **p. 370**
    Recognition: An introduced low shrub with *wedge-shaped* leaves and *very tough* bark whose nature becomes apparent when an attempt is made to break a twig. Leaves 3″–4″. Height to 3′. Flowers purplish, in small side clusters, April–May. Fruits red, single-seeded, Aug.–Sept.
    Similar species: Only Leatherwood (Plate 59) has a similarly

tough bark. It has circular leaf scars and more than 3 bundle scars.

MOUNTAIN-HOLLY   p. 370
Nemopanthus mucronata (L.) Trel.
  Recognition: A shrub with rather small leaves. Leaves more or less elliptic but often with parallel sides, typically *bristle-tipped;* rarely with some small teeth. Buds have 2–3 exposed scales; somewhat long-pointed; end buds true. Older branches gray. Though related to hollies (Plate 61), stipules absent. Leaves 1″–2½″. Height to 10′. Flowers yellowish, small, single or clustered, May–June. Fruits dull red, rarely yellow, several-seeded, Aug.–Sept.
  Similar species: Oblong, bristle-tipped leaves and long-pointed buds separate this from other 1-bundle-scar shrubs with tooth-less foliage.

STAGGERBUSH   *Lyonia mariana* (L.) D. Don   p. 370
  Recognition: A slender shrub. Leaves rather nondescript, egg-shaped to elliptic, hairless or hairy only on veins beneath. Buds have *4–5 visible scales;* ball-shaped to short cone-shaped. End buds false. Twigs grayish. Leaves 1″–3″. Height to 7′. Flowers white to pink, bell-shaped, in open clusters on older branches, May–June. Fruits dry, urn-shaped, 5-parted capsules.
  Similar species: Other nonevergreen shrubs with 1 bundle scar and untoothed leaves have hairy twigs, diaphragmed pith, or other distinctive characteristics. Leaf shape and dry fruits of Staggerbush are shared with next 2 species, but (1) Zenobia has only 2–3 bud scales and reddish twigs and (2) Minniebush has large true end buds present.
  Remarks: Foliage may be poisonous to lambs and calves.

ZENOBIA   *Zenobia pulverulenta* (Bartr.) Pollard   Not illus.
  Recognition: A shrubby heath with *leathery,* wavy-edged leaves and *white-powdered* hairless foliage and twigs. Twigs reddish to brown. Buds have 2–3 visible scales but otherwise much like those of last species. Leaves 1″–3″. Height to 10′. Flowers white, in short clusters, June. Fruits dry, ball-shaped, 5-parted capsules. Pine woods; se. Virginia, e. N. Carolina, and ne. S. Carolina.

MINNIEBUSH   *Menziesia pilosa* (Michx.) Juss.   p. 370
  Recognition: A low Appalachian shrub. Leaves elliptic, hairy above; *obvious glands* along midrib beneath. Foliage clustered near twig tips. Side buds 2- to 3-scaled, egg-shaped; end buds true and usually much larger. Twigs somewhat bristly-hairy, older bark shreddy. Leaves 1″–2″. Height to 6′. Flowers white

to purplish, small, bell-shaped, May–June. Fruits dry 4-parted capsules.
Similar species: No other shrub with 1 bundle scar has such leaf glands on leaf undersides, though (1) American Silverberry has brown scales on midrib. In winter, large true end buds also occur among 1-bundle-scar plants only in azaleas (Plate 64) and pepperbushes (Plate 66); azaleas have tighter bark and pepperbushes have hairy outer end bud scales. (2) See also Staggerbush.

WHIN   *Genista tinctoria* L.   **Not illus.**
Recognition: A low weak shrub with narrow stalkless leaves and twigs that are finely grooved lengthwise (see Chinese Matrimony-vine, p. 190). Leaf scars small; bundle scars single, though often indistinct. Leaves ½″–1″. Flowers yellow, June–July. Fruits flat several-seeded pods. A European importation; poor soils, s. Maine, Massachusetts, and Michigan to District of Columbia.

ANDRACHNE   **Not illus.**
Andrachne phyllanthoides (Nutt.) Muell. Arg.
  Recognition: Low shrub with leaves small, elliptic, nearly stalkless, and finely bristle-tipped. Twigs somewhat 5-angled, 5-lined, often slightly hairy. Branchlets shiny. Bud scales 3–4; edges hairy. Leaves under 1″. Height to 3′. Flowers small, May–Oct. Fruits dry capsules. Dry soils, s. Missouri to Texas.

PONDSPICE   *Litsea aestivalis* (L.) Fern.   **p. 370**
Recognition: A rare southern shrub much like the related spicebushes (Plate 59). Leaves rather narrow, hairless, and leathery. Crushed leaves and twigs *aromatic*. Buds conical; leaf scars somewhat raised. Leaves 1″–3″. Height to 9′. Flowers yellow, small, March–April. Fruits single-seeded.

OILNUT   *Pyrularia pubera* Michx.   **p. 370**
Recognition: A *parasitic* Appalachian shrub growing on roots of various trees and shrubs. Leaves thin, broadly elliptic, often soft and hairy, with tiny *transparent dots* visible when held up to light. Twigs fine-hairy; buds large and greenish. Leaves 2″–6″. Height to 13′. Flowers in end clusters, May–June. Fruits pear-shaped, inch-long, Sept.

REDBAY   *Persea borbonia* (L.) Spreng.   **p. 370**
Recognition: A Coastal Plain tree. Leaves narrow, *shiny, leathery, evergreen,* pale beneath. Twigs angled. Bark dark *reddish, deeply grooved.* Leaves 3″–6″. Height to 50′ or 70′; diameter to 3′. Flowers May–July. Fruits blue or black, single-seeded, in red-stemmed clusters, Aug.–Sept.

TITI   *Cyrilla racemiflora* L.   **p. 370**
   Recognition: A southern shrub. Leaves *shiny, blunt-tipped, evergreen, and leathery,* but thin in var. *subglobosa* Fern. (se. Virginia). Leaves 2″–4″. Height to 20′ (to 35′ in South). Flowers white, in long end clusters, June–July. Fruits yellow, Aug.–Sept.

Broad-leaved Plants with Alternate Simple Leaves

(Key, pages 168–174; text, pages 168–296)

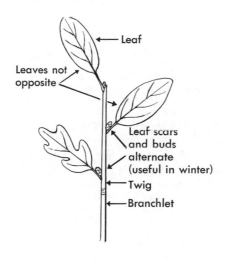

Leaf

Leaves not opposite

Leaf scars and buds alternate (useful in winter)

Twig

Branchlet

OVER one-half of our woody plants fall in this category. Although a number of species therefore resemble one another in having alternate simple leaves, the separation of the group into subdivisions aids in their identification. The outline in the text (p. 168) indicates the major characteristics used in subdividing the group. It may be used as a general guide to identification. In identifying specimens note cross references in the text discussion of each species.

LOW CREEPING AND TRAILING SHRUBS

with alternate and (except Sand Cherry and
dwarf willows) leathery, evergreen leaves.

Ⅴ CRANBERRIES and Relatives, *Vaccinium* spp.   pp. 175–77
  (A) NORTHERN MOUNTAIN-CRANBERRY, (B) CREEP-
  ING BLUEBERRY, (C) SMALL CR., (D) LARGE CR.
Ⅴ SNOWBERRY WINTERGREEN, *Gaultheria hispidula* p. 177
  Mossy woods; Newfoundland, Labrador, and British Colum-
  bia to New England, Pennsylvania (and in mts. to N. Caro-
  lina), Michigan, Minnesota, and Idaho.
  Ⅴ SMOOTHLEAF DRYAS   p. 177
  Dryas integrifolia (not illus.)
  Ⅴ TOOTHLEAF DRYAS, *D. drummondii* (not illus.)   p. 177
Ⅴ RHODODENDRON ROSEBAY   p. 177
  Rhododendron lapponicum
  Tundras and rocky areas; Arctic south to Newfoundland, e.
  Quebec, mts. of Maine, New Hampshire, and New York; also
  Dells of Wisconsin River.
Ⅴ EVERGREEN BEARBERRY, *Arctostaphylos uva-ursi*   p. 178
  Tundras and rocky and sandy areas; Arctic south to w.
  Newfoundland, Long Island, Virginia, Indiana, n. Illinois, n.
  Minnesota, S. Dakota, New Mexico, and n. California.
  Ⅴ ALPINE BEARBERRY, *A. alpina* (not illus.)   p. 178
  Ⅴ RED BEARBERRY, *A. rubra* (not illus.)   p. 178
Ⅴ REDBERRY WINTERGREEN, *Gaultheria procumbens* p. 178
  Woods, openings; Newfoundland and Manitoba to New Eng-
  land, Wisconsin, Minnesota, in mts. to Georgia and Alabama.
  Ⅴ PIPSISSEWAS   p. 179
  Chimaphila umbellata, C. maculata (not illus.)
Ⅴ TRAILING ARBUTUS, *Epigaea repens*   p. 179
  Woods; Labrador and Saskatchewan to Florida and Iowa.
Ⅴ SAND CHERRY, *Prunus depressa*   p. 179
  Beaches, rocks; New Brunswick, e. Quebec, and sw. Ontario
  to w. Massachusetts, e. Pennsylvania, New York, Wisconsin.
Ⅴ DWARF WILLOWS, *Salix* spp.   p. 179
  (A) WIDELEAF DWARF WILLOW, (B) BEARBERRY
  DWARF WILLOW. For these and others see pages 180–81.

CRANBERRY SNOWBERRY WINTERGREEN RHODODENDRON ROSEBAY REDBERRY WINTERGREEN TRAILING ARBUTUS

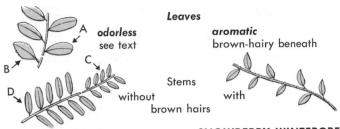

Leaves

odorless
see text

aromatic
brown-hairy beneath

Stems

without
brown hairs

with

CRANBERRIES

SNOWBERRY WINTERGREEN

Leaves odorless,
hairless

yellow
beneath

green
beneath

Stems

with brown
and yellow scales

somewhat
hairy

RHODODENDRON ROSEBAY

EVERGREEN BEARBERRY

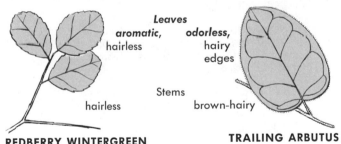

Leaves

aromatic,
hairless

odorless,
hairy
edges

Stems

hairless

brown-hairy

REDBERRY WINTERGREEN

TRAILING ARBUTUS

Leaves thin,
not evergreen,
not aromatic

Older bark
not speckled

speckled

SAND CHERRY

DWARF WILLOWS

GREENBRIERS

Green-stemmed, often evergreen, mostly thorny, vines climbing by tendrils attached to the persistent bases of the leafstalks.

§ LAUREL GREENBRIER, *Smilax laurifolia*   p. 182
   Swamps and bottomlands; New Jersey and Tennessee to Florida and Texas.

§ REDBERRY GREENBRIER, *Smilax walteri*   p. 182
   Sandy and boggy places; Coastal Plain from Louisiana and Florida to New Jersey.

§ BRISTLY GREENBRIER   p. 182
   Smilax tamnoides var. *hispida*
   Fertile soils; New York, s. Ontario and S. Dakota to Florida and Texas.
   § HELLFETTER GREENBRIER   p. 182
   S. tamnoides (not illus.)

§ GLAUCOUS GREENBRIER, *Smilax glauca*   p. 183
   Woods and thickets; s. New England, se. New York, e. Pennsylvania, W. Virginia, s. Ohio, s. Illinois, and se. Missouri to Florida and Texas.

§ BULLBRIER GREENBRIER, *Smilax bona-nox*   p. 183
   Woods and thickets; se. Massachusetts, Delaware, Maryland, Kentucky, se. Indiana, s. Illinois, Missouri, and Kansas to Florida and Texas.

§ COMMON GREENBRIER, *Smilax rotundifolia*   p. 183
   Woods and thickets; Nova Scotia, s. Maine, s. New Hampshire, New York, s. Ontario, s. Michigan, Illinois, se. Missouri, and Oklahoma to Florida and Texas.

Typical Greenbrier berries

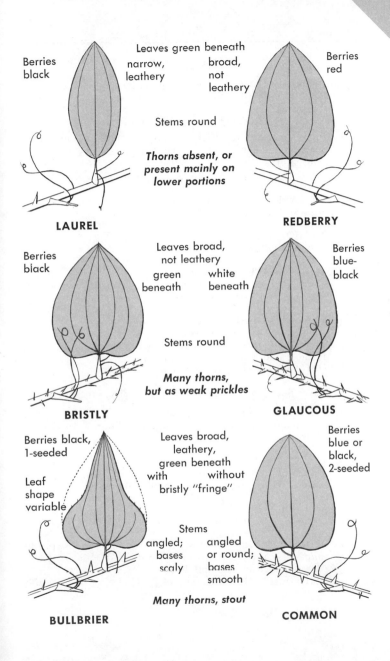

Berries black

Leaves green beneath
narrow, leathery

broad, not leathery

Berries red

Stems round

Thorns absent, or present mainly on lower portions

LAUREL

REDBERRY

Berries black

Leaves broad, not leathery
green beneath

white beneath

Berries blue-black

Stems round

Many thorns, but as weak prickles

BRISTLY

GLAUCOUS

Berries black, 1-seeded

Leaf shape variable

Leaves broad, leathery, green beneath
with   without
bristly "fringe"

Berries blue or black, 2-seeded

Stems
angled; bases scaly

angled; or round; bases smooth

Many thorns, stout

BULLBRIER

COMMON

GRAPES (1)

Dark-stemmed, thornless vines climbing by tendrils. Leaves variable, often deeply lobed; bases not remaining in winter.

GROUP I (Group II, Plate 35)

Twigs round, brown; older bark shreddy; pith not continuous; no tendrils opposite each 3rd leaf (except in Fox Grape and New England Grape, which have tendrils opposite most leaves).

Ia — Leaves red-woolly or very white beneath.

ʃ FOX GRAPE, *Vitis labrusca* p. 184
   Fertile soils; s. Maine and s. Michigan to Georgia and Tennessee.
   ʃ NEW ENGLAND GRAPE p. 185
   V. novae-angliae (not illus.)

ʃ SUMMER GRAPE, *Vitis aestivalis* p. 185
   Dry woods; Massachusetts, New York, Ohio, Michigan, and Wisconsin to Georgia and Texas.

ʃ SILVERLEAF GRAPE p. 185
   Vitis aestivalis var. *argentifolia*
   Woods; New Hampshire and s. Minnesota to se. Virginia. Alabama, and Kansas.
   ʃ POSTOAK GRAPE, *V. lincecumii* (not illus.) p. 185

Ib — Leaves not woolly, though sometimes hairy, green beneath.

ʃ FROST GRAPE, *Vitis vulpina* p. 185
   Bottomlands; se. New York, Illinois, and e. Kansas to Florida and Texas.

ʃ RIVERBANK GRAPE, *Vitis riparia* p. 186
   Streambanks; New Brunswick, Quebec, Manitoba, and Montana to n. Virginia, W. Virginia, Tennessee, and New Mexico.
   ʃ DUNE GRAPE p. 186
   V. riparia var. *syrticola* (not illus.)

ʃ SAND GRAPE, *Vitis rupestris* p. 186
   Sandy soils; Maryland, s. Pennsylvania, and Missouri to w. N. Carolina, Arkansas, and Texas.
   ʃ BUSH GRAPE, *V. acerifolia* (not illus.) p. 186

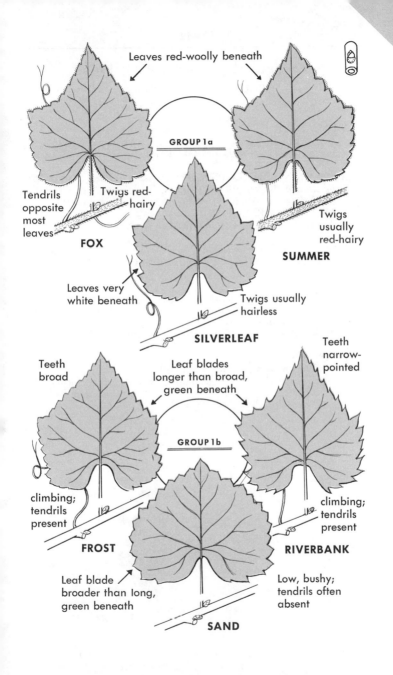

Leaves red-woolly beneath

GROUP 1a

Tendrils opposite most leaves

Twigs red-hairy

FOX

Twigs usually red-hairy

SUMMER

Leaves very white beneath

Twigs usually hairless

SILVERLEAF

Teeth broad

Leaf blades longer than broad, green beneath

Teeth narrow-pointed

GROUP 1b

climbing; tendrils present

FROST

climbing; tendrils present

RIVERBANK

Leaf blade broader than long, green beneath

Low, bushy; tendrils often absent

SAND

GRAPES (2), AMPELOPSIS, ETC.

GROUP II (Group I, Plate 34)

Twigs or stems distinctively marked as indicated.

ʃ MUSCADINE GRAPE, *Vitis rotundifolia*   p. 187
   Woods and thickets; s. Delaware, Virginia, W. Virginia, s.
   Indiana, se. Missouri, and Oklahoma to Florida and Texas.

ʃ AMERICAN AMPELOPSIS, *Ampelopsis cordata*   p. 187
   Fertile woods; Virginia, s. Ohio, s. Illinois, and se. Nebraska
   to Florida and Mexico, rarely north to Massachusetts.
   ʃ ASIATIC AMPELOPSIS   p. 187
   A. brevipedunculata (not illus.)

ʃ CAT GRAPE, *Vitis palmata*   p. 187
   Wet thickets and woods; s. Indiana, Illinois, and se. Iowa to
   Louisiana and Texas.

ʃ WINTER GRAPE, *Vitis cinerea*   p. 187
   Bottomlands; se. Virginia, s. Ohio, Illinois, Iowa, and Nebraska to Florida and e. Texas.
   ʃ POSSUM GRAPE, *V. baileyana* (not illus.)   p. 188

ʃ BOSTON IVY   p. 188
   Parthenocissus tricuspidata (not illus.)
   Buildings and trees; occasionally escapes from cultivation.

Typical Wild Grape

MOONSEEDS

Thornless, nonevergreen vines, usually with lobed or nearly
lobed leaves, which climb by green twining stems.

§ REDBERRY MOONSEED, *Cocculus carolinus* p. 188
Thickets; se. Virginia, Illinois, Missouri, and se. Kansas to
Florida and Texas.

§ CUPSEED, *Calycocarpum lyoni* p. 188
Fertile soils; Kentucky, s. Illinois, and e. Kansas to Florida
and Louisiana.

§ CANADA MOONSEED, *Menispermum canadense* p. 189
Streambanks; w. New England, w. Quebec, and se. Manitoba
to Georgia, Alabama, Arkansas, and Oklahoma.

CANADA MOONSEED

Tendrils not forked, sometimes few

Leaves hairless

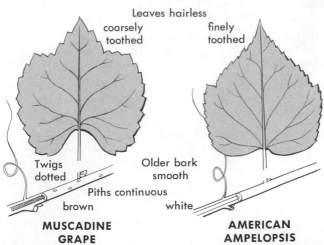

coarsely
toothed

finely
toothed

Twigs
dotted

Older bark
smooth

Piths continuous

brown

white

**MUSCADINE
GRAPE**

**AMERICAN
AMPELOPSIS**

Tendrils forked, only every 3rd one lacking

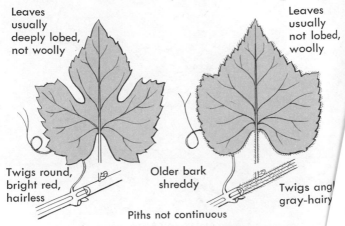

Leaves
usually
deeply lobed,
not woolly

Leaves
usually
not lobed,
woolly

Twigs round,
bright red,
hairless

Older bark
shreddy

Twigs angl
gray-hairy

Piths not continuous

CAT GRAPE

WINTER GRAPE

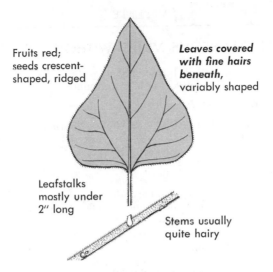

Fruits red; seeds crescent-shaped, ridged

Leaves covered with fine hairs beneath, variably shaped

Leafstalks mostly under 2" long

Stems usually quite hairy

REDBERRY MOONSEED

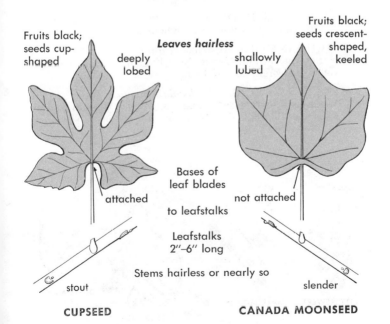

Fruits black; seeds cup-shaped

Leaves hairless

deeply lobed

shallowly lobed

Fruits black; seeds crescent-shaped, keeled

Bases of leaf blades to leafstalks

attached

not attached

Leafstalks 2"–6" long

Stems hairless or nearly so

stout

slender

CUPSEED

CANADA MOONSEED

MISCELLANEOUS VINES WITHOUT TENDRILS

Vines that climb by twining stems or aerial rootlets
or scramble overground.

§ ENGLISH IVY, *Hedera helix* (not illus.)   p. 189

§ AMERICAN BITTERSWEET, *Celastrus scandens*   p. 189
    Fencerows and woods; s. Quebec and s. Manitoba to Georgia,
    Louisiana, and Oklahoma.
   § ASIATIC BITTERSWEET   p. 190
    C. orbiculatus (not illus.)

§ SUPPLEJACK, *Berchemia scandens*   p. 190
    Bottomlands; Virginia, Tennessee, and Missouri to Florida and
    Texas.

§ EUROPEAN MATRIMONY-VINE   p. 190
    Lycium halimifolium
    Waste ground; local from s. Canada southward.
   § CHINESE MATRIMONY-VINE   p. 190
    L. chinense (not illus.)

§ BITTER NIGHTSHADE, *Solanum dulcamara*   p. 190
    Waste areas near houses; throughout our area.

§ DUTCHMAN'S-PIPE, *Aristolochia durior*   p. 191
    Fertile Appalachian forests; New England and sw. Pennsyl-
    vania to Georgia and Alabama.

§ WOOLLY PIPE-VINE, *Aristolochia tomentosa*   p. 191
    Woods; N. Carolina, sw. Indiana, s. Illinois, Missouri, and se.
    Kansas to Florida and e. Texas; naturalized in w. New York.

BITTERSWEET **MATRIMONY-VINE**

NIGHTSHADE

**DUTCHMAN'S-
PIPE**

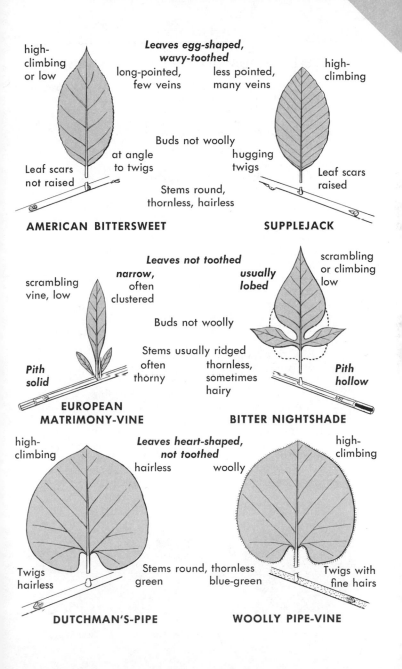

high-climbing or low

Leaves egg-shaped, wavy-toothed

long-pointed, few veins

less pointed, many veins

high-climbing

Buds not woolly

Leaf scars not raised

at angle to twigs

hugging twigs

Leaf scars raised

Stems round, thornless, hairless

AMERICAN BITTERSWEET

SUPPLEJACK

scrambling vine, low

Leaves not toothed

narrow, often clustered

usually lobed

scrambling or climbing low

Buds not woolly

Pith solid

Stems usually ridged
often thorny

thornless, sometimes hairy

Pith hollow

EUROPEAN MATRIMONY-VINE

BITTER NIGHTSHADE

high-climbing

Leaves heart-shaped, not toothed

hairless

woolly

high-climbing

Twigs hairless

Stems round, thornless green

blue-green

Twigs with fine hairs

DUTCHMAN'S-PIPE

WOOLLY PIPE-VINE

MISCELLANEOUS UPRIGHT THORNY PLANTS

whose leaves are mostly not lobed. They may be clustered on short "spur" branches (right) except in Firethorn and Devil's-club (see text). Also see Autumn-olive, (p. 293). Plums are the only plants of this group with glands frequently present on the leafstalks (see text).

↟ OSAGE-ORANGE, *Maclura pomifera*   p. 191
    Thickets; s. New England, New York, Iowa, and e. Kansas to Georgia and Texas; also Washington and Oregon.

↟ᐯ EASTERN BUMELIA, *Bumelia lycioides*   p. 192
    Coastal Plain bottomlands; se. Virginia to n. Florida, west to e. Texas, and north in Mississippi Valley to s. Indiana, s. Illinois, and se. Missouri.

  ᐯ SMALL BUMELIA, *B. smallii* (not illus.)   p. 192
↟ᐯ WOOLLY BUMELIA, *B. lanuginosa* (not illus.)   p. 192

ᐯ FIRETHORN, *Cotoneaster pyracantha*   p. 192
    Thickets; escape, Pennsylvania to Florida and Louisiana.

ᐯ AMERICAN BARBERRY, *Berberis canadensis*   p. 193
    Dry woods; w. Virginia and se. Missouri to Georgia.
  ᐯ EUROPEAN BARBERRY, *B. vulgaris* (not illus.)   p. 193
  ᐯ JAPANESE BARBERRY, *B. thunbergii* (not illus.)   p. 193

↟ᐯ AMERICAN PLUM, *Prunus americana*   p. 194
    Thickets; Massachusetts, New York, s. Ontario, s. Manitoba and w. Montana to nw. Florida and New Mexico.
  ↟ᐯ CANADA PLUM, *P. nigra* (leaf edge illus.)   p. 195
  ↟ᐯ CHICKASAW PLUM, *P. angustifolia* (not illus.)   p. 195
  ↟ᐯ BULLACE PLUM, *P. insititia* (not illus.)   p. 195
  ↟ᐯ SLOE PLUM, *P. spinosa* (not illus.)   p. 195

↟ᐯ AMERICAN CRABAPPLE, *Pyrus coronaria*   p. 196
    Rich woods, thickets; centr. New York, s. Ontario, and e. Kansas to w. S. Carolina and n. Alabama.
    For other native crabapples not illustrated, see pages 195–97.

ᐯ DEVIL'S-CLUB, *Oplopanax horridus* (not illus.)   p. 197

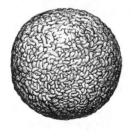

OSAGE-ORANGE   **AMERICAN PLUM**   **CRABAPPLE**

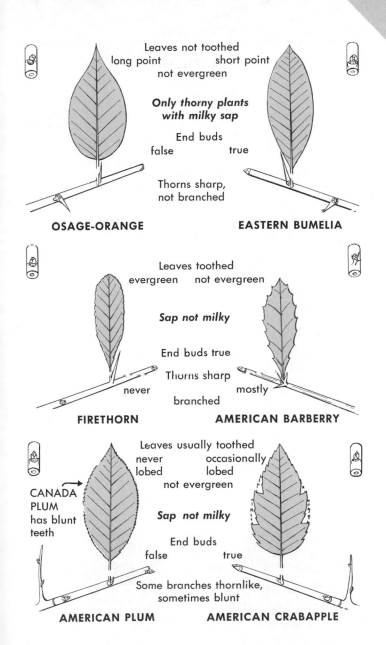

Leaves not toothed
long point   short point
not evergreen

*Only thorny plants
with milky sap*

End buds
false   true

Thorns sharp,
not branched

OSAGE-ORANGE   **EASTERN BUMELIA**

Leaves toothed
evergreen   not evergreen

Sap not milky

End buds true

Thorns sharp
never   mostly

branched

FIRETHORN   **AMERICAN BARBERRY**

Leaves usually toothed
never   occasionally
lobed   lobed
not evergreen

CANADA
PLUM
has blunt
teeth

Sap not milky

End buds
false   true

Some branches thornlike,
sometimes blunt

AMERICAN PLUM   **AMERICAN CRABAPPLE**

HAWTHORNS

(p. 197)

Very dense, usually long-thorny shrubs or small trees. The only
simple-leaved plants with nonleafy thorns mostly over 1 inch long.
Spur branches may be present. Leaves toothed, variable, either
not lobed or feather-lobed (rarely fan-lobed).

♠W These plants, distinctive though they are as a group, are virtually indistinguishable as species to all except the few botanists
who have given the genus special study. Frequent hybridization complicated by great individual variation confounds accurate identification.

The number of species of hawthorns (*Crataegus*) in this
country has been variously determined as over 1000 and as less
than 100. In this book, therefore, no attempt is made to differentiate between the many species of hawthorns. The drawings
opposite serve only to indicate the major leaf types as an aid
to identification of the genus.

For the amateur it seems best simply to call them hawthorns
and not attempt to be more specific.

Flowers

Fruit

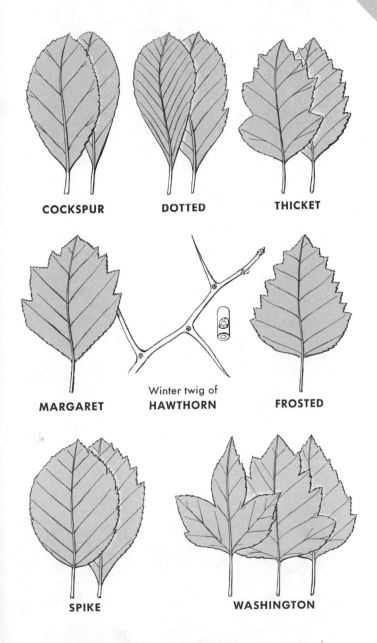

COCKSPUR

DOTTED

THICKET

MARGARET

Winter twig of
HAWTHORN

FROSTED

SPIKE

WASHINGTON

THORNY CURRANT AND GOOSEBERRIES

The only common thorny shrubs with alternate, fan-lobed leaves.
These may be clustered on short "spur" branches.
Thorns are present at the buds.

Ⅴ BRISTLY BLACK CURRANT, *Ribes lacustre*   p. 199
   Low woods and bogs; Newfoundland and Alaska to Nova
   Scotia, n. New England, w. Massachusetts, New York, n. Ohio,
   Michigan, Minnesota, Colorado, and California; in Appala-
   chians to Tennessee.
   Ⅴ CANADA GOOSEBERRY   p. 199
   R. oxyacanthoides (not illus.)
   Ⅴ ROCK GOOSEBERRY, *R. setosum* (not illus.)   p. 199

Ⅴ PASTURE GOOSEBERRY, *Ribes cynosbati*   p. 200
   Open woods; w. New Brunswick, s. Quebec, and Manitoba
   to w. N. Carolina, n. Alabama, and Missouri.

Ⅴ MISSOURI GOOSEBERRY, *Ribes missouriense*   p. 200
   Fields and woods; Connecticut, Michigan, and S. Dakota to
   Tennessee, Arkansas, and Kansas.

Ⅴ EUROPEAN GOOSEBERRY, *Ribes grossularia*   p. 200
   An escape from gardens in scattered localities.

Ⅴ ROUNDLEAF GOOSEBERRY, *Ribes rotundifolium*   p. 200
   Rocky fields and openings; w. Massachusetts to W. Virginia
   and w. N. Carolina.

Ⅴ SMOOTH GOOSEBERRY, *Ribes hirtellum*   p. 200
   Swamps and openings; Newfoundland, s. Labrador, n. On-
   tario, and N. Dakota to New England, Pennsylvania, W.
   Virginia, n. Ohio, n. Illinois, and N. Dakota.

BRISTLY BLACK CURRANT

PASTURE
GOOSEBERRY

SMOOTH
GOOSEBERRY

Berries black, bristly
Many long prickles always *present between thorns* sometimes
Berries red, spiny

Leaves almost hairless — soft-hairy

BRISTLY BLACK CURRANT

PASTURE GOOSEBERRY

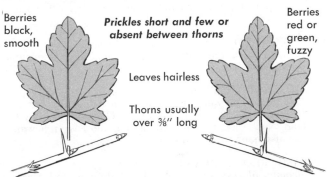

Berries black, smooth
Prickles short and few or absent between thorns
Berries red or green, fuzzy

Leaves hairless

Thorns usually over ⅜" long

MISSOURI GOOSEBERRY

EUROPEAN GOOSEBERRY

Berries black, smooth
Prickles short and few or absent between thorns
Berries black, smooth

Leaves mostly hairless

All thorns under ⅜" long

Leaf lobes obtusely pointed

Leaf lobes acutely pointed

ROUNDLEAF GOOSEBERRY

SMOOTH GOOSEBERRY

THORNLESS CURRANTS

Low shrubs with alternate, fan-lobed leaves, which
may be clustered on short "spur" branches.

Ⅴ AMERICAN BLACK CURRANT, *Ribes americanum*   p. 201
   Floodplains and woods openings; w. New Brunswick and
   Alberta to Delaware, w. Virginia, Nebraska, and New Mexico.

Ⅴ EUROPEAN BLACK CURRANT, *Ribes nigrum*   p. 201
   Escaped from gardens; locally established in wild.
   Ⅴ CANADIAN BLACK CURRANT   p. 201
   R. hudsonianum (not illus.)

Ⅴ GOLDEN CURRANT, *Ribes odoratum*   p. 202
   Rocky places; Minnesota and S. Dakota to Missouri, Arkansas,
   and Texas, but cultivated in the East.

Ⅴ GARDEN RED CURRANT, *Ribes sativum*   p. 202
   Escaped from cultivation to fields and woods openings;
   throughout n. U.S. and s. Canada.

Ⅴ SKUNK CURRANT, *Ribes glandulosum*   p. 202
   Low wet woods and boggy spots; Newfoundland, Labrador,
   Northwest Territories, and n. British Columbia to New Eng-
   land, New York, n. Ohio, Minnesota, and Saskatchewan; in
   Appalachians to N. Carolina.

Ⅴ SWAMP RED CURRANT, *Ribes triste*   p. 202
   Swampy places; Newfoundland, s. Labrador, and Alaska to
   n. New Jersey, ne. Pennsylvania, w. New York, s. Ontario,
   Michigan, S. Dakota, and Oregon; in mts. to W. Virginia.

GARDEN RED CURRANT

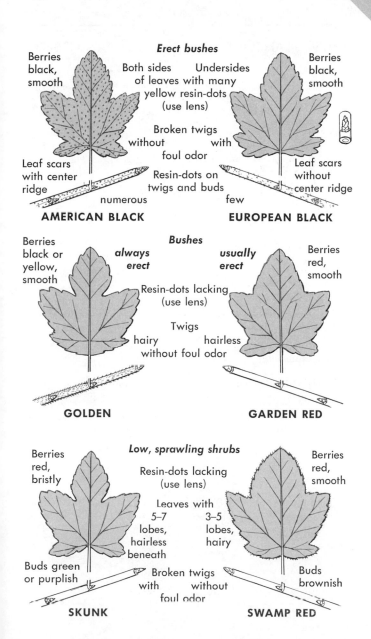

Erect bushes

Berries black, smooth

Both sides of leaves with many yellow resin-dots (use lens)

Undersides

Berries black, smooth

Broken twigs without / with foul odor

Leaf scars with center ridge

Resin-dots on twigs and buds

numerous   few

Leaf scars without center ridge

AMERICAN BLACK   **EUROPEAN BLACK**

Berries black or yellow, smooth

Bushes

always erect   *usually erect*

Resin-dots lacking (use lens)

Berries red, smooth

Twigs

hairy   hairless

without foul odor

GOLDEN   **GARDEN RED**

Berries red, bristly

Low, sprawling shrubs

Resin-dots lacking (use lens)

Leaves with 5–7 lobes, hairless beneath

3–5 lobes, hairy

Berries red, smooth

Buds green or purplish

Broken twigs with / without foul odor

Buds brownish

SKUNK   **SWAMP RED**

MISCELLANEOUS PLANTS WITH FAN-LOBED LEAVES

With the currants, the only thornless species whose alternate leaves are all of this type. Mulberries and Sassafras (Plate 43) usually have some fan-lobed leaves.

⚰ TULIP-TREE, *Liriodendron tulipifera*   p. 203
   Fertile woods; Massachusetts, s. Vermont, s. Ontario, s. Michigan, and s. Illinois, to centr. Florida, Louisiana, and e. Arkansas.

⚰ SWEETGUM, *Liquidambar styraciflua*   p. 203
   Wet woods; s. Connecticut, se. New York, W. Virginia, s. Ohio, s. Illinois, se. Missouri, and se. Oklahoma to centr. Florida and e. Texas.

⚰ SYCAMORE, *Platanus occidentalis*   p. 204
   Streambanks and bottomlands; sw. Maine, New York, s. Ontario, centr. Michigan, Iowa, and e. Nebraska to nw. Florida and centr. Texas.

Ⅴ ROSE-OF-SHARON, *Hibiscus syriacus*   p. 205
   Roadsides and thickets; an escape; Connecticut, New York, Ohio, and Missouri to Florida and Texas.

Ⅴ FLOWERING RASPBERRY, *Rubus odoratus*   p. 205
   Openings and fields; Nova Scotia, s. Quebec, and s. Ontario to Long Island, Georgia, and Tennessee.
   Ⅴ THIMBLEBERRY, *R. parviflorus* (not illus.)   p. 205

Ⅴ NINEBARK, *Physocarpus opulifolius*   p. 205
   Open areas; Quebec, n. Ontario, Minnesota, and Colorado to S. Carolina, Tennessee, and Arkansas.

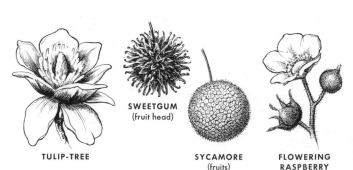

SWEETGUM
(fruit head)

TULIP-TREE   **SYCAMORE**   **FLOWERING**
                        (fruits)   **RASPBERRY**

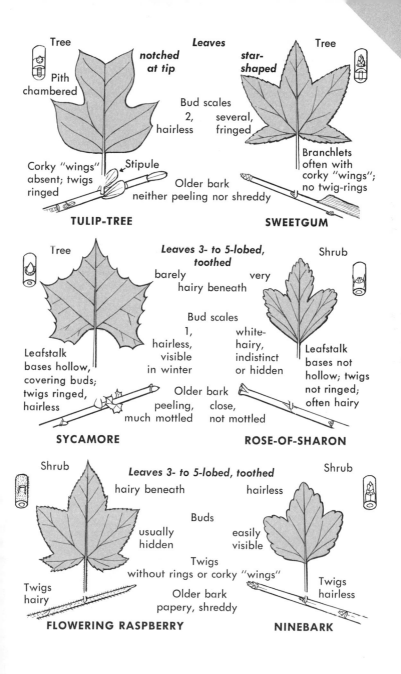

Tree

Pith chambered

Leaves

notched at tip

Bud scales 2, hairless

Corky "wings" absent; twigs ringed — Stipule

Older bark neither peeling nor shreddy

TULIP-TREE

Tree

star-shaped

Bud scales several, fringed

Branchlets often with corky "wings"; no twig-rings

SWEETGUM

Tree

Leaves 3- to 5-lobed, toothed

barely hairy beneath

Bud scales 1, hairless, visible in winter

Leafstalk bases hollow, covering buds; twigs ringed, hairless

Older bark peeling, much mottled

SYCAMORE

Shrub

very hairy beneath

white-hairy, indistinct or hidden

Leafstalk bases not hollow; twigs not ringed; often hairy

close, not mottled

ROSE-OF-SHARON

Shrub

Leaves 3- to 5-lobed, toothed

hairy beneath

Buds usually hidden

Twigs without rings or corky "wings"

Older bark papery, shreddy

Twigs hairy

FLOWERING RASPBERRY

Shrub

hairless

Buds easily visible

Twigs hairless

NINEBARK

LEAVES FAN-LOBED OR FAN-VEINED

Plants whose leaves have 3–5 main veins meeting near their bases.
Unlobed leaves mostly heart-shaped or triangular.
Note: The sap of the leafstalks and twigs of the 3 mulberries is
milky; that of the others is clear.

↟ PAPER-MULBERRY, _Broussonetia papyrifera_   p. 206
  Thickets and young woods; s. New England, Missouri, and
  se. Kansas to Florida and s. Texas.

↟ RED MULBERRY, _Morus rubra_   p. 206
  Fertile soils; Massachusetts, sw. Vermont, New York, s.
  Ontario, se. Minnesota, and se. Nebraska to s. Florida and
  centr. Texas.

↟ WHITE MULBERRY, _Morus alba_   p. 207
  Rich soils; Maine and Ontario to Florida and Texas.

↟ AMERICAN BASSWOOD, _Tilia americana_   p. 207
  Moist woods; New Brunswick, s. Quebec, and Manitoba to
  Florida and Texas.
  ↟ FLORIDA BASSWOOD, _T. floridana_ (not illus.)   p. 207
  ↟ HOARY BASSWOOD, _T. neglecta_ (not illus.)   p. 207
  ↟ WHITE BASSWOOD, _T. heterophylla_ (not illus.)   p. 207

↟ SASSAFRAS, _Sassafras albidum_   p. 208
  Old fields and woods; sw. Maine, s. Vermont, New York, s.
  Ontario, centr. Michigan, and se. Iowa to centr. Florida and
  e. Texas.

↟ REDBUD, _Cercis canadensis_   p. 208
  Fertile woods; Connecticut, s. New York, s. Ontario, s. Wisconsin, and s. Nebraska to n. Florida and w. Texas.

↟ AMERICAN HACKBERRY, _Celtis occidentalis_   p. 209
  Woods and open places; more common southward, sw. Que-
  bec and Idaho to n. Florida, Arkansas, Oklahoma, and Utah.
  ↟ UPLAND HACKBERRY, _C. tenuifolia_ (not illus.)   p. 209
  ↟ LOWLAND HACKBERRY, _C. laevigata_ (not illus.)   p. 209

⩔ NEW JERSEY TEA, _Ceanothus americanus_   p. 209
  Dry, open woods; centr. Maine, s. Quebec, and s. Manitoba
  to Florida and Texas.
  ⩔ REDROOT, _C. ovatus_ (leaf illus.)   p. 210
  ⩔ WILD-LILAC, _C. sanguineus_ (not illus.)   p. 210

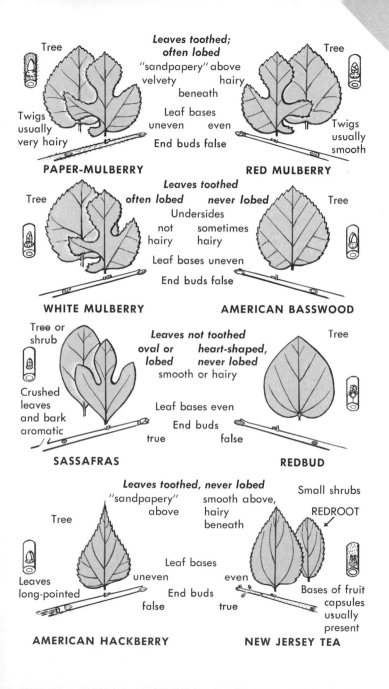

**Leaves toothed;
often lobed**

"sandpapery" above
velvety   hairy
      beneath

Leaf bases
uneven   even

End buds false

Tree

Twigs
usually
very hairy

PAPER-MULBERRY

Tree

Twigs
usually
smooth

RED MULBERRY

**Leaves toothed
often lobed   never lobed**
Undersides
not   sometimes
hairy   hairy

Leaf bases uneven

End buds false

Tree

Tree

WHITE MULBERRY

AMERICAN BASSWOOD

Leaves not toothed
oval or   heart-shaped,
lobed   never lobed
smooth or hairy

Leaf bases even

End buds
true   false

Tree or
shrub

Crushed
leaves
and bark
aromatic

SASSAFRAS

Tree

REDBUD

Leaves toothed, never lobed
"sandpapery"   smooth above,
above   hairy
      beneath

Leaf bases
uneven   even

End buds
false   true

Tree

Leaves
long-pointed

Small shrubs

REDROOT

Bases of fruit
capsules
usually
present

AMERICAN HACKBERRY

NEW JERSEY TEA

POPLARS

Trees with toothed, mostly triangular leaves, usually with 3–5 main veins meeting near their bases. Leafstalks quite long (not shown). Lowermost bud scale exactly above leaf scar.

⭘ WHITE POPLAR, *Populus alba*   p. 211
   Spreading from cultivation; throughout our area.
⭘ GRAY POPLAR, *P. canescens* (not illus.)   p. 211

⭘ BIGTOOTH ASPEN, *Populus grandidentata*   p. 211
   Dry soils and burns; Nova Scotia, e. Quebec, Ontario, and se. Manitoba to Maryland, w. Virginia, w. N. Carolina, Kentucky, w. Tennessee, and ne. Iowa.

⭘ COMMON COTTONWOOD, *Populus deltoides*   p. 211
   Rich soils; New Hampshire, sw. Quebec, and s. Saskatchewan to nw. Florida, centr. Texas, and w. Kansas.

⭘ LOMBARDY POPLAR, *Populus nigra* var. *italica*   p. 212
   Escaped from cultivation; local.

⭘ QUAKING ASPEN, *Populus tremuloides*   p. 212
   Dry woods and burns; Newfoundland, Labrador, and Alaska to New Jersey, n. Virginia, W. Virginia, Ohio, ne. Missouri, e. S. Dakota, sw. Nebraska, Colorado, w. Texas, and s. California.

⭘ SWAMP COTTONWOOD, *Populus heterophylla*   p. 212
   Coastal Plain bottomlands; Connecticut and se. Pennsylvania to nw. Florida, west to Louisiana, and north to Mississippi Valley to Ohio, s. Michigan, and se. Missouri.

⭘ BALSAM POPLAR, *Populus balsamifera*   p. 213
   Bottomlands; Newfoundland, Labrador, and Alaska to Maine, New York, s. Ontario, Minnesota, nw. Nebraska, Colorado, Idaho, and British Columbia.

⭘ BALM-OF-GILEAD, *Populus gileadensis*   p. 213
   Spreading from cultivation; Newfoundland and Ontario to n. U.S.

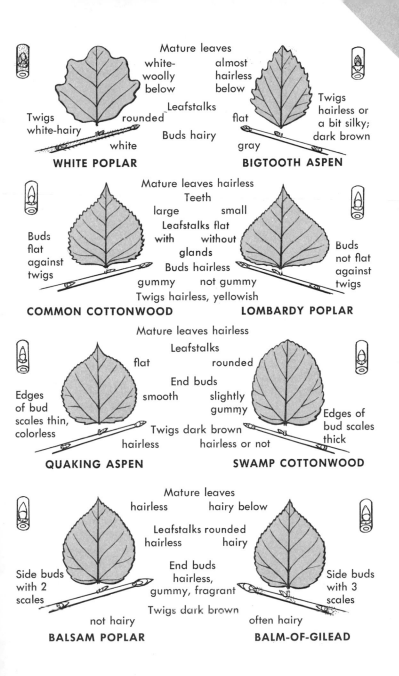

WHITE POPLAR
Twigs white-hairy
Leafstalks rounded
white
Mature leaves white-woolly below
Buds hairy

BIGTOOTH ASPEN
Mature leaves almost hairless below
Leafstalks flat
Twigs hairless or a bit silky; dark brown
gray

COMMON COTTONWOOD
Buds flat against twigs
Mature leaves hairless
Teeth large
Leafstalks flat with glands
Buds hairy gummy
Twigs hairless, yellowish

LOMBARDY POPLAR
Teeth small
Leafstalks flat without glands
Buds not gummy
Buds not flat against twigs

QUAKING ASPEN
Edges of bud scales thin, colorless
Mature leaves hairless
Leafstalks flat
End buds smooth
Twigs dark brown
hairless

SWAMP COTTONWOOD
Leafstalks rounded
End buds slightly gummy
Edges of bud scales thick
hairless or not

BALSAM POPLAR
Side buds with 2 scales
Mature leaves hairless
Leafstalks rounded hairless
End buds hairless, gummy, fragrant
Twigs dark brown
not hairy

BALM-OF-GILEAD
Mature leaves hairy below
Leafstalks rounded hairy
Side buds with 3 scales
often hairy

OAKS (1) — LEAVES LOBED WITHOUT BRISTLE-TIPS

Only oaks have leaves of this "feather-lobed" type, but not all oaks have such leaves (see Plates 47 and 48). Buds are clustered at tips of twigs. Oaks usually can be identified by differences in leaf shapes, bud types, and acorns. In winter, and when in doubt, consult the text.

↟ WHITE OAK, *Quercus alba*   p. 216
    Dry or moist woods; centr. Maine, s. Quebec, s. Ontario, and
    Minnesota to nw. Florida and e. Texas.

↟ OVERCUP OAK, *Quercus lyrata*   p. 216
    Coastal Plain swamp forests; s. New Jersey to n. Florida, west
    to e. Texas, and north in the Mississippi drainage to sw.
    Indiana, s. Illinois, se. Missouri, and se. Oklahoma.

↟ POST OAK, *Quercus stellata*   p. 216
    Dry soils; se. Massachusetts, se. New York, se. Pennsylvania,
    W. Virginia, centr. Ohio, s. Indiana, s. Iowa, and w. Oklahoma
    to centr. Florida and centr. Texas.

↟ MOSSYCUP OAK (BUR OAK), *Quercus macrocarpa*   p. 217
    Rich woods, prairie borders; New Brunswick, s. Quebec,
    s. Ontario, n. Michigan, and se. Saskatchewan to w. New
    England, Maryland, W. Virginia, Alabama, and centr. Texas.

WHITE   OVERCUP   POST   MOSSYCUP

ACORNS

LEAVES LOBED WITHOUT BRISTLE-TIPS

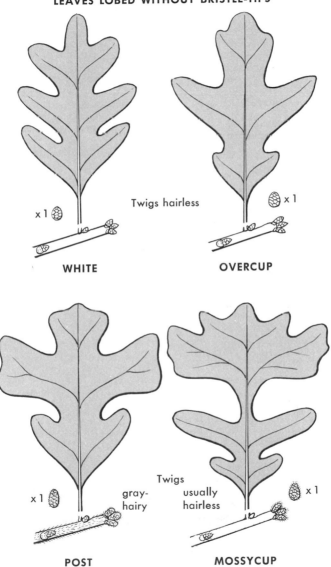

x 1

Twigs hairless

x 1

WHITE

OVERCUP

x 1

gray-hairy

Twigs usually hairless

x 1

POST

MOSSYCUP

OAKS (2) — LEAVES LOBED WITH BRISTLE-TIPS

↟ SCARLET–PIN OAK GROUP (see acorns and buds below)
  ↟ SCARLET OAK, *Quercus coccinea*   p. 217
  Dry soils; sw. Maine, s. Ontario, s. Michigan, and se. Missouri
  to nw. New Jersey, w. Maryland, n. Georgia, n. Mississippi,
  and ne. Arkansas.
  ↟ PIN OAK, *Q. palustris*   p. 217
  Bottomlands and moist woods; centr. Massachusetts, se. New
  York, s. Ontario, s. Michigan, se. Iowa, and e. Kansas to
  N. Carolina, Tennessee, and ne. Oklahoma.
  ↟ JACK OAK, *Q. ellipsoidalis*   p. 217
  Dry soils; n. Ohio, centr. Michigan, and s. Manitoba to n.
  Indiana, n. Missouri, and Iowa.
  ↟ NUTTALL OAK, *Q. nuttallii*   p. 218
  Low woods; w. Tennessee, se. Missouri, and se. Oklahoma
  to Alabama and e. Texas.
  ↟ SHUMARD OAK, *Q. shumardii*   p. 218
  Bottomlands and moist soils, mostly Coastal Plain; s. Pennsyl-
  vania, nw. Ohio, and se. Kansas to n. Florida and centr. Texas.

↟ BLACK OAK, *Quercus velutina*   p. 218
  Dry soils; s. Maine, New York, s. Ontario, s. Minnesota, and
  se. Nebraska to nw. Florida and e. Texas.

↟ RED OAK, *Quercus rubra*   p. 218
  Woods; Nova Scotia, s. Quebec, n. Michigan, n. Minnesota,
  and e. Nebraska to Georgia and se. Oklahoma.

↟ SPANISH OAK, *Quercus falcata*   p. 219
  Woods; se. New York, s. Ohio, s. Illinois, and s. Missouri to
  n. Florida and e. Texas.
  ↟ TURKEY OAK, *Q. laevis* (not illus.)   p. 219

↟ BLACKJACK OAK, *Quercus marilandica*   p. 219
  Dry barren soils; se. New York, New Jersey, s. Michigan, and
  s. Iowa to ne. Florida and centr. Texas.

↟ SCRUB OAK, *Quercus ilicifolia*   p. 219
  Dry slopes; se. Maine and New York to Maryland, w. N.
  Carolina, and W. Virginia.

SCARLET   PIN   JACK   SHUMARD
ACORNS AND BUDS OF SCARLET–PIN OAK GROUP

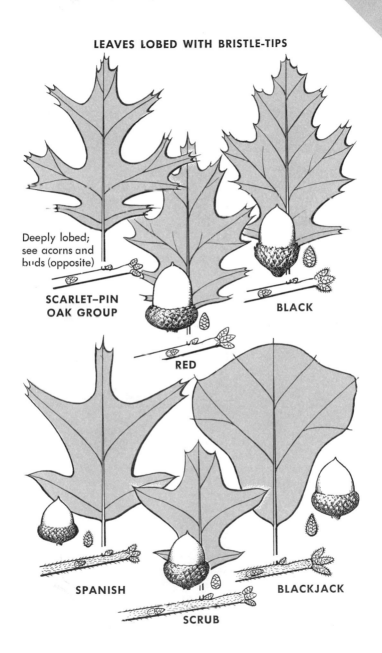

LEAVES LOBED WITH BRISTLE-TIPS

Deeply lobed;
see acorns and
buds (opposite)

**SCARLET–PIN
OAK GROUP**

BLACK

RED

SPANISH

SCRUB

BLACKJACK

OAKS (3) — LEAVES TOOTHED OR WAVY-EDGED

⬥ SWAMP OAK, *Quercus bicolor*   p. 220
    Low woods; sw. Maine, sw. Quebec, s. Ontario, and se.
    Minnesota to Maryland, n. Virginia, w. N. Carolina, Tennessee, and Arkansas.

⬥ CHESTNUT OAK, *Quercus prinus*   p. 220
    Dry woods; sw. Maine, New York, and s. Ontario to se.
    Virginia, nw. Georgia, n. Alabama, ne. Mississippi, and s.
    Illinois.
    ⬥ BASKET OAK, *Q. michauxii* (leaf edge illus.)   p. 220

⬥ CHINQUAPIN OAK, *Quercus muehlenbergii*   p. 220
    Dry woods especially on limestone soils; Connecticut, nw.
    Vermont, s. Ontario, s. Wisconsin, and se. Nebraska to nw.
    Florida, centr. Texas, and ne. New Mexico.

⋁ DWARF OAK, *Quercus prinoides*   p. 221
    Dry barrens; sw. Maine, Minnesota, and Nebraska to se.
    Virginia, Alabama, and Texas.

SWAMP   CHESTNUT   CHINQUAPIN

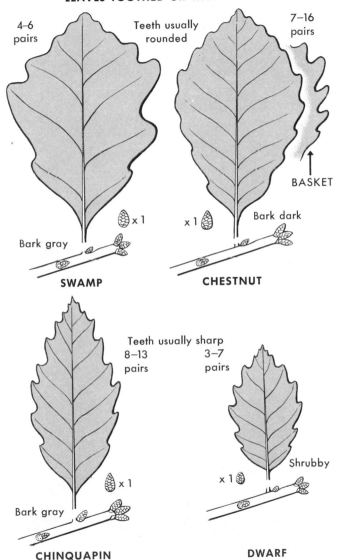

LEAVES TOOTHED OR WAVY-EDGED

4–6 pairs

Teeth usually rounded

7–16 pairs

BASKET

Bark gray

× 1

× 1

Bark dark

SWAMP

CHESTNUT

Teeth usually sharp
8–13 pairs

3–7 pairs

Bark gray

× 1

× 1

Shrubby

CHINQUAPIN

DWARF

OAKS (4) — LEAVES NOT LOBED, TOOTHED, OR WAVY-EDGED

⬧ SHINGLE OAK, *Quercus imbricaria*   p. 221
    Fertile woods; New Jersey, Pennsylvania, s. Michigan, and
    Iowa to S. Carolina, Tennessee, Louisiana, and se. Kansas.
    ⬧ LAUREL OAK, *Q. laurifolia* (not illus.)   p. 221

⬧ WILLOW OAK, *Quercus phellos*   p. 222
    Coastal Plain uplands; se. New York to nw. Florida, west to
    e. Texas, and north in Mississippi Valley to s. Illinois, se.
    Missouri, and se. Oklahoma.
    ⬧ SAND OAK, *Q. incana* (not illus.)   p. 222

⬧ WATER OAK, *Quercus nigra*   p. 222
    Coastal Plain and adjacent areas; s. New Jersey to centr.
    Florida, west to e. Texas, and north in Mississippi Valley to
    se. Missouri and e. Oklahoma.

⬧ LIVE OAK, *Quercus virginiana*   p. 222
    *Coastal Plain soils except toward Southwest, where it also
    occurs inland;* se. Virginia to s. Florida, west to centr. Texas
    and sw. Oklahoma.
    ⬧ DARLINGTON OAK, *Q. hemisphaerica* (not illus.)   p. 222

SHINGLE   **WILLOW**   **WATER**   **LIVE**

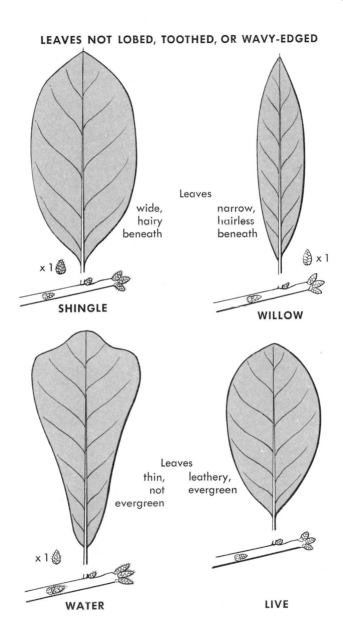

LEAVES NOT LOBED, TOOTHED, OR WAVY-EDGED

Leaves wide, hairy beneath

×1

SHINGLE

Leaves narrow, hairless beneath

×1

WILLOW

Leaves thin, not evergreen

×1

WATER

Leaves leathery, evergreen

LIVE

MAGNOLIAS

Trees with leaves not toothed; twigs ringed; buds with a
single bud scale; end buds large; bundle scars many.

↟⋁ SWEETBAY MAGNOLIA, *Magnolia virginiana*   p. 223
   Swamps and damp woods; e. Massachusetts, New Jersey,
   Pennsylvania, and Arkansas to Florida and Texas.

↟ CUCUMBER MAGNOLIA, *Magnolia acuminata*   p. 223
   Mature woods; w. New York, s. Ontario, s. Illinois, and
   s. Missouri to Georgia, Louisiana, and se. Oklahoma.

↟ BIGLEAF MAGNOLIA, *Magnolia macrophylla*   p. 224
   Mature forests; S. Carolina, W. Virginia, s. Ohio, and Arkansas
   to nw. Florida and Louisiana.

↟ EARLEAF MAGNOLIA, *Magnolia fraseri*   p. 224
   Swamps and mountain streamsides; w. Virginia, W. Virginia,
   and e. Kentucky to n. Georgia and n. Alabama.

↟ UMBRELLA MAGNOLIA, *Magnolia tripetala*   p. 224
   Mountain streamsides; s. Pennsylvania, Ohio, Kentucky, and
   Missouri to Georgia, Arkansas, and se. Oklahoma.

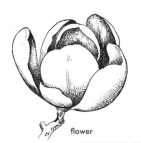

flower   fruit
                "cone"

SWEETBAY MAGNOLIA

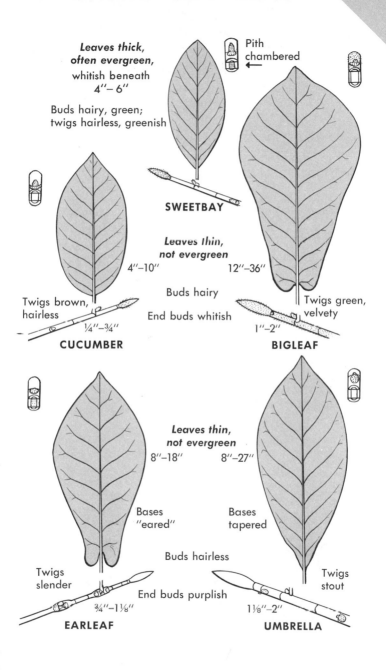

Leaves thick, often evergreen, whitish beneath 4″– 6″

Buds hairy, green; twigs hairless, greenish

Pith chambered ←

SWEETBAY

Leaves thin, not evergreen

Buds hairy

End buds whitish

12″–36″

Twigs green, velvety

1″–2″

BIGLEAF

Twigs brown, hairless

¼″–¾″

4″–10″

CUCUMBER

Leaves thin, not evergreen 8″–18″

Bases "eared"

Twigs slender

Buds hairless

End buds purplish

¾″–1⅛″

EARLEAF

8″–27″

Bases tapered

Twigs stout

1⅛″–2″

UMBRELLA

ELMS AND WATER-ELM

Trees mostly with double-toothed, feather-veined leaves.
Leaf bases usually uneven. Buds many-scaled,
the scales in 2 regular rows.

⚶ WINGED ELM, *Ulmus alata*   p. 225
    Mostly bottomlands; Virginia, s. Indiana, s. Illinois, and
    Missouri to Florida and Texas.
  ⚶ SEPTEMBER ELM, *U. serotina* (not illus.)   p. 225

⚶ ROCK ELM, *Ulmus thomasi*   p. 225
    Deep soils and rocky uplands; w. New England, s. Quebec,
    centr. Michigan, and se. S. Dakota to Tennessee, nw. Arkan-
    sas, and e. Kansas.

⚶ AMERICAN ELM, *Ulmus americana*   p. 226
    Mostly bottomlands; Newfoundland, Nova Scotia, e. Quebec,
    and Saskatchewan to n. Florida and Texas.

⚶ ENGLISH ELM, *Ulmus procera*   p. 226
    European; an escape, from New England and New York to
    Virginia.
  ⚶ WITCH ELM, *U. glabra* (not illus.)   p. 226

⚶ SLIPPERY ELM, *Ulmus rubra*   p. 226
    Fertile soils; New England, sw. Quebec, s. Ontario, and
    N. Dakota to nw. Florida and Texas.
  ⚶ᵥ SIBERIAN ELM, *U. pumila* (not illus.)   p. 227

⚶ WATER-ELM, *Planera aquatica*   p. 227
    Coastal Plain swamps; se. N. Carolina to n. Florida, west to
    Texas and north in Mississippi Valley to s. Illinois, se.
    Missouri, and se. Oklahoma.

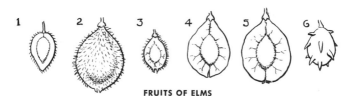

FRUITS OF ELMS

(1) Winged, (2) Rock, (3) American, (4) English, (5) Slippery, (6) Water

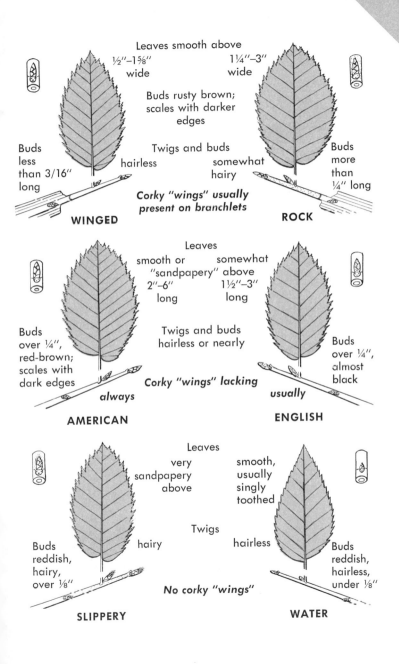

Leaves smooth above

½"–1⅝" wide   1¼"–3" wide

Buds rusty brown; scales with darker edges

Buds less than 3/16" long

hairless   Twigs and buds somewhat hairy

Buds more than ¼" long

Corky "wings" usually present on branchlets

WINGED   **ROCK**

Leaves

smooth or "sandpapery" above   2"–6" long   somewhat hairy above   1½"–3" long

Buds over ¼", red-brown; scales with dark edges

Twigs and buds hairless or nearly

Buds over ¼", almost black

Corky "wings" lacking

always   *usually*

AMERICAN   **ENGLISH**

Leaves

very sandpapery above   smooth, usually singly toothed

Twigs

hairy   hairless

Buds reddish, hairy, over ⅛"

Buds reddish, hairless, under ⅛"

No corky "wings"

SLIPPERY   **WATER**

IRONWOOD, HORNBEAM, HAZELNUTS, ALDERS

Trees and shrubs with mostly double-toothed leaves. Leaf bases even. Buds characteristic as on plate opposite. In all species the twigs are variably hairy or hairless.

⬥ IRONWOOD, *Carpinus caroliniana*   p. 227
Bottomlands and other rich soils; New England, s. Quebec, s. Ontario, and e. Minnesota to Florida and Texas.

⬥ HORNBEAM, *Ostrya virginiana*   p. 228
Fertile woods; Nova Scotia and s. Manitoba to Florida and Texas.

⩔ AMERICAN HAZELNUT, *Corylus americana*   p. 228
Woods borders and thickets; Maine and Saskatchewan to Georgia, Missouri, and Oklahoma.
⩔ BEAKED HAZELNUT, *C. cornuta* (fruit illus.)   p. 228

⬥ EUROPEAN BLACK ALDER, *Alnus glutinosa*   p. 229
Wet soils; escape, Newfoundland and Illinois to Delaware and Pennsylvania.
⬥ EUROPEAN WHITE ALDER   p. 229
A. incana (not illus.)
⬥⩔ SEASIDE ALDER, *A. maritima* (twig illus.)   p. 229

⬥⩔ SMOOTH ALDER, *Alnus serrulata*   p. 229
Streambanks and swamp borders; sw. Nova Scotia, centr. Vermont, New York, s. Michigan, Illinois, Missouri, and se. Oklahoma to nw. Florida and Louisiana.

⬥⩔ SPECKLED ALDER, *Alnus rugosa*   p. 230
Streambanks and swampy places; Newfoundland, Labrador, and Saskatchewan to Massachusetts, Pennsylvania, w. Maryland, W. Virginia, n. Ohio, n. Indiana, and ne. Iowa.
⩔ MOUNTAIN ALDER, *A. crispa* (twig illus.)   p. 230

IRONWOOD   HORNBEAM   AMERICAN HAZELNUT   BEAKED HAZELNUT   ALDERS

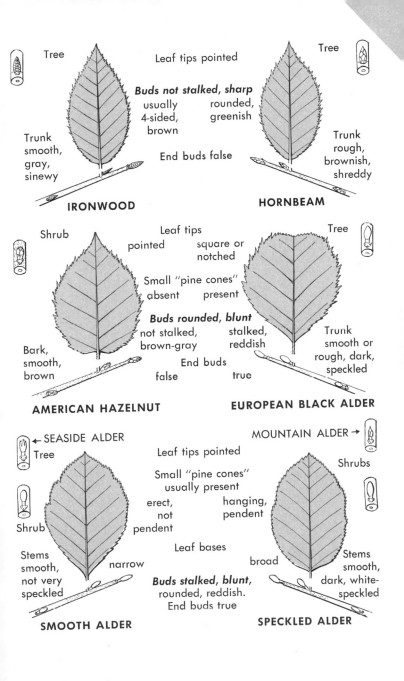

Tree

Leaf tips pointed

Buds not stalked, sharp

usually 4-sided, brown   rounded, greenish

Trunk smooth, gray, sinewy

End buds false

IRONWOOD

Tree

Trunk rough, brownish, shreddy

HORNBEAM

Shrub

Leaf tips pointed   square or notched

Small "pine cones" absent   present

Buds rounded, blunt

not stalked, brown-gray   stalked, reddish

Bark, smooth, brown

End buds false   true

AMERICAN HAZELNUT

Tree

Trunk smooth or rough, dark, speckled

EUROPEAN BLACK ALDER

← SEASIDE ALDER

Tree

Shrub

Stems smooth, not very speckled

MOUNTAIN ALDER →

Shrubs

Leaf tips pointed

Small "pine cones" usually present

erect, not pendent   hanging, pendent

Leaf bases

narrow   broad

Buds stalked, blunt, rounded, reddish. End buds true

SMOOTH ALDER

Stems smooth, dark, white-speckled

SPECKLED ALDER

BIRCHES

Trees and shrubs with mostly double-toothed leaves. Bark
with narrow cross stripes. Buds with 2–3 scales.

⬆ AMERICAN WHITE BIRCH, *Betula papyrifera*   p. 231
   Young forests; Newfoundland, Labrador, and Alaska to New
   England, Pennsylvania, W. Virginia, n. Ohio, n. Illinois, n.
   Iowa, and S. Dakota; in mts. to N. Carolina.
   ⬆ EUROPEAN WHITE BIRCH, *B. alba* (not illus.)   p. 232
   ⬆ EUROPEAN WEEPING BIRCH   p. 232
   B. pendula (not illus.)
   ⬆ BLUELEAF BIRCH   p. 232
   B. caerulea-grandis (not illus.)

⬆ GRAY BIRCH, *Betula populifolia*   p. 232
   Poor soils; Prince Edward I. and w. Quebec to Delaware,
   w. Virginia, n. Ohio, n. Indiana, and sw. Ontario.

⬆ BLACK BIRCH, *Betula lenta*   p. 233
   Mature forests; sw. Maine, s. Quebec, and e. Ontario to
   Delaware, Maryland, and e. Ohio; in mts. to n. Georgia and
   n. Alabama.
   ⬆ VIRGINIA BIRCH, *B. uber* (not illus.)   p. 233

⬆ YELLOW BIRCH, *Betula lutea*   p. 233
   Moist forests; Newfoundland, s. Labrador, and se. Manitoba
   to Delaware, Maryland, n. Indiana, n. Illinois, and ne. Iowa;
   in mts. to N. Carolina and Georgia.

⬆ RIVER BIRCH, *Betula nigra*   p. 234
   Bottomlands; se. New Hampshire, e. New York, Indiana, se.
   Minnesota, and se. Kansas to n. Florida and Texas.

⬇ SWAMP BIRCH, *Betula pumila*   p. 234
   Bogs and swamps; Newfoundland, Labrador, Ontario, and
   British Columbia to n. New Jersey, New York, n. Ohio, n.
   Indiana, Wisconsin, and Montana.
   ⬆⬇ NORTHERN BIRCH, *B. borealis* (not illus.)   p. 234
   ⬇ NEWFOUNDLAND DWARF BIRCH   p. 234
   B. michauxii (not illus.)
   ⬇ TUNDRA DWARF BIRCH   p. 235
   B. glandulosa (twig illus.)
   ⬇ MINOR BIRCH, *B. minor* (not illus.)   p. 235

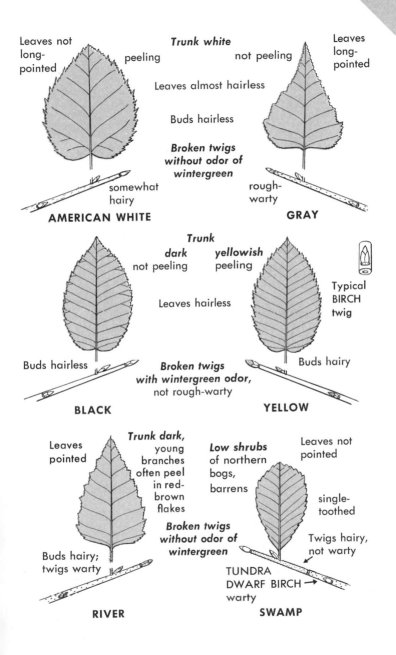

Leaves not long-pointed **Trunk white** peeling not peeling Leaves long-pointed

Leaves almost hairless

Buds hairless

Broken twigs without odor of wintergreen

somewhat hairy rough-warty

AMERICAN WHITE **GRAY**

Trunk dark yellowish not peeling peeling

Typical BIRCH twig

Leaves hairless

Buds hairless Buds hairy

Broken twigs with wintergreen odor, not rough-warty

BLACK **YELLOW**

Leaves pointed **Trunk dark,** young branches often peel in red-brown flakes **Low shrubs** of northern bogs, barrens Leaves not pointed

single-toothed

Broken twigs without odor of wintergreen

Twigs hairy, not warty

Buds hairy; twigs warty TUNDRA DWARF BIRCH → warty

RIVER **SWAMP**

CHERRIES AND THORNLESS PLUMS

Trees and shrubs mostly with single-toothed leaves. Leafstalks mostly with glands. Trunk bark with narrow cross stripes. Buds with many scales. The white flowers and dark fruits are in long grapelike clusters in the top 2 species, in short umbrellalike clusters in the others.

↟ BLACK CHERRY, *Prunus serotina*   p. 236
  Woods and thickets; Nova Scotia, s. Quebec, s. Ontario, and N. Dakota to Florida, Texas, and Arizona.

↟∀ CHOKE CHERRY, *Prunus virginiana*   p. 236
  Young woods and thickets; Newfoundland, Labrador, and British Columbia to Maryland, nw. Georgia, e. Kentucky, Illinois, Kansas, New Mexico, and s. California.

↟∀ EUROPEAN BIRD CHERRY   p. 237
  P. padus (not illus.)

↟∀ FIRE CHERRY (PIN CHERRY)   p. 237
  Prunus pensylvanica
  Burned areas, thickets, and young woods; Newfoundland, s. Labrador, n. Ontario, and British Columbia to New York, Pennsylvania, Iowa, n. Indiana, S. Dakota, and Colorado; in mts. to n. Georgia and e. Tennessee.

↟ PEACH, *P. persica* (twig illus.)   p. 237

∀ EASTERN DWARF CHERRY   p. 237
  Prunus susquehanae
  Sandy and acid soils; sw. Maine, sw. Quebec, and se. Manitoba to Virginia, Illinois, and Minnesota.

∀ NORTH. DWARF CHERRY, *P. pumila* (not illus.)   p. 238
∀ WEST. DWARF CHERRY, *P. besseyi* (not illus.)   p. 238

↟ SWEET CHERRY, *Prunus avium*   p. 238
  Locally common, escaped from cultivation; Nova Scotia and s. Ontario to Florida and westward.

↟∀ SOUR CHERRY, *Prunus cerasus*   p. 238
  Old World; established locally in thickets from Prince Edward I. and Michigan southward.

↟∀ MAHALEB CHERRY, *P. mahaleb* (twig illus.)   p. 239

∀ BEACH PLUM, *Prunus maritima*   p. 239
  Sandy coastal areas; Maine to e. Pennsylvania and Delaware.

∀ GRAVES PLUM, *P. gravesii* (not illus.)   p. 239

↟∀ GOOSE PLUM, *Prunus hortulana*   p. 239
  Escaped; s. Indiana and Iowa to Alabama and Oklahoma.

↟∀ MUNSON PLUM, *P. munsoniana* (not illus.)   p. 240
↟∀ ALLEGHANY PLUM   p. 240
  P. alleghaniensis (not illus.)

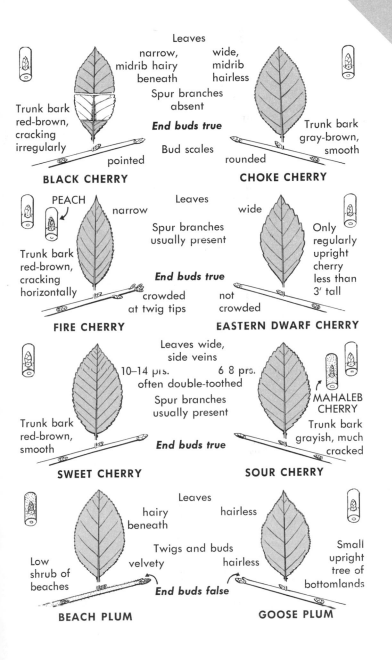

Leaves
narrow, midrib hairy beneath   wide, midrib hairless

Spur branches absent

Trunk bark red-brown, cracking irregularly

End buds true

Bud scales

pointed

BLACK CHERRY

Trunk bark gray-brown, smooth

rounded

CHOKE CHERRY

PEACH   narrow   Leaves   wide

Spur branches usually present

Trunk bark red-brown, cracking horizontally

End buds true

crowded at twig tips   not crowded

FIRE CHERRY

Only regularly upright cherry less than 3' tall

EASTERN DWARF CHERRY

Leaves wide, side veins

10–14 prs.   6 8 prs.

often double-toothed

Spur branches usually present

Trunk bark red-brown, smooth

End buds true

SWEET CHERRY

MAHALEB CHERRY

Trunk bark grayish, much cracked

SOUR CHERRY

Leaves
hairy beneath   hairless

Twigs and buds

Low shrub of beaches

velvety   hairless

End buds false

BEACH PLUM

Small upright tree of bottomlands

GOOSE PLUM

JUNEBERRIES

Also called SHADBUSH and SERVICEBERRY. Trees and shrubs with toothed leaves. Buds slender, reddish; scales black-tipped, often twisted. Clusters of white flowers in early spring; dark fruits like huckleberries.

♠♥ DOWNY JUNEBERRY, *Amelanchier arborea*   p. 241
     Woods; sw. New Brunswick, sw. Quebec, s. Ontario, n. Michigan, ne. Minnesota to n. Florida, Louisiana, e. Texas.
♠♥ SMOOTH JUNEBERRY, *Amelanchier laevis*   p. 242
     Thickets, woods borders; Newfoundland, Ontario, and Minnesota to Delaware, Ohio, s. Indiana, Missouri, and e. Kansas; in mts. to Georgia and Alabama.
  ♠♥ INLAND JUNEBERRY, *A. interior* (not illus.)   p. 242
♠♥ SWAMP JUNEBERRY, *Amelanchier intermedia*   p. 242
     Swamps and thickets; Newfoundland and n. Minnesota to Virginia, w. N. Carolina, Michigan, and s. Minnesota.
♥ BARTRAM JUNEBERRY, *Amelanchier bartramiana*   p. 242
     Newfoundland, Labrador, and w. Ontario to ne. Pennsylvania, s. Ontario, n. Michigan, n. Wisconsin, and n. Minnesota.
♥ RUNNING JUNEBERRY, *Amelanchier stolonifera*   p. 242
     Dry soils; Newfoundland and w. Ontario to Virginia, Michigan, and Minnesota.
  ♥ COASTAL JUNEBERRY, *A. obovalis* (not illus.)   p. 243
  ♥ NANTUCKET JUNEBERRY   p. 243
     A. nantucketensis (not illus.)
  ♥ NOVA SCOTIA JUNEBERRY   p. 243
     A. lucida (not illus.)
  ♥ FERNALD JUNEBERRY, *A. fernaldii* (not illus.)   p. 243
♠♥ OBLONGLEAF JUNEBERRY   p. 243
   Amelanchier canadensis
     Damp thickets; centr. Maine, sw. Quebec, and w. New York to Georgia.
♥ LOW JUNEBERRY, *Amelanchier humilis*   p. 244
     Usually dry soils; sw. Quebec and w. Ontario to Vermont, Pennsylvania, Ohio, Michigan, and S. Dakota.
  ♥ ALDERLEAF JUNEBERRY, *A. alnifolia* (not illus.) p. 244
  ♥ GASPE JUNEBERRY, *A. gaspensis* (not illus.)   p. 244
♥ ROUNDLEAF JUNEBERRY, *Amelanchier sanguinea* p. 245
     Thickets and woods; Maine, s. Quebec, w. Ontario, and n. Minnesota to New Jersey, n. Ohio, s. Michigan, and n. Iowa; in mts. to N. Carolina.
  For the following juneberries not illustrated, see page 245:
  LARGE-FLOWERED, *A. amabilis;* HURON, *A. huronensis;* WIEGAND, *A. wiegandii;* MINNESOTA, *A. mucronata.*

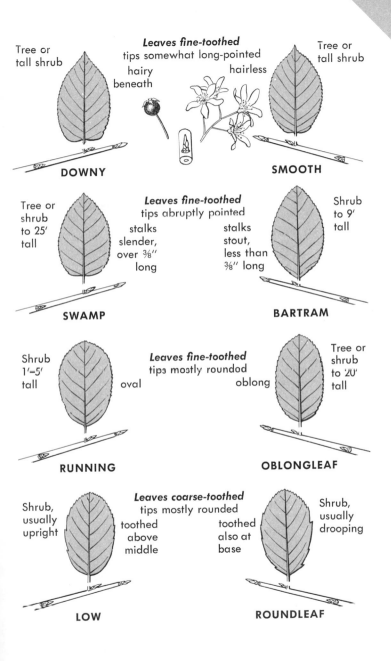

DOWNY
Tree or tall shrub

Leaves fine-toothed
tips somewhat long-pointed
hairy beneath   hairless

SMOOTH
Tree or tall shrub

SWAMP
Tree or shrub to 25' tall

Leaves fine-toothed
tips abruptly pointed
stalks slender, over ⅜" long   stalks stout, less than ⅜" long

BARTRAM
Shrub to 9' tall

RUNNING
Shrub 1'–5' tall

Leaves fine-toothed
tips mostly rounded
oval   oblong

OBLONGLEAF
Tree or shrub to 20' tall

LOW
Shrub, usually upright

Leaves coarse-toothed
tips mostly rounded
toothed above middle   toothed also at base

ROUNDLEAF
Shrub, usually drooping

WILLOWS (1)

Trees and shrubs, mostly with long, narrow, usually toothed leaves. Buds with a single bud scale.

Ⅴ TALL PRAIRIE WILLOW, *Salix humilis*   p. 250
   Dry thickets; Newfoundland, Labrador, n. Ontario, and Minnesota to Florida and e. Texas.

Ⅴ DWARF PRAIRIE WILLOW   p. 251
   Salix humilis var. *microphylla*
   Dry sites; se. Maine and s. Minnesota to ne. Virginia and inland in Piedmont and mts. to nw. Florida, La., Oklahoma. Other gray-hairy and nontoothed willows are not illustrated and will be found in the text, pages 251–54.

Ⅴ HOARY WILLOW, *Salix candida*   p. 254
   Damp soils; Newfoundland, Labrador, and British Columbia to New Brunswick, w. New England, n. New Jersey, Pennsylvania, n. Illinois, n. Iowa, S. Dakota, and Colorado.

↟Ⅴ BEBB WILLOW, *Salix bebbiana*   p. 254
   Thickets; Newfoundland, Labrador, and Alaska to Maryland, Ohio, Iowa, Nebraska, New Mexico, Arizona, Calif.
   ↟Ⅴ GOAT WILLOW, *S. caprea* (not illus.)   p. 255
    Ⅴ SANDDUNE WILLOW, *S. syrticola* (not illus.) p. 255
   ↟Ⅴ EUROPEAN GRAY WILLOW   p. 255
    S. cinerea (not illus.)
    Ⅴ NORTHERN GRAY WILLOW   p. 255
    S. paraleuca (not illus.)

↟Ⅴ SANDBAR WILLOW, *Salix interior*   p. 255
   Stream bars and alluvium; New Brunswick, e. Quebec, and Alaska to Maryland, Kentucky, Louisiana, Texas, se. New Mexico, and e. Montana.

↟Ⅴ BLACK WILLOW, *Salix nigra*   p. 256
   Damp soils; New Brunswick, s. Quebec, s. Ontario, and Minnesota to n. Florida and Texas.
   ↟ CRACK WILLOW, *S. fragilis* (not illus.)   p. 256

↟Ⅴ SHINING WILLOW, *Salix lucida*   p. 256
   Wet ground; Newfoundland, se. Labrador, n. Manitoba, and Saskatchewan to Delaware, Maryland, Iowa, S. Dakota.
   ↟Ⅴ BAYLEAF WILLOW, *S. pentandra* (not illus.) p. 256

Ⅴ HEARTLEAF WILLOW, *Salix cordata*   p. 256
   Sandy and rocky soils; Newfoundland, se. Labrador, and n. Ontario to e. Massachusetts, n. New York, and s. Ontario.
   Ⅴ RIGID WILLOW, *S. rigida* (not illus.)   p. 257
   ↟Ⅴ BALSAM WILLOW, *S. pyrifolia* (not illus.)   p. 257
   Ⅴ MYRTLELEAF WILLOW, *S. myrtillifolia* (not illus.) p. 257
   Ⅴ BLUNTLEAF WILLOW, *S. obtusata* (not illus.) p. 257

Leaves not toothed, gray-hairy, at least beneath

Leaves not toothed,
gray-hairy,
edges rolled

Typical
willow
twig

Leaves
wedge-
shaped, wavy,
more than 2" long

TALL PRAIRIE

Leaves
less
than
2" long

DWARF PRAIRIE

Leaves

not toothed,
narrow

toothed,
wide

edges

rolled   flat

white-**woolly**

HOARY

gray-hairy

BEBB

Leaves toothed, hairless or slightly silky, green beneath

Leaves narrow

teeth
coarse

teeth
fine

Base
tapered

Base
rounded

SANDBAR

BLACK

Leaves wider

extremely   moderately
long-pointed

leathery

Twigs hairless

SHINING

not
leathery

Twigs hairy

HEARTLEAF

WILLOWS (2)

Trees and shrubs, mostly with long, narrow, usually
toothed leaves. Buds with a single bud scale.

Ⅴ BASKET WILLOW, *Salix purpurea*   p. 258
   Damp soils; European; Newfoundland, Ontario, and Wisconsin to Virginia, W. Virginia, Ohio, and Iowa.

ⅣⅤ PUSSY WILLOW, *Salix discolor*   p. 258
   Damp soils; Newfoundland, Labrador, and British Columbia
   to Delaware, Maryland, Missouri, and Idaho; south in mts.
   to w. N. Carolina and e. Tennessee.

ⅣⅤ PEACHLEAF WILLOW, *Salix amygdaloides*   p. 258
   Lowlands; sw. Quebec, Vermont, s. Ontario, s. Manitoba, and
   se. British Columbia to Massachusetts, Kentucky, Missouri,
   Texas, Arizona, and Washington.
   ⅄ WARD WILLOW, *S. caroliniana* (not illus.)   p. 258
   ⅄ MISSOURI WILLOW, *S. eriocephala* (not illus.)   p. 259

⅄ WEEPING WILLOW, *Salix babylonica*   p. 259
   Shorelines; an escape throughout our area in U.S. and Canada.

Ⅴ SILKY WILLOW, *Salix sericea*   p. 259
   Damp soils; Nova Scotia, s. Quebec, s. Wisconsin, and e. Iowa
   to Georgia, Tennessee, and Missouri.
   Ⅴ ROUNDLEAF WILLOW, *S. vestita* (not illus.)   p. 259
   Ⅴ FELTED WILLOW, *S. coactilis* (not illus.)   p. 260
   Ⅴ WOOLLY WILLOW, *S. cryptodonta* (not illus.)   p. 260

⅄ WHITE WILLOW, *Salix alba*   p. 260
   Planted and escaped; Nova Scotia and Ontario to N. Carolina,
   Tennessee, and Iowa.

Ⅴ MEADOW WILLOW, *Salix gracilis*   p. 260
   Lowlands; New Brunswick and Alberta to n. New Jersey,
   centr. Pennsylvania, Indiana, n. Iowa, n. Nebraska, and centr.
   Colorado.
   ⅣⅤ BROADLEAF WILLOW   p. 261
   S. glaucophylloides (not illus.)
   ⅣⅤ YELLOW WILLOW, *S. lutea* (not illus.)   p. 261

Ⅴ AUTUMN WILLOW, *Salix serrissima*   p. 261
   Wet places; Newfoundland and Alberta to n. New Jersey, n.
   Ohio, n. Indiana, N. Dakota, and Colorado.

Leaves toothed, hairless and whitened or white-hairy beneath

Teeth lacking near leaf bases

Leaves often nearly opposite

BASKET

Leaves alternate

PUSSY

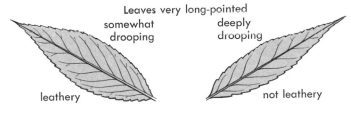

Leaves very long-pointed
somewhat drooping

leathery

PEACHLEAF

deeply drooping

not leathery

WEEPING

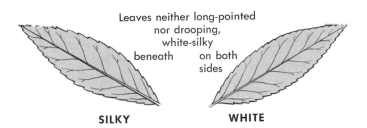

Leaves neither long-pointed nor drooping, white-silky beneath

SILKY

on both sides

WHITE

Leaves neither long-pointed nor drooping
hairless or rusty-silky

Twigs clustered at branchlet tips

MEADOW

hairless, leathery

Twigs not clustered

AUTUMN

MISCELLANEOUS PLANTS
WITH 3 BUNDLE SCARS (1)

"Bundle scars" are small marks within a leaf scar (see p. xxiv). The leaves of these plants are mostly toothed or wavy-edged.

Ѵ SWEETGALE, *Myrica gale*   p. 262
 Swamps; Newfoundland, Labrador, and Alaska to n. New Jersey, e. Pennsylvania, Michigan, Minnesota, and Oregon; in mts. to N. Carolina and Tennessee.

Ѵ COMMON WAXMYRTLE, *Myrica cerifera*   p. 262
 Coastal Plain, sandy and gravelly soils; s. New Jersey to Florida, west to e. Texas, and north to Oklahoma and Arkansas.

Ѵ DWARF WAXMYRTLE, *M. pusilla* (not illus.)   p. 262
Ѵ NORTHERN BAYBERRY, *Myrica pensylvanica*   p. 262
 Poor soils, mostly near coast and Great Lakes; s. Newfoundland, e. New Brunswick, and n. Ohio to N. Carolina.

Ѵ BLACK BAYBERRY, *M. heterophylla* (not illus.)   p. 263
Ѵ SWEETFERN, *Comptonia peregrina*   p. 263
 Dry soils; Nova Scotia and Manitoba to Virginia, W. Virginia, Ohio, nw. Indiana, ne. Illinois, and Minnesota; in mts. to n. Georgia.

♠ BEECH, *Fagus grandifolia*   p. 263
 Rich mature soils; Nova Scotia, Prince Edward I., s. Ontario, and e. Wisconsin to n. Florida and Texas.

♠Ѵ COMMON WITCH-HAZEL, *Hamamelis virginiana*   p. 263
 Woods; Nova Scotia, s. Ontario, centr. Michigan, and se. Minnesota to centr. Florida and e. Texas.

Ѵ SPRINGTIME WITCH-HAZEL   p. 264
 H. vernalis (not illus.)

Ѵ WITCH-ALDER, *Fothergilla gardeni* (not illus.)   p. 264
♠ CHESTNUT, *Castanea dentata*   p. 264
 Well-drained forests; s. Maine, New York, s. Ontario, and s. Michigan to Georgia and ne. Mississippi.

♠Ѵ EASTERN CHINQUAPIN, *C. pumila* (not illus.)   p. 265
♠ OZARK CHINQUAPIN, *C. ozarkensis* (not illus.)   p. 265

BAYBERRY   **BEECH**   **WITCH-HAZEL**   **CHESTNUT**

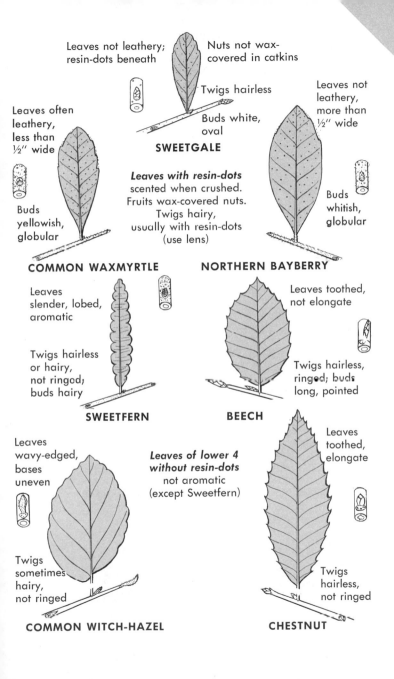

Leaves not leathery; resin-dots beneath

Nuts not wax-covered in catkins

Twigs hairless

Buds white, oval

SWEETGALE

Leaves often leathery, less than ½″ wide

Buds yellowish, globular

COMMON WAXMYRTLE

Leaves not leathery, more than ½″ wide

Buds whitish, globular

NORTHERN BAYBERRY

Leaves with resin-dots scented when crushed. Fruits wax-covered nuts. Twigs hairy, usually with resin-dots (use lens)

Leaves slender, lobed, aromatic

Twigs hairless or hairy, not ringed; buds hairy

SWEETFERN

Leaves toothed, not elongate

Twigs hairless, ringed; buds long, pointed

BEECH

Leaves wavy-edged, bases uneven

Twigs sometimes hairy, not ringed

COMMON WITCH-HAZEL

Leaves of lower 4 without resin-dots not aromatic (except Sweetfern)

Leaves toothed, elongate

Twigs hairless, not ringed

CHESTNUT

MISCELLANEOUS PLANTS
WITH 3 BUNDLE SCARS (2)

"Bundle scars" are small marks within a leaf scar (see p. xxiv).

♦Ѵ RED CHOKEBERRY, *Pyrus arbutifolia*   p. 266
    Wet or dry thickets; Nova Scotia, s. Ontario, Michigan, and
    Missouri to Florida and e. Texas.
  Ѵ PURPLE CHOKEBERRY, *P. floribunda* (not illus.)   p. 266

Ѵ BLACK CHOKEBERRY, *Pyrus melanocarpa*   p. 266
    Wet or dry thickets; Newfoundland, nw. Ontario, and Minne-
    sota to S. Carolina and Tennessee.

Ѵ ALDERLEAF BUCKTHORN, *Rhamnus alnifolia*   p. 266
    Thickets and woods; Newfoundland and British Columbia to
    n. New Jersey, W. Virginia, n. Indiana, n. Illinois, Minnesota,
    Nebraska, Wyoming, and California.
  Ѵ LANCELEAF BUCKTHORN   p. 267
    R. lanceolata (leaf & twig illus.)
    Thickets; s.-centr. Pennsylvania, W. Virginia, s. Ohio, s.
    Wisconsin, and Nebraska to Alabama and Texas.

♦Ѵ CAROLINA BUCKTHORN, *Rhamnus caroliniana*   p. 267
    Woods; w. Virginia, W. Virginia, s. Ohio, s. Illinois, Missouri,
    and Nebraska to Florida and Texas.
  Ѵ EUROPEAN BUCKTHORN, *R. frangula* (leaf illus.) p. 267
    Thickets; Nova Scotia, s. Quebec, s. Ontario, and Minnesota
    to New Jersey, Ohio, and Illinois.

♦ DOMESTIC APPLE, *Pyrus malus*   p. 267
    Spread from cultivation; throughout our area in the U.S. and
    s. Canada.
  ♦ CHINESE APPLE, *P. prunifolia* (not illus.)   p. 268
  ♦ SIBERIAN CRABAPPLE, *P. baccata* (not illus.)   p. 268
  ♦ DOMESTIC PEAR   p. 268
    P. communis (leaf & twig illus.)
    Spread from cultivation; ne. U.S. and s. Canada.
  ♦ CHINESE PEAR, *P. pyrifolia* (not illus.)   p. 268

Ѵ GROUNDSEL-TREE, *Baccharis halimifolia*   p. 268
    Coastal salt marshes and adjacent areas; e. Massachusetts to
    Florida and s. Texas.

Fruits of typical **CHOKEBERRY** (left) and **BUCKTHORN** (right)

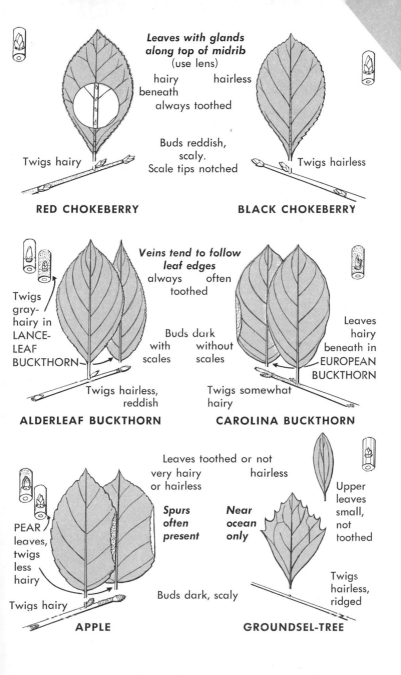

Leaves with glands along top of midrib (use lens)

hairy   hairless
beneath
always toothed

Twigs hairy

Buds reddish, scaly. Scale tips notched

Twigs hairless

RED CHOKEBERRY   **BLACK CHOKEBERRY**

Veins tend to follow leaf edges
always   often
toothed

Twigs gray-hairy in LANCE-LEAF BUCKTHORN

Buds dark with scales   without scales

Leaves hairy beneath in EUROPEAN BUCKTHORN

Twigs hairless, reddish

Twigs somewhat hairy

ALDERLEAF BUCKTHORN   **CAROLINA BUCKTHORN**

Leaves toothed or not
very hairy   hairless
or hairless

Spurs often present   *Near ocean only*

PEAR leaves, twigs less hairy

Twigs hairy

Buds dark, scaly

Upper leaves small, not toothed

Twigs hairless, ridged

APPLE   **GROUNDSEL-TREE**

MISCELLANEOUS PLANTS WITH
3 (OR MORE) BUNDLE SCARS (3)

All but the top 2 plants have 3 bundle scars; all
but 1 have leaves that are never toothed.

Ⅴ LEATHERWOOD, *Dirca palustris*   p. 269
     Rich woods; New Brunswick, Ontario, and Minnesota to
     n. Florida and Louisiana.

⬆Ⅴ TALL PAWPAW, *Asimina triloba*   p. 269
     Bottomlands; New Jersey, w. New York, s. Ontario, s. Michi-
     gan, se. Iowa, and se. Nebraska to n. Florida and e. Texas.
     Ⅴ DWARF PAWPAW, *A. parviflora* (not illus.)   p. 270

⬆ SOUR-GUM, *Nyssa sylvatica*   p. 270
     Lowlands and swamps; centr. Maine, s. Ontario, s. Michigan,
     and centr. Missouri to Florida and e. Texas.
     ⬆ TUPELO, *N. aquatica* (not illus.)   p. 270

Ⅴ SWEET-SPIRES, *Itea virginica*   p. 271
     Swamps and wet ground; Florida and Texas north along coast
     to New Jersey and e. Pennsylvania; in Mississippi Valley to
     Kentucky, s. Illinois, Missouri, and Oklahoma.

Ⅴ COMMON SPICEBUSH, *Lindera benzoin*   p. 271
     Wooded bottomlands; sw. Maine, s. Ontario, s. Michigan,
     Iowa, and se. Kansas to Florida and Texas.
     Ⅴ HAIRY SPICEBUSH, *L. melissaefolium* (not illus.)   p. 271

⬆Ⅴ ALTERNATE-LEAF DOGWOOD   p. 271
     Cornus alternifolia
          Upland woods; Newfoundland, s. Ontario, se. Manitoba, and
          e. Minnesota to nw. Florida, Alabama, and n. Arkansas.

⬆Ⅴ SMOKETREE, *Cotinus obovatus*   p. 272
     Limestone woods and cliffs in 3 scattered localities; s.-centr.
     Tennessee to nw. Alabama, sw. Missouri, and nw. Arkansas
     to e. Oklahoma and s.-centr. Texas. Also reported in Davies
     County, Kentucky.

⬆Ⅴ CORKWOOD, *Leitneria floridana*   p. 272
     Swamps in scattered localities; se. Georgia and n. Florida,
     e. Texas and se. Arkansas; and ne. Arkansas and s. Missouri.

Shrub

Bark very
tough and
fibrous

Buds
hidden
beneath
leaf bases

Pith
never
frequently
chambered

LEATHERWOOD

Leaves
regularly
over
6″ long

Shrub
or tree

End buds
without
scales,
dark-woolly

TALL PAWPAW

Tree

never
toothed

Leaves

always
toothed

Shrub

Dry fruit
clusters
present
in winter

Twigs

brown

green

Buds in 2's
or more

Pith chambered
distinctly ← **sometimes faintly** →

SOUR-GUM

SWEET-SPIRES

Shrub

and twigs
very spicy,
aromatic

Buds on
stalks or
with 2 to 3
scales

Leaves

hairy
beneath,
veins
follow
edges

Shrub
or tree

Bud scales 2

Pith not chambered

**COMMON
SPICEBUSH**

**ALTERNATE-LEAF
DOGWOOD**

Shrub
or tree

single

Side
bud scales
2 to 4

usually

End buds

clustered

Side buds

long-pointed

never

Shrub
or tree

Side
bud scales
2 or 3

Pith not chambered

SMOKETREE

CORKWOOD

SPIREAS

Shrubs generally with toothed leaves, papery bark, raised
leaf scars. Umbrella- or cone-like heads of small dry
fruits usually present.

V STEEPLEBUSH SPIREA, *Spiraea tomentosa*　　　　p. 273
　　Moist meadows; Prince Edward I., e. Quebec, s. Ontario, and
　　Manitoba, to e. Virginia, n. Georgia, Tennessee, and Arkansas.

V NARROWLEAF SPIREA (MEADOWSWEET)　　　　p. 273
　　Spiraea alba
　　Damp meadows; nw. Vermont, sw. Quebec, and Saskatchewan to Delaware, w. N. Carolina, Ohio, n. Missouri, and
　　N. Dakota.

V BROADLEAF SPIREA (MEADOWSWEET)　　　　p. 273
　　Spiraea latifolia
　　Damp meadows and tundras; Newfoundland, s. Labrador,
　　n. Quebec, and Michigan to Long Island, New York, and
　　interior N. Carolina.

V DWARF SPIREA, *Spiraea corymbosa*　　　　p. 273
　　Mountains; n. New Jersey and Pennsylvania to Kentucky and
　　Georgia.

V VIRGINIA SPIREA, *Spiraea virginiana*　　　　p. 273
　　Damp rocky slopes; W. Virginia, w. N. Carolina, and Tennessee.

V JAPANESE SPIREA, S. *japonica* (not illus.)　　　　p. 273

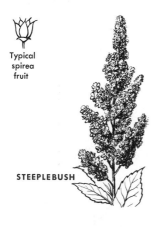

Typical
spirea
fruit

STEEPLEBUSH

BROADLEAF
SPIREA
(MEADOWSWEET)

Leaves coarse-toothed

Flowers and fruits in long, erect clusters

Only spirea with twigs and under- sides of leaves woolly

STEEPLEBUSH

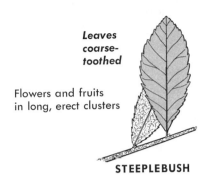

Leaves

fine- toothed ⅜"–¾" wide

coarse- toothed ⅝"–1⅛" wide

Flowers and fruits in long, erect clusters

Twigs yellow- brown

Buds

pointed, silky

short, hairless

Twigs red or purplish brown

NARROWLEAF

BROADLEAF

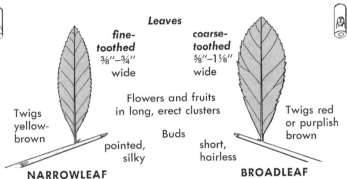

Leaves coarse-toothed

above middle; 1"–2" wide

or not toothed; ¼"–¾" wide

Flowers, fruits in flat-topped clusters

Twigs dark purple

Buds hairless

short, stubby

often longer

Twigs yellow- brown to gray

DWARF

VIRGINIA

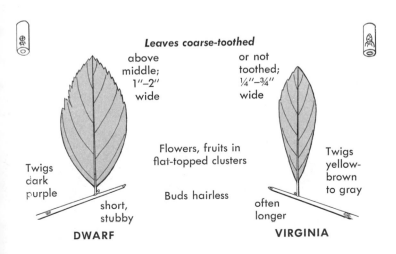

HOLLIES

Trees and shrubs mostly with toothed or thorny leaves. Very tiny, black, sharp stipules on either side of most leaf scars (use lens.).

♦ AMERICAN HOLLY, *Ilex opaca*   p. 274
    Moist woods; e. Massachusetts, se. New York, e. Pennsylvania, s. Ohio, se. Missouri, and Oklahoma to Florida and Texas.

Ѵ LOW GALLBERRY HOLLY, *Ilex glabra*   p. 274
    Sandy and peaty soils; Nova Scotia to Florida and Louisiana.
  Ѵ TALL GALLBERRY HOLLY   p. 275
    I. coriacea (leaf illus.)
  ♦Ѵ YAUPON HOLLY, *I. vomitoria* (leaf illus.)   p. 275

♦Ѵ DECIDUOUS HOLLY, *Ilex decidua*   p. 275
    Woods and thickets; Coastal Plain and Piedmont Plateau, Maryland to Florida, west to s. Texas, and north in Mississippi Valley to sw. Indiana, s. Illinois, Missouri, se. Kansas, and e. Oklahoma.
  Ѵ JUNEBERRY HOLLY, *I. amelanchier* (not illus.)   p. 275

♦Ѵ LARGELEAF HOLLY, *Ilex montana*   p. 276
    Wet slopes and bottomlands; sw. Massachusetts and w. New York to nw. Florida and Louisiana.
  Ѵ GEORGIA HOLLY, *I. longipes* (not illus.)   p. 276

Ѵ COMMON WINTERBERRY HOLLY   p. 276
  Ilex verticillata
    Wet thickets and swamps; Newfoundland and Minnesota to Georgia, Tennessee, and Missouri.

♦Ѵ SMOOTH WINTERBERRY HOLLY, *Ilex laevigata*   p. 276
    Lowland thickets and swamps; mostly Coastal Plain, s. Maine. and New York to n. Georgia.

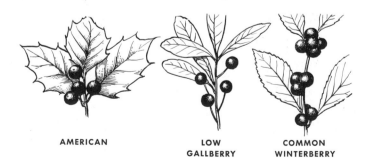

AMERICAN   LOW   COMMON
                GALLBERRY   WINTERBERRY

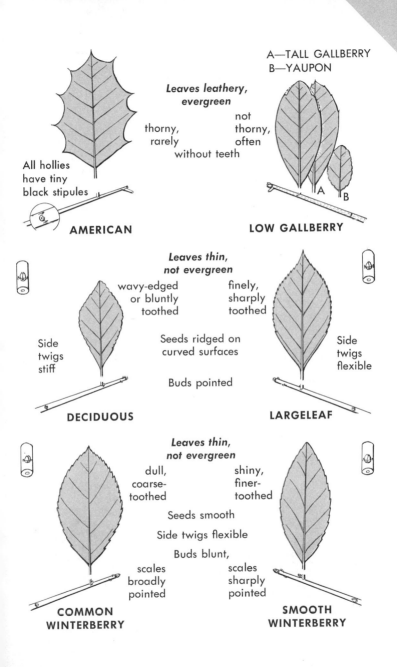

A—TALL GALLBERRY
B—YAUPON

AMERICAN

All hollies have tiny black stipules

Leaves leathery, evergreen

thorny, rarely
not thorny, often
without teeth

LOW GALLBERRY

Leaves thin, not evergreen

wavy-edged or bluntly toothed
finely, sharply toothed

Seeds ridged on curved surfaces

Buds pointed

Side twigs stiff

Side twigs flexible

DECIDUOUS

LARGELEAF

Leaves thin, not evergreen

dull, coarse-toothed
shiny, finer-toothed

Seeds smooth

Side twigs flexible

Buds blunt,

scales broadly pointed
scales sharply pointed

COMMON WINTERBERRY

SMOOTH WINTERBERRY

BLUEBERRIES

Shrubs with small leaves and green or reddish twigs covered
with tiny "warts" (obscured if twigs hairy).

ᐯ VELVETLEAF BLUEBERRY, *Vaccinium myrtilloides*　p. 277
　　Woods and swamps; Newfoundland, Quebec, and British
　　Columbia to Nova Scotia, w. New England, Pennsylvania,
　　w. Virginia, n. Ohio, n. Illinois, ne. Iowa, and Montana.
ᐯ BLACK HIGHBUSH BLUEBERRY　　　　　　p. 277
　　Vaccinium atrococcum
　　Wet or barren sites; New England, New York, and s. Ontario
　　to n. Florida and Arkansas.
　ᐯ COASTAL HIGHBUSH BLUEBERRY　　　　p. 278
　　　V. caesariense (not illus.)
ᐯ COMMON HIGHBUSH BLUEBERRY　　　　　p. 278
　　Vaccinium corymbosum
　　　Acid soils; Nova Scotia, s. Quebec, and Wisconsin to Florida
　　　and Louisiana.
　ᐯ ELLIOTT BLUEBERRY, *V. elliottii* (not illus.)　　p. 278
ᐯ EARLY LOW BLUEBERRY, *Vaccinium vacillans*　　p. 278
　　Dry woods and thickets; w. Nova Scotia, s. Ontario, Michi-
　　gan, ne. Iowa, and e. Kansas to Georgia and Missouri.
　ᐯ SLENDER BLUEBERRY, *V. tenellum* (not illus.)　　p. 279
ᐯ LATE LOW BLUEBERRY, *Vaccinium angustifolium*　p. 279
　　Tundras, bogs, and barrens; Newfoundland, Labrador, n.
　　Ontario, and Minnesota to Delaware, Maryland, w. Virginia,
　　W. Virginia, Ohio, and ne. Iowa.
ᐯ SOUTHERN LOW BLUEBERRY　　　　　　p. 279
　　Vaccinium pallidum
　　　Dry woods; se. Virginia, W. Virginia, and Missouri to
　　　Georgia, Alabama, and Arkansas.

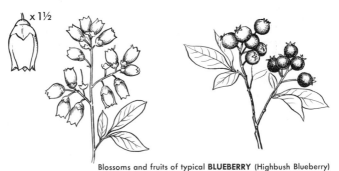

Blossoms and fruits of typical **BLUEBERRY** (Highbush Blueberry)

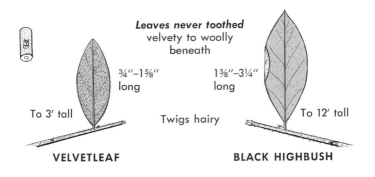

Leaves never toothed
velvety to woolly
beneath

¾"–1⅝"
long

1⅝"–3¼"
long

To 3' tall

Twigs hairy

To 12' tall

VELVETLEAF

BLACK HIGHBUSH

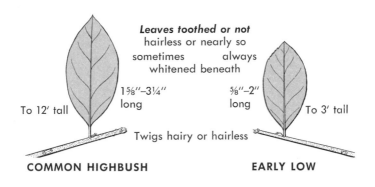

Leaves toothed or not
hairless or nearly so
sometimes   always
whitened beneath

1⅝"–3¼"
long

⅝"–2"
long

To 12' tall

To 3' tall

Twigs hairy or hairless

COMMON HIGHBUSH

EARLY LOW

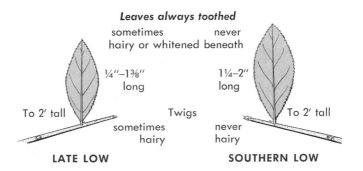

Leaves always toothed
sometimes   never
hairy or whitened beneath

¼"–1⅜"
long

1¼–2"
long

To 2' tall

Twigs

To 2' tall

sometimes
hairy

never
hairy

LATE LOW

SOUTHERN LOW

HUCKLEBERRIES, BILBERRIES, ETC.

Shrubs mostly with small leaves. Twigs not covered
with fine "warts."

Ꝟ DWARF HUCKLEBERRY, *Gaylussacia dumosa*   p. 280
   Sandy soils and bogs, mostly near coast; Newfoundland, e.
   New Brunswick, e. Pennsylvania, and Tennessee to Florida
   and Mississippi.
   Ꝟ TALL HUCKLEBERRY, *G. frondosa* (not illus.)   p. 280
Ꝟ BLACK HUCKLEBERRY, *Gaylussacia baccata*   p. 280
   Woods and swamps; Newfoundland and Saskatchewan to
   Georgia and Louisiana.
Ꝟ TALL DEERBERRY, *Vaccinium stamineum*   p. 280
   Woods and openings; Massachusetts, s. Ontario, Indiana,
   Missouri, and Kansas to Florida and Louisiana.
   Ꝟ LOW DEERBERRY, *V. caesium* (not illus.)   p. 281
Ꝟ TUNDRA BILBERRY, *Vaccinium uliginosum*   p. 281
   Tundras, bogs, and stony ground; Arctic to Newfoundland,
   n. New England, n. New York, n. Michigan, and n. Minnesota.
   Ꝟ OVALLEAF BILBERRY, *V. ovalifolium* (not illus.)   p. 281
Ꝟ SQUARE-TWIG BILBERRY   p. 281
   Vaccinium membranaceum
      Thickets; w. Ontario and n. Michigan; sw. S. Dakota; also
      s. British Columbia to California.
   Ꝟ NEWFOUNDLAND BILBERRY   p. 282
   V. nubigenum (not illus.)
Ꝟ DWARF BILBERRY, *Vaccinium cespitosum*   p. 282
   Poor soils; Newfoundland, Labrador, and Alaska to n. New
   England, n. New York, n. Michigan, n. Minnesota, Colorado,
   and California.
   Ꝟ SOUTHERN MOUNTAIN-CRANBERRY   p. 282
   V. erythrocarpum (not illus.)
Ꝟ BOX HUCKLEBERRY, *Gaylussacia brachycera*   p. 282
   Dry woods; local, Delaware, and W. Virginia to Tennessee.
↟Ꝟ FARKLEBERRY, *Vaccinium arboreum*   p. 282
   Dry Coastal Plain woods; se. Virginia to Florida, west to
   centr. Texas, and north in Mississippi Valley to s. Indiana,
   s. Illinois, Missouri, and se. Kansas.

| BLACK | TALL | FARKLEBERRY | DWARF |
| HUCKLEBERRY | DEERBERRY | | BILBERRY |

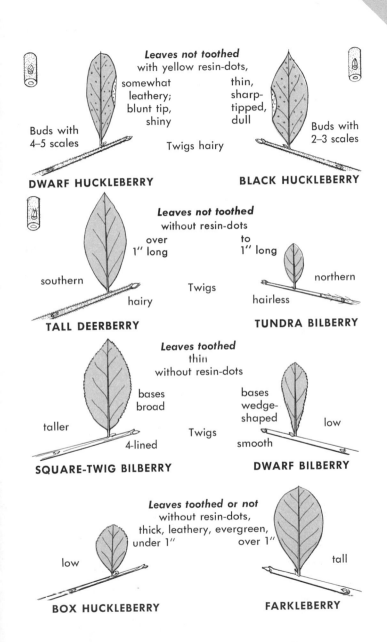

Leaves not toothed
with yellow resin-dots,

somewhat
leathery;
blunt tip,
shiny

thin,
sharp-
tipped,
dull

Buds with
4–5 scales

Twigs hairy

Buds with
2–3 scales

DWARF HUCKLEBERRY

BLACK HUCKLEBERRY

Leaves not toothed
without resin-dots

over
1" long

to
1" long

southern

northern

Twigs

hairy

hairless

TALL DEERBERRY

TUNDRA BILBERRY

Leaves toothed
thin
without resin-dots

bases
broad

bases
wedge-
shaped

taller

low

Twigs

4-lined

smooth

SQUARE-TWIG BILBERRY

DWARF BILBERRY

Leaves toothed or not
without resin-dots,
thick, leathery, evergreen,
under 1"   over 1"

low

tall

BOX HUCKLEBERRY

FARKLEBERRY

AZALEAS

Leaves and buds clustered near the twig tips, and often with several twigs originating from an old end-bud cluster. Leaves with hairy edges (use lens); end buds often large; fruits long capsules.

ᐯ SMOOTH AZALEA, *Rhododendron arborescens*   p. 283
  Rich soils; Pennsylvania and Kentucky to Georgia and Alabama.
  ᐯ PINKSHELL AZALEA, *R. vaseyi* (not illus.)   p. 283

ᐯ RHODORA AZALEA, *Rhododendron canadense*   p. 284
  Poor soils and acid bogs; Newfoundland and s.-centr. Quebec to n. New Jersey and ne. Pennsylvania.
  ᐯ JAPANESE AZALEA, *R. japonicum* (not illus.)   p. 284

ᐯ EARLY AZALEA, *Rhododendron roseum*   p. 284
  Rocky slopes and woods; sw. Maine and sw. Quebec to the mts. of Virginia, Tennessee, and Missouri.
  ᐯ WOOLLY AZALEA, *R. canescens* (not illus.)   p. 284

ᐯ FLAME AZALEA, *Rhododendron calendulaceum*   p. 284
  Wooded slopes; sw. Pennsylvania, se. Ohio, and W. Virginia to Georgia and Alabama.
  ᐯ CUMBERLAND AZALEA   p. 285
  R. cumberlandense (not illus.)

ᐯ SWAMP AZALEA, *Rhododendron viscosum*   p. 285
  Wet thickets and woods; sw. Maine and ne. Ohio to S. Carolina and e. Tennessee.
  ᐯ TOOTHED AZALEA, *R. serrulatum* (not illus.)   p. 285

ᐯ PINK AZALEA, *Rhododendron nudiflorum*   p. 285
  Woods; Massachusetts and New York to s. S. Carolina, Tennessee, and s. Ohio.
  ᐯ DWARF AZALEA, *R. atlanticum* (not illus.)   p. 285

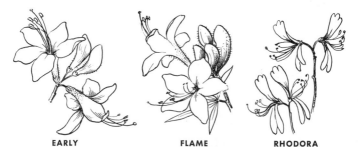

EARLY   FLAME   RHODORA

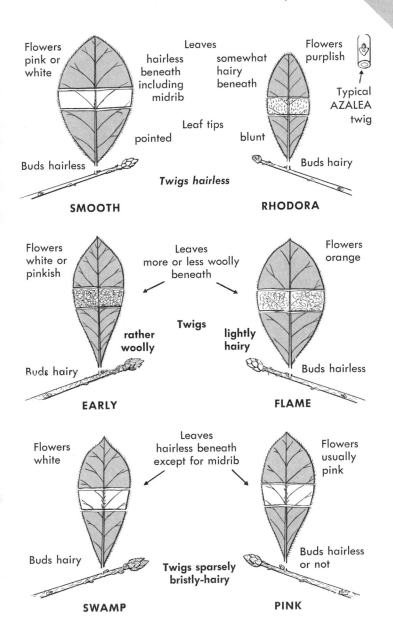

SMOOTH
Flowers pink or white
Leaves hairless beneath including midrib
Leaf tips pointed
Buds hairless
Twigs hairless

RHODORA
Flowers purplish
Typical AZALEA twig
Leaves somewhat hairy beneath
Leaf tips blunt
Buds hairy

EARLY
Flowers white or pinkish
Leaves more or less woolly beneath
Twigs rather woolly
Buds hairy

FLAME
Flowers orange
Twigs lightly hairy
Buds hairless

SWAMP
Flowers white
Leaves hairless beneath except for midrib
Buds hairy
Twigs sparsely bristly-hairy

PINK
Flowers usually pink
Buds hairless or not

EVERGREEN HEATHS

Leaves leathery, evergreen, mostly not toothed.
The fruits are dry capsules.

♠Ⅴ GREAT RHODODENDRON p. 286
Rhododendron maximum
Damp thickets; sw. Maine, New York, s. Ontario, and Ohio
to w. S. Carolina, Georgia, and n. Alabama.
♠Ⅴ CATAWBA RHODODENDRON p. 286
R. catawbiense (leaf illus.)

Ⅴ MOUNTAIN LAUREL, *Kalmia latifolia* p. 287
Rocky woods and swamps; New Brunswick, Maine, s. Ontario,
Ohio, s. Indiana, and w. Kentucky to nw. Florida and se.
Louisiana.

Ⅴ FETTERBUSH, *Lyonia lucida* (leaf illus.) p. 287

Ⅴ LABRADOR TEA, *Ledum groenlandicum* p. 287
Bogs and peat soils; Greenland and Alaska to n. New Jersey,
Ohio, Michigan, Minnesota, Alberta, and Washington.

Ⅴ LEATHERLEAF, *Chamaedaphne calyculata* p. 287
Bogs and peat soils; Newfoundland and Alaska to Long Island,
New York, n. Indiana, n. Illinois, n. Iowa, Alberta, and British
Columbia; in mts. to Georgia.

Ⅴ PIERIS, *Pieris floribunda* p. 288
Damp mountain slopes; Virginia to Georgia.

Ⅴ SWEETBELLS, *Leucothoë* (2 species, not illus.) p. 288

Ⅴ BOG ROSEMARY, *Andromeda glaucophylla* p. 288
Bogs and peat soils; sw. Greenland, Labrador, and e. Mani-
toba to n. New Jersey, W. Virginia, Indiana, Wisconsin, and
Minnesota.

**GREAT
RHODODENDRON**   **MOUNTAIN
LAUREL**   **LABRADOR
TEA**

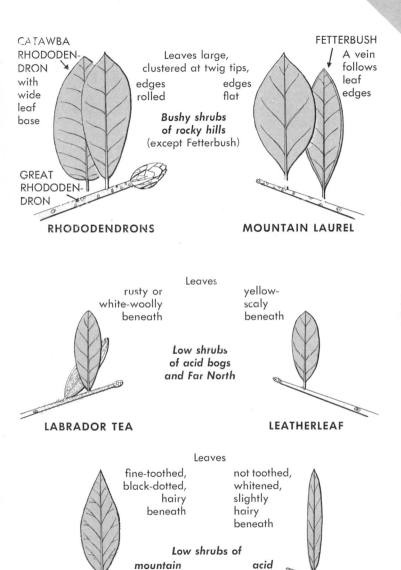

CATAWBA RHODODENDRON with wide leaf base

GREAT RHODODENDRON

Leaves large, clustered at twig tips, edges rolled / edges flat

Bushy shrubs of rocky hills (except Fetterbush)

FETTERBUSH
A vein follows leaf edges

RHODODENDRONS

MOUNTAIN LAUREL

Leaves

rusty or white-woolly beneath

yellow-scaly beneath

Low shrubs of acid bogs and Far North

LABRADOR TEA

LEATHERLEAF

Leaves

fine-toothed, black-dotted, hairy beneath

not toothed, whitened, slightly hairy beneath

Low shrubs of mountain slopes / acid bogs

PIERIS

BOG ROSEMARY

NONEVERGREEN HEATHS

With thin, mostly toothed leaves. Fruits are dry capsules.

⬆ SOURWOOD, *Oxydendrum arboreum*   p. 289
   Rich woods; New Jersey, s. Pennsylvania, s. Ohio, and s.
   Illinois to Florida and se. Louisiana.

⩔ MALEBERRY, *Lyonia ligustrina*   p. 289
   Swampy thickets and sandy soils; New England, New York,
   and Kentucky to Florida, Louisiana, and Arkansas.

⩔ MOUNTAIN PEPPERBUSH, *Clethra acuminata*   p. 289
   Mountain woods; w. Virginia and W. Virginia to n. Georgia
   and n. Alabama.

⩔ COAST PEPPERBUSH, *Clethra alnifolia*   p. 290
   Swamps and sandy soils; s. Maine, s. New Hampshire, se.
   New York, and e. Pennsylvania to Florida and e. Texas.

⩔ SWAMP SWEETBELLS, *Leucothoë racemosa*   p. 290
   Swampy thickets; Massachusetts, se. New York, and e. Pennsylvania to Florida and Louisiana.

⩔ MOUNTAIN SWEETBELLS, *Leucothoë recurva*   p. 290
   Dry mountain slopes; Virginia to Alabama.

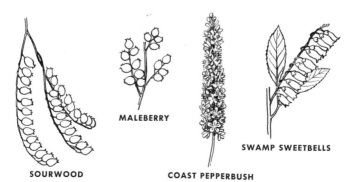

MALEBERRY

SWAMP SWEETBELLS

SOURWOOD   COAST PEPPERBUSH

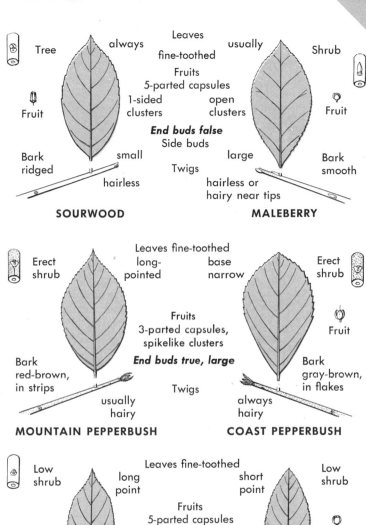

Tree   always

Leaves   usually   Shrub

fine-toothed

Fruits

5-parted capsules

Fruit   1-sided   open   Fruit
clusters   clusters

End buds false

Side buds

Bark   small   large   Bark
ridged   Twigs   smooth

hairless   hairless or
hairy near tips

SOURWOOD   **MALEBERRY**

Erect   Leaves fine-toothed   Erect
shrub   long-   base   shrub
pointed   narrow

Fruits

Fruit   3-parted capsules,   Fruit
spikelike clusters

End buds true, large

Bark   Bark
red-brown,   gray-brown,
in strips   Twigs   in flakes

usually   always
hairy   hairy

MOUNTAIN PEPPERBUSH   **COAST PEPPERBUSH**

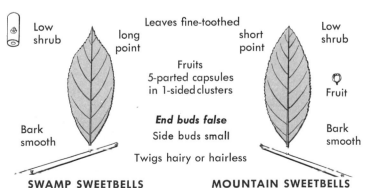

Low   Leaves fine-toothed   Low
shrub   long   short   shrub
point   point

Fruits

5-parted capsules

in 1-sided clusters   Fruit

Fruit

End buds false

Side buds small

Bark   Bark
smooth   smooth

Twigs hairy or hairless

SWAMP SWEETBELLS   **MOUNTAIN SWEETBELLS**

MISCELLANEOUS PLANTS
WITH 1 BUNDLE SCAR (1)

"Bundle scars" are small marks within a leaf scar (see p. xxiv). These species have limited ranges (below) and have leaves that are sometimes or always toothed. Fruits variable.

♦∀ SWEETLEAF, *Symplocos tinctoria*   p. 291
   Swampy or sandy woods; mostly Coastal Plain, Delaware to
   w. N. Carolina and n. Florida, west to e. Texas, and north
   in Mississippi Valley to se. Tennessee, s. Arkansas, and se.
   Oklahoma.

♦∀ SILVERBELL-TREE, *Halesia carolina*   p. 291
   Bottomlands and rich soils; Virginia, s. W. Virginia, s. Ohio,
   s. Illinois, se. Missouri, and se. Oklahoma to Florida and e.
   Texas.

∀ AMERICAN SNOWBELL, *Styrax americana*   p. 291
   Wet Coastal Plain woods; se. Virginia to Florida, west to
   Texas, and north in Mississippi Valley to s. Ohio, s. Indiana,
   and s. Illinois, and se. Missouri.

♦∀ BIGLEAF SNOWBELL, *Styrax grandifolia*   p. 291
   Coastal Plain bottomlands; s. Virginia to Florida, west to
   Louisiana, and north to w. Tennessee and Arkansas.

∀ SILKY-CAMELLIA, *Stewartia malachodendron*   p. 291
   Fertile Coastal Plain woods; e. Virginia to w. Florida and
   w. Louisiana; north in Mississippi Valley to w. Tennessee and
   e. Arkansas.

∀ MOUNTAIN-CAMELLIA, *Stewartia ovata*   p. 292
   Bottomlands in mountain forests; Virginia and se. Kentucky
   to centr. N. Carolina, n. Georgia, and n. Alabama.

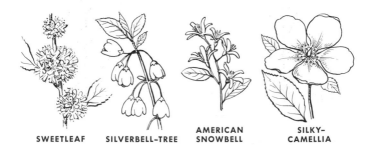

SWEETLEAF   SILVERBELL-TREE   AMERICAN   SILKY-
                                    SNOWBELL   CAMELLIA

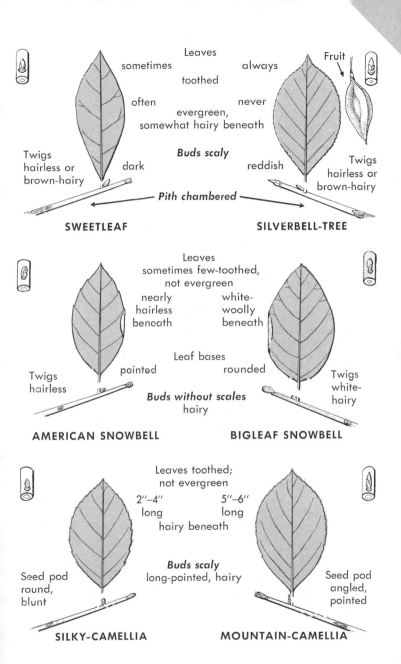

Leaves
sometimes   always
toothed
often   never
evergreen,
somewhat hairy beneath

Buds scaly

Twigs
hairless or   dark   reddish   Twigs
brown-hairy   hairless or
                                              brown-hairy

Fruit

⟵ *Pith chambered* ⟶

SWEETLEAF   **SILVERBELL-TREE**

Leaves
sometimes few-toothed,
not evergreen
nearly   white-
hairless   woolly
beneath   beneath

Leaf bases
pointed   rounded

Twigs   Twigs
hairless   *Buds without scales*   white-
                   hairy   hairy

AMERICAN SNOWBELL   **BIGLEAF SNOWBELL**

Leaves toothed;
not evergreen
2"–4"   5"–6"
long   long
hairy beneath

Buds scaly
long-pointed, hairy

Seed pod   Seed pod
round,   angled,
blunt   pointed

SILKY-CAMELLIA   **MOUNTAIN-CAMELLIA**

MISCELLANEOUS PLANTS
WITH 1 BUNDLE SCAR (2)

"Bundle scars" are small marks within a leaf scar (see p. xxiv).
These trees and shrubs have leaves wavy-edged or not toothed.

♠ PERSIMMON, *Diospyros virginiana*   p. 292
   Old fields and barren woods; Connecticut, s. New York,
   Pennsylvania, Ohio, Illinois, Missouri, and e. Kansas to Flor-
   ida and e. Texas.
Ⅴ AMERICAN SILVERBERRY   p. 293
   Elaeagnus commutata
      Dry soils; e. Quebec and Alaska to sw. Quebec, Minnesota,
      S. Dakota, and Utah.
   Ⅴ AUTUMN-OLIVE, *E. umbellata* (not illus.)   p. 293
Ⅴ DAPHNE, *Daphne mezereum*   p. 293
      Escaped, especially on limestone soils; Newfoundland and s.
      Ontario to New England, New York, and Ohio.
Ⅴ MOUNTAIN-HOLLY, *Nemopanthus mucronata*   p. 294
      Damp thickets and swamps; Newfoundland and Minnesota
      to w. Virginia, W. Virginia, Indiana, and n. Illinois.
Ⅴ STAGGERBUSH, *Lyonia mariana*   p. 294
      Sandy or peaty soils; s. Rhode Island, se. New York, e. Penn-
      sylvania, and Arkansas to Florida and e. Texas.
   Ⅴ ZENOBIA, *Zenobia pulverulenta* (not illus.)   p. 294
Ⅴ MINNIEBUSH, *Menziesia pilosa*   p. 294
      Wooded slopes; Pennsylvania and W. Virginia to Georgia.
   Ⅴ WHIN, *Genista tinctoria* (not illus.)   p. 295
   Ⅴ ANDRACHNE, *Andrachne phyllanthoides* (not illus.) p. 295
Ⅴ PONDSPICE, *Litsea aestivalis*   p. 295
      Swamps; se. Virginia and Tennessee to Florida and Louisiana.
Ⅴ OILNUT, *Pyrularia pubera*   p. 295
      Mountain woods; Pennsylvania, W. Virginia, to Georgia and
      Alabama.
♠ REDBAY, *Persea borbonia*   p. 295
      Coastal swamps; s. Delaware to Florida and west to Texas.
Ⅴ TITI, *Cyrilla racemiflora*   p. 296
      Coastal swamps; se. Virginia to Florida and west to Texas.

PERSIMMON   SILVERBERRY   MOUNTAIN-HOLLY   STAGGERBUSH

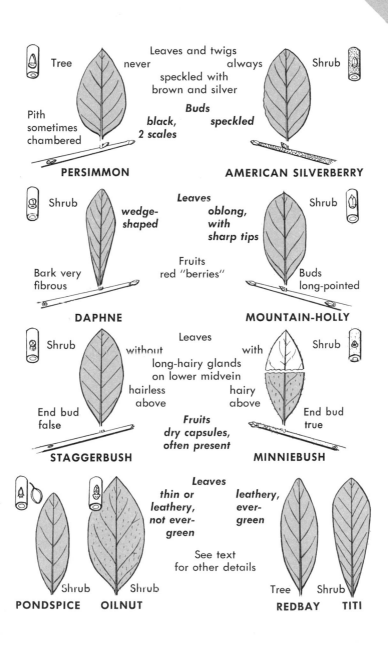

Tree — Leaves and twigs never always speckled with brown and silver — Shrub

Buds **black, 2 scales** | *Buds* **speckled**

Pith sometimes chambered

PERSIMMON | **AMERICAN SILVERBERRY**

Shrub — *Leaves oblong, with sharp tips* — Shrub

wedge-shaped

Bark very fibrous | Fruits red "berries"

Buds long-pointed

DAPHNE | **MOUNTAIN-HOLLY**

Shrub — Leaves without / with long-hairy glands on lower midvein — Shrub

hairless above / hairy above

End bud false | *Fruits dry capsules, often present* | End bud true

STAGGERBUSH | **MINNIEBUSH**

Leaves thin or leathery, not ever-green / *leathery, ever-green*

See text for other details

Shrub | Shrub | Tree | Shrub

PONDSPICE | **OILNUT** | **REDBAY** | **TITI**

Appendixes
Index

APPENDIX A

Winter Key to Plants with Opposite Leaf Scars

(Nonevergreen species of Sections II and III)

How to use a key is explained in the introduction, "How to Use This Book." See subheading "Identifying Unknown Plants" (p. xxvii). Plate numbers in parentheses indicate that the plants are included but not illustrated in connection with the plate specified.

	Name	*Plate*
1. Plants creeping or climbing, not erect:		
2. Creeping or trailing shrubs		12
2. Climbing vines:		
3. Branchlets with hollow pith (see also Silkvine, p. 70)		
	HONEYSUCKLES (1)	13
3. Branchlets with solid pith	**CLEMATIS, etc.**	7
1. Plants erect; trees or shrubs:		
4. Leaf scars with 4 to many bundle scars, often large:		
5. Central bud missing; a pair of buds present at twig tip:		
6. Leaf scars circular or nearly so **PRINCESS-TREE, etc.**		18
6. Leaf scars 4-sided to crescent-shaped:		
7. Pith slender; fruits balloonlike	**BLADDERNUT**	8
7. Pith thick; fruits berries	**ELDERBERRIES**	8
5. 1 or 3 buds present at twig tip:		
8. End buds with only 2–3 pairs of scales, mostly dark-velvety; not gummy; buds and twigs hairy or hairless:		
9. Twigs neither velvety-hairy nor white-powdered (see also Japanese Corktree, p. 52)	**ASHES (1)**	9
9. Twigs velvety-hairy or white-powdered	**ASHES (2)**	10
8. End bud with many smooth, overlapping scales, sometimes gummy; buds and twigs mostly hairless		
	BUCKEYES	11
4. Leaf scars with 1 or 3 bundle scars, small to moderate size:		
10. Bundle scar 1:		
11. Twigs covered with silver, brown, or gray scaly particles; buds with 2 bud scales or none:		
12. Granular twig scales brown and/or silver		
	BUFFALOBERRIES	17
12. Granular twig scales grayish	**BEAUTYBERRY**	(19)
11. Twigs not covered with scaly particles; buds variable:		
13. Twigs bright green or red **BURNINGBUSH, etc.**		19
13. Twigs more somberly colored:		
14. Scales present at twig bases		
	CORALBERRY, etc.	17

Name   *Plate*

14. Scales not present at twig bases:
    15. Twigs thorn-tipped   **COMMON BUCKTHORN**   **19**
    15. Twigs not thorn-tipped:
        16. Buds globular; plants either parasitic or semi-aquatic:
            17. Parasites on tree roots; s. Appalachians:
                18. Twigs hairy; branchlets pale brown
                        BUCKLEYA   (16)
                18. Twigs hairless; branchlets dark gray
                        NESTRONIA   (16)
            17. Growing in shallow water or on wet soils:
                19. Leaf scars and buds often in whorls of 3's; opposing leaf scars connected by lines; buds single above leaf scars:
                    20. Twigs rounded and smooth
                        BUTTONBUSH   **16**
                    20. Twigs angular and ridged
                        SWAMP LOOSESTRIFE   (16)
                19. Leaf scars and buds paired; leaf scars not connected by lines; buds often several above leaf scars   **FORESTIERAS**   **19**
        16. Buds elongate; nonparasitic upland plants:
            21. Bud scales thick, fleshy; side buds with only 2–3 scales   **LILACS**   **18**
            21. Bud scales papery; side buds with 4 or more scales:
                22. Twigs slender, 1/16″ or under; leaf scars much raised   **PRIVETS**   **16**
                22. Twigs stout, over 1/16″ thick; leaf scars not raised (at least top edges about flush with twigs)   **FRINGE-TREE**   **16**
10. Bundle scars 3:
    23. Side buds hidden beneath leaf scars or bark:
        24. Leaf scars raised above the twigs; bark of branchlets tight; tree   **FLOWERING DOGWOOD**   **15**
        24. Leaf scars not raised (at least upper edges about flush with twigs); bark of branchlets usually flaky; shrubs:
            25. Plants of upland sites; twigs neither branched nor striated   **MOCK-ORANGES**   **19**
            25. Plants of coastal salt marshes and shores; twigs branched, finely lined   **MARSH-ELDER**   (19)
    23. Side buds visible:
        26. Upper leaf scars meeting in raised points (in salt marshes, see also Sea-oxeye, p. 81)   **ASHLEAF MAPLE**   **10**
        26. Upper leaf scars not meeting in raised points:
            27. Paired leaf scars not connected by lines:
                28. Twig tips usually thorny; inner bark yellow
                        COMMON BUCKTHORN   **19**
                28. Twig tips not thorny; inner bark not yellow:
                    29. Broken twigs with a spicy odor; twigs swollen near buds   **ALLSPICES**   **16**
                    29. Broken twigs without a spicy odor; twigs not much swollen at buds:

Name   Plate

30. Central end bud lacking, only a pair of buds at twig tips:
   31. Pith white, bud scales 2–4, fruits balloonlike capsules
                             BLADDERNUT   8
   31. Pith brown, bud scales many, fruits small and juicy,
       berrylike   **RED ELDERBERRY**   8
30. Central end bud present; 1 or 3 buds present at twig tips:
   32. Bud scale 1; fruits small capsules containing many
       tiny, silky seeds   **BASKET WILLOW**   56
   32. Buds without scales or, if scaly, with 2 or more scales:
      33. Bud scales more than 2:
         34. Bud scales 6 or less (usually 4 or less); fruits
            fleshy with single flat seeds **VIBURNUMS (2)**   21
         34. Bud scales mostly 6 or more; fruits dry,
            winged   **MAPLES**   22
      33. Bud scales 2 or none:
         35. Leaf scars not U-shaped, nearly enclosing the
            buds   **JAPANESE CORKTREE**   (10)
         35. Leaf scars U-shaped, adjacent to the buds:
           36. Twigs hairy or trunk bark white-striped;
              bud scales 2; fruits dry, winged **MAPLES**   22
           36. Twigs not hairy; trunk not white-striped;
              bud scales 2 or none; fruits fleshy, with
              single flat seeds   **VIBURNUMS (1)**   20
27. Paired leaf scars connected by lines:
   37. Papery scales present at twig bases:
      38. Thin, hairy ridges descending along sides of twigs;
        bark not papery   **BUSH-HONEYSUCKLES**   19
      38. Twigs not ridged; bark papery:
         39. Twigs stout, relatively inflexible; umbrellalike
            dried fruit clusters usually present in winter; low
            shrubs   **HYDRANGEAS**   19
         39. Twigs slender, relatively flexible; fruits are
            berries; low or tall shrubs **HONEYSUCKLES (2)**   14
   37. No papery scales present at the bases of the twigs:
      40. Bud scales more than 2:
         41. Mostly shrubs; fruits fleshy with single flat seeds;
            bud scales 6 or less (usually 4 or less)
                           VIBURNUMS (2)   21
         41. Mostly trees; fruits dry, winged; bud scales mostly
            6 or more   **MAPLES**   22
      40. Bud scales 2 or none:
         42. Leaf scars raised above the twigs; bud scales 2
                           DOGWOODS   15
         42. Leaf scars usually not much raised above the
            twigs:
           43. Twigs hairy or trunk bark white-striped; bud
              scales 2; fruits dry, winged   **MAPLES**   22
           43. Twigs not hairy; trunk not white-striped; bud
              scales 2 or none; fruits fleshy with single flat
              seeds   **VIBURNUMS (1)**   20

APPENDIX B

Winter Key to Plants with Alternate Leaf Scars

(Nonevergreen species of Sections I, IV, and V)

BECAUSE of the large number of plants in this group, it is broken into 6 divisions. Plate numbers in parentheses indicate that the plants are included but not illustrated in connection with the plate specified.

Creeping, trailing, matted or otherwise flattened shrubs	Division A, below
Climbing or sprawling vines	Division B, p. 379
Upright trees and shrubs with twigs spiny, thorny, or prickly	Division C, p. 380

Upright trees and shrubs; twigs without spines, thorns, or prickles:

Leaf scars with 4 or more bundle scars	Division D, p. 381
Leaf scars with 3 bundle scars	Division E, p. 383
Leaf scars lacking or with 1 bundle scar	Division F, p. 386

Within each division, the key will help identify an unknown specimen by naming the species or the group of species containing the unknown. Confirmation and further identification should be undertaken by reference to the plate and text listed. Note that Divisions D, E, and F of the above Winter Key do not correspond with those subdivisions of the Summer Key, pages 168–74.

DIVISION A

Creeping, trailing, matted, or otherwise flattened shrubs

	Name	Plate
1. Plants prickly, trailing	**DEWBERRIES**	23

1. Plants not prickly:
    2. Leaf scars with 1 bundle scar:
        3. Older bark shreddy   **SHRUBBY CINQUEFOIL**   30
        3. Older bark not shreddy:
            4. Older bark smooth; without "warty" spurs on twigs
                              BEARBERRIES   32
            4. Older bark scaly; "warty" spurs on twigs
                           AMERICAN LARCH   2
    2. Leaf scars with 3 bundle scars:

Division A (*contd.*)   *Name*   *Plate*

5. Buds covered by a single scale   **DWARF WILLOWS**   32
5. Buds covered by more than 1 scale:
  6. Buds covered by 2–3 scales   **BIRCHES**   52
  6. Buds covered by more numerous scales:
    7. End buds false   **PLUMS**   53
    7. End buds true:
      8. Older bark usually shreddy; leaf scars very narrow;
        broken twigs mostly with foul odor; mostly in swamps
           CURRANTS   41
      8. Older bark not shreddy; leaf scars not very narrow:
        9. Twigs speckled; broken twigs with sour odor
           SAND CHERRY   32
        9. Twigs not speckled; broken twigs without sour
          odor   **MOUNTAIN ALDER**   51

DIVISION B

Climbing or sprawling vines

(CAUTION: Watch for Poison-ivy)

10. Vines climbing by aerial rootlets; *poisonous*   **POISON-IVY**   25
10. Vines without aerial rootlets; nonpoisonous:
  11. Vines climbing by tendrils:
    12. Tendrils attached to old leaf bases; twigs green and
      without distinct pith; stems mostly prickly or bristly
           GREENBRIERS   33
    12. Tendrils attached to twigs; twigs not green; pith
      distinct; stems not prickly:
      13. Pith brown, woody partitions usually present
           GRAPES (1), (2), etc.   34, 35
      13. Pith white, without pith partitions:
        14. Tendrils not forked
           AMPELOPSIS   35
        14. Tendrils forked:
          15. Tendril tips very slender, often disk-
            tipped   **BOSTON IVY, CREEPERS** (35), 30
          15. Tendril tips stout; not disk-tipped:
            16. Tendrils present mostly near the
              branch tips   **PEPPER VINE**   31
            16. Tendrils more frequent   **CISSUS**   (25)
  11. Vines without tendrils:
    17. Prickly; trailing or climbing   **BRAMBLES**   23
    17. Not prickly; climbing by twining stems:
      18. Leaf scars flanked by knobby growths   **WISTERIAS**   30
      18. Leaf scars not so flanked:
        19. Leaf scars with more than 3 bundle scars
           MOONSEEDS   36
        19. Leaf scars with 1–3 bundle scars
           MISCELLANEOUS   37

DIVISION C

Upright trees and shrubs with spiny, thorny, or prickly twigs

	Name	Plate

20. Shrubs with leaf scars lacking:
    21. Arching, rambling shrubs with old leafstalk bases remaining   **BRAMBLES**   **23**
    21. Small shrubs with leaves triangular and thornlike   **GORSE**   **6**
20. Shrubs or trees with leaf scars evident:
    22. Leaf scars with more than 3 bundle scars:
        23. Sap milky; twigs slender; end buds false   **OSAGE-ORANGE**   **38**
        23. Sap not milky; twigs stout; end buds true:
            24. South and mostly east of Great Lakes   **HERCULES-CLUB, etc.**   **24**
            24. North and west of Great Lakes   **DEVIL'S-CLUB**   **(38)**
    22. Leaf scars with 1–3 bundle scars:
        25. Twigs and thorns bright green; thorns long; single bundle scar scarcely evident; southern   **TRIFOLIATE ORANGE**   **(24)**
        25. Twigs and thorns or prickles not green; bundle scars more obvious:
            26. Leaf scars with 1 bundle scar:
                27. Twigs covered with brown and silver scales   **AUTUMN-OLIVE**   **(68)**
                27. Twigs not scaly:
                    28. Twigs ridged; plant bushy   **MATRIMONY-VINES**   **37**
                    28. Twigs not ridged; a tree   **OSAGE-ORANGE**   **38**
            26. Leaf scars with 3 bundle scars:
                29. Thorns or prickles in pairs, flanking buds and leaf scars:
                    30. Buds located above leaf scars; end buds true   **PRICKLY-ASHES**   **24**
                    30. Buds hidden beneath leaf scars; end buds false   **BLACK LOCUSTS**   **24**
                29. Thorns or prickles not paired:
                    31. Buds hidden beneath or surrounded by leaf scars; thorns several inches long   **HONEY LOCUSTS**   **24**
                    31. Buds located above the leaf scars:
                        32. Thorns usually over 1″; thorns without buds; buds almost spherical; leaf scars not ridged   **HAWTHORNS**   **39**
                        32. Prickles under ½″, often triple; buds long-pointed; prominent ridges from leaf scars   **GOOSEBERRIES**   **40**
                        32. Thorns or prickles short, or if long then with buds; buds mostly not spherical; leaf scars without prominent ridges   **MISCELLANEOUS**   **38**

DIVISION D

*Upright trees and shrubs with nonthorny twigs and with
leaf scars that have 4 or more bundle scars (these may be in
3 groups, which are not to be confused with Division E plants)*

(CAUTION: Watch for Poison-ivy, Poison-oak, and Poison Sumac)

	Name	*Plate*

33. Buds narrowed at base (stalked):
    34. Buds without scales, hairy:
        35. End buds not much if any larger than side buds;
           poisonous   **POISON-IVY, POISON-OAK**   25
        35. End buds much larger than side buds; not poisonous
                                    PAWPAWS   59
    34. Buds with 2–3 smooth, usually reddish scales; not
        poisonous   **ALDERS**   51
33. Buds not narrowed at base:
    36. Twigs "ringed," or nearly completely encircled by narrow lines (stipule scars) beneath buds:
        37. Buds with only 1 bud scale:
            38. Leaf scars surrounding buds   **SYCAMORE**   42
            38. Leaf scars adjacent to buds   **MAGNOLIAS**   49
        37. Buds with more than 1 bud scale:
            39. Twigs partially encircled by broader leaf (not
                stipule) scars; wood yellow   **YELLOWROOT**   31
            39. Twigs completely ringed by stipule scars:
                40. Buds long-pointed, many-scaled; pith solid
                                   BEECH   57
                40. Buds blunt, 2-scaled; pith chambered
                             TULIP-TREE   42
    36. Twigs without encircling stipule scars:
        41. Buds clustered at enlarged twig tips:
            42. Buds large, distinct, or if small then not woolly
                             OAKS (1–4)   45–48
            42. Buds small, indistinct, white-hairy
                       ROSE-OF-SHARON   42
        41. Buds not clustered at twig tips:
            43. Leaf scars large, triangular or shield-shaped;
                twigs stout; trees:
                44. End buds true:
                    45. Pith chambered; buds woolly **WALNUTS**   27
                    45. Pith continuous; buds hairy or hairless
                         HICKORIES (1), (2) 28, 29
                44. End buds false; buds woolly:
                    46. Buds sunken in bark, often one above the
                        other   **COFFEE-TREE**   31
                    46. Buds not sunken, 1 per leaf scar:
                      47. Leaf scars 3-lobed; bundle scars in 3
                        groups   **CHINABERRY** (31)
                    47. Leaf scars deeply triangular; bundle
                      scars scattered **TREE-OF-HEAVEN**   27
            43. Leaf scars small or narrow; twigs stout or not;
                trees or shrubs:
                48. Side buds hidden beneath nearly circular
                    leaf scars   **FRAGRANT SUMAC**   25

Division D (contd.)   *Name*   *Plate*

48. Side buds not so hidden:
  49. Leaf scars nearly encircling twigs; wood yellow
                                        YELLOWROOT   31
  49. Leaf scars restricted to half the twig circumference or
  less; wood rarely yellow (see Yellowwood):
    50. Buds nearly or completely surrounded by leaf scars:
      51. Buds completely surrounded by leaf scars; bark
      very tough and leathery   **LEATHERWOOD**   59
      51. Buds nearly surrounded by deeply U- or V-shaped
      leaf scars; bark normal:
        52. Bundle scars usually 5, projecting; sap not
        milky; wood of twigs yellow **YELLOWWOOD**   30
        52. Bundle scars more than 5, not projecting;
        sap milky; wood of twigs not yellow **SUMACS**   26
    50. Buds located above leaf scars:
      53. End buds without scales and much larger than
      side ones; buds wine-red   **PAWPAWS**   59
      53. Buds scaly:
        54. Visible bud scales only 2–3:
          55. Twigs stout, relatively inflexible; end
          buds false:
            56. Leaf scars 3-lobed   **CHINABERRY**   (31)
            56. Leaf scars crescent-shaped; *poisonous*
                          POISON SUMAC   26
          55. Twigs slender, flexible; end buds true or
          false:
            57. Pith partitioned near each leaf scar:
              58. Twigs smooth or shreddy; mostly
              vines   **GRAPES** (1), (2)   34, 35
              58. Twigs with sandpapery surfaces;
              shrub or tree **PAPER-MULBERRY**   43
            57. Pith solid:
              59. Leaf scars narrow; bundle scars
              in a line; end buds true
                        MOUNTAIN-ASHES   27
              59. Leaf scars oval or triangular;
              bundle scars not in a line; end
              buds false:
                60. Buds red or green, usually
                sharp; inner bark fibrous
                        BASSWOODS   43
                60. Buds brownish, usually blunt;
                inner bark weak **CHESTNUTS**   57
        54. Buds with 4 or more visible scales:
          61. Stems very long-bristly or bristly-hairy;
          end buds true **BRISTLY SARSAPARILLA**   24
          61. Stems not bristly, though some hairy:
            62. End buds true; twigs with lines lead-
            ing from leaf scars   **NINEBARK**   42
            62. End buds false; twigs not lined:
              63. Bud scales in 2 rows; sap milky
                        MULBERRIES   43
              63. Bud scales not in 2 rows or lower
              2 paired; sap clear **HAZELNUTS**   51

DIVISION E

Upright trees and shrubs with nonthorny twigs and leaf scars
with 3 bundle scars (see Division D for plants with
numerous bundle scars collected in 3 groups)

	Name	Plate

64. Pith chambered:
  65. Twigs stout; leaf scars large, shield-shaped   **WALNUTS**   27
  65. Twigs slender; leaf scars small, not shield-shaped:
    66. Twigs green; fruits small dry pods in clusters; shrub   **SWEET-SPIRES**   59
    66. Twigs brownish; fruits berrylike; trees:
      67. End buds false; fruits dry when ripe **HACKBERRIES**   43
      67. End buds true; fruits fleshy   **SOUR-GUMS**   59
64. Pith continuous:
  68. Buds without scales; hairy:
    69. Buds stalked, with slender bases:
      70. Fruit pods in short clumps   **WITCH-HAZELS**   57
      70. Fruit pods in long clusters   **WITCH-ALDER**   (57)
    69. Buds not stalked   **BUCKTHORNS**   58
  68. Buds with 1 or more scales:
    71. Twigs with small yellow resin-dots evident (use lens):
      72. Buds short, blunt   **WAXMYRTLES**   57
      72. Buds long, slender   **CURRANTS**   41
    71. Twigs without resin-dots (use lens):
      73. Leaf scars like a narrow line half encircling twigs;
      plants bramblelike   **ROSES**   23
      73. Leaf scars wider; plants not bramblelike:
        74. End buds true:
          75. Buds with 1–3 visible scales (or if 4 scales,
          then buds somewhat long-pointed):
            76. Buds with single caplike scale
            WILLOWS (1), (2)   **55, 56**
            76. Buds with more than 1 scale:
              77. Buds narrowed conspicuously at
              base (stalked); bud scales 2–3,
              reddish   **ALDERS**   51
              77. Buds not stalked (sessile):
                78. Older branchlets with leaf-
                scar-crowded spur branches;
                bud scales 2–3, not paired:
                  79. Bark usually with narrow
                  cross stripes   **BIRCHES**   52
                  79. Bark not striped   **APPLES**   58
                78. Older branchlets without spur
                branches; bud scales 2–4, paired
                (see also Bladder-senna, p. 144)
                  80. Bud scales 2; leaf scars
                  crowded toward twig tips
        ALTERNATE-LEAF DOGWOOD   59
                  80. Bud scales 2 or 4, somewhat
                  long-pointed; leaf scars not
                  crowded toward twig tips
                  SMOKETREE   59
         75. Buds with 4 or more visible scales:

Division E (contd.)   *Name*   *Plate*

81. Buds ball-shaped, some thorns over 1″ usually present
                                        HAWTHORNS   39
81. Buds longer than broad:
  82. Buds with lowermost scale immediately above leaf
    scar; bark often smooth and greenish on young
    trunks and branches; trees   **POPLARS**   44
  82. Lowest bud scale not so aligned:
    83. Branchlets often with corky "wings"; bud scales
      hairy-fringed; tree   **SWEETGUM**   42
    83. Branchlets without corky wings:
      84. Twigs nearly encircled by narrow stipule scars
        near leaf scars; buds very long, slim   **BEECH**   57
      84. Twigs without encircling stipule scars:
        85. End buds much larger than side buds
          and clustered at twig tips; s. Missouri
          southward   **CORKWOOD**   59
        85. End buds about same size as side buds,
          clustered only in some cherries:
          86. Twigs with obvious long lines lead-
            ing from each end of the leaf scar
            and bark papery, shreddy:
            87. Twigs with 3 lines descending
              from each leaf scar; yellow resin-
              dots lacking   **NINEBARK**   42
            87. Twigs with only 2 descending
              lines or if with 3 then with resin-
              dots (use lens)   **CURRANTS**   41
          86. Twigs without long (but sometimes
            with short) lines from leaf scars; bark
            not papery or shreddy:
            88. Buds reddish, slender:
              89. Bud scales often twisted with
                black tips (use lens); shrubs
                or small trees **JUNEBERRIES**   54
              89. Bud scales not twisted but
                with tips notched (use lens);
                shrubs   **CHOKEBERRIES**   58
            88. Buds not reddish or, if so, then
              stout, or at least not slender:
              90. Older bark usually with nar-
                row cross stripes; trees or
                shrubs   **CHERRIES**   53
             90. Older bark not cross-striped:
              91. Bud scales paired, 2–4
             B.-SENNA, SMOKETREE   (30), 59
              91. Bud scales not paired:
                92. Leaf scars narrow;
                trees or shrubs
                      APPLES   38, 58
              92. Leaf scars deeper;
                northern shrub
                MOUNTAIN ALDER   51
74. End buds false:
  93. Buds with 2–3 visible scales:

Division E (contd.)   Name   Plate

94. Twigs stout; leaf scars large; buds small, round; trees (see also Hoptree and Albizzia, below):

95. Buds often several at each leaf scar, 1 above another:

96. Buds imbedded in bark; twigs whitish; pith pink
                              COFFEE-TREE   31

96. Buds raised; twigs not whitish; pith whitish
                      WESTERN SOAPBERRY   (30)

95. Buds single; raised; leaf scar 3-lobed; pith white
                              CHINABERRY   (31)

94. Twigs slender; leaf scars smaller; buds various; trees and shrubs:

97. Broken twigs spicy-aromatic; buds clustered
                              SPICEBUSHES   59

97. Broken twigs not aromatic:

98. Leaf scars U-shaped; buds hairy   **HOPTREE**   25

98. Leaf scars otherwise:

99. Twigs deeply grooved; occurring at edges of salt water   **GROUNDSEL-TREE**   58

99. Twigs not grooved; mostly on uplands:

100. Twigs usually red or green; inner bark tough and fibrous   **BASSWOODS**   43

100. Not as above:

101. Buds as wide as long   **ALBIZZIA**   31

101. Buds considerably longer than broad:

102. Pith irregular in cross section
                              CHESTNUTS   57

102. Pith nearly circular or oval in cross section **INDIGOBUSHES**   30

93. Buds with 4 or more visible scales:

103. Broken twigs with spicy odor; twigs hairy; low shrub
                              SWEETFERN   57

103. Broken twigs not spicy-aromatic:

104. Buds short, blunt, ball-like; plant usually long-thorny   **HAWTHORNS**   39

104. Buds mostly longer, not ball-like; not thorny:

105. Dry clustered remains of tiny fruit capsules usually present; twigs and buds hairy; low shrubs   **NEW JERSEY TEAS**   43

105. Fruit remains, if present, larger, not capsular:

106. Leaf scars raised with 2 obvious longish lines leading from sides of their bases:

107. Leaf scars with upper edge often fringed; some buds narrow at base; a 3rd line sometimes leading from centers of leaf-scar bases   **REDBUD**   43

107. Leaf scars not fringed; buds not stalked; only 2 lines:

108. Buds narrow, often sharp; broken twigs with sour odor; trunk bark often with cross stripes   **PLUMS**   38, 53

108. Buds broad, mostly blunt; broken twigs without sour

Division E (contd.)   *Name*   *Plate*
   odor; trunk bark not striped   **APPLES, PEARS**   38, 58
106. Leaf scars not raised or at least without obvious lines leading from them:
    109. Scales of buds in regular vertical rows:
       110. Bud scales in 2 rows; buds round in cross section;
some species with "winged" branchlets; trunk
ridged   **ELMS**   50
       110. Bud scales in 4 rows; buds 4-angled; branchlets
not winged; trunk smooth, "muscular" **IRONWOOD** 51
    109. Scales of buds not in regular rows; buds round in
cross section:
       111. Buds pressed tightly against twigs; pith some-
times chambered   **HACKBERRIES** 43
       111. Buds not tightly pressed; pith continuous:
          112. Leaf scars in 2 regular rows along twigs:
             113. Buds sharp; scales finely grooved (use
lens); trunk scaly; tree   **HORNBEAM** 51
             113. Buds blunt; bud scales not grooved
(use lens); stems not scaly; shrubs
HAZELNUTS 51
          112. Leaf scars less regularly placed:
             114. Bud scales blackish, dark **BUCKTHORNS** 58
             114. Bud scales brown, lighter   **PLUMS**   38, 53

DIVISION F

*Upright trees and shrubs with nonthorny twigs and with
leaf scars either lacking or with 1 bundle scar*

115. Leaf scars lacking:
    116. Trees with fibrous bark; twigs and needlelike foliage
dropping in winter leaving no leaf scars; fruits ball-
shaped cones   **BALDCYPRESS**   3
    116. Shrubs, rambling and thornless with thin flaky bark;
leaves breaking off above base, 3 bundle scars evident
only if leaf base is cut transversely
FLOWERING RASPBERRIES   42
115. Leaf scars present, with 1 bundle scar:
    117. Leaves needlelike, clustered, falling in winter; "warty"
spur branches present; fruits cones   **LARCHES**   2
    117. Leaves not needlelike but falling in winter; fruits not
cones:
       118. Pith chambered:
          119. Buds with only 2 visible scales, blackish
PERSIMMON 68
          119. Buds with more than 2 visible scales:
             120. Bark white-striped; buds reddish
SILVERBELL-TREE 67
             120. Bark not striped; buds dark
SWEETLEAF 67
       118. Pith continuous:
          121. Twigs covered with silver and brown scales
SILVERBERRIES 68

Division F (contd.)   *Name*   *Plate*

121. Twigs without such scales:
    122. Broken twigs with very tough leathery bark **DAPHNE** 68
    122. Twig bark not especially tough:
        123. Buds without scales **SNOWBELLS** 67
        123. Buds covered by scales:
            124. Broken twigs spicy-aromatic:
                125. In southern swamps; twigs not branched **PONDSPICE** 68
                125. In uplands, widespread; twigs often branched **SASSAFRAS** 43
            124. Broken twigs not spicy-aromatic:
                126. End buds false:
                    127. Twigs covered with numerous, fine, granular speckles (sometimes partly obscured by hairiness); twigs usually green or reddish; buds mostly with 2–3 visible scales; shrubs **BLUEBERRIES** 62
                    127. Twigs not warty-granular:
                        128. Buds with 2 visible scales:
                            129. Buds blackish; pith spongy or chambered **PERSIMMON** 68
                            129. Buds not blackish; pith continuous:
                                130. Fruits fleshy berries; twigs hairy or flattened and ridged or older bark shreddy **HUCKLEBERRIES** 63
                                130. Fruits dry capsules; twigs neither hairy nor flattened and ridged; older bark not shreddy:
                                    131. Buds blunt **ZENOBIA** (68)
                                    131. Buds mostly sharp **MALEBERRY** 66
                        128. Buds, 3 or more visible scales:
                            132. Leaf scars conspicuously raised, often with descending lines at sides; twigs very slender; clustered small dry fruits common at twig tips **SPIREAS** 60
                            132. Leaf scars not conspicuously raised, without lines at sides:
                                133. Tree; buds small; ball-shaped; fruits small dry capsules **SOURWOOD** 66

Division F (contd.)   *Name*   *Plate*
  133. Shrubs:
      134. Twigs usually with reddish, catkinlike bud clus-
          ters; fruits dry capsules   **SWEETBELLS** **66**
      134. Twigs without catkinlike bud clusters:
          135. Buds ball-shaped or conical; fruits dry cap-
              sules:
              136. Twigs grayish   **STAGGERBUSH** **68**
              136. Twigs reddish   **ZENOBIA** **(68)**
          135. Buds longer; fruits not capsules:
              137. Southwestern; fruits beanlike pods
                         PRAIRIE ACACIA **(31)**
              137. Widespread; fruits fleshy berries
                         HUCKLEBERRIES **63**
126. End buds true:
      138. End buds much larger than side buds; buds usually
          clustered toward twig tips; side buds with 2–3 scales;
          shrubs:
          139. Outer bud scales of end buds about as long as
              buds, hairy, often falling early **PEPPERBUSHES** **66**
          139. Outer bud scales shorter than buds, not falling
              early:
              140. Branchlets with shreddy bark **MINNIEBUSH** **68**
              140. Branchlets with tight bark   **AZALEAS** **64**
      138. End buds about size of side buds:
          141. Spur branches usually present; very tiny,
              black, sharp stipules flanking each leaf scar
              (use lens); buds often clustered toward twig
              tips; trees or shrubs   **HOLLIES** **61**
          141. Spur branches and stipules of this type
              absent; buds variable; shrubs:
              142. Buds with 2–3 visible scales:
                 143. Twigs angled with long ridges:
                    144. Usually scrambling, vinelike
                       MATRIMONY-VINES **37**
                    144. Upright shrubs
                       WHIN, ANDRACHNE **(68)**
                 143. Twigs neither angled nor ridged:
                    145. Buds hairy, tapering; Vir-
                      ginia southward
                  SILKY-, MOUNTAIN-CAMELLIAS **67**
                    145. Buds hairless
                        BLADDER-SENNA **(30)**
                        MOUNTAIN-HOLLY **68**
              142. Buds with 4 or more visible scales:
                 146. Twigs sharply ridged, green, often
                    dying at tips:
                 147. Dense bushy shrub
                        SCOTCH BROOM **25**
                 147. Weak slender shrub
                        BICOLOR LESPEDEZA **(25)**
              146. Twigs not ridged:
                 148. Buds clasped at base by
                    raised leaf scars and stipules
                 SHRUBBY CINQUEFOIL, etc. **30**

Division F (contd.)   *Name*   *Plate*

148. Buds not clasped at base:

    149. Twigs very slender, often tipped with flat or cone-shaped clusters of small dry fruits; clumped shrubs

                                      SPIREAS   **60**

    149. Twigs less slender; clusters of dry fruits may be present:

        150. Buds large, greenish; plants parasitic on roots of other shrubs or trees; fruits large, nutlike; Appalachians **OILNUT**   **68**

        150. Buds small, not greenish; plants not parasitic; fruits small, dry capsules   **NEW JERSEY TEAS**   **43**

APPENDIX C

Key to Trees
in Leafy Condition

FOR USE only in identifying specimens at least 25 feet tall, thus excluding shrubs. Plate numbers in parentheses indicate that the plants are included but not illustrated in connection with the plate specified.

	Name	Plate

1. Leaves needlelike or very small and scalelike; mostly cone-bearers (Section I):
   2. Leaves long, needlelike:
      3. Needles in bundles or groups along twigs
                                          PINES, LARCHES **1, 2**
      3. Needles occurring singly:
         4. Needles blunt, flat   **FIRS, etc.** **3**
         4. Needles sharp:
            5. Needles 4-sided, neither in opposing pairs nor in whorls of 3   **SPRUCES** **4**
            5. Needles 3-sided; either in opposing pairs or in whorls of 3   **JUNIPERS** **5**
   2. Leaves very small and scalelike, hugging twigs:
      6. Leaves blunt; conifers   **WHITE CEDARS** **5**
      6. Leaves sharp; a flowering tree   **TAMARISK** **(6)**
1. Leaves broad; flowering plants:
   7. Leaves opposite:
      8. Leaves compound (Section II):
         9. Leaves with only 3 leaflets, or twigs large, pithy
                                BLADDERNUT, etc. **8**
         9. Leaves with 5–11 (rarely 3) leaflets; twigs if large, not pithy:
            10. Leaves feather-compound:
               11. Twigs neither densely velvety nor white-powdered (see also Japanese Corktree, p. 52)   **ASHES (1)** **9**
               11. Twigs either densely velvety or white-powdered   **ASHES (2), etc.** **10**
            10. Leaves fan-compound   **BUCKEYES** **11**
      8. Leaves simple (Section III):
         12. Leaves not toothed:
            13. Leaves not heart-shaped:
               14. Leaves with veins that strongly tend to follow leaf edges   **DOGWOODS** **15**
               14. Leaves with veins only slightly if at all following leaf edges:
                   15. Leaves thick, leathery   **DEVILWOOD** **(16)**
                   15. Leaves thin, not leathery **FRINGE-TREE** **16**

                                               Name   *Plate*
    13. Leaves heart-shaped   **PRINCESS-TREE, etc.** 18
  12. Leaves toothed:
    16. Leaves not lobed:
      17. Twigs 4-lined or buds globular
              MISCELLANEOUS 19
      17. Twigs not 4-lined; buds not globular
              VIBURNUMS (1) 20
    16. Leaves lobed   **MAPLES** 22
7. Leaves alternate:
  18. Leaves compound (Section IV):
    19. Twigs thorny   **LOCUSTS, etc.** 24
    19. Twigs thornless:
      20. Leaves only once-compound (*leaflets* not divided):
        21. Leaflets 3   **HOPTREE** 25
        21. Leaflets more than 3:
          22. Leaflets toothed (in Tree-of-Heaven with
             only 1 basal pair of glandular teeth):
            23. Leaflets 11–41 (rarely 7 or 9):
               24. Buds nearly hidden beneath leaf-
                  stalk bases; sap often milky **SUMACS** 26
               24. Buds easily visible (or in Tree-of-
                  Heaven partly hidden):
                  25. Buds white-woolly, brown-
                      woolly, or red-gummy
                        WALNUTS, etc. 27
                  25. Buds yellow-hairy or brown-
                      hairless
                  PECAN, WATER HICKORY 28
             23. Leaflets 5–9:
               26. Leaflets mostly 5–7: **HICKORIES (1)** 28
               26. Leaflets mostly 7–9: **HICKORIES (2)** 29
           22. Leaflets not toothed:
             27. Bundle scars more than 5   **SUMACS** 26
             27. Bundle scars 5   **YELLOWWOOD** 30
      20. Leaves twice- or thrice-compound
              COFFEE-TREE, etc. 31
  18. Leaves simple (Section V):
    28. Twigs thorny:
      29. Thorns less than 1″, or if longer then buds not
        ball-shaped   **OSAGE-ORANGE, etc.** 38
      29. Thorns mostly over 1″, buds ball-shaped
                  HAWTHORNS 39
    28. Twigs thornless:
      30. Leaves lobed:
        31. Leaves fan-lobed:
          32. Plants with all leaves lobed
                  MISCELLANEOUS 42
         32. Plants with some leaves not lobed
                  MULBERRIES, etc. 43
        31. Leaves feather-lobed   **OAKS (1), (2)** 45, 46
      30. Leaves not lobed:
        33. Leaf scars with more than 1 bundle scar:
          34. Leaves mostly heart-shaped or triangular,
             with 3–5 stout veins meeting near leaf base:

35. Bundle scars 3; leaves toothed; bark of young trunks usually smooth whitish- or greenish-yellow; lowermost bud scale in outside position squarely above leaf scar
POPLARS 44

35. Bundle scars 1 to many, or if 3, then leaves not toothed or pith usually chambered; bark and bud scales not as above **MISCELLANEOUS** 43

34. Leaves neither heart-shaped nor triangular, or if so, with only a single main vein:

  36. Twigs with clustered (true) end buds:

    37. Acorns or their cups usually present on twigs or on ground; bundle scars 4 or more   **OAKS** (3), (4) **47, 48**

    37. Acorns absent; bundle scars 3:

      38. Leafstalks with glands; broken twigs with peculiar sour odor; trunk often with narrow cross stripes   **FIRE CHERRY** 53

      38. Without these characteristics; swamps from sw. Missouri southward only   **CORKWOOD** 59

  36. Twigs with single end buds (either true or false end buds):

    39. Twigs with completely encircling lines or rings (stipule scars):

      40. Leaves not toothed   **MAGNOLIAS** 49

      40. Leaves toothed   **BEECH** 57

    39. Twigs without completely encircling lines:

      41. Leaves not toothed and not definitely wavy-edged:

        42. Buds with a single scale; leaves mostly narrow   **WILLOWS** (1), (2) **55, 56**

        42. Buds without scales or with more than 1 scale; leaves various:

          43. Buds without scales:

            44. Leaves usually under 6″ long, more or less elliptic or egg-shaped
BUCKTHORNS 58

            44. Leaves usually over 6″ long, wedge-shaped   **PAWPAWS** 59

          43. Buds with 2 or more scales:

            45. Leaf bases uneven
UPLAND HACKBERRY (43)

            45. Leaf bases even **MISCELLANEOUS** 59

      41. Leaves with definite teeth or distinctly wavy-edged:

        46. Leaves with distinct double teeth:

          47. Leaf bases mostly uneven, 1 side much lower than other; buds many-scaled, scales in 2 even rows:

            48. Leaves quite long-pointed and usually triangular   **HACKBERRIES** 43

            48. Leaves not long-pointed, mostly egg-shaped   **ELMS** 50

          47. Leaf bases mostly even, both sides similar or only slightly uneven:

            49. Buds with 2–3 scales, neither hairy

Name   Plate

nor narrowed at base; older bark often conspicuously
streaked horizontally **BIRCHES** 52
49. Buds with 2 or more scales, hairy or narrowed at
base:
    50. Leafstalks near leaf base without glands; older
    bark not, or slightly, streaked **IRONWOOD, etc.** 51
    50. Leafstalks near leaf base with small paired glands;
    older bark usually streaked horizontally **CHERRIES** 53
46. Leaves with single teeth or definite wavy edges:
    51. Bark of upper branches and young trunks often
    smooth and whitish- or greenish-yellow: lowermost
    bud scales located in outside position squarely above
    leaf scar; leafstalk often much flattened **POPLARS** 44
    51. Bark not of this type; bud scales, if present, not as
    above; leafstalks not much flattened:
        52. Leafstalks mostly with pair of minute swollen
        glands near leaf bases; broken twigs with unique
        strong odor; older bark often striped horizontally
        CHERRIES 53
        52. Leafstalks without glands; twigs without peculiar
        "cherry" odor; older bark striped or not:
            53. Buds long, slender, the several reddish scales
            with tiny dark tips and often twisted; trunk
            bark smooth and often twisted **JUNEBERRIES** 54
            53. Buds with a single scale; leaves usually long
            and slender **WILLOWS** (1), (2) 55, 56
            53. Buds otherwise:
                54. Leaves spicy-scented when crushed, yel-
                low resin-dotted (use lens) **BAYBERRIES** 57
                54. Leaves otherwise:
                    55. End buds false; southern swamps
                    WATER-ELM 50
                    55. End buds true; uplands **CHESTNUTS** 57
33. Leaf scars with only 1 bundle scar:
    56. Leaves leathery, evergreen:
        57. End buds true; spur branches usually present; tiny
        black thornlike stipules flanking each leaf scar (use
        lens) **HOLLIES** 61
        57. End buds false; spur branches absent; stipules of
        above type lacking:
            58. Fruits fleshy berries **FARKLEBERRY** 63
            58. Fruits dry capsules **RHODODENDRONS, etc.** 65
    56. Leaves thin, not evergreen:
        59. Spur branches usually present; tiny black thornlike
        stipules flanking leaf scars (use lens); end buds true;
        fruits fleshy; leaves toothed **HOLLIES** 61
        59. Spur branches and stipules of above type absent;
        end buds true or false; fruits dry or fleshy; leaves
        toothed or not:
            60. Pith chambered or buds without scales:
                61. Buds with 2 scales, dark; trunk bark divided
                into small squares **PERSIMMON** 68
                61. Buds and bark otherwise
                MISCELLANEOUS (1) 67

Name   Plate

60. Pith not chambered and buds scaly:

    62. Leaves toothed   **SOURWOOD**   66

    62. Leaves not toothed:

        63. Leaves mostly triangular, with 3–5 main veins meet-
ing near leaf base   **NEW JERSEY TEAS**   43

        63. Leaves otherwise   **MISCELLANEOUS**   68

APPENDIX D

Key to Trees
in Leafless Condition

FOR USE only in identifying specimens at least 25 feet tall, thus excluding shrubs. Plate numbers in parentheses indicate that the plants are included but not illustrated in connection with the plate specified.

	Name	Plate

1. Leaf scars lacking, twigs and needlelike foliage dropping in winter, leaving no leaf or bundle scars; fruits ball-shaped cones **BALDCYPRESS** 3
1. Leaf scars present:
  2. Leaf scars opposite (Sections II and IV):
    3. Leaf scars with 4 to many bundle scars, often large:
      4. Central bud missing, a single pair of buds present at twig tip):
        5. Leaf scars 4-sided to crescent-shaped **BLADDERNUT, etc.** 8
        5. Leaf scars circular or nearly so **PRINCESS-TREE, etc.** 18
      4. 1 or 3 buds present at twig tip:
        6. Twigs moderately slender; end bud of moderate size, with only 2–3 pairs of scales; buds and twigs hairy or hairless:
          7. Twigs neither velvety-hairy nor white-powdered (see also Japanese Corktree, p. 52) **ASHES (1)** 9
          7. Twigs velvety-hairy or white-powdered **ASHES (2)** 10
        6. Twigs stout; end bud often very large, with many scales, and often gummy; buds and twigs mostly hairless **BUCKEYES** 11
    3. Leaf scars with 1 or 3 bundle scars:
      8. Bundle scar 1:
        9. Twigs bright green or red, 4-lined **BURNINGBUSH, etc.** 19
        9. Twigs more somberly colored:
          10. Buds ball-shaped **FORESTIERAS** 19
          10. Buds longer than broad **FRINGE-TREE** 16
      8. Bundle scars 3:
        11. Upper leaf scars meeting in raised points **ASHLEAF MAPLE** 10
        11. Upper leaf scars not meeting in raised points:
          12. Leaf scars much raised above twigs; buds hidden beneath leaf scars in 1 species **DOGWOODS** 15
          12. Leaf scars not much raised; buds visible:

Name   *Plate*

13. Central bud missing, a single pair of buds at twig tips
  BLADDERNUT, etc.   8
13. 1 or 3 buds present at twig tips:
  14. Buds with a single caplike scale   **BASKET WILLOW**   56
  14. Buds with 2 or more scales:
    15. Bud scales 2:
      16. Fruits dry, winged; twigs hairy or trunk bark
        white-striped   **MAPLES**   22
      16. Fruits fleshy; twigs not hairy; trunk not white-
        striped:
        17. Leaf scars deeply U-shaped
          JAPANESE CORKTREE   (10)
        17. Leaf scars not U-shaped   **VIBURNUMS** (1)   20
    15. Bud scales 4 or more   **MAPLES**   22
2. Leaf scars alternate (Sections I, III, and IV):
  18. Twigs thorny or bristly:
    19. Leaf scars with 1 or with more than 3 bundle scars
      OSAGE-ORANGE, etc.   38
    19. Leaf scars with 3 bundle scars:
      20. Thorns in pairs or buds hidden beneath or sur-
        rounded by leaf scars   **LOCUSTS**, etc.   24
      20. Thorns not paired; buds above leaf scars
        HAWTHORNS   39
  18. Twigs thornless:
    21. Leaf scars with 4 or more bundle scars:
      22. Buds narrowed at base (stalked):
        23. Buds without scales, red-brown, hairy, end
          buds longer   **PAWPAWS**   59
        23. Buds with 2–3 smooth, usually reddish, scales,
          end buds not conspicuously larger than side
          buds   **ALDERS**   51
      22. Buds not conspicuously narrowed at base:
        24. Twigs completely encircled by narrow lines
          (stipule scars) beneath buds:
          25. Buds with only 1 bud scale or none:
            26. Leaf scars entirely surrounding buds
              SYCAMORE   42
            26. Leaf scars, buds adjacent   **MAGNOLIAS**   49
          25. Buds with more than 1 bud scale:
            27. Buds long-pointed, many-scaled, not
              aromatic   **BEECH**   57
            27. Buds blunt, 2-scaled, spicy-scented
              when crushed   **TULIP-TREE**   42
        24. Twigs without encircling stipule scars:
          28. Buds clustered at enlarged twig tips
            OAKS (1)-(4)   45-48
          28. Buds not clustered at twig tips:
            29. Leaf scars large, triangular or shield-
              shaped; twigs stout:
              30. End buds true:
                31. Pith chambered; buds woolly
                  WALNUTS   27
                31. Pith continuous; buds hairy or
                  not   **HICKORIES** (1), (2)   28, 29

Name   *Plate*

30. End buds false; buds woolly:

    32. Buds sunken in bark, often one above the other
                                 COFFEE-TREE   31

    32. Buds not sunken, 1 per leaf scar:

        33. Leaf scar 3-lobed; bundle scars in 3 groups
                                 CHINABERRY   (31)

        33. Leaf scars deeply triangular; bundle scars
             scattered   **TREE-OF-HEAVEN**   27

29. Leaf scars small or narrow; twigs stout or not:

    34. Twigs sandpaper-rough; pith partitioned near each
        leaf scar   **PAPER-MULBERRY**   43

    34. Twigs and pith not as above:

        35. Buds nearly encircled by U- or V-like leaf scars:

            36. Bundle scars usually 5; sap not milky
                               YELLOWWOOD   30

            36. Bundle scars more than 5; sap milky
                                 SUMACS   26

        35. Buds located above leaf scar:

            37. Buds with 4 or more visible scales; sap milky
                               MULBERRIES   43

            37. Buds with only 2–3 visible scales; sap not
               milky:

                38. Leaf scars narrow; bundle scars in a line;
                    end buds true   **MOUNTAIN-ASHES**   27

                38. Leaf scars oval or triangular; bundle scars
                    not in a line; end buds false:

                    39. Twigs stout   **CHINABERRY**   (31)

                    39. Twigs slender:

                        40. Buds red or green, usually moder-
                          ately sharp; inner bark fibrous
                                   BASSWOODS   43

                      40. Buds brownish, usually blunt;
                        inner bark weak   **CHESTNUTS**   57

21. Leaf scars with less than 4 bundle scars:

    41. Leaf scars with 3 bundle scars (*for alternate 41* see
        p. 400):

        42. Pith chambered:

            43. Twigs stout; leaf scars large, shield-shaped
                               WALNUTS   27

            43. Twigs slender; leaf scars small, not shield-
               shaped:

                44. End buds false; fruits dry when ripe
                               HACKBERRIES   43

                44. End buds true; fruits fleshy   **SOUR-GUMS**   59

        42. Pith continuous:

            45. Buds without scales, hairy:

                46. Buds narrowed at base   **WITCH-HAZELS**   57
                46. Buds not stalked   **BUCKTHORNS**   58

            45. Buds with 1 or more scales:

                47. Twigs with small yellow resin-dots evident
                    (use lens)   **WAXMYRTLES**   57

                47. Twigs without resin-dots (use lens):

                    48. End buds true:

                      49. Buds with 1–3 visible scales:

Name   *Plate*

50. Buds with a single caplike scale   **WILLOWS** (1), (2)   **55, 56**
50. Buds with more than 1 bud scale:
  51. Buds stalked, reddish; woody conelike catkins usually
    present   **ALDERS**   **51**
  51. Buds without narrow, constricted base:
    52. Leaf scars crowded toward twig tips; bud scales
      2, paired   **ALTERNATE-LEAF DOGWOOD**   **59**
    52. Leaf scars distributed more evenly along twigs:
      53. Buds long-pointed, with 2–4 paired scales;
        spur branches absent   **SMOKETREE**   **59**
      53. Buds blunt or merely sharp, with 2–3 scales;
        spur branches often present:
        54. Buds hairless; young bark usually with
          prominent horizontal stripes   **BIRCHES**   **52**
        54. Buds usually hairy or woolly; bark not
          striped   **APPLES**   **58**
49. Buds with 4 or more visible scales:
  55. Buds ball-shaped; long thorns usually present
                                             HAWTHORNS   **39**
  55. Buds longer:
    56. Buds clustered at twig tips:
      57. End buds much larger than side buds; s. Missouri
        southward   **CORKWOOD**   **59**
      57. End buds about same size as side buds; wide-
        spread   **FIRE CHERRY**   **53**
    56. Buds not clustered at twig tips:
      58. Buds with the lowermost scale centered directly
        above leaf scar; bark often smooth and greenish
        on young trunks and branches; trees   **POPLARS**   **44**
      58. Buds with lowermost scale not centered directly
        above leaf scar:
        59. Buds quite long and slender:
          60. Twigs nearly encircled by narrow lines
            near leaf scars; tree   **BEECH**   **57**
          60. Twigs without encircling stipule scars;
            shrubs or small trees:
            61. Buds brownish; bud scales paired
                                         SMOKETREE   **59**
            61. Buds reddish; bud scales not paired:
              62. Bud scales often twisted, with
                black unnotched tips; 2nd bud
                scale usually less than half length
                of bud; small trees or shrubs
                                     JUNEBERRIES   **54**
              62. Bud scales not twisted, with
                notched undarkened tips (use
                lens); 2nd bud scale about half
                length of bud or longer; shrubs
                                   CHOKEBERRIES   **58**
        59. Buds relatively short and stout, blunt to
          sharp but not long-pointed:
          63. Branchlets usually with corky "wings";
            bud scales hairy-fringed (use lens); tree
                                         SWEETGUM   **42**

Name   Plate

63. Branchlets and buds otherwise:
    64. Older bark usually with narrow cross stripes; broken twigs with unique almondlike odor
        CHERRIES   53
    64. Older bark not cross-striped; broken twigs without special odor   **APPLES**   38, 58
48. End buds false:
    65. Buds with 2–3 visible scales:
        66. Twigs stout, relatively inflexible; leaf scars large; buds small, round:
            67. Buds often several at each leaf scar, above one another:
                68. Buds imbedded in bark; twigs whitish; pith pink   **COFFEE-TREE**   31
                68. Buds raised; twigs not whitish; pith whitish
                    WESTERN SOAPBERRY   (30)
            67. Buds single, raised; leaf scar 3-lobed; pith white
                CHINABERRY   (31)
        66. Twigs slender, relatively flexible; leaf scars smaller; buds various:
            69. Leaf scars U-shaped; buds hairy   **HOPTREE**   25
            69. Leaf scars not U-shaped; buds hairy or not:
                70. Inner bark of branches tough and fibrous; twigs mostly red or green   **BASSWOODS**   43
                70. Inner bark of branches not especially fibrous; twigs brownish:
                    71. Buds as wide as long   **ALBIZZIA**   31
                    71. Buds longer than broad   **CHESTNUTS**   57
    65. Buds with 4 or more visible scales.
        72. Buds short, blunt, ball-shaped   **HAWTHORNS**   39
        72. Buds mostly longer, not ball-shaped:
            73. Leaf scars raised, with 2 obvious lines leading down from sides of their bases:
                74. Leaf scars with upper edge often fringed with hairs; some buds narrow at base; a 3rd line sometimes leading from centers of leaf-scar bases   **REDBUD**   43
                74. Leaf scars not fringed; buds not stalked; only 2 lines present:
                    75. Buds narrow, often sharp; broken twigs with sour odor; trunk bark often with cross stripes   **PLUMS**   38, 53
                    75. Buds broad, mostly blunt; broken twigs without sour odor; trunk bark not striped
                      PEARS   58
            73. Leaf scars not raised, or at least without obvious lines leading from them:
                76. Scales of buds in regular vertical rows:
                  77. Bud scales in 2 rows; buds round in cross section; some species with "winged" branchlets; trunk ridged   **ELMS**   50
                  77. Bud scales in 4 rows; buds 4-angled; branchlets not winged; trunk smooth, gray, "muscular"   **IRONWOOD**   51

Name   *Plate*

76. Scales of buds not in regular rows; buds round in cross section:

    78. Buds pressed tightly against twigs; pith sometimes chambered   **HACKBERRIES**   43

    78. Buds not tightly pressed; pith continuous:

        79. Leaf scars in 2 regular rows along twigs; bud scales finely grooved (use lens)   **HORNBEAM**   51

        79. Leaf scars less regularly placed; bud scales not grooved (use lens)   **PLUMS**   38, 53

41. Leaf scars with 1 bundle scar:

    80. Spur branches usually present:

        81. Fruits fleshy, berrylike; tiny black thornlike stipules flanking leaf scars (use lens)   **HOLLIES**   61

        81. Fruits dry cones   **LARCHES**   2

    80. Spur branches absent; fruits dry or fleshy:

        82. Pith chambered or buds without scales:

            83. Buds with 2 scales, dark; trunk bark divided into small squares   **PERSIMMON**   68

            83. Buds and bark otherwise   **MISCELLANEOUS**   67

        82. Pith not chambered; buds with scales:

            84. Buds with several scales, ball-shaped; fruits dry   **SOURWOOD**   66

            84. Buds with 2 scales, not ball-shaped; fruits fleshy   **PERSIMMON**   68

APPENDIX E

Plant Relationships

ALTHOUGH field identification does not require a knowledge of major classification groups or even of family or scientific names, it is desirable to know the general relationships of the various plants. The following list indicates the family relationships of the genera of woody plants. All are members of the Division Spermatophyta, bearing embryo-containing seeds. The closeness of the relationships of the several families is further indicated by the ordinal, subclass, class, and subdivisional groupings. This classification is the one of Engler and Prantl, which is followed by Fernald (see Preface) and other standard references. All major and many minor botanical subdivisions are based mainly on flower and fruit structures. Family names are those ending in *aceae;* names of the orders are here standardized by use of the ending *ales.*

Subdivision GYMNOSPERMAE

Order CONIFERALES

TAXACEAE:	*Taxus*
PINACEAE:	*Pinus, Larix, Picea, Abies, Tsuga, Taxodium, Chamaecyparis, Thuja, Juniperus*

Subdivision ANGIOSPERMAE

Class MONOCOTYLEDONEAE

Order LILIALES

LILIACEAE:	*Smilax*

Class DICOTYLEDONEAE
Subclass Archichlamydeae

Order SALICALES

SALICACEAE:	*Salix, Populus*

Order MYRICALES

MYRICACEAE:	*Myrica, Comptonia*

Order LEITNERIALES

LEITNERIACEAE:	*Leitneria*

401

Order JUGLANDALES

JUGLANDACEAE: *Juglans, Carya*

Order FAGALES

CORYLACEAE: *Corylus, Ostrya, Carpinus, Betula, Alnus*
FAGACEAE: *Fagus, Castanea, Quercus*

Order URTICALES

ULMACEAE: *Ulmus, Planera, Celtis*
MORACEAE: *Morus, Broussonetia, Maclura*

Order SANTALALES

SANTALACEAE: *Pyrularia, Nestronia, Buckleya*
LORANTHACEAE: *Phoradendron, Arceuthobium*

Order ARISTOLOCHIALES

ARISTOLOCHIACEAE: *Aristolochia*

Order RANALES

RANUNCULACEAE: *Clematis, Xanthorhiza*
BERBERIDACEAE: *Berberis*
MENISPERMACEAE: *Cocculus, Menispermum, Calycocarpum*
MAGNOLIACEAE: *Magnolia, Liriodendron*
CALYCANTHACEAE: *Calycanthus*
ANNONACEAE: *Asimina*
LAURACEAE: *Persea, Sassafras, Litsea, Lindera*

Order ROSALES

SAXIFRAGACEAE: *Philadelphus, Decumaria, Hydrangea, Itea, Ribes*
HAMAMELIDACEAE: *Hamamelis, Fothergilla, Liquidambar*
PLATANACEAE: *Platanus*
ROSACEAE: *Physocarpus, Spiraea, Pyrus, Amelanchier, Crataegus, Cotoneaster, Potentilla, Dryas, Rubus, Rosa, Prunus*
LEGUMINOSAE: *Acacia, Albizzia, Gymnocladus, Gleditsia, Cercis, Cladrastis, Genista, Cytisus, Ulex, Amorpha, Robinia, Wisteria, Colutea, Lespedeza*

Order GERANIALES

RUTACEAE: *Xanthoxylum, Phellodendron, Ptelea, Poncirus*
SIMAROUBACEAE: *Ailanthus*
MELIACEAE: *Melia*
EUPHORBIACEAE: *Andrachne*

Order SAPINDALES

EMPETRACEAE: *Empetrum, Corema*
ANACARDIACEAE: *Cotinus, Rhus*

Order Sapindales (contd.)

CYRILLACEAE:	*Cyrilla*
AQUIFOLIACEAE:	*Ilex, Nemopanthus*
CELASTRACEAE:	*Euonymus, Pachistima, Celastrus*
STAPHYLACEAE:	*Staphylea*
ACERACEAE:	*Acer*
HIPPOCASTANACEAE:	*Aesculus*
SAPINDACEAE:	*Sapindus*

Order RHAMNALES

RHAMNACEAE:	*Berchemia, Rhamnus, Ceanothus*
VITACEAE:	*Ampelopsis, Cissus, Parthenocissus, Vitis*

Order MALVALES

TILIACEAE:	*Tilia*
MALVACEAE:	*Hibiscus*

Order PARIETALES

THEACEAE:	*Stewartia*
GUTTIFERAE:	*Ascyrum, Hypericum*
TAMARICACEAE:	*Tamarix*
CISTACEAE:	*Hudsonia*

Order MYRTALES

THYMELAEACEAE:	*Dirca, Daphne*
ELAEAGNACEAE:	*Eleagnus, Shepherdia*
LYTHRACEAE:	*Decodon*
NYSSACEAE:	*Nyssa*

Order UMBELLALES

ARALIACEAE:	*Aralia, Oplopanax, Hedera*
CORNACEAE:	*Cornus*

Subclass **Metachlamydeae**

Order ERICALES

CLETHRACEAE:	*Clethra*
PYROLACEAE:	*Chimaphila*
ERICACEAE:	*Ledum, Rhododendron, Menziesia, Leiophyllum, Loiseleuria, Kalmia, Phyllodoce, Andromeda, Zenobia, Pieris, Lyonia, Leucothoë, Oxydendrum, Chamaedaphne, Cassiope, Epigaea, Gaultheria, Arctostaphylos, Calluna, Erica, Gaylussacia, Vaccinium*

Order EBENALES

SAPOTACEAE:	*Bumelia*
EBENACEAE:	*Diospyros*
SYMPLOCACEAE:	*Symplocos*
STYRACACEAE:	*Halesia, Styrax*

Order OLEALES

OLEACEAE: *Fraxinus, Syringa, Forestiera, Chionanthus, Osmanthus, Ligustrum*

Order GENTIANALES

LOGANIACEAE: *Gelsemium*
ASCLEPIADACEAE: *Periploca*

Order POLEMONIALES

VERBENACEAE: *Callicarpa*
SOLANACEAE: *Solanum, Lycium*
SCROPHULARIACEAE: *Paulownia*
BIGNONIACEAE: *Campsis, Bignonia, Catalpa*

Order RUBIALES

RUBIACEAE: *Mitchella, Cephalanthus*
CAPRIFOLIACEAE: *Diervilla, Lonicera, Symphoricarpos, Linnaea, Viburnum, Sambucus*

Order CAMPANULALES

COMPOSITAE: *Baccharis, Iva, Borrichia*

The Meaning of Botanical Terms

(some with technical equivalents)

SEE ALSO diagrams and text (pp. xx–xxiii) in "How to Use This Book" chapter.

Aerial rootlet (vine). Small rootlike organs along stems of some climbing vines. See Poison-ivy, Plate 25.
Alternate (leaves, buds). Not opposite, but arranged singly at intervals along twigs.
Angled (twig, bud). With evident ridges; not smoothly rounded.
Aromatic. Having a spicy odor, at least when crushed.

Base (leaf). The lower portion, toward the leafstalk.
Berry (fruit). Strictly speaking, a fleshy fruit that contains small seeds (such as a grape). "Berry" or berrylike fruits are mentioned, indicating fleshy fruits that are not true berries.
Blade (leaf). The broad expanded portion.
Bloom (twig, leaf, fruit, etc.). A whitish powdery coating.
Bract. A somewhat leaflike, petal-like, or woody structure occurring beneath a flower or fruit or their clusters.
Branchlet. Except for the twig, the youngest and smallest division of a branch.
Bristle. A stiff hair, sometimes pricklelike.
Bundle scars. Tiny, somewhat circular dots within the leaf scar, caused by the breaking of bundles of ducts leading into the leafstalk. Sometimes elongate or curved.

Capsule. A dry fruit that splits partly open at maturity.
Catkin. A cluster of tiny flowers or fruits, usually fuzzy and caterpillar-shaped, often drooping. They occur in willows and relatives. Where containing flowers of only 1 sex, male catkins usually are larger.
Chambered (pith). Pith divided crosswise by numerous plates or membranes. Term is here used broadly to include all types of segmented and transversely divided pith (diaphragmed, partitioned). When the twig is cut lengthwise, such a pith looks ladderlike.
Coarse-toothed (leaf edge). With large teeth; dentate, serrate.
Compound (leaf). Divided into leaflets, each of which usually has the general appearance of a leaf. See page xx.

Deciduous (leaf, stipule, bud scale, etc.). Falls off seasonally, usually in autumn.
Double-toothed (leaf edge). Each tooth bearing smaller teeth.

Egg-shaped (leaf). Broader near the base than at the tip, the base broadly rounded (but leaf tip is sharper than apex of an egg); ovate.

Elliptic (leaf). Widest in the middle and tapering evenly to both ends like the cross section of a football.

End bud (twig). True end bud or sometimes several, clustered, located at the precise end of the twig. False end bud occurs in some species when the end bud is shed and a nearby side bud acts as end bud. A scar marks the site of the shed bud and lies beside the false end bud. See illustration, page xxiv.

Fan-compound (leaf). A compound leaf with leaflets radiating from a point; palmate-compound.

Fan-lobed (leaf). Major lobes radiating from a point; palmate-lobed.

Fan-veined (leaf). Main veins radiating from a point; palmate-veined.

Feather-compound (leaf). Midribs of main leaflets branching from a central main midrib at several points in a featherlike pattern; pinnate-compound.

Feather-lobed (leaf). The main lobes more or less at right angles to the midrib, not radiating from a central point; pinnate-lobed.

Feather-veined (leaf). The main veins more or less at right angles to a main midrib; pinnate-veined.

Fine-toothed (leaf edge). With small teeth; denticulate or serrulate.

Form. Used in this volume to include all populations of plants of the same species which vary slightly from the typical, whether such variation is limited geographically (see *Variety*) or not; forma.

Four-lined (twig). With 4 more or less equidistant lines running lengthwise along the twig.

Four-sided (twig; bud). Approximately square in cross section.

Fruit. The seed-bearing portion of a plant with its associated structures. The term does not imply that it is either fleshy or edible.

Genus. A group of species sufficiently closely related to be given the same generic name.

Gland. Strictly speaking, a surface or protuberance that secretes a substance; but generally any small knob or wart that is a normal part of the plant and has no other known function.

Glandular-toothed (leaf). Bearing teeth that bear glands. See Tree-of-Heaven, Plate 27.

Hairy. Covered with hairs; pubescent, hirsute, etc.

Heart-shaped (leaf). The shape of the valentine heart; cordate.

Hollow (pith). Twig actually without pith, but with the space present.

Hybrid. The offspring of a cross between 2 species.

Involucre. A circle or cluster of bracts beneath flowers or fruits.

Lateral (bud). To the side rather than at the end of twig or branchlet.

Leaf scar. The mark left on the twig at the point of attachment of a leafstalk when the leaf falls.

Leaflet. A leaflike subdivision of a compound leaf.

Leafstalk. The stalk supporting a leaf; petiole.

Leathery (leaf). Of a smoothly tough texture; coriaceous.

Legume. A plant of the pea family or the 1- to many-seeded podlike fruit of a pea-family plant.

Lenticel. A corky spot on the bark originating as a breathing pore and either circular or somewhat stripelike (see Cherries).

Lobed (leaf, flower petal, sepal). Divided into rounded, incompletely separated sections.

Long-pointed (leaf). The tip gradually tapering to a point; acuminate.

Midrib (leaf, leaflet). The central rib or main vein.

Naked (bud). Without bud scales.

Narrow (leaves). Shaped like the top view of a canoe; slender and pointed at each end. Often slightly wider near the base; lanceolate.

Net-veined (leaf). With a network of veins.

Node. The place, sometimes swollen, on a stem or twig where a leaf is attached or a leaf scar occurs.

Oblong (leaf). Longer than broad, with the longer sides parallel.

Once-compound (leaf). A compound leaf with a single set of undivided leaflets (see *Twice-compound*).

Opposite (leaves, leaf scars, buds). Two at a node; in opposing pairs.

Ovary. The ovule-bearing (egg-bearing) portion of the flower.

Ovule. See *Ovary*.

Palmate. See various *Fan* prefixes.

Parasitic (plant). Growing on another plant and deriving food from it.

Partitioned (pith). The pith divided crosswise by woody plates, usually near the leaf scars.

Persistent (scales, fruits, leaves). Remaining attached.

Petal (flower). One of a circle of modified leaves immediately outside the reproductive organs; usually brightly colored.

Petiole. See *Leafstalk*.

Pinnate. See various *Feather* prefixes.

Pith. The spongy or hollow center of twig or some stems.

Pod. The dryish fruit of some plants, especially legumes, containing one to many seeds and usually flattened, splitting down 1 or both sides; see *Legume*.

Prickle. A small, sharp outgrowth involving only the outer epidermal layer; generally more slender than a thorn. But in this book no stress is placed on the technical distinctions between prickles and thorns. See also *Bristle*.

Prostrate. Flat on the ground.

Reclining (stem). The lower portion somewhat flattened along the ground but the upper parts curving upward.

Resin-dot. Tiny circular or globular yellow spots, usually not obvious except under magnification.

Ridged (twig). Angular, with lengthwise lines.

Ringed (twig). With narrow encircling stipule scars at leaf scars.

Rolled (leaf edge). Curled under; revolute.

Runner (branch). A lower branch that takes root; stolon.

Scale (bud, leaf, twig). (1) A thin, membranelike covering of the bud or twig base, or (2) a fine, grainlike surface material.

Seed. That portion of the ripened fruit which contains the embryo and its closely associated essential coats.

Sepal (flower). One of the outermost circle of modified leaves surrounding the reproductive organs; usually green.

Sheath (conifer needle). Thin tissues present at needle bases and binding the needle bundles.

Short-pointed (leaf tip). Abruptly constricted and sharply pointed; not gradually tapering.

Shreddy (bark). Dividing into fragile, thin, narrow sheets.

Shrub. A woody plant usually growing with several equally strong stems and less than about 15 feet maximum height.

Side (buds). In a lateral, not end, position.

Simple (leaf). Composed of only a single blade, though frequently lobed.

Single-toothed (leaf edge). Bearing only a single set of teeth. See also *Double-toothed*.

Sinus (leaf). The indentation between 2 leaf lobes.

Solid (pith). Smoothly pithy, the twig center neither chambered nor hollow.

Species. For practical purposes here: populations whose individuals freely breed with one another and vary only slightly from one another.

Spicy-scented. See *Aromatic*.

Spike (flowers, fruits). A cluster with a narrow, fingerlike shape, the individual flowers or fruits without separate stalks, or with only very short ones.

Spine. A thorn.

Spur branch. A stubby branchlet with densely crowded leaves and leaf scars. See drawing, Plate 38.

Stalked (buds). Having a narrow necklike base.

Sterile (flower). Infertile, unproductive.

Stipule. A growth at the base of the leafstalk, usually small and in pairs, leaving scars on the twig when they drop. See also *Ringed*.

Stolon. See *Runner*.

Straggling. Semi-upright.

Tendril (vine). A clasping, twining, slender outgrowth of the stem.

Thorn (twig, branchlet, branch, stem). A stout, sharp, woody outgrowth of the stem. Technically, prickles are of different origin, but this book does not require a distinction to be made.

Thrice-compound (leaf). Divided into leaflets that in turn are divided into leaflets, and they further divided into subleaflets; an uncommon type.

Tip (leaf). The apex.

Trailing (stem). Lying prostrate on the surface or on other vegetation.

Tree. A woody plant usually with a single main stem and generally growing more than 20 feet tall.

Trunk. The large main stem of a tree.

Tubular (flower). With the basal portion hollow and tubelike.

Tundra. Vegetation type of very cold climates, especially in Far North, overlying permafrost and consisting of lichens, sedges, mosses, grasses, and low woody plants.

Twice-compound (leaf). With the leaflets again divided into leaflets.

Twig. The end subdivision of a branch; the current year's growth.

Twining (stem, leafstalk). Clasping by winding around.

Variety. That portion of a species which in a certain geographic area differs slightly from the remainder of the species elsewhere.

Wavy-edged (leaf edge). With shallow, rounded undulations.

Wavy-toothed (leaf edge). Wavy-edged but with more toothlike projections; crenate.

Wedge-shaped (leaves, leaf bases, leaf tips). With narrow, tapering bases or, less often, tips (cuneate, acute).

Whorled (leaves, leaf scars). Arranged in circles around the twigs.

Winged (leafstalk, twig). With projecting thin flat membranes or corky outgrowths.

Woody plant. With the stems and limbs containing lignin (wood).

APPENDIX G

Table for Converting Inches to Millimeters

Inches	Mm.	Inches	Mm.	Inches	Mm.
1/32	0.8	1/2	12.7	1	25.4
1/16	1.6	9/16	14.3	2	50.8
1/8	3.2	5/8	15.9	3	76.2
3/16	4.8	11/16	17.5	4	101.6
1/4	6.4	3/4	19.1	5	127.0
5/16	7.9	13/16	20.6	6	152.4
3/8	9.5	7/8	22.2	7	177.8
7/16	11.1	15/16	23.8	8	203.2

Index

This index refers to silhouettes (*italic* numbers), text descriptions (roman lightface), and legend pages opposite the Plates (**boldface**); silhouettes are listed only after the common names. Alternate vernacular names are given as *See* references. Each species or group of similar plants also is mentioned in the Key at the beginning of its Section (I–V). Broad-leaved plants also are listed either in Appendix A or B, and if they are trees are further included in either Appendix C or D. All such Key references are by common name and are not included in the index. Generic names are classified according to taxonomic relationship in Appendix E. Names of families and higher categories, as well as plants mentioned under the *Similar species* subentry but not described elsewhere in the book, are included in the index.

Abies
> *balsamea*, *21*, **38**
> *fraseri*, 21
Acacia, Prairie, 148
acacia, Rose-. *See* Bristly Locust, 128
Acacia angustissima var. *hirta*, 148
Acer
> *barbatum*, 98
> *campestre*, 98
> *ginnala*, 96
> *negundo*, *52*, **62**
> *nigrum*, 98, **120**
> *pensylvanicum*, *96*, **120**
> *platanoides*, 98, **120**
> *pseudo-platanus*, 97
> *rubrum*, 96, **120**
> *saccharinum*, 97, **120**
> *saccharum*, 97, **120**
> *spicatum*, *96*, **120**
Aceraceae, 403
Aesculus
> *discolor*, 54
> *glabra*, 53, **64**
> *hippocastanum*, 53, **64**
> *octandra*, 53, **64**
> *pavia*, 54
> *sylvatica*, 54
Ailanthus. *See* Tree-of-heaven, 136, 158
Ailanthus altissima, 136, **158**
Albizzia, 147, **166**

Albizzia julibrissin, 147, **166**
Alder(s), 227, **336**
> European Black, 229, **336**
> European White, 229
> Mountain, 230, **336**
> Seaside, 229, **336**
> Smooth, 229, **336**
> Speckled, 229, **336**
alder, Witch-, 264
Allspice
> Hairy, 81
> Smooth, 81, **108**
Alnus
> *crispa*, 230, **336**
> *glutinosa*, 229, **336**
> *incana*, 229
> *maritima*, 229, **336**
> *rugosa*, 230, **336**
> *serrulata*, 229, **336**
Alpine-azalea, 69, **100**
Amelanchier
> *alnifolia*, 244
> *amabilis*, 245
> *arborea*, 241, **342**
> *bartramiana*, 242, **342**
> *canadensis*, 243, **342**
> *fernaldii*, 243
> *gaspensis*, 244
> *humilis*, 244, **342**
> *huronensis*, 245
> *interior*, 242

411

Amelanchier (contd.)
   intermedia, 242, **342**
   laevis, 242, **342**
   lucida, 243
   mucronata, 245
   nantucketensis, 243
   obovalis, 243
   sanguinea, 245, **342**
   stolonifera, 242, **342**
   wiegandii, 245
Amorpha
   brachycarpa, 144
   canescens, 144, **164**
   fruticosa, 143, **164**
   nana, 144, **164**
   nitens, 143
Ampelopsis
   American, 187, **304**
   Asiatic, 187
Ampelopsis
   arborea, 146, **166**
   brevipedunculata, 187
   cordata, 187, **304**
Anacardiaceae, 402
Andrachne, 295
Andrachne phyllanthoides, 295
Andromeda glaucophylla, 288, **364**
Angiospermae, 401
Annonaceae, 402
Apple
   Chinese, 268
   Domestic, 267, **350**
   Siberian Crab, 268
Aquifoliaceae, 403
Aralia
   hispida, 128, **152**
   spinosa, 128, **152**
Araliaceae, 403
Arbor Vitae. *See* Northern White
   Cedar, 25, **42**
Arbutus, Trailing, 179, **298**
Arceuthobium pusillum, 30
Archichlamydeae, 401
Arctostaphylos
   alpina, 178
   rubra, 178
   uva-ursi, 178, **298**
Aristolochia
   durior, 191, **308**
   tomentosa, 191, **308**
Aristolochiaceae, 402
Aristolochiales, 402
Arrowwood
   Northern, 93, **118**

   Shortstalk, 93, **118**
   Softleaf, 94, **118**
   Southern, 93, **118**
Artemesia, xi n.
Arundinaria, xi n.
Asclepiadaceae, 404
Ascyrum
   hypericoides, 67, **100**
   stans, 68, **100**
Ash(es), 49, **60, 62**
   Biltmore, 51, **62**
   Black, 50, **60**
   Blue, 49, **60**
   Green, 50, **60**
   Pumpkin, 51, **62**
   Red, 51, **62**
   Water, 52, **62**
   White, 7, 50, **60**
ash, Mountain-
   American, 137, **158**
   European, 137
   Northern, 137, **158**
ash, Prickly-
   Northern, 129, **152**
   Southern, 129, **152**
Asimina
   parviflora, 270
   triloba, 269, **352**
Aspen
   Bigtooth, 211, **322**
   Quaking, *10,* 212, **322**
Autumn-olive, 293
Azalea(s), 283, **362**
   Cumberland, 285
   Dwarf, 285
   Early, 284, **362**
   Flame, 284, **362**
   Japanese, 284
   Pink, 285, **362**
   Pinkshell, 283
   Rhodora, 284, **362**
   Smooth, 283, **362**
   Swamp, 285, **362**
   Toothed, 285
   Woolly, 284
azalea, Alpine-, 69, **100**

Baccharis halimifolia, 268, **350**
Baldcypress, 5, 22, **38**
Balm-of-Gilead, 213, **322**
Barberry
   American, 193, **310**
   European, 193
   Japanese, 193

Basswood(s), 207, **320**
    American 207, **320**
    Florida, 207
    Hoary, 207
    White, 207
Bayberry
    Black, 263
    Northern, 262, **348**
Bearberry
    Alpine, 178
    Evergreen, 178, **298**
    Red, 178
Beautyberry, 89
Beech, *10*, 263, **348**
Beech, Blue. *See* Remarks under
    Ironwood, 227
Berberidaceae, 402
Berberis
    canadensis, 193, **310**
    thunbergii, 193
    vulgaris, 193
Berchemia scandens, 190, **308**
Betula
    alba, 232
    borealis, 234
    caerulea-grandis, 232
    glandulosa, 235, **338**
    lenta, 233, **338**
    lutea, 233, **338**
    michauxii, 234
    minor, 235
    nigra, 234, **338**
    papyrifera, 231, **338**
    pendula, 232
    populifolia, 232, **338**
    pumila, 234, **338**
    uber, 233
Bignonia capreolata, 47, **56**
Bignoniaceae, 404
Bilberry(ies), 279, **360**
    Dwarf, 282, **360**
    Newfoundland, 282
    Ovalleaf, 281
    Square-twig, 281, **360**
    Tundra, 281, **360**
Birch(es), 231, **338**
    American White, 231, **338**
    Black, 233, **338**
    Blueleaf, 232
    European Weeping, 232
    European White, 232
    Gray, *10*, 232, **338**
    Minor, 235
    Newfoundland Dwarf, 234

    Northern, 234
    River, 234, **338**
    Swamp, 234, **338**
    Tundra Dwarf, 235, **338**
    Virginia, 233
    White (American), 231
    Yellow, 233, **338**
Bittersweet
    American, 189, **308**
    Asiatic, 190
Blackberry, 125, **150**
Blackhaw
    Rusty, 92, **116**
    Smooth, 91, **116**
Bladdernut, 48, **58**
Bladder-senna, 143
Blasphemy-vine. *See under* Green-
    briers, 181
Blueberry(ies), 277, **358**
    Black Highbush, 277, **358**
    Coastal Highbush, 278
    Common Highbush, 278, **358**
    Creeping, 176, **298**
    Early Low, 278, **358**
    Elliott, 278
    Late Low, 279, **358**
    Slender, 279
    Southern Low, 279, **358**
    Velvetleaf, 277, **358**
Bodarc, Bodock, Bois d'arc. *See*
    Remarks under Osage-orange, 191
Borrichia frutescens, 81
Box Elder. *See* Ashleaf Maple, 52, **62**
Brambles, Prickly, 123, **150**
Broom, Scotch, 132, **154**
Broom-crowberry, 29, **44**
Broussonetia papyrifera, 206, **320**
Brunnichia, xi n.
Buckeye(s), 52, **64**
    Dwarf, 54
    Ohio, 53, **64**
    Particolored, 54
    Red, 54
    Sweet, 53, **64**
Buckleya, 80
Buckleya distichophylla, 80
Buckthorn
    Alder. *See* European Buck-
        thorn, 267, **350**
    Alderleaf, 266, **350**
    Carolina, 267, **350**
    Common, 88, **114**
    European, 267, **350**
    Lanceleaf, 267, **350**

Buckwheat-vine, xi n.
Buffaloberry
    Canada, 83, **110**
    Silver, 84
Bumelia
    Eastern, 192, **310**
    Small, 192
    Woolly, 192
Bumelia
    lanuginosa, 192
    lycioides, 192, **310**
    smallii, 192
Burningbush, 87, **114**
Bush-honeysuckle
    Northern, 86, **114**
    Southern, 86
Butternut, *8*, 135, **158**
Buttonbush, 80, **108**

Calfkill. *See* Sheep Laurel, 78, **108**
Callicarpa americana, 89
Calluna vulgaris, 28, **44**
Calycanthaceae, 402
Calycanthus
    fertilis, 81, **108**
    floridus, 81
Calycocarpum lyoni, 188, **306**
camellia, Mountain-, 292, **368**
camellia, Silky-, 291, **368**
Campanulales, 404
Campsis radicans, 47, **56**
canes, xi n.
Caprifoliaceae, 404
Carpinus caroliniana, 227, **336**
Carya
    aquatica, 139, **160**
    cordiformis, 141, **162**
    glabra, 140, **160**
    illinoensis, 139, **160**
    laciniosa, 142, **162**
    ovalis, 140, **160**
    ovata, 139, **160**
    pallida, 141, **162**
    texana, 141
    tomentosa, 141, **162**
Cassiope, 29, **44**
Cassiope hypnoides, 29, **44**
Castanea
    dentata, 264, **348**
    ozarkensis, 265
    pumila, 265
Catalpa
    Chinese, 86
    Common, *6*, 85, **112**

Catalpa
    bignonioides, *6*, 85, **112**
    ovata, 86
    speciosa, 85
Catawba-tree, 85
Ceanothus
    americanus, 209, **320**
    ovatus, 210, **320**
    sanguineus, 210
Cedar
    Atlantic White, 25, **42**
    Northern White, *4*, 25, **42**
    Red, *4*, 26, **42**
cedar, Salt-. *See* Tamarisk, 28
Cedrus, 25
Celastraceae, 403
Celastrus
    orbiculatus, 190
    scandens, 189, **308**
Celtis
    laevigata, 209
    occidentalis, 209, **320**
    tenuifolia, 209
Cephalanthus occidentalis, 80, **108**
Cercis canadensis, 208, **320**
Chamaecyparis thyoides, 25, **42**
Chamaedaphne calyculata, 287, **364**
Cherry(ies), 235, **340**
    Bird. *See* Fire Cherry, 237,
        340
    Black, *13*, 236, **340**
    Choke, 236, **340**
    Eastern Dwarf, 237, **340**
    European Bird, 237
    Fire, 237, **340**
    Mahaleb, 239, **340**
    Northern Dwarf, 238
    Pin. *See* Fire Cherry, 237, **340**
    Sand, 179, **298**
    Sour, 238, **340**
    Sweet, 238, **340**
    Western Dwarf, 238
Chestnut, 264, **348**
Chestnut, Horse, 53, **64**
Chimaphila
    maculata, 179
    umbellata, 179
Chinaberry, 147
Chinquapin
    Eastern, 265
    Ozark, 265
Chionanthus virginicus, 81, **108**
Chokeberry
    Black, 266, **350**

Chokeberry (contd.)
    Purple, 266
    Red, 266, **350**
Cinquefoil, Shrubby, 143, **164**
Cissus, 132
Cissus incisa, 132
Cistaceae, 403
Cladrastis lutea, 142, **164**
Clematis, Purple, 47, **56**
Clematis
    orientalis, 47
    verticillaris, 47, **56**
    viticella, 47
Clethra
    acuminata, 289, **366**
    alnifolia, 290, **366**
Clethraceae, 403
Climbing-dogbane, xi n.
Cocculus carolinus, 188, **306**
Coffee-tree, 147, **166**
Colutea arborescens, 143
Compositae, 404
Comptonia peregrina, 263, **348**
Coniferales, 401
Coralberry, 82, **110**
Corema conradii, 29, **44**
Corktree, Japanese, 52
Corkwood, 272, **352**
Cornaceae, 403
Cornus
    alternifolia, 271, **352**
    amomum, 77, **106**
    drummondi, 77, **106**
    florida, 76, **106**
    foemina, 77
    obliqua, 77
    priceae, 78
    racemosa, 76, **106**
    rugosa, 75, **106**
    stolonifera, 76, **106**
Corylaceae, 402
Corylus
    americana, 228, **336**
    cornuta, 228, **336**
Cotinus
    coggygria, 272
    obovatus, 272, **352**
Cotoneaster pyracantha, 192, **310**
Cottonwood
    Common, 5, 211, **322**
    Swamp, 212, **322**
Crabapple(s), 195, **310**
    American, 196, **310**
    Narrowleaf, 197

    Prairie, 197
    Siberian, 268
Cranberry(ies), 175, **298**
    Large, 177, **298**
    Small, 176, **298**
cranberry, Highbush-. *See* Cran-
    berry Viburnum, 94, **118**
cranberry, Mountain-
    Northern, 176, **298**
    Southern, 282
Crataegus, 197, **312**
    crus-galli, 198
    margaretta, 198
    pedicellata, 198
    phaenopyrum, 198
    pruinosa, 198
    punctata, 198
    succulenta, 198
Creeper
    Thicket, 144, **164**
    Trumpet, 47, **56**
    Virginia, 144, **164**
Cross Vine, 47, **56**
Crowberry
    Black, 29, **44**
    Purple, 30
    Rock, 30
crowberry, Broom-, 29, **44**
Cupseed, 188, **306**
Currant(s), 198, 201, **314**, **316**
    American Black, 201, **316**
    Bristly Black, 199, **314**
    Canadian Black, 201
    European Black, 201, **316**
    Garden Red, 202, **316**
    Golden, 202, **316**
    Skunk, 202, **316**
    Swamp Red, 202, **316**
Cypress, Bald, 5, 22, **38**
Cyrilla racemiflora, 296, **370**
Cyrillaceae, 403
Cytisus scoparius, 132, **154**

Daphne, 293, **370**
Daphne mezereum, 293, **370**
Decodon verticillatus, 80
Decumaria, 70
Decumaria barbara, 70
Deerberry
    Low, 281
    Tall, 280, **360**
Devil's-club, 197
Devilwood, 79

Dewberry
    Bristly, 125, **150**
    Prickly, 125, **150**
Diapensia, xi n.
Dicotyledoneae, 401
Diervilla
    lonicera, 86, **114**
    sessilifolia, 86
Diospyros virginiana, 292, **370**
Dirca palustris, 269, **352**
Dogwood(s), 75, **106**
    Alternate-leaf, 271, **352**
    Flowering, *11*, 76, **106**
    Narrowleaf, 77
    Price, 78
    Red-osier, 76, **106**
    Red-panicle, 76, **106**
    Roughleaf, 77, **106**
    Roundleaf, 75, **106**
    Silky, 77, **106**
    Stiff, 77
dogwood, Poison-. *See* Poison Sumac, 134, **156**
Dryas
    Smoothleaf, 177
    Toothleaf, 177
Dryas
    drummondii, 177
    integrifolia, 177
Dutchman's-pipe, 191, **308**
Dwarf Willows, 179, **298**

Ebenaceae, 403
Ebenales, 403
Elaeagnaceae, 403
Elaeagnus
    angustifolia, 293
    commutata, 293, **370**
    multiflora, 293
    umbellata, 293
Elder, Box. *See* Ashleaf Maple, 52, **62**
elder
    Marsh-, 90
    Poison-. *See* Poison Sumac, 134, **156**
Elderberry
    Common, 48, **58**
    European, 48
    Red, 49, **58**
Elm(s), 224, **334**
    American, *6*, *9*, 226, **334**
    English, 226, **334**
    Rock, 225, **334**
    September, 225

    Siberian, 227
    Slippery, 226, **334**
    Winged, 225, **334**
    Witch, 226
elm, Water-, 227, **334**
elm, Yoke-. *See* Hornbeam, 228, **336**
Empetraceae, 402
Empetrum
    atropurpureum, 30
    eamesii, 30
    nigrum, 29, **44**
Epigaea repens, 179, **298**
Erica
    cinerea, 29
    tetralix, 29
    vagans, 29
Ericaceae, 403
Ericales, 403
Euonymus, Climbing, 70
Euonymus
    americanus, 68, **100**
    atropurpureus, 87, **114**
    europaeus, 88
    fortunei, 70
    obovatus, 68, **100**
Euphorbiaceae, 402

Fagaceae, 402
Fagales, 402
Fagus grandifolia, 263, **348**
False-spirea, xi n.
Farkleberry, 282, **360**
Fern, Sweet, 263, **348**
Fetterbush, 287, **364**
Fir
    Balsam, *4*, 21, **38**
    Fraser, 21
Firethorn, 192, **310**
Forestiera
    Swamp, 88, **114**
    Upland, 88
Forestiera
    acuminata, 88, **114**
    ligustrina, 88
Fothergilla gardeni, 264
Fraxinus
    americana, 50, **60**
    americana var. *biltmoreana*, 51, **62**
    caroliniana, 52, **62**
    nigra, 50, **60**
    pennsylvanica, 51, **62**
    pennsylvanica var. *subintegerrima*, 50, **60**
    quadrangulata, 49, **60**

Fraxinus (contd.)
  tomentosa, 51, **62**
Fringe-tree, 81, **108**

Gallberry Holly
  Low, 274, **356**
  Tall, 275, **356**
Gaultheria
  hispidula, 177, **298**
  procumbens, 178, **298**
Gaylussacia
  baccata, 280, **360**
  brachycera, 282, **360**
  dumosa, 280, **360**
  frondosa, 280
Gelsemium sempervirens, 70
Genista tinctoria, 295
Gentianales, 404
Geraniales, 402
Gleditsia
  aquatica, 127, **152**
  triacanthos, 126, **152**
Gooseberry(ies), 198, **314**
  Canada, 199
  European, 200, **314**
  Missouri, 200, **314**
  Pasture, 200, **314**
  Rock, 199
  Roundleaf, 200, **314**
  Smooth, 200, **314**
Gorse, 30, **44**
Grape(s), 184, **302, 304**
  Bush, 186
  Cat, 187, **304**
  Dune, 186
  Fox, 184, **302**
  Frost, 185, **302**
  Muscadine, 187, **304**
  New England, 185
  Possum, 188
  Postoak, 185
  Riverbank, 186, **302**
  Sand, 186, **302**
  Silverleaf, 185, **302**
  Summer, 185, **302**
  Winter, 187, **304**
Greenbrier(s), 181, **300**
  Bristly, 182, **300**
  Bullbrier, 183, **300**
  Common, 183, **300**
  Glaucous, 183, **300**
  Hellfetter, 182
  Laurel, 182, **300**
  Redberry, 182, **300**
Groundsel-tree, 268, **350**

Guelder-rose, 95
Gum
  Black. *See* Sour-gum, 270, **352**
  Sweet, *13,* 203, **318**
gum, Sour-, 270, **352**
Gutierrezia, xi n.
Guttiferae, 403
Gymnocladus dioica, 147, **166**
Gymnospermae, 401

Hackberry
  American, 209, **320**
  Lowland, 209
  Upland, 209
Halesia carolina, 291, **368**
Hamamelidaceae, 402
Hamamelis
  vernalis, 264
  virginiana, 263, **348**
haw
  Possum-. *See* Deciduous Holly,
    275, **356**
  Rusty Black-, 92, **116**
  Smooth Black-, 91, **116**
Hawthorn(s), 197, **312**
  Cockspur, 198, **312**
  Dotted, 198, **312**
  Frosted, 198, **312**
  Margaret, 198, **312**
  Spike, 198, **312**
  Thicket, 198, **312**
  Washington, 198, **312**
Hazelnut(s), 227, **336**
  American, 228, **336**
  Beaked, 228, **336**
Heath(s), 286, 289, **364, 366**
  Cornish, 29
  Crossleaf, 29
  Scotch, 29
heath, Mountain-, 30, **44**
Heather, 28, **44**
Hedera helix, 189
Hellfetter. *See under* Greenbriers,
  181
Hemlock
  Carolina, 22
  Eastern, *4,* 21, **38**
Hercules-club, 128, **152**
Hibiscus syriacus, 205, **318**
Hickory(ies), 138, 141, **160, 162**
  Black, 141
  Bitternut, 141, **162**
  Mockernut, 141, **162**
  Pale, 141, **162**
  Pignut, *8,* 140, **160**

Hickory (contd.)
    Shagbark, 8, 139, **160**
    Shellbark, 142, **162**
    Sweet Pignut, 140, **160**
    Water, 139, **160**
Hippocastanaceae, 403
Hobblebush, 91, **116**
Holly(ies), 274, **356**
    American, 274, **356**
    Common Winterberry, 276, **356**
    Deciduous, 275, **356**
    Georgia, 276
    Juneberry, 275
    Largeleaf, 276, **356**
    Low Gallberry, 274, **356**
    Mountain. *See* Largeleaf Holly,
        276, **356**
    Smooth Winterberry, 276, **356**
    Tall Gallberry, 275, **356**
    Yaupon, 275, **356**
holly, Mountain-, 294, **370**
Honeysuckle(s), 70, 72, **102**, **104**
    Bella, 74
    Canada, 75, **104**
    European, 73, **104**
    Four-lined, 74, **104**
    Hairy, 71, **102**
    Japanese, 71, **102**
    Japanese, 71, **102**
    Morrow, 73
    Mountain, 71, **102**
    Northern, 74, **104**
    Pale, 72
    Rock, 72, **102**
    Standish, 75
    Swamp, 74, **104**
    Tartarian, 73, **104**
    Trumpet, 72, **102**
    Woodbine, 71
    Yellow, 72, **102**
Hoptree, 132, **154**
Hornbeam, 228, **336**
    American. *See* Remarks under
        Ironwood, 227
    Hop. *See* Remarks under Iron-
        wood, 227
Horsechestnut, 53, **64**
Huckleberry(ies), 279, **360**
    Black, 280, **360**
    Box, 282, **360**
    Dwarf, 280, **360**
    Tall, 280
Hudsonia
    Downy, 28, **44**

    Woolly, 28, **44**
Hudsonia
    ericoides, 28, **44**
    tomentosa, 28, **44**
Hydrangea
    Asiatic, 87
    Oakleaf, 87
    Wild, 87, **114**
Hydrangea
    arborescens, 87, **114**
    paniculata, 87
    quercifolia, 87
Hypericum
    densiflorum, 83, **110**
    frondosum, 83
    kalmianum, 82, **110**
    spathulatum, 83, **110**

Ilex
    amelanchier, 275
    coriacea, 275, **356**
    decidua, 275, **356**
    glabra, 274, **356**
    laevigata, 276, **356**
    longipes, 276
    montana, 276, **356**
    opaca, 274, **356**
    verticillata, 276, **356**
    vomitoria, 275, **356**
Indigobush
    Downy, 144, **164**
    Dull-leaf, 143, **164**
    Fragrant, 144, **164**
    Missouri, 144
    Shining, 143
Inkberry. *See* Low Gallberry Holly,
    274, **356**
Ironwood, 227, **336**
Itea virginica, 271, **352**
Iva frutescens, 90
Ivy
    Boston, 188
    English 189
ivy, Poison-, 130, **154**

Jessamine, False, 70
Juglandaceae, 402
Juglandales, 402
Juglans
    cinerea, 135, **158**
    nigra, 135, **158**
Juneberry(ies), 240, **342**
    Alderleaf, 244
    Bartram, 242, **342**

Juneberry (contd.)
    Coastal, 243
    Downy, 241, **342**
    Fernald, 243
    Gaspé, 244
    Huron, 245
    Inland, 242
    Large-flowered, 245
    Low, 244, **342**
    Minnesota, 245
    Nantucket, 243
    Nova Scotia, 243
    Oblongleaf, 243, **342**
    Roundleaf, 245, **342**
    Running, 242, **342**
    Smooth, 242, **342**
    Swamp, 242, **342**
    Wiegand, 245
Juniper
    Dwarf, 26, **42**
    Mexican, 27
    Trailing, 27, **42**
Juniperus
    communis, 26, **42**
    horizontalis, 27, **42**
    mexicana, 27
    virginiana, 26, **42**

Kalmia
    angustifolia, 78, **108**
    latifolia, 287, **364**
    polifolia, 79, **108**
Kudzu-vine, xi n.

Lambkill. *See* Sheep Laurel, 78, **108**
Larch(es), 20, **36**
    American, 5, 20, **36**
    European, 20, **36**
Larix
    decidua, 20, **36**
    laricina, 20, **36**
Lauraceae, 402
Laurel
    Mountain, 287, **364**
    Pale, 79, **108**
    Sheep, 78, **108**
Leadplant. *See* Downy Indigobush,
    144, **164**
Leatherleaf, 287, **364**
Leatherwood, 269, **352**
Ledum groenlandicum, 287, **364**
Leguminosae, 402
Leiophyllum buxifolium, 84, **110**
Leitneria floridana, 272, **352**

Leitneriaceae, 401
Leitneriales, 401
Lespedeza, Bicolor, 132
Lespedeza bicolor, 132
Leucothoë
    axillaris, 288
    editorum, 288
    racemosa, 290, **366**
    recurva, 290, **366**
Ligustrum
    amurense, 79
    obtusifolium, 80
    ovalifolium, 79
    vulgare, 79, **108**
Lilac
    Common, 84, **112**
    Persian, 85
lilac, Wild-, 210
Liliaceae, 401
Liliales, 401
Linden. *See* Basswoods, 207
Lindera
    benzoin, 271, **352**
    melissaefolium, 271
Linnaea borealis var. *americana*, 68,
    100
Liquidambar styraciflua, 203, **318**
Liriodendron tulipifera, 203, **318**
Litsea aestivalis, 295, **370**
Locust
    Black, 12, 127, **152**
    Bristly, 128, **152**
    Clammy, 128, **152**
    Downy, 128
    Honey, 12, 126, **152**
    Water, 127, **152**
Loganiaceae, 404
Loiseleuria procumbens, 69, **100**
Lonicera
    canadensis, 75, *104*
    dioica, 71, **102**
    flava, 72, **102**
    flavida, 72
    hirsuta, 71, **102**
    involucrata, 74, **104**
    japonica, 71, **102**
    morrowi, 73
    morrowi × *bella*, 74
    oblongifolia, 74, **104**
    periclymenum, 71
    prolifera, 72, **102**
    sempervirens, 72, **102**
    standishii, 75
    tatarica, 73, **104**

Lonicera (contd.)
  villosa, 74, **104**
  xylosteum, 73, **104**
Loosestrife, Swamp, 80
Loranthaceae, 402
Lycium
  chinense, 190
  halimifolium, 190, **308**
Lyonia
  ligustrina, 289, **366**
  lucida, 287, **364**
  mariana, 294, **370**
Lythraceae, 403

Maclura pomifera, 191, **310**
Magnolia(s), 223, **332**
  Bigleaf, 224, **332**
  Cucumber, 223, **332**
  Earleaf, 224, **332**
  Sweetbay, 223, **332**
  Umbrella, 224, **332**
Magnolia
  acuminata, 223, **332**
  fraseri, 224, **332**
  macrophylla, 224, **332**
  tripetala, 224, **332**
  virginiana, 223, **332**
Magnoliaceae, 402
Maleberry, 289, **366**
Malvaceae, 403
Malvales, 403
Maple(s), 95, **120**
  Ashleaf, 52, **62**
  Black, 98, **120**
  Florida, 98
  Hedge, 98
  Mountain, 96, **120**
  Norway, 98, **120**
  Red, 7, 96, **120**
  Siberian, 96
  Silver, 97, **120**
  Striped, 96, **120**
  Sugar, *6*, 7, 97, **120**
  Sycamore, 97
Marsh-elder, 90
Matrimony-vine
  Chinese, 190
  European, 190, **308**
Meadowsweet. *See* Narrowleaf and
  Broadleaf Spireas, 273, **354**
Melia azedarach, 147
Meliaceae, 402
Menispermaceae, 402
Menispermum canadense, 189, **306**
Menziesia pilosa, 294, **370**

Metachlamydeae, 403
Minniebush, 294, **370**
Mistletoe
  American, 69
  Dwarf, 30
Mitchella repens, 68, **100**
Mock-orange
  Common, 89, **114**
  Garden, 89
  Gray, 90
  Hairy, 89
Monocotyledoneae, 401
Moonseed(s), 188, **306**
  Canada, 189, **306**
  Redberry, 188, **306**
Moosewood. *See* Striped Maple,
  96, **120**
Moraceae, 402
Morus
  alba, 207, **320**
  rubra, 206, **320**
Mountain-ash
  American, 137, **158**
  European, 137
  Northern, 137, **158**
Mountain-camellia, 292, **368**
Mountain-cranberry
  Northern, 176, **298**
  Southern, 282
Mountain-heath, 30, **44**
Mountain-holly, 294, **370**
Mulberry
  Red, 206, **320**
  White, 207, **320**
mulberry, Paper-, 206, **320**
Myrica
  cerifera, 262, **348**
  gale, 262, **348**
  heterophylla, 263
  pensylvanica, 262, **348**
  pusilla, 262
Myricaceae, 401
Myricales, 401
Myrtales, 403
Myrtle, Sand, 84, **110**
Myrtle, Wax
  Common, 262, **348**
  Dwarf, 262

Nannyberry, 92, **116**
Nemopanthus mucronata, 294, **370**
Nestronia, 80
Nestronia umbellula, 80
Nightshade, Bitter, 190, **308**

Ninebark, 205, **318**
Nyssa
    aquatica, 270
    sylvatica, 270, **352**
Nyssaceae, 403

Oak(s), 213, **324, 326, 328, 330**
    Basket, 220, **328**
    Black, 218, **326**
    Blackjack, 219, **326**
    Bur. *See* Mossycup Oak, *9*, 217,
        324
    Chestnut, 220, **328**
    Chinquapin, 220, **328**
    Darlington, 222
    Dwarf, 221, **328**
    Dwarf Chinquapin. *See* Dwarf
        Oak, 221
    Jack, 217, **326**
    Laurel, 221
    Live, 222, **330**
    Mossycup, *9*, 217, **324**
    Nuttall, 218, **326**
    Overcup, 216, **324**
    Pin, *9*, 217, **326**
    Post, 216, **324**
    Red, 218, **326**
    Sand, 222
    Scarlet, 217, **326**
    Scrub, 219, **326**
    Shingle, 221, **330**
    Shumard, 218, **326**
    Spanish, 219, **326**
    Swamp, 220, **328**
    Swamp White. *See* Swamp
        Oak, 220, **328**
    Turkey, 219
    Water, 222, **330**
    White, *5, 9*, 216, **324**
    Willow, 222, **330**
oak, Poison-, 131
Oilnut, 295, **370**
Oleaceae, 404
Oleales, 404
olive
    Autumn-, 293
    Russian-. *See under* American
        Silverberry, 293
Oplopanax horridus, 197
Opuntia, xi n.
Orange, Trifoliate, 129
Osage-orange, *13*, 191, **310**
Osmanthus americanus, 79
Ostrya virginiana, 228, **336**

oxeye, Sea-, 81
Oxydendrum arboreum, 289, **366**

Pachistima, 69, **100**
Pachistima canbyi, 69, **100**
Pachysandra, xi n.
Paper-mulberry, 206, **320**
Parietales, 403
Parthenocissus
    inserta, 144, **164**
    quinquefolia, 144, **164**
    tricuspidata, 188
Partridgeberry, 68, **100**
Paulownia tomentosa, 85, **112**
Pawpaw
    Common. *See* Tall Pawpaw,
        269, **352**
    Dwarf, 270
    Tall, 269, **352**
Peach, 237, **340**
Pear
    Chinese, 268
    Domestic, 268, **350**
pears, prickly-, xi n.
Pecan, 139, **160**
Pecan, Bitter. *See* Water Hickory,
    139, **160**
Pepperbush
    Coast, 290, **366**
    Mountain, 289, **366**
Pepper Vine, 146, **166**
Periploca graeca, 70
periwinkles, xi n.
Persea borbonia, 295, **370**
Persimmon, 292, **370**
Phellodendron japonicum, 52
Philadelphus
    coronarius, 89
    hirsutus, 89
    inodorus, 89, **114**
    pubescens, 90
Phoradendron flavescens, 69
Phyllodoce caerulea, 30, **44**
Physocarpus opulifolius, 205, **318**
Picea
    abies, 24, **40**
    glauca, 24, **40**
    mariana, 24, **40**
    rubens, 23, **40**
Pieris, 288, **364**
Pieris floribunda, 288, **364**
Pinaceae, 401
Pine(s), 16, **34, 36**
    Jack, 19, **36**

Pine (contd.)
  Loblolly, 2, 18, **34**
  Longleaf, 18, **34**
  Mountain, 19, **36**
  Norway. *See* Red Pine, 2, 18, **36**
  Pitch, 2, 17, **34**
  Red, 2, 18, **36**
  Scotch, 19, **36**
  Scrub, 19, **36**
  Shortleaf, 18, **36**
  Swamp, 17, **34**
  White, 2, 17, **34**
Pinus
  australis, 18, **34**
  banksiana, 19, **36**
  echinata, 18, **36**
  pungens, 19, **36**
  resinosa, 18, **36**
  rigida, 17, **34**
  serotina, 17, **34**
  strobus, 17, **34**
  sylvestris, 19, **36**
  taeda, 18, **34**
  virginiana, 19, **36**
Pipe-vine, Woolly, 191, **308**
Pipsissewa
  Common, 179
  Mottled, 179
Planera aquatica, 227, **334**
Plane-tree. *See under* Sycamore, 204
Platanaceae, 402
Platanus occidentalis, 204, **318**
Plum(s), 194, 235, **310, 340**
  Alleghany, 240
  American, 194, **310**
  Beach, 239, **340**
  Bullace, 195
  Canada, 195, **310**
  Chickasaw, 195
  Goose, 239, **340**
  Graves, 239
  Munson, 240
  Sloe, 195
  Wild, 194, **310**
Poison-dogwood. *See* Poison Sumac, 134, **156**
Poison-elder. *See* Poison Sumac, 134, **156**
Poison-ivy, 130, **154**
Poison-oak, 131
Polemoniales, 404
Poncirus trifoliata, 129

Pondspice, 295, **370**
Poplar(s), 210, **322**
  Balsam, 213, **322**
  Black. *See under* Lombardy Poplar, 212
  Gray, 211
  Lombardy, 6, 212, **322**
  White, 211, **322**
  Yellow. *See* Tulip-tree, 7, 203, **318**
Populus
  alba, 211, **322**
  balsamifera, 213, **322**
  canescens, 211
  deltoides, 211, **322**
  gileadensis, 213, **322**
  grandidentata, 211, **322**
  heterophylla, 212, **322**
  nigra, 212
  nigra var. *italica*, 212, **322**
  tremuloides, 212, **322**
Possum-haw. *See* Deciduous Holly, 275, **356**
Potentilla fruticosa, 143, **164**
Prickly-ash
  Northern, 129, **152**
  Southern, 129, **182**
prickly-pears, xi n.
Princess-tree, 85, **112**
Privet
  Amur, 79
  California, 79
  Common, 79, **108**
  Regal, 80
Prunus, 194
  alleghaniensis, 240
  americana, 194, **310**
  angustifolia, 195
  avium, 238, **340**
  besseyi, 238
  cerasus, 239, **340**
  depressa, 179, **298**
  gravesii, 239
  hortulana, 239, **340**
  insititia, 195
  mahaleb, 239, **340**
  maritima, 239, **340**
  munsoniana, 240
  nigra, 195, **310**
  padus, 237
  pensylvanica, 237, **340**
  persica, 237, **340**
  pumila, 238
  serotina, 236, **340**

Prunus (contd.)
  spinosa, 195
  susquehanae, 237, **340**
  virginiana, 236, **340**
Ptelea trifoliata, 132, **154**
Pueraria, xi n.
Pyrolaceae, 403
Pyrularia pubera, 295, **370**
Pyrus
  americana, 137, **158**
  angustifolia, 197
  arbutifolia, 266, **350**
  aucuparia, 137
  baccata, 268
  communis, 268, **350**
  coronaria, 196, **310**
  decora, 137, **158**
  floribunda, 266
  ioensis, 197
  malus, 267, **350**
  melanocarpa, 266, **350**
  prunifolia, 268
  pyrifolia, 268
Pyxidanthera, xi n.
Pyxie moss, xi n.

Quercus
  alba, 216, **324**
  bicolor, 220, **328**
  coccinea, 217, **326**
  ellipsoidalis, 217, **326**
  falcata, 219, **326**
  hemisphaerica, 222
  ilicifolia, 219, **326**
  imbricaria, 221, **330**
  incana, 222
  laevis, 219
  laurifolia, 221
  lyrata, 216, **324**
  macrocarpa, 217, **324**
  marilandica, 219, **326**
  michauxii, 220, **328**
  muehlenbergii, 220, **328**
  nigra, 222, **330**
  nuttallii, 218, **326**
  palustris, 217, **326**
  phellos, 222, **330**
  prinoides, 221, **328**
  prinus, 220, **328**
  rubra, 218, **326**
  shumardii, 218, **326**
  stellata, 216, **324**
  velutina, 218, **326**
  virginiana, 222, **330**

raisin, Wild-
  Northern, 92, **116**
  Southern, 92, **116**
Ranales, 402
Ranunculaceae, 402
Raspberry
  Black, 125, **150**
  Flowering, 205, **318**
  Red, 124, **150**
  Wine, 125
Redbay, 295, **370**
Redbud, 208, **320**
Redroot, 210, **320**
Rhamnaceae, 403
Rhamnales, 403
Rhamnus
  alnifolia, 266, **350**
  caroliniana, 267, **350**
  cathartica, 88, **114**
  frangula, 267, **350**
  lanceolata, 267, **350**
Rhododendron
  Catawba, 286, **364**
  Great, 286, **364**
Rhododendron
  arborescens, 283, **362**
  atlanticum, 285
  calendulaceum, 284, **362**
  canadense, 284, **362**
  canescens, 284
  catawbiense, 286, **364**
  cumberlandense, 285
  japonicum, 284
  lapponicum, 177, **298**
  maximum, 286, **364**
  nudiflorum, 285, **362**
  roseum, 284, **362**
  serrulatum, 285
  vaseyi, 283
  viscosum, 285, **362**
Rhus
  aromatica, 131, **154**
  copallina, 133, **156**
  glabra, 135, **156**
  radicans, 130, **154**
  toxicodendron, 131
  typhina, 134, **156**
  vernix, 134, **156**
Ribes
  americanum, 201, **316**
  cynosbati, 200, **314**
  glandulosum, 202, **316**
  grossularia, 200, **314**
  hirtellum, 200, **314**

Ribes (contd.)
   hudsonianum, 201
   lacustre, 199, **314**
   missouriense, 200, **314**
   nigrum, 201, **316**
   odoratum, 202, **316**
   oxyacanthoides, 199
   rotundifolium, 200, **314**
   sativum, 202, **316**
   setosum, 199
   triste, 202, **316**
Robinia
   elliottii, 128
   hispida, 128, **152**
   pseudo-acacia, 127, **152**
   viscosa, 128, **152**
Rosa, 126, **150**
   multiflora, 126
   setigera, 126
Rosaceae, 402
Rosales, 402
Rose(s), 126, **150**
   Multiflora, 126
   Prairie, 126
rose, Guelder-, 95
Rose-acacia. *See* Bristly Locust,
   128, **152**
Rosebay, Rhododendron, 177, **298**
Rosemary, Bog, 288, **364**
Rose-of-Sharon, 205, **318**
Rubiaceae, 404
Rubiales, 404
Rubus
   allegheniensis, 125, **150**
   flagellaris, 125, **150**
   hispidus, 125, **150**
   idaeus, 124, **150**
   occidentalis, 125, **150**
   odoratus, 205, **318**
   parviflorus, 205
   phoenicolasius, 125
Rue, xi n.
Russian-olive. *See under* American
   Silverberry, 293
Ruta, xi n.
Rutaceae, 402

St. Andrew's Cross, 67, **100**
St. Johnswort
   Dense, 83, **110**
   Golden, 83
   Kalm, 82, **110**
   Shrubby, 83, **110**
St. Peterswort, 68, **100**

Salicaceae, 401
Salicales, 401
Salicornia, xi n.
Salix, 179, **298**
   alba, 260, **346**
   amoena, 253
   amygdaloides, 258, **346**
   ancorifera, 253
   arctica, 181
   arctophila, 180
   argyrocarpa, 252
   babylonica, 259, **346**
   bebbiana, 254, **344**
   brachycarpa, 251
   calcicola, 253
   candida, 254, **344**
   caprea, 255
   caroliniana, 258
   chlorolepis, 253
   cinerea, 255
   coactilis, 260
   cordata, 256, **344**
   cordifolia, 252
   cryptodonta, 260
   discolor, 258, **346**
   eriocephala, 259
   fragilis, 256
   glaucophylloides, 261
   gracilis, 260, **346**
   hebecarpa, 254
   herbacea, 180, **298**
   humilis, 250, **344**
   humilis var. *microphylla,* 251,
     344
   interior, 255, **344**
   jejuna, 180
   laurentiana, 251
   leiolepis, 180
   lucida, 256, **344**
   lutea, 261
   myrtillifolia, 257
   nigra, 256, **344**
   obtusata, 257
   paraleuca, 255
   pedicellaris, 254
   pedunculata, 253
   pellita, 252
   pentandra, 256
   planifolia, 253
   purpurea, 258, **346**
   pyrifolia, 257
   reticulata, 180
   rigida, 257
   sericea, 259, **346**

Salix (contd.)
    serissima, 261, **346**
    syrticola, 255
    uva-ursi, 180, **298**
    vestita, 259
    viminalis, 252
    wiegandii, 181
Salt-cedar. *See* Tamarisk, 28
Saltwort, xi n.
Sambucus
    canadensis, 48, **58**
    nigra, 48
    pubens, 49, **58**
Sandmyrtle, 84, **110**
Santalaceae, 402
Santalales, 402
Sapindaceae, 403
Sapindales, 402
Sapindus drummondi, 145
Sapotaceae, 403
Sarsaparilla, Bristly, 128, **152**
sarvis. *See under* Juneberries, 240
Sassafras, *13*, 208, **320**
Sassafras albidum, 208, **320**
Saxifragaceae, 402
Scotch Broom, 132, **154**
Scrophulariaceae, 404
Sea-oxeye, 81
senna, Bladder-, 143
serviceberries, shadblows, shadbushes. *See under* Juneberries, 240
Sheepkill. *See* Sheep Laurel, 78, **108**
Shepherdia
    argentea, 84
    canadensis, 83, **110**
Silkvine, 70
Silky-camellia, 291, **368**
Silverbell-tree, 291, **368**
Silverberry
    American, 293, **370**
    Asiatic. *See* Autumn-olive, 293
    Japanese. *See* Autumn-olive, 293
    Many-flowered. *See under* American Silverberry, 293
Simaroubaceae, 402
Smilax
    bona-nox, 183, **300**
    glauca, 183, **300**
    laurifolia, 182, **300**
    rotundifolia, 183, **300**
    tamnoides, 182
    tamnoides var. *hispida*, 182, **300**
    walteri, 182, **300**

Smoketree, 272, **352**
Snowbell
    American, 291, **368**
    Bigleaf, 291, **368**
Snowberry, 82, **110**
Snowberry, Creeping. *See* Snowberry Wintergreen, 177, **298**
soapberries. *See* Remarks under Canada Buffaloberry, 83
Soapberry, Western, 145
Solanaceae, 404
Solanum dulcamara, 190, **308**
Sorbaria, xi n.
Sour-gum, 270, **352**
Sourwood, 289, **366**
Spermatophyta, 401
Spicebush
    Common, 271, **352**
    Hairy, 271
Spindletree, European, 88
Spiraea
    alba, 273, **354**
    corymbosa, 273, **354**
    japonica, 273
    latifolia, 273, **354**
    tomentosa, 273, **354**
    virginiana, 273, **354**
Spirea(s), 272, **354**
    Broadleaf, 273, **354**
    Dwarf, 273, **354**
    Japanese, 273
    Narrowleaf, 273, **354**
    Steeplebush, 273, **354**
    Virginia, 273, **354**
spirea, False-, xi n.
Spruce(s), 23, **40**
    Black, *3*, 24, **40**
    Norway, *3*, 24, **40**
    Red, *3*, 23, **40**
    White, *3*, 24, **40**
Squashberry, 95, **118**
Staggerbush, 294, **370**
Staphylaceae, 403
Staphylea trifolia, 48, **58**
Stewartia
    malachodendron, 291, **368**
    ovata, 292, **368**
Strawberry-bush
    American, 68, **100**
    Running, 68, **100**
Styracaceae, 403
Styrax
    americana, 291, **368**
    grandifolia, 291, **368**

"sugarberries." *See under* American Hackberry, 209
Sumac(s), 133, **156**
    Fragrant, 131, **154**
    Poison, 134, **156**
    Smooth, 135, **156**
    Staghorn, *12*, 134, **156**
    Winged, 133, **156**
Supplejack, 190, **308**
Sweetbells
    Coastal, 288
    Mountain, 290, **366**
    Swamp, 290, **366**
    Upland, 288
Sweetfern, 263, **348**
Sweetgale, 262, **348**
Sweetgum, *13*, 203, **318**
Sweetleaf, 291, **368**
Sweet-spires, 271, **352**
Sycamore, *10*, 204, **318**
Symphoricarpos
    albus, 82, **110**
    occidentalis, 82
    orbiculatus, 82, **110**
Symplocaceae, 403
Symplocos tinctoria, 291, **368**
Syringa
    persica, 85
    vulgaris, 84, **112**

Tamarack. *See* American Larch, 5, 20, **36**
Tamaricaceae, 403
Tamarisk, 28
Tamarix gallica, 28
Taxaceae, 401
Taxodium distichum, 22, **38**
Taxus canadensis, 22, **38**
Tea
    Labrador, 287, **364**
    New Jersey, 209, **320**
Teaberry. *See* Redberry Wintergreen, 178, **298**
Theaceae, 403
Thimbleberry, 205
Thuja occidentalis, 25, **42**
Thymelaeaceae, 403
Tilia, 207
    americana, 207, **320**
    floridana, 207
    heterophylla, 207
    neglecta, 207
Tiliaceae, 403

Titi, 296, **370**
Trachelospermum, xi n.
Tramps' Troubles. *See under* Greenbriers, 181
Tree-of-Heaven, *12*, 136, **158**
Trumpet Creeper, 47, **56**
Tsuga
    canadensis, 21, **38**
    caroliniana, 22
Tulip-tree, *7*, 203, **318**
Tupelo, 270
Twinflower, 68, **100**

Ulex europaeus, 30, **44**
Ulmaceae, 402
Ulmus
    alata, 225, **334**
    americana, 226, **334**
    glabra, 226
    procera, 226, **334**
    pumila, 226
    rubra, 226, **334**
    serotina, 225
    thomasi, 225, **334**
Umbellales, 403
Urticales, 402

Vaccinium
    angustifolium, 279, **358**
    arboreum, 282, **360**
    atrococcum, 277, **358**
    caesariense, 278
    caesium, 281
    cespitosum, 282, **360**
    corymbosum, 278, **358**
    crassifolium, 176, **298**
    elliottii, 278
    erythrocarpum, 282
    macrocarpon, 177, **298**
    membranaceum, 281, **360**
    myrtilloides, 277, **358**
    nubigenum, 282
    ovalifolium, 281
    oxycoccus, 176, **298**
    pallidum, 279, **358**
    stamineum, 280, **360**
    tenellum, 279
    uliginosum, 281, **360**
    vacillans, 278, **358**
    vitis-idaea var. *minus*, 176, **298**
Verbenaceae, 404
Viburnum(s), 90, 93, **116**, **118**
    Cranberry, 94, **118**

Viburnum (contd.)
    Mapleleaf, 95, **118**
    Siebold, 94
Viburnum
    acerifolium, 95, **118**
    alnifolium, 91, **116**
    cassinoides, 92, **116**
    dentatum, 93, **118**
    edule, 95, **118**
    lantana, 91, **116**
    lentago, 92, **116**
    molle, 94, **118**
    nudum, 92, **116**
    opulus, 95
    prunifolium, 91, **116**
    rafinesquianum, 93, **118**
    recognitum, 93, **118**
    rufidulum, 92, **116**
    sieboldii, 94
    trilobum, 94, **118**
Vinca, xi n.
Virginia Creeper, 144, **164**
Virgin's Bower. *See under* Purple
    Clematis, 47
Vitaceae, 403
Vitis
    acerifolia, 186
    aestivalis, 185, **302**
    aestivalis var. *argentifolia*, 185,
        302
    baileyana, 188
    cinerea, 187, **304**
    labrusca, 184, **302**
    lincecumii, 185
    novae-angliae, 185
    palmata, 187, **304**
    riparia, 186, **302**
    riparia var. *syrticola*, 186
    rotundifolia, 187, **304**
    rupestris, 186, **302**
    vulpina, 185, **302**

Walnut(s), 135, **158**
    Black, 8, 135, **158**
    White. *See* Butternut, 135, **158**
Water-elm, 227, **334**
Waxmyrtle
    Common, 262, **348**
    Dwarf, 262
Wayfaring-tree, 91, **116**
Whin, 295
Wild-lilac, 210
Wild-raisin
    Northern, 92, **116**

    Southern, 92, **116**
Willow(s), 246, **344**, 346
    Arctic Dwarf, 181
    Autumn, 261, **346**
    Balsam, 257
    Basket, 258, **346**
    Bayleaf, 256
    Bearberry Dwarf, 180, **298**
    Bebb, 254, **344**
    Belle Isle Dwarf, 180
    Black, *11*, 256, **344**
    Bluntleaf, 257
    Bog, 254
    Broadleaf, 261
    Canada, 251
    Crack, 256
    Dwarf, 179, **298**
    Dwarf Prairie, 251, **344**
    European Gray, 255
    Felted, 260
    Flatleaf, 253
    Goat, 255
    Heartleaf, 256, **344**
    Hoary, 254, **344**
    Limestone, 253
    Meadow, 260, **346**
    Missouri, 259
    Mount Albert, 253
    Myrtleleaf, 257
    Netvein Dwarf, 180
    Newfoundland, 253
    Northern Gray, 255
    Ontario, 252
    Osier, 252
    Peachleaf, 258, **346**
    Pussy, *11*, 258, **346**
    Quebec, 251
    Rigid, 257
    Roundleaf, 259
    Sandbar, 255, **344**
    Sanddune, 255
    Shining, 256, **344**
    Silky, 259, **346**
    Silverleaf, 252
    Smooth Dwarf, 180
    Spreading, 254
    Tall Prairie, 250, **344**
    Taller, 181
    Tundra Dwarf, 180
    Ungava, 252
    Ward, 258
    Weeping, *11*, 259, **346**
    White, 260, **346**
    Wideleaf Dwarf, 180, **298**

Willow (contd.)
   Wiegand Dwarf, 181
   Woolly, 260
   Yellow, 261
Winterberry Holly
   Common, 276, **356**
   Smooth, 276, **356**
Wintergreen
   Redberry, 178, **298**
   Snowberry, 177, **298**
   Spotted. *See* Mottled Pipsis-
     sewa, 179
Wisteria
   American, 145, **164**
   Chinese, 145
   Japanese, 145
   Kentucky, 145
Wisteria
   floribunda, 145
   frutescens, 145, **164**
   macrostachya, 145
   sinensis, 145

Witch-alder, 264
Witch-hazel
   Common, 263, **348**
   Springtime, 264
Wolfberry, 82
wormwoods, xi n.

Xanthorhiza simplicissima, 146, **166**
Xanthoxylum
   americanum, 129, **152**
   clava-herculis, 129, **152**

Yellowroot, 146, **166**
Yellowwood, 142, **164**
Yew, American, 22, **38**
Yoke-elm. *See under* Hornbeam,
   228
Yucca, xi n.

Zenobia, 294
Zenobia pulverulenta, 294